D0448243

EYEWITNESS **COMPANIONS**

Film

RONALD BERGAN

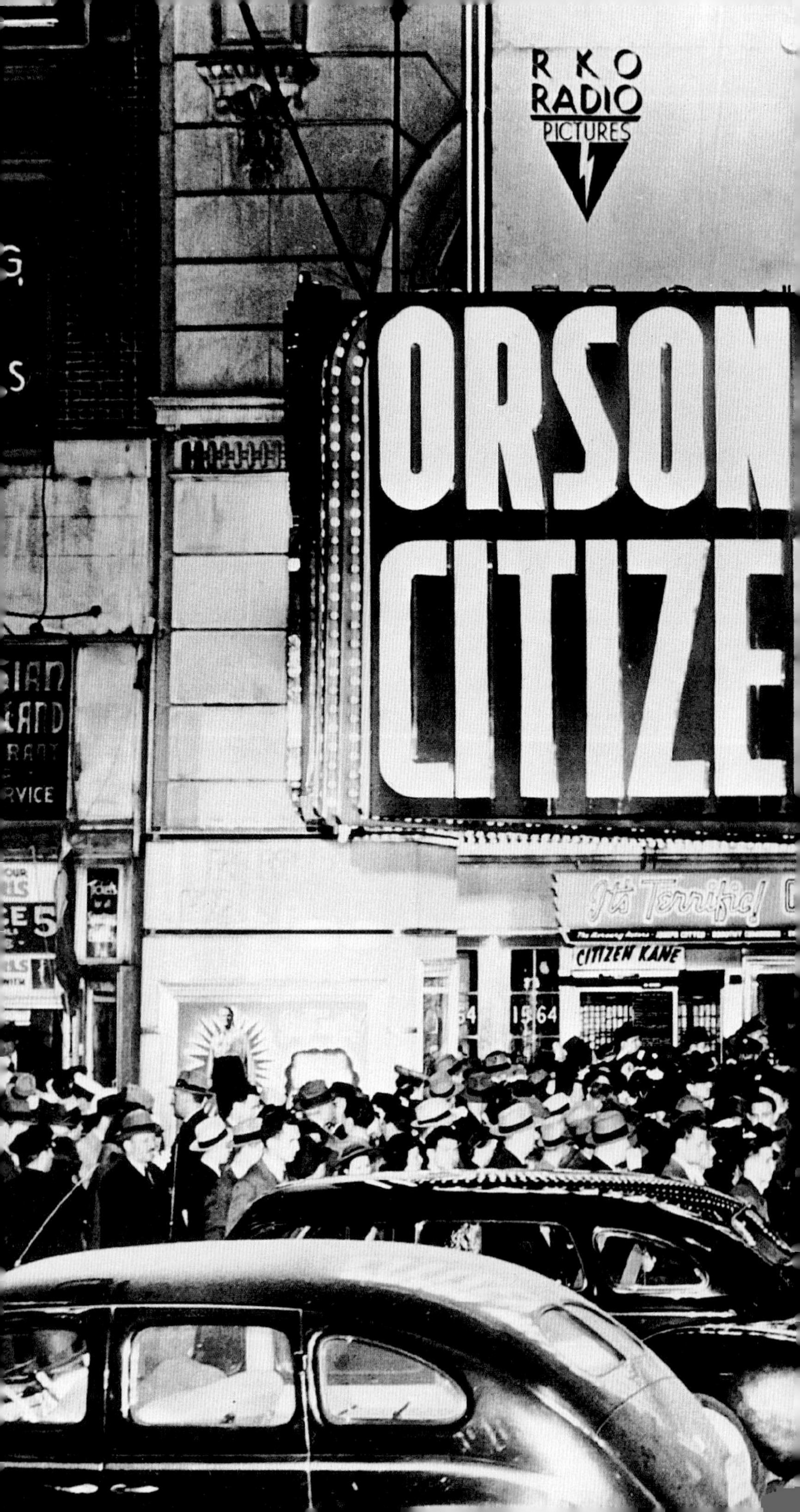
RKO
RADIO
PICTURES
ORSON
CITIZE
It's Terrific!
CITIZEN KANE
1564

RKO
RADIO
PICTURES
WELLES
KANE
ON WELLES CITIZEN KANE

LONDON, NEW YORK, MUNICH, MELBOURNE, AND DELHI

Senior Editor Sarah Larter
Project Editors Nicola Hodgson, Marie Greenwood
Additional text contributions Melinda Corey, Tom Charity
Senior Art Editor Alison Gardner
DTP Designer John Goldsmid
Production Controller Rita Sinha
Managing Editor Debra Wolter
Managing Art Editor Karen Self
Publisher Jonathan Metcalf
Art Director Bryn Walls

First published in 2006 by
DK Publishing
375 Hudson Street, New York, NY 10014

06 07 08 09 10 9 8 7 6 5 4 3 2 1

A CIP cataloging-in-publication record for this book is available from the Library of Congress

ISBN-13: 978-0-67091-573-6
ISBN-10: 0-75662-203-4

Color reproduction by GRB, Italy
Printed and bound in China by Leo

Discover more at
www.dk.com

CONTENTS

In the US, movies began in the penny arcade kinetoscopes of the 1890s. You dropped a penny in a slot and peered through a viewer to watch the delights of Fatima, the belly dancing sensation of Chicago's World Fair in 1896. Who could have predicted that this new medium would become the largest entertainment industry the world has ever known or that it was to be the new art form of the 20th century?

From its very beginnings, the cinema provided romance and escapism for millions of people all over the globe. It was the magic carpet that took people instantly away from the harsh realities of life. The movies offered a panacea in the Depression years, was the opium of the people through World War II, and continued to waft the public away from reality throughout the following decades. It was Hollywood, California, known as "the Dream Factory," which eventually supplied most of "the stuff that dreams are made of".

But, as the following pages will reveal, although Hollywood has dominated the film industry world-wide from the 1920s, it is not the only "player" in a truly global market. What makes film the most international of the arts is the vast range of films that come from more than 50 countries — films that are as multifaceted as the cultures that produce them. More and more countries, long ignored as film-making nations, have produced films that have entered the international bloodstream.

Certainly in the last few decades, creative cinema has spread from the US and Europe to Central and Eastern Asia, and also to the Developing World, the most amazing amazing example of which is Iran. African nations have given birth to directors of unique imagination, such as Ousmane Sembene and Souleymane Cissé. China, Hong Kong, Taiwan, and Korea have produced films of spectacular visual quality as well as absorbing content. There has been a huge revival in Spain and the Latin American countries. Denmark, neglected as a film-making country since the days of the great director Carl Dreyer, started to experience a renaissance in the late 1980s.

The barriers between English-language films and the rest of the world are disappearing daily as witnessed by the cultural cross-fertilization of stars and directors. A child in the US is just as likely to watch Japanese "anime" films as Walt Disney cartoons, and young people in the west are as familiar with Asian martial arts films or Bollywood as audiences in the east are with US movies.

However, not only does cinema provide pure entertainment world-wide, it is also known as "the seventh art." Writing about film as early as 1916, the German psychiatrist Hugo Münsterberg discussed the unique properties of cinema, and its capacity

An exuberant Gene Kelly *in a publicity still from* Singin' in the Rain *(1952), a musical which affectionately satirizes the early days of sound.*

"Another fine mess!" *The matchless comic duo Stan Laurel and Oliver Hardy in a characteristically perilous situation in one of their many silent shorts.*

to reformulate time and space. Riccioto Canudo, the Italian-born French critic, argued in 1926 that cinema must go beyond realism and express the film-makers' emotions as well as the characters' psychology, and even their unconscious. These possibilities of cinema were expressed by French "impressionist" film-makers and theorists, Louis Delluc and Jean Epstein, and were underlined by the montage theory that was expounded by the great Russian film-makers of the 1920s. They disturbed the accepted continuity of chronological development and attempted new ways of tracing the flow of characters' thoughts, replacing straightforward storytelling with fragmentary images and multiple points of view.

Film began to equal other arts in seriousness and depth, not only with so-called "art cinema," but also in mainstream filming, in which such pioneers as D.W. Griffith, Fritz Lang, Charlie Chaplin, Busby Berkeley, Walt Disney, Jean Renoir, Orson Welles, John Ford, and Alfred Hitchcock can be counted. Technical advances, such as fast film, sound, Technicolor, CinemaScope, and lightweight camera equipment, were used to look into new

Maggie Cheung *as Flying Snow in Zhang Yimou's spectacular* Hero *(2002), an example of an Asian martial arts film entering the mainstream of western cinema.*

Edmund (Skandar Keynes) *is confronted by the CGI-created lion Aslan, in* The Chronicles of Narnia: The Lion, the Witch and the Wardrobe *(2005).*

ways of expression on the big screen. In the last decade of the 20th century, CGI (computer generated imagery) continued this exploration, while digital cameras enabled more people to make features than ever before. With the emergence of videos and DVDs, and the downloading of movies from the internet, films can be viewed in a variety of ways. As British director Peter Greenaway has said, "More films go to people nowadays than people go to films." Directors are learning to come to terms with these new ways of watching films. Yet, whatever technical advances have been made, no matter where and how we watch films, whether seen on a cell phone or on a giant screen, whether an intimate drama in black-and-white or a spectacular epic in Technicolor, it is the intrinsic quality of the film – the direction, the screenplay, the cinematography, and the acting – that continues to astonish, provoke, and delight audiences.

We have attempted to make this guide to cinema as objective as possible, and to include films and directors that have made a difference to cinema, although some subjective selectivity is unavoidable.

A note about foreign-language titles: in many cases, both the English title and the original title of the film is given. However, when the title of the film has never been translated or the film is best known under its original title (e.g. *La Dolce Vita* rather than *The Sweet Life)*, the original title is used. If the film is better known by its English title (e.g. *In the Mood For Love* rather than *Fa yeung nin wa*), we give the English version only.

THE STORY OF CINEMA

1895–1919 The Birth of Cinema

In 1995 the world celebrated the centenary of cinema, marking the date the Lumière brothers had patented a device that displayed moving images. From the late 19th century into the first decades of the 20th century, the love affair with cinema grew.

Why did the world celebrate the centenary of cinema in 1995? Thomas Alva Edison patented his invention of the Kinetoscope in 1891. This was first shown publicly in 1893. It was a peep-show device in which a 50 ft loop of film gave continuous viewing. The first pictures were of dancing girls, performing animals, and men at work. But one could go even further back than this. Film — photographic images printed on a flexible, semitransparent celluloid base, and cut into strips — was devised by Henry M. Reichenbach for George Eastman's Kodak company in 1889. It was based on inventions variously attributed to the brothers J.W. and I.S. Hyatt (1865), to Hannibal Goodwin (1888), and to Reichenbach himself.

However, this would be dating the cinema from its conception rather than its birth and is only one step along the road to film as we know it.

The Arrival of a Train at a Station *(L'Arivée d'un Train en Gare de la Ciotat, 1895) was a single-shot sequence lasting 50 seconds, filmed by Louis Lumière. The audience ducked under their seats, convinced that the train was real.*

The Lumières' first showing *of the Cinématographe Lumière attracted little attention, but the crowds swelled and soon more than 2,000 people were lining up daily.*

1895–1919

1895
The Lumière brothers patent and demonstrate the Cinématographe.

1897
Méliès builds a studio at Montreuil-sous-Bois, near Paris, where he eventually produces more than 500 films.

1899
Humphrey Bogart, Fred Astaire, James Cagney, Noel Coward, and Alfred Hitchcock born.

1900
At the World Fair in Paris, 1.5 million gaze at a giant Cinématographe.

1903
The Great Train Robbery released, launching the Western movie genre.

1905
The first Nickelodeon opens in Pittsburgh, USA, seating 100.

1905
American entertainment trade journal *Variety* begins publication.

NICKELODEONS

The first cinemas were called nickelodeons. The price of a ticket was just a nickel, and "odeon" is the Greek word for theater. They seated about 100, and showed films continuously, ensuring a steady flow of spectators. The first was built in the US in 1905 and, by 1907, around two million Americans were going to nickelodeons every day. But the boom was short-lived. By 1910, theatres with larger seating capacity, capable of showing longer films, were starting to replace them.

In 1908, there were *around 8,000 nickelodeons throughout the US. The Comet Theatre in New York City was one of them.*

THE LUMIÈRE BROTHERS

In France, brothers Auguste and Louis Lumière were working in their father Antoine's photographic studio in Lyons. In 1894, Edison's Kinetoscope was shown in Paris and, in the same city, Louis Lumière began work on a machine to compete with Edison's device. The Cinématographe, initially a camera and projector in one, was patented in the brothers' names on February 13, 1895.

The first public performance of the Cinématographe took place on December 28, 1895 at the Salon Indien in the Grand Café on the Boulevard des Capucines in Paris. It was a 20-minute program of ten films recorded with an immobile camera with occasional panning. The first film seems to have been *Workers Leaving the Lumière Factory* (1895) in which a few hundred people pour out of the gates, including a man on a bicycle, a dog, and a horse. Some have argued that the film was staged because none of the workers look at the camera or walk toward it.

A Trip to the Moon (Le Voyage dans la Lune, 1902) *was one of Georges Méliès' fantastical films.*

Other Lumière films shown at this first cinema show included *The Demolition of a Wall* (1895), in which reverse motion was used to "rebuild" a wall, thus making this the first film with special effects.

A film called *Watering the Gardener* (1895) is considered the first film comedy. It shows a gardener receiving a jet of water in the face when a naughty boy steps on a hose and then releases it.

Among the audience at this Cinématographe presentation was Georges Méliès. He was a conjurer, cartoonist, inventor, and mechanic, and was greatly excited by what he

1908
The first movie star, Florence Lawrence, appears in 38 films.

1911
Credits begin to appear at the beginning of films.

1914
The first "picture palace," The Strand, opens at New York's Times Square. It seats 3,300.

1915
D.W Griffith's 3-hour epic, *The Birth of a Nation* premieres.

1910

1915

1906
The Story of the Kelly Gang premieres in Melbourne, Australia. At 70 minutes, it is the longest feature film to date.

1913
"Hollywood"'s name formally adopted, and becomes the center of the film industry.

1914
Charlie Chaplin makes his first appearance as the "Little Tramp" character in the Keystone Studios' *Kid Auto Races at Venice.*

THE FIRST BOX OFFICE HITS

1	FR	Workers Leaving the Lumière Factory, 1895
2	FR	The Demolition of a Wall, 1895
3	FR	Watering the Gardener, 1895
4	FR	A Trip to the Moon, 1902
5	US	The Great Train Robbery, 1903
6	FR	The Melomanic, 1903
7	FR	20,000 Leagues Under the Sea, 1907
8	FR	The Tunnel Under the English Channel, 1907
9	US	The Squaw Man, 1913
10	US	The Birth of a Nation, 1915

saw. On April 4, 1896, Méliès opened his Théatre Robert Houdin as a cinema. In 1898, the shutter of his camera jammed while he was filming a street scene. This incident made him realize the potential of trick photography to create magical effects. He went on to develop many devices, such as superimposition and stop motion. For example, in *The Melomanic* (1903), Méliès plays a music master who removes his head, only for it to be replaced by another and another. As the music master throws each head onto a telegraph wire, they form a series of musical notes.

FANTASY AND REALITY

Film scholars have pointed out that the films of the Lumière brothers and of Méliès reveal the distinction between documentary and fiction films. The Lumières employed cameramen to travel the world, while Méliès remained in his studio making his fantastic films. Among the hundred or so Méliès films still in existence are two adaptations of novels by Jules Verne, *A Trip to the Moon* (1902) and *20,000 Leagues Under the Sea* (1907).

THE BIRTH OF HOLLYWOOD CINEMA

In the early 20th century, American movie production companies were situated in New York. Biograph Studios (est. 1896) was an early home of many major silent film creative forces. Slapstick pioneer Mack Sennett worked there and at another New York studio, Keystone (est. 1912). There Charlie Chaplin also made movies,

The Squaw Man (1913), *a Western adapted from the stage and directed by Cecil B. DeMille, was the first feature-length film to be produced in Hollywood.*

until, already famous, he was lured away to Essanay (est. 1907) in 1915.

But the man with the greatest influence on the movies as an art form was David Wark (D.W.) Griffith. From his first film, *The Adventures of Dollie* (1908), he transformed the medium. Originally an actor, he learned about film-making from his employer, Edwin S. Porter, whose movie *The Great Train Robbery* (1903), was the first to convey a defined story, and use long-shot and a final close-up (of a shot fired at the audience). Between 1908 and 1913, he directed 450 titles, in which he developed film grammar and camera placement, and learned to elicit naturalistic acting from his players. The biblical spectacle *Judith of Bethulia* (1914) was the first American four-reeler and *The Birth of a Nation* (1915) was its first masterpiece.

Cleopatra (1917) *starred Theda Bara, aka Theodosia Goodman from Cincinnati. Her pseduonym was an anagram of "Arab Death".*

Just before World War I, a number of independent producers moved to a small suburb to the west of Los Angeles; Hollywood, as we know it today, began to take shape. More and more films were shot there because of the space and freedom the area provided; in 1913, Cecil B. DeMille directed *The Squaw Man* there. In March 1915, Carl Laemmle opened the Universal Studios at a cost of $165,000. A pioneering role can be ascribed to Thomas Ince, who devised the standard studio system. This system concentrated production into vast factory-like studios.

At the same time, the star system was developed and refined. The first performer to lay claim to the title of film star was Florence Lawrence, "The Biograph Girl." Theda Bara was the subject of the first full publicity campaign to create a star image. Her background was tailored to fit the role of the exotic "vamp." At the same time, other stars were gaining influence. Three of the most famous worldwide were Mary Pickford, Douglas Fairbanks, and Charlie Chaplin. Pickford, who made her name as "Little Mary," made enormous amounts of money with films like *Little Rich Girl* and *Rebecca of Sunnybrook Farm* (both 1917). In 1920 she married Fairbanks, who gained a following after several satires on American life. On January 15, 1919, unhappy with the lack of independence in working under contract to others, Chaplin, Pickford, Fairbanks, and D.W. Griffith founded the United Artists Corporation. United Artists, unlike the other big companies, owned no studio of its own, and rented the studio space required for each production. It had no cinema holdings and had to arrange distribution of its products with cinemas or circuits. Despite these drawbacks, United Artists survived.

This silent movie camera *stands on top of a sturdy tripod, and was cranked by hand.*

1920–1929 Silence is Golden

The Silent Film Era saw the consolidation of the studio system that was to endure into the 1950s. The 1920s was also a decade in which the first great stars lit up the screen, including Garbo and Dietrich. But, by 1929, a technological innovation had changed the course of cinema.

In the economic boom that followed World War I, cinema moguls Carl Laemmle, Adolph Zukor, William Fox, Louis B. Mayer, Sam Goldwyn, and Jack Warner with his brothers Harry, Albert, and Sam (all European Jewish emigrants), increased their grip on the film industry.

GENRES AND STARS

The studios began to turn out stories that repeated themes and structures, forming what would later be dubbed "genres." Westerns became a staple of the

Rudolph Valentino (1895–1926), *supreme Latin lover, in a scene from one of his greatest hits,* Blood and Sand *(1922) in which he played a hot-blooded matador.*

Film poster, *1926*

1920–1929

1920
The "marriage of the century" takes place between stars Douglas Fairbanks and Mary Pickford. He buys her a lodge called Pickfair.

1921
Fatty Arbuckle aquitted of the rape and manslaughter of Virginia Rappe.

1922
Robert Flaherty releases *Nanook of the North*, about the life of an Eskimo family, the first film to be called a documentary.

1922
Rin Tin Tin becomes cinema's first canine star, helping save Warner Bros. from bankruptcy.

1924
Metro-Goldwyn-Mayer (MGM) is founded by the merging of three production companies.

STAR SCANDALS

During the 1920s, a rash of scandals broke out among members of the Hollywood community. There was the unsolved murder of director William Desmond Taylor, involving film star Mabel Normand (the lover of Mack Sennett); the mysterious death of Thomas Ince aboard newspaper tycoon William Randolph Hearst's yacht, and the trial for rape and murder of comedian Roscoe "Fatty" Arbuckle.

Fatty Arbuckle (1887–1933) *was cleared of the charges against him, but his career was finished.*

studios in the 1920s, making good use of Californian locations. Cowboy stars, who seldom deviated from their established screen roles, included W.S. Hart, Tom Mix and Hoot Gibson. James Cruze's *The Covered Wagon* (1923) and John Ford's *The Iron Horse* (1924) both showed the epic and artistic possibilities of the genre.

But, during the Silent Film Era, it was American comedy that reached the widest audiences worldwide. This was due mainly to the comic genius of Charlie Chaplin, Buster Keaton, Harold Lloyd, Harry Langdon, and Stan Laurel and Oliver Hardy, all of whom reached their apogee in the 1920s.

The studios also recognized the value of typecasting, so that the audience quickly identified the persona of the stars by the roles they played. One of the biggest of these stars was Rudolph Valentino. Valentino came to the US from Italy in 1913 as a teenager. After becoming a professional dancer in the cafés of New York, he ventured out to California in 1917. In 1921, he appeared as the playboy hero in Rex Ingram's *The Four Horseman of the Apocalypse*, and became the unrivalled Latin lover of the screen, the male equivalent of the vamp. *The Sheik* (also 1921) sealed his seductive image forever.

In the optimism and materialism of the 1920s, Hollywood began to represent glamour, as well as a defiance of conventional morality. Because of

> **"Collective madness, incarnating the tragic comedy of a new fetishism."**
>
> **THE VATICAN,** 1926, *on the orgy of mourning following the death of Valentino*

BOX OFFICE HITS OF THE 1920s

1	US	The Big Parade, 1925
2	US	The Four Horsemen of the Apocalypse, 1921
3	US	Ben-Hur, 1925
4	US	The Ten Commandments, 1923
5	US	What Price Glory, 1926
6	US	The Covered Wagon, 1923
7	US	Way Down East, 1920
8	US	The Singing Fool, 1928
9	US	Wings, 1927
10	US	The Gold Rush, 1925

1925
The Phantom of the Opera is released, starring Lon Chaney in his most notable role.

1925
Charlie Chaplin's *The Gold Rush* is released.

1926
Don Juan released by Warner Bros. with sound effects and music but no dialogue.

1926
Rudolph Valentino dies at 31. Some 100,000 fans attend his funeral, and suicide attempts are reported.

1927
Fox's *Movietone* newsreel, the first sound news film, released.

1928
Mickey Mouse appears for the first time in *Steamboat Willie.*

May, 1929
The first Academy Awards ceremony held in Hollywood.

1929
George Eastman demonstrates his first film in Technicolor.

concerns over the immorality of the film business both off and on screen, in 1921 the Motion Picture Producers and Distributors of America (MPPDA) was founded as a self-regulating body. Former Post-Master General, Will H. Hays, became its first president, serving until his retirement in 1945. Hays tried to mold the Hollywood product into a wholesome and totally inoffensive form of family entertainment. His singular power led to the MPPDA being generally known as the Hays Office and the Production Code on matters of morality was called the Hays Code.

Pola Negri (1894–1987) *started her career in Germany before coming to Hollywood with Ernst Lubitsch in the 1920s.*

SIN AND SOPHISTICATION

Nevertheless, "It Girl" Clara Bow and "Flapper" Joan Crawford were seen as freewheeling symbols of the jazz age, replacing the post-Victorian ideals of womanhood as exemplified by Mary Pickford, Lillian and Dorothy Gish, and Bessie Love. D.W. Griffith's melodramas, *Broken Blossoms* (1919) and *Way Down East* (1920) marked the end of an era, while Cecil B. DeMille made a series of risqué domestic comedies that tested limits. Six of these moral tales, such as *Male and Female* (1919), starred Gloria Swanson as an extravagantly gowned sophisticate, more sinned against than sinning. European sophistication was offered by Erich von Stroheim, who built almost the whole of Monte Carlo on the Universal backlot for *Foolish Wives* (1921). Among the marital comedies of manners that Ernst Lubitsch directed at Warner Bros. were *The Marriage Circle* (1924) and *Lady Windermere's Fan* (1925). At the time, Lubitsch admitted that he had been inspired by Charlie Chaplin's *Woman of Paris* (1923), in which Edna Purviance, Chaplin's leading lady in almost 30 comedies, played a high-class prostitute. The studios, now strongly established in Hollywood, started to buy up talented directors from Europe. These included Ernst Lubitsch and F. W. Murnau from Germany, Michael Curtiz from Hungary, and Mauritz Stiller and Victor Sjostrom from Sweden. There were also leading players to enrich the star system, such as the Polish-born Pola Negri. She was the first European star to be given the full Hollywood star treatment. Another European-born star was the imposing Swiss-born Emil Jannings, who arrived in Hollywood from Germany in 1927. He was the first to win the Best Actor Oscar twice, for *The Way of All Flesh* (1927) and *The Last Command* (1928).

PICTURE PALACES

They heyday of the picture palaces was roughly the period spanning the two world wars. During these years, many hundreds of movie houses were built all over the world, with splendid foyers, imposing staircases, and mighty Wurlitzer organs. On average, picture palaces were capable of seating about 2,000 people, and they ran three or four shows every day. Many were masterpieces of Art Deco architecture. These opulent pleasure palaces insulated the public from the harsh outside world and were as much a part of the experience of movie-going as the film itself. However, by the end of the 1930s, box office returns were failing to keep pace with the vast investment required by the studios to keep up the lavish picture palaces

Illustration *of London's Art Deco Regal Cinema (1929).*

Flesh and the Devil (1926) *was the first and most memorable of the three silent films in which Greta Garbo and her lover John Gilbert were paired. Garbo, at her most seductive, plays a femme fatale.*

GARBO AND GILBERT

The Swedish-born Greta Gustafsson (1905–90) was brought to Hollywood by Louis B. Mayer in 1925 with her mentor, Mauritz Stiller, who had renamed her Garbo, made her lose 22 pounds and created her mystique. However, Stiller was not chosen to direct her first American film, *The Torrent* (1925), and was replaced by Clarence Brown (1890–1987) after only ten days on her second film, *Flesh and the Devil* (1926).

The urgency of her love scenes with John Gilbert, with whom she was involved off-screen, conveyed a mature sexuality and vulnerability never before seen in American films. The cinematographer William Daniels, who shot nearly all her Hollywood films, devised a subtle romantic lighting for her that did much to enhance her screen image.

Garbo and Gilbert were paired for the last time in *Queen Christina* (1933). Whereas the film launched Garbo into a series of tragic roles on which her reputation as an actress rests, Gilbert made just one further picture before dying of a heart attack brought on by excessive drinking.

ACTION AND HORROR

Home-grown talent was also in evidence in Hollywood. Lon Chaney was justly famed for his make-up skills and was known as "The Man With a Thousand Faces." However, his portrayal of a series of grotesques in such films as *The Hunchback of Notre Dame* (1923) and *The Phantom of the Opera* (1925) was based not only on external distortion but sensitive acting, that brought a quality of humanity even to these most warped and terrifying characters.

Also hugely popular was the derring-do of Douglas Fairbanks, who went from strength to strength in *The Mark of Zorro* (1920), *Robin Hood* (1922), *The Thief of Bagdad* (1924), and *The Black Pirate* (1926), all vehicles built around the star's muscular athleticism. Fairbanks had a hand in every aspect of film-making, and was particularly interested in set design.

EUROPE AND RUSSIA

After World War I, the prosperity of the film industry in France and Italy was eclipsed by increased imports of American films. Nevertheless, despite the flood of Hollywood films, Europe would continue to produce films of great artistic quality. Among the masterpieces were Abel Gance's *Napoléon* (1927) and Carl Dreyer's *The Passion of Joan of Arc* (1928) from France, and G.W. Pabst's *Pandora's Box* (1929) and Fritz Lang's *Metropolis* (1926) from Germany. In the Soviet Union, the release of Sergei Eisenstein's *The Strike* (1924) opened one of the most exciting periods of experimentation and creative freedom in the history of Soviet cinema.

THE COMING OF SOUND

In contrast, despite notable exceptions such as F.W. Murnau's *Sunrise* (1927), Frank Borzage's *Seventh Heaven (*1927) – which won three of the very first Oscars — and King Vidor's *The Crowd* (1928), Hollywood production was unremarkable in the late 1920s. Conditions were ripe for radical innovation. In August 1926, Warner Bros., ailing financially, presented the first synchronized program using a sound-on-disc system called Vitaphone. Their main intention was to offer cinema owners a substitute for the live performers in their programs, in particular the cinema orchestra and the stage show.

The final shot of *Raoul Walsh's spectacular* The Thief of Bagdad *(1924) shows Douglas Fairbanks in the title role and his princess (Julanne Johnston) sailing over the rooftops on a magic carpet.*

Because of this, their first feature film with sound, *Don Juan* (1926), starring John Barrymore, was not a talking picture at all. It used only a musical score, recorded on discs, to accompany the silent images, thus saving the extra cost of hiring an orchestra.

The breakthrough came in October 1927 when Warner Bros. launched the first commercially successful sound feature film, *The Jazz Singer*, this time featuring lip-synch recordings of songs as well as some dialogue.

The success of *The Jazz Singer* gave impetus to the installation of sound recording and projection equipment in studios and cinemas.

In May 1928, after thorough examination of the different sound techniques, almost all the studios decided to adopt Western Electric's more flexible sound-on-film recording process. This meant the end of Warner's Vitaphone. By 1929, thousands of cinemas were equipped with sound, and dozens of silent films had added talking sequences.

The German poster *for* Pandora's Box (1929) *shows the unique allure of Louise Brooks.*

During the filming of Stroheim's *Queen Kelly* (1928), starring Gloria Swanson, the producers (including Swanson herself and Joseph P. Kennedy, father of the future US president) called a halt. They claimed that, with a third of the film shot without sound, it was impossible to reshoot it with sound, and therefore the film was redundant. In reality, it was because Swanson and Kennedy came to consider the subject matter of the film too shocking. *Queen Kelly* was hastily edited, given an arbitrary ending and a music track was added. Swanson's luminous career survived the arrival of sound; but *Queen Kelly*, although released in Europe, never secured a commercial release in the US.

Twenty-two years later, Swanson and Stroheim would come together again in Billy Wilder's *Sunset Boulevard*, about a forgotten star of silent films. In this film, the sequences screened by

An unemployed man *appeals for help in the soulless big city in King Vidor's silent, poignant masterpiece,* The Crowd (1928).

New Yorkers queue to see *The Jazz Singer* (1927), eager to experience the novelty of synchronized sound — the "talkies" — for the first time.

Norma Desmond (Swanson) at her home are from *Queen Kelly*, and there are other allusions to Stroheim's unfinished and largely unseen sado-masochistic masterpiece.

MGM interfered with the editing and added a sound track to Victor Sjöström's finest achievement in the US, *The Wind* (1928). This film featured Lillian Gish, one of the greatest of silent screen stars, giving the performance of her life. There were some directors in Hollywood who were able to use the new technology creatively. Rouben Mamoulian, on his first film, *Applause* (1929), insisted on using two microphones on certain scenes, later mixing the sound.

THE BIRTH OF RKO

Sound led to the creation of a new major studio, Radio-Keith-Orpheum or RKO in 1928, whose trademark was a pylon transmitting radio signals on a globe. It also led to a new genre — the musical. It was MGM's *The Broadway Melody* (1929), which won the Academy Award for Best Film, that opened the floodgates for other musicals, dozens of which appeared before the decade was out.

The Broadway Melody (1929), *was the first "100% All-Talking, All-Singing, All-Dancing, Motion Picture".*

THE SCRAMBLE FOR SOUND

The coming of sound was as seismic in other countries as in the US. In Great Britain, the success of "talkies" from the US resulted in a wild scramble to wire studios and cinemas for the new techniques. Other countries started to demand dialogue in their own languages, which led to the disintegration of the international film market, dominated by Hollywood for more than a decade. It split into as many markets as there were languages.

Some experiments in producing multi-lingual films were tried, such as E.A. Dupont's *Atlantic* (1929). The film was shot in English, French, and German, with three different casts. It was a very expensive solution. Sound affected not only film content and style, but the structure of the industry. The artistic effect of this was to immobilize the camera and to freeze the action in the studio.

"You ain't heard nothing yet!"

AL JOLSON, 1927, *The Jazz Singer*

Most of the early talkies were successful at the box-office, but many of them were of poor quality — dialogue-dominated play adaptations, with stilted acting (from inexperienced performers) and an unmoving camera or microphone. (The period of Hollywood's transition to talkies was wittily re-created in *Singin' in the Rain*, 1952, see page 436.)

Screenwriters were required to place more emphasis on characters in their scripts, and title-card writers became unemployed. Most of the entries were literal transcriptions of Broadway shows put on the screen. However, gradually directors and studio technicians learned how to mask camera noise, free the camera and mobilize the microphones and sound recording equipment. The technology became subservient to the direction and not vice versa. From this period onwards, there was no looking back. The talkies were here to stay.

1930–1939 The Cinema Comes of Age

Besides changing the shape of the whole film industry, the coming of sound affected the careers of many directors and actors. During the 1930s many genres went from strength to strength, and a new generation of stars, including Fred Astaire and Ginger Rogers, Joan Crawford, Spencer Tracy, and Clark Gable, transfixed viewers.

Three of the four founders of United Artists, Douglas Fairbanks, Mary Pickford, and D.W. Griffith, made unsuccessful attempts at the talkies. Griffith, one of the most important figures in the history of film, became one of the most old-fashioned almost overnight. Fairbanks and Pickford, teaming up for the only time in *The Taming of the Shrew* (1929), revealed their vocal deficiencies, and the film flopped. Only Chaplin survived into the sound era, deciding to ignore spoken dialogue until *The Great Dictator* (1940). He sensed rightly that words would weaken the international appeal and effectiveness of much of his comedy. Thus in *City Lights* (1931), perhaps the peak of his career, Chaplin used only music and realistic sound effects. In the mid and late 1920s, the Hungarian-born Vilma Banky was one of Hollywood's most bankable stars, but her Hungarian accent was deemed too thick for the talkies. Norma Talmadge retired after *Du Barry, Woman of Passion* (1930) when certain critics reviled her Brooklyn accent – rather out of keeping with the 18th-century costumes. John Gilbert, who had costarred with Greta Garbo in several films, is chiefly remembered as one of the casualties of sound. When dialogue was added to *His Glorious Night* (1929), his high-pitched voice was ridiculed by critics. His various attempts at a comeback failed, despite his efforts as Garbo's leading man in Rouben Mamoulian's *Queen Christina* (1933) — the sexual electricity was no

Garbo talks! *The Swedish star made a smooth transition to sound in* Anna Christie *(1930).*

> **"Give me a whiskey, ginger ale on the side – and don't be stingy, baby."**
>
> **GRETA GARBO,** *Anna Christie,* 1930

The supreme dancing duo *of Fred Astaire and Ginger Rogers perform in* Top Hat *(1935). The film is perhaps the most popular of their nine black-and-white musicals.*

1930–1939

1930
Debut issue of *The Hollywood Reporter,* published. The daily trade paper would become an institution.

1930
The movie industry begins to dub in dialogue of films exported to foreign markets.

1931
Fritz Lang's influential *M* appears, the first psychodrama about a serial killer.

1932
Four-year-old Shirley Temple is signed to 20th-Century Fox.

1933
The first drive-in movie theatre opens in New Jersey, US.

1933
King Kong released, featuring stop-motion special effects.

1934
A new Motion Picture Production Code, or the Hays Code, established.

1935
It Happened One Night (1934) becomes the first film to sweep the Oscars, winning five major awards, a feat unrepeated until 1975.

1937
The first US full-length animated feature, Disney's *Snow White and the Seven Dwarfs*, released.

1939
Gone With the Wind premieres.

1936

1938

1934
Warner Bros. shuts down its German distribution office in protest against Nazi anti-semitic practices.

1936
Chaplin's *Modern Times*, a comment on the Depression, is released.

1938
African-American leaders challenge the Hays Office to make roles other than servants and menials available to blacks.

Jean Gabin *gives a spellbinding performance of tragic stature in* Daybreak (Le Jour Se Lève, *1939), Marcel Carné's masterpiece of "poetic realism."*

longer there. Garbo herself had little trouble making the transition. Her deep, accented voice was immediately acceptable from the moment she spoke her first line in *Anna Christie* (1929). Similarly the celebrated husky contralto of Marlene Dietrich was heard in six baroque erotic dramas directed by Josef von Sternberg in Hollywood. The director had made her a star overnight in Germany's first talking picture, *The Blue Angel* (1930).

Some directors really came into their own with the talkies: Frank Capra and Howard Hawks with their machinegun dialogue, George Cukor with his glossy, literate films at MGM, and Ernst Lubitsch, who was able to demonstrate his cynical wit and sophistication in films such as *Trouble in Paradise* (1932) as well as in musicals starring Maurice Chevalier.

EUROPEAN FILM IN THE 1930s

In France, René Clair and Jean Renoir made good use of sound. Clair's first sound film, *Sous les Toits de Paris* (*Under the Roofs of Paris*, 1930) used songs and street noises with a minimum of dialogue. Renoir's *La Chienne* (*The Bitch*, 1931) made brilliant use of direct sound. Renoir also made two of the most important films of this rich period in French cinema, *La Grande Illusion* (1937) and *La Règle du Jeu* (1939). In 1936, the Cinémathèque Française was founded by Henri Langlois, Jean Mitry and Georges Franju. Its immediate task was to save old films from destruction.

In 1935, the famous studio Cinecittá was built on the outskirts of Rome, supported by Mussolini. But the quality of the films, grandiose propaganda epics and "white telephone" films — unreal, glamorous tales set in elegant surroundings – was low. Until the Nazis came to power in Germany, films there showed an awareness of social and political trends, most notably G.W. Pabst's *Westfront 1918* (1930) and *Kameradschaft* (1931), and Fritz Lang's *M* (1931).

Socialist realism, a strictly ideological interpretation of history told in an unimaginative and straightforward style, was becoming entrenched in the Soviet Union, and all artists had to toe the party line.

In Great Britain, the outstanding figure in the industry at the time was Hungarian emigré Alexander Korda, who settled in England in 1931 and formed his own production company London Films. Denham Studios was built in an attempt to rival Hollywood.

BOX OFFICE HITS OF THE 1930s

1	US	Gone With the Wind, 1939
2	US	Snow White and the Seven Dwarfs, 1937
3	US	The Wizard of Oz, 1939
4	US	Frankenstein, 1931
5	US	King Kong, 1933
6	US	San Francisco, 1936
7=	US	Hell's Angels, 1930
=	US	Lost Horizon, 1937
=	US	Mr. Smith Goes to Washington, 1939
8	US	Maytime, 1937

BOOM AND BUST

Meanwhile, the Hollywood studio system, having recovered from the Wall Street Crash of 1929, was reaching its apogee. First there was a "talkie boom" at the end of the 1920s, and the American movie industry enjoyed its best year ever in 1930 as theater admissions and studio profits reached record levels. Then, in 1931, the Depression caught up with the movie industry, and profits fell drastically.

The rapid rise of the double feature with a cheaply made second, or "B-movie," was a direct result of the Depression. To attract patrons in those troubled times, most of the theaters offered two features in each program,

The celebrated *"Battle on the Ice" sequence, in which the invading Teutonic knights are lured by Russian forces onto the ice, which then melts and drowns them, from Sergei Eisenstein's* Alexander Nevsky *(1938). The spectacular tour de force is enhanced by Prokofiev's pulsating music.*

and changed the programs they offered two or three times a week. As a result, "Poverty Row" studios, such as Monogram and Republic, could specialize in B-movies, usually Westerns or action adventures.

MAJOR HOLLYWOOD STUDIOS

In the 1930s, the greatest asset of Columbia Pictures, which grew from a Poverty Row company into a major contender under the dictatorial Harry Cohn (1891–1958), was Frank Capra. The director made a succession of films that earned critical acclaim and secured Capra an unusual degree of independence. These included *It Happened One Night* (1934), *Mr. Deeds Goes to Town* (1936), and *Mr. Smith Goes to Washington* (1939).

Universal Pictures, which started the decade with Lewis Milestone's celebrated antiwar film *All Quiet on the Western Front* (1930), established itself as the horror movie studio by producing all the early classics of the genre. These included *Frankenstein* (1931) and *The Bride of Frankenstein* (1935), both directed by James Whale, and both with Boris Karloff (born William Henry Pratt in London) as the monster. The studio also produced Tod Browning's *Dracula* (1931) starring the Hungarian-born Bela Lugosi in the role that typecast him for the rest of his career. In the mid-1930s, wholesome teenage soprano Deanna Durbin almost single-handedly rescued the studio from bankruptcy with ten lighthearted, economical musicals, all produced by Hungarian-born Joe Pasternak (1901–91), the most successful purveyor of popular classics in the movies.

James Whale's *Frankenstein* *(1931), marked the beginning of Universal Pictures' horror movie output.*

RKO, born with the coming of sound, produced nine chic Fred Astaire-Ginger Rogers musicals from *Flying Down to Rio* (1933) to *The Story of Vernon and Irene Castle* (1939), and Katharine Hepburn's earlier films, including Howard Hawks' *Bringing Up Baby* (1938), one of the four films she made with Cary Grant. The groundbreaking *King Kong* (1933) was also a monster hit for RKO *(see page 410)*.

Twentieth Century Fox was a latecomer among the major Hollywood studios. It was formed in 1935 by a merger of two companies: Twentieth Century Pictures and Fox Film Corporation. Twentieth Century Pictures was set up in 1933 by Darryl F. Zanuck (1902–79), one of the very few American-born Hollywood moguls, and Joseph Schenck (1877–1961) who was married to actress Norma Talmadge. The Fox Film Corporation had been in the business since 1915, but had been in financial straits since William Fox himself was ousted in 1930.

Filmgoing *became a weekly ritual for the majority of city dwellers during the1930s, when the distinctive product of the studios was immediately identifiable.*

Leo the lion *poses for MGM's studio logo, which is still in use today; on the circle framing Leo was the MGM motto: "Ars Gratia Artis" — art for art's sake.*

The company's impressive trademark — searchlights scanning the heavens above futuristic skyscraping letters spelling the company's name – became synonymous with big-feature entertainment. But the company only really started to make its mark at the start of the 1940s.

Warner Bros. became associated with gangster pictures, often starring James Cagney, Edward G. Robinson, and George Raft. Also on their roster were Bette Davis, Humphrey Bogart (mostly performing as a heavy throughout the decade), and Errol Flynn, who was at his swashbuckling best in *Captain Blood* (1935), *The Charge of the Light Brigade* (1936), and *The Adventures of Robin Hood* (1938), all three directed by Hungarian-born Michael Curtiz. Another European emigré at Warner was the German-born William Dieterle, who directed two successful "biopics" (biographical pictures, *see page 123*) starring Paul Muni as Louis Pasteur and Emile Zola.

Warner Bros. musicals were grittier than those of other studios, but they also contained the most fantastic cinematic numbers ever committed to film, by the dance director Busby Berkeley *(see page 259)*. His most characteristic work — the famous kaleidoscopic effects —was done at Warners between 1933 and 1937.

If Warner Bros. could be considered working-class, then, in sharp contrast, MGM, with its logo of a roaring lion, could be considered middle-class. Driven by Louis B. Mayer and, until his premature death, "Boy Wonder" Irving Thalberg (1899–1936), MGM operated on a lavish budget making "beautiful pictures for beautiful people." MGM had Garbo, Jean Harlow, Norma Shearer (Thalberg's wife), Joan Crawford, Clark Gable, Spencer Tracy, William Powell, and Myrna Loy. Powell and

Loy were very popular as the husband-wife detective team in the "Thin Man" series which ran for six films. Olympic swimmer Johnny Weissmuller made his debut for MGM as the vine-swinging hero in *Tarzan the Ape Man* (1932), which led to a string of sequels.

MGM devised the formula of providing idealistic folksy films of Americana, and glamourous and prestigious romantic screen classics, such as George Cukor's *David Copperfield* (1934). Other hits for the studio were *Mutiny on the Bounty* (1935), *The Great Ziegfeld* (1936), the longest Hollywood talkie released up to that time, at 2 hours, 59 minutes, *Captains Courageous* (1937), and *Boys Town* (1938), which won Spencer Tracy consecutive Best Actor Oscars.

If MGM encapsulated middle-class values, then Paramount had aristocratic pretensions. Run by Adolph Zukor, it had Lubitsch's elegance, Sternberg's exoticism, and DeMille's extravagance. Players under contract to Paramount included Dietrich, Gary Cooper, Claudette Colbert, the Marx Brothers (until 1933), W.C. Fields, and Mae West, whose saucy humor was partly responsible for the creation of the Legion of Decency in 1934.

Tarzan the Ape Man *(1932) introduced Johnny Weissmuller, the most successful Tarzan of them all. Jane was played by Maureen O'Sullivan.*

SEAL OF APPROVAL

In September 1931, the Production Code was considerably tightened, and submission of scripts to the Hays Office was made compulsory. By 1934, with the cooperation of the largely Catholic Legion of Decency, members pledged to condemn "all motion pictures except those which did not offend decency and Christian morality." The PCA (Production Code Administration) was set up to give a Seal of Approval on every print of a film, with most studios agreeing not to release a film without this certificate. As a result, a number of films were withheld from release, and drastic reconstruction undertaken. The conversion of Mae West's *It Ain't No Sin* into the innocuous *Belle of the Nineties* (1934) was the most prominent. The Production Code even found the cartoon character Betty Boop immoral and demanded that her sexiness be hidden. Among the proscriptions were: profanity, nudity, sexual perversion, miscegenation,

Clark Gable and Claudette Colbert *share a motel room in* It Happened One Night *(1934). The screwball comedy was a surprise hit, winning five Oscars.*

and scenes of childbirth. The Code also suggested that respect must be shown to the flag, no sympathy for criminals must be shown, a man and woman, even if married, must not be shown in bed together. The Code amounted to a form of censorship. Though it inhibited some film-makers, it did help to ensure a steady flow of high quality family entertainment.

The films of 1939 – a golden year for Hollywood — included *Mr. Smith Goes to Washington*, *The Wizard of Oz*, John Ford's mold-breaking Western *Stagecoach*, *Dark Victory*, with Bette Davis, *Goodbye Mr. Chips*, starring Robert Donat, (who won the Best Actor Oscar); Lewis Milestone's *Of Mice and Men*, Lubitch's *Ninotchka* (publicized by "Garbo laughs!"), and *Gone With the Wind*. We will not see its like again.

GLORIOUS TECHNICOLOR

By the 1930s, Technicolor had become such a successful cinematography process that it was often used as the generic name for any color film. Walt Disney (1901–66) enjoyed the exclusive rights to make animated films in color from 1932–35, producing Oscar-winning shorts, such as *Flowers and Trees* (1932) and *The Three Little Pigs* (1933). By the mid-1930s, color was no longer a novelty, but was being used for about 20 percent of the Hollywood output. Technicolor reached its zenith at the end of the decade with two expensive MGM movies, *The Wizard of Oz* and *Gone With the Wind*, both credited to Victor Fleming.

Technicolor cameras, *here with film rolls on top, were mainly used in studios.*

Hollywood's *first full-length feature film photographed entirely in three-strip Technicolor was Rouben Mamoulian's* Becky Sharp *(1935) — an adaptation of William Thackeray's Napoleonic-era novel* Vanity Fair.

1940–1949 The Cinema Goes to War

The outbreak of World War II in Europe finally brought the economic problems of the 1930s to an end in the US. There was a return to full employment, which led to a boom in film attendance. During the post-war years, the studios were troubled by union problems and strikes, followed by the notorious anti-Communist "Hollywood witch-hunt."

In October 1940, the *New York Herald Tribune* wrote, "The incomparable Charles Chaplin is back on the screen in an extraordinary film. *The Great Dictator* is a savage comic commentary on a world gone mad. It has a solid fabric of irresistible humor and also blazes with indignation." Chaplin's first talkie, a thinly disguised satire on Nazi Germany, earned more money than any of his other pictures. However, he, and the world, had much to be indignant about.

William Wyler's Mrs. Miniver *(1942), showed how an upper middle-class English family bore up bravely during World War II.*

FILM FIGHTS FASCISM

Although the US was neutral in the war until the bombing of Pearl Harbor by Japan on December 7, 1941, Hollywood seemed to be on prewar alert with several related films made before the attack. Howard Hawks' *Sergeant York*, starring Gary Cooper, though set in the First World War, was an attack on isolationism. Other calls for America to take up arms, and which extolled the virtues of democracy over the brutality of Fascist regimes, were William Wyler's *Mrs. Miniver*, Michael Curtiz's *Casablanca*, set in 1941 war-time Morocco, and Ernst Lubitsch's *To Be or Not To Be*. Tragically, Carole Lombard, the star of the latter, didn't live to see its release. In early 1942, while on a War Bond tour, she was killed in a plane crash, at just 34 years old.

The outbreak of war in Europe threatened to devastate Hollywood's vital overseas trade. The studios' exports to the Axis nations – principally Germany, Italy, and Japan – had declined to almost nil in 1937–8, but Hollywood still derived about one third of its total revenue from overseas markets, the United Kingdom in particular. By late 1940, Britain stood alone as Hollywood's significant remaining overseas market.

1940–1949

1940 · 1942 · 1944

1940
Alfred Hitchcock's first American film, *Rebecca*, released. It will win Best Picture Oscar.

1941
Citizen Kane, directed by Orson Welles, released. It is to become one of the most highly regarded films in cinema history.

1941
Bette Davis becomes the first female president of the Motion Picture Academy of Arts and Sciences.

1941
The Maltese Falcon, directed by John Huston, is the first of the classic film noir.

1942
Paul Robeson leaves the industry because of the lack of quality roles for black actors.

1944
The first TV ad for a film is broadcast by Paramount.

In Britain, more than half the studio space was taken up by the making of propaganda films for the government. Many were of real merit, like *London Can Take It* (1940), *The Foreman Went to France* (1941), and *The First of the Few* (1942). The movement also produced Humphrey Jennings, a poet of the documentary, whose best work, *Listen to Britain* (1941) and *Fires Were Started* (1943), summed up the spirit of Britain at war. Laurence Olivier's *Henry V* (1944), made on the eve of Britain's invasion of occupied France, used the patriotic fervor of the Shakespeare play to good effect. Weekly attendances by wartime British audiences tripled from 1939 to 1945.

In France, in 1940, the French film industry fell under Nazi control and all English-language films were banned. René Clair and Jean Renoir left for Hollywood. To avoid censorship, directors chose nonpolitical subjects, though Marcel Carné's *Les Visiteurs du Soir* (*The Devil's Envoys*, 1942) was seen by the French as an allegory of their situation, with the Devil (played with relish by Jules Berry) seen as Hitler. Henri-Georges Clouzot's *Le Corbeau* (*The Raven*, 1943) made by a German-run company, was temporarily banned after Liberation.

Other films were more overlty pro-Axis. Jean Delannoy's *L'Eternel Retour* (*Love Eternal*, 1943), with a screenplay by Jean Cocteau, was an update of the Tristan and Isolde legend featuring Aryan lovers, which was pleasing to the Occupiers. In all, Germany made 1,100 feature films under the Nazi regime, many of them harmless entertainments, with anti-Semitic propaganda films among the dross. Emil Jannings, who had

BOX OFFICE HITS OF THE 1940s

1	US	Bambi, 1942
2	US	Pinocchio, 1940
3	US	Fantasia, 1940
4	US	Song of the South, 1946
5	US	Mom and Dad, 1945
6	US	Samson and Delilah, 1949
7	US	The Best Years of Our Lives, 1946
8	US	The Bells of St. Mary's, 1945
9	US	Duel in the Sun, 1946
10	US	This is the Army, 1943

Humphrey Jennings' *beautifully photographed documentary,* Fires Were Started *(1943), depicts the National Fire Service at work during the London Blitz.*

1945
Roberto Rossellini's Italian realist masterpiece *Open City* is released.

1946
The Cannes Film Festival debuts on the French Riviera.

1947
As a result of HUAC investigations, The "Hollywood Ten" are jailed for refusing to cooperate.

1946

1948

1945
Restrictions on the allocation of raw film stock ends with the War's finish.

1946
The Jolson Story, a popular biopic of Al Jolson, is released.

1949
The US Supreme Court rules that Hollywood-based studios must end monopolization of US movie-making, heralding the end of the studio system.

returned to Germany from Hollywood to costar with Marlene Dietrich in *The Blue Angel*, and remained there, was appointed head of the country's biggest studio, UFA, in 1940. In the following year, he played the title role of *Ohm Krüger*, an anti-British film set in the Boer War. Because of his co-operation with the Nazi Ministry of Propaganda he was blacklisted by the Allies and spent his last years in retirement in Austria.

STUDIO FARE

Back in Hollywood, to meet the increased demand for top features, studios either turned to independent producers, whose ranks grew rapidly in the 1940s, or granted their own contract talent greater freedom over their productions. At Paramount, Cecil B. DeMille was granted the status of "in-house independent" producer, which got him a profit participation deal on his pictures.

The growing power of the independent film-makers and top contract talent in the early 1940s was reinforced by the rise of the talent guilds — The Screen Writers Guild, The Screen Directors Guild, The Screen Actors Guild — which provided a serious challenge to studio control, particularly in terms of the artists' authority over their work. Moreover, top contract talent was going freelance. This further undermined the established contract system which was a crucial factor in studio hegemony.

Despite the success of Walt Disney's *Fantasia* and Alfred Hitchcock's first American film, *Rebecca* (both 1940), RKO was in serious financial difficulties. RKO's distribution was seriously affected when Walt Disney, David O. Selznick (who had brought Hitchcock to Hollywood), and Sam Goldwyn set up their own releasing companies. Looking for a quick return, RKO took a chance on the 26-year-old Orson Welles with *Citizen Kane* (1941), but, though it brought them prestige, it didn't bring in funds. They had more success with Val Lewton, who produced a series of subtle, low-budget psychological thrillers, such as Jacques Tourneur's *Cat People* (1942).

HOLLYWOOD'S WAR EFFORT

Ironically, the war years were comparatively good times for Hollywood. With America suddenly engaged in a global war, Hollywood's social, economic, and industrial fortunes changed virtually overnight. The government now saw "the national cinema" as an ideal source of diversion, information, morale boosting, and propaganda for citizens and soldiers alike. Within a year of Pearl Harbor, nearly one-third

Simone Simon *played a feline heroine in Jacques Tourneur's* Cat People *(1942), afraid that an ancient curse would turn her into a panther when sexually aroused.*

ENTERTAINING THE TROOPS

Big name stars who enlisted in the US Army included James Stewart and Clark Gable, while others performed for the forces at military bases, or contributed to the war effort in other ways. Some of Hollywood's best directors – John Ford, Frank Capra, John Huston, and William Wyler – made war-related documentaries or training films. The US Government's Office of War Information (OWI), formed in 1942, served as an important propaganda agency during World War II, and co-ordinated its efforts with those of the film industry.

Marlene Dietrich *became less mysterious when she helped the Allied cause by entertaining US troops.*

of Hollywood's feature films were war-related. The studios reasserted their hold over the industry and enjoyed record revenues, while playing a vital role in the war effort.

The US film industry was extremely prolific, affluent, powerful, and productive during the 1940s, while European film production suffered because of the impact of hostilities. Hollywood film production reached its peak during the years 1943 to 1946 with cinema attendance at pre-Depression levels. The Big Five studios radically reduced their output from an average of 50 films a year to 30, concentrating on bigger pictures which played longer runs.

Motion pictures offered the masses an easy, inexpensive, and accessible means of escape from long working hours, austerity, and the horrifying news from abroad. Westerns, Technicolor musicals, and sophisticated comedies were perfect tranquilizers. As a gesture toward topicality, the established genres, like the gangster movie and the thriller, often substituted a Nazi or a Fifth Columnist for the traditional underworld baddie. But wartime audiences also wanted to be uplifted by the movies, and dramas, such as *Casablanca* (1942) and *Mrs. Miniver* (1942), were immensely popular.

A WOMAN'S PLACE

America's entry into the war in 1942 meant big changes in the position of women in society. Traditional models for representing male-female relationships came into increasing conflict with the realities of the world where women were doing men's jobs and looking after the home alone while

The Saturday morning matinee *was a staple of kids' film-going from the 1940s to the 1960s. The program was mostly cartoons, serials, and B-Westerns.*

the men were away fighting. Many of the films of the time reflected this, with forceful female stars, such as Barbara Stanwyck, Bette Davis, and Joan Crawford in powerful melodramas, including *Now, Voyager* (1942) and *Mildred Pierce* (1945).

Michael Curtiz's *Mildred Pierce (1945) gave Joan Crawford, playing a self-sacrificing mother, her only Oscar.*

SHOOTING STARS

Despite losing Gable and others to the armed services, and Garbo to permanent retirement from the screen in 1941 at age 36, MGM could still boast of "more stars than there are in the heavens." Throughout the 1940s, songwriter Arthur Freed (1894–1973) headed MGM's top musical production unit, making the studio synonymous with the best screen musicals. Among the talents Freed gathered were Gene Kelly, Fred Astaire, Frank Sinatra, Judy Garland, and June Allyson; directors Vincente Minnelli, Stanley Donen, George Sidney, and Charles Walters; lyricists Betty Comden, Adolph Green, and Alan Jay Lerner. Freed also signed Lena Horne, the first African-American woman to have a long-term contract with a major studio. Horne negotiated a clause that prevented her from playing domestics, jungle natives, or other racial stereotypes. However, she was used as a speciality performer, so that her numbers could be edited out for theaters in the Southern states.

Columbia was fortunate in having the flame-haired sex goddess Rita Hayworth under contract. Charles Vidor, the Hungarian-born director brought out the best in her in *Cover Girl* (1944) and *Gilda* (1946). In the latter, she "sings" (dubbed by Anita Ellis) "Put the Blame on Mame," peeling off her long gloves, as Glenn Ford – and millions of hot-blooded men — lusted after her. The biggest wartime star at 20th-Century Fox was leggy blonde

John Mills (right) *as Pip and Alec Guinness as Herbert Pocket in David Lean's* Great Expectations *(1946), perhaps the finest of all Dickens screen adaptations.*

Betty Grable, a favorite forces pinup, who appeared in several highly Technicolored musicals. However, when studio head Darryl F. Zanuck returned after his war service, he made Fox's output more serious-minded.

POST-WAR BOOM

In 1940s Great Britain, the average annual cinema attendance reached 1,462 million. In 1947, the new Labour Government imposed a 75 per cent tax on foreign film imports; the US responded by placing an embargo on the export of films to Britain. The sudden shortage of American films

> **"Every man I knew had fallen in love with Gilda and wakened with me."**
>
> **RITA HAYWORTH,** 1946, *Gilda*

was a challenge to the British film industry. When an agreement was signed with the Motion Picture Association of America in 1948, a flood of Hollywood films hit the market and, at the same time, Americans were obliged to spend 75 percent of their British earnings to make American films in British studios. In the late 1940s, the Rank Organization owned the two largest studios in Britain, Denham and Pinewood, and several smaller ones.

The War's end brought rapid changes in the industry, particularly with the application of the antitrust legislation that signaled the end of the old Hollywood. Forced by law to divest themselves of financial control of the theaters, the major studios lost the guaranteed outlets for their products just as the audience started to decline in numbers. France reinforced the quota system on American films. It

Rita Hayworth *in Charles Vidor's* Gilda *(1946), the role with which she was most identified, epitomized 1940s Hollywood glamour.*

"How Would You Like To Tussle With Russell" *was the slogan for* The Outlaw *(1943), dreamt up by the producer-director Howard Hughes, who discovered Jane Russell.*

also initiated coproductions between France and Italy, which helped to finance independent production.

The most important aesthetic change that took place in films at the time was Italian neorealism, a term first applied to Luchino Visconti's *Ossessione* (1942), shown only clandestinely at the time, but which had a profound influence on other young Italian directors, such as Roberto Rossellini and Vittorio De Sica, and those in other countries.

Split into two countries, East and West Germany had two separate film industries. A certain number of directors who worked during the Nazi era, such as Leni Riefenstahl, were blacklisted. In East Germany, Russian films dominated the cinemas while, in the West, mostly American films were shown with the aim, it was stated, of aiding de-Nazification. Similarly, Japan was flooded with American films that were supposed to show the people a modern democratic society.

CHALLENGING AUTHORITY

The release of the Billy the Kid Western, *The Outlaw*, by the maverick millionaire Howard Hughes, caused a huge censorship uproar. The film was withdrawn after it finally got a general release in 1946, although it had been completed in 1941. The delay was a result of the producer Hughes challenging the legal authority of the Production Code when the film was refused a Seal of Approval, mainly for "glamourizing crime and immorality." It could have had more to do with Jane Russell's cantilevered bra, specially designed for her by Hughes.

More realistic representations of sexual and psychological problems and psychopathic behavior could be found in the film noir genre, as well as movies such as Elia Kazan's *Gentleman's Agreement* and Edward Dmytryk's *Crossfire* (both 1947), about anti-semitism in the US. Kazan's *Pinky* and Clarence Brown's *Intruder in the Dust* (both 1949) dealt with racial prejudice, while Billy Wilder's *The Lost Weekend* (1945) explored alcoholism.

However, this willingness to engage in serious confrontations with social problems and religious and racial bigotry emerged just as the House of Representatives UnAmerican Activities Committee (HUAC), spurred on by Senator Joseph McCarthy, began its investigations into alleged Communist infiltration of the motion picture industry. After declaring that Hollywood film-makers "employed subtle techniques in pictures glorifying the Communist system," the HUAC held public hearings in October 1947 to question "friendly" witnesses (friendly to the purposes of the committee), who included Adolph

Menjou, Ronald Reagan, Robert Taylor, and Gary Cooper. Ten so-called "unfriendly" witnesses were subpoenaed. The Hollywood Ten, as they were called, were imprisoned after claiming that the Fifth Amendment of the US Constitution gave them the right to refuse to answer the question of whether or not they had been Communists. One of them, director Edward Dmytryk, later recanted. Eventually more than 300 film artists and technicians were blacklisted, their contracts terminated and their careers finished. Some worked under assumed names or went abroad. Others, including Larry Parks (who had risen to fame in *The Jolson Story*, 1946, one of the most popular biopics), Lee J. Cobb, Budd Schulberg, and Elia Kazan were so afraid of going to prison, they named people who had been members of left-wing groups. It was one of the shabbiest periods in the history of Hollywood, and sapped its creative spark into the 1950s.

"Are you now or have you ever been a member of the Communist Party?"

HUAC 1947

The mid-1940s also saw the emergence in Britain of Ealing Studios, a team of directors, writers, and technicians who believed that the way to an international market was to capture and exploit the British spirit with all its oddities and humor. It could be described as a genuine indigenous school of film-making.

Humphrey Bogart *and his wife, Lauren Bacall, leading a line of Hollywood artists, scriptwriters and directors, march in protest against the McCarthy witch-hunts.*

1950–1959 The Cinema Fights Back

The 1950s gave cinema a rival — television. Throughout the decade cinema attendence dropped as people tuned in to the small black-and-white screens in their living rooms. The big Hollywood studios responded by developing a series of devices and new tricks to tempt audiences back in front of the silver screen.

In the early 1950s, the House Committee on Un-American Activities (HUAC) was at its peak, interrogating Americans about their Communist connections and distributing millions of pamphlets to the American public with titles such as "One Hundred Things You Should Know About Communism." The second wave of HUAC hearings began in 1951 with Republican Senator Joseph McCarthy leading the charge. Over the next three years McCarthy subpoenaed some of the most prominent entertainers of the era. But, in 1954, with the help of Edward Murrow's unedited footage of the hearings (the subject of George Clooney's *Good Night and Good Luck*, 2005), the public was able to see McCarthyism for what it really was — a witch-hunt.

While Senator McCarthy was seeing Reds under every bed, film moguls saw the box in people's living rooms as the real enemy. Although cinema's audience figures had already started to decline in 1947, the main cause for the drastic reduction in cinema admissions was blamed on the television sets that were proliferating in homes across the USA. In the first years of the 1950s, 50 percent of US homes had at least one TV set, a number that was set to grow

Ernest Borgnine *played a Bronx butcher, a role that revealed his tender side, in* Marty *(1955), a film that began a vogue for dramas about ordinary people.*

1950–1959

1950
Gloria Swanson, and other actors from the silent screen, play aspects of themselves in *Sunset Boulevard*.

1951
HUAC opens a second round of hearings in Hollywood, and blacklists 212 people.

1952
A Streetcar Named Desire is the first film to win three acting Oscars, for Vivien Leigh, Karl Malden, and Kim Hunter.

1952
MGM releases *Singin' in the Rain*, perhaps the best-loved film musical of all.

1953
Single- or multi-film contracts replace seven-year contracts for actors.

1953
The Academy Awards are televized for the first time.

1954
Akira Kurosawa's influential epic, *The Seven Samurai*, released.

1950 1952 1954

AT THE DRIVE-IN

Outdoor drive-ins, first introduced in the USA in 1933, flourished in the 1950s. Patrons watched a film from their own cars, parked in a semi-circle around a giant screen. The sound was supplied by small speakers attached inside each car. Drive-ins attracted families with small children, avoiding the need for a babysitter, and young couples. With the latter in mind, many of the drive-ins showed "B" horror movies, dubbed "drive-in fodder".

Some 4,000 drive-ins *were constructed across America but, in the 1960s, their popularity started to decline. Today only a few still exist, frequented by nostalgic audiences.*

dramatically. As Samuel Goldwyn commented, "Why should people go out and pay money to see bad films when they can stay at home and see bad television for nothing?"

Jack Warner stipulated that no TV set was to be seen in a Warner Bros. movie. Television, which was added to the list of taboos, was seldom mentioned in films except in a satirical context as in the MGM musical *It's Always Fair Weather* (1955) and Elia Kazan's *A Face in the Crowd* (1957), a biting attack on the manipulation of the masses by TV.

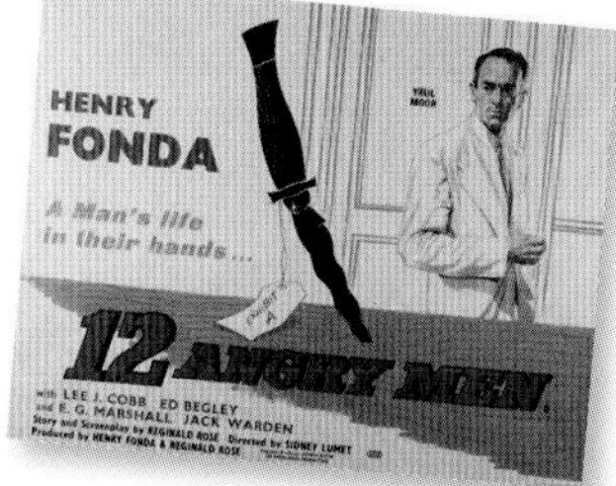

Most of *Sidney Lumet's* 12 Angry Men *(1957) takes place in a jury room, creating an intimate, claustrophobic atmosphere.*

Ironically, the arch-enemy provided Hollywood with some of the best screenplays of the era, as well as the first generation of directors to come to the movies via the TV studio. These included John Frankenheimer who made *The Manchurian Candidate* (1962), Sidney Lumet, Robert Mulligan (best known for *To Kill A Mockingbird*, 1962), and Delbert Mann. Mann's *Marty* (1955), based on a Paddy Chayefsky teleplay about a lonely, unattractive butcher from the Bronx (movie heavy Ernest Borgnine, cast against type, winning the Best Actor Oscar), was the "sleeper" of the decade. As a result, other intimate, realistic television dramas such as Lumet's *12 Angry Men* (1957) were successfully adapted for the big screen.

A LION IN YOUR LAP

The existence of a financial competitor to Hollywood stimulated all sorts of movie innovations. One novelty that had mixed results was

1955
James Dean is killed in a car accident.

1955
RKO sells its film library to television.

1957
The first kiss between a black man and a white woman (Harry Belafonte and Joan Fontaine) is featured in *Island in the Sun*.

1956

1958

1955
On the Waterfront sweeps the Academy Awards, winning eight Oscars.

1956
Cecil B. DeMille remakes his own silent epic, *The Ten Commandments*. It is nominated for seven Oscars.

1958
Horror film *The Fly* appears.

1959
Release of Hitchcock's *North by Northwest*.

3-D movie-making. The first color feature-length Hollywood film made in Natural Vision (soon to be dubbed 3-D), was *Bwana Devil* (1952); the film's publicity slogan was "A Lion in your lap." Arch Oboler, who produced, directed, and wrote it, made a huge profit on his comparatively small investment, due to the novelty value of the film's pioneering technique. However, these films, which could only be seen through cheap cardboard Polaroid spectacles, were still fairly crude, with images changing in quality and causing "ghosts" on the screen. Nevertheless, Hollywood began making about 30 3-D films a year, with audiences being subjected to all sorts of missiles hurtling towards them. Gradually, the glasses became an increasing annoyance, and many

The only distinguishing feature *of* Bwana Devil *(1952), an African adventure shot in the Californian hills, was the novelty value of 3-D.*

The 3-D experience *was uncomfortable for those who already wore glasses, headaches were common, and the novelty soon wore thin.*

good films produced in 3-D such as MGM's *Kiss Me Kate* (1953) and Alfred Hitchcock's *Dial M For Murder* (1954) were released as ordinary "flat" films.

STRETCHING THE SCREEN

In 1952 a film was released showing how a technology called Cinerama could make films more realistic by involving viewers' peripheral vision. *This is Cinerama* informed its audiences that "you will be gazing at a movie screen — you'll find yourself swept right into the picture, surrounded by sight and sound." A series of short subjects followed, including scenes of a roller coaster, a bullfight, and Niagara Falls. The process had three 35mm projectors, three screens curved to cover 140 degrees, as well as stereophonic sound. However, theatres that showed films in this new way were required to employ three full-time projectionists and invest thousands of dollars in new equipment, and Cinerama's popularity was short-lived.

Todd-AO was developed in the early 1950s to produce a wide screen image by photographing on 65mm and printing on a 70mm positive. The remaining space at the side of the print allowed room for six Stereophonic soundtracks. The process was developed by the American Optical Company (hence AO) for showman Mike Todd. Todd-AO was successfully used for *Oklahoma!* (1955) and the star-studded *Around the World in Eighty Days* (1956). Todd married Elizabeth Taylor in 1956, but their stormy marriage was cut short when he was killed in a plane crash.

How To Marry A Millionaire *(1953) tried to prove that CinemaScope could be as effective for comedy as for spectacles.*

In 1953, 20th Century Fox unveiled CinemaScope, a process that used an anamorphic (distortable) lens to expand the size of the image. *The Robe*, a biblical epic starring British actor Richard Burton, was the first CinemaScope feature. By the end of 1953, every major studio except Paramount — whose rival VistaVision process had a 35mm film running horizontally instead of vertically — was making films in CinemaScope.

Richard Burton and Jean Simmons *starred in Henry Koster's CinemaScope spectacle* The Robe *(1953). The sequel,* Demetrius and the Gladiators, *followed in 1954.*

The size of the screen, to a large extent, dictated the content of the movies, so that *Knights of the Round Table* (1953), *Land of the Pharoahs* (1955), and *Helen of Troy* (1955) filled the screens, if not the theatres. The need to cram every inch of the screen with spectacle was an expensive operation, and CinemaScope films seldom recouped their costs. Exceptions included Elia Kazan's *East of Eden* (1955), Nicholas Ray's *Rebel without a Cause* (1955), Vincente Minnelli's *Lust for Life* (1956), and Otto Preminger's *River of No Return* (1954).

THE MOVIES MATURE

There was a more interesting device for getting people to leave their TV sets for a movie theater: controversial

Carroll Baker *plays the virgin bride in Elia Kazan's* Baby Doll *(1956), a film that scandalized puritan America because of provocative poses such as this.*

and adult subjects deemed unsuitable by TV's sponsors for family viewing at home. So if someone wanted to hear the words "virgin" and "seduce," they would have to go out to the movies to see Preminger's *The Moon is Blue* (1954), which was released without the Production Code's Seal of Approval. This film helped to create a permissiveness that wrested Hollywood from the puritan values that had gripped it for so long.

Independent producers were also breaking the hold of the major studios, and tackled more daring subjects, delving into areas that Hollywood had previously avoided. Movies such as Kazan's *Baby Doll* (1956) led to revisions of the Production Code, after which "mature" subjects such as prostitution, drug addiction, and miscegenation could be shown if "treated within the limits of good taste."

BOX OFFICE HITS OF THE 1950s

1	US	Lady and the Tramp, 1955
2	US	Peter Pan, 1953
3	US	Cinderella, 1950
4	US	The Ten Commandments, 1956
5	US	Ben-Hur, 1959
6	US	Sleeping Beauty, 1959
7	US	Around the World in Eighty Days, 1956
8	US	This is Cinerama, 1952
9	US	South Pacific, 1958
10	US	The Robe, 1953

HOLLYWOOD THEMES

Despite the Communist witch-hunts, against the background of the Cold War Hollywood continued to explore liberal themes. Native Americans were, for the first time, sympathetically treated in films like Delmer Daves' *Broken Arrow* (1950) and Robert Aldrich's *Apache* (1954). Racial intolerance was examined in Joseph Mankiewicz's *No Way Out* (1950) and Stanley Kramer's *The Defiant Ones* (1958). Juvenile delinquency was explored in Richard Brooks' *The Blackboard Jungle* (1955), the first major Hollywood film to use rock 'n' roll on its soundtrack. Preminger's *The Man with the Golden Arm* (1955) and Fred Zinnemann's *A Hatful of Rain* (1957) tackled the subject of drug addiction with a frankness hitherto unknown. With the Korean War over and wounds beginning to heal, Stanley

Kubrick was able to make *Paths of Glory* (1957), one of the screen's most powerful anti-militarist statements.

The steep decline in weekly theatre attendance forced studios to find creative ways to make money from the new medium. Converted Hollywood studios were beginning to produce more hours of film for TV than for feature films. The vast studio structure was weakened, but the studios still had a certain identity, and kept turning out good films under their banners.

This classic poster *for Otto Preminger's* The Man With The Golden Arm *(1955) was created by Saul Bass; the film starred Frank Sinatra as a professional gambler hooked on narcotics.*

At MGM the artistic status of the musical was raised by Vincente Minnelli's *An American in Paris* (1951) and Gene Kelly and Stanley Donen's *Singin' in the Rain* (1952). Although Republic Pictures produced some of their best films — Nicholas Ray's *Johnny Guitar* (1954), and John Ford's *Rio Grande* (1950) and *The Quiet Man* (1952) — the company abandoned making films in 1958. RKO, which businessman Howard Hughes had bought in 1948 for $9 million, and later paid $23 million for ownership of the subsidiaries, ceased production in 1953. The studio was sold to Desilu Productions in 1957, a TV company owned by Lucille Ball.

Columbia recovered in the early 1950s, with the help and support of independent producers, David Lean (*The Bridge on the River Kwai*, 1957), Elia Kazan (*On the Waterfront*, 1954), and Fred Zinnemann (*From Here To Eternity*, 1953). The latter was notable for casting the usually ladylike Deborah Kerr in an adulterous affair with Burt Lancaster, and for reviving Frank Sinatra's flagging career. Lancaster emerged, with Kirk Douglas, as the most versatile and adventurous of the stars of the 1950s.

Alec Guinness *(right) is the stubborn English POW colonel in the seven Oscar-winning* The Bridge on the River Kwai *(1957). The bridge is in the background.*

In fact, they were among those performers who gained greater independence by going freelance, and becoming producers themselves. Other stars, such as Bette Davis, successfully reinvented themselves.

> **"I don't believe you want to go to the theater to see somebody you can see next door."**
>
> **JOAN CRAWFORD,** 1950

HIP NEW STARS

With youth culture beginning to infiltrate the movies in the 1950s, it was now possible for young people to identify with certain stars. Joan Crawford, a remnant of past glamour, was scathing about the "ordinary" characters in films that were becoming popular with young people. But it was precisely because of their youth that audiences could imagine the new stars living next door and that made them attractive.

Marlon Brando projected an anticonformist image, especially in *The Wild One* (1954), the film noted for a line of dialogue that typified his attitude. "What are you rebelling against?' Brando is asked. "Whaddaya got?," he replies.

James Dean (1931–55), who starred in only three films, *Rebel without a Cause* (1955), *East of Eden* (1955), and *Giant* (1956), was the personification of adolescent rebellion and despair. On September 20, 1955, Dean died when the silver Porsche Spyder he was driving was involved in a head-on collision with another vehicle. It resulted in a level of hysteria not seen since the untimely death of Rudolph Valentino in 1926. Dean has since become one of those stars whose popularity is not diminished by death.

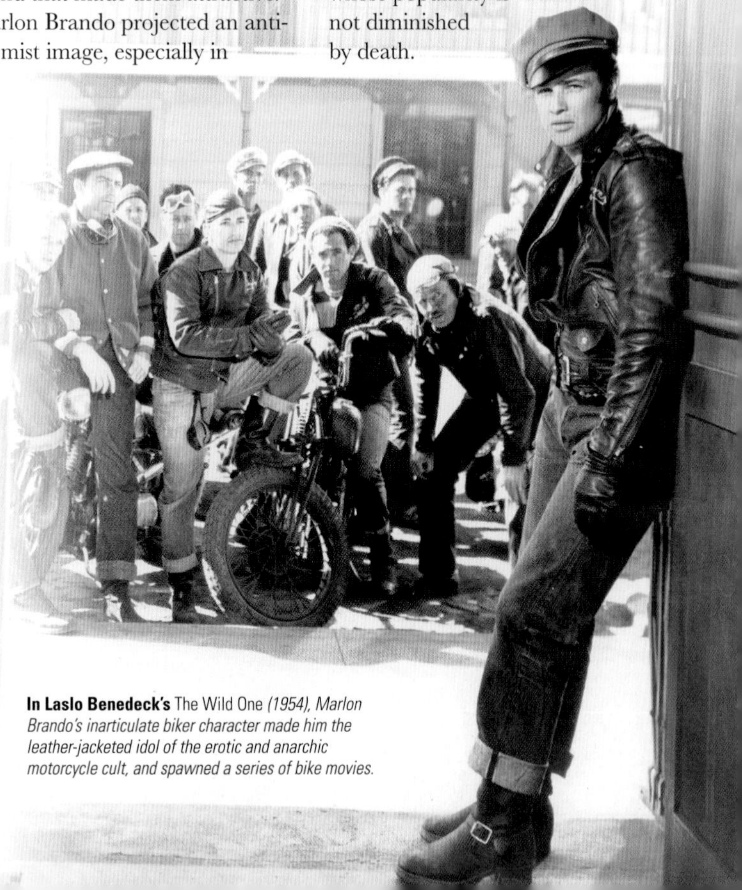

In Laslo Benedeck's The Wild One *(1954), Marlon Brando's inarticulate biker character made him the leather-jacketed idol of the erotic and anarchic motorcycle cult, and spawned a series of bike movies.*

James Dean, Elizabeth Taylor, and Rock Hudson, *three of the biggest stars of the 1950s, are pictured on the set of George Stevens'* Giant *(1956), which was Dean's last film.*

What Brando and Dean were able to do was attract a new type of youngster to the cinema — those who preferred their heroes to be more nonconformist than the clean-cut, studio-bred idols of the 1930s and '40s.

THE LEGACY OF THE 1950s

Away from the new wave of anarchic performers, there were still a number of stars in the glamorous Hollywood tradition, such as Ava Gardner, Susan Hayward, Elizabeth Taylor, Grace Kelly, Rock Hudson, and Audrey Hepburn. Three names from an earlier era made sensational comebacks: Bette Davis played a fading actress in *All About Eve (*1950), Judy Garland played her greatest role in *A Star is Born* (1954), and Ingrid Bergman returned to Hollywood to win an Oscar for *Anastasia* (1956). However, the predominant US movie symbols of the 1950s remain Brando in leather astride a motorcycle in *The Wild One*, the boyish blond features of rebellious James Dean, and the wide eyes of pin-up idol Marilyn Monroe, who did not live much beyond the end of the decade. The ghosts of the 1950s are still there to haunt us.

"THE METHOD"

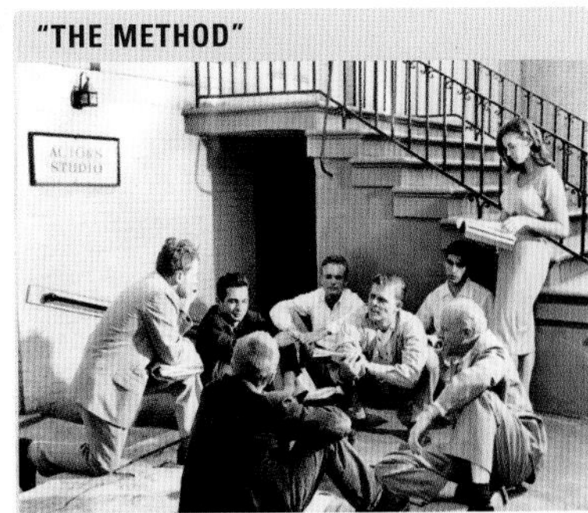

A "Method" session *takes place at the Actors' Studio; founded by Elia Kazan and Cheryl Crawford, its most famous teacher was Lee Strasberg.*

"The Method" was advanced by a group of actors and directors at the Actors Studio in New York in 1948. It was influenced by the teachings of the Russian stage director, Konstantin Stanislavsky, who stressed a more instinctive approach to acting than had been popular until that time. Marlon Brando (1924–2004) typified this style of acting. Many thought there was madness in "The Method" and it became the most caricatured of all acting styles with its mumbled delivery, shrugging of shoulders, fidgeting, and scratching. Humphrey Bogart commented, "I came out here with one shirt and everyone said I looked like a bum. Twenty years later Marlon Brando comes out with only a sweatshirt and the town drools over him. That shows how much Hollywood has progressed."

In From Here To Eternity *(1953), the fact that the hitherto ladylike Deborah Kerr played the adulterous army wife caught up in an affair with Burt Lancaster added to the frisson felt by audiences— especially evident during the celebrated erotic beach scene.*

1960–1969 The New Wave

Much was changing as the new decade dawned. America had a dynamic new leader, John F. Kennedy, and in Europe more liberated attitides to sex, fashion, and politics filtered into books, art, and movies. In the film world, the first rumblings of change came about in France with the New Wave, whose influence reached as far as Hollywood.

At the start of 1960, the Writers' Guild of America went on strike for more equitable contracts and a share of the profits of films sold to TV. The Screen Actors' Guild of America demanded a raise in minimum salaries and a share in TV residuals. Both the writers and the actors won their cases, victories that became a contributory factor in pushing Hollywood to the brink of economic disaster.

Due to various insecurities and financial difficulties the studios were quickly taken over by multi-national companies. Paramount was rescued by Gulf + Western Industries; Warner Bros. merged with Seven Arts Ltd, a TV company, to become Warner Bros.–Seven Arts; MGM shifted its interests to real estate; and MCA (the Music Corporation of America) acquired Universal-International Studios. The Bank of America absorbed United Artists through its Transamerica Corporation subsidiary. Even without huge overheads and star salaries, this studio continued to attract many leading independent producers and directors such as Stanley Kramer. He had his greatest ever success with *It's a Mad, Mad, Mad, Mad World* (1963) — a $10 million earner. United Artists also had directors Billy Wilder (*The Apartment*, 1960), Norman Jewison (*In the Heat of the Night*, 1967), John Sturges

Shirley MacLaine and Jack Lemmon *star in Billy Wilder's comedy* The Apartment *(1960), the last black-and-white film to win the Best Picture Oscar, until Steven Spielberg's* Schindler's List *(1993).*

BOX OFFICE HITS OF THE 1960s

1	US	One Hundred and One Dalmatians, 1961
2	US	Jungle Book, 1967
3	US	The Sound of Music, 1965
4	UK	Thunderball, 1965
5	US	Goldfinger, 1964
6	US	Doctor Zhivago, 1965
7	UK	You Only Live Twice, 1967
8	US	The Graduate, 1967
9	US	Butch Cassidy and the Sundance Kid, 1969
10	US	Mary Poppins, 1964

1960–1969

1960

1960
Alfred Hitchcock's *Psycho* terrifies audiences for the first time.

1961
West Side Story receives 11 Oscar nominations. In the event, it wins all but one.

1962

1962
Marilyn Monroe is found dead of a drug overdose at her home in Los Angeles.

1962
The first James Bond film, *Dr No*, is released.

1963
Sidney Poitier becomes the first black actor to win a Best Actor Oscar, for *Lilies of the Field.*

1963
The first video recorder is sold for $30,000.

1964

(*The Great Escape*, 1963), and Blake Edwards. The latter, with *The Pink Panther* (1963), initiated a slapstick comedy series starring Peter Sellers as the incompetent Inspector Clouseau.

On the whole, while the studios became administrative centres organizing finance and distribution, they were losing their individual stamp. To fill the gap, independent producers became more common to the movie-making package. They would come to the studio with a package consisting of director, script, writers, and marketable stars.

Although the structure of the industry had changed drastically, most of the pictures still followed the genre pattern initiated by the studios in their heyday. There were musicals: Robert Wise and Jerome Robbins' *West Side Story* (1961), George Cukor's *My Fair Lady* (1964)

The 1961 *screen version of the landmark Broadway musical* West Side Story *features finger-snapping, high-kicking street gangs.*

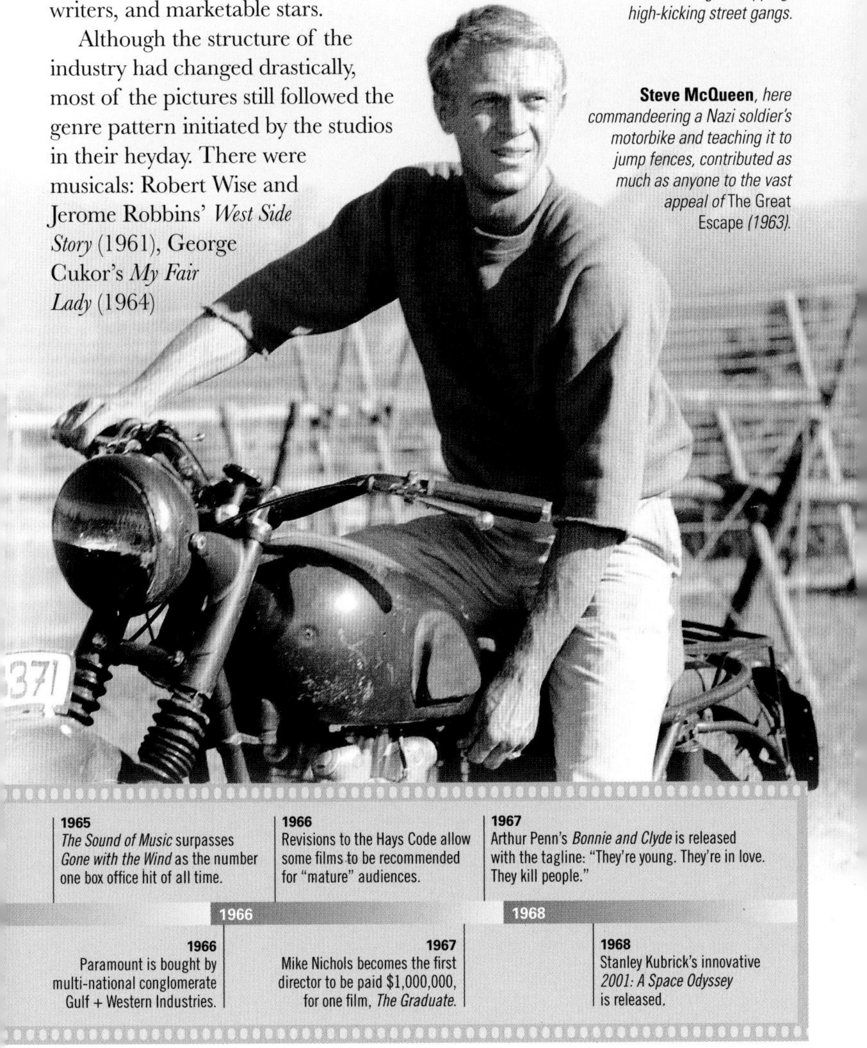

Steve McQueen, *here commandeering a Nazi soldier's motorbike and teaching it to jump fences, contributed as much as anyone to the vast appeal of* The Great Escape *(1963).*

1965
The Sound of Music surpasses *Gone with the Wind* as the number one box office hit of all time.

1966
Revisions to the Hays Code allow some films to be recommended for "mature" audiences.

1967
Arthur Penn's *Bonnie and Clyde* is released with the tagline: "They're young. They're in love. They kill people."

1966

1968

1966
Paramount is bought by multi-national conglomerate Gulf + Western Industries.

1967
Mike Nichols becomes the first director to be paid $1,000,000, for one film, *The Graduate*.

1968
Stanley Kubrick's innovative *2001: A Space Odyssey* is released.

Richard Burton (Marc Antony) *and Elizabeth Taylor (Cleopatra) caused a scandal with their highly publicized off-screen love affair during the making of* Cleopatra *(1962) as they were both married to other people at the time.*

and William Wyler's *Funny Girl* (1968), all derived from Broadway shows; Westerns, notably from veterans John Ford and Howard Hawks with *The Man Who Shot Liberty Valance* (1962) and *El Dorado* (1966) respectively, and newcomer Sam Peckinpah with *Ride the High Country* (1962), all of them valedictions to the Old West; and romantic comedies like the popular Doris Day—Rock Hudson cycle.

THE MOVIE-GOING HABIT

As movie-going had ceased to be a habit, each film had to attract its own audience, and extravagant advertising campaigns accompanied the many million-dollar spectacles that pushed their way onto the screens, among them Anthony Mann's *El Cid* (1961) and *The Fall of the Roman Empire* (1964); Nicholas Ray's *King of Kings* (1961) and *55 Days at Peking* (1963); and George Stevens' *The Greatest Story Ever Told* (1965). All of them were shot in Spain or Italy, further diminishing Hollywood as a production centre. Movies shot on location in Europe in the 1950s such as *Roman Holiday* were considered novel and were successful; these later features were not.

Cleopatra (1962), shot on location in Rome, nearly bankrupted 20th Century Fox. Starring Elizabeth Taylor, already the highest-paid performer in the history of Hollywood at $1 million, as the Queen of Egypt, and future husband Richard Burton as Marc Anthony, it cost a record $44 million. Fox then regained a fortune with Robert Wise's *The Sound of Music* (1965) and then lost it all again with Richard Fleisher's *Dr. Dolittle* (1967) and Wise's *Star!* (1968).

The concurrence of Fox's failure, and the success of more youth-oriented movies, proved to be a major turning point in Hollywood history. In the mid-1960s, Hollywood found itself with a new audience drawn mainly from the 16–24 age bracket. With different tastes from their elders,

MULTIPLEX CINEMAS

From the mid-1960s, the traditional picture palace with one auditorium was largely replaced by multiplex cinemas. These comprised a single utilitarian building divided into a number of cinemas and about six to eight screens (most of them smaller than the old auditoria). Ostensibly, this gives distributors a wider choice of outlets and audiences a wider choice of films and times. In the 1990s, many multiplexes grew into megaplexs with 20 or more screens, some screens showing the same presentations.

One of the Virgin Megaplex *cinemas in the UK boasts 20 screens and has seating capacity for up to 5,000 people.*

this younger generation expressed a growing aversion to traditional values. Hollywood needed to tap in to this new audience and its adult tastes. Instead of paying huge amounts to respected and experienced directors like Robert Wise and Richard Fleischer, it suddenly seemed reasonable to take a risk on younger, more experimental directors.

SEX AND VIOLENCE

With the demise of the Production Code in the US, the limits of language, topics, and behavior were considerably widened, almost enough to satisfy young audiences craving for sex and violence. Films started to depict violence in a more brutal and graphic manner, notably Robert Aldrich's *The Dirty Dozen* (1966), Arthur Penn's *Bonnie and Clyde* (1967), and Peckinpah's *The Wild Bunch* (1969).

Though it made no reference to civil rights or Vietnam, Mike Nichols' *The Graduate* (1967) was taken as a symbol of the counterculture of the time. The title character of Benjamin Braddock (played by Dustin Hoffman) had a great appeal among middle-class college kids and the use of Simon & Garfunkel songs such as *Mrs. Robinson* instead of an orchestral music score

Playing the title role *of* The Graduate *(1967), Dustin Hoffman is on the verge of being seduced by his parents' friend, Mrs. Robinson (Anne Bancroft). The film's frank treatment of sex appealed to young audiences.*

added to the film's attraction for young people. It also initiated the trend for pop-song soundtracks in the movies.

It was only after Hoffman came along that the names and faces of movie stars reflected more accurately the diversity of ethnic groups in America, opening up the floodgates for Barbra Streisand, Al Pacino, Elliott Gould, Robert De Niro, and Richard Dreyfuss.

"Their Credo is Violence... Their God is Hate..."

THE WILD ANGELS 1966

Roger Corman — who since 1953, had been making "Z movies" (films on a tiny budget and in rented studios) — formed American International. It produced *The Wild Angels* (1966), a low-budget biker picture, and *The Trip* (1967), the title referring to a psychedelic LSD "trip." Both films starred Peter Fonda (son of Henry, brother of Jane, and father of Bridget), who produced, cowrote and featured in *Easy Rider* (1969). This inexpensive bike movie, directed by Dennis Hopper, earned around $35 million.

ANGRY YOUNG MEN

In the late 1950s and early 1960s, there emerged in England a movement of playwrights, novelists, and film-makers who were labelled "Angry Young Men." Many of their works dealt honestly and vigorously with working-class life. As such, many contained an overt criticism of the "never had it so good" philosophy of the Conservative government of the day. Karel Reisz's *Saturday Night and Sunday Morning* (1960), Tony Richardson's *A Taste of Honey* (1961) and *The Loneliness of the Long Distance Runner* (1962), and Lindsay Anderson's *This Sporting Life* (1963) made important contributions to this movement.

In contrast to these grimey "kitchen sink" dramas, the "sparkle" of Swinging London was depicted in a whole series of films that showed trendy young people living it up in affluent surroundings. Actually, the phrase "Swinging London" originated from the New York TV columnist John Crosby, who had grown disenchanted with America and come to London in 1964 looking for a job. He wrote an article for *The Daily Telegraph*'s color supplement in which he used this phrase for the first time, describing London as being more "swinging" than New York.

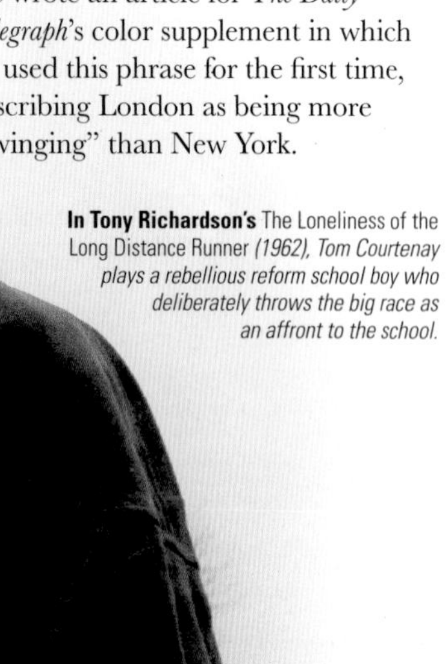

In Tony Richardson's The Loneliness of the Long Distance Runner *(1962), Tom Courtenay plays a rebellious reform school boy who deliberately throws the big race as an affront to the school.*

Sean Connery and *Ursula Andress starred in* Dr. No *(1962), a successful Bond recipe of sex, violence, and camp humor.*

Curiously, it was an adaptation of a classic 18th-century novel, Henry Fielding's *Tom Jones* (1963), directed by Tony Richardson and written by *Look Back in Anger* playwright, John Osborne, that triggered the vogue for "Swinging London" films. Their apotheosis was reached by Italian Michelangelo Antonioni's *Blow-Up* (1966), in which swinging London society is seen through foreign eyes.

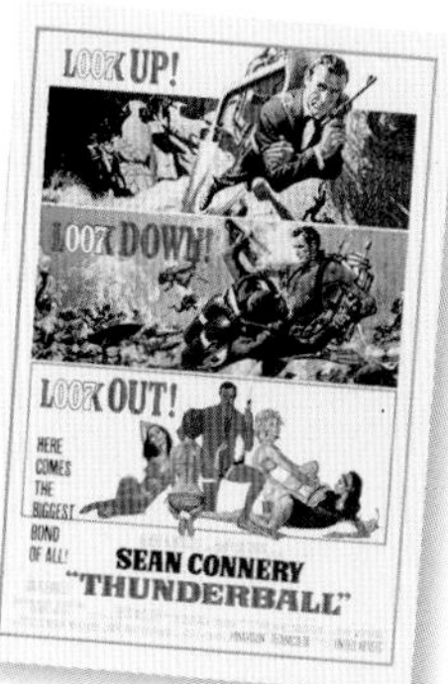

***Thunderball* film poster**

BOND AND SPAGHETTI

With the high cost of producing and making films in Hollywood and the shrinking of studio size, many studios reduced their internal production and increased movie-making outside the country, mostly in Britain (an economically advantageous production base), making big-budget films there.

For example, there was the creation of the most durable series in the history of cinema, the string of 007 James Bond movies. The first, *Dr. No* (1962), was made for less than $1 million. The Bond films got progressively more expensive as they took more at the box office. *Thunderball* (1965) became the sixth-highest earning movie of the decade from any source, pulling in nearly $26 million. The Bond producers with the gold fingers were US agronomist, Albert R. "Cubby" Broccoli, and Canadian-born Harry Saltzman. They set up Eon productions in England, from where all the Bond features have originated, although the film locations ranged far and wide.

It took three years before the Italian-made Western Sergio Leone's *A Fistful of Dollars* (1964) was picked up for distribution in the US in 1967, although it had been a hit in Italy. It started a whole spate of Spaghetti Westerns, and made Clint Eastwood, after small parts in ten movies, and seven years in TV's *Rawhide* series, an international superstar at the age of 37. The plot was taken from *Yojimbo* (1961), directed by Akira Kurosawa, whose *The Seven Samurai* (1954) was remade as *The Magnificent Seven* (1960) by John Sturges.

FRENCH NEW WAVE

Perhaps the main impetus for the change in the way films were made came with the New Wave in France.

"La Nouvelle Vague" managed to revitalize French cinema when it had been in danger of being totally ossified. Several young critics on the influential magazine *Cahiers du Cinéma* decided to take practical action in their battle against the staid content of French productions by making films themselves. The leading figures of the group were François Truffaut, Jean-Luc Godard, Alain Resnais, Claude Chabrol, Jacques Rivette, Eric Rohmer and Louis Malle.

The French New Wave directors turned their backs on conventional filming methods. They took to shooting in the streets with hand-held cameras and a very small team, using jump cuts, improvisation, deconstructed narratives, and quotes from literature and other films. The young directors, producers, and actors captured the life of early 1960s France — especially Paris — as it was lived by its young people.

Although the films represented a radical departure from traditional cinema, and were aimed at a young, intellectual audience, many of them achieved a measure of critical and financial success, gaining a wide audience both in France and abroad. Their methods and subject matter were taken up and adapted by young directors in other countries — especially the UK and Czechoslovakia — and eventually opened the way for the American indie movement.

Blow-Up (1966) was *director Michelangelo Antonioni's first international commercial success. In it, David Hemmings plays a fashion photographer.*

The film poster for A Fistful of Dollars *(1964), starring Clint Eastwood as the impassive, laconic, poncho-clad loner, constantly smoking a cheroot.*

In 1960 alone, some 18 directors had made their first features in France. At the same time, Italian cinema had its own new wave with Federico Fellini, Luchino Visconti, Pier Paolo Pasolini, Michelangelo Antonioni, and Bernardo Bertolucci. Winners at the 1960 Cannes film festival included Fellini's *La Dolce Vita* (1960), Kon Ichikawa's *Kagi* (1959), Antonioni's *L'Avventura* (1959), Ingmar Bergman's *The Virgin Spring* (1959), and Luis Buñuel's *The Young One* (1960), all of which were films that were not afraid to enter unchartered territory.

But towards the end of the decade the mood began to change. At the Cannes Film Festival in May 1968, as French workers went on strike and students in Paris were setting cars alight, digging up the paving stones on the Left Bank, and confronting the riot police, French cinema's ruling body adopted a motion demanding that the festival be cancelled as a sign of solidarity with the workers and students. "We refuse to be of service to a brutal capitalist society which we put in question," it stated. Protestors led by Louis Malle, François Truffaut, and Jean-Luc Godard prevented the showing of Carlos Saura's *Peppermint Frappé*, with the help of its director and star, Geraldine Chaplin. The jury resigned and the festival was aborted. Neither France nor French cinema would be the same again.

After 1968 the experimental elements of the French New Wave were already starting to become assimilated into mainstream cinema. Many of the technical and conceptual advances of the New Wave were transformed into the clichés of film-making. Truffaut incorporated more traditional elements in his films, while Godard became increasingly political and radical in his film-making. Chabrol continued to make genre thrillers of varying quality, and Rohmer pursued his own obsession with the behavior of young people.

CENSORSHIP

In the same year, 1968, the Russian invasion of Prague interrupted one of the most creative periods of film-making that part of the world had ever known. Rigid censorship was returned to Eastern Europe. In Poland, the purges that followed the student demonstrations in March 1968 hit the cinema harder than any other art or industry. Every aspect of cinema came under official attack.

In Latin America, political repression intensified and the most famous of Brazil's Cinema Novo directors, Glauber Rocha, went into exile in protest. In the US, the anti-Vietnam war protests grew. However, it took Hollywood almost ten years to address these issues.

Sami Frey, Anna Karina, *and Claude Brasseur, three petty crooks in Jean-Luc Godard's* Bande à Part *(1964), do a spontaneous synchronized dance in a café – a scene to which Quentin Tarantino paid homage in* Pulp Fiction *(1994).*

1970–1979 Independence Days

An estimated 43.5 million Americans visited cinemas each week in 1960, compared with only 15 million a decade later. However, when there were pictures that the public really wanted to see — blockbusters like *Star Wars* and *Jaws* — then cinema attendance shot up, and profits soared once again.

The result of this pattern was that certain films grossed a fortune, while many others barely recouped their costs. Escalating production expenses made film-making a risky business.

But Hollywood, as ever, recovered well, managing to pour out a stream of pictures that for richness, variety, and intelligence compared with the very best of the past. Francis Ford Coppola's success with *The Godfather* (1972) was seminal. Following in his footsteps were Martin Scorsese, Steven Spielberg, George Lucas, Michael Cimino, Brian De Palma, Peter Bogdanovich, Paul Schrader, John Milius, John Carpenter, and many others. These directors ushered in the New Hollywood.

Spectral pirates *on a ghost ship get ready to terrorize a coastal town in John Carpenter's chiller* The Fog *(1979).*

THE MOVIE BRATS

Many of these "movie brats," as they were dubbed, were graduates from film schools, a new phenomenon. Born in the 1940s, they had grown up with cinema and had a passion for the films of classical Hollywood. They had also studied, and were influenced by, the masters of foreign cinema. For example, Lucas's *Star Wars* (1977) was influenced by Akira Kurosawa's *The Hidden Fortress* (1958). The resemblance between the two buffoon farmers in *The Hidden Fortress* and the two talkative droids, C-3P0 and R2-D2, in *Star Wars* is apparent. Even the name Ben Obi-Wan Kenobi (played by Alec Guinness) is Japanese-sounding. Of course, such cinephilia had no effect on the film's immense popularity, and *Star Wars* succeeded in grossing more than $164 million in only two years in the USA. The merchandising of this film was also hugely lucrative. Both Spielberg's *Jaws* (1975) and *Star Wars* were the first films to earn more than $100 million in video rentals.

"Don't go in the water" *was a tagline of* Jaws *(1975), Steven Spielberg's incredibly successful horror-disaster film, which made beach-goers around the globe hesitate before plunging into the water.*

1970–1979

1970
CBS hold a demonstration of colour video-recording in New York.

1970
The IMAX wide-screen format premieres in Japan.

1971
The Beatles last film *Let It Be* released.

1971
Melvin Van Peebles' *Sweet Sweetback's Baad Asssss Song* kicks off the blaxploitation genre.

1972
Two years after *Airport*, the disaster movie trend continues with *The Poseidon Adventure*.

1973
The Exorcist, inspired by a true story about a girl possessed by a demon, shocks audiences.

1973
Universal turns down George Lucas's idea for *Star Wars* – and Fox picks it up.

1974
Roman Polanski's thriller *Chinatown*, starring Jack Nicholson, is a big hit.

1970 — 1972 — 1974

1975
Jaws is released and becomes a worldwide phenomenon.

1975
Robert Altman's *Nashville*, a complex, epic study of US culture, appears.

1976
Dolby stereo is used in films.

1976

1977
Close Encounters of the Third Kind released.

1977
Star Wars grosses almost $200 million on its first release, and receives 10 Oscar nominations.

1978
Woody Allen's 1977 film *Annie Hall* wins the Best Picture Oscar.

1978

1978
Marlon Brando is paid more than $3million, plus royalties, for a four-minute appearance in *Superman*.

1979
Miramax Films set up by brothers Bob and Harvey Weinstein.

It was Lucas's *American Graffiti* (1973) that spawned many "rites of passage" films. This dreamy, rock 'n' roll-driven vision of adolescent life in a small Californian town in 1962, before the Vietnam War and the drugs scene, cost $750,000 and made $55 million at the box office. It helped boost the careers of Harrison Ford, Richard Dreyfuss, and Ron (cast as Ronny) Howard. The film's success convinced producer Garry Marshall to reconsider a failed pilot for a TV series eventually called *Happy Days*, featuring 20-year-old Howard. Harrison Ford went on to establish himself as Han Solo in the *Star Wars* cycle. Dreyfuss' fame grew in two Spielberg blockbusters: as an ichthyologist somewhat out-acted by "Bruce," the shark machine in *Jaws,* and as the representative of ordinary mid-western manhood chosen by little green men to take off with them in their flying saucer in *Close Encounters of the Third Kind* (1977).

Woody Allen and Diane Keaton, *real-life lovers at the time, starred in* Manhattan *(1979), a sparkling romantic comedy in which Allen's heart is in every frame.*

Most of Spielberg's films were aimed primarily at teenagers, whereas the films of Woody Allen were directed at more mature audiences.

Annie Hall (1977), which won him the Best Picture and Best Director Academy Awards, was a breakthrough, capitalizing on the vogue for sexual anxiety and the tendency for self-examination — frequently on the analyst's couch.

ANGST AND MACHISMO

If Allen represented New York Jewish angst, Scorsese explored the close-knit Italian-American community with the underlying rigid and sentimental codes of masculinity, also evident in Coppola's *The Godfather*. As a result of these two Italian-American directors, Al Pacino and Robert De Niro became two of the key stars of the decade. Their

Close Encounters of the Third Kind *(1977) was the first of Steven Spielberg's science fiction movies, a favourite genre of the director.*

acting style was derived from their "Method" predecessors like Marlon Brando, whose character of Don Corleone, ironically, De Niro plays as a young man in *The Godfather II* (1975). Brando proved he was still a force to be reckoned with in the '70s in Bertolucci's *Last Tango in Paris* (1972), Coppola's *The Godfather*, and *Apocalypse Now* (1979).

Marlon Brando *plays the crazed Colonel Kurtz in Francis Coppola's* Apocalypse Now *(1979).*

The latter was one of a number of films on the Vietnam War. Hollywood had initially been reluctant to come to grips with the war, which had ended in 1975, probably because it was an issue

Dustin Hoffman and Robert Redford *play Washington Post investigative reporters in Alan J. Pakula's* All the President's Men *(1976).*

that divided the nation. In commercial terms, the subject was therefore bound to offend and alienate a large part of the potential audience. The film-making community split itself between the hawks like John Wayne, whose *The Green Berets* (1968) had been contrary to the zeitgeist, and doves such as Jane Fonda, who made her documentary *Vietnam Journey* (1974) on behalf of the anti-war movement.

THE VEXING ISSUE OF VIETNAM

Hollywood could no longer turn a blind eye to the war in Vietnam as a major subject. 1978 was the year when both Michael Cimino's *The Deer Hunter* and Hal Ashby's *Coming Home* appeared. Each reveals the scars, both physical and mental, left behind by the war and the extent to which US soldiers' experiences there had entered the national consciousness. At the Oscar ceremony of that year, Francis Ford Coppola presented Cimino with the Oscar for Best Director. *The Deer Hunter* also won Best Picture, while Jon Voight and Jane Fonda won Oscars for Best Actor and Best Actress respectively for *Coming Home*.

At the same ceremony, there was a poignant moment when the Old Hollywood made way for the New. John Wayne, who was fighting his last battle with cancer, presented Cimino with the Best Film award. Wayne got the biggest cheer of the evening as, gaunt with illness, he tottered up the Academy staircase and said, "Oscar first came to the Hollywood scene in 1928. So did I. We're both a little weatherbeaten but we're still here and plan to be around a whole lot longer." Wayne died a few months later.

Coming Home (1978) was instigated by its anti-Vietnam War star, Jane Fonda. The film tells of the love affair between a volunteer (Fonda) at a Vietnam veteran's hospital and an ex-soldier confined to a wheelchair by war injuries (Jon Voight).

The Vietnam War and the Watergate Scandal of 1974 fuelled

an American malaise which was reflected in a spate of so-called "conspiracy" movies that explored the nation's dark underside. The best of these were Alan J. Pakula's *The Parallax View* (1974), Sydney Pollack's *Three Days of the Condor* (1975), and *All the President's Men* (1976), all of which exposed government cover-ups. Coppola's *The Conversation* (1974) was a post-Watergate thriller about a professional eavesdropper (Gene Hackman) being bugged himself.

Warner Bros. *withdrew* Clockwork Orange *from UK distribution at Kubrick's request.*

VIOLENCE ON SCREEN

Vietnam was the first war to be consistently reported on television. It was one of the many reasons why violence in the movies would increase (race riots and campus unrest were two others). The moral ambiguity of Don Siegel's *Dirty Harry* (1971) — Clint Eastwood's first incarnation of the cold-blooded rogue cop Harry Callahan — John Boorman's *Deliverance* (1972), Scorsese's *Taxi Driver* (1976) and Tobe Hooper's *The Texas Chainsaw Massacre* (1974) worried many. Stanley Kubrick's *A Clockwork Orange* (1971), "being the adventures of a young man whose principal interests are rape, ultra-violence, and Beethoven" did nothing to alleviate these concerns.

The British Board of Film Classification passed the film with an X certificate, claiming that it was "...an important social document of outstanding brilliance and quality." But a group calling itself The Festival of Light found it "sickening and disgusting" and tried to stop it being shown. However, a spate of copycat violence, plus threats against Kubrick's own family, forced the director himself to request a UK ban. *A Clockwork Orange* was not seen again by British film-goers for another 27 years, until Kubrick's sudden death in 1999.

The dispute over *A Clockwork Orange* never reached the same pitch in the United States but, in 1973, for its

In Don Siegel's Dirty Harry *(1971), Clint Eastwood stars as Harry Callahan, a dedicated cop who has no time for the niceties of the law.*

American release, Kubrick cut about 30 seconds of footage to win an R rating. In 1968, the Motion Picture Producers and Distributors of America superseded the Production Code and incorporated a series of ratings for films. These included G for general audiences, M for mature audiences, R for ages 17 and over, and X for over-18s only. The rating system then had minor revisions in 1970, 1972, 1984, and 1990.

Brooke Shields and Susan Sarandon *feature in Louis Malle's* Pretty Baby *(1978), which captures the tragi-comic life of prostitutes in a brothel.*

SEX ON SCREEN

The market for mainstream films showing sex scenes expanded in the 1970s. There was also a more outspoken approach to sex in films which came to the US from abroad: *Last Tango in Paris* (1972), with its explicit sex scenes; *Emmanuelle* (1974) by Just Jaeckin, in which bored bourgeois wife Sylvia Kristel explores all the possibilities of sex; Pier Paulo Pasolini's *Salo* (1975), an updating of a Marquis de Sade novel; and Nagisa Oshima's *Ai No Corrida* (1976), featuring a gangster and a geisha acting out their sexual fantasies. *Pretty Baby* (1978), Louis Malle's first US film, featured a 12-year-old girl (Brooke Shields) being brought up in a turn-of-the-century New Orleans brothel. Public disquiet became vocal and there was again agitation for federal legislation on censorship. In Europe, Spain, Portugal, and the Communist countries there was some relaxation on censorship. Many of the technical and conceptual advances of the French, Italian, Czech, British, and other New Waves soon became assimilated into mainstream cinema. Rainer Werner Fassbinder, Werner Herzog, and Wim Wenders brought a brief New Wave to German cinema in the 1970s. There were a few other individuals who made an impact, such Andrei Tarkovsky and Sergei Paradjanov in the USSR and Andrzej Wajda and Krzysztof Kieslowski in Poland, but Eastern European cinema gradually lost its way. Milos Forman had fled Czechoslovakia in 1968, but his US career really took off with *One Flew Over the Cuckoo's Nest* (1975). Based on a cult novel of the '60s, it became the first film in 41 years (since *It Happened One Night*) to fly off with all five major Oscars, and raked in $56.5 million.

BOX OFFICE HITS OF THE 1970s		
1	US	Star Wars, 1977
2	US	Jaws, 1975
3	US	Grease, 1978
4	US	Close Encounters of the Third Kind, 1977
5	US	The Exorcist, 1973
6	US	Superman, 1978
7	US	Saturday Night Fever, 1977
8	US	Jaws 2, 1978
9	UK	Moonraker, 1979
10	UK	The Spy Who Loved Me, 1977

STALLONE AND TRAVOLTA

This sum was almost equalled by *Rocky* (1976), the archetypal rags-to-riches story of the decade. Producer Irwin Winkler recalled: "In comes this big lug who weighed 220 lb, didn't talk well, and acted slightly punch drunk. He said he had an idea for a boxing script and wanted to star in it." The "lug" was Sylvester Stallone.

Jack Nicholson *cheers up his fellow inmates in a state mental hospital in Milos Forman's* One Flew Over the Cuckoo's Nest *(1975).*

It is by now Hollywood folklore how Stallone, with only $106 in his bank account and three bad movies to his debit, turned down a one-off payment of $265,000 and instead secured $70,000, a percentage of the profits, and the lead role. *Rocky* became a box-office hit and won Oscars for Best Picture (the first sports film to do so), and Best Director (John G. Avildsen).

Another of the crop of Italian-Americans who made it big in the 1970s was John Travolta, who gave male dancing the on-screen kiss of life in *Saturday Night Fever* (1977), at the height of the disco craze.

One of the most significant developments of the decade was when Sony brought out the home video-cassette recorder in 1975; it cost around $2,000 and had a recording time of up to one hour. Its future impact on viewing habits could hardly be imagined at the time.

In Saturday Night Fever *(1977), John Travolta showed the acrobatic exuberance of Gene Kelly, and a strut reminiscent of Fred Astaire — but his riveting dancing was all his own.*

1980–1989 The International Years

In the 1980s, the Hollywood machine reasserted itself. The movie brats lost their way as the studios consolidated everything they had learned from the *Star Wars* phenomenon, marshalling the power of TV advertising to sell high-concept movie packages, pushing up the cost of marketing, and raising the stakes across the board.

Martin Scorsese began the 1980s with *Raging Bull* (1980) and the '90s with *GoodFellas* (1990). But Scorsese's high-caliber output was the exception — and even he talked about giving up the fight in the 1980s. The 1970s "Hollywood Renaissance" proved to be a flash in the pan. The power enjoyed by the movie brats reached its apogee with the epic western *Heaven's Gate* (1980), directed by Michael Cimino with such perfectionism that the budget rocketed 500 per cent to about $44 million. Modest by today's standards, these figures were enough to bring United Artists to the brink of bankruptcy.

In Raging Bull *(1984), Robert De Niro gained 60 lb to play boxer Jake LaMotta in middle age; his reward was one of the film's disappointing haul of just two Oscars.*

Slow and anti-heroic, this was perhaps the most radical of all the revisionist westerns but, when the film was previewed at a running time of 219 minutes, the American critics were merciless. The studio panicked, and *Heaven's Gate* was cut to 149 minutes — a desecration comparable to the treatment RKO had meted out to Orson Welles' *The Magnificent Ambersons* (1942) four decades earlier. The shorter cut did nothing to salvage the film's commercial prospects. It grossed only $1.5 million. United Artists' illustrious name was history. The studio was sold in 1981, merging with another fallen giant, MGM.

Heaven's Gate effectively finished off the western for at least a decade. (The next significant contributions to the genre would be TV's *Lonesome Dove* in 1989 and Kevin Costner's *Dances with Wolves* in 1990.) More than that, it became a watchword for unchecked

1980–1989

1980 Alfred Hitchcock, master of suspense, dies age 80.

1980 Sherry Lansing becomes the first female president of a major studio (20th Century Fox).

1981 Ronald Reagan becomes the first movie-star president.

1981 Katharine Hepburn wins her fourth Best Actress Oscar for *On Golden Pond.*

1981 *Raiders of the Lost Ark* marks the first collaboration betwen Steven Spielberg and George Lucas.

1982 Ridley Scott's *Blade Runner* opens.

1982 Princess Grace of Monaco, formerly actress Grace Kelly (*High Noon, Rear Window)* dies in a car crash.

1984 The US Supreme Court rules that home videotaping does not violate copyright laws.

1980 · 1982 · 1984

directorial megalomania — a widespread condition in the late 1970s and early '80s (the subject of Peter Biskind's well-sourced history of the period, *Easy Riders, Raging Bulls*).

Francis Ford Coppola had got away with his vastly over-budget *Apocalypse Now*, but his bold dreams of a film-makers' studio, Zoetrope, foundered on *One from the Heart* (1982), an innovative but expensive exercise in digital cinema that didn't connect with critics or audiences. Its failure plunged him into debt and pulled the plug on a studio that at one point housed such eclectic talents as Jean-Luc Godard, Wim Wenders, Gene Kelly, Michael Powell, and Tom Waits.

Such spectacular failures curtailed artistic ambition in American cinema. When a film of real daring did come along, Hollywood seemed bent on suppressing it. Sergio Leone's magnificent gangster opus *Once Upon a Time in America* (1984) was hacked back from 229 minutes to 139 for its US release, in spite of the fact that the film performed well in Europe. Universal sat on Terry Gilliam's *Brazil* (1985) for a year, preparing their own edit, before the film-maker shamed them into releasing his cut. The motto RKO had

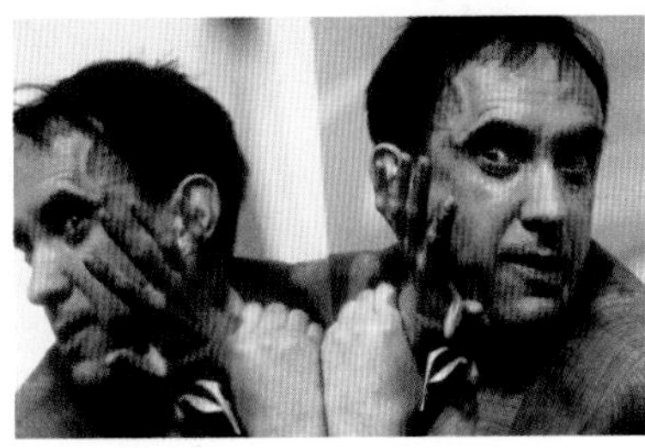

Jonathan Pryce *plays day-dreaming bureaucrat Sam Lowry pursuing his ideal woman in the weird, totalitarian future of Terry Gilliam's* Brazil *(1985).*

Sergio Leone's *gangster epic* Once Upon a Time in America *(1984) was a violent requiem for the immigrant's dream. It was Leone's last film.*

1985 The first Blockbuster video store opens in Dallas, Texas.

1986 Film star Rock Hudson dies of AIDS and the epidemic begins to be acknowledged.

1986 Media mogul Ted Turner buys MGM's film library and begins "colourizing" its black and white films.

1987 The first Disney tie-in with McDonalds: a Happy Meals toy based on *Duck Tales.*

1988 Video sales of *E.T. The Extra-Terrestrial* exceed 15 million.

1988 Martin Scorsese's *The Last Temptation of Christ* is released despite objections by some Christians.

1989 Warner Communications merges with Time, Inc to become the biggest media company in the world.

adopted after ridding themselves of Orson Welles in the 1940s applied across the board in the 1980s: "Showmanship, not genius."

If the balance of power shifted definitively away from the directors (and the big directors' vanity and self-indulgence didn't help their cause), the studios themselves were in a state of flux. Increasing competition from independent production companies like Cannon, DEG, Orion, and Tri-Star had, by 1986, knocked the major studios' share of the US box office to a low of 64 percent.

Increasingly, the real power fell to the talent agencies. The largest was Creative Artists Agency (CAA), which represented numerous A-list stars, writers, and directors. They began to pitch studios pre-packaged deals: scripts with their clients already attached. CAA president, Michael Ovitz, became the most feared and courted man in Hollywood, and star salaries rose steeply, pushing up the average cost of a movie even as admissions continued to flatline. For the agents, the deal was the be-all and end-all.

It's not that there weren't box-office hits. Steven Spielberg's *Raiders of the Lost Ark* (1981) and *E.T. The Extra-Terrestrial* (1982) consolidated his reputation as the man with the Midas touch. As the decade progressed, Hollywood channeled more and more of its resources into supporting

In the 1980s, *popcorn entertainment came back into style. Steven Spielberg's* Indiana Jones and the Temple of Doom *(1984) epitomized the return to mainstream blockbusters.*

BOX OFFICE HITS OF THE 1980s		
1	US	E.T. The Extra-Terrestrial, 1982
2	US	Return of the Jedi, 1983
3	US	The Empire Strikes Back, 1980
4	US	Indiana Jones and the Last Crusade, 1989
5	US	Rain Man, 1988
6	US	Raiders of the Lost Ark, 1981
7	US	Batman, 1989
8	US	Back to the Future, 1985
9	US	Who Framed Roger Rabbit 1988
10	US	Top Gun, 1986

blockbuster "event" movies, generally released on public holiday weekends with saturation marketing campaigns. These, in turn, aggravated inflationary pressures across the business.

The rewards were phenomenal, not only in box office terms, but also in ancillary merchandising deals. But in this model there was less and less room for the adult dramas that had always been Hollywood's mainstay. Teenagers became the prime audience — the 12–20 age group constituted 48 percent of box-office in 1980.

Sylvester Stallone's *John Rambo went from underdog in* First Blood *(1982) to killing machine in the eponymous sequels.*

Slasher horror movies and risqué adolescent comedies were the new staples: *Friday the 13th* (1980) would spawn more than a dozen sequels stretching into the new millennium; *Porky's* (1982) would beget innumerable imitators.

While established stars like Robert Redford and Clint Eastwood continued to write their own ticket, the teen audience fostered its own stars. The "Brat Pack" included Molly Ringwald, Rob Lowe, Emilio Estevez, Charlie Sheen, and Andrew McCarthy. Some other actors of the 1980s, such as Tom Cruise, Demi Moore, Matt Dillon, and John Cusack, have since enjoyed long film careers, while some were not so fortunate.

BIRTH OF THE ACTION HERO

Reports of video-savvy audiences ("tape-heads") shouting "Fast forward" at the screen may have been apocryphal, but it's arguably true that the 1980s refined the movie with action sequences into a new genre: the action film. In 1982 it was still possible for Sylvester Stallone to star in a passably serious, if formulaic, thriller about a Vietnam war veteran failing to adapt to life back home (*First Blood*). But three years later, by the time of *Rambo: First Blood, Part II* (1985), the character had been transformed into an invulnerable one-man army, and any vestiges of realism had been obliterated. By *Rambo III* (1988) he was battling the Soviets in Afghanistan — and Stallone was earning $20 million for the picture. The same trajectory is obvious in Stallone's *Rocky* films. A credible underdog in the first movie, he became a pumped-up American champ in the later sequels, a warrior wrapped up in the patriotism of Ronald Reagan's presidency.

Even then, another action star was poised to outgun Stallone. Former bodybuilder Arnold Schwarzenegger, probably the most iconic star of the era, had been hanging around Hollywood since the early 1970s. With his thick Austrian accent, negligible acting ability, and a physique memorably described by journalist Clive James as "like a walnut wearing a condom," he was an unlikely superstar. John Milius cast him as *Conan the Barbarian* (1982), and he then played a taciturn robot assassin in James Cameron's *The Terminator* (1984). Even though the character was the villain — literally a killing machine — audiences adored the film, and Schwarzenegger was made.

With the exception of Sigourney Weaver in *Alien* (1979) and *Aliens* (1986), women in action films of this era are usually relegated to supporting bit roles. These films are characterized by bombast and machismo — explosions, fusillades of bullets, fireballs, and car chases, all as

Tom Cruise attracts *Kelly McGillis in* Top Gun *(1986), a typical high-velocity movie from US über-producers Jerry Bruckheimer and Don Simpson.*

destructive as demolition derbies. The genre was aimed primarily at young men, and translated well into the increasingly important overseas markets — not least because the films had very little meaningful dialogue. The best action films have an exhilarating cinematic dynamic: Paul Verhoeven's *Robocop* (1987), John McTiernan's *Die Hard* (1988), and James Cameron's *Terminator* films (1984 and 1991) are as accomplished as slapstick comedies of the 1920s or musicals from the 1950s. Directors had always shot action sequences from multiple angles and, as action sequences became longer and more elaborate, this aesthetic infected Hollywood's visual language. Shot durations shrank, and visual continuity was handled by back-lighting and design. The aesthetic was often attributed to the influence of MTV. Music television's non-stop diet of pop promos, with their rapid-fire backbeat montage, became popular with the spread of cable television in the early 1980s, and music promo directors sometimes graduated to feature films. More came from advertising, with their visual skills honed in 30-second segments. The Britons Ridley and Tony Scott, Adrian Lyne, Hugh

"You have twenty seconds to comply."

ROBOCOP 1987

THE VIDEO REVOLUTION

In 1982, MPAA industry spokesman Jack Valenti told a US Senate committee that "the VCR is to the American film producer and the American public as the Boston strangler is to the woman home alone." Valenti's concerns about copyright infringement devastating the Hollywood industry were misplaced.

VHS beat out Betamax in the videotape wars, in large part because it courted Hollywood. And the video rental market proved to be manna for film producers.

Video stores flourished, granting audiences unparalleled control over what they watched and how: rewind, replay, and fast forward buttons were the first step toward viewer interactivity.

A by-product of the success of video was that cinemas shrank, as single-screen venues were halved and quartered to allow for more flexible programing. Across the US, drive-in theaters closed (more than 1000 in the 1980s) and were replaced with ever more multiplexes housed in suburban malls. A whole sector of films would henceforth find their audience at home, on video, instead of on the big screen.

Hudson, and Alan Parker all came up through advertising. Between them Tony Scott and Adrian Lyne directed *Top Gun* (1986), *Beverly Hills Cop 2* (1987), *Flashdance* (1983), *9½ Weeks* (1986), and *Fatal Attraction* (1987), some of the biggest hits of the decade. These were quintessential "high concept" movies: films that could be pitched and sold in 30 words or less.

OUTSIDE HOLLYWOOD

There was a related fashion in France, where Jean-Jacques Beineix pioneered what critic Serge Daney dubbed "le cinéma du look" with the flamboyant *Diva* (1981) and *Betty Blue* (1986). Luc Besson (*Subway*, 1985) and former critic Leos Carax (*Boy Meets Girl*, 1984) represented the extremes of the style, the first a resolute populist, the second a confrontational intellectual. Aging practitioners of the "nouvelle vague" continued to work: Jean-Luc Godard returned to cinema after a flirtation with video, as did Maurice Pialat, whose intense emotional authenticity inspired a generation of 1990s film-makers. But in 1981 French cinema was rocked by the suicide of director Jean Eustache. The New German Cinema was, likewise, knocked off course by the death, in 1982, of its most prolific talent, Rainer Werner Fassbinder, aged just 36. Wim Wenders had a tough Hollywood initiation with *Hammett* (1982), but recovered with *Paris, Texas* (1984). He returned to Berlin for *Wings of Desire* (1987). Some of the best international cinema of this time came from further east: from China's Fifth Generation film-makers (Chen Kaige and his erstwhile cameraman Zhang Yimou); from Hong Kong (where Tsui Hark, John Woo, and Stanley Kwan were making their names); and especially from Taiwan, where Hou Hsaio-hsien and Edward Yang were constructing a cinematic identity reflecting Taiwan's own complex self-image. Hou's films were the antithesis of Hollywood's faster, faster approach. Languorous meditations on the recent past, they were often composed of scenes filmed in a single, unobtrusive master shot.

Designer cinema *even prevailed in France, where films like Jean-Jacques Beineix's* Betty Blue *(1986) privileged style over content.*

1990– Celluloid to Digital

After a century of celluloid, a radical technological shift began to take effect in the 1990s with the advent of digital film-making. While the studios increasingly concentrated their resources on blockbusters like *Titanic*, the independents made intelligent, adult drama and reached wider audiences than ever before with movies like *Pulp Fiction*.

One hundred years after Pierre and Auguste Lumière screened their first one-reelers in Paris, 40 of the world's leading film-makers took up the challenge of making a film using the original cinematographe camera to create a silent, monochrome movie with no cuts, in natural light, and lasting no more than 52 seconds.

Lumière and Company (1996) showed both how much and how little cinema had changed over the course of its short history. For all the innovations of sound and color, the various refinements of film stock and size, in essence, the technology remained the same: strips of celluloid pulled through a shutter to be exposed to light for a fraction of a second.

By the dawn of the 21st century, that technology was superseded with the transition from analogue to digital systems. The cutters were the first to switch, moving from moviolas to computers. This shift was partly necessitated by the increasingly frenetic montage techniques popularized by film-makers such as Martin Scorsese in films like *GoodFellas* (1990), and his one-time pupil Oliver Stone in *JFK* (1991) and *Natural Born Killers* (1994). The first 35mm feature with a digital soundtrack was *Dick Tracy* (1990).

Tom Hanks' *Forrest Gump crosses paths with JFK, President Nixon, and Elvis Presley through the magic of CGI.*

The groundbreaking animation *Toy Story* (1995) was the first feature film made entirely on computer, but *Jurassic Park* (1993) and *Forrest Gump* (1994) had already integrated computer-generated imagery (CGI) into live action films. This technique opened up new avenues for the later spectacular historical epics — *Titanic* (1997) and *Gladiator* (2000) — and fantasy films such as the *Lord of the Rings* trilogy (2001–03) and the *Harry Potter* series (2001–). These movies dominated the box office, ringing up billion-dollar receipts worldwide.

1990–2006

1990 | 1993 | 1996

1990
Macaulay Culkin becomes a child star in *Home Alone.*

1990
Cyrano de Bergerac, starring Gérard Depardieu, wins a record ten César Awards.

1993
Disney buys Miramax Films for $80 million, considered a bargain price.

1993
Actor Brandon Lee (son of Bruce) is killed by a faulty prop gun during filming of *The Crow* (1994).

1994
The first new major studio in more than 50 years, Dreamworks SKG, is announced by Steven Spielberg, Jeffrey Katzenberg, and David Geffen.

1994
Spielberg's 1993 film about the Holocaust, *Schindler's List*, wins seven Oscars.

The more gradual transition to digital cameras was anticipated by a new generation of improved, lightweight video cameras. Although they could not match the aesthetic quality of film, video cameras had one key advantage: they were much cheaper to use.

DIGITAL FILM-MAKING

Shrewd low-budget film-makers in the early 1990s capitalized on the digital camera's limitations and a fashion for extreme handheld cinema-verité style camerawork set by Woody Allen's *Husbands and Wives* (1992), Mathieu Kassovitz's *La Haine* (1995), and Lars

Going against the grain of the CGI spectacular, The Shawshank Redemption *(1994) was a slow-paced, old-fashioned prison drama that could have been made any time in the last 30 years. Significantly, it was only a minor hit on theatrical release, but became an all-time favourite when audiences saw it on video and DVD.*

1997
The most expensive film ever, *Titanic*, also becomes the highest grossing.

1998
Saving Private Ryan wins Steven Spielberg his second Best Director Oscar.

1999
The first of three prequels, *Star Wars: Episode I – The Phantom Menace*, makes $100 million in a record five days.

2000
Crouching Tiger, Hidden Dragon is the first Asian action film to find US commercial and critical success.

2001
The final episode of Peter Jackson's critically acclaimed *Lord of the Rings* trilogy released.

2002
Halle Berry is the first black actress to win Best Actress Oscar. African-American actor Denzel Washington also wins Best Actor.

2003
Arnold Schwarzenegger becomes Governor of California

By shooting in black and white, *the talented young French director Mathieu Kassovitz gave his angry youth movie* La Haine *a patina of realism. The film graphically illustrates the racial divisions that would erupt across France ten years later.*

von Trier's *Breaking the Waves* (1996), as well as TV shows like *NYPD Blue*. In this idiom, poor image quality translated as gritty realism. No film exemplified this better than *The Blair Witch Project* (1999). It purported to be discovered footage shot on camcorder and 16mm film by a student research team who got lost in the woods and disappeared while investigating a local legend. This simple scenario was augmented by an elaborate internet campaign fostering the notion the film was, in fact, a documentary. *The Blair Witch Project* cost approximately $35,000 and made a staggering $248 million worldwide. A sequel followed two years later, but it was a flop.

The Coen brothers' comic thriller Fargo *(1996) stars William H. Macy in a biting moral fable set in a wintery US midwest.*

DOGME 95

With developments encouraging more elaborate fantasies and facilitating back-to-basics realism, four Danish directors seized the moment to announce the Dogme 95 Manifesto. "Today a technological storm is

raging, the result of which will be the ultimate democratization of the cinema," they claimed. "For the first time, anyone can make movies..." They went on to stress the importance of the avant-garde and denounce the superficial, cosmetic aspects of the Hollywood mainstream.

Emily Watson *gives a bravura performance as a giddy modern-day saint in Lars von Trier's vertiginous* Breaking the Waves *(1996).*

Signed by the controversial director Lars von Trier, the document concluded with ten "Vows of Chastity" designed to return cinema to its roots in realism: film-makers pledged to shoot on actual locations, using only the props that belonged there; to avoid period and genre films; to dispense with optical effects and "superficial action; "to use a handheld camera; and no postrecorded music.

Contentious and at least partly tongue in cheek, the Dogme 95 movement nevertheless struck a chord. Thomas Vinterberg's *Festen* (*The Celebration*) was the first film to be released under the banner in 1998, and won the Jury Prize at Cannes. Like von Trier's *The Idiots*, released the same year, and contrary to the vows' diktats, it was shot on video.

THE INDEPENDENTS

By 2005 there would be over 50 official Dogme films, but that was just a drop in the ocean compared to the booming American independent film scene.

James Cameron's Titanic *(1997) cost $200 million to make and, despite rocky reviews, became the first film to gross over one billion dollars. It ensured mainstream stardom for Leonardo DiCaprio and Kate Winslet.*

The Usual Suspects *(1995) was a lower-budget independent movie that was a box office hit. The stylized, edgy thriller had powerful performances from the "line-up" of hoodlums, and a plot that twisted and turned.*

As soon as the technology became available, Digital Video (DV) cameras made an immediate impact — in the year 2000, twice as many independent features were made as in the preceding year.

Among the first major film-makers to go digital were Mike Figgis, who ran four cameras concurrently and quartered the screen in the real time drama *Timecode* (2000). Spike Lee used digital technology for his close-to-home racial satire *Bamboozled* (2000), while Eric Rohmer recreated Revolutionary France by using digital paintings as backdrops in *The Lady and the Duke* (2001). Zacharias Kunuk's digital *Atanarjuat: The Fast Runner* (2001) was the first native Inuit feature, and Michael Mann mixed digital and celluloid in *Ali* (2001). Mann went on to exploit digital's superior night vision for *Collateral* (2004). Meanwhile, artist David Fincher, who had started out in a special effects production company, showed how seamlessly CGI could be integrated into traditional film drama in the anarchic *Fight Club* (1999).

David Fincher marked the millennium *with the subversive black comedy* Fight Club *(1999), starring Brad Pitt and Edward Norton. Critics recoiled from the film but it became a cult hit on DVD.*

The indie boom had started in the 1980s, partly due to the proliferation of film festivals like Sundance, and perhaps because Hollywood films had become conservative and formulaic, and so removed from the realities of American life.

A piecemeal movement sprang up around role models John Sayles (social conscience liberalism) who made *Silver City* (2004), *Casa de los Babys* (2003), and *Sunshine State* (2002), and Jim Jarmusch (minimalist cool) director of films including *Coffee and Cigarettes* (2003), *Ghost Dog: The Way of the Samurai* (1999), and *Mystery Train* (1989).

Primarily centred on the US east coast, the 1980s independents produced breakthrough films about African-Americans (Spike Lee's *She's Gotta Have It*, 1986), gays and lesbians (Sayles' *Lianna*, 1983, and Gus Van Sant's *Mala Noche*, 1988), and about women (Susan Seidelman's *Desperately Seeking Susan*, 1985). These films found critical support and developed their own art-house

Octogenarian Eric Rohmer *embraced the latest technology to fashion* The Lady and the Duke *(2001), a portrait of Revolutionary France that resembled a painting brought to life.*

DVDs

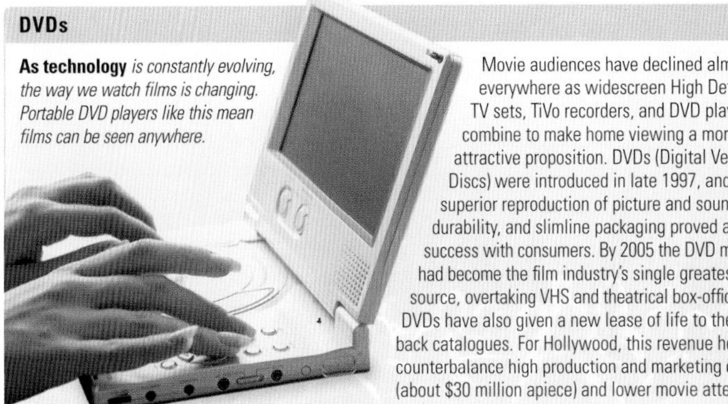

As technology *is constantly evolving, the way we watch films is changing. Portable DVD players like this mean films can be seen anywhere.*

Movie audiences have declined almost everywhere as widescreen High Definition TV sets, TiVo recorders, and DVD players combine to make home viewing a more attractive proposition. DVDs (Digital Versatile Discs) were introduced in late 1997, and their superior reproduction of picture and sound, durability, and slimline packaging proved a runaway success with consumers. By 2005 the DVD market had become the film industry's single greatest revenue source, overtaking VHS and theatrical box-office. DVDs have also given a new lease of life to the studios' back catalogues. For Hollywood, this revenue helps to counterbalance high production and marketing costs (about $30 million apiece) and lower movie attendance.

audience. Steven Soderbergh's *sex, lies and videotape* (1989) was a landmark, making $24.7 million in the US, and another $30 million internationally. It was the biggest hit to date for New York "speciality" distribution company, Miramax, and the first American indie to break out of the art-house circuit and into the multiplexes.

Soderbergh immediately landed a studio contract and would become one of the most successful directors of the era, nabbing two Oscar nominations in the same year for *Erin Brockovich* and *Traffic* in 2000. He was not alone in embracing the mainstream for most, "independence" was a transitional station on the way to a Hollywood career. Jim Jarmusch was an exception, finding funding out of Japan that allowed him to retain copyright to his cool bohemian doodles. Hal Hartley was another who preferred to work cheaply without watering down his deadpan neo-Godardian comedies, such as *Flirt* (1995) and *Henry Fool* (1997). Soderbergh himself stepped out of the Hollywood mainstream on occasion to recharge his creative batteries with avant-garde experiments like *Schizopolis* (1996). And Gus Van Sant went from the art house (*My Own Private Idaho*, 1991) to the multiplex (*Good Will Hunting*, 1997) and back again (*Elephant*, 2003). But most found they could co-exist with the studios — in general, this was not an era of confrontational political film-making or challenging formal innovation.

THE NEW INDIES

Quite a few of the talented young film-makers who emerged from the indie sector contented themselves with working clever, ironic variations on classical Hollywood genres.

After two Hollywood flops, Alfonso Cuarón *put his career back on track by returning to his native Mexico to make the earthy sex comedy* Y Tu Mamá También *(2001).*

Joel and Ethan Coen, for example, invested some ethical complexity in a series of stylish pastiches on the worlds of James M. Cain, Dashiell Hammett, Raymond Chandler, Clifford Odets, and Preston Sturges.

QUENTIN TARANTINO

Cult heroes the Coens were rudely trumped when Quentin Tarantino unleashed his more visceral brand of souped-up cinephilia with *Reservoir Dogs* in 1992. Born in 1963, Tarantino had grown up in the video age. In fact, he worked as a clerk in a video store before Harvey Keitel showed interest in his script about an undercover cop infiltrating a gang of jewel thieves. A magpie talent, Tarantino's influences were legion: Hong Kong thrillers (*Reservoir Dogs* borrowed from a Ringo Lam thriller, *City on Fire*, 1987); Jean-Luc Godard; Jean-Pierre Melville; Stanley Kubrick; and Sam Fuller.

In synthesizing them, Tarantino also forged something new and arresting: a pop post-modernism that spoke for the young people novelist Douglas Coupland called "Generation X" and film-maker Richard Linklater dubbed "Slackers". Non-conformists but avid consumers, this generation was media-savvy, ironic about relationships, cynical about politics, but inclined toward liberal multi-culturalism.

Tarantino's second film, *Pulp Fiction* (1994) rocked Hollywood with its audacious approach to narrative structure, outrageously casual violence, and flip, funny dialogue. Produced by Miramax, it became the first "indie" movie to break $100 million at the US box office. To the dismay of the old guard, it even walked away with the Palme d'Or at Cannes, depriving Polish auteur Krzysztof Kieslowski

BOX OFFICE HITS OF THE 1990s–2000s

1	US	Titanic, 1997
2	US	The Lord of the Rings: The Return of the King, 2003
3	US	Harry Potter and the Philosopher's Stone, 2001
4	US	Star Wars: Episode 1 – The Phantom Menace, 1999
5	US	The Lord of the Rings: The Two Towers, 2002
6	US	Jurassic Park, 1993
7	US	Harry Potter and the Goblet of Fire, 2005
8	US	Shrek 2, 2004
9	US	Harry Potter and the Chamber of Secrets, 2002
10	US	Finding Nemo, 2003

of a third straight festival triumph for his *Three Colours* trilogy.

Tarantino's success — and the disproportionate influence it bestowed on Miramax — has been criticised for "mainstreaming" art-house and independent film. Conversely, he could be credited for pushing the borders of the commercial film, breaking ground for the wider acceptance of independent-minded artists like Richard Linklater, Paul Thomas Anderson, David O. Russell, Spike Jonze, and Sofia Coppola, who became the first American woman to earn an Oscar nomination for Best Director with *Lost in Translation* (2003). Tarantino was the most important American film-maker of the 1990s.

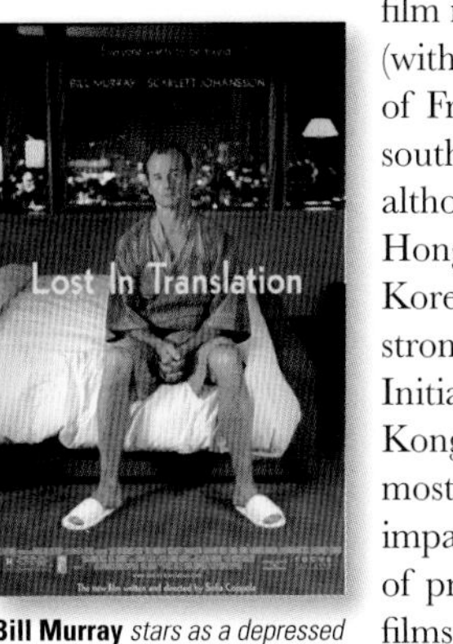

Bill Murray *stars as a depressed movie star, Bob Harris, in Tokyo in* Lost in Translation *(2003).*

WORLD CINEMA

Beyond US borders, Hollywood continued to exert a strong grip on film markets in Europe (with the partial exception of France), Asia, and the southern hemisphere, although India, China, Hong Kong, and South Korea all maintained strong local industries. Initially it was Hong Kong that made the most international impact, with a series of prestigious art house films from Wong Kar-Wai (*Chungking Express*, 1994) and a cycle of stylish, souped-up urban crime thrillers like John Woo's *A Better Tomorrow* (1986),

Working stylish variations on the classic cops *and robbers formula, Hong Kong thriller* Infernal Affairs *(2002) was a smash hit at home and abroad. Two equally inventive sequels followed soon after.*

The popularity of J.K. Rowling's *Harry Potter books translated into mega box office for Warner Bros. The recipe was fidelity to the source, expert British character acting, and — the magic ingredient — dazzling CGI*

Ringo Lam's *Full Contact* (1993), and Wai Keung Lau and Siu Fai Mak's *Infernal Affairs* (2002). Woo and Lam both went on to Hollywood careers, while Martin Scorsese directed Leonardo DiCaprio in a remake of *Infernal Affairs* (*The Departed*, 2006).

Hollywood continues to draw fresh blood from the thriving Asian horror market, remaking Japanese hits, such as *Ring* (1998) and *The Grudge* (2003), and enticing their directors — Hideo Nakata and Takasha Shimizu respectively — to America.

Elsewhere, Mexico produced the thrilling *Amores Perros* (2000) and *Y Tu Mamá También* (2001), and Brazil came up with the incendiary *favela* story *City of God* (2002, *see page 490*). Isolated from American culture, Iran produced a refracted, poetic take on neo-realism through film-makers like Mohsen Makmalbaf, Jafar Panahi and the minimalist master Abbas Kiarostami (A *Taste of Cherry*, 1997).

Lacking a strong home market for genre films, and failing to compete with Hollywood production values, European cinema seems largely irrelevant to most audiences most of the time. Aside from a few art-house stalwarts like Pedro Almodóvar (*All About My Mother*, 1999), Michael Haneke (*Caché*, 2005), and Lars von Trier (*Dogville*, 2003), there is no guarantee of widespread international distribution beyond the film festival circuit and DVD.

DIGITAL DOWNLOADS

Today the industry is just beginning to face up to its next great challenge: the internet. Digital downloads of feature films and streamed video-on-demand are becoming a reality, raising the spectres of widespread piracy and the collapse of theatrical exhibition. Yet Hollywood has survived such scares before, adapting to new technologies and ultimately profiting from them.

The worldwide web holds out promises too: a video jukebox with an infinite range of choice, virtually no delivery costs, and an audience that would have been unimaginable at any time before in the art form's history.

Crash (2005) *was a suprise winner over Ang Lee's* Brokeback Mountain *(2005) at the 2006 Academy Awards, scooping the prize for Best Film. Set in Los Angeles it highlights racial tensions and the assumptions strangers make about each other.*

sandra bullock
don cheadle
matt dillon
jennifer esposito
brendan fraser
terrence howard
chris "ludacris" bridges
thandie newton
ryan phillippe
larenz tate
michael peña
a film by PAUL HAGGIS
crash
Moving at the speed of life, we are bound to collide with each other.
www.crashfilm.com

HOW MOVIES ARE MADE

End-of-movie credits run for minutes, and rightly so. It takes many dozens of creative, technical, publicity, and distribution talents to take a movie from idea to screen. *The Godfather* (1972) had crews across several continents; *Gone With the Wind* (1939) had multiple crews in the studio. Most movies are less complicated to make than these films, but still follow the same gestation process and have similar types of players.

The basic stages of making a movie remain the same whatever the size of the budget or the cast. The process begins with pre-production, then moves through production, and post-production. The players in pre-production and production include the producers, directors, screenwriters, and actors, who constitute the "above-the-line" people who generally have higher status and wildly varying payment. Below-the-line players generally include the production department, cinematographers, composers, editors, costume designers, production designers, stuntpeople, and sound crew. Their costs are generally lower and more predictable.

After the movie is made, the post-production begins. Its players include the editor, sound editor, composer, and special effects crew. The final part of post-production involves getting the movie to its audience, and entails the steps of distribution and exhibition. The movie that has completed post-production work and is a finished product goes into the hands of the distributors and exhibitors. The distributors decide when the movie will be released and get it to the cinemas, and the exhibitors show it.

The Perils of Pauline *(1914) made farmer's daughter Pearl White a star and honed the elements of action films — danger, stunts, and suspense.*

Anecdotes about how actors, directors, producers, and screenwriters collaborate are legion. The inception of a film may be straightforward — as with the concept for *It's a Wonderful Life* (1946), which was transmitted from Frank Capra to James Stewart — or it may be long and involved, as in the search for the new James Bond, Daniel Craig. Equally intricate is the work of technical staff, such as costume designers, who come up with ways to make the fashions of the Roman empire look authentic, as in *Gladiator* (2000). Dazzling special effects combine computer-generated images and old-fashioned physical trickery to enliven a story of a giant gorilla or a galaxy far, far away.

After the movie is made, it has to reach the viewer. Distributors set up showing periods with cinemas, then alter the time if a film is a surprise hit or underperforms. Deals are also made for international markets, where established stars can save a movie that flounders in its home country. Finally, there is the video market, where all movies end up, often (as with children's classics) to healthy profit.

The complexity of the movie-making process gives the lie to silent star Norma Desmond's (Gloria Swanson) contention in *Sunset Boulevard* (1950) that "I am big. It's the pictures that got small."

Pre-production

The pre-production stage of making a movie usually begins with a conversation. Held anywhere, it will mark the first time producers, screenwriters, and studio executives discuss the concept and potential actors for their movie.

THE "PITCH" AND THE PRODUCER

As captured in movie lore and skewered in Robert Altman's *The Player* (1992), a movie pitch is a short encapsulization of a movie idea which, if it succeeds, pleases a studio executive or other powerful individuals. Some ideas get the go-ahead but fail in execution, such as the remake of *Sabrina* (1995). Other ideas, such as James Cameron's premise for *Titanic* (1997) as primarily a love story, can result in a film classic.

From the beginning, the producer is central to the making of the movie. He may be a forceful, creative type or he may be part of a group of investors who has a more distant relationship with the industry but knows the star. Since the days of the Hollywood studio stystem, the definition of a producer has become increasingly fluid and many are now seeking to have the tasks of producers defined more clearly. But traditionally, a producer is responsible for securing the money to make the movie.

In most cases, the money for a movie comes from the studio executives. As with producers, the studio executives vary in the scope of their power. Wherever they fit, they will provide money and will be highly involved with the screenwriter and with the producer through the next stage of the movie's development.

Director Nicholas Ray *(left) discusses a project with screenwriter Philip Yordan. The two collaborated on* Johnny Guitar *in 1954.*

THE DEVELOPMENT STAGE

In restaurants and offices, producers and movie executives cook up a deal and talk it through. At this stage a screenwriter will also produce a draft of the script. The screenwriter is usually known to the producers or executives through past work with them or experience on similar types of projects. Whatever the screenwriter's stature, the script is very often rewritten again and again to please the producers and studios in a process known as development, which, if tortured enough, may even earn the name "development hell." When the script is finished and believed to represent a potentially profitable venture, studio executives "green light" the picture and pre-production begins.

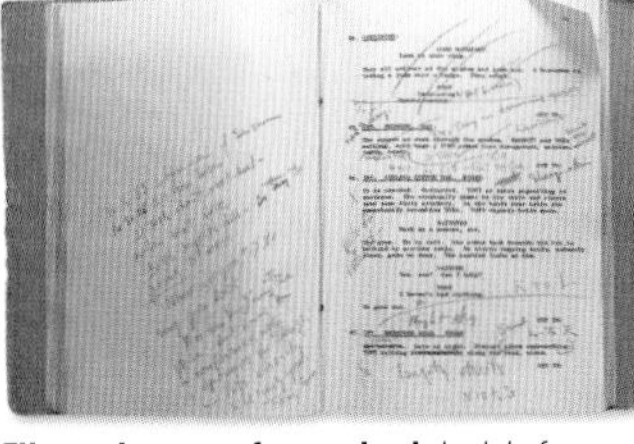

Film scripts are often revised, *both before and during filming. This is a marked-up script by Harold Pinter for* The Servant *(1963).*

The actors may be involved at the development stage. This is even more likely to be the case if the script is being written as a vehicle for a particular actor, or is attached to a well-known actor-director/producer team (such as James Cameron/Arnold Schwarzenegger in the 1980s and 1990s). Another situation where this may be the case is if the actor is the director himself (such as Clint Eastwood or Mel Gibson). Often, stars that are big in the box office are involved during development to secure the necessary funding for a big film. A top US star can command $30 million per movie — and may also receive a percentage of the gross profit. Less well-known actors are usually signed up during the pre-production stage.

Pre-production encompasses the activities necessary to get a movie ready for production, that is, filming. These activities include casting, scouting locations, doing historical research, and storyboarding.

Storyboards *help the director visualize each scene — these are from* The Wizard of Oz *(1939).*

PRODUCER AND PRODUCTION CREW

Depending on his level of involvement, the producer may be responsible for choosing locations, setting up a shooting schedule and budget, and hiring the crew, which includes a director of photography, a production designer, a costume designer, a composer, and an editor. At the pre-production stage there is work for the practical members of the production department, who calculate the cost of the preparation for, and the shooting of, the film. At this stage the location scout will also search for the best locations for the movie. These may be real locations, for example, New York for *On the Town* (1949), or a convincing substitute, such as using Italy for 19th-century New York

WHO'S WHO ON SET

Best boy	Assistant to the gaffer
Boom operator	Positions and operates the microphone
Chief/key/head grip	Moves the camera
Continuity person (script supervisor)	Ensures make-up, costumes etc. don't change between scenes
Director of photography (cinematographer/ first cameraman/ lighting cameraman)	Responsible for lighting, composition, choice of camera, lens, and film — in fact, the "look" of the film
First assistant cameraman (focus puller)	Maintains camera, changes lenses and magazines, operates focus control
Gaffer	Chief electrician
Grip	Moves equipment on set
Location manager	Finds suitable locations and clears their use with owner
Mixer (sound recordist)	Person on set in overall charge of sound recording
Production manager (line producer)	Person who controls the day-to-day budget
Second assistant cameraman (clapper loader)	Loads magazines, operates clapperboard, and performs other camera tasks
Set decorator	Finds props and decorates the set
Set designer	Designs the set using sketches and models
Stills person	Takes still photographs of the production
Wardrobe	Responsible for care and repair of costumes throughout the production.

The Living Daylights (1987), *in which Timothy Dalton made his debut as James Bond, was shot in Europe, the US, and in the studio. Here, the crane allows for a panoramic view of the set.*

streets in *Gangs of New York* (2002). To film the 16th-century feudal Japan of Akira Kurosawa's *Throne of Blood* (1957), the director commissioned a castle to be built. The 19th-century story of love and obsession on the British coast, Karel Reisz's *The French Lieutenant's Woman* (1981) was filmed in part on location, in a British town largely untouched by time (Lyme Regis).

CREATIVE CREW

To sign actors, casting directors break down a script to see what roles have to be cast. In the US, he or she may use the private company Breakdown Services, which distributes daily lists, or "breakdowns" of available roles to Screen Actors Guild (SAG, the major actors' association) franchised agents and personal managers. The agents and managers then submit names of clients who might be right for the part. Following auditions and hiring, the casting director negotiates the contract with the actor.

Additionally, the cinematography, production design, and editing components of the movie are set up. The director and director of photography, or DP, may discuss the intended look for the film and how to achieve it. The DP may also confer with the production designer and crew to make sure that the cameras can be accommodated in the set design. When planning the shoot, the scenes are not shot in order, for example all the action in one location will be filmed together, even though it might be viewed at different times in the final version. The editor will put it all together logically in post-production.

Polish director Andrzej Wajda *casts for the film* Pan Tadeusz: The Last Foray in Lithuania, *1999.*

Production

As immortalized in movies about the movies, such as *Singin' in the Rain* (1952), production is the shooting of the movie. It occurs after pre-production is completed and includes the crafts of acting, cinematography, costume design, directing, lighting, and design.

CINEMATOGRAPHY

Lighting and photographing a film is called cinematography, and is the responsibility of the DP, also known as the cinematographer. Although they are responsible for how the film is lit and photographed, they do not run the camera or set up the lights. Instead, under the supervision of the DP, these activities are done by members of the cinematographic crew. The camera operator runs the camera. The electrical crew is under the guidance of the gaffer or chief electrician.

Director David Lean *often discussed the overall look of particular shots with cinematographers, as here in* Ryan's Daughter *(1970).*

In all phases of making the movie, the DP is a craftsman and an artist. He or she uses knowledge of many kinds of technology, such as film stocks and printing processes, cameras, lenses, and filters; they apply artistic sensibilities to place the camera and compose the picture in the

Girl with a Pearl Earring *(2003) required cinematographer Eduardo Serra to recreate artist Johannes Vermeer's esthetic sensibility.*

Alex McDowell's set *for* Charlie and the Chocolate Factory *(2005) involved merging the imaginative views of children's novelist Roald Dahl and director Tim Burton.*

frame. Nearly every day, the DP reviews the "rushes" or daily footage and discusses it with the director to make sure the movie has the director's desired approach.

In the US, some cinematographers are invited to become members of the professional society called the American Society of Cinematographers. DPs belonging to the society appear in the film credits with an ASC after their name.

PRODUCTION DESIGN

The physical world to be photographed in a movie is created by the production designer. He or she acts as architect, decorator, and visionary to create everything from elaborate sets to small props that may become totemic items, like the light sabers of *Star Wars* (1977). Among the production designer's duties are designing and overseeing the construction of sets and scenery; designing props and overseeing their purchase or rental; and working with the costume designer to make sure the actors' wardrobe coordinates with the rest of the film's look. The production designer usually has knowledge of architecture, engineering, painting, drawing, and theater and film arts. He or she applies this background to research the historical period of the movie and the material world of its inhabitants, or to realize an imaginary culture. The range encompasses the look of an Elizabethan theater in *Shakespeare in Love* (1998) and the futuristic world of *Gattaca* (1997).

Active in both the pre-production and production stages, the production designer works with the director and producer to create sketches of sets. Implementing these ideas requires adhering to budgets, time constraints, and the vision of the director. It also requires a staff, known as the art department, including the art director, set designer, set decorator, scenic artist, property master, construction coordinator, and landscaper.

A member of the art department *paints a background for an imaginary, historical, or inaccessible location. The department works under the production designer.*

ACTING

Once signed, actors prepare for their roles. They develop the appropriate characteristics for their character, such as gaining weight, as Robert De Niro did to play Jake LaMotta in *Raging Bull* (1980), or finding a walk, as Alec Guinness is said to have done for each of his roles. Some immerse themselves in the period of the film. But nearly all serious actors have prepared beforehand through training in acting. One of the best known schools for actors has been the Actors Studio in New York City. Founded in 1947 and led by Lee Strasberg, the Actors Studio has stressed having actors develop a deep understanding of their characters' motivations. Famous actors who have used the Actors Studio "Method" style include Marlon Brando, Robert De Niro, Dustin Hoffman, and Marilyn Monroe. Notable university acting programs include the Yale School of Drama in the US, while drama schools such as The Royal Academy of Dramatic Arts (RADA) in London have trained many well-known faces. Internationally, drama schools abound. In Paris, there is France's national drama and theater school, the Conservatoire National Supérieur d'Art Dramatique. Germany has the Berlin University of the Arts, Spain has the Septima Ars School of Cinema and TV. Finland has its Theater Academy, and in New Delhi, India, there is the Imago School of Acting.

Clint Eastwood attended acting classes *when he came to Hollywood in 1955; his first break was the television series* Rawhide.

While audiences are no longer shocked by variances from an actor's persona, as they were with aspects of James Stewart's performance in *Anatomy of a Murder* (1959), actors still manage their careers effectively by remaining consistent with the sensibilities they have established in their films. Thus, Tom Hanks is likely to continue to represent the decent everyman, while Julia Roberts will doubtless remain the accessible, practical everywoman.

FILM ACTOR IN ACTION

On the set, actors endure challenges and advantages unique to the form. Unlike the stage, the set offers no live audience for reaction and support; but it does allow the actor to redo a line or scene they are not happy with. Movies are a medium

Joseph Fiennes, *himself a stage-trained actor, plays the title role in* Shakespeare in Love *(1998), which celebrates stage-trained actors from the Elizabethan era.*

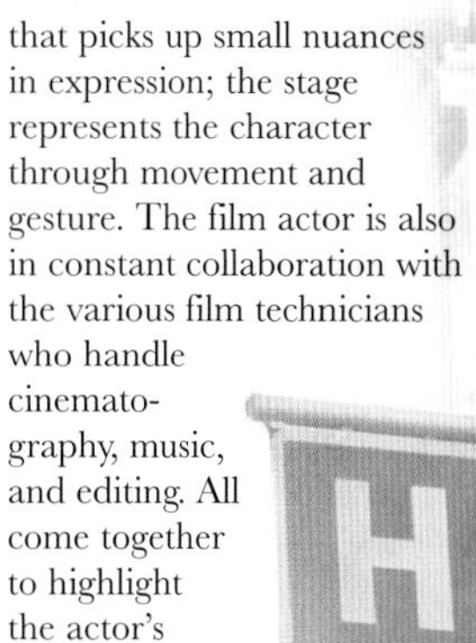

that picks up small nuances in expression; the stage represents the character through movement and gesture. The film actor is also in constant collaboration with the various film technicians who handle cinematography, music, and editing. All come together to highlight the actor's performance. Charlton Heston's Moses in *The Ten Commandments* (1956) is accorded stature by the forceful color on screen and Cecil B. DeMille's direction, which defines Heston's powerful character through sweeping gestures.

In the US, actors are members of the Screen Actors Guild, which has established a minimum payment for its actors. More established or in-demand actors get salaries far beyond scale, but for many actors, the rate is scale plus ten (ten percent for the agent).

STUNT PERFORMERS

The players who substitute for principals and perform acts of derring-do are the stunt performers. These trained men and women are largely unknown to the movie-going audience, but their presence in fires, explosions, or chase scenes is essential. They are chosen for their general resemblance to the star and are dressed to match him or her.

Although some actors do at least some of their own stunts, stunt doubles replace actors when the stunt is considered too dangerous for anyone but a trained person. In part, the stunt performer is used for economic reasons: to keep the actor in sufficiently good health to complete the movie and make good on the investment. If the stunt is considered too dangerous for a human, the effects are done by digital imagery and long-established tricks of photography. In using stunt performers, the goal is to avoid mishaps such as the injury sustained by silent comic actor Harold Lloyd, who lost a thumb and forefinger while filming *Haunted Spooks* (1920).

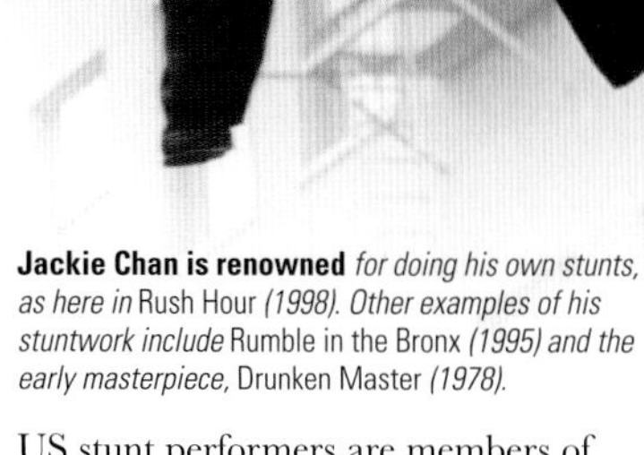

Jackie Chan is renowned *for doing his own stunts, as here in* Rush Hour *(1998). Other examples of his stuntwork include* Rumble in the Bronx *(1995) and the early masterpiece,* Drunken Master *(1978).*

US stunt performers are members of the Stuntmen's Association of Motion Pictures and the Screen Actors Guild. A few are so accomplished that they receive industry accolades. Perhaps the most honored was Western and action movie stuntman Yakima Canutt (1895–1986), who appeared in *Stagecoach* (1939), and who received a special Academy Award for his extraordinary stuntwork in 1966.

Shirley Temple was by 1938 *the top box-office draw in Hollywood, delivering cheer during the Depression in movies such as* Bright Eyes *(1934) and* Dimples *(1936).*

ANIMALS AND CHILDREN

While digital effects and animatronics can be used to create an animal, or at least place it where the director wants it to be, real animals are still effective additions to many movies, particularly family-oriented ones. To circumvent some of the troubles in dealing with animals, multiple look-alike animals are sometimes used, each performing a different set of scenes. Or animals may be made to perform by a trainer dangling food before its eyes. In some films, the animals themselves are the stars. Notable examples include Lassie, whose first big-screen feature, *Lassie Come Home* (1943), was actually Oscar-nominated, and the killer whale Willy, who makes friends with a young boy in the heart-warming *Free Willy* (1993).

Children are also big draws for the movie-goer seeking familiarity. On the set, child actors pose many of the same challenges as animals, and are dealt with in the same way. Multiple child actors are chosen for a role (such as twins or triplets in a movie calling for a baby), and they perform for only limited periods. In most countries, child labor laws regulate how long child actors may remain on the set. Furthermore, school-age children are usually tutored when they are not filming.

Whether child or animal, the non-adult actor will, through natural affinity to the camera, forever frustrate the trained adult actor by stealing the movie.

SOUND

Sound is crucial to a film, helping to create the required atmosphere as, for example, in *Jaws* (1975).

Sound in film is made up of three parts — the dialogue, sound effects, and music — and is created and implemented by three talents — the mixer, sound editor, and composer. The sound components appear on separate tracks, recorded separately, but run together in the movie. The sound crew works on the film during both the production and post-production phases of making a film.

The first of two phases of creating a movie's sound occurs during the production stage. This is when most of the dialogue and some sound effects are recorded on the set. The person in charge at this point is the floor mixer, who ensures that the recording is clear and in balance. The dialogue takes priority over background sounds, since the latter can always be dubbed in later. A guide track is used to dub dialogue and background sounds if necessary.

The many tasks involved in creating the sound mix are done by the sound crew: its members include the sound mixer (or floor mixer or recordist), who is responsible for the sound recording on the set and directs the rest of the crew. Other sound crew members include the sound recorder, boom opearator, cablemen, and playback operators.

In producing the voiceover *for Princess Fiona in* Shrek *(2001), Cameron Diaz continued the venerable tradition of having notable stage and screen voices feature in an animated film.*

Racing Stripes *(2005) brings the animal/animatronics film into the 21st century but relies on a classic story of outsized wishes coming true as a zebra (voice of Frankie Muniz) believes he is a racehorse and comes to race with thoroughbreds.*

COSTUMES, MAKEUP, AND HAIR

Just as the production designer creates a world on the set or location of a film, the costume designer, makeup artist, and hairstylist create a vision on the actors. They change the actors' clothes and their overall appearance so that they fit into the world that is being created onscreen.

The costume designer works closely with the director, cinematographer, and production designer to design a wardrobe. Part of the job is to research the period covered in the film for clothing style, color, fabric composition, and fit on the body. The different jobs that may be included within this area are costume supervisor, costumer/stylist, set costumer, tailor/seamstress, wig master or mistress, and wardrobe attendant. Wardrobe pieces that can be purchased off-the-rack (from a shop) may be obtained by the stylist.

Many of the top costume designers have become known for the looks they create, the actors they have dressed, or the stories they generate. The broad-shouldered look that Adrian created for Joan Crawford was embraced (in modified form) for ladies' wear during the 1940s. Givenchy was the man who dressed Audrey Hepburn, Travis Banton dressed Marlene Dietrich. Consummate studio designer Edith Head dressed just about everyone — stories and anecdotes abounded about her famous clients' attributes and habits, such as Barbara Stanwyck's tiny waist or Paul Newman and Robert Redford's unfussy ways.

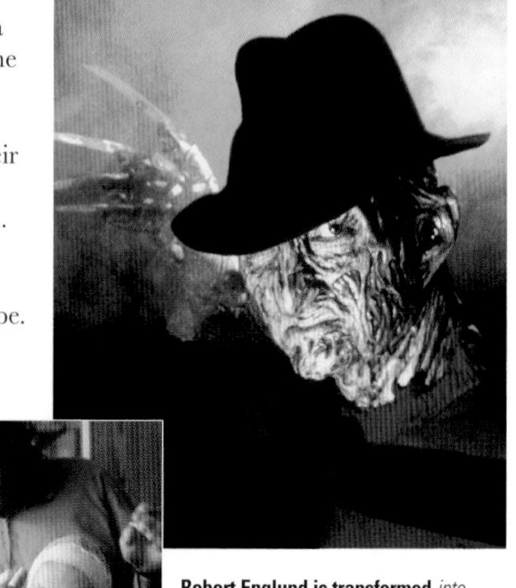

Robert Englund is transformed *into Freddy Krueger, the horribly scarred dream monster of* A Nightmare on Elm Street *(1984) and its sequels. Creature make-up typically requires several hours daily for application and removal of latex appliances.*

Even more than the costume designer, the makeup artist develops a close relationship with the actors. The makeup artist is responsible for conveying the actor's sensibility for the film by preparing the actor's face, neck, forearms, and hands. The work is redone at least once a day and must remain consistent throughout shooting. Members of the makeup team include the makeup artist and his or her assistant.

If relevant to the film, there may also be a body makeup artist, who applies special effects makeup.

There has been a separate category for makeup in the Academy Awards since 1981. Awards have been given to such diverse films as *Frida* (2002) and *The Chronicles of Narnia: The Lion, the Witch and the Wardrobe* (2005).

Elizabeth Taylor is fitted *into costume for* Cleopatra *(1963). Designer Irene Sharaff created costumes for later Taylor movies, including* The Taming of the Shrew *(1967).*

A huge version of Mount Rushmore *was created in a studio as a menacing backdrop to Cary Grant and Eva Marie Saint in* North by Northwest *(1959). The US government forbade the use of the real monument.*

Jaws (1975) used *an animatronic shark to bring to life the killer fish of Peter Benchley's novel. The shark proved memorable on screen.*

SPECIAL EFFECTS

Beyond the ability of the stuntperson or makeup artist lies special effects. In a huge ranges of movie genres, including drama, epic and horror, special effects are manufactured illusions that can be imagined, but are impossible to film without trickery. Examples include the sinking of the *Titanic* in James Cameron's spectacular fim of the same name, and the transformation of mad scientist, Seth Brundle, (Jeff Goldblum) into a horrific giant man/fly hybrid in *The Fly* (1986). In many cases, special effects are used to reduce costs. A matte painting is less costly than filming with live actors upon a huge national monument (such as Mount Rushmore in *North by Northwest*). It also gives the illusion of filming on-site when, in fact, a location is off-limits to filming. There are two kinds of special effects (abbreviated as FX, SFX, SPFX or EFX). They are visual

or photographic effects, which are achieved by manipulating the film image, and mechanical or physical effects, achieved through the use of mechanical devices on the set. (While a physical effect may be simple, such as using an unseen rope to move or knock over a prop, special effects today are usually much more complicated.) In this book, the term "special effects" refers to both visual and mechanical effects.

Visual effect techniques include computer-generated imagery (CGI), digital compositing, digital matte paintings, green screen technology, miniatures, morphing, motion-capture, rotoscopes, and traveling mattes.

Mechanical effects include animatronic puppets, explosions, full-scale mock-ups, rain and snow machines, squibs that replicate bloody bullet hits, and wires attached to actors. A complicated FX sequence may include a variety of visual and mechanical effects.

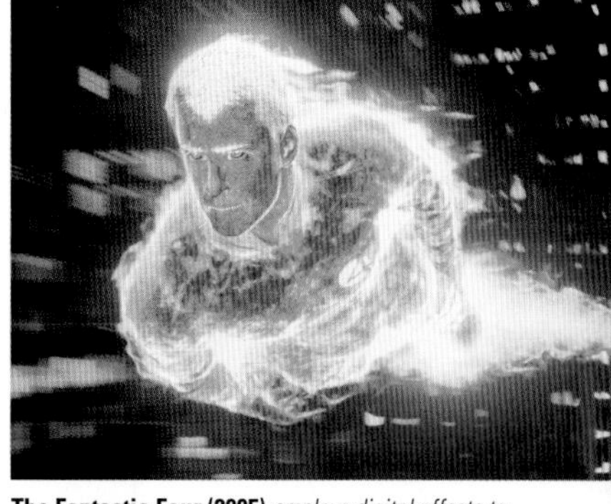

The Fantastic Four (2005) *employs digital effects to transform a 3D laser scan of actor Chris Evans into the Human Torch. The fiery effect was a highlight of the film.*

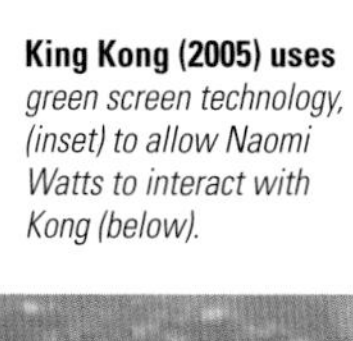

King Kong (2005) uses *green screen technology, (inset) to allow Naomi Watts to interact with Kong (below).*

TECHNOLOGICAL ADVANCES

The technology for special effects is changing so rapidly that many long-standing practices, such as brush-and-canvas matte paintings, and rear projection have now fallen out of use. Even animatronics, used (with difficulty) for the shark in *Jaws* (1975) and refined in the films of the 1980s and 1990s, is less widely used today. Yet some established technologies are still used, such as rain and snow machines, which permit filming even when the weather is uncooperative. Some digital effects, such as morphing (a computer-generated effect in which one image is transformed into another), have been around so long they are almost considered old-fashioned.

Current technologies include motion-capture, in which an actor's movements are translated to a computer-graphics model. Motion-capture can be blended with digital animation to create realistic virtual creatures, such as the giant gorilla in *King Kong* (2005).

Green screens are green fabric backgrounds positioned behind actors that allow CGI to be integrated into the scene. Green screens have largely superseded blue screens because the green delivers finer outlines.

The 2005 stop-motion feature, Corpse Bride, *uses puppets made of stainless steel covered by silicone skin. Directed by Tim Burton and Mike Johnson, it is the first feature to use digital still, not film, cameras.*

Post-production

A crucial part of the movie-making process begins once filming is finished. Thousands of frames of film must be assembled into an order that conveys a story, and the scenes may be shortened or reordered so that the finished product reflects the director's vision.

EDITING

Most films are shot out of sequence. During filming, it is the editor's job to begin assembling the pieces of film into the order that they will be seen in the final film. The editor talks with the director about the previous day's filming, known as rushes. The film shot may be transferred to videotape or digital format for ease in rearranging or selecting. The film construction made at this point is called the assembly. The bulk of the editing is done during post-production.

Charlie Chaplin editing a film. *He also wrote, directed and acted in his films in a 50-year career.*

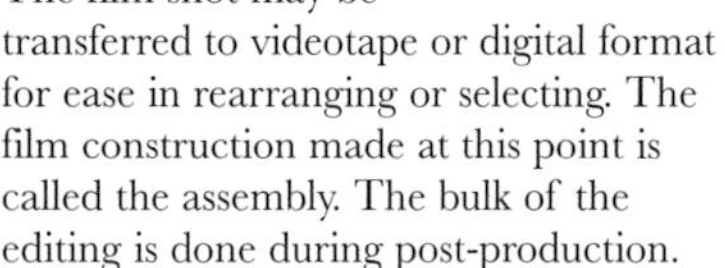

The film editor carries out many different stages of editing to shape the final arrangement of shots that makes a finished film. First, they work with the director to refine the assembly of all the different sections of the film into a rough cut, the first fully edited work print. This includes the soundtrack to the film. But the individual shots are not completely determined at this stage. This version of the film is dominated by the director's vision and is known as the director's cut. During post-production, the DP and the director also work together to oversee the timing of the first print. Among the tasks in this stage are correcting density and color balance. Following repeated consultation with the director, the editor assembles the shots with visual effects into the fine cut. It runs to the length the director, editor, and producer have decided.

The sound mixing desk *is where the various tracks of human dialogue, sound effects, and music are combined to create an original to transfer to the film negative.*

Composer John Williams *has won Academy Awards for best score for* Jaws *(1975),* Star Wars *(1977),* E.T. The Extra-Terrestrial *(1982), and* Schindler's List *(1993).*

For the first hundred years of film-making, film editing meant physically cutting and reassembling the edited film reel itself. Today, however, much film editing is done electronically, using video and digital technology. Films are transferred to videotape and digital format, and are computer coded; this allows the editor to edit scenes on screen. Using the fine cut as a guide, the original negative is cut.

POST-PRODUCTION SOUND

There are four post-production stages that go into creating the movie's sound. These include dialogue and sound effects, composed music, the sound mix, and transferring the original sound mix on to the film negative.

Firstly, the sound editor, or sound effects editor, works with the director and editor to create the soundtracks. Additional sounds are created by a foley artist or from film library stock.

A composer (such as John Williams or Danny Elfman) is used if the film requires an original score. A music editor will then edit the music to fit the film. For existing music under copyright, rights managers arrange fees for its use in the film. A recording or rerecording mixer works with the director to blend together the many tracks of different sound. The finished mix is transferred on to the original negative. The film sound is recorded with a digital system and reproduced as an optical sound track. It is then read as synchronized sound when it is sent through the loudspeakers during an audience showing.

RELEASE PRINTS

Color testing follows the making of the original negative. Once all phases of the movie are completed, the movie is previewed with audiences; depending on their reaction, final cuts are made.

When the original negative is finalized, master prints are made from the original negative. Duplicate negatives are made from that to produce release prints.

US stars, such as Tom Cruise, *agree to do publicity to promote their recent releases, as here on Jay Leno's late-night talk show.*

DISTRIBUTION AND EXHIBITION

Once a movie is completed, the distributor gets it to cinemas and exhibitors make sure that it is shown. The distributor is usually the movie studio that financed the film. The distributor plans the release date, licenses movies to cinemas, arranges to have prints of the film sent to exhibitors, and creates a marketing and advertising programme for the film. The exhibitor negotiates a financial deal with the distributor for the financial take at the cinema on the film, including paying advance money to secure an expected hit.

The studio is also responsible for advertising and publicizing the film. This includes market research, advertisements (television, radio, newspaper, and online), "coming attractions" trailers in cinemas, posters, lobby cards, and stills.

Other aspects of publicity include press kits and press releases to the media, and booking stars for media interviews and general exposure.

THEATRICAL RELEASE

Once the film is in the cinema, it has only a short time to earn its money as a theatrical release. After a few weeks or

Charlize Theron on the red carpet *at the 57th Cannes Film Festival Award Ceremony. In recent years, awards ceremonies have set fashion trends as well as invigorating takings at the box office.*

(if the movie is a blockbuster or an Academy Award winner) months, attendance will diminish. The days of one film (such as *The Sound of Music*, 1965) playing at the same cinema for a year are gone, and unlikely to return. Therefore, distributors have to judge box office receipts carefully and recalibrate the number of cinemas showing a film. A movie with good word-of-mouth and sustained interest (such as *March of the Penguins* in 2005) will be shown on more screens. If it is underperforming, it may need a different advertising campaign (as with *Munich*, 2005) or be withdrawn altogether.

Movie merchandise, such as *this toy from the 1963 film* The Great Escape, *is a multi-million dollar industry and can generate more income than the film itself.*

After the domestic theatrical release, a film's earning potential is extended by its release in overseas cinemas. There is also revenue to come from the home-video/DVD sales and the licensing to a variety of television rights, including pay-per-view, premium cable channels, basic cable channels, and terrestrial television. The distributor can also extend a film's life by licensing merchandising rights to makers of toys, mugs, T-shirts, recordings, and video games. Since the release of the first *Star Wars* film in 1977, and the highly successful accompanying figurines and book tie-ins, merchandising has taken on a new importance. Many products relating to a film are now sold even before the release of the film.

THE ROLE OF THE FILM CRITIC

Good planning and deal-making does not ensure a movie hit. Neither does advance audience interest. Often, a film's success begins (or ends) with the film critics.

Film critics are the first to slot a movie into its place in the film canon. They pre-screen the movie and tell the audience whether they believe it is worth the price of admission. Despite the critics, however, the strongest force for the popularity of a movie is the audience. Based on the film's stars, subject matter, director, time of year, and the cultural atmosphere of the time, the public decides whether to go and see a film or not. Audiences are affected by timing: *Jaws* worked well as a summer blockbuster. They also want an element of familiarity: *Shakespeare in Love* works, but *Marlowe in Love* probably wouldn't. Finally, the time has to be right culturally: the gay cowboy movie *Brokeback Mountain* was very successful when released in 2005; but 20 years ago, it may have been an art-house staple.

MOVIE GENRES

When a film is labelled a Western, a musical or a romantic comedy, audiences already have certain preconceptions and expectations about what genre, or kind, of film it is. Although within each category films differ in many respects, they share comparable, recognizable patterns in terms of theme, period and setting, and plot, and in their use of iconography, or symbols, and the type of characters portrayed.

The concept of genre really began during the Hollywood studio period. It helped production decisions and made a film easier to market. Also, during Hollywood's golden era, when the studios were turning out hundreds of films at a rapid rate, the generic concept provided script writers with a template on which to work.

Each studio specialized in a particular genre: Universal (horror), Warner Bros. (gangster), MGM (musical), and Paramount (comedy). Some directors became connected with a specific genre: John Ford (Westerns), Cecil B. DeMille (epics), Alfred Hitchcock (thrillers), Vincent Minnelli (musicals), and Douglas Sirk (melodrama). But it was with the stars that the public most associated certain types of pictures: James Cagney, Edward G. Robinson (gangsters), Joan Crawford, Barbara Stanwyck (melodrama), Fred Astaire, Betty Grable (musicals), John Wayne, Randolph Scott (Westerns), and Boris Karloff, Bela Lugosi (horror). Performers were so closely linked with certain genres that it became an event when they departed from the norm. "Garbo Laughs!" was the publicity line for Ernst Lubitsch's *Ninotchka* (1939), which prepared audiences to accept Greta Garbo, previously seen only in melodramas, in a comedy.

Janet Leigh *about to be stabbed in the shower in Alfred Hitchcock's* Psycho *(1960), one of the most famous and shocking scenes in cinema history.*

Today, genres and actors have become more flexible, though stars such as Bruce Willis and Sylvester Stallone remain linked in the public's mind with action movies and Jim Carrey and Adam Sandler with comedies. There are still directors who specialize in certain genres: John Hughes in teen movies, Woody Allen with comedy, John Woo with action, and Wes Craven with horror.

Over the years, the well-loved conventions became clichés, such as the good cowboy and the villain having a showdown on a dusty street. So traditional genres began to be reinterpreted, challenged or satirised. Sam Peckinpah and Sergio Leone's Westerns can be termed revisionist, as can the film noirs of the Coen Brothers. Audiences are familiar enough with genres to enjoy lampoons, such as Mel Brooks' *Blazing Saddles* (1974) and the Austin Powers movies of the late 1990s, directed by Jay Roach. Despite *auteur* cinema (the personal expression of a director) being the antithesis of genre cinema, directors such as Jean-Luc Godard, Jean-Pierre Melville and Wong Kar-Wai have used established genres for their own purposes.

Action-adventure

"Lights, camera, action" is the command given by the director at the beginning of each shot. Action films — often linked to adventure — tend to be real crowd-pleasers, with their combination of exciting storylines, physical action, and special effects.

Action-adventure encompasses several genres — Westerns, war films, crime pictures, and even comedies. The style is associated with nonstop action —dramatic chases, shoot-outs, and explosions — often centered around a male hero struggling against terrible odds. Action films offer pure escapism and entertainment for the audience and are often big box office hits.

It was in the 1980s that the action-adventure genre became established. The style inherited the law-and-order ideology from the "rogue cop" films of Clint Eastwood — such as the Dirty Harry films — and the vigilante movies of Charles Bronson in the late 1960s and 1970s. Hollywood's big action films became increasingly gung-ho with *Top Gun* (1986) as the apotheosis of renewed American confidence and power in the Reagan era. Among the action men who

WHAT TO WATCH

1920	The Mark of Zorro (US)
1938	The Adventures of Robin Hood (US)
1954	The Seven Samurai (*Shichi-nin no Samurai*, Jap)
1986	Top Gun (US)
1987	Lethal Weapon (US)
1991	Thelma and Louise (US)
1996	Mission: Impossible (US)

Errol Flynn (right) faces Basil Rathbone *as Sir Guy of Gisbourne at the exciting climax of Michael Curtiz's classic swashbuckler,* The Adventures of Robin Hood *(1938). The film was a huge hit for Warner Bros.*

Bruce Willis *as one-man army John McClane survives various hair-raising stunts in the explosive action thriller* Die Hard *(1988).*

Belmondo carried on the tradition. In Japan, Toshiro Mifune starred in numerous samurai films, or *jidai-keki*, filled with furious swordplay.

dominated the genre in the 1980s were Harrison Ford (*Raiders of the Lost Ark*, 1981), Bruce Willis (*Die Hard*, 1988), and Mel Gibson (*Lethal Weapon*, 1987).

ACTION HEROES

No hero came larger or more testosterone-filled than former Mr. Universe, Arnold Schwarzenegger. Schwarzenegger made an impact in sword-and-sorcery fantasies (*Conan the Barbarian*, 1982), science fiction action (*Terminator*, 1984), and military movies (*Commando*, 1985). An equally macho fantasy figure was Sylvester Stallone as a Vietnam vet in the jingoistic *Rambo* cycle. These films glorified the power of the individual to solve political and social problems through a combination of excessive musculature and firearms.

Pre-1960s action heroes were far more moral. Their code was to kill only in self-defense. Costume epics featured flamboyant characters played by actors such as Douglas Fairbanks. He swashbuckled his way supremely though *The Mark of Zorro* (1920), *The Three Musketeers* (1921), and *Robin Hood* (1922). Fairbanks' worthy successors were Errol Flynn, Tyrone Power, and Stewart Granger in the US, while in France, Jean Marais, Gérard Philipe, and Jean-Paul

Film poster, *1981*

GENDER ROLES

Traditionally, action-adventure movies were aimed mostly at male audiences in their teens to mid-30s. Women are generally shown as either having a restraining influence or fueling men's violence. However, in the 1990s a new style of action-adventure film began to appear where women played roles traditionally taken by men. In Ridley Scott's *Thelma and Louise* (1991) two women go on a crime spree. *Lethal Weapon 3* (1992) added a tough, female martial-arts expert to the buddy-buddy formula. However, the genre is still male-dominated, and although the heroes are more clean-cut and cocky, such as Tom Cruise (*Mission: Impossible*, 1996) and Keanu Reeves (*The Matrix*, 1999), they are equally lethal.

TOM CRUISE

Tom Cruise (born 1962), one of the most successful stars in movie history, first leapt into stardom in *Risky Business* (1983), in which he dances in his underwear. The versatile Cruise appeared in some of the top box-office films of the 1980s, including *Top Gun* (1986), *Rain Man* (1988), *and Born on the Fourth of July* (1989), in which he played a paraplegic Vietnam vet. Other demanding roles were in *Interview with the Vampire* (1994), *Jerry Maguire* (1996), *Eyes Wide Shut* (1999), and *Collateral* (2004).

Animation

Film animation encompasses a multitude of styles, themes, and techniques. From the simplest drawing by hand to images created using the most up-to-date digital technology, it has always aimed to appeal to the widest possible age range.

In the middle of the 19th century, long before the invention of cinema, devices to give drawings the illusion of movement were in use. In 1832, the Belgian Joseph Plateau invented an apparatus that produced an apparently moving picture from a series of drawings. The action was viewed through slits on a revolving disc. In 1882, Emile Reynaud introduced his Praxinoscope, using perforated film, which projected images on a screen to a theater audience at the Musée Grevin in Paris. However, when live action cinema was invented, animation was neglected until 1908, when it was almost reinvented by the American J. Stuart Blackton. He pioneered stop-motion photography, a technique which was taken up by Émile Cohl in France. Cohl made more than 100 brief animated films between 1908 and 1918, and created the first regular cartoon character.

Gene Kelly and Tom and Jerry *dance together, combining animation with live-action in* Anchors Aweigh *(1945).*

In 1909 Winsor McCay, an American cartoonist, created Gertie the Dinosaur using simple line drawing. It was the first animated cartoon to be shown as part of a theatrical program in the US. In 1919 he made probably the first animated feature, *The Sinking of the Lusitania.*

The years 1919–20 saw the emergence of the first cartoon production units. These turned out one-reel films about ten minutes long, which supported cinema programs. This was possible due to the labor-saving method of "cel" animation, allowing the tracing of moving parts of characters on celluloid sheets without having to redraw the entire character and background for every frame of film. In the 1920s, Pat Sullivan's Felix the Cat reigned supreme — his witty thoughts given in bubbles — until the coming of sound transformed animated films.

Walt Disney's *Steamboat Willie* (1928) was the first sound cartoon. It demonstrated the force of music,

WHAT TO WATCH

1928	Steamboat Willie (US)
1937	Snow White and the Seven Dwarfs (US)
1940	Pinocchio (US)
1968	Yellow Submarine (UK)
1988	Akira (Japan)
1995	Toy Story (US)
2001	Spirited Away (Japan)
2003	Belleville Rendez-vous (France)
2005	Wallace and Gromit: The Curse of the Were-Rabbit (UK)

Mickey Mouse is the sorcerer's apprentice *in one of the most memorable of the musical sequences in Walt Disney's* Fantasia *(1940).*

not as background accompaniment, but as an element intrinsic to the film's structure and visual rhythm. From 1928, cartoon characters such as Max Fleisher's Betty Boop and Disney's Mickey Mouse, Donald Duck, and Goofy became as well known as film stars. Disney's studio, which streamlined cartoon production, dominated Hollywood animation in the 1930s, consolidating its position with the hugely successful animation features, *Snow White and the Seven Dwarfs* (1937), *Pinocchio* (1940), *Fantasia* (1940 — the first film to use stereo sound commercially), *Dumbo* (1941), and *Bambi* (1942). Dave Fleisher, whose

Plasticine buddies — *the cheese-loving Wallace and his faithful dog Gromit, the lovable Oscar-winning creations of Nick Park and Aardman Animations.*

Sylvain Chomet's *Belleville Rendez-vous* *(2003) proved a huge success for French animation. Here, the aged song-and-dance team make a comeback.*

Popeye shorts proved very popular from 1933 to 1947, tried to rival Disney's full-length cartoons with *Gulliver's Travels* (1939) and *Hoppity Goes To Town* (1941), but they were perhaps too sophisticated for children to have been commercial successes. In the 1940s, MGM made headway with William Hanna and Joe Barbera's cartoon shorts featuring Tom and Jerry, which had jazzy sound effects, little dialogue, and zany violence as frustrated cat Tom eternally pursued resourceful mouse Jerry. Also at MGM, Tex Avery's anarchism was given free rein in a series of crazy cartoons that exploded the boundaries of the genre, among the best of which were *Screwball Squirrel* (1944) and *King Sized Canary* (1947).

At Warner Bros., Chuck Jones helped to create Porky Pig, Daffy Duck, and Bugs Bunny. Jones was also responsible for the Roadrunner/ Coyote series in the 1950s, noted for its speed and devastating use of the desert landscape. Another major force was UPA (United Productions of America), set up in 1948 by a breakaway group of Disney animators. In reaction to the naturalistic graphic style and sentimentality of Disney, UPA developed freer, more economical, contemporary art styles. Among their most famous creations was Mr. Magoo. All this inventive cartoon work was halted with the proliferation of television, when studios began to devote their output almost entirely to low budget mass-produced cartoons.

ANIMATION ABROAD

While America was developing animation, other countries were experimenting with the genre. In Canada, Norman McLaren used many techniques, such as drawing directly on film, mixing live action and drawings, and pixillation (the use of a stop frame camera to speed up and distort movement). In Great Britain, Len Lye painted directly onto film stock, while John Halas and Joy Batchelor made *Animal Farm* (1954), the first British animated feature film.

But it wasn't until the 1990s that British animation was really put on the map by Aardman Animations with their plasticine characters Wallace and Gromit. After Nick Park and his team won the Oscar for best short animation with *The Wrong Trousers*

(1993), they were able to raise the finances to make the features *Chicken Run* (2000) and *Wallace and Gromit: The Curse of the Were-Rabbit* (2005). France also came up with a winner in Sylvain Chomet's exhilarating *Belleville Rendez-vous* (2003).

In Czechoslovakia, celebrated puppet animator Jiri Trnka made his feature-length *A Midsummer Night's Dream* (1958), without dialogue, and Karel Zeman made ten features, some of them combining live actors with animated models and drawings. Jan Svankmajer, a graphic artist and puppeteer, made the weird *Alice (Neco z Alenky*, 1988), which follows Lewis Carroll's heroine (played by an actress) through an animated land of wonders. The Zagreb animation studio in Croatia, which was formed in 1950, turned out a string of witty and inventive satires while Polish Walerian Borowczyk made bitterly ironic animated films such as *Mr. and Mrs. Kabal's Theatre* (1967).

Film poster, *2001*

NEW TALENT

In the US, after a decline in the quality of Disney animated features, there was a revival by a new crew of younger talents, who produced a string of hits unequalled since the 1940s. Among them were *Beauty and the Beast* (1991) and *The Lion King* (1994). A new golden age of animation dawned at the beginning of the 21st century, leading to the creation of an Oscar for the Best Animated Feature. In 2003, it was awarded to Hayao Miyazaki's inventive *Spirited Away*. In 2004 Pixar Animation Studios took the Oscar for *The Incredibles* (2004).

The green troll and the talkative donkey *were voiced by Mike Myers and Eddie Murphy respectively in the computer-animated* Shrek *(2001), which won the first Oscar for Best Animated Feature.*

Avant-Garde

Avant-garde is a term applied to any experimental movement in the arts that is in opposition to conventional forms. In cinema, it specifically refers to a group of influential and radical film-makers who were active throughout Europe from the end of World War I.

In 1918, French poet Louis Aragon wrote that "cinema must have a place in the avant-garde's preoccupations... if one wants to bring some purity to the art of movement and light." Critic Riccioto Canudo argued in 1926 that cinema should express the film-maker's emotions as well as a character's psychology and even their unconscious. The formalist possibilities of cinema were expounded by the French film-makers and theorists Louis Delluc and Jean Epstein, and underlined by the montage theory of the great Russian film-makers in the 1920s.

Avant-garde films disturbed the accepted continuity of chronological development and attempted new ways of tracing the flow of characters' thoughts. Collages of fragmentary images, complex allusions, and multiple points of view replaced logical explanation of meaning. Avant-garde artists, such as Man Ray, Hans Richter, Fernand Léger, Oskar Fischinger, and Walter Ruttmann, made films influenced by such movements as German expressionism, Russian constructuralism, surrealism, and Dadaism. Salvador Dali's contribution to Luis Buñuel's *Un Chien Andalou* (1928) and *L'Age d'Or* (1930) was invaluable. Marcel L'Herbier, with *L'Inhumaine* (1924) and *L'Argent* (1928), hoped to create "visual music" by using sets created by modernist artists.

WHAT TO WATCH

1924	L'Inhumaine (France)
1928	Un Chien Andalou (France)
1930	L'Age d'Or (France)

Each set for Marcel L'Herbier's L'Inhumaine *(1924) was created by a different designer, including Fernand Léger.*

By the 1930s, Hollywood film-makers were experimenting too. Director and editor Slavko Vorkapich called his montage sequences "symphonies of visual movement," and dance director Busby Berkeley used overhead shots, *trompe l'oeil*, superimposition, trick photography, and surreal settings in his musicals.

The spirit of the avant-garde movement lived on in the American Underground and in the films of Jean-Luc Godard, Chris Marker, and Jean-Marie Straub and his wife Danièle Huillet. The latter couple in particular have never swerved from making films that break away from accepted notions of realism, disengage from bourgeois values, and question the primacy of narration.

Biopic

By its very nature, the biopic (biographical picture) exists in all genres. Examples include a war film, *Patton* (1970), an epic, *Lawrence of Arabia* (1962), and a melodrama, *Mommie Dearest* (1981). Yet there are characteristics that mark the biopic out as a genre of its own.

On the whole, a biopic is a rather fanciful dramatized portrayal of the life of a famous figure. There are certain narrative principles that govern the conventional biopic: the protagonist risks all for success, endures a period of neglect, then achieves success, before experiencing personal conflict or becoming afflicted in some way. Typically, the protagonist falls from the height of fame and makes a triumphant comeback.

It was German-born William Dieterle who set the pattern with numerous biopics. His most successful starred Paul Muni behind heavy makeup in *The Story of Louis Pasteur* (1936), *The Life of Emile Zola* (1937), and *Juarez* (1939). The most archetypal of the genre to follow were *The Story of Alexander Bell* (1939) with Don Ameche; *Young Tom Edison* and *Edison the Man* (both 1940); *Yankee Doodle Dandy* (1942) with James Cagney as composer-entertainer George M. Cohan; *The Jolson Story* (1946); and Cornel Wilde as Chopin in *A Song to Remember* (1945).

A close resemblance between the actor and the real-life figure was achieved by Henry Fonda in John Ford's *Young Mr. Lincoln* (1939), Kirk Douglas as Van Gogh in *Lust for Life* (1956), Ben Kingsley in *Gandhi* (1982), and Anthony Hopkins in *Nixon* (1995). Jamie Foxx provided the right gestures for singer Ray Charles in Taylor Hackford's *Ray* (2004).

WHAT TO WATCH

1939	Young Mr. Lincoln (US)
1982	Gandhi (UK)
2004	The Aviator (US)

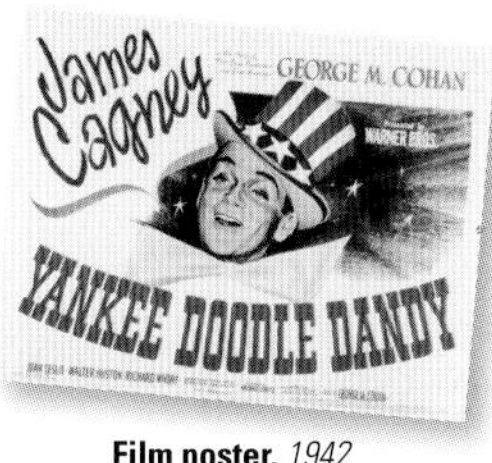

Film poster, *1942*

Joaquin Phoenix *plays the country music legend Johnny Cash, and Reese Witherspoon plays singer June Carter in* Walk the Line *(2005)*

Comedy

In its various forms, from visual slapstick to verbal repartee, comedy has been part of cinema ever since a naughty boy stepped on a hose in the Lumière Brothers' *Watering the Gardener* in 1895. Since then, many stars have employed many different ways of making us laugh.

The Keystone Kops, *the famous slapstick troupe, pose for the camera in 1912. Many famous faces started their careers in the Kops, including Fatty Arbuckle, far right.*

Comedy is one of the oldest of theatrical genres. Originally derived from the *commedia dell'arte* and the burlesque, circus, and vaudeville traditions, comedy found a more natural home in silent cinema than tragedy, the reverse mask. Slapstick, which derives its name from the wooden sticks that circus clowns slapped together to promote audience applause, was predominant in the earliest silent films, since it didn't need sound to be effective.

Charlie, The Little Tramp, *struggles to survive in one of Chaplin's best-loved shorts,* A Dog's Life *(1918).*

FIRST FILM COMICS

Most of the earliest comedies were made by the French and, in 1907, the Pathé Company launched a series of comedies featuring the character Boireau, played by the comedian André Deed, cinema's first true comic star. Other comedians followed both in France and Italy, each with their own specific character. The most gifted and influential of all the comic artists was Max Linder from France. Charlie Chaplin called him "the Professor to whom I owe everything."

While the other comic stars were manic and grotesque, Linder adopted the character of a handsome young boulevardier, a bemused dandy with sleek hair, trimmed moustache, and a silk hat that survived all catastrophes. By 1910, Linder was making one film a week playing the character of a wealthy

bachelor in hopeless pursuit of well-bred pretty ladies. Just a year later he was the highest paid entertainer of the time, writing and directing his own films and enjoying fame throughout Europe.

EARLY US COMICS

It was not until 1912 that US comedy emerged with Mack Sennett's films for the Keystone company and, famously, the Keystone Kops. In five years, Sennett established the type of rapid, irreverent comedy forever associated with his name. Using sped-up action, reverse motion, and other camera and editing tricks, the films usually ended with a chase of death-defying thrills, with many stunts executed by the comics themselves. Sennett filmed the throwing of the first custard pie by Mabel Normand at Fatty Arbuckle in *A Noise from the Deep* (1913). He also made the first feature-length comedy, *Tillie's Punctured Romance* (1914), which starred Marie Dressler and Charlie Chaplin.

The four giants of American silent film comedy, Chaplin, Buster Keaton, Harold Lloyd, and Harry Langdon, all emerged from one- or two-reelers to make features in the 1920s. Whereas Chaplin was cocky, Keaton stoical, and Lloyd foolhardy, Langdon cultivated the character of what the writer and film critic James Agee called "an elderly baby." With his white moon face, and innocent and morose demeanour, he seldom instigated any of the chaos around him. With *Safety Last* (1923), Harold Lloyd introduced a comedy of thrills by hanging precariously on the side of a skyscraper. Although he is now best known for these feats, of the 300 films he made, only five contain such sequences.

Harold Lloyd, *who did most of his athletic stunts without a double, keeps his balance in a highly dangerous situation in* Safety Last *(1923).*

LAUREL AND HARDY

The English-born Stan Laurel (1890–1965) and the American Oliver Hardy (1892–1957) are the most famous and best-loved comedy team ever. They are at their hilarious best in more than 60 short films that they made together from 1927, such as *The Music Box* (1932), in which they try to deliver a piano up a huge flight of stairs. Their bowler hats and suits are symbols of their pretentions to middle-class respectability, but their innocence, Stan's clumsiness, Ollie's delusions of grandeur, and their constant squabbling, mark them out as overgrown children.

Stan and Ollie *established their complementary characters early on, with Hardy's famous glare at the camera, and baffled Laurel scratching his head and crying.*

VISUAL GAGS

Although the coming of sound diminished slapstick comedy, the tradition of sight gags was continued by the teams of Stan Laurel and Oliver Hardy in the 1930s, Bud Abbott and Lou Costello in the 1940s, and Dean Martin and Jerry Lewis in the 1950s. Peter Sellers fell about as the maladroit Inspector Clouseau in Blake Edwards' *Pink Panther* series begun in the 1960s, while in France, the pratfall tradition was carried on by Jacques Tati, Pierre Etaix, and Louis De Funes, and in Italy by Toto. More recent examples include the *Police Academy* movies, containing typical doses of 1980s crude visual gags, Jim Carrey in *Ace Ventura, Pet Detective* (1993) and *The Mask* (1994), and the so-called "gross out" comedies of the Farrelly Brothers, Bobby and Peter, such as *There's Something About Mary* (1998).

Film poster, *1978*

THE BIRTH OF THE WISECRACK

The leading exponent of the wise-cracking comedies, which inevitably came with the talkies, was the irascible, bibulous, raspy-voiced W.C. Fields, two of his best films being *The Bank Dick* (1940) and *Never Give a Sucker an Even Break* (1941). Fields costarred with Mae West in *My Little Chickadee* (1940), a spoof Western, in which they exploited their unique comic personae. West, with her ample hourglass figure, was a sashaying parody of a sex symbol and the mistress of sexual innuendo, and one of the few comediennes to make it big in the movies. Her racy wisecracks in *She Done Him Wrong* and *I'm No Angel* (both 1933) resulted in the formation of the Motion Picture Production Code. West responded by resorting to double-entendre to make her comedy a little less direct. The Marx Brothers broke into cinema in 1929 with *The Cocoanuts*, but they had been performing on stage long before that. The four brothers – Groucho, Harpo, Chico, and Zeppo – had been in vaudeville since childhood and, by the 1920s, had become one of the most popular theatrical acts in the US. Uninhibited and irrepressible, the Marx Brothers conveyed a sense of spontaneity as they disrupted all around them with their unique brand of surreal, madcap humor. Although

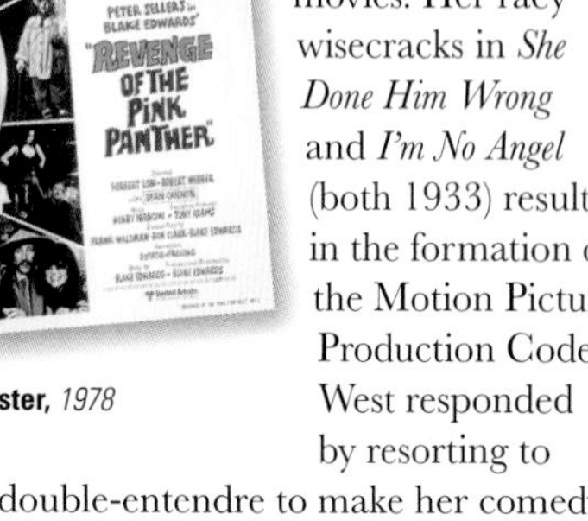

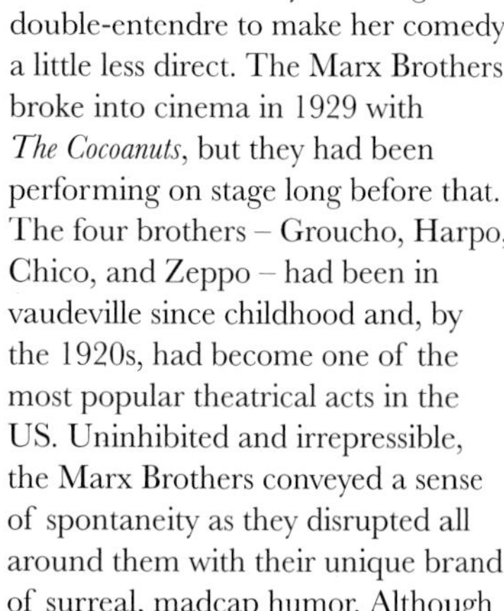

there were four brothers originally, it was three that took centre stage – and Groucho's witticisms, Harpo's dumb show, and Chico's massacre of the English language combined several traditions of comedy. *Duck Soup* (1933), directed by Leo McCarey, an anarchic spoof on warfare, is considered by many to be their finest film. Their last film together was *Love Happy* (1949).

In 1940, Bob Hope teamed up with Bing Crosby and Dorothy Lamour to make seven hilarious *Road To...* pictures. Both Groucho Marx and Bob Hope were plainly potent influences on Woody Allen.

Film poster, *1949*

SCREWBALL COMEDY

Screwball comedy was a unique creation of Hollywood in the 1930s; its main elements were irreverent humor, fast-paced action and dialogue, and eccentric characters, generally the idle rich. The improbable plots commonly focused on the battle of the sexes. An archetypal film is Gregory La Cava's *My Man Godfrey* (1936), which tells of a man (William Powell) from a shantytown who becomes butler to a wealthy family, straightens out their lives, and marries their scatterbrained daughter (Carole Lombard). Other screwball comedy gems were Frank

The Marx Brothers demonstrate *their musical skills in an MGM studio publicity still — Harpo on harp, Chico on piano, and Groucho on trombone.*

In Pillow Talk *(1959), Doris Day's and Rock Hudson's first outing as a winning romantic comedy team, Day's character bravely defends her virginity.*

Capra's five-Oscar winning *It Happened One Night* (1934), about a wacky runaway heiress (Claudette Colbert) with a hard-boiled reporter (Clark Gable) on her tail; Mitchell Leisen's *Easy Living* (1937) and *Midnight* (1939), and Leo McCarey's *The Awful Truth* (1937). Howard Hawks directed, among others, the madcap *Bringing Up Baby* (1938) with Cary Grant and Katharine Hepburn — the title role being taken by a leopard — and the irreverent, fast-paced *His Girl Friday* (1940), also starring Cary Grant. Preston Sturges's social comedies continued in a similar vein into the 1940s, but with the advent of World War II, frivolity and social ridicule seemed inappropriate.

The 1950s saw more sophisticated harder-edged comedies such as Joseph Mankiewicz's *All About Eve* (1950) and several Katharine Hepburn–Spencer Tracy vehicles in which they brought the battle of the sexes to a new level, particularly in George Cukor's *Adam's Rib* (1949). The latter could be seen as forerunners of the glossy Rock Hudson–Doris Day movies: *Pillow Talk* (1959), *Lover Come Back* (1961), and *Send Me No Flowers* (1964), and other romantic comedies of the 1960s and beyond. The formula for these "rom-coms" or "chick flicks," as they would be dubbed a few decades later, was "boy meets girl, boy loses girl, boy gets girl." This was a durable formula, as evidenced by modern variations such as Rob Reiner's *When Harry Met Sally* (1989), Gerry Marshall's *Pretty Woman* (1990), Nora Ephron's *Sleepless in Seattle* (1993), James L. Brooks' *As Good as It Gets* (1997), and the British hit, *Four Weddings and a Funeral* (1994).

Renée Zellweger *as the eponymous heroine in* Bridget Jones's Diary *(2001), about a 32-year-old single girl's misadventures with men and life.*

EALING COMEDY

Long before British comedies became internationally popular in the 1990s, Britain had provided the delightful Ealing comedies from the mid-1940s to the mid-1950s, including Charles Crichton's *The Lavender Hill Mob* (1951), Alexander MacKendrick's *The Man in the White Suit* (1951) and *The Ladykillers* (1955), and Robert Hamer's *Kind Hearts and Coronets* (1949). All starred Alec Guinness, the latter in eight different roles. *The Ladykillers* was remade in 2004 by the Coen Brothers.

SATIRE

Parallel to Hollywood romantic comedies were black comedies, such as Stanley Kubrick's *Dr Strangelove* (1964) and Robert Altman's *M*A*S*H* (1970); the more genial genre spoofs of Mel Brooks' *Blazing Saddles* (1974) and *Young Frankenstein* (1974); the wacky humour of Jim Abrahams' and the Zucker brothers' *Airplane!* (1980) and *The Naked Gun* series (1988–91); as well as the deliciously silly Mike Myers' Austin Powers movies (1999–2002), parodies of James Bond films.

Although a number of "naughty" French comedies were shown widely in the 1960s, one had to wait for *La Cage aux Folles* (1978) — Edouard Molinaro's drag queen farce — to break all box-office records in the US for a foreign language film to that date. Hollywood remade it as *The Birdcage* (1996), along with a number of other French comedies, such as Coline Serreau's *Three Men and a Cradle* (*Trois Hommes et un Couffin*, 1985), which became *Three Men and a Baby* (1987). Italian comedy became popular abroad after the success of Mario Monicelli's *Big Deal on Madonna Street* (*I Soliti Ignoti*, 1958) about a group of useless crooks trying to carry out a heist. It was remade by Louis Malle as *Crackers* (1984), given a California setting, and was the inspiration behind Woody Allen's *Small Time Crooks* (2000).

US comedians that came to the fore in the 1980s and 90s included Eddie Murphy (*Trading Places*, 1983), Steve Martin (*L.A. Story*, 1991), and Jim Carrey (*The Cable Guy*, 1996), each in their own way continuing the genre, and displaying a flair for visual comedy rather than elegant, verbal wit.

WHAT TO WATCH

1927	The General (US)
1937	Duck Soup (US)
1940	His Girl Friday (US)
1955	The Ladykillers (UK)
1963	The Pink Panther (US)
1977	Annie Hall (US)
1980	Airplane! (US)
1994	Four Weddings and a Funeral (UK)
1997	The Full Monty (UK)
2000	Meet the Parents (US)

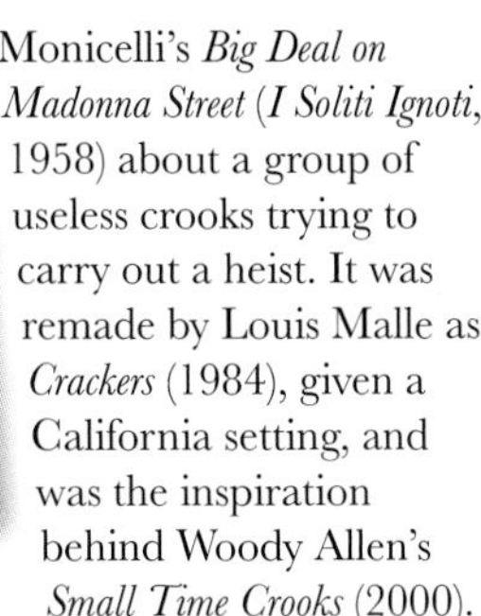

Film poster, *1979*

Michel Serrault camps it up in La Cage aux Folles *(1978), a French farce set in St Tropez, which was transplanted to Miami in the remake,* The Birdcage *(1996).*

Costume Drama

The classic costume drama, or period piece, derives from literary sources. The best examples of the genre are typified by lavish costumes and design, which succeed in capturing the ambience of the particular era in which they are set in meticulous detail.

Becky Sharp (1935) was the first Technicolor feature film and the sixth adaptation of William Makepeace Thackeray's novel *Vanity Fair*. The most visually striking moment in the film was the ball scene, which showed off the women's gorgeous gowns and the soldiers' red uniforms to great effect. Technicolor and costume dramas were made for each other, but the marriage was only consummated in 1939 with *Gone With the Wind*.

A year earlier, Bette Davis had won the Best Actress Oscar for her performance as the spoiled Southern Belle Julie Marsden in William Wyler's *Jezebel* (1938), set in pre-Civil War New Orleans. The role was compensation for not getting the part of Scarlett O'Hara in *Gone With the Wind*. In one great scene in *Jezebel*, Davis arrives at a ball — at which unmarried girls traditionally wear white — dressed in a scarlet gown, in order to scandalize the assembled company. The impact of this single splash of color was brilliantly suggested by Ernest Haller's black-and-white photography.

WHAT TO WATCH

1938	Jezebel (US)
1945	Les Enfants du Paradis (France)
1954	Senso (Italy)
1975	Barry Lyndon (UK)
1988	Dangerous Liaisons (US)
1992	Howards End (UK)
1995	Sense and Sensibility (UK/US)

Miriam Hopkins *plays the title role of Rouben Mamoulian's* Becky Sharp *(1935).*

MELODRAMA

Gainsborough Pictures in England made a series of melodramatic period pieces in the 1940s with a list of stars headed by Margaret Lockwood, James Mason, Stewart Granger, and Phyllis Calvert. Two of the most popular films were directed by Leslie Arliss: *The Man in Grey* (1943) and *The Wicked Lady* (1945), both with Mason and Lockwood relishing respectively the roles of sadistic lover and sexy villainess. Two decades later, Tony Richardson's bawdy four-Oscar-winning version of Henry Fielding's *Tom Jones* (1963) captured a similar spirit. In the 1980s, James Ivory made a number of refined costume dramas, which were adapted from the novels of Henry James and E.M. Forster.

ACROSS THE WORLD

Martin Scorsese uncharacteristically entered Ivory territory with *The Age of Innocence* (1993), adapted from Edith Wharton's novel. Other leading directors who made rare, and usually successful, ventures into the genre were Stanley Kubrick with Thackeray's *Barry Lyndon* (1975); Ingmar Bergman with *Fanny and Alexander* (1982); Peter Greenaway with *The Draughtsman's Contract* (1982); Stephen Frears with *Dangerous Liaisons* (1988), and Mike Leigh with *Topsy-Turvy* (1999).

In Italy, former Neo-Realist film-maker, Luchino Visconti, made two lush historical romances, *Senso* (1954) and *The Leopard* (1963). France, which has always produced fine costume dramas, turned out a string of successful historical romances in the 1990s, including Jean-Paul Rappeneau's *Cyrano de Bergerac* (1990) and *The Horseman on the Roof* (1995), and Patrice Chéreau's *La Reine Margot* (1994).

Pride and Prejudice *(2005) stars Keira Knightley as heroine Elizabeth Bennet and Matthew Macfadyen as her love interest, Mr. Darcy.*

JANE AUSTEN MANIA

The 1990s also saw a resurgence of interest in the six novels of Jane Austen. Over a few years, Roger Mitchell's *Persuasion* (1995), Ang Lee's *Sense and Sensibility* (1995), Douglas McGrath's *Emma* (1996), Patricia Rozema's *Mansfield Park* (1999), and Joe Wright's *Pride and Prejudice* (2005) were released as well as a Bollywood version of the latter, Gurinder Chadha's *Bride and Prejudice* (2004). Coincidentally, the Indian-born Mira Nair directed the seventh version of *Vanity Fair* (2004).

The Catholic Marguerite de Valois *(Isabelle Adjani) marries the Protestant Henri de Navarre (Daniel Auteuil) in a sumptuous scene from Patrice Chéreau's* La Reine Margot *(1994).*

Cult Movies

The term cult movie denotes any film that, for a reason unallied to its intrinsic artistic quality, has attracted obsessive devotion from a group of fans. The expression "so bad it's good" is often used to describe many cult movies.

Considered one of the worst film directors of all time, Edward D. Wood has gathered a cult following. So cheap were Wood's films that the spaceships in *Plan 9 from Outer Space* (1958) were represented by spinning hubcaps and paper plates.

Reefer Madness (1936) was a propaganda film made by a religious group to warn of the dangers of marijuana. In the film, a group of dope peddlers turn clean-cut teenagers into raving lunatics by giving them a puff of "the demon weed." *Reefer Madness* remained in obscurity for nearly 40 years until it was re-released in 1972. The film became a camp hit, especially among the pot-smoking young, the very people it had aimed to alarm.

The Rocky Horror Picture Show (1975), combining the conventions of science fiction, musicals, and horror films with elements of transvestism and homosexuality, attracted fans to midnight screenings dressed as characters from the film. Russ Meyer's "nudie-cutie" films also gained a cult following, especially *Faster, Pussycat! Kill! Kill!* (1965). Gaining more of a following among gay audiences was John Waters' *Pink Flamingos* (1972), starring drag superstar Divine.

The poster for Attack of the 50ft. Woman *(1957) shows Allison Hayes turned into a giant; she wreaks havoc and eventually crushes her cheating husband to death.*

Cultists revel in films with ludicrous titles such as *Santa Claus Conquers the Martians* (1964) or *Attack Of the 50ft. Woman* (1957). Occasionally a more mainstream film would catch the imagination of a group of fans, such as *This Is Spinal Tap* (1984), Rob Reiner's hilarious mockumentary send-up of the rock'n'roll industry, and Bruce Robinson's acidly witty *Withnail and I* (1987), about two "resting" young actors in the 1960s.

Christopher Guest plays Nigel Tufnel, *co-lead guitarist of an ageing British rock group on tour in the US in Rob Reiner's* This Is Spinal Tap *(1984).*

WHAT TO WATCH

1958	Plan 9 from Outer Space (US)
1965	Faster, Pussycat! Kill! Kill! (US)
1972	Pink Flamingos (US)
1975	The Rocky Horror Picture Show (UK)
1987	Withnail and I (UK)

Disaster

The heyday of the disaster movie was the 1970s, the decade in which this sub-genre of action movies reached its zenith. A string of films were released, featuring stellar casts threatened by earthquakes, sinking ships, fires, air crashes, tidal waves, and other catastrophes.

The success of *Airport* (1970) – in which an airliner comes under threat from a bomb – spawned three sequels and the spoof *Airplane!* (1980). It also initiated a cycle of disaster movies that included *Earthquake* (1974), a film made in "Sensurround," which gave audiences the sensation of a minor tremor at certain climactic moments.

Taking advantage of this vicarious enjoyment of others in peril, and the latest special effects, was the producer Irwin Allen, dubbed "The Master of Disaster". In *The Poseidon Adventure* (1972), Gene Hackman, Shelley Winters, and Ernest Borgnine, among others, try to escape from a capsized luxury liner, while in *The Towering Inferno* (1974), Paul Newman and Steve McQueen battle the flames to rescue various well-known faces from a burning 138-story hotel.

These films actually formed part of a second wave of disaster movies. The first wave included *San Francisco* (1936), *In Old Chicago* (1937), and *The Rains Came* (1939); in these, an earthquake, a fire, and a flood featured as the respective climaxes of each film — unlike the films of the 1970s where the disasters were central to the plot. The genre faded after Allen followed his triumphs with the laughable *The Swarm* (1978), in which Michael Caine battles killer bees, and *Beyond The Poseidon Adventure* (1979), featuring Caine again, now trying to loot the ship.

There was a revival of disaster movies from the mid-1990s with *Independence Day* (1996), *Titanic* (1997), *Armageddon* (1998), and *The Day After Tomorrow* (2004), all benefitting from the arrival of Computer Generated Imagery (CGI).

WHAT TO WATCH

1970	Airport (US)
1972	The Poseidon Adventure (US)
1974	The Towering Inferno (US)
1996	Independence Day (US)
1997	Titanic (US)

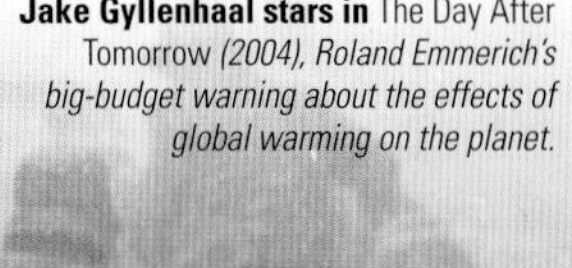

Jake Gyllenhaal stars in The Day After Tomorrow *(2004), Roland Emmerich's big-budget warning about the effects of global warming on the planet.*

Documentary

The documentary, or non-fiction film, goes back to the very beginning of cinema history. Since undergoing a rennaissance and becoming more popular than ever at the beginning of the 21st century, the genre could be considered the most enduring of all film forms.

John Grierson, the leading force behind the British documentary movement in the 1930s, defined documentary as "the creative treatment of actuality."

Documentaries dominated the cinema in its early years but, after 1908, they became subsidiary to fiction films. Documentary films began to be taken seriously immediately after the Russian Revolution (1917), when propaganda pictures were sent across the vast country on "agitprop" trains to educate the masses about communism. Dziga Vertov edited a series of "agitprop" films between 1922–25 called *Kino-Pravda* (Cinema Truth). These were created from newsreel sequences to which he added slow or reverse motion, animation, texts, and still photographs.

In contrast to the didactic Russian films were American Robert Flaherty's ethnological documentaries, such as *Nanook of the North* (1922). The future directors of *King Kong* (1933), Merian C. Cooper and Ernest B. Schoedsack, directed two exotic adventure–travel films: *Grass* (1925), following a Persian tribe during their annual migration, and *Chang* (1927) about a Thai family's struggle to survive life with a herd of elephants.

Impoverished fisherman *Colman "Tiger" King and his family struggle to survive in Robert Flaherty's* Man of Aran *(1934).*

Memphis Belle: A Story of a Flying Fortress (1944) *was William Wyler's record of a B-17's last bombing mission over Germany in World War II.*

In Germany, Walter Ruttmann's *Berlin: Symphony of a Great City* (1927), an impressionistic view of a day in the life of the German capital, was shot using cameras concealed in a removal van and in suitcases to catch people unawares. Vertov's *Man with a Movie Camera* (1929), a filmed poem of a Soviet city, displayed all the techniques of the cinema at his disposal. These experimental films were part of an effort to distance documentaries from the style of fiction films.

SOCIAL COMMENT

In western Europe and the US, documentaries highlighted social and environmental problems. In the UK, the Crown Film Unit developed under Grierson, who believed that film should have a social purpose. The unit produced some of the most outstanding documentaries of the 1930s, including Alberto Cavalcanti's *Coal Face* (1935) and Basil Wright and Harry Watt's *Night Mail* (1936), both of which included W.H. Auden's verse and Benjamin Britten's music.

In the US, Pare Lorentz's *The River* (1938) showed the effects of soil erosion in the Mississippi Basin. The film won the best documentary award at the Venice Festival in competition with Leni Riefenstahl's *Olympia* (1938), which was about the 1936 Berlin Olympics. Dutch-born Joris Ivens' *The Spanish Earth* (1937), with a commentary written and spoken by Ernest Hemingway, was one of several films that supported the Republican cause during the Spanish Civil War (1936–9). The outbreak of World War II took both documentary and fiction film-makers, on both sides, into the field of propaganda. The end of the war saw a drop in the output of documentary films in the west. Firstly, they had become too closely associated with wartime propaganda, and secondly, television documentaries were taking their role. It took more than 15 years for the crisis to pass.

FILMS OF TRUTH

In late 1950s England, the so-called Free Cinema — a series of shorts describing mostly working-class people

Man with a Movie Camera, *Russian film poster, 1929*

and places — launched the careers of Lindsay Anderson, Tony Richardson, and Karel Reisz. In France, Alain Resnais' career began with several remarkable short art films, among them *Van Gogh* (1948), *Guernica* (1950), and *Night and Fog* (1955), his devastating documentary about Nazi concentration camps. Georges Franju's powerful *Blood of the Beasts* (*Le Sang des Bêtes*, 1949) showed the daily slaughter of animals in an abattoir juxtaposed with everyday life in Paris. Other film-makers who have contributed to the *cinéma verité* (the cinema of truth) movement include Chris Marker and Jean Rouch. The latter believed that the camera's intervention stimulated people to greater spontaneity.

Bob Dylan, *holding the lyrics of "Subterranean Homesick Blues", is the subject of D.A. Pennebaker's documentary,* Don't Look Back *(1967).*

In the US, Direct Cinema was developed in the early 1960s by a group of film-makers, notably Richard Leacock, D.A. Pennebaker, and the Maysles brothers, Albert and David. Like the *cinéma verité* film-makers, exponents of Direct Cinema also believed that the camera should unobtrusively record the "truth." Fred Wiseman, a leading exponent of Direct Cinema, eavesdropped on many institutions such as *High School* (1968), *Juvenile Court* (1973), and *Welfare* (1975). Pennebaker's *Don't Look Back* (1967) — a behind-the-scenes look at Bob Dylan's British concert tour — started a trend for "rockumentaries." In this vein, Michael Wadleigh's *Woodstock* (1970) stands out, winning the Oscar for Best Documentary Feature.

WHAT TO WATCH

1929	Man with a Movie Camera (USSR)
1955	Night and Fog (France)
1967	Don't Look Back (US)
1969	The Sorrow and the Pity (France)
2003	Capturing the Friedmans (US)

REPORTAGE

Beginning in the late 1960s, there was a gradual move away from *cinéma verité* and the recording of reality toward historical reporting and investigative exposés. These included films such as Marcel Ophüls' four-and-half-hour *The Sorrow and the*

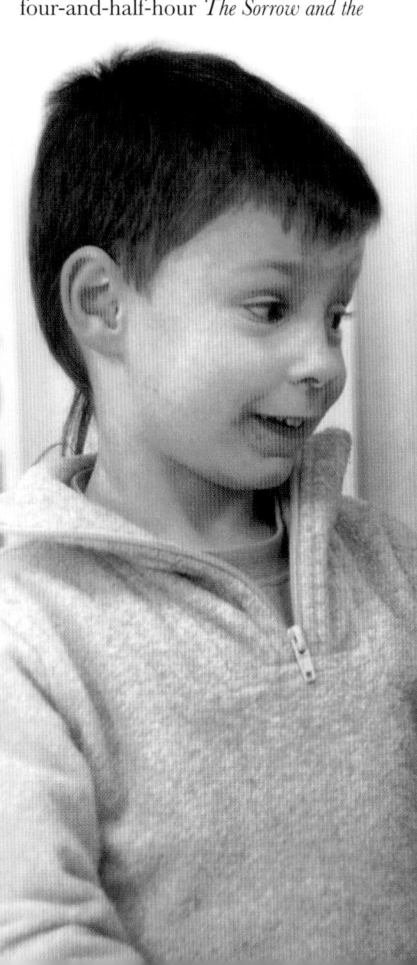

Pity (1969), which builds up a complex picture of France under the Occupation. By the same director, *Hotel Terminus: The Life and Times of Klaus Barbie (1988)* was a discomforting portrait of the "Butcher of Lyons," and Claude Lanzmann's *Shoah* (1985) gave an insight into the Holocaust. Errol Morris's investigation into a 1976 murder, *The Thin Blue Line* (1988), helped free an innocent man from death row, and his *Fog of War* (2003) put in the confessional the man who was US Defense Secretary during the Vietnam conflict.

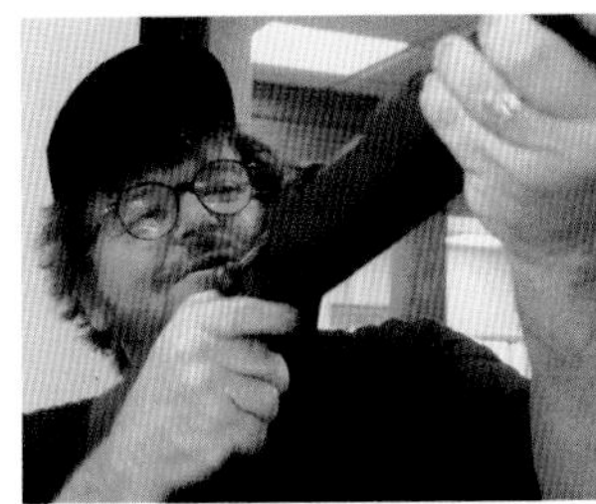

Michael Moore, *a sharpshooter literally and figuratively, narrates* Bowling for Columbine *(2002), his Oscar-winning exposé of America's love affair with guns.*

No less serious were Michael Moore's examinations of the dark side of America: *Roger and Me* (1989), *Bowling for Columbine* (2002), and *Fahrenheit 9/11* (2004).

Documentaries now compete with fiction films at the box office. *Être et Avoir* (2002), the story of an inspirational rural school teacher in France, *Spellbound* (2002), about children competing in the US National Spelling Bee, and *Super Size Me* (2004), Morgan Spurlock's take on fast-food and obesity in the US, were all international commercial hits.

Nicolas Philibert's Être et Avoir (2002) *is a delightful portrait of George Lopez, a dedicated rural schoolmaster, seen here with the impish Jojo.*

Epics

Narratives in the epic tradition surpass the ordinary in scale, and are of heroic proportions. This applies to the film genre, too. Epic movies typically feature vast panoramas with hundreds of extras, and are likely to be historical or biblical stories containing spectacular scenes.

The first film to be worthy of the title of epic was *Cabiria* (1914), a huge spectacle made in Italy following the adventures of a slave girl during the Second Punic War, in about 200 BCE. Its great success in America inspired D.W. Griffith to embark on his large-scale productions of *The Birth of a Nation* (1915) and *Intolerance* (1916). But it was Cecil B. DeMille who became most associated with epics, in a series of films that started with *The Ten Commandments* (1923) and ended with his 1956 remake of the film. Fred Niblo's *Ben-Hur* (1926) featured a spectacular sea battle and a breathtaking chariot race (replicated in William Wyler's version of 1959).

Cleopatra *(1963) was panned by critics and avoided by film-goers but made its money back.*

POLITICS AND EPICS

Sometimes, epic films had a topicality. In the USSR, Sergei Eisenstein's *Alexander Nevsky* (1938), made under the threat of a Nazi invasion, told how the hero defended Holy Russia in the 13th century against brutal Teutons. The film inspired Laurence Olivier's *Henry V* (1944), made when Britain was preparing to launch an invasion of German-occupied France.

In the 1940s, MGM head Dore Schary was eager to film a novel about Roman dictator Nero, in order to equate Nero with modern dictators. But the hit $8 million movie *Quo Vadis* was not made until 1951.

WHAT TO WATCH

1915	The Birth of a Nation (US)
1938	Alexander Nevsky (USSR)
1953	The Robe (US)
1956	The Ten Commandments (US)
1959	Ben-Hur (US)
1960	Spartacus (US)
1965	Doctor Zhivago (US)
2000	Gladiator (US)

FILLING THE SCREEN

It was appropriate that the first feature film in CinemaScope was *The Robe* (1953), a biblical epic that began a renaissance of epics that filled the vast screen. Among the biggest and best were Howard Hawks's *Land of the Pharaohs* (1955), King Vidor's *War and Peace* (1956), Stanley Kubrick's *Spartacus* (1960), and Anthony Mann's *El Cid* (1961). From 1958, Italy turned out numerous "sword and sandals" movies starring famous bodybuilders such as American-born Steve Reeves, who played Hercules among other mythological heroes.

EPIC COSTS

Cleopatra (1963) took over four years to shoot in Rome at a cost of around $40 million and nearly bankrupted 20th Century Fox. Yet studios were still willing to invest in epics.

Akira Kurosawa's *epic* Kagemusha *(1980) follows a thief who poses as a clan leader to confuse his enemy. It was the most expensive Japanese movie of the time.*

David Lean made the leap from small black-and-white British pictures to long, lavish films such as *Doctor Zhivago* (1965). Akira Kurosawa's impressive *Kagemusha* (1980), was completed only with the assistance of his American producers. Michael Cimino's *Heaven's Gate* (1980) was the biggest flop of all time, costing United Artists $44 million and earning only $1.5 million at the box office. A new cycle of epics kicked off with Mel Gibson's *Braveheart* (1995) and continued with Ridley Scott's *Gladiator* (2000) and Wolfgang Petersen's *Troy* (2004), both of which included computer-generated effects.

In the celebrated *20-minute chariot race in* Ben-Hur *(1959), Charlton Heston, playing the title role, was watched by 8,000 extras in an 18-acre set.*

Film Noir

Film noir is a term that French film critics originally applied to the dark, doom-laden, black-and-white Hollywood crime dramas of the 1940s, such as *The Maltese Falcon* (1941), which were only seen in French cinemas for the first time after World War II.

The roots of film noir can be seen in the German expressionist films of the 1920s and 1930s, such as *The Cabinet of Dr. Caligari* (1919) and Fritz Lang's *M* (1931). The style and subject matter were also influenced by certain French films of the 1930s, including Jean Renoir's *La Chienne* (1931) and *La Bête Humaine* (1938). Both were remade by Fritz Lang as noirs in Hollywood, as *Scarlet Street* (1945) and *Human Desire* (1954) respectively.

NOIR IN AMERICAN SOCIETY

The low-key lighting, off-center camera angles, and shadowy, claustrophobic atmosphere were imported to the US by emigré film-makers, such as Lang, Robert Siodmak (*Phantom Lady*, 1944), Jacques Tourneur (*Out of the Past*, 1947), Otto Preminger (*Fallen Angel*, 1945), Billy Wilder (*Double Indemnity*, 1944), and Edgar Ulmer (*Detour*, 1945), who all made among the best film noirs. The style may have originated in Europe, but the subject matter was found in urban America and inspired by hard-boiled crime writers like James M. Cain, Raymond Chandler, Dashiell Hammett, and Cornell Woolrich.

Film poster, *1944*

Jane Greer plays a femme fatale *who has caught Robert Mitchum in her web in* Out of the Past *(1947), which was released in the UK as* Build My Gallows High.

WHAT TO WATCH

1944	Double Indemnity (US)
1945	Fallen Angel (US)
1946	The Big Sleep (US)
1955	Kiss Me Deadly US)
1958	Touch of Evil (US)
1974	Chinatown (US)
1997	L.A. Confidential (US)

Film noir developed during and after World War II in the context of post-war anxiety and cynicism. The almost exclusively male anti-heroes of the genre, many of whom were private eyes, shared this malaise. They were disillusioned loners moving through dark alleyways, rundown hotels, cheerless bars, and gaudy nightclubs. The detectives, the police, and the villains were all as corrupt and mercenary as each other.

Film poster, *1997*

HARD-BOILED ANTI-HEROES

Alan Ladd made a name for himself as the baby-faced killer in *This Gun for Hire* (1942), his first film opposite vampish Veronica Lake. The couple teamed up again in *The Glass Key* (1942), based on Dashiell Hammett's novel, and *The Blue Dahlia* (1946), scripted by Raymond Chandler. Chandler's cynical private eye Philip Marlowe was portrayed most memorably by Humphrey Bogart in Howard Hawks's *The Big Sleep* (1946).

Chandler also cowrote the script for *Double Indemnity*, the archetypal noir, in which an insurance salesman, Fred McMurray, is led into fraud and murder by the amoral and seductive Barbara Stanwyck. Many film noirs center around a weak man whose life is ruined when caught up in a web of passion, deceit, and murder by a beautiful and charming — but amoral and double-dealing — *femme fatale.*

POSTNOIR AND NEONOIR

By the early 1950s, the classic period of film noir had ended, but there were isolated examples of the genre still being made, such as Robert Aldrich's *Kiss Me Deadly* (1955) and Orson Welles's *Touch of Evil* (1958). In the 1960s, Jean-Pierre Melville kept film noir alive in France with his crime thrillers and, some years later, a number of post- and neo-noirs appeared in the US, notably Robert Altman's *The Long Goodbye* (1973), Roman Polanski's *Chinatown* (1974), Lawrence Kasdan's *Body Heat* (1981), the Coen brothers' *Blood Simple* (1983), and Curtis Hanson's *L.A. Confidential* (1997), all of them paying homage to film noirs of the past.

CHIAROSCURO

The word *chiaroscuro* comes from the Italian *chiaro* (bright) and *oscuro* (dark). It was first used to refer to the use of light and shade in paintings. The bold contrast between light and shade in cinematography gave film noirs their look and atmosphere. The effect is seen here in a scene from *The Killers* (1946), featuring Burt Lancaster and Ava Gardner.

Gangster

The gangster movie came into being as a distinct genre in Prohibition America of the 1920s, when alcohol was banned and racketeers flourished. The crime films of the late 1920s and 1930s were updated with dramatic effect in the 1970s and 1990s mob movies.

Although the gangster film only came into its own with the introduction of sound — guns blazing, cars screeching, and the fast-paced, tough, and slangy dialogue — urban crime had provided material for the cinema from the earliest days. One of the first was D.W. Griffith's 17-minute *The Musketeers of Pig Alley* (1912) set in a New York slum. A former assistant to D.W. Griffith, Raoul Walsh's first feature film, *Regeneration* (1915), was about a New York street gang. The film was shot on location in the Bowery in New York. Later, in Germany, Fritz Lang's *Dr. Mabuse, the Gambler* (1922), about a master criminal who tries to take over the world, foreshadowed the coming of Hitler. However, the first true gangster movies were Josef von Sternberg's *Underworld* (1927), starring George Bancroft, and Lewis Milestone's *The Racket* (1928), both of which dealt with organized crime. Sternberg followed up with two more crime pictures featuring Bancroft, *The Dragnet* (1928) and *Thunderbolt* (1929), his first sound

Film poster, *1931*

James Cagney stars as "Rocky" Sullivan, *a hoodlum who proves to be a bad influence on the Dead End Kids in* Angels With Dirty Faces *(1938)*.

Alain Delon plays Jeff Costello, *a cold-blooded hired killer, in his last hours of life, in Jean-Pierre Melville's ultra-stylish* Le Samurai *(1967).*

film. Rouben Mamoulian's *City Streets* (1931), with Gary Cooper as an innocent drawn into the underworld, featured the first sound flashback.

NEW REALISM

It was the cycle of gangster movies that Warner Bros. produced that achieved a new realism. Some of them were based on real incidents and living hoodlums. Mervyn LeRoy's *Little Caesar* (1931), depicting the rise and fall of a gang boss, was closely modelled on Al Capone. The final line, "Mother of Mercy, is this the end of Rico?" spoken by the dying Edward G. Robinson, was just the beginning of a Hollywood crime wave – 50 gangster movies were made in 1931 alone. *Little Caesar* made Robinson into a star. James Cagney achieved the same status for William Wellman's *Public Enemy* (1931), which includes the celebrated scene in which Cagney shoves half a grapefruit into Mae Clarke's kisser.

There were complaints that these films endowed gangsters with a certain kind of glamour. When Howard Hawks' *Scarface* (1932) was released, it immediately ran into trouble with the censors. Some of the violent scenes had to be cut and the subtitle "Shame of the Nation" added. One of the great classics of the genre, *Scarface,* starred Paul Muni as a brutish, childish, and arrogant racketeer. Brian De Palma directed a violent remake in 1983.

In 1934, the puritanical Production Code was enforced, stating that "crime will be shown to be wrong and that the criminal life will be loathed and that

WHAT TO WATCH

1931	Little Caesar (US)
1931	Public Enemy (US)
1938	Angels With Dirty Faces (US)
1967	Bonnie and Clyde (US)
1972	The Godfather (US)
1990	GoodFellas (US)
1994	Pulp Fiction (US)

Al Pacino plays the ruthless Cuban refugee *turned cocaine-smuggler in* Scarface *(1983), Brian De Palma's powerful and violent update of Howard Hawks' 1932 classic of the same name.*

Takeshi Kitano, *the director and star of* Fireworks (Hana-Bi, *1997), plays a hard-boiled cop who faces numerous tragedies in his life.*

the law will at all times prevail." Villains could no longer be protagonists, but gangster films were Hollywood's most profitable movies. So the studios switched to making law enforcement officers the heroes. Cagney and Robinson changed sides, though the films were still about gangsters and no less violent.

William Wyler's *Dead End* (1937) and Michael Curtiz's *Angels With Dirty Faces* (1938) both showed the bad influence a gangster can have on kids. The stars of these films, Humphrey Bogart and James Cagney, faced each other in Raoul Walsh's *The Roaring*

Joe Pesci (centre left) *plays a brutal gangster in Martin Scorsese's* GoodFellas *(1990). His ruthlessness impresses small-time crook Ray Liotta (foreground).*

Twenties (1939), the Prohibition-era, documentary-style culmination of the Hollywood gangster cycle.

END OF THE ERA

World War II saw the demise of the gangster film, which reappeared in the 1940s in the guise of film noir *(see pages 140–1)*. Henry Hathaway's *Kiss of Death* (1947) introduced Richard Widmark to the screen as a giggling psychopath killer. Walsh and Cagney were reunited in *White Heat* (1949), with the latter playing a mother-fixated murderer. Roger Corman picked up the genre in the late 1950s and 1960s with *Machine-Gun Kelly* (1958), with Charles Bronson, and *The St. Valentine's Day Massacre* (1967). In France, Jacques Becker's influential *Hands off the Loot!* (*Touchez pas au Grisbi*, 1954), starring the magisterial Jean Gabin as an ageing gangster, looked forward to Jean-Pierre Melville's crime dramas of the 1960s. In 1960, both Jean-Luc Godard and François Truffaut paid homage to the American gangster movie in *Breathless (A Bout de Souffle)* and *Shoot the Pianist* respectively.

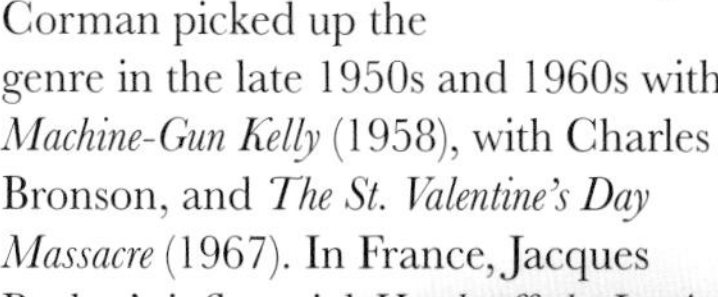

Film poster, *1994*

Akira Kurosawa did the same in Japan with his two adaptations from Ed McBain cop novels, *The Bad Sleep Well* (1960) and *High and Low* (1963). There were also the *yakuza* (Japanese organized crime) films, such as Seijun Suzuki's *Tokyo Drifter* (1966), Kinji Fukasaku's *Battles Without Honour and Humanity* (1973), and Takeshi Kitano's *Fireworks (Hana-Bi*, 1997).

In the US, Arthur Penn's *Bonnie and Clyde* (1967) and Francis Ford Coppola's *The Godfather* (1972) gave a new direction to the gangster genre. *Mean Streets* (1973), featuring a group of small-town hoods, established Martin Scorsese's reputation. He went on to make *GoodFellas* (1990), *Casino* (1995), and *Gangs of New York* (2002), which took street gang warfare in 19th-century New York as its subject.

Other directors, such as Sergio Leone (*Once Upon a Time in America*, 1984), Warren Beatty (*Bugsy*, 1991), and the Coen brothers (*Miller's Crossing*, 1990) ventured successfully into traditional film gangsterdom, while the UK's Guy Ritchie, with *Lock, Stock and Two Smoking Barrels* (1998), started a trend of British crime movies.

Quentin Tarantino made most impact in the genre with *Reservoir Dogs* (1992) and *Pulp Fiction* (1994), both of which looked back to early Warner Bros. heist classics like John Huston's *The Asphalt Jungle* (1950).

Horror

Horror movies tap into our deepest fears and anxieties, and what is suggested is often more frightening than what is revealed. The German expressionist films of the 1920s, influenced by the English Gothic novel, were among the first examples of the genre.

Boris Karloff stars as the monster *in James Whale's* Frankenstein *(1931), a performance that was both touching and poetic. The striking make-up was devised by Jack Pierce.*

The high watermark of Hollywood horror was the 1930s. The films of the period were informed by a crystallization of influences, which included Mary Shelley's *Frankenstein,* Bram Stoker's *Dracula,* and Robert Louis Stevenson's *Dr. Jekyll and Mr. Hyde*; German expressionist films such as *The Cabinet of Dr. Caligari* (1919) and *Nosferatu* (1922); and, from the mid-1920s, the emigration of European film-makers to Hollywood. However, the two most influential films, both made in 1931, were directed by an American, Tod Browning, and an Englishman, James Whale. Browning's *Dracula,* helped by Bela Lugosi's chilling performance, and Whales's *Frankenstein,* starring Boris Karloff, set the style for a cycle of horror films, mainly from Universal Studios.

WHAT TO WATCH

1922	Nosferatu (Germany)
1935	The Bride of Frankenstein (US)
1942	Cat People (US)
1968	The Night of the Living Dead (US)
1973	The Exorcist (US)
1978	Halloween (US)
1998	Ring (Ringu) (Japan)
1999	The Blair Witch Project (US)

CLASSIC CHILLERS

Browning had previously made eight horror movies with Lon Chaney. Whale was to contribute two more classic horrors to the genre, *The Old Dark House* (1932) and *The Bride of Frankenstein* (1935). The former was another strand of the horror genre — the haunted-house movie, one of the first being *The Cat and The Canary* (1927) directed by German-born Paul Leni. The studio also created a new creature in *The Werewolf of London* (1935) and *The Wolf Man* (1941), the latter with the hulking Lon Chaney Jr., who was to reprise the role three more times.

Arguably the best of the *Dr. Jekyll and Mr. Hyde* films was Rouben Mamoulian's 1931 version (the fifth) starring Fredric March. The same year also saw the release of the Danish Carl Dreyer's *Vampyr,* which had an eerie, dreamlike quality.

During the 1940s, the real horrors of World War II made monster movies seem innocuous in comparison. The chillers produced by Val Lewton at RKO relied on a suggestion of horror rather than its depiction. An underlying fear of the supernatural invested each scene in Jacques Tourneur's *Cat People* (1942) and *I Walked with a Zombie* (1943), and Mark Robson's *The Seventh Victim* (1943).

LOW-BUDGET SCARE

Britain's Hammer Studios brought all the notorious monsters back to life in gory Technicolor in the 1950s and 1960s. They made stars of Christopher Lee and Peter Cushing in a number of *Dracula* and *Frankenstein* films. Also in England in the 1960s, Roger Corman produced a series of garish adaptations of Edgar Allen Poe's short stories, taking their tone from Vincent Price's ghoulish hamming. Following Corman's low-budget independent example was George A. Romero, whose horror movies were full of slavering zombies, from *Night of the Living Dead* (1968) to *Land of the Dead* (2005).

In the 1960s and 1970s, Italy produced a stream of startling baroque horror flicks directed by Mario Bava and Dario Argento.

The 1970s saw a number of gory horrors, including Tobe Hooper's exploitative *The Texas Chainsaw Massacre* (1974) and William Friedkin's horror hit *The Exorcist* (1973). John Carpenter's *Halloween* (1978), Sean Cunningham's *Friday the 13th* (1980), and Wes Craven's

Film poster, *1931*

Frances Dee features in *Jacques Tourneur's* I Walked with a Zombie *(1943), an example of RKO's horror output of the 1940s. The atmosphere, lighting, and exotic setting of Haiti contributed to the film's disturbing mood.*

A Nightmare on Elm Street (1984) all featured terrorized teens and spawned endless inferior sequels.

The Blair Witch Project (1999) showed what could be achieved with a tiny budget, with the protagonists filming on two video cameras as if it were a real documentary *(see page 78)*. The one country that has produced more horror films than any other is Japan, which has almost redefined the genre. The most successful of its films was Hideo Nakata's *Ring* (*Ringu*, 1998), about a video tape that shocks to death those who watch it. The film was remade in the US in 2002 as *The Ring*.

A woman has a look of pure shock *and fear on her face after viewing a mysterious video tape in Hideo Nakata's* Ring (Ringu, *1998).*

Old favourites such as *The Mummy*, which first terrified film-goers in 1932, continue to be revisited. The 1999 version benefits from the use of CG1 technology.

Martial Arts

The popularity of martial arts movies grew in the early 1970s due to a growing interest in the west in Eastern philosophy, and the star presence of Bruce Lee. In recent years the genre has been discovered again through films such as *Hero* (2002).

Martial arts movies typically include a series of brilliantly choreographed fights in which the hero is outnumbered by his or her enemies, armed with knives or clubs, and defeats them with his bare hands. The plots are usually simple affairs of good versus evil.

The most well-known actor in this field was Bruce Lee, whose reputation is based on only four films: *Fists of Fury* (1971); *The Chinese Connection* (1972); *Way of the Dragon* (1972), which he wrote and directed himself; and *Enter the Dragon* (1973), in which he and two others manage to free hundreds of prisoners from an island fortress over which an evil warlord holds sway. *Enter the Dragon* was Lee's last completed film before his mysterious death at the age of 32. It was given the Hollywood treatment and made a fortune for Warner Bros.

From the 1980s, a plethora of martial arts films appeared, such as *The Karate Kid* (1984) for younger audiences, and those starring Jean-Claude Van Damme (known as "the muscles from Brussels"); Chuck Norris; Steven Seagal; and Jackie Chan, whose comic take on the genre earned him the nickname the "Buster Keaton of Kung-Fu." But Bruce Lee's true successor was Jet Li, who began a new wave of kung fu movies in China in the 1990s, such as *Once Upon a Time in China* (1991).

Jackie Chan is a fan *of both Buster Keaton and Bruce Lee, and successfully combines physical comedy with action.*

Using outstanding special effects, the martial arts movie *Crouching Tiger, Hidden Dragon* (2000) became the highest grossing foreign-language film ever released in America.

Bruce Lee prepares for action *in* Enter the Dragon *(1973), which was the first American-produced martial arts film. It made its star a legend and inspired a generation of film-makers.*

WHAT TO WATCH

1971	Fists of Fury (Hong Kong)
1972	The Chinese Connection (Hong Kong)
1973	Enter the Dragon (Hong Kong/US)
1984	The Karate Kid (US)
1991	Once Upon a Time in China (Hong Kong)
2000	Crouching Tiger, Hidden Dragon (Taiwan/H.Kong/US)
2002	Hero (China/Hong Kong)
2003	Kill Bill Volume 1 (US)

Melodrama

In between the male-orientated war films, Westerns, and action movies that Hollywood turned out in the 1930s and 1940s, there was what was called "the woman's picture." The genre continued with success into the 1950s and 1960s, with a slightly more feminist slant.

The term "melodrama" is often used when referring to Hollywood tearjerkers, whose plots revolve around a woman who is the victim of adultery, unrequited love, or a family tragedy. The heroine would overcome these difficulties or, at least, learn to cope with them. British dramas were often too restrained to become melodramas, though David Lean's heartbreaking *Brief Encounter* (1945), about an illicit, seemingly unconsummated affair, comes close. Among the American directors who instigated these high-class soap operas were Frank Borzage, Edmund Goulding, and John M. Stahl. Borzage's forte was sentimental romances with sweet and innocent Janet Gaynor (*Seventh Heaven*, 1927; *Street Angel*, 1928) and the delicate

Trevor Howard bids Celia Johnson *goodbye on the platform where they first met in David Lean's* Brief Encounter *(1945), written by Noël Coward.*

WHAT TO WATCH

1934	Imitation of Life (US)
1937	Stella Dallas (US)
1942	Now Voyager (US)
1945	Mildred Pierce (US)
1952	The Life of Oharu (Japan)

Julianne Moore *stars as a repressed 1950s suburban housewife who falls for her black gardener in Todd Haynes' Douglas Sirk pastiche* Far from Heaven *(2002).*

and tragic Margaret Sullavan in four movies including *Little Man, What Now?* (1934), about young lovers fighting against adversity. Goulding, at Warner Bros., provided Bette Davis with four of her best and most typical melodramas including *Dark Victory* (1939), in which Davis goes blind before dying radiantly. Stahl pulled out all the stops for *Leave Her to Heaven* (1945), a lurid tale of a woman (Gene Tierney) whose jealousy ruins all those around her. Stahl also directed three elegant weepies, *Magnificent Obsession* (1935), *Imitation of Life* (1934), and *When Tomorrow Comes* (1939), all three remade (the latter as *Interlude*, 1957) by Douglas Sirk, whose films of the 1950s provided the peak of Hollywood melodrama.

Film poster, *1939*

The German Rainer Werner Fassbinder and the Spanish Pedro Almodóvar, both gay, embraced the flamboyant style and plot absurdities of the Sirkian soaps, while commenting upon them. In 2002, Todd Haynes made the perfect Sirk pastiche, *Far from Heaven.*

Much of these melodramas depended on the leading lady. Barbara Stanwyck (King Vidor's *Stella Dallas*, 1937), Bette Davis (Irving Rapper's *Now Voyager*, 1942), and Joan Crawford (Michael Curtiz's *Mildred Pierce*, 1945) reigned supreme among the soap queens, all three sacrificing themselves for others in the films mentioned and many more. While India (Nargis), France (Arletty), Greece (Melina Mercouri), and Italy (Anna Magnani) all produced their own stars, arguably the greatest actress in screen melodrama was Kinuyo Tanaka of Japan. She featured in 14 of Kenji Mizoguchi's films, including *The Life of Oharu* (1952) and *Sansho, the Bailiff* (1954), period films that transcended the genre.

JOAN CRAWFORD

Joan Crawford (1904–77) was a major star for more than 30 years. With her shoulder pads, enormous eyes, and large mouth widened into "The Crawford Smear", she often portrayed a woman from the wrong side of the tracks who claws her way to the top, sacrificing love and happiness to stay there.

Musicals

Born with the coming of sound, the movie musical had its base in vaudeville and in opera. With its brazen blending of fantasy and reality, the musical provided audiences with an accessible and immediate escape from life in the Great Depression, and then beyond.

In *The Pirate* (1948), Judy Garland says, "I know there is a real world and a dream world and I shan't confuse them." This is exactly what this and other musicals set out to do, and it was this unreality that gave directors, cameramen, and designers most creative scope within the commercial structure of Hollywood. Musicals could also more easily circumvent censorship than other genres. Scantily dressed women and sexual innuendo almost went unnoticed by the censors

WHAT TO WATCH

1931	Le Million (France)
1933	42nd Street (US)
1934	The Merry Widow (US)
1935	Top Hat (US)
1944	Meet Me in St. Louis (US)
1952	Singin' in the Rain (US)
1958	Gigi (US)
1961	West Side Story (US)
1972	Cabaret (US)

Lucille Ball, *bedecked in plumes of feathers, cracks a whip at a posse of girls dressed as black cats performing a feline dance from* Ziegfeld Follies *(1946).*

Dance director *Busby Berkeley's water sprites in "By a Waterfall", a typically extravagant number from the film* Footlight Parade *(1933).*

when within the seemingly harmless confines of the musical. It was the studio system of the 1930s, '40s, and '50s that enabled these lavish dreams to take shape. Each major studio stamped its product with distinguishing aesthetic trademarks, emphasized by their own particular stars, dance directors, designers, and orchestrators.

EUROPEAN STYLE

In the late 1920s and early 1930s, artists and technicians from Europe flooded into Hollywood, bringing with them a cosmopolitan style and approach. Their musical theatre background was opera and operetta. They knew little of the American tradition of vaudeville, the inspiration behind so many "backstage" musicals. And they did not perceive America as a glamorous enough setting for musical comedy

Paris was the glittering backdrop of three musicals the German Ernst Lubitsch made for Paramount — the most European of the studios — which starred Jeanette MacDonald and Maurice Chevalier. Chevalier's gallic charm and MacDonald's Anglo-Saxon reserve and self-mockery produced a seductive, piquant combination. *The Love Parade* (1929), distinguished by its lavish settings, songs integrated into the scenario, and sexual innuendo, set a pattern for screen operettas. At MGM, Lubitsch directed Chevalier and MacDonald again in *The Merry Widow* (1934), a film that moves from one wondrous moment to the next. Russian-born Rouben Mamoulian directed the couple in the witty and stylish *Love Me Tonight* (1932).

BACKSTAGE MUSICALS

Coming from the American vaudeville tradition, *The Broadway Melody* (1929) invented the backstage musical, which was to dominate the genre, on and off, for decades to come. It was also the first all-talking, all-singing, all-dancing movie and the first sound film to win an Oscar for Best Picture. The plots of backstage musicals revolved around

FRED ASTAIRE

Fred Astaire (1899–1987), born Frederick Austerlitz, was the supreme screen dancer who simply "reeked of class." He walked with a jaunty dance-like strut, and his light, carefree singing voice inspired top songwriters. Teamed with Ginger Rogers for the first time in *Flying Down to Rio* (1933), there followed another eight black-and-white RKO musicals. Besides the superb dance duets were Astaire's magical solos. Later, he moved with exceptional ease into the MGM Technicolor musical, his most memorable being *The Band Wagon* (1953).

The cast of On the Town *(1949) included Frank Sinatra and Gene Kelly.*

the problems of putting on a show. They followed the auditions, the rehearsals, the bickering, the wise-cracking chorus girls, the out-of-town tryouts, the financial difficulties, and the final, spectacular production; this often featured a youngster taking over the lead at the last moment and achieving instant stardom. Unlike in operettas, people only sang and danced within the confines of the show.

Another formula was to dispense with plot altogether in favor of a string of statically filmed numbers. The first of these was *Hollywood Revue of 1929* in which the song by Arthur Freed and Nacio Herb Brown called "Singin' in the Rain" was first heard. MGM paid three extravagant tributes to Broadway impresario Florenz Ziegfeld: *The Great Ziegfeld* (1936), which featured a gigantic revolving wedding cake; *Ziegfeld Girl* (1941), which, with clever editing, shows Judy Garland on top of the same wedding cake set; and *Ziegfeld Follies* (1946), featuring the studio's biggest stars of the period including Fred Astaire and Gene Kelly.

Cyd Charisse *plays the tantalizing gangster's moll and Fred Astaire is a private eye in the "Girl Hunt" ballet from* The Band Wagon *(1953).*

Film poster, *1955*

GREAT DANCERS

Astaire was the greatest dancer in the history of cinema. He remains unsurpassed in invention, virtuosity, and elegance. Although he tried various cinematic forms, they never hindered the purity of his dancing, either solo or with his many dancing partners, the most famous and durable of whom was Ginger Rogers. They danced through nine RKO musicals between 1933 and 1939 — all light-hearted comedies of errors set against

JUDY GARLAND

Born Frances Gumm, Judy Garland (1922–69) gained an MGM contract at the age of 13. She had an early success as Dorothy in the perennial favorite, *The Wizard of Oz* (1939). After a series of "juvenile" musicals with Mickey Rooney, Garland gained maturity in future husband Vincente Minnelli's *Meet Me in St. Louis* (1944). She was fired by MGM, but made a triumphant comeback in *A Star is Born* (1954).

sophisticated, cosmopolitan settings. As a dancer, choreographer, and director, Gene Kelly became one of the most creative forces in the heyday of the musical in the 1950s. Kelly experimented with slow motion, multiple images, animation, and trick photography to extend the appeal of dancing. He showed two sides of his dancing skills in the 18-minute ballet that ends Vincente Minnelli's *An American in Paris* (1951), and in the exuberant title number of *Singin' in the Rain* (1952), co-directed by Kelly and Stanley Donen.

What distinguished the films that burst forth from MGM by directors such as Donen, Kelly, and Minnelli was the integration of musical numbers into the film's narrative theme — in these features, song, dance, and music no longer punctuated the story, but actually worked to advance the plot.

Minnelli's sumptuous *Gigi* (1958) was among the very last musicals especially written for the screen, excepting the stream of colorful Elvis Presley vehicles in the 1960s.

The girls sing an exuberant *number from* Grease *(1978), the popular nostalgic high-school musical set in the 1950s, starring John Travolta and Olivia Newton-John.*

STAGE ADAPTATIONS

In the early days of the musical, studios lavished fortunes on celluloid versions of Broadway shows in the hope of repeating their success, but these bore little resemblance to the stage originals. More faithful adaptations began in 1950, with MGM's *Annie Get Your Gun. Guys and Dolls* (1955), *Oklahoma!* (1955), *The King and I* (1956), *South Pacific* (1958) and, in the '60s, *West Side Story* (1961), *My Fair Lady* (1964), and *The Sound of Music* (1965) followed. However, after the flop of *Hello, Dolly* (1969), the musical — like the Western — became a rare phenomenon. A limited revival of the genre came in the 1970s with Bob Fosse's *Cabaret* (1972), which captured the essence of Berlin in the early '30s, and *Saturday Night Fever* (1977) and *Grease* (1978), the films in which John Travolta made his name.

MUSICALS ABROAD

The Hollywood musical had a little influence on the few notable musicals made outside the US. In the Soviet Union in the 1930s, Grigori Alexandrov made four Hollywood-style musicals, the best known being *Jazz Comedy* (1934). Jacques Demy's *The Young Girls of Rochefort*

In Moulin Rouge *(2001), Ewan McGregor is a poet and Nicole Kidman a courtesan, both singing 20th century pop music in the Paris of 1899.*

(1967) was a direct homage to the MGM musical — Gene Kelly was persuaded to feature — but his *The Umbrellas of Cherbourg* (1964), in which all the dialogue was sung, was intrinsically French.

Up until the mid-1960s, British musicals were mostly rather genteel affairs that had little impact outside the UK. That all changed with US-born Richard Lester's two Beatles' movies, *A Hard Day's Night* (1964) and *Help!* (1965). There followed Carol Reed's Oscar-winning *Oliver!* (1968), Ken Russell's Busby Berkeley parody *The Boy Friend* (1971), and Alan Parker's *Bugsy Malone* (1976). Other examples were few and far between until Parker's *Evita* (1996).

Interest in the American musical was retained in Baz Luhrmann's visually extravagant *Moulin Rouge* (2001), and in further reproductions of Broadway hits such as *Chicago* (2002) and *The Producers* (2005). Sadly, musicals written directly for the screen, which made it a cinematic genre independent of the theatre, have become almost obsolete.

Catherine Zeta-Jones *plays murderous, vampish flapper Velma Kelley in Rob Marshall's adaptation of Bob Fosse's jazz-stage Broadway musical* Chicago *(2002).*

Propaganda

Produced with the intention of persuading viewers of a particular belief or ideology, propaganda films have been used by governments around the world since the early 20th century. Though documentary is the most popular form, drama is also used to convey a "message."

The manipulative power of film was recognized from the earliest days of cinema; part of its effectiveness came from the mistaken belief that the camera cannot lie. Propaganda films came of age during World War I, when every major belligerent power commissioned official films showing its enemy in an unfavorable light.

Westfront 1918 *(1930), directed by G.W. Pabst, focuses on the lives of four World War I soldiers and highlights the reality of life at the front.*

POLITICAL AIMS

Vladimir Lenin, the head of the Soviet state, realized at the beginning of the Russian Revolution of 1917 that film was the most important of all the arts because it could educate the masses — many of whom were illiterate — to support Bolshevik aims. Almost all the great silent Soviet films of the 1920s by Sergei Eisenstein, V.I. Pudovkin, and Alexander Dovzhenko, as well as Dziga Vertov's *Kino-Pravda* (literally Cinematic Truth) newsreels *(see page 134)* were made for propaganda purposes. At the same time, the films were revolutionary in form. Between the wars, many British documentaries explored social evils, such as *Housing Problems* (1935). In the US, the state tried to sell the New Deal — the reform of the economy during the Depression — to the public with Pare Lorentz's *The Plow that Broke the Plains* (1936). In Germany, *Kuhle Wampe* (1932), which was co-written by playwright Bertolt Brecht, focused

In To Whom Does the World Belong? *(Kuhle Wampe, 1932), children from Berlin's tent city look up to see an unemployed young man about to throw himself off a building. The film was banned by the Nazis.*

Film poster, *1943*

on the effects of unemployment, while G.W. Pabst's *Westfront 1918* (1930) showed the horror of life in the trenches. However, after the Nazis took over the film industry in 1934, anti-Semitic films serving the government's policies became *de rigueur.* Leni Riefenstahl's documentary of the 1934 Nuremberg Rally, *The Triumph of the Will* (1935), earned her the reputation of Germany's foremost ideological propagandist.

WORLD WAR II AND BEYOND

During World War II, the British director Humphrey Jennings made documentaries about the effect of the war on ordinary people. His *London Can Take It!* (1940) and *Listen To Britain* (1942) did much to influence public

"Cinema is not an extension of revolutionary action. Cinema is and must be revolutionary action in itself."

CUBAN FILM-MAKER SANTIAGO ÁLVAREZ

opinion in America. When the US entered the war in 1941, a stream of anti-Nazi dramas were produced, with titles such as *Hitler's Madmen* (Douglas Sirk, 1943) and *Hitler's Children* (Edward Dmytryk, 1943). Tarzan, Sherlock Holmes, and even Donald Duck were recruited into battle against the enemy in Walt Disney's *Der Fuehrer's Face* (1943).

Frank Capra, John Huston, William Wellman, William Wyler, and John Ford all served with the American Office of War Information, making important contributions to the war effort, most importantly in Capra's series *Why We Fight* (1942–45). During the Cold War, the efforts of the US Information Service to make anti-Soviet documentaries, and the various crude fiction films that replaced Nazis with communists, had little effect in the liberal climate of the 1960s and 1970s. In fact, some of the most effective propaganda films of the period were anti-American, including the shorts by Cuban Santiago Álvarez, such as *Hanoi, Tuesday 13th* (1967).

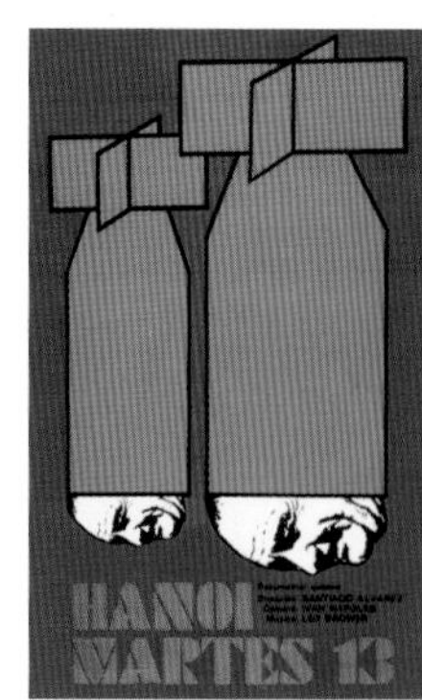

Film poster, *1967*

WHAT TO WATCH

1935	The Triumph of the Will (Germany)
1936	The Plow that Broke the Plains (US)
1943	Der Fuehrer's Face (US)

Science Fiction and Fantasy

In science fiction and fantasy films, imaginary worlds and scenarios are constructed — often with the aid of special effects — to enable the improbable to become possible. Themes within these films include alien life forms, space/time travel, and futuristic technology.

Jean Cocteau, who directed the magical *Beauty and the Beast* (*La Belle et la Bête*, 1946), remarked that "the cinema is a dream we all dream at the same time." This is no more so than in science fiction (sci-fi) and fantasy films. *The Wizard of Oz* (1939) makes the distinction between reality and fantasy by showing Dorothy's dream domain in glorious Technicolor and her home in Kansas in monochrome. Yet the message of the film is, "there's no place like home." Fantasy adventures go beyond the limitations of our minds to an imagined, but not always preferable, world. Similarly, the worlds that science fiction creates are often warped.

Johnny Depp plays the naïve *man-made boy in* Edward Scissorhands *(1990), Tim Burton's comic-tragic satire, hatched from an idea the director had as a child.*

WHAT TO WATCH

1926	Metropolis (Germany)
1939	The Wizard of Oz (US)
1960	The Time Machine (US)
1968	2001: A Space Odyssey (US)
1972	Solaris (Russia)
1977	Star Wars (US)
1999	The Matrix (US)

Many fantasy adventures are about displacement, where a character is in the wrong place at the wrong time. Examples include Nicolas Roeg's *The Man Who Fell to Earth* (1976), Steven Spielberg's *E.T. The Extra-Terrestrial* (1982), and Tim Burton's *Edward Scissorhands* (1990).

SPECIAL EFFECTS

To quote the motto of the *Star Trek* series, both science fiction and fantasy films "boldly go where no man has gone before" and, as a result, are more reliant than any other genre on special effects (SFX). In the wake of *Star Wars* (1977), the art of special effects entered a new age. Computer-generated imagery (CGI) soon dominated most of the science fiction and fantasy American blockbusters from the 1980s, often becoming their *raison d'être.* Ironically, the Wachowski Brothers' *The Matrix* (1999), heavily dependent on CGI, is a cautionary tale about a world taken over by computers.

EARLY SCI-FI

Nonetheless, audiences still delight in films from the pre-digital days of cinema. The space travel genre was launched by George Méliès's *A Trip*

to the Moon (1902), based on a story by Jules Verne *(see page 18)*. Méliès went on to film more of Verne's visionary novels, many of which — such as *Twenty Thousand Leagues under the Sea* and *A Journey To The Center of the Earth* — were filmed and refilmed over the years.

Film poster, *1956*

Russian cinema's first venture into science fiction was Yakov Protazanov's *Aelita* (1924), a delightful didactic comedy-drama featuring two Russians who land on Mars and organize a Soviet-style revolution against the autocratic Queen Aelita. It would be many years before Russia returned to the genre with Andrei Tarkovsky's *Solaris* (1972) and *Stalker* (1979), which both manage to be technologically convincing with only minimum special effects.

In France, René Clair's first film, *The Crazy Ray* (*Paris Qui Dort*, 1923), tells of a mad scientist who utilizes a magic ray (an effect created with stop-motion photography) on the citizens of Paris, causing them to freeze in different positions.

After the influential *Metropolis* (1926), Fritz Lang embarked on *The Woman in the Moon* (1929), about a scientist who believes the moon is rich in gold and tries to corner the market. Raoul Walsh's *The Thief of Bagdad* (1924), starring Douglas Fairbanks, set new Hollywood standards for special effects; which still astonish despite Alexander Korda's impressive 1940 Technicolor remake. Fairbanks climbs a magic rope, braves the Valley of Monsters, rides a flying horse, and sails over the rooftops on a magic carpet.

Michael Rennie as Klaatu is *brought back to life by his robot Gort, watched by earthling Patricia Neal in* The Day the Earth Stood Still *(1951).*

The starship Enterprise in Star Trek: The Motion Picture *(1979), the first of a successful run of ten movies derived from the cult TV series.*

H.G. WELLS

The 1930s and 1940s were not very rich in science fiction or fantasy movies. However, there were three superlative adaptations of H.G. Wells novels: James Whale's *The Invisible Man* (1933), in which Claude Rains made his first screen (dis)appearance; William Cameron Menzies' *Things to Come* (1936), about an apocalyptic world war and the undemocratic society that results; and Lothar Mendes' *The Man Who Could Work Miracles* (1936), in which a bashful clerk is granted the power to do what he wishes by the gods. H.G. Wells also provided the source material for *War of the Worlds* (1953) — remade by Spielberg in 2005 — and *The Time Machine* (1960). Both were produced by Hungarian-born special-effects expert George Pal, whose *Destination Moon* (1950) began a stream of Hollywood sci-fi movies in the 1950s, many of them metaphors for the Cold War. Robert Wise's *The Day the Earth Stood Still* (1951), an intelligent, anti-war sci-fi classic, features an alien who warns that, unless nuclear weapons are destroyed, his race will annihilate Earth.

"Get ready to crumble," *as Godzilla battles with a UFO that turns into a strange monster in Takao Okawara's* Godzilla, 2000.

MONSTER MOVIES

In Japan, a decade after the horrors of Hiroshima and Nagasaki, *Godzilla* (1954) was the first of a series of *Godzilla* movies in which many of the creatures were the result of nuclear radiation. They were influenced by *The Beast from 20,000 Fathoms* (1953), about a dinosaur revived by an atomic blast, which spawned countless imitations. The monster was animated by Ray Harryhausen, the most celebrated of all SFX men, whose crowning achievement was *Jason and the Argonauts* (1963).

SCI-FI WRITERS

Unlike the low-budget sci-fi that dominated the 1950s, Stanley Kubrick's *2001: A Space Odyssey* (1968) revolutionized space travel films with its dazzling technology. The screenplay was written by Arthur C. Clarke, and adapted from one of his short stories.

Other science fiction writers whose novels have been adapted into films include Ray Bradbury (*Fahrenheit 451*, 1966), Stanislaw Lem (*Solaris*, 1972), and Isaac Asimov (*I, Robot*, 2004). Many of the novels and short stories of the prolific Philip K. Dick have become films, including *Blade Runner* (1982) and *Minority Report* (2002).

Time travel became popular in the 1980s with Terry Gilliam's *Time Bandits* (1981) — the first in a fantasy trilogy with *Brazil* (1985) and 1988's *The Adventures of Baron Munchausen* — James Cameron's *The Terminator* (1984), and Robert Zemeckis's *Back to the Future* (1985), paradigms for future science fiction and fantasy movies.

Alien tripod fighting machines *invade the Earth in* War of the Worlds *(2005), Steven Spielberg's version of H.G. Wells's classic 1898 futuristic novel.*

Serials

The serial was a multi-episode, usually action-adventure, film. It was shown in cinemas in weekly instalments, and each chapter ended on a cliffhanger. It is the only obsolete cinematic genre, though some of its features are evident in television soap operas and mini-series.

WHAT TO WATCH

1914	The Perils of Pauline
1936	Flash Gordon
1938	The Lone Ranger

"Buster" Crabbe's most famous role was as Flash Gordon, *whose adventures in outer space thrilled audiences through three serials in 1936, 1938, and 1940.*

From the earliest days of film, serials were an important ingredient of cinema programs. *The Adventures of Kathlyn* (1913) was the first true serial, but a year later director Louis Gasnier caused a sensation with *The Perils of Pauline* (1914), starring Pearl White. As the most famous of "serial queens," she endured all sorts of indignities from villains, such as being tied to a railroad track.

In France, Louis Feuillade was directing serials such as *Fantômas* (1913–14), about a master criminal. His greatest triumph was *Les Vampires* (1915–16), which had a dreamlike quality that was admired as much by the general public as by the surrealists. In Germany, Fritz Lang made his reputation with *The Spiders* (1919–20), which featured the use of mirrors, hypnosis, underground chambers, and arch criminals, elements that would often reappear throughout his *oeuvre.*

In the US, 28 serials were made in 1920 alone. With the coming of sound, the main studios started producing serials of better quality. These included Universal's *Flash Gordon* (from 1936) with Larry "Buster" Crabbe in the title role, battling his nemesis Ming the Merciless (Charles Middleton). At $350,000, it was the most expensive serial ever made, three times the average serial budget. Crabbe also starred in *Buck Rogers Conquers the Universe* (1939).

Film poster *(1938)*

Other hit serials of the 1930s were *Dick Tracy*, *Zorro*, *The Lone Ranger*, and *Hawk of the Wilderness*. During World War II, *Captain America*, *Superman*, and *Batman* all faced German or Japanese villains. In the 1950s, mainly thanks to the advent of television, the output of serials began to diminish. The Western serial *Blazing the Overland Trail* was the last serial ever produced, in 1956.

Series

Series can either be sequels (*The Godfather: Part II*), prequels (the *Star Wars* saga), or films with different plots but the same characters (the *Harry Potter* cycle). The convention of putting numerals after film titles, as in *Spider-Man 2* (2004), did not begin until the 1970s.

Before the 1970s, feature film sequels were rare, yet favorite characters kept on reappearing in numerous films. One of the first was Tarzan, who initially swung into view in 1918 played by Elmo Lincoln in *Tarzan of the Apes*. Several other silent Tarzans appeared before Johnny Weissmuller's famous yodelling call was heard in *Tarzan the Ape Man* (1932). Weissmuller, a former US Olympic swimming champion, went on to make 19 Tarzan movies over the next 16 years.

Series made up a significant proportion of Hollywood's B picture output from the 1930s. Among the longest running were *Andy Hardy* (1938–58), *Sherlock Holmes* (1939–46), *Dr. Kildare* (1938–47), *Charlie Chan* (1931–49), and the gang of lovable juvenile delinquents in their various incarnations as *The Dead End Kids*, *The East Side Kids*, and *The Bowery Boys* (1938–58). Notable series from the 1960s onwards included *The Pink Panther* and *Planet of the Apes*.

The French-Italian co-produced series *Don Camillo* (1951–65), the story of a parish priest in conflict with a communist mayor, was a major international hit. In England, the broad *Carry On...* farces ran from 1958–78, while the James Bond thriller series began with *Dr. No* in 1962, making it the longest ever continuing series in the English language. The ingredients of the successful Bond recipe, which remains virtually unchanged to this date, are exotic locales, a bevy of (mostly treacherous) beautiful women, and an evil genius who wishes to take over the world. But in terms of sheer numbers, you can't beat the Japanese series *Zatoichi*, in which the hero, a blind swordsman, featured in 27 films between 1962 and 2003.

WHAT TO WATCH

1931–49	Charlie Chan films
1951–65	Don Camillo films
1962–89	Zatoichi films
1962–	James Bond films

Harrison Ford as the eponymous hero *(right) and his archeologist father, Sean Connery, are bound together in Steven Spielberg's* Indiana Jones and the Last Crusade *(1989), Jones' third adventure.*

Teen Movies

In the 1950s, producers first recognized a market for youth-oriented films, the number of which grew steadily until a dramatic increase in the 1980s. Often set in a school, these movies invariably showed teens trying to attract the opposite sex and attempting to escape adult control.

Teenagers were typically patronized and ridiculed in films made before the 1950s. An example was the extremely popular *Andy Hardy* series of the 1930s and early 1940s, which starred Mickey Rooney as a happy-go-lucky adolescent getting into scrapes.

The growing teen audience of the 1950s began to identify with new stars like Marlon Brando (*The Wild One*, 1954) and James Dean (*Rebel Without a Cause*, 1955). In the next decade, a series of "beach party" movies came out, while Roger Corman's bike and LSD films appealed to a hipper youth audience. In the 1970s, George Lucas' seminal *American Graffiti* (1973) sparked off other "rites-of-passage" pictures. Then came the so-called "Brat Pack," a group of young actors associated with the films of writer director John Hughes, including *The Breakfast Club* (1985) and *Pretty in Pink* (1986).

Although most teen stars fade from view as they (and their fans) mature, a few have gone on to productive careers, including Demi Moore, Rob Lowe, and James Spader. Actors such as Drew Barrymore and Scarlett Johansson have established themselves as bone fide 21st-century stars. But already Lindsay Lohan is beating a path for the next generation...

WHAT TO WATCH

1955	Rebel Without a Cause (US)
1973	American Graffiti (US)
1985	The Breakfast Club (US)

Film poster, *1959*

Judd Nelson, Emilio Estevez, *Ally Sheedy, Molly Ringwald, and Anthony Michael Hall star in John Hughes' Brat Pack flick,* The Breakfast Club *(1985).*

Thrillers

Thrillers are gripping yarns of suspense, where the tension is created by placing one or more characters in a threatening situation from which they have to escape. This type of film can cross several genres to produce action, science fiction, and even Western thrillers.

It was Alfred Hitchcock, "The Master of Suspense," who perfected one of the fundamental thriller types in *North by Northwest* (1959): the picaresque pursuit. This is usually a mystery involving spies or terrorists, in which the protagonist is the pursued or the pursuer, attempting to solve a crime or prevent a disaster. Among the large number of films that could be called Hitchcockian are Carol Reed's *The Third Man* (1949), Stanley Donen's *Charade* (1963) and *Arabesque* (1966), and several thrillers by Brian De Palma, particularly *Obsession* (1976).

Matt Damon and Franka Potente *star in* The Bourne Supremacy *(2004), the second thriller in the series about special agent Jason Bourne.*

Another Hitchcockian theme is the "woman-in-peril" psychological thriller as epitomized by *Psycho*, (1960). Other potent examples include *Gaslight* (1940 and 1944), in which a husband drives his wife slowly insane in order to gain an inheritance; Anatole Litvak's *Sorry, Wrong Number* (1948), featuring an invalid (Barbara Stanwyck) who overhears a murder plot on the phone — against herself; Terence Young's *Wait Until Dark* (1967), in which Audrey Hepburn plays a blind woman left alone in an apartment and terrorized by gangsters; and Phillip Noyce's *Dead Calm* (1989), where Nicole Kidman fights for her life on a yacht after picking up a crazed castaway.

Film poster, *1966*

In the 1970s, there emerged a number of post-Watergate conspiracy thrillers, including Alan Pakula's *The Parallax View* (1974), a disturbing no-holds-barred look at a political assassination cover-up. The conspiracy thriller reappeared in the 1990s with films such as Phillip Noyce's *Patriot Games* (1992) and *Clear and Present Danger* (1994), both with Harrison Ford as an intrepid CIA agent. It continued with Doug Liman's *The Bourne Identity* (2002) and its sequel, starring Matt Damon as an amnesiac agent, as well as Fernando Meirelles' *The Constant Gardener* (2005).

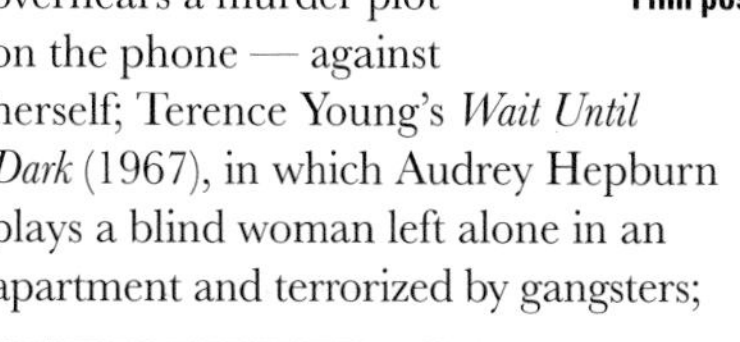

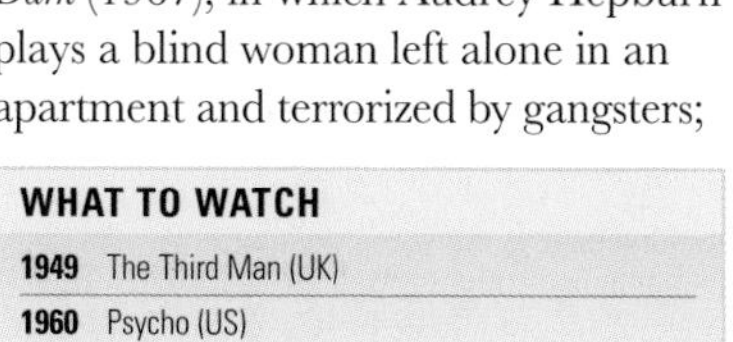

WHAT TO WATCH

1949	The Third Man (UK)
1960	Psycho (US)
1991	The Silence of the Lambs (US)
2005	The Constant Gardener (UK/Germany)

Cary Grant is pursued *by a mysterious crop-dusting plane that suddenly appears from nowhere in* North by Northwest *(1959), one of Alfred Hitchcock's most celebrated set pieces.*

Underground

The term "underground" as a film genre originated in the US toward the end of the 1950s. It applied to US experimental film-making, which was rooted in the European avant-garde but was strongly connected to the American Beat movement that emerged at that time.

In the 1940s, a period of experimental film-making began in the US. Encouragement came from a number of artists and film-makers from Europe, among them the New York-based Hans Richter and Marcel Duchamp, and Oskar Fischinger in Los Angeles.

Maya Deren's *Meshes of the Afternoon* (1943) was one of the first independent underground films. Dealing with a suicide, it is famous for its four-stride sequence: from beach to grass to mud to pavement to rug. In the early 1950s, younger directors such as Stan Brakhage emerged, working in a similar mode. The films they made are often described as "psychodramas."

In 1955, the magazine *Film Culture* was of crucial importance to the new US cinema. *Guns of the Trees* (1964) was one of a number of feature-length films that was inspired by the French New Wave. Toward the end of 1960, the New American Cinema Group was formed, favoring films that were "rough, unpolished but alive." Many of them, such as Jack Smith's *Flaming Creatures* (1963) embraced Hollywood even as it defied its narrative traditions by using clips of "tits 'n' sand" movies. The mode for campiness was exploited by Andy Warhol in films such as *Blow Job* (1963). A year later, Kenneth Anger's gay biker film *Scorpio Rising* was released, and it became a seminal movie in US underground cinema.

In films such as *Wavelength* (1967), Michael Snow attempted to redefine our way of seeing by exploring new time and space concepts.

Maya Deren stars *in her own* Meshes of the Afternoon *(1943), a study of feminine angst. The film rejects the traditional narrative structure in favour of a dream logic.*

WHAT TO WATCH

1943	Meshes of the Afternoon (US)
1967	Wavelength (Canada/US)
1968	Flesh (US)

War

Battle scenes and war have been the subject of films since the beginning of cinema, but as a genre, war movies came of age during World War I. Often, they take an anti-war stance, but equally they can be made to stir up popular support and even serve as propaganda.

War films emerged as a major film genre after the outbreak of World War I. The most significant was D.W. Griffith's *Hearts of the World* (1918), which used documentary material and a studio reconstruction of a French village occupied by "beastly huns" led by ruthless German officer Erich von Stroheim.

Charlie Chaplin's *Shoulder Arms* (1918), set partly in the trenches, was released only a few weeks before the armistice, drawing howls of protest. Yet it was Chaplin's biggest triumph up to that time, proving that comedy could provide a much-needed release from tragic events.

After the armistice, war films all but ceased. Exceptions were Abel Gance's *J'Accuse* (1919), described by the director as "a human cry against the bellicose din of armies." The film that launched Rudolph Valentino as a great star, Rex Ingram's *The Four Horsemen of the Apocalypse* (1921), had a strong anti-war message. However, it was also so anti-German that some thought it incited hatred between nations, and the film was banned in Germany and withdrawn from circulation for years.

Film poster, *1927*

War films were revived in the mid-1920s with King Vidor's *The Big Parade* (1925), Raoul Walsh's *What Price Glory?* (1926), and William Wellman's *Wings* (1927), the first film to win the Best Picture Oscar. At the beginning of sound, cinemas were flooded with war films, and in 1930 alone there appeared Howard Hawks' *The Dawn Patrol*, Howard Hughes' *Hell's Angels*, James Whale's *Journey's End*, and Lewis Milestone's *All Quiet*

A soldier stands *in the war cemetery before the dead of World War I rise up from their graves to accuse the living in Abel Gance's* J'Accuse *(1919).*

A Royal Air Force *aircraft in action in* The Battle of Britain *(1969), Guy Hamilton's all-star tribute to the 1942 film* The First of the Few.

on the Western Front, a portrayal from the German perspective. In Germany itself, G.W. Pabst's *Westfront 1918* (1930) depicted the futility of life in the trenches. But as the memories of the war and the mood of anti-militarism that marked these films began to fade, so the subject became less popular. Jean Renoir's *La Grande Illusion* (1937), the first war film for some years, was a moving anti-war statement that did not actually include any fighting.

Hawks' *Sergeant York* (1941), based on the true story of World War I's most decorated US soldier (played by Oscar winner Gary Cooper), was intended to inspire American audiences as the country emerged from isolationism to join the fight against the Axis powers.

World War II has always been the most popular period for war genre film-makers because the issues seemed more straightforward than in most wars. After the US entered the war, Hollywood turned out a stream of flag-waving action features, as did the UK. British films like Noël Coward's *In Which We Serve* (1942) and Carol Reed's *The Way Ahead* (1944) were deemed more realistic but more class-conscious than their US counterparts.

Unlike the usual war saga, Wellman's *The Story of G.I. Joe* (1945) concentrated on the fatigue and anxiety that the common soldier suffered. The heroics were left to Errol Flynn and John Wayne, who were depicted winning the war almost single-handedly.

Film poster for *Peter Weir's WWII drama* Gallipoli *(1981)*

Post-war films were allowed to be a little more critical of the military establishment. Mark Robson's *Home of the Brave* (1949) courageously took on the subject of racism in the US army, while few punches were pulled in *Attack!* (1956), Robert Aldrich's powerful indictment of life in the military.

Japan, which had made jingoistic films during the war, concentrated on more pacifist themes after it, almost as an act of atonement. One of the first, Kon Ichikawa's *The Burmese Harp* (1956), is a cry of anguish for those that suffered during World War II. A year later, Stanley Kubrick's anti-militarism was revealed in the bitterly ironic and moving World War I drama, *Paths of Glory*. In contrast, the 1960s saw a number of war epics celebrating Allied victories, such as *The Longest Day* (1962), *The Battle of the Bulge* (1965), and *The Battle of Britain* (1969).

WHAT TO WATCH

1919	J'Accuse (France)
1957	Paths of Glory (US)
1979	Apocalypse Now (US)
1981	Das Boot (Germany)
1987	Full Metal Jacket (US)
1998	Saving Private Ryan (US)

George Clooney, *Mark Wahlberg, and Ice Cube star in David O. Russell's* Three Kings *(1999), set during the 1991 Gulf War.*

Robert Altman's iconoclastic *M*A*S*H* (1970), though set in Korea, was plainly a reference to the Vietnam War. The only US film on the subject made during the Vietnam War was *The Green Berets* (1968), a gung-ho action movie starring John Wayne. It was only in the 1970s that the conflict was properly explored in movies. Among the most effective of these films were Michael Cimino's *The Deer Hunter (*1978), Francis Ford Coppola's *Apocalypse Now* (1979), Oliver Stone's *Platoon* (1986), and Kubrick's *Full Metal Jacket* (1987).

However, film-makers constantly returned to World War II for inspiration. From Germany, there came Wolfgang Petersen's *Das Boot* (1981), which followed the efforts of a U-boat crew to survive, and the spectacular *Stalingrad* (1993). Russia, which had earlier produced such remarkable war films as Grigori Chukrai's *The Ballad of a Soldier* (1959) and Andrei Tarkovsky's *Ivan's Childhood* (1962), continued the tradition with Elem Klimov's powerful *Come and See* (1985). In America, there was an 18-year gap between Sam Fuller's tough, symbolic *The Big Red One* (1980) and other distinguished WWII dramas such as Terrence Malick's *The Thin Red Line* and Steven Spielberg's *Saving Private Ryan,* with its opening 30-minute soldier's eye view of battle.

The 1991 Gulf War was examined in Edward Zwick's *Courage Under Fire* (1996), and in David O. Russell's *Three Kings* (1999). Whichever conflict is being portrayed, the eternal truths of war lend a similarity to all war movies.

The American soldiers' *assault on a Normandy beach is realistically filmed in the celebrated opening sequence from Steven Spielberg's* Saving Private Ryan *(1998).*

Westerns

The Western is not only the oldest of all film genres, but it is the only home-grown American art form. From the 1920s to the early 1960s, it was the Western's popularity that consolidated Hollywood's dominance of the global film market.

The historical setting of the Western is traditionally the 1850s to the 1890s, a period that saw the California and Dakota gold rushes, the American Civil War, the building of the transcontinental railway, the Indian wars, the opening up of the cattle ranges, the range wars, and the steady spread westwards of homesteaders, farmers, and immigrants. It also saw the virtual extermination of the buffalo and most of the indigenous Native American tribes.

Film poster *for the first Western, released in 1903*

John Ford's Stagecoach (1939) *was a milestone in the history of the Western and was the first to be shot in Utah's Monument Valley.*

However, some Westerns extend back to the time of America's colonial era or forward to the mid-20th century. The geographical location is usually west of the Mississippi river, north of the Rio Grande river, and south to the border with Mexico.

The most fundamental theme of the Western is the civilizing of the wilderness — the taming of nature, lawbreakers, and "savages" (usually "Red Indians"). Among the iconic elements are remote forts and vast ranches, and the small-town saloon, jail, and main street — where the inevitable showdown between

The patriarchal John Wayne *and his adopted son Montgomery Clift (in his first film) have an uncomfortable relationship in Howard Hawks'* Red River *(1948).*

hero and villain takes place. However, many of the best Westerns have a psychological complexity that stretches beyond the simplistic good versus evil premise towards the dimensions of Greek tragedy.

BIRTH OF THE WESTERN

Before the beginning of cinema in 1895, there were the popular Wild West shows of "Buffalo Bill" Cody, the frontier stories of Zane Grey, Owen Wister's influential *The Virginian* — the first modern Western novel, published in 1902 — and dime novels that narrated the exploits of heroes on both sides of the law: Wyatt Earp, Doc Holliday, Wild Bill Hickok, Calamity Jane, Bat Masterson, the James Brothers, and Billy the Kid. As the newspaperman says in John Ford's *The Man Who Shot Liberty Valance* (1962), "When the legend becomes fact, print the legend." So, by the time of the first narrative screen Western, Edward S. Porter's *The Great Train Robbery* (1903), the legends of the West had already become embedded in American popular culture.

That ten-minute film launched the film career of "Bronco Billy" Anderson, who became the first Western hero. Other cowboy stars followed, the most famous being W.S. Hart and Tom Mix. Also in the early 1900s, D.W. Griffith was making Westerns, mainly featuring red devils thirsty for the blood of whites, such as the two-reeler *The Battle of Elderbush Gulch* (1913). The next year, Cecil B. DeMille's first film, *The Squaw Man*, became the first feature shot entirely

Clint Eastwood stars as "Blondie" *in* The Good, the Bad and the Ugly *(1966), the third and last of the Spaghetti Westerns he made for Sergio Leone.*

in Hollywood. More crucial to the development of the genre was James Cruze's *The Covered Wagon* (1923), an epic, two-and-a-half-hour long reconstruction of one of the great 19th-century treks across America. Its huge success led to the increase of Western production, and allowed John Ford to make the far superior and even longer *The Iron Horse* the following year, which was shot mainly on location in Nevada.

A GOLDEN AGE

Westerns were enhanced by the coming of sound, but the golden age began with John Ford's *Stagecoach* (1939), beautifully shot in the now familiar Monument Valley, Utah. It raised the genre to artistic status, stamped Ford as one of the great directors of Westerns, and ensured John Wayne's rise from B-movie obscurity to A-list stardom.

Most of the leading Hollywood directors made Westerns, including the German-born Fritz Lang with *The Return of Frank James* (1940), *Western Union* (1941), and *Rancho Notorious* (1952); and Hungarian-born Michael Curtiz with *Dodge City* (1939), *Virginia City* (1940), and *Santa Fe Trail* (1940), all three starring Errol Flynn.

In this rich period, Ford made his resplendent Cavalry trilogy: *Fort Apache* (1948), *She Wore a Yellow Ribbon* (1949), and *Rio Grande* (1950), romantic visions of the Old West with John Wayne at their centre. Wayne also starred in Howard Hawks' *Red River* (1948), in which his muscular macho security was contrasted with Montgomery Clift's nervy angularity, creating a special tension. Hawks went on to make three more fine Westerns with Wayne, the best being *Rio Bravo* (1959). Anthony Mann's five films starred a new, tougher James Stewart, and included *Bend of the River* (1952) and *The Man from Laramie* (1955); these were among the most distinguished Westerns of the 1950s. Others include Bud Boetticher's seven taut Westerns with Randolph Scott, one of which was *Seven Men from Now* (1956); Henry King's *The Gunfighter* (1950), Fred Zinnemann's *High Noon* (1952); George Stevens's *Shane* (1953); William Wyler's *The Big Country* (1958); and a very few in which Native Americans were treated sympathetically, such as

Film poster, *1952*

WHAT TO WATCH

1939	Stagecoach (US)
1955	The Man From Laramie (US)
1956	The Searchers (US)
1960	The Magnificent Seven (US)
1962	The Man who Shot Liberty Valance (US)
1969	The Wild Bunch (US)
1969	Once Upon a Time in the West (Italy/US)
1992	Unforgiven (US)

Delmer Daves's *Broken Arrow* (1950) and Robert Aldrich's *Apache* (1954).

Director and star Kevin Costner *carries his dead wife (Mary McDonnell) in* Dances with Wolves *(1990), in which Costner's Unionist soldier is adopted by a Sioux tribe.*

DECLINE OF THE GENRE

In 1950, Hollywood produced 130 Westerns. A decade later this was down to 28. There are several explanations for this decline: the increase in Western television series, which replaced the many B-Western features produced for the cinema; the fact that the ideology that formed the Western was becoming outmoded in the new permissive society; and the rise of the more violent Spaghetti Westerns, which brought stardom for Clint Eastwood. These Italian-produced films were influenced in plot and tone by Japanese samurai films, as was John Sturges' *The Magnificent Seven* (1960), a transplanting of Akira Kurosawa's *The Seven Samurai* (1954).

The genre was kept alive by Sam Peckinpah's nostalgic but harsh views of the Old West, and revisionist Westerns like Arthur Penn's *Little Big Man* (1970). However, studios considered the Western a moribund genre, which accounts for Kevin Costner's long battle to make *Dances with Wolves* (1990). His patience paid off, however, when it won seven Academy Awards including Best Picture. Two years later, Clint Eastwood's *Unforgiven* also won the Best Picture award. In a modern twist on the genre, *Brokeback Mountain* (2005) features two cowboys in love.

Jake Gyllenhaal (left) and Heath Ledger *star in Ang Lee's* Brokeback Mountain *(2005), based on E. Annie Proulx's short story.*

WORLD CINEMA

In an age of internationalism, the cinema has proved itself the most international of the arts. Just as more and more people are visiting the Taj Mahal, the Kremlin, the Eiffel Tower, Mount Fuji, and the Sistine Chapel, so growing numbers of movie lovers have come to appreciate Indian, Russian, French, Japanese, and Italian films, not to mention the rich output of China, South America, Spain, Scandinavia, and Iran.

In the 1890s, early cinema came into being almost simultaneously in the US, Great Britain, France, and Germany. Within 20 years, cinema had spread to all parts of the globe, had developed a sophisticated technology, and become a major industry. Today, both the sheer diversity of world cinema and the number of films produced is staggering. This chapter attempts to cover as many countries and as many significant films as possible but a book of any size cannot hope to include everything. (The omission of countries, such as the Netherlands and some from South-East Asia, is addressed in this introduction.)

In the 1920s, the general public went to see silent movies from many parts of the world. But a wider appreciation of world cinema by western audiences really began after World War II, when Italian, Japanese, German, and French motion pictures were once more available. The increasing awareness of the quality of these films was aided by the recognition given each year by the Academy of Motion Picture Arts and Sciences. Vittorio De Sica's *Shoeshine* (1946) was the first to receive a special award in 1947. In 1956, Federico Fellini's *La Strada* (1954) became the first winner of the new Academy Award for the Best Foreign Language (as in non-English language) Film.

Rosario Flores plays the bullfighter, Lydia, *who is badly gored in a corrida and remains in a coma in Pedro Almodóvar's sensitive and intriguing* Talk To Her *(2002).*

In the last few decades, it has gradually become recognized that entertainment is not the preserve of Hollywood. Gangster movies, horror films, whodunits, Westerns, war epics, melodramas, musicals, and love stories are produced all over the globe. A glance at the long list of American remakes of "foreign" films will confirm that Hollywood has drawn inspiration from world cinema. Neither is it one-way traffic. There are film noirs of Jean-Pierre Melville that are based on the American model, and countless quotes in French New Wave films that come from Hollywood movies. Witness the popularity of Spaghetti Westerns and the influence of US movies on German directors Wim Wenders and Rainer Werner Fassbinder.

From its earliest days, Hollywood has benefited from an influx of gifted stars from abroad. From Sweden came Greta Gustafsson (Garbo) and Ingrid Bergman (mother of Isabella Rossellini). From Germany came Maria Magdelena Von Losch (Marlene Dietrich) and from Austria, Hedy Kiesler (Hedy Lamarr). Italy gave America Sofia Scicolone (Sophia Loren), while Egypt supplied Michel

The blind toddler *in Kurdish-Iranian Bahman Ghobadi's devastating picture of the effects of war (in this case the second Gulf War) on children in* Turtles Can Fly *(2004).*

Shahoub (Omar Sharif). From Brazil came Maria do Carmo Miranda Da Cunha (Carmen Miranda). Over the past few decades we have grown used to seeing stars like Burt Lancaster, Donald Sutherland, Nastassja Kinski, Isabella Rossellini, Gérard Depardieu, Charlotte Rampling, Antonio Banderas, Juliette Binoche, Penelope Cruz, Audrey Tatou, and Jackie Chan move with ease between English-speaking and foreign films

Directors, too, brought their expertise to Hollywood: Victor Sjöström (Sweden), Fritz Lang (Germany), Billy Wilder (Austria), Jean Renoir (France), Miloš Forman (Czechoslovakia) to name but a few. One of the first European directors to have careers on two continents was Louis Malle, who made *Atlantic City* (1981) in the United States and returned to his native France for *Au Revoir Les Enfants* (1987). In recent years, there has been even more cross-fertilization: a New Zealander, Peter Jackson, directed *The Lord of the Rings* trilogy; and a Mexican, Alfonso Cuarón, directed *Harry Potter and the Prisoner of Azkaban* (2004). The supreme example is the Taiwanese-born Ang Lee, who has made films that are typically English (*Sense and Sensibility*, 1995), Asian (*Crouching Tiger, Hidden Dragon*, 2000), and American (*Brokeback Mountain*, 2005).

Film poster *for the moving* Sansho Dayu *(*Sansho the Bailiff*, 1954) by Japanese director Kenji Mizoguchi.*

Brigitte Lin plays *the mysterious drug dealer in Wong Kar Wai's* Chungking Express *(1994), which has two unconnected stories set in Hong Kong.*

Dutch director Paul Verhoeven made successful erotic thrillers in his homeland such as *Spetters* (1980) and *The Fourth Man* (1983) before crossing the Atlantic to make major hits such as *RoboCop* (1987), *Total Recall* (1990), and *Basic Instinct* (1991). Other notable directors to come from the Netherlands were the documentary film-makers Joris Ivens and Bert Haantra, and Fons Rademakers, who directed *The Assault* (1986), winner of the Best Foreign Film Oscar. From Belgium came André Delvaux, whose films, merging dream and reality, put him in the tradition of other Belgian artists like René Magritte. Most conspicuous are the Belgian Dardenne Brothers, Jean-Pierre (born 1951) and Luc (born 1954), whose international reputation has grown over the years with such realistic dramas as *The Promise* (1996), *Rosetta* (1999), *The Son* (2002), and *The Child* (2005).

In South-East Asia, Indonesia is mostly known for popular teenage films and musicals. Since 1998, a new generation of film-makers has emerged that includes as many female as male directors, writers, and producers. The majority of Thai films are made for entertainment, mixing comedy, melodrama, and music. Wisit Sasanatieng's *Tears of the Black Tiger* (2000) was a successful pastiche of such films. Pen-Ek Ratanaruang's musical *Monrak Transistor* (2001) was another Thai film that did well internationally, as did the bizarre *Tropical Malady* (2004), directed by Apichatpong Weerasethakul. Tran Anh Hung is Vietnam's most celebrated director whose *The Scent of Green Papaya* (1993), *Cyclo* (1995) and *The Vertical Rays of the Sun* (2000) were shown worldwide. In the Philippines, Lino Brocka broke new ground for his country's cinema when his films *Insiang* (1976), *Jaguar* (1979), and *Bona* (1980) were acclaimed at the Cannes Film Festival.

In fact, it could be said that the centre of cinema has had a major shift from its traditional bases of the US and Europe to Asia and beyond.

Aoua Sangare *stars in Yeleen* (Brightness, *1987), the Malian Souleymane Cisse's magical film, drawing on African ritual with elemental imagery of water, fire, and earth.*

Gael García Bernal *plays the young Che Guevara with Roderigo de la Serna as Alberto Granado in* The Motorcycle Diaries *(2004).*

Africa

There are three distinct areas of film production on the African continent, all rising out of centuries of colonialism, and mostly divided linguistically into films in Arabic, French, and English. In recent years there have been more big-budget hits seen by western audiences.

Many African nations did not have a film industry before they became independent of colonial rule in the 1960s and 1970s. Since then, film has begun to flourish and productions have attracted international attention. France has been a major provider of financial resources for African filmmakers, many of whom have received training at cinema schools in Europe.

From the 1930s, Arab cinema became synonymous with Egyptian cinema. What was to become the pre-eminent genre, the Egyptian musical, made its first appearance in 1932 with *The Song of the Heart*, directed by the Italian Mario Volpi. However, production of films made in North Africa, as a whole, remained very low until well after World War II. It was only with the emergence of Youssef Chahine that Egyptian cinema began to be taken seriously internationally.

WHAT TO WATCH

1968	The Money Order (Ousmane Sembene, Senegal)
1969	The Night of Counting the Years (Shadi Abdelsalam, Egypt)
1974	Xala (Ousmane Sembene, Senegal)
1975	Chronicle of the Burning Years (Mohammed Lakhdar-Hamina, Algeria)
1978	Alexandria... Why? (Youssef Chahine, Egypt)
1986	Man of Ashes (Nouri Bouzid, Tunisia)
1987	Yeelen (Souleymane Cissé, Mali)
1989	Yaaba (Idrissa Ouadragoa, Burkina Faso)
1994	The Silences of the Palace (Moufida Tlatli, Tunisia)
2002	Heremakono (Abderrahmane Sissako, Mauritania)

Chahine's *Cairo Station* (1958) focused on the dispossessed. Chahine would alternate between big-budget productions such as *Alexandria... Why?* (1978) and *Adieu Bonaparte* (1984), and patently political films, such as *The Sparrow* (1973), which deals with Egypt's Six-Day War against Israel. Chahine's films and Shadi

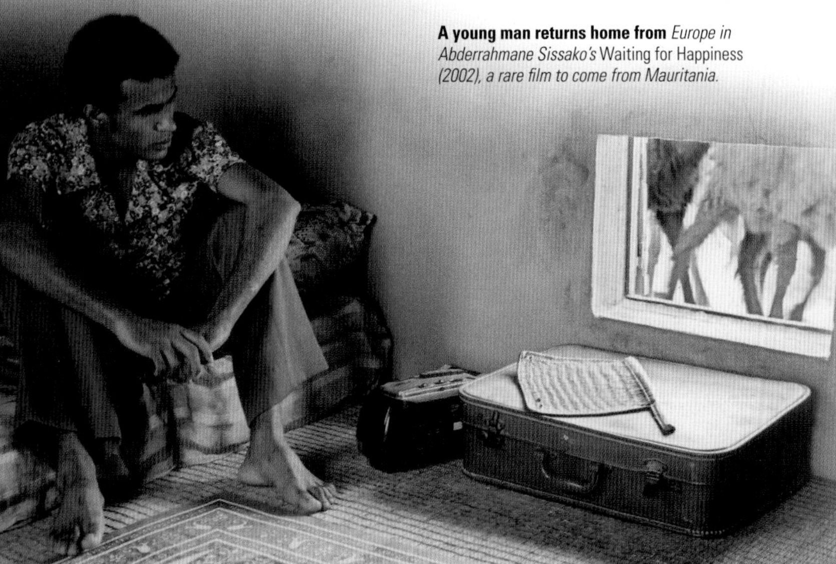

A young man returns home from *Europe in Abderrahmane Sissako's* Waiting for Happiness *(2002), a rare film to come from Mauritania.*

Tsotsi (2005), *which follows the life of a violent gang leader in Johannesburg, South Africa, won Best Foreign Language Film at the 2006 Academy Awards.*

Abdelsalam's *The Night of Counting the Years* (1969), about the robbing of mummies' tombs, all stood out from the commercial dross of the Egyptian film industry.

In the Maghreb, Algeria's first films of independence reflected the struggle for liberation, the most famous being Gillo Pontecorvo's *The Battle of Algiers* (1966), an Italian-Algerian co-production. Mohammed Lakhdar-Hamina's *Chronicle of the Burning Years* (1975), which traces the history of Algeria from 1939 to 1954, was one of the most expensive productions to come out of the Developing World. Algeria, Morocco, and Tunisia have all produced award-winning films over the years, such as the Tunisian Moufida Tlatli's *The Silences of the Palace* (1994), an emotionally powerful look at the role of women in a changing world, a rare feature by a woman film-maker working in a male-dominated Arab country. The pre-eminent director of sub-Saharan African cinema is Ousmane Sembene of Senegal. Thanks to his pioneering work, younger African film directors, such as Souleymane Cissé from Mali and Idrissa Ouedragoa from Burkina Faso, were able to make their mark. The most famous African film festival, which is held biannually in Ougadougou, Burkina Faso, since 1969, has been a wonderful shop window for sub-Saharan cinema.

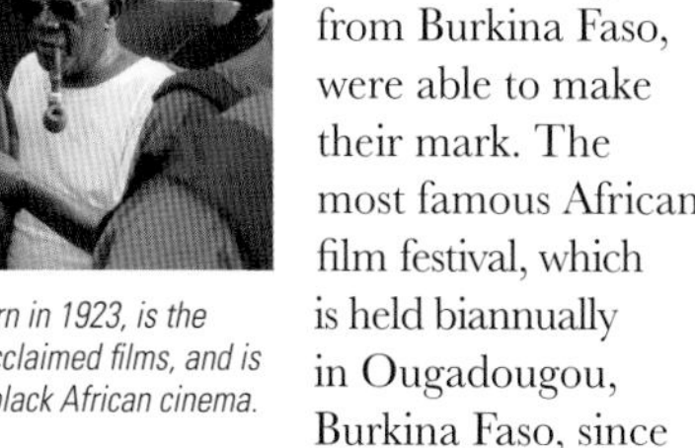

Ousmane Sembene, *born in 1923, is the director of a number of acclaimed films, and is considered the father of black African cinema.*

Under the years of apartheid, South Africa produced very little of worth. Many films post-apartheid continued to look back on that period. *Mapantsula* (1988) by Oliver Schmitz and Graham Hood's Oscar-winning *Tsotsi* (2005), about black-on-black violence, look at the present day.

The Middle East

Although the cinema of this region has been dominated by films from North Africa, particularly Egypt and the Maghreb, there have been significant films made in the Middle East, many based on the political tensions in the area.

In Lebanon, before the long civil war started in 1975, cinema attendance was the highest in the Arab world (though the country produced few features of its own). Syria and Iraq made a number of strong documentaries but, like their neighbors, turned out few feature films.

Hany Abu-Assad's Paradise Now *(2005) tells of two friends recruited for a suicide bombing in Tel Aviv.*

However, at the beginning of the 21st century, the tragic situation in the Middle East, particularly the tensions between Israel and Palestine, gave rise to some of the best films to come from that area. Palestinian writer-director Elia Suleiman's *Divine Intervention* (2002) brilliantly chooses to look at the situation at an Israeli-Palestinian checkpoint with black humor. *The Syrian Bride* (2004), by the Israeli director Eran Riklis, is also set in no-man's land, an arid area between checkpoints at the Israeli and Syrian borders. The first feature by Palestinian director Tawfik Abu Wael, *Thirst* (2004) is a beautifully composed film about an Arab family living in an abandoned village in a dusty corner of Israel.

The best-known Israeli director internationally, Amos Gitai, made *Free Zone* (2005), in which three women — an American, an Israeli, and a Palestinian — become traveling companions in a remote area of Jordan. The controversial Foreign Film Academy Award nominee, *Paradise Now* (2005), traces 24 hours in the lives of two Palestinian suicide-bombers. The director, Hany Abu-Assad, is a Palestinian born in Israel, and he made the story an exciting thriller, while at the same time perceptively revealing the minds of these "martyrs."

WHAT TO WATCH

2002	Divine Intervention (Elia Suleiman, Palestine)
2004	The Syrian Bride (Eran Riklis, Palestine)
2004	Thirst (Tawfik Abu Wael, Palestine)
2005	Paradise Now (Hany Abu-Assad, Palestine)

Free Zone *(2005) stars Nathalie Portman as an American woman in Jordan trying to establish her identity in the dramatic landscape of the country.*

Iran

In the 1990s, the cinema of Iran entered the world stage with the gradual thaw in the country's strictly controlled popular culture. What was revealed was a most original and vibrant national cinema.

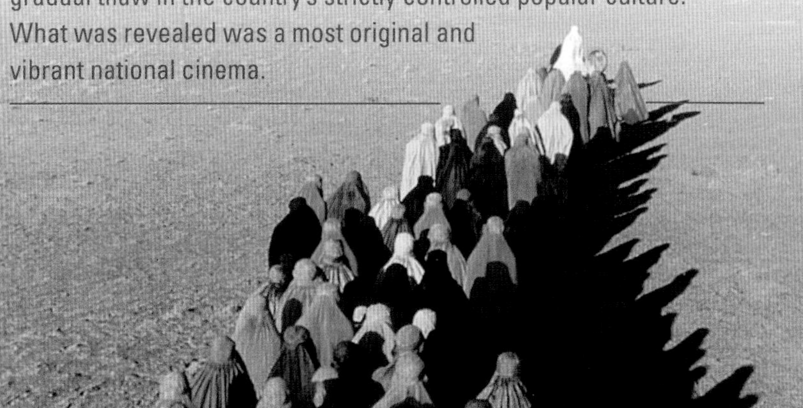

Women in their colourful *but imprisoning burqas make a journey in Afghanistan in Mohsen Makhmalbaf's hotly topical* Kandahar *(2001).*

Iran, under its various authoritarian regimes, has produced only a few notable films over the years. But, in the 1960s, a handful of Iranian films began to be seen abroad. Among the first was Dariush Mehrjui's *The Cow* (1968), about a farmer who loses his beloved cow, assumes the animal's identity, and slides into madness. This minutely observed study of village life and its sparse style presaged later Iranian movies.

Two young girls, *kept locked up by their parents, are released into society for the first time in* The Apple *(1998).*

After the Islamic Revolution of 1979, cinema was condemned for its perceived western values. Nevertheless, in 1983, a Cinema Foundation was established to encourage films with "Islamic values." As a result, freed from the burdens of the past, new directors such as Mohsen Makhmalbaf and Abbas Kiarostami emerged with a number of cinematic masterpieces. There followed many more, including Jafar Panahi, Majid Majidi, Marzieh Meshkini, Babak Payami, and Makhmalbaf's daughter, the extraordinary Samira Makhmalbaf. At 18, Samira directed her first feature, *The Apple* (1998), which launched her as a leading figure in world cinema.

Despite the restrictions imposed by the fundamentalist Islamic regime, most Iranian cinema — one of the most subtly feminist in the world — has managed to find ingenious ways of making profound statements about the human condition.

WHAT TO WATCH

1968	The Cow (Dariush Mehrjui)
1995	The White Balloon (Jafar Panahi)
1997	Taste of Cherry (Abbas Kiarostami)
1997	The Children of Heaven (Majid Majidi)
2000	Blackboards (Samira Makhmalbaf)
2000	The Day I Became a Woman (Marzieh Meshkini)
2001	Secret Ballot (Babak Payami)
2001	Kandahar (Mohsen Makhmalbaf)
2004	Turtles Can Fly (Bahman Ghobadi)

Eastern Europe

The histories of Poland, Hungary, and Czechoslovakia in the 20th century, and their film industries, follow certain similar patterns — independence followed by Nazi subjugation, then repressive Communism, liberalization, a hardening of the regime, and freedom.

The first studio built in Poland was in Warsaw in 1920, two years after independence. In 1929, a group of avant-garde film-makers formed START, a society for the devotees of artistic film. Alexander Ford, the best known of them, became a key figure in Polish cinema. His most important "socially useful" films were *Legion of the Streets* (1932) and *People of the Vistula* (1936).

During World War II, film-making was permitted in countries under German occupation, except Poland for fear of a subtle use of patriotic references. The devastation of the war forced the film industry to begin from scratch. The majority of postwar films tended to deal with the Nazi occupation, the horrors of the ghetto and the heroes of the resistance. Alexander Ford's *Border Street* (1948) was one of the first of a cluster of Polish films that emerged from the rubble of the war. It follows the lives of several families from different social classes in prewar Warsaw whose lives are changed by the tragic events of the period. Ford's *Five Boys From Barska Street* (1953), the first major Polish film in color, was about juvenile delinquency. The assistant on the film was Andrzej Wajda, whose first feature, *A Generation*, the following year, was to give a very different view of Polish youth. Followed by *Kanal* (1957) and *Ashes and Diamonds* (1958), Wajda's war trilogy brought Polish cinema to the world's attention as never before.

Kanal (1957), *about the 1944 Warsaw uprising, shows how Polish partisans were pursued and trapped in the sewers by Nazi soldiers.*

The late 1950s and 1960s was a fertile period for Polish cinema, which produced Andrzej Munk's *Eroica* (1957), Jerzy Kawalerowicz's *Mother Joan of the Angels* (1961), set in a 17th century convent and one of the first Polish films seen in the west not dealing with a war theme, Roman Polanski's *Knife in the Water* (1962), Wojciech Has' *The Saragossa Manuscript* (1964) and Jerzy Skolimowski's *Walkover* (1965). Many of these directors were graduates of the excellent film school in Lodz. However, after 1968, political repression and censorship, as in neighboring Hungary and Czechoslovakia, limited freedom of expression and the cinema suffered.

WHAT TO WATCH

1962	Knife in the Water (Roman Polanski, Poland)
1965	The Shop on the High Street (Ján Kádar, Czechoslovakia)
1965	The Round-Up (Miklós Janscó, Hungary)
1965	Loves of a Blonde (Miloš Forman, Czechoslovakia)
1966	Daisies (Vera Chytilova, Czechoslovakia)
1966	Closely Observed Trains (Jirí Menzel, Czechoslovakia)
1976	Man of Marble (Andrzej Wajda, Poland)
1993/4	The Three Colors trilogy (Krzysztof Kieslowski, Poland)
2000	The Werckmeister Harmonies (Bela Tarr, Hungary)
2000	Divided We Fall (Jan Hrebejk, Czech Republic)

In the mid-1970s, in the face of censorship, a new trend called Cinema of Moral Concern surfaced, characterized by sensitivity to ethical problems and a focus on the relationship between the individual and the state. Examples are Andrej Wajda's *Man of Marble* (1976), Krzsztof Zanussi's satires *Camouflage* (1977) and *Constans* (1981), Agnieszka Holland's *Provincial Actors* (1979), and Krzysztof Kieslowski's *No End* (1984).

Zygmunt Malanowicz *and Jolanta Umecka embrace in Roman Polanski's first feature,* Knife in the Water *(1962). An absurdist drama of sexual rivalry and the generation gap, it gained an Oscar nomination and brought Polanski immediate fame.*

HUNGARY

Hungary became the first country to nationalize its film industry, doing so several months before the Soviet Union under its brief period of Communism in 1919. When Horthy's fascist government came into power in 1920, it was put back into private ownership, and Alexander Korda, Mihaly Kertesz (Michael Curtiz), Paul Fejos and the film theoretician Bela Balazs, all of whom had made valuable contributions to Hungarian film, were forced to leave the country. The quality of films was at its lowest during Hungary's alliance with the Axis powers during World War II. The first important postwar success

In Miklós Jancsó's The Round-Up *(1965), a group of peasants is tortured in an attempt to find the leader of a partisan movement.*

was Géza von Radványi's *Somewhere in Europe* (1947), which marked the return of Balazs as screenwriter, and led to the renationalization of the film industry. In the late 1950s, a younger generation of film-makers made their mark, helped by the setting up of the Balazs Bela Studio: Miklós Jancsó (*The Round-Up*, 1965), István Szabó (*Father*, 1967), and István Gaál (*The Falcons*, 1970). The latter film draws an impressive analogy between the taming of wild birds and a way of life that requires blind obedience. Pal Gábor's *Angi Vera* (1979), which eloquently conveys the repressive climate of Stalinist Hungary in the late 1940s, surprised and impressed critics in the west. Márta Mészáros, formerly married to Miklós Jancsó, also made a reputation with her intimate films on the female condition, most particularly her three-part "Diary" (1982–90), *Diary for My Children*, *Diary for My Loves*, and *Diary for My Mother and Father*. Bela Tarr emerged in the 1990s as one of the most remarkable of European directors with his seven-and-a-half-hour *Satanango* (1994) and *Werckmeister Harmonies* (2000), in which the long take is stretched to its limits.

Klaus Maria Brandauer (right) *plays an actor who sells his soul when working under the Nazis in Szabo's Oscar-winning* Mephisto *(1981).*

In Jan Hrebejk's black comedy Divided We Fall *(2000), Boleslav Polivka (center) is an unlikely hero who hides a Jewish friend, an escapee from a concentration camp, in his house under the nose of a Nazi sympathizer, who also lives in the house.*

CZECHOSLOVAKIA

Czechoslovakia became an independent nation in 1918, though competition from German and US films limited independent Czech cinema for some time. Two films stood out during the end of the silent era: Gustav Machaty's *Erotikon* (1929), which achieved much of its erotic effect by symbolic imagery, and Curt Junghan's *Such Is Life* (1929), which dealt with conditions of working-class life in Prague. But Machaty's greatest claim to fame was *Ecstasy* (1933), in which the nude scenes played by Hedy Kiesler (later Lamarr) caused a furor. The Pope protested when it was shown at the Venice Film Festival, the nude scenes were cut in the US, and Hedy's husband tried to buy up all the prints. Despite the protests, the film is, in fact, full of pastoral beauty.

Five-year-old *Andrei Chalimon attempts to imitate his musician stepfather in the title role of Jan Sverák's charming Oscar-winning* Kolya *(1996).*

In 1933, the Barrandov studios, one of the best equipped in Europe, then as now, opened in a suburb of Prague. During the war, the Germans took it over, which interrupted any advance in the industry. After the war, the national film school FAMU was set up in Prague, and a new generation of directors emerged from it, notably Ivan Passer, Jirí Menzel, Vera Chytilová, and Miloš Forman. Ján Kadár's *The Shop on the High Street* (1965) was the first Czech film to win a Foreign Film Oscar, while Menzel's *Closely Watched Trains* (1966) soon became the second. The 1968 Russian invasion ended this exciting period of activity. Kádar, Passer and Forman left for the US. Chytilová, whose *Daisies* (1966) was the most adventurous and anarchic film of the period, was silenced. The animosity toward the Russians is dealt with in *Kolya* (1996), in which a Czech finds himself with a Russian stepson, who he learns to love.

Film censorship was less rigorous in Slovakia and, directors, such as Stefan Uher, Dusan Hanák, and Juraj Jakubisko, were able to pursue their careers relatively freely. Since the breakup of Czechoslovakia into the Czech Republic and Slovakia in 1993, the film industries have developed their own distinct characters.

The Balkans

Given the political upheavals that this region of Europe has suffered since cinema was invented, it is not surprising that film production has been sporadic and often traditionalist. However, a number of talented film-makers have come from these countries in recent years.

YUGOSLAVIA

In Yugoslavia, the best of the small output of pre-World War II feature films was Mihailo-Miko Popovic's *With Faith in God* (1934), a Serbian World War I epic. After 1945, Yugoslavian films dealt almost exclusively with the war, such as in the popular "partisan" movies. But it was animation films that made an impact abroad, especially through the work of the Zagreb school, whose style was a refreshing alternative to Walt Disney.

The best known Yugoslavian directors are Dusan Makavejev, officially disapproved of at home, and Aleksandar Petrovic, whose films, *Three* (1965) and *I Even Met Happy Gypsies* (1967), were nominated two years running for the Best Foreign Film Oscar. The Bosnian Emir Kusturica burst on to the scene in 1981, winning prestigious awards with each new film.

BULGARIA

In 1915, seven years after independence, Bulgaria produced its first feature, *The Bulgarian is Gallant.* It starred and was directed by Vassil Gendov, who also directed Bulgaria's first talkie, *The Slaves' Revolt* (1933). During World War II, only propaganda films were allowed, and then under Communist rule, features focussed on the Soviet socialist realism model. As elsewhere in Europe, there was an improvement from the 1960s, with Vulo Radev's *The Peach Thief* (1964) being among the first internationally important productions. Metodi Andonov's *The Goat Horn* (1972) — remade by Nikolai Volev in 1994 — became the most critically acclaimed Bulgarian film of the time.

Underground *(1995) is directed by celebrated Bosnian director, Emir Kusturica, and is an epic portrait of Yugoslavia from 1941 to the present. Kusturica won Best Director at Cannes for* Time of the Gypsies *(1989).*

Anthony Quinn in Zorba the Greek *(1964), directed by Michael Cacoyannis, one of the few Greek directors to gain international recognition for his work.*

ROMANIA

Romania took a long time to build the semblance of a film industry, which has produced about 15 films a year from the 1960s. A breakthrough was made with Liviu Ciulei's *Forest of the Hanged* (1965), which won Best Director at Cannes. This anti-war drama achieved an understated quality, and contrasted with the propaganda epics that preceded it. Lucian Pintilie, the best-known Romanian director, made his very first feature, *Sunday at Six,* in the same year.

Yol *shows Turkey through the eyes of five prisoners.*

GREECE

Although the first Greek film appeared in 1912, long periods of instability crippled any attempts at forming a film industry, and few features were produced until the 1950s when Michael Cacoyannis became the embodiment of Greek cinema, reaching the peak of his popularity with *Zorba the Greek* (1964). Since then, Theo Angelopoulos *(see page 255)* began to loom impressively in the 1970s.

TURKEY

Omer Lutfi Akad was the D.W. Griffith of Turkish cinema. His feature, *In the Name of the Law* (1952), marked a departure from the number of cheap melodramas being made. But it was almost three decades before Yilmaz Güney became the most influential and internationally acclaimed director Turkey has ever produced. However, several of his best films, including *Yol* (1982), were directed by proxy as he languished in prison for his left-wing political activities. Since Güney, there has been an impressive string of Turkish films including Yesim Ustaoglu's *Journey to The Sun* (1999), Nuri Bilge Ceylan's *Uzak* (2002), and Semih Kaplanoglu's *Angel's Fall* (2005).

WHAT TO WATCH

1957	A Matter of Dignity (Michael Cacoyannis, Greece)
1967	I Even Met Happy Gypsies (Aleksandar Petrovic, Yugoslavia)
1972	The Goat Horn (Metodi Andonov, Bulgaria)
1982	Yol (Serif Gören, Yilmaz Güney, Turkey)
1995	Underground (Emir Kusturica, Yugoslavia)
1998	Eternity and a Day (Theo Angelopoulos, Greece)
2002	Uzak (Nuri Bilge Ceylan, Turkey)

Russia

In the 1920s, Russian cinema was the most exciting and experimental in the world until the heavy hand of Stalinism held it down. Despite occasional masterpieces, it would be many years before Russia reemerged to take its place among the great cinematic nations.

There was little of cinematic interest in pre-revolutionary Russia as it was impossible to deal with contemporary issues under strict Tsarist censorship. Films depended heavily on adaptations from literature or the theater and, until World War I, foreign films dominated the Russian market. The leading director was Yakov Protazanov, who directed more than 40 films between 1909 and 1917. He was one of the few members of the old guard to remain in Russia after the revolution in October 1917. Protazanov went on to make the Soviet Union's first science-fiction movie, *Aelita* (1924).

In their first days of power, the Bolsheviks established a State Commission of Education, which included an important subsection devoted to cinema. As the new Soviet leader, Lenin realized the immense value of film as propaganda, and early Soviet cinema played an important role in getting the revolutionary message across to the population all over the vast country, usually carried by "agit-prop" trains. Film schools were set up in Moscow and Petrograd (later Leningrad) in 1918 and the film industry was nationalized a year later. However, because of the Civil War and the foreign blockade of films, film stock, and equipment, it took a few years before it could start producing more than a handful of feature films.

A gang of thieves is surprised *by Mr. West and his faithful cowboy aide in* The Extraordinary Adventures of Mr. West In the Land of the Bolsheviks (1924).

Things started to change in 1924 as the economy improved and the Soviet government declared that the state would not interfere in matters of artistic style — even non-naturalistic and avant-garde expression — but that the films should have a revolutionary content. Thus began an exciting and fruitful period of film-making. Lev Kuleshov, one of the first theorists of the cinema, put his researches at the services of his first feature, the gag-filled satire, *The Extraordinary Adventures of Mr. West in the Land of the Bolsheviks* (1924). Using mobile cameras, quick cutting, and sequences derived from American chase films, the film managed to deride the west's stereotyped view of "mad, savage Russians" while creating its own stereotyped American — the Harold-Lloyd type Mr. West.

SILENT MASTERPIECES

There followed the silent masterpieces of Sergei Eisenstein, Vsevolod Pudovkin, Alexander Dovzhenko, Boris Barnet, Abram Room, Dziga Vertov, and the directing duo of Leonid Trauberg and Grigori Kozintsev, all bursting with creative enthusiasm. Leading the way was Eisenstein's *Strike* (1924), for which he used the "dynamic montage," that is, visual metaphors and shock cuts. This reached its peak in *The Battleship Potemkin* (1925), with its memorable Odessa Steps sequence *(see page 401)*, and *October* (1928).

Taking the same subject as *October* (the 1917 Russian Revolution), Pudovkin showed a different slant in *The End of St. Petersburg* (1927), while Dovzhenko made *Earth* (1930), a pastoral symphony dedicated to his native Ukraine.

WHAT TO WATCH

1925	The Battleship Potemkin (Sergei Eisenstein)
1928	Storm Over Asia (Vsevolod Pudovkin)
1929	The Man with the Movie Camera (Dziga Vertov)
1930	Earth (Alexander Dovzhenko)
1944/6	Ivan the Terrible Parts I and II (Sergei Eisenstein)
1957	The Cranes Are Flying (Mikhail Kalatozov)
1959	Ballad of a Soldier (Grigori Chukrai)
1969	The Color of Pomegranates (Sergei Paradjanov)
1985	Come and See (Elem Klimov)
2002	Russian Ark (Alexander Sokurov)

Barnet made a number of delightfully fresh satirical comedies such as *The Girl With the Hatbox* (1927) and *The House on Trubnaya* (1928). Abram Room's *Bed and Sofa* (1927) dealt with a ménage-à-trois with warmth and humor. Trauberg and Kozintsev's *The New Babylon* (1929), set in Paris at the time of the Commune in 1871, brilliantly used montage and lighting to contrast the rich and the poor. In contrast, Vertov *(see page 377)*, continued to make documentaries, culminating with *The Man with the Movie Camera* (1929).

A poster for Dovzhenko's *poetic film* Earth *(1930) shows a brave peasant representing the face of collectivization.*

Tragically, this great period of Russian experimentation came to an end as Stalin strengthened his hold. More and more of the best films, especially those of Eisenstein, were attacked for being "bourgeois" due to their use of symbolism and modernistic visual style. By the end of 1932, the slogan "socialist realism," a phrase attributed to Stalin himself, was *de rigueur* in all the arts. Socialist realism was opposed to "formalism," or art that put style above content. Soviet art had to be optimistic and understandable and loved by the masses. This meant that the experimentation that had made Soviet cinema great was now reined in.

Counterplan (1932), directed by Lev Arnshtam, Fridrikh Ermler, and Sergei Yutkevich, about the foiling of a sabotage attempt on a steel plant, was, according to one writer, "the first victory of socialist realism in the Soviet cinema."

Nevertheless, in the period before World War II, the Soviet Union did produce some films that can still be enjoyed today, such as the Hollywood-style musicals, *Jazz Comedy* (1934) and *Volga-Volga* (1938), made by Grigori Alexandrov, a former colleague of Eisenstein. Mark Donskoi's "Gorky trilogy" — *The Childhood of Maxim Gorky* (1938), *My Apprenticeship* (1939), and *My Universities* (1940) — was rich in incident, character, and period detail; it was one of the few masterpieces of socialist realism. Another was Eisenstein's first sound film, *Alexander Nevsky* (1938), with a wonderful score by Russian composer Sergei Prokofiev.

Innokenti Smoktunovsky *stars as the Prince of Denmark (left), and Viktor Kolpakov plays the Gravedigger in* Hamlet *(1964).*

THE DEATH OF STALIN

During World War II, the film industry concentrated mainly on morale-boosting documentaries. One of the few features made was Eisenstein's *Ivan The Terrible* (1944), which was made in two parts: the first was approved by Stalin, the second was banned and not released until 1958. The post-war years represented a low point in Soviet cinema both in quality and quantity. It was only after Stalin's death in 1953, and Khrushchev's famous speech in 1956 which attacked aspects of Stalinism, that it began to pick up. The result of this "thaw" was a number of films that merited international successes. Mikhail Kalatozov's *The Cranes Are Flying* (1957), a lyrical love story, won the Best Film at Cannes and Grigori Chukrai's *Ballad of a Soldier* (1959), an unrhetorical and moving view of everyday life in wartime Russia, won a Special Jury Prize at Cannes.

This relative freedom of expression continued into the mid-1960s with some notable films such as Josef Heifits' *The Lady With the Little Dog* (1959), Kozintsev's *Hamlet* (1964), Andrei Tarkovsky's *Ivan's Childhood* (1962), and Sergei Paradjanov's *Shadows of our Forgotten Ancestors* (1964), before repression set in again. Tarkovsky's *Andrei Rublev* (1966) and Paradjanov's *The Color of*

Two young Russian women *confide in one another in Vladimir Menshov's Oscar-winning* Moscow Does Not Believe in Tears *(1979).*

Pomegranates (1969) were both shelved. Despite some exceptions, including Sergei Bondarchuk's remarkable eight-hour *War and Peace* (1966–7), good films were few and far between until the late 1970s when *Moscow Does Not Believe in Tears* (1979), a romantic comedy-drama, won the Best Foreign Film Oscar in that year.

THE POST-COMMUNIST ERA

After the fall of communism, there was a phase when most Russian films were either kitsch or imitations of American action movies. However, after the initial reaction against the past, Russia once again became one of the leading cinematic countries with films such as Pavel Chukhrai's *The Thief* (1997), Alexander Sokurov's *Russian Ark* (2002), Andrei Zvyagintsev's *The Return* (2003), Alexei German Jr's *The Last Train,* and Boris Khlebnikov and Aleksei Popogrebsky's *Koktebel* (all 2003). The breakup of the USSR meant that the former Soviet republics were able to establish a characteristic cinema, good examples of which are cosmopolitan Georgian director Otar Iosseliani's *Brigands — Chapter VII* (1996) and Jamshed Usmonov's *Angel on the Right* (Tajikistan, 2002).

Tsar Nicholas II and the Russian *royal family take tea on the eve of the Revolution in Alexander Sokurov's extraordinary one-take* Russian Ark *(2002), filmed entirely in the Hermitage in St. Petersburg.*

The Nordic Countries

Considering the small size of their populations, the contribution to the art of cinema of the Nordic countries, led by Sweden and Denmark, has been phenomenal. From Ingmar Bergman to Lars von Trier, many directors from this part of Europe have been highly influential.

In 1906 the Nordisk film company (the oldest film company in the world still in existence) provided the impetus for the rise of Danish cinema. Some of the early Danish films went in for "shocking" subjects in films with such titles as *The White Slave Trade* (1910), *The Morphine Takers* (1911), and *Opium Dreams* (1914). Production dropped severely after World War I and it took a long time to recover, thus forcing Denmark's two most famous directors, Carl Dreyer and Benjamin Christensen, to seek work in other countries. In Sweden, Dreyer shot *The Parson's Widow* (1920) and Christensen made his most famous film, *Witchcraft Through the Ages* (1922), a semi-documentary made up of a series of tableaux inspired by the artists Hieronymus Bosch and Pieter Bruegel. Dreyer returned to Denmark during World War II, where he directed one of his greatest films, *Day of Wrath* (1943). But fearing imprisonment by the Nazi authorities for what were seen as allusions to the tyranny of the Occupation in the film, Drêyer fled to Sweden and returned only after the war. Among the light comedies and soft porn produced in Denmark in the 1950s, only Dreyer's *Ordet* (1954), which won the Golden Bear in Berlin, stood out.

A couple of notable Danish films from the 1960s were Palle Kjærulff-Schmidt's *Once There Was a War* (1966), a tale of an adolescent boy in Copenhagen during the Occupation, and Henning Carlsen's *Hunger* (1966), an atmospheric adaptation of Knut Hamsen's famous first novel about a penniless writer.

Three great Swedes in Hollywood: *directors Victor Sjöström (renamed Victor Seastrom by MGM) and Mauritz Stiller with Greta Garbo, at the start of her career in the US.*

WHAT TO WATCH

1921	The Phantom Carriage (Victor Sjöström, Sweden)
1943	Day of Wrath (Carl Dreyer, Denmark)
1966	Persona (Ingmar Bergman, Sweden)
1987	Babette's Feast (Gabriel Axel, Denmark)
1998	Festen (Thomas Vinterberg, Denmark)
1998	The Idiots (Lars Von Trier, Denmark)

SWEDISH CINEMA

In Sweden in 1907, the Svenska Bio studio was founded, and two years later Charles Magnussen joined as production manager. In 1912, Magnussen signed up two directors, Victor Sjöström and Mauritz Stiller, who were to transform Swedish cinema. In the same year, Magnussen and Julius Jaenzon co-directed *The Vagabond's Galoshes*, based on a Hans Christian Andersen fairy tale, which had sequences shot on location in France and the US, and included an early tracking shot.

Bibi Andersson (left) and *Liv Ulmann as women who exchange identities in Ingmar Bergman's* Persona *(1966).*

Mauritz Stiller made sophisticated, ironic sex comedies, such as *Love and Journalism* (1916) and *Erotikon* (1920), before moving nearer the more sombre Swedish literary tradition with films based on the novels of Selma Lagerlöf. Sjöström, with *Karin, Daughter of Ingmar* (1920) and *The Phantom Carriage* (1921), and Stiller, with *Sir Arne's Treasure* (1919) and Greta Garbo's first feature film, *The Saga of Gosta Berling* (1923), gave Sweden a reputation for making films of high artistic quality. When Sjöström, Stiller, and Garbo left for Hollywood in the mid-1920s, Swedish cinema suffered.

The only director of note in the 1930s was Gustaf Molander, whose most famous film was *Intermezzo* (1936), a weepie in which the young Ingrid Bergman had her first starring role. David O. Selznick saw it and offered Bergman a contract and a remake of the film Hollywood-style two years later. One of the most significant Swedish films of the 1940s was Alf Sjöberg's *Frenzy* (1944), about misunderstood youth. It not only launched 26-year-old Ingmar Bergman — whose first screenplay this was — and the teenage actress Mai Zetterling, but instigated the renaissance of Swedish cinema. From his debut film, *Crisis* (1946), Bergman's talent was immediately recognized, and from the 1950s he personified Swedish cinema. Lesser figures, such as Arne Mattsson (*One Summer of Happiness*, 1951) and Arne Sucksdorff (*The Great Adventure*, 1953) gained some recognition abroad.

In the 1960s, a younger generation of directors emerged such as Bo Widerberg, most renowned for the

In a portrayal that won her *Best Actress at Cannes, Pia Degermark stars in the title role of Bo Widerberg's lyrically photographed* Elvira Madigan *(1967), set to the strains of Mozart's Piano Concerto No.21.*

One of the inept Soviet *rock musicians in* Leningrad Cowboys Go America *(1989), a typically idiosyncratic film by Finnish director Aki Kaurismäki.*

tragic love story *Elvira Madigan* (1967) and Vilgot Sjöman, who caused a scandal with *I Am Curious Yellow* (1967) and *I Am Curious Blue* (1968), both containing explicit sex. Mai Zetterling's first two films as director, *Loving Couples* (1964) and *Night Games* (1966), were wickedly sensuous Strinbergian dramas with a feminist twist.

However, Ingmar Bergman continued to cast his shadow. Following his classics of the 1950s, notably *The Seventh Seal* *(see page 443)* and *Wild Strawberries* (both 1957), he made a series of psychodramas in the 1960s, most of them starring Liv Ullmann. (In 2000, Ullmann would direct *Faithless*, a compelling film written by Bergman about their relationship.) She also starred in Jan Troell's *The Emigrants* (1972) and *The New Land* (1973), two heartfelt sagas of Swedes who emigrated to the US in the 19th century. Ullmann had her first starring role in *The Wayward Girl* (1959). This tale of sexual liberation was the last film by Edith Carlmar, Norway's first female director, who made ten features between 1949 and 1959. In 1957, another Norwegian film had made an impact internationally — Arne Skouen's *Nine Lives* was based on the real-life experience of resistance fighter Jan Baalsrud.

Finland's film of note in the 1950s was Edvin Lane's *The Unknown Soldier* (1956), still the country's highest-grossing film ever. Jorn Donner made many films dealing with sexuality. Donner was Finland's best-known director until the arrival of the idiosyncratic Aki Kaurismäki, who put Finland firmly on the cinematic map in the 1980s. Kaurismäki's best-known film is probably *The Man Without a Past* (2002).

Like Kaurismäki, Fridrik Thor Fridriksson is the sole international representative of his country, Iceland, though he started to get widely well-known in the 1990s with off-beat films like *Cold Fever* (1994) and *Devil's Island* (1996).

Films from the Baltic countries, emerging from Soviet domination,

tentatively began to be recognized abroad after 2000. These included Kristijonas Vildzhiunas's *The Lease* (2002, Lithuania), Laila Pakalnina's *The Python* (2003, Latvia), and Jaak Kilmi and René Reinumägi's *Revolution of Pigs* (2004, Estonia).

A CREATIVE EXPLOSION

The 1980s onwards have been a time of great creativity in the Nordic countries. In Denmark, it began when Danish films won Best Foreign Film Oscars two years in succession, Gabriel Axel's *Babette's Feast* (1987) and Bille August's *Pelle the Conqueror* (1987). In 1995, Lars von Trier and Thomas Vinterberg jointly formulated the artistic manifesto Dogme 95, which turned low-budget film aesthetics into a rich cinematic principle. Among the Dogme films to make a huge impact were Vinterberg's *Festen* (*The Celebration*), von Trier's *The Idiots* (both 1998), Søren Kragh-Jacobsen's *Mifune* (1999), Lone Scherfig's *Italian For Beginners* (2000) and Annette Olesen's *Minor Mishaps* (2002).

In a remote and austere Danish town, *guests enjoy a sumptuous once-in-a-lifetime meal prepared by a French cook (Stéphane Audran) in* Babette's Feast *(1987).*

Notable Swedish films were Lukas Moodysson's comedy-drama *Together* (2000), Roy Andersson's weird *Songs from the Second Floor* (2000), and Björn Runge's *Daybreak* (2003). Norway had hits with Ola Solum's *Orion's Belt* (1985), Nils Gaup's *Pathfinder* (1987), and the life-enhancing documentary about a male choir, Knut Erik Jensen's *Cool and Crazy* (2001).

Swedish experts come to *examine the domestic habits of Norwegian bachelors in Bent Hamer's quirky satire* Kitchen Stories *(2003).*

Germany

Despite the considerable contribution that Germany has made to the history of film, there was a wide gap between its greatest period – the silent era — and the new dawn of German cinema in the 1970s, almost half a century later.

"Never before and in no other country have images and language been abused so unscrupulously as here. Nowhere else have people suffered such a loss of confidence in images of their own, their own stories and myths, as we have," proclaimed German director Wim Wenders in 1977. Wenders is referring to the fatal legacy of Nazism, which permeated so many German films, whether from the Federal Republic (West Germany) or the Democratic Republic (East Germany). This took place mainly between 1949 and 1989, but also before and after that period.

Much of this is expounded by the critic Siegfried Kracauer in his book, *From Caligari to Hitler* (1947), which analyzed the German psyche through German films. The starting point of the book is Robert Wiene's *The Cabinet of Dr. Caligari* (1919, *see page 399*), which was to become a trademark of German cinema of the 1920s with its stylized, distorted studio sets, artificial lighting and shadows.

THE SILENT AGE

Before World War I, there were 2,000 cinemas and two large film studios near Berlin. Most German films were farcical comedies and static adaptations from literature and the stage. Nevertheless, there were a few films that anticipated the expressionist style of *Dr. Caligari*, such as the first of three versions of *The Student of Prague* (1913), an early spark that ignited German

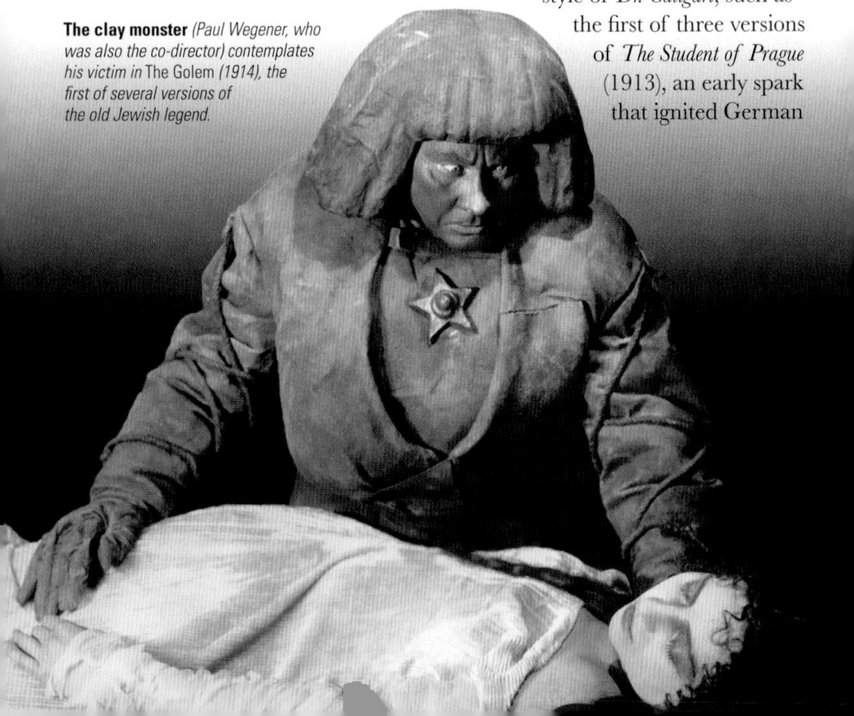

The clay monster *(Paul Wegener, who was also the co-director) contemplates his victim in* The Golem *(1914), the first of several versions of the old Jewish legend.*

cinema's love of supernatural subjects, leading in turn to the making of classics of expressionism. It starred Paul Wegener, who sells his reflection to obtain the means to woo the girl of his choice. Wegener also played the monster in *The Golem* (1914), which he co-directed (with Henrik Galeen).

Film production dramatically increased during World War I because films from enemy countries — the US, France, and England — were not shown in Germany. The renowned UFA (Universum Film Aktien Gesellschaft) film company was formed in 1917 and remained the dominant force in the industry until the end of World War II. Among the directors that emerged at this period were F.W. Murnau, Paul Leni, Fritz Lang, and Ernst Lubitsch. Murnau's *Nosferatu* (1922), Leni's *Waxworks* (1924), and Lang's two-part *Dr. Mabuse, the Gambler* (1922) and *Metropolis* (1927), were expressionistic masterpieces. Lubitsch was also directing lavish, ironical historical romances, such as *Madame Du Barry* (1919), *Anne Boleyn* (1920), and *Pharoah's Wife* (1922).

Emil Jannings as the proud hotel doorman *who loses his job and is reduced to lavatory attendant in F. W. Murnau's* The Last Laugh *(1924).*

At the same time, there were the *kammerspiel* (chamber play) films, chiefly Lupu Pick's *Shattered* (1921) and Murnau's *The Last Laugh* (1924). There were also two other popular genres: "street films" like G.W. Pabst's *The Joyless Street* (1925), with 20-year-old Greta Garbo (in her last European film), and "mountain films," which focussed on man's battle against Nature. The latter was exemplified by the films of Arnold Fanck, the best being *The White Hell of Pitz Palu* (1929). Appearing in four of Fanck's films was director Leni Riefenstahl (*see page 355*), whose first feature as a director, *The Blue Light* (1932) was a similar "mountain film."

END OF THE GOLDEN AGE

Before the Golden Age was terminated by Hitler, there were a number of significant sound films: Josef von Sternberg's *The Blue Angel* (1930), Pabst's *Westfront 1918* (1930) and *The Threepenny Opera* (1931), and Leontine Sagan's *Madchen in Uniform* (1931), about a lesbian relationship. Fritz Lang's *M* (1931) with Peter Lorre as a child killer, and his *Testament of Dr. Mabuse* (1933) were also made during this period. The latter, made as Hitler seized power, had the mad villain expressing sentiments too close for Nazi comfort, thus provoking Joseph Goebbels, the Minister of Propaganda, to ask Lang to change the last reel.

WHAT TO WATCH

1924	The Last Laugh (F.W. Murnau)
1928	Pandora's Box (G.W. Pabst)
1930	The Blue Angel (Josef von Sternberg)
1931	M (Fritz Lang)
1959	The Bridge (Bernhard Wicki)
1975	Kings of the Road (Wim Wenders)
1978	The Marriage of Maria Braun (Rainer Werner Fassbinder)
1979	The Tin Drum (Volker Schlöndorff)
1981	Das Boot (Wolfgang Peterson)
1998	Run Lola Run (Tom Tykwer)

Lang declined and fled the country. All filming now came under the control of Goebbels, who purged Jews from the industry. Over 1,000 films were made under the Nazis, most of them frivolous comedies and musicals, balanced with a number of anti-Semitic propaganda pieces, including *Jew Süss* and *The Eternal Jew* (both 1940). Other propaganda films were *Hitlerjunge Quex* (1933), and Riefenstahl's *Triumph of the Will* (1935) and *Olympia* (1938). One of the few films to survive the period was *The Adventures of Baron Munchhausen* (1943), an elaborate fantasy, superbly photographed in Agfacolor, which was made to celebrate the 25th anniversary of UFA studios.

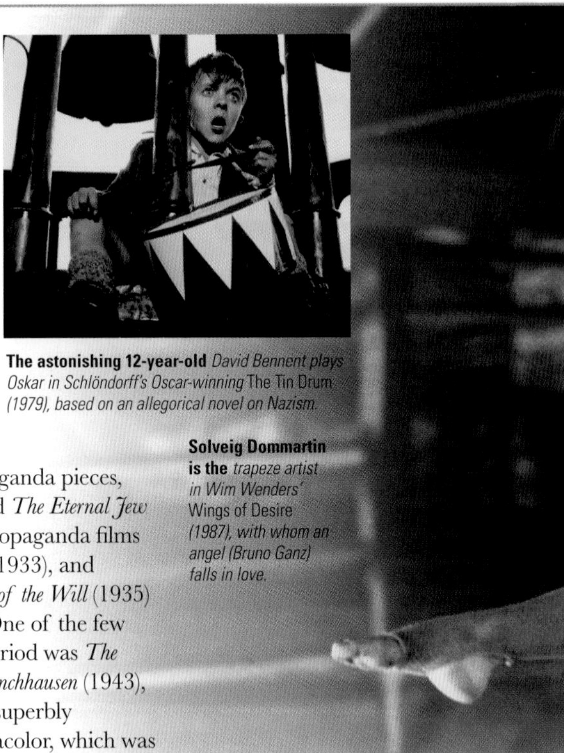

The astonishing 12-year-old *David Bennent plays Oskar in Schlöndorff's Oscar-winning* The Tin Drum *(1979), based on an allegorical novel on Nazism.*

Solveig Dommartin is the *trapeze artist in Wim Wenders'* Wings of Desire *(1987), with whom an angel (Bruno Ganz) falls in love.*

After the war, it took just as long to rebuild the film industry as it did to rebuild the now Allied-occupied country. Almost all the production facilities, including UFA and Tobis studios, were in the Russian zone, and were taken over by DEFA, the newly formed State film company. Most of the postwar films (known as "rubble films") in both East and West Germany were marked by strong sociological content, in an attempt to come to terms with bitter reality. After the division of Germany in 1949, the two film industries developed separately, East Germany made films with a heavy political slant, while West Germany, in contrast, turned out more escapist entertainment.

A SLOW REBIRTH

The 1950s was a fallow period for German films, although they produced several stars, such as Romy Schneider, Horst Buchholz, Curd Jürgens, and Maria Schell, all of whom became internationally recognized. The only film of much note was Bernhard Wicki's *The Bridge* (1959), about seven schoolboys drafted into the dregs of Hitler's army in 1945 who are asked to defend a bridge against American tanks, which they do to the death.

In the early 1960s, the West German film-maker Alexander Kluge wrote a manifesto demanding subsidies and the setting up of a film school. It paved the way for a new wave of directors including Volker Schlöndorff, Rainer Werner Fassbinder, Werner Herzog, and Wim Wenders. There followed Hans-Jürgen Syberberg, with his attempts to demystify Germany's cultural and historical past, Edgar Reitz, whose *Heimat* (1983–2005) mirrored modern German history, and feminist film-makers Margarethe von Trotta and Helga Sanders Brahms.

Wolfgang Peterson's *Das Boot* (1981), Oliver Hirschbiegel's *Downfall* (2004), and Wolfgang Becker's *Good Bye, Lenin!* (2003) came to terms with recent German history.

As the Nazi period — a subject that dominated much German cinema from the 1960s — recedes into the past, a new, more confident German cinema has emerged, typified by Tom Tykwer's *Run Lola Run* (1998), which cleverly covers the same time span in three different ways, Hans Weingartner's *The Edukators* (2004), about a group of anarchists, and German-born Turk Fatih Akin's *Head-On* (2004), a cry of rage on behalf of Turkish immigrants.

Lola (Franka Potente) *has 20 minutes to find 100,000 Deutschmarks to stop her boyfriend robbing a grocery store in Tom Tykwer's fast-paced hit film* Run Lola Run *(1998).*

France

No other country, except the US, has contributed so much to the technical and artistic development of film than France. However, it could be argued that France has an even more enviable record, consistently producing films of both commercial and artistic merit.

Louis Feuillade's five-episode Fantômas *(1913–14) puts the arch criminal and master of disguise (René Navarre) in a variety of tricky situations.*

There is still a dispute as to which country invented cinema. What is certain is that the Lumière brothers of France were the first to exploit it commercially. They first showed their films to the general public in Paris on December 28, 1895, the date generally acknowledged as marking the birth of cinema. Not long after this, film producers Leon Gaumont and Charles Pathé, realizing the commercial potential of the new medium, began to build their movie empires. Alice Guy-Blaché, in charge of production at Gaumont, became the first woman director with *La Fee Aux Chou (The Good Fairy and the Cabbage Patch*, 1902).

Some of the earliest French films, besides the magic cinematic tricks of Georges Méliès, were reproductions of classic plays, typically made up in a series of tableux. Early stars included the legendary stage actress Sarah Bernhardt who starred in *Queen Elizabeth* (1912), which was distributed successfully in the US. But the most famous French name in the US was the elegant comedian Max Linder, who influenced Charlie Chaplin and other great comics of the silent screen. At the same time, Louis Feuillade was making his serials, *Fantômas* (1913–14), about a diabolical criminal, and *Les Vampires* (1915–16).

World War I disrupted French film production, allowing American film to

become more dominant in Europe. After the war, the French developed film as an art form. The film theoretician Ricciotto Canuda referred to film as "The Seventh Art" and one of the first serious critics, Louis Delluc, an important director in his own right, coined the word *cinéaste* meaning a film-maker. (The Prix Louis Delluc has been awarded annually since 1937 to the best French film of the year.) Germaine Dulac directed *The Seashell and the Clergyman* (1928), which was probably the first surrealist film, while Dulac's *The Smiling Madame Beudet* (1922) is recognized as the first feminist film. Other firsts include the use of slow motion in Jean Epstein's *The Fall of the House of Usher* (1928), and the blurred image (*flou*) in Marcel L'Herbier's *El Dorado* (1921). Abel Gance was a towering figure who was already using split-screen techniques in *J'accuse!* (1919) before his masterpiece *Napoléon* (1927).

WHAT TO WATCH

1927	Napoléon (Abel Gance)
1934	L'Atalante (Jean Vigo)
1937	La Grande Illusion (Jean Renoir)
1939	Le Jour se Lève (Marcel Carné)
1951	Diary of a Country Priest (Robert Bresson)
1959	Hiroshima Mon Amour (Alain Resnais)
1962	Jules et Jim (François Truffaut)
1968	Weekend (Jean-Luc Godard)
1995	La Haine (Mathieu Kassovitz)
2000	The Taste of Others (Agnès Jaoui)

The great Jean Gabin, *as a thief hiding in the Algerian Casbah, is confronted by his jealous mistress (Line Noro) in Julien Duvivier's fatalistic romance* Pépé le Moko *(1936).*

THE COMING OF SOUND

From the 1930s, Jean Renoir, Marcel Pagnol and Sacha Guitry relished using dialogue, while René Clair made musicals. This period was characterized by "poetic realism" in the work of Marcel Carné (*Le Jour se Lève*, 1939), Jean Renoir (*La Bête Humaine*, 1938) and Julien Duvivier (*Pépé le Moko*, 1936); all three films starred the charismatic actor Jean Gabin. The German Occupation of France in 1940 sent Renoir, Clair, Duvivier and the German-born Max Ophüls into self-exile in Hollywood.

Carné remained in France, as did Jean Cocteau, Jacques Becker, Claude Autant-Lara, Henri Clouzot and Robert Bresson, all making escapist films that avoided propaganda and the censor. However, after Liberation, Cocteau, Clouzot, Becker and Bresson made their best films while Renoir, Clair and Ophüls made welcome returns.

In 1946, the Centre National du Cinéma Français (CNC) was set up. One of its first actions was to protect the French film industry against the influence of foreign films, particularly American, by limiting the

Claude Laydu in the title role of *Robert Bresson's poignant* Diary of a Country Priest *(1951), plays a man isolated and assailed by self-doubt.*

Jacques Tati as Monsieur Hulot *finds it difficult to enter the ultra-modern house of his brother-in-law (Jean-Pierre Zola) in* Mon Oncle (My Uncle, *1958).*

number of foreign films shown. It also helped finance independent productions, many of which reflected the social and political climate of the post-war years, with a return to realism and film noir, of which Jean-Pierre Melville was the master.

Yet, in the 1950s, there was still a dominance of veteran directors. Some, such as Marcel Carné, who had made the internationally acclaimed *Les Enfants du Paradis* (1945) during the Occupation, saw their reputations gradually decline. Many of them succumbed to the lure of commercial cinema, turning out lavish but uninspired color movies, often in lucrative co-productions with Italy.

There was also a literary tradition pursued by Claude Autant-Lara, who adapted Stendhal, Maupassant and Dostoevsky to the screen. The French stars of the 1950s were, to a great extent, the French stars of the 1930s and '40s – Jean Gabin, Fernandel, Edwige Feuillère, Gérard Philipe, Danielle Darrieux and Pierre Fresnay.

The first rumblings of discontent were given influential expression in 1948 by Alexandre Astruc in an article called The Birth of the New Avant-Garde: Le Camera Stylo which fulminated against the assembly-line method of producing films, which the French industry had inherited from Hollywood, and where front-office interference ensured that maverick films were tailored to fit tried-and-tested formulas.

JULIETTE BINOCHE

Believed to be the highest-paid actress in French film history, Juliette Binoche (born 1964) came to international attention in *The Unbearable Lightness of Being* (1988). She starred in Krzysztof Kieslowski's *Three Colors: Blue* (1993), playing a woman painfully trying to come to terms with the death of her husband and daughter. Binoche continues to move easily between prestigious French films like *The Horseman on the Roof* (1995), co-productions like *Caché* (2005) and Hollywood productions such as *The English Patient* (1996) and *Chocolat* (2000).

directors initially collaborated and assisted each other. This helped in the development of a common and distinct use of form, style, and narrative, making their work instantly recognizable. Their influence is still felt throughout the film world.

In the 1980s, three young directors — Jean-Jacques Beinex, Luc Besson, and Leos Carax — gave a new "postmodern" face to French cinema, deriving their aesthetics for their cool thrillers from commercials and pop videos. Women directors have also been among the first rank of French directors. After Agnès Varda and Marguerite Duras had become established, there followed Yannick Bellon, Nelly Kaplin, Coline Serreau, Diane Kurys, and Claire Denis. And excellent new French films and directors continue to emerge. Sophisticated comedies: Agnès Jaoui's *The Taste of Others* (2000) and *Look at Me* (2004); affecting personal dramas: François Ozon's *Five Times Two* (2004) and *Time To Leave* (2005); social satires: Laurent Cantet's *Human Resources* (1999) and *Time Out* (2001); films of urban decay: Mathieu Kasovitz's *La Haine* (1995); sexual explorations: Catherine Breillat's *Romance* (1999) and Gaspard Noé's *Irreversible* (2002); and romantic comedies: *Amélie* (2001) by Jean-Pierre Jeunet.

CAHIÉRS DU CINEMA

In 1951, film critic André Bazin founded *Cahiérs du Cinéma*, the most influential of film magazines. Several young critics on the magazine decided to take practical action in their battle against traditional, literary French film, or "Cinéma du Papa," by making films themselves, taking advantage of the film subsidies bought in by the Gaullist government. The leading figures of this movement, which became known as the "French New Wave," were François Truffaut, Jean-Luc Godard, Alain Resnais, Claude Chabrol, Jacques Rivette, Eric Rohmer, and Louis Malle. The core group of

Romain Duris *is torn between becoming a pianist (here being coached by Linh Dan Pham) and a gangster like his father, in* The Beat That My Heart Skipped *(2005).*

Italy

Italy has had a profound influence on cinema style, particularly within three periods: pre-World War I with mammoth epics, the immediate post-World War II of the neorealists, and from 1960 to the mid-1970s, the "second film renaissance" led by Federico Fellini.

One of the huge sets built for *Giovanni Pastrone's pioneering epic* Cabiria *(1914), which took six months to shoot in studios and on location.*

In 1905, the first Italian studios were built, owned by two of the largest production companies, Cines and Itala, both of which made successful costume dramas. At Cines, Mario Caserini directed *Giovanna d'Arco* (1908), and Ubaldo Maria del Colle made *The Last Days of Pompeii* (1913), while at Itala, Giovanni Pastrone made *The Fall of Troy* (1910) and, most significantly, the monumental *Cabiria* (1914). The adventures of a Sicilian slave girl accompanied by strongman Maciste took over six months to shoot and contained technical innovations such as dolly and crane shots. Its great success in the US inspired D.W. Griffith and Cecil B. DeMille to embark on large-scale productions. These early spectacles would be the prototypes for "peplum" ("Sword and Sandal") epics, popular in the 1950s.

World War I and competition from the US put an end to big production spectacles, and all the studios had closed down by 1922. Ironically, it was Mussolini's Fascist regime that revived Italian cinema. The film school, Centro Sperimentale di Cinematografica, was founded in 1935, and the Cinecitta studios (soon to be known as "Hollywood on the Tiber") was opened by Mussolini.

Although Italian cinema in the 1930s was dominated by "White Telephone" films, superficial tales of the wealthy, and propaganda films that looked back on the glory that was Rome, such as *Scipio l'Africano* (1937), there were some notable exceptions. Mario Camerini's *What Scoundrels Men Are!* (1932), the first Italian film to be shot entirely on location, and Alessandro Blasetti's *Four Steps in the Clouds* (1942), anticipated neorealism by using humble characters and ordinary backgrounds.

THE NEOREALIST MOVEMENT

Luchino Visconti's *Ossessione* (1942, *see page 426*), is regarded by many as the first neorealist film. This label was applied to any film, made after Liberation, which dealt with the working class, and was shot on location, whether with actors or non-actors. One of the key figures of the movement was Cesare Zavattini, who wrote scripts for almost all of Vittorio De Sica's films from 1944–73, including *Bicycle Thieves* (1948, *see page 430*) and *The Garden of the Finzi-Continis* (1970). Although the world praised

Sophia Loren in Vittorio de Sica's Two Women *(1960) for which she gained the rare distiction of winning a Best Actress Oscar in a foreign-language film.*

Italian Neo-Realist films, they only constituted a small percentage of production. After the war, Italian audiences preferred escapist entertainment, such as comedies starring Toto and Alberto Sordi. By 1950, Italian Neo-Realism began to decline, though De Sica's *Umberto D* (1952) and *The Roof* (1956), continued the tradition, and some younger directors, such as Pier Paolo Pasolini in his first film *Accatone* (1961), showed its influence, as did some films from countries as diverse as Brazil and Iran. Roberto Rossellini, whose *Rome, Open City* (1945) and *Paisà* (1946) are among the best examples of neorealism, began to move away from the style with spiritual melodramas starring Ingrid Bergman; and both Visconti and De Sica abandoned many of the principles of neorealism. The 1950s was the time of "peplum" movies and frivolous vehicles for international stars such as Sylvana Mangano, Gina Lollobrigida, and Sophia Loren.

The climactic wedding celebration *from* Amarcord *(1973), Federico Fellini's affectionate, often dreamlike, semi-autobiographical memoir of Rimini, his home town.*

WHAT TO WATCH

1950	The Flowers of St Francis (Roberto Rossellini)
1952	Umberto D. (Vittorio De Sica)
1961	La Notte (Michelangelo Antonioni)
1963	The Leopard (Luchino Visconti)
1964	The Gospel According to St. Matthew (Pier Paolo Pasolini)
1973	Amarcord (Federico Fellini)
1977	1900 (Bernardo Bertolucci)
1994	Il Postino (Michael Radford)
2003	The Best of Youth (Marco Tullio Giordana)

The 1960s heralded a golden age of Italian cinema. The watershed year was 1960, which saw the release of Federico Fellini's *La Dolce Vita* (*see page 449*), Luchino Visconti's *Rocco and His Brothers,* and Michelangelo Antonioni's *L'Avventura* (*see page 451*). Then came a flood of remarkable films from these three masters as well as from Pasolini, Bernardo Bertolucci (*The Conformist,* 1970, *see page 459*), Marco Bellocchio, Ermano Olmi, Ettore Scola, Francesco Rosi, and the Taviani Brothers. At the same time, Sergio Leone and others were making "Spaghetti Westerns," injecting new life into the genre. There was also the Italian horror cinema whose leading practitioners were Mario Bava and Dario Argento.

Following a lull in the 1980s, the industry was given a boost by a wave of films by new directors. At the forefront of these were Giuseppe Tornatore with *Cinema Paradiso* (1989, *see page 478*), Gabriele Salvatores and *Mediterraneo* (1991), and Roberto Benigni with *Life Is Beautiful* (1997). All won Best Foreign Film Oscars. There were many other films of quality that kept interest in Italian cinema alive, notably Gianni Amelio's *Open Doors* (1990) and *The Keys to the House* (2004), *Il Postino* (1994) by Michael Radford, Nani Moretti's *The Son's Room* (2000), and Marco Tullio Giordana's *The Best Of Youth* (2003).

Jasmine Trinca *and Luigi Lo Cascio in the 383-minute* The Best of Youth *(2003).*

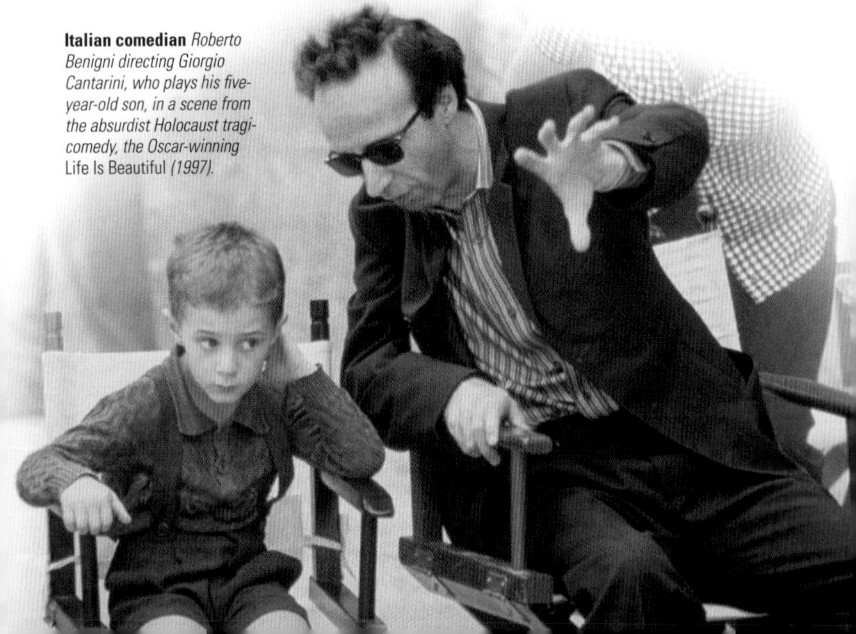

Italian comedian *Roberto Benigni directing Giorgio Cantarini, who plays his five-year-old son, in a scene from the absurdist Holocaust tragi-comedy, the Oscar-winning* Life Is Beautiful *(1997).*

United Kingdom

Despite overwhelming competition from US films, British cinema has managed to survive under the shadow of its perceived rival in Hollywood. British cinema has created films with a distinctly British flavor, and continues to export its talented directors and stars.

One of the first British production companies was founded as early as 1898 by an American, Charles Urban, one of many emigrés to play a part in British cinema. Cecil Hepworth was one of the first English directors to realize the imaginative possibilities of the medium, his most famous film being *Rescued by Rover* (1905), a seven-minute thriller made on a budget of $40 (£8). Two directors of the silent era who stood out were George Pearson, who made 11 films with the cockney comedienne Betty Balfour, and Maurice Elvey, whose career spanned 40 years, during which time he made over 300 features.

Although the 1920s were rather barren, some soon-to-be important figures started making films in that decade: the producer Michael Balcon, who would be the main force behind the films produced at Ealing Studios, Alfred Hitchcock, who already was making a reputation as a master of suspense with films like *The Lodger* (1926), Victor Saville, who later directed three musicals with Britain's top musical-comedy star Jessie Matthews in the 1930s, and Herbert Wilcox who directed many of his wife Anna Neagle's films in the 1930s and 1940s. In an effort to counteract the dominance of American films, a British quota system was introduced in 1927, under which exhibitors were obliged to show a 5 percent quota of British films, increasing by annual stages to 20 percent by 1935. It resulted in an increase in the production of British films, but also had the adverse effect of encouraging cheap and inferior films, known as "quota quickies."

The first British talkie was *Blackmail* (1929), directed by Alfred Hitchcock, who would go on to make some of the best British films of the 1930s. Alexander Korda, a Hungarian emigré,

A sequence from Cecil Hepworth's Rescued by Rover *(1905), which follows the rescue by a collie dog of a baby abducted by gypsies.*

WHAT TO WATCH

1938	The Lady Vanishes (Alfred Hitchcock)
1945	Brief Encounter (David Lean)
1947	Odd Man Out (Carol Reed)
1947	Black Narcissus (Michael Powell and Emeric Pressburger)
1949	Whisky Galore (Alexander MacKendrick)
1963	The Servant (Joseph Losey)
1968	If (Lindsay Anderson)
1983	Local Hero (Bill Forsyth)
1985	Brazil (Terry Gilliam)
2000	Billy Elliot (Stephen Daldry)

formed London Films and built Denham Studios. He directed *The Private Life of Henry VIII* (1933), which broke US box-office records and which gave Charles Laughton the first Best Actor Oscar in a British film.

During World War II, there were excellent morale-boosting features and documentaries. Among the directors at work were Humphrey Jennings, whose documentaries such as *London Can Take It* (1940) showed the effect of the war on ordinary people, Carol Reed (*The Way Ahead*, 1944), David Lean and Noël Coward (*In Which We Serve*, 1942), Laurence Olivier who made *Henry V* (1944) into a patriotic pageant, and Powell and Pressburger (*Colonel Blimp*, 1943).

After the war, entertainment was richly provided by the Ealing Comedies, many of them starring Alec Guinness, who played eight roles in Robert Hamer's *Kind Hearts and Coronets* (1949). However, war films continued to be made like Michael Anderson's *The Dam Busters* and Guy Hamilton's *The Colditz Story* (both 1954). In the late

Vivien Leigh and Laurence Olivier, *the most glamorous couple in British cinema, in their first of three films together,* Fire Over England *(1937).*

1950s, dissatisfaction grew among younger film-makers who felt British films were not addressing contemporary issues. The change came about with Jack Clayton's *Room at the Top* (1958), which treated class and sex with a refreshing frankness. There followed a series of "kitchen sink" films of working-class life, outstanding among them were Karel Reisz's *Saturday Night and Sunday Morning* (1960, *see page 450*), Tony Richardson's *A Taste of Honey* (1961), Lindsay Anderson's *This Sporting Life* (1963), and John Schlesinger's *A Kind of Loving* (1962). These soon gave way to more escapist "Swinging London" films, and the cycle of James Bond movies, beginning with *Dr. No* (1962).

Jamie Bell plays the title role in Stephen Daldry's Billy Elliot *(2000), a boy torn between his love of ballet and the prejudices of his father.*

SWINGING LONDON

London became the most fashionable capital in the world and a number of foreign directors made films there, such as Michelangelo Antonioni (*Blow Up*, 1966), Roman Polanski (*Repulsion*, 1965), François Truffaut (*Fahrenheit 451*, 1966) and Stanley Kubrick, who settled in England. Two other American-born directors, Richard Lester (two Beatles films: *A Hard Day's Night*, 1964, and *Help!*, 1965) and Joseph Losey (*The Servant*, 1963, and *Accident*, 1967), also made an impact.

Quality began to decline in the 1970s, to be revived in the 1980s by Hugh Hudson's *Chariots of Fire* (1981) and Richard Attenborough's *Gandhi* (1982), both of which won Best Picture Oscars, Bill Forsyth's *Gregory's Girl* (1980), Peter Greenaway's *The Draughtsman's Contract* (1982) and Terry Gilliam's *Brazil* (1985). The huge success of Mike Newell's romantic-comedy, *Four Weddings and a Funeral* (1996), Danny Boyle's *Trainspotting* (1996), Peter Cattaneo's social-comedy *The Full Monty* (1997), and Guy Ritchie's gangster movie *Lock, Stock and Two Smoking Barrels* (1998), generated a string of lesser imitations.

Poster *for the film,* Trainspotting *(1996).*

Ben Cross *as Harold Abrahams trains for the 1924 Paris Olympics in* Chariots of Fire *(1981), Hugh Hudson's hymn to physical endeavor.*

Spain

For 36 years, under Franco's repressive regime, it was almost impossible for Spain to create a vibrant film industry and for talented film-makers to express themselves freely. However, after Franco, Spanish films became among the best in the world.

Any chance that Spain would have had in developing its small film industry in the early 20th century was dashed by the military dictatorship of Primo de Rivera from 1923–30. The arrival of sound coincided with the election of a democratic government in 1931 and an attempt was made to build up a film industry. Several studios were built and the first big production and distribution company, CIFESA, was founded in 1934. However, many gifted film-makers, most notably Luis Buñuel, went to Hollywood to work on Spanish-language versions of American films. Before that, Buñuel made *Land Without Bread* (1932), the first of only three films he was to make in his native country. This stark documentary on the poverty of peasants in a barren area of Spain was so effective in revealing this social evil that it was promptly banned by the government.

Elderly but fit, Don Anselmo *(José Isbert) wants to own a motorized wheelchair to go on outings in* The Wheelchair *(1960), Marco Ferreri's black comedy.*

When the Nationalists came to power after the Spanish Civil War, they immediately brought the film industry under government control, imposing strict moral and political guidelines. The fact that José Luis Sáenz de Heredia's fascistic *Raza* (1942), which is based on an autobiographical novel by General Franco, is regarded as one of the outstanding Spanish films of the 1940s, says a lot about Spanish cinema of the period. However, in the next decade, despite restrictions, a distinctive Spanish cinema emerged, led by Juan Antonio Bardem and Luis García Berlanga. They co-directed *This Happy Pair* (1953) about a young couple's financial struggles. Berlanga's *Welcome Mr. Marshall* (1953) is a sardonic look at the effect on a small Spanish town of the possibility of American aid, and, despite cuts,

Luis Buñuel's third *and last film made in Spain,* Tristana *(1970) starred Catherine Deneuve, and was set in the Spain of the 1920s.*

***In The Spirit of the Beehive* (1973),** *Ana (Ana Torent) hands an apple to a fugitive who she relates to the monster in the film* Frankenstein.

El Verdugo (Not on Your Life, 1964) contains social criticism spiked with gallows humor. Bardem's *Death of a Cyclist* (1955), in which the milieu of the rich and the contrasting poor districts of Madrid are well caught in this bitter comment on contemporary Spain, won the Grand Prix at Cannes. Bardem also bravely produced *Viridiana* (1961), which marked Buñuel's return to Spain after 29 years. The film's savage attack on the mentality and rituals of the Catholic church led to it being banned outright in Spain. Buñuel returned to Spain in slightly more liberal times to make *Tristaña* (1970).

The Italian Marco Ferreri directed three films in Spain in the 1960s, the best being *The Wheelchair* (1960) a black comedy in the Buñuel vein. Carlos Saura was the first Spanish director to deal with the Spanish Civil War and its aftermath. Saura's films contain an oblique criticism of Franco's regime and analyse the bourgeoisie, the church, the army, and sexual taboos. *The Hunt* (1966) was the first film of many to feature his future wife, Geraldine Chaplin. Saura's later films such as *Cria Cuervos* (1976) and *Elisa, My Life* (1977) have a shifting chronology and an obsession with childhood.

The remarkable child actress Ana Torrent appeared in the latter two films after making her mark in Victor Erice's *The Spirit of the Beehive* (1973) about an 8-year-old girl who becomes obsessed with Boris Karloff's good-bad monster in James Whale's

WHAT TO WATCH

1953	Welcome Mr. Marshall (Luis García Berlanga)
1955	Death of a Cyclist (Juan Antonio Bardem)
1961	Viridiana (Luis Buñuel)
1973	The Spirit of the Beehive (Victor Erice)
1976	Cria Cuervos (Carlos Saura)
1996	Tierra (Julio Medem)
2002	Talk to Her (Pedro Almodóvar)
2004	The Sea Inside (Alejandro Amenábar)

Frankenstein. This impressive debut feature can be read partly as an allegorical account of a country living under the shadow of an authoritarian regime. Erice has completed only three films in a career spanning nearly three decades, the other two being *El Sur* (1983), about a young girl's relationship with her father, and *Quince Tree of the Sun* (1992), one of the very best films on the creative process. José Luis Borau's *Furtivos* (1975), which exposes the harsh reality of Franco's Spain, opened two months before the death of the Generalissimo. It was the first film to be distributed in Spain without a license from the censors. But the expected burst of creativity in the new era had to wait until Pedro Almodóvar came on the scene in the 1980s with his outrageously campy melodramas. Almodóvar's *All About My Mother* (1999) won a Best Foreign Film Oscar, as did Fernando Trueba's *Belle Epoque* (1992) and Alejandro Amenábar's *The Sea Inside* (2004). Other first-class directors are Bigas Luna (*Jamón, Jamón*, 1992, and *The Tit and The Moon*, 1994), Julio Medem (*Tierra*, 1996, *Sex and Lucia*, 2001), and the Mexican-born Guillermo del Toro (*The Devil's Backbone*, 2001). Trueba (*Two Much*, 1995) and Amenábar (*The Others*, 2001) have made the trip to Hollywood, while stars such as Javier Bardem, Penélope Cruz, and Antonio Banderas have become famous. Veteran directors such as Carlos Saura and Mario Camus, whose *The Holy Innocents* (1984) is one of the best Spanish films of the last few decades, continue to remain active.

Javier Bardem is a paraplegic *who wants to die, but is shown he has reasons to live, in Alejandro Amenábar's* The Sea Inside *(2004).*

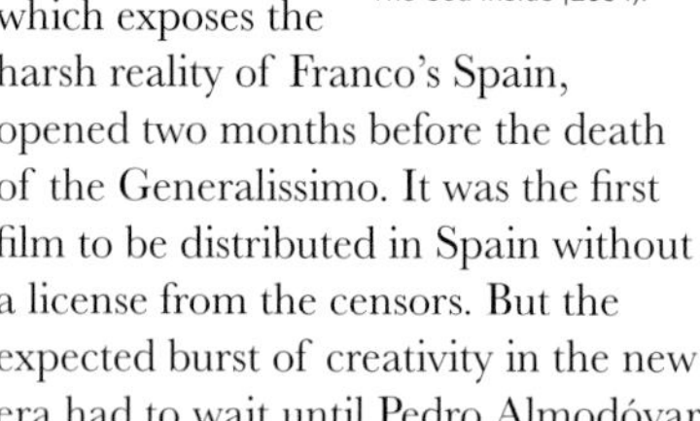

Fernando (Jorge Sanz), *a deserter from the army during the Spanish Civil War, has to decide between three women, daughters of his best friend, in* Belle Epoque *(1992).*

Portugal

Portugal has never had a large indigenous film industry, making only an average of 10 films annually. But the country has attracted foreign film-makers and produced a great film director in Manoel de Oliveira, who has put Portuguese cinema on the map.

João César Monteiro, *as a manager of an ice cream parlour, fantasizes about his young female employees in* God's Comedy *(1995), which he also directed.*

In the late 1920s, Portugal produced a number of remarkable films under the influence of various European avant-garde movements: José Leitão de Barros's *Maria do Mar* (1930), Jorge Brum do Canto's beautiful documentaries and especially Manoel de Oliveira's *Working on the Douro River* (1931), a series of images of the fishermen and assorted workers of the director's home town of Oporto. In 1942, Oliveira made his first feature, the neorealistic *Aniki Bóbó*, following the adventures of street urchins growing up in the slums of Oporto. He was not to make another feature for 21 years, after which he would make one film a year into his 90s, creating a synthesis of literary, theatrical, musical, and visual material. Perhaps his most accessible film is *Abraham's Valley* (1993), a sensual and understated variation on *Madame Bovary*.

Leonor Silveira *plays the sensuous Ema in Manoel de Oliveira's* Abraham Valley *(1993), from the novel by Agustina Bessa-Luís.*

Other Portuguese directors of stature include António de Macedo (*A Sunday Afternoon*, 1966), Fernando Lopes (*On The Edge of the Horizon*, 1993), João Botelho (*A Portuguese Goodbye*, 1986; *Hard Times*, 1988), Paulo Rocha (*River Of Gold*, 1998; *The Heart's Root*, 2000), and Teresa Villaverde (*Três Irmãos*, 1994). Another notable figure was João César Monteiro, who starred in and directed *God's Comedy* (1995), which won the Special Jury Prize in Venice. Monteiro himself appeared in many of his own long, observant, and often bizarre films.

WHAT TO WATCH

1988	Hard Times (João Botelho)
1993	Abraham's Valley (Manoel de Oliveira)
1995	God's Comedy (João César Monteiro)
1998	River of Gold (Paulo Rocha)
2002	O Delfim (Fernando Lopes)

Canada

Despite its close proximity to the US, and the cultural gulf between the French and the English speaking populations, a Canadian film industry and identity took shape, especially in animation, and has developed over the decades, particularly since the 1970s.

The Canadian Pacific railway set up a film unit as early as 1900, but it was only in 1939, when the National Film Board of Canada was established under John Grierson to counteract the dominance of Hollywood, that Canadian films began to make some impression worldwide. The NFB built up a strong animation department, where Norman McLaren was able to experiment with the art form. Michael Snow was prominent in avant-garde circles with his "abstract" films.

After World War II, Francophone Canadians began making films, many of them *cinema-verité* documentaries influenced by French director Jean Rouch. Among the leading figures in Canada were Pierre Perrault and Michel Brault. Gradually, French Canadian directors became the prime force in the Canadian film industry.

Marie-Josée Croze *is among a group of people trying to offer comfort to a man dying of cancer in Denys Arcand's bleak and funny* The Barbarian Invasions *(2003).*

Nick Stahl (left) plays *Dodge and Joshua Close plays Oliver in Jacob Tierney's* Twist *(2003), a gay take on Charles Dickens'* Oliver Twist *set in the hustler district of Toronto.*

Claude Jutra (*My Uncle Antoine*, 1971), Gilles Carle (*The True Nature of Bernadette*, 1972) and especially Denys Arcand, made their marks in the 1970s. The elder Arcand, known as "the Godfather of the New Canadian cinema," has continued to make trenchant satires on Quebec society, which include *Jesus of Montreal* (1989) and *The Barbarian Invasions* (2003). It was easier and more likely that Anglophone directors, like Ted Kotcheff and Norman Jewison, could work in Hollywood. However, two English Canadian directors, David Cronenberg and Atom Egoyan, although they have worked abroad, remain resolutely Canadian in their different idiosyncratic ways.

WHAT TO WATCH

1971	My Uncle Antoine (Claude Jutra)
1972	The True Nature of Bernadette (Gilles Carle)
1974	The Apprenticeship of Duddy Kravitz (Ted Kotcheff)
1986	The Decline of the American Empire (Denys Arcand)
1987	I've heard the Mermaids Singing (Patricia Rozema)
1988	Dead Ringers (David Cronenberg)
1989	Jesus of Montreal (Denys Arcand)
1994	Exotica (Atom Egoyan)
1997	The Sweet Hereafter (Atom Egoyan)
2003	The Barbarian Invasions (Denys Arcand)

Mia Kirshner is a sensitive stripper *and Bruce Greenwood is an obsessive client in Atom Egoyan's erotic thriller,* Exotica *(1994).*

Central America

Mexico has always been the leading producer of feature films in Latin America. Post-revolutionary Cuba, which once produced more than 10 features a year, has gradually turned to digital film-making, the only solution for poor film-producing countries in Central America.

Until Sergei Eisenstein's *Que Viva Mexico* (1931), Mexican audiences were exposed to popular melodramas, crude comedies, as well as Spanish-language versions of Hollywood movies. Eisenstein's visit to Mexico inspired directors like Emilio Fernández and cameraman Gabriel Figuero, and the number of Mexican-made films increased and improved.

Maria Candelaria (1944), which was directed by Fernández and shot by Figuero, and starred prestigious Hollywood actor Dolores del Rio, won the best film at Cannes. The Spanish exile Luis Buñuel made most of his films in Mexico from 1946 to 1960, perhaps the best being *Los Olvidados* (*The Young and the Damned*, 1950) about slum kids in Mexico City. Figuera, who shot most of Buñuel's Mexican films, also worked for John Ford (*The Fugitive*, 1947) and John Huston (*Night of the Iguana*, 1964). During World War II, movie production in Mexico tripled. The fact that Argentina and Spain had fascist governments made the Mexican movie industry the world's largest producer of Spanish-language films in the 1940s. Although the Mexican government was reactionary, it

A poor couple, Pedro Armendáriz *and Maria Elena Marqués, find a very valuable pearl in Emilio Fernandez's* La Perla *(1947), based on the John Steinbeck story.*

In Lucía (1969), Raquel Revuelta *is one of three women called Lucía from different epochs, each demonstrating women's changing role in a macho society.*

encouraged the production of films that would help articulate a true Mexican identity, in contrast to the view often seen in Hollywood movies.

Indigenous cinema suffered through the 1960s and 1970s, until government sponsorship of the industry and the creation of state-supported film helped create *Nuevo Cine Mexicano* (New Mexican Cinema) in the 1990s. Alfonso Arau's *Like Water For Chocolate* (1992) led the way for Alejandro Gonzáles Iñárritu's *Amores Perros* (2001) and Alfonso Cuaron's *Y Tu Mamá También* (2001).

In prerevolutionary Cuba, films were mostly light musicals and comedies. Shortly after Castro took power in 1959, the Cuban Institute of Cinematic Art and Industry (ICAIC) was set up to control the country's production and distribution. One of its founders was Tomás Gutiérrez Alea, who made some of Cuba's finest films. Humberto Solás reinvented the historical epic with *Lucía* (1969) and Santiago Álvarez, imprisoned more than once under Batista's regime, made weekly newsreels. In the 1960s, using newsreel footage, stills, cartoons, and various other devices, Alvarez made a name as a leading exponent of short agit-prop documentaries. The Vietnam war provided him with the material for *Hanoi, Tuesday 13th* (1967) and *LBJ* (1968).

The Cuban Revolution attracted foreign directors such as French film-makers Chris Marker (*¡Cuba Si!*, 1961) and Agnès Varda (*Salut les Cubains*, 1963) to Cuba. One of the most remarkable films made in Cuba was a Soviet-Cuban co-production, *I Am Cuba* (1964), a propagandist piece flamboyantly directed by Mikheil Kalatozishvili. Wim Wenders' colorful Oscar-nominated documentary, *Buena Vista Social Club* (1999) about the aging, home-grown musicians of the title was shot in Havana, Cuba.

Haiti, although it does not have a film industry to speak of, has been the subject of a number of documentaries. It is also the setting for several feature films, from Jacques Tourner's fanciful *I Walked with a Zombie* (1943) to Laurence Cantet's *Vers le Sud* (2005), which is about sexual tourism.

Marco Leonardi as Pedro and Lumi Cavazos *as Tita, lovers forbidden to marry, in Alfonso Arau's landmark film,* Like Water For Chocolate *(1992), all about love, desire, rebellion...and food.*

WHAT TO WATCH

1943	Maria Candelaria (Emilio Fernández)
1947	The Pearl (Emilio Fernández)
1950	Los Olvidados (Luis Buñuel)
1964	I Am Cuba (Mikhail Kalatozov)
1968	Memories of Underdevelopment (Tomás Gutiérrez Alea)
1969	Lucia (Humberto Solás)
1992	Like Water For Chocolate (Alfonso Arau)
2001	Y Tu Mamá También (Alfonso Cuarón)
2001	Amores Perros (Alejandro Gonzáles Iñárritu)

South America

Politics have never been far away from South American cinema. The 1960s saw a new wave of political protest movies and, by the end of the 20th century, this had broadened into mainstream success, particularly for Argentinean and Brazilian directors.

Film-making in South America was extremely parochial and unsophisticated during the silent era when local products were eclipsed by foreign films. Sound helped to advance the Argentinean and Brazilian film industries. During the 1930s, Argentina rivalled Mexico in the Latin-American market with its "gaucho" and tango movies, the most successful being directed by José A. Ferreya and starring the tango singer Libertad Lamarque.

In Brazil, the large number of illiterate people led the studios to quickly equip themselves to make sound films. One of the earliest was *Alô, Alô, Brazil?* (1935), a musical which launched Carmen Miranda's career. The most important figure in early Brazilian cinema was Humberto Mauro, who tried to elevate the poor quality of local production with such serious films as *Ganga Bruta* (1933), probably the first great Brazilian film.

In the 1940s, film production in Brazil was down to its lowest level. At this time, Alberto Cavalcanti returned to his native land after a successful cosmopolitan career (particularly at Ealing Studios in England) to become head of production of the Vera Cruz film company. The first Brazilian film to become internationally known, Lima Barreto's *O Cangaceiro* (*The Bandit*, 1953), a poetic Robin Hood-type adventure, was made under Cavalcanti's aegis.

Cinema languished in Argentina during the Peronist era (1946–55), until Leopoldo Torre Nilsson emerged as the most famous of all Argentinean directors. The son of the prolific director Leopoldo Torres Rios, he began working with his father at the age of 15, and was scriptwriter and assistant on many of his father's films. His own

A self-styled black saint gains a *following in Glauber Rocha's Black God White Devil (1964) set in the sertão, the parched land of north-east Brazil.*

films, most of them adaptations from the novels of his wife, Beatriz Guido, broke away from the staple Argentinean product of superficial comedies and melodramas. *House of the Angel* (1957), *The Fall* (1959), and *The Hand in the Trap* (1961) are studies of a bourgeoisie repressed by a suffocating Catholic Church and its effect on adolescents. The gothic claustrophobia of these films echoes the work of Spanish director Luis Buñuel without the biting irony. *Summerskin* (1961) and *The Terrace* (1963) show teenagers creating a world of their own away from the stifling mansions of their parents. Unfortunately, by the mid-1960s, Torre Nilsson found it increasingly difficult to make the films he wanted because of the political and economic climate of his country.

NEW WAVE AND LIBERATION

Brazilian film finally matured in the 1960s with *Cinema Nôvo*, a New Wave movement of young political film-makers. The main figures were Glauber Rocha (*Black God White Devil*, 1964), Ruy Guerra (*The Guns*, 1963), Carlos Diegues (*Ganga Zumba*, 1963) and Nelson Pereira Dos Santos (*Barren Lives*, 1963). Made under repressive

A hired killer (Mauricio do Valle) *in Glauber Rocha's political allegory,* Antonio Das Mortes *(1969), ends up siding with the peasants against the brutal landowners.*

conditions following the military coup in 1964, *Antonio Das Mortes* (1969) was Rocha's last radical cry from Brazil before almost 10 years in exile.

In Argentina, a group of film-makers set up the independent *Cine Liberacion*. A leading figure was Fernando Solanas. His *The Hour of the Furnaces* (1968), a three part masterpiece co-directed with Octavio Getino, presents a dazzling array of interviews, intertitles, songs, poems, footage from other films, and new material bearing witness to the negative effects of neo-colonialism. This devastating film, made clandestinely, ends with a two-minute

WHAT TO WATCH

1961	The Hand in the Trap (Leopoldo Torre Nilsson, Argentina)
1963	Barren Lives (Nelson Pereira Dos Santos, Brazil)
1969	Antonio Das Mortes (Glauber Rocha, Brazil)
1968	The Hour of the Furnaces (Fernando Solanas, Argentina)
1975/79	The Battle of Chile (Patricio Guzmán, Chile)
1985	The Official Version (Luis Puenzo, Argentina)
1998	Central Station (Walter Salles, Brazil)
2002	City of God (Fernando Meirelles, Brazil)

A former teacher, Dora (Fernanda Montenegro), *waits with Josué (Vinícius de Oliveira) during a quest for the boy's father in* Central Station *(1998).*

close-up of the dead Che Guevara to whom the film is dedicated along with "all who died fighting to liberate Latin America." The film was partly responsible for new and rigorous censorship laws.

In the same year, Miguel Littin's *The Jackal of Nahueltoro* (1969) was released. It was one of the best films to come from Chile in the creative period just before and during the presidency of Salvador Allende. Based on a real case, it tells the story of an illiterate peasant murderer, who is taught to read and to understand social values in prison, only to be executed by firing squad. Patricio Guzmán's *The Battle of Chile* (1975–79), a powerful documentary on the events leading up to the overthrow of the Allende government by the CIA and the forces of General Pinochet, was smuggled out of the country into Cuba, where it took over four years to edit. The events of the bloody military coup in Chile on September 11, 1973, are seen through the eyes of two young boys in Andrés Wood's *Machuca* (2004).

LATIN RESURGENCE

The 1980s saw a renaissance of Argentinean cinema. *Funny Dirty Little War* (1983), Hector Olivera's black comedy of Peronist militants in the early 1970s, was a fast, furious, and

funny political satire. Luis Puenzo's moving *The Official Version* (1985) was about the fate of the children of the Disappeared — when thousands of Argentinain citizens vanished during the "Dirty War" (1976–83). This courageous film won the Best Foreign Film Oscar. The next year, María Luisa Bemberg's *Camila*, an indictment of oppression during the dictatorship of 1847, was read as a criticism of modern Argentina.

Gael García Bernal *(front) as the young Che Guevara with Rodrigo De la Serna as Alberto Granado in* The Motorcycle Diaries *(2004).*

Carlos Sorin made the fascinating *A King and His Movie* (1986), about the difficulties of a director trying to make an historical film in Argentina. He followed this with the gently humorous road movie *Historias Minimas* (2002), and the canine comedy, *Bombon, the Dog* (2004). Among the other first-rate Argentinean films of this later period were Fabián Bielinsky's *Nine Queens* (2000) and Pablo Trapero's cop thriller *El Bonaerense* (2002). Other recent successes included the semi-documentary *Familia Rodante* (2005) and Lucrecia Martel's *The Holy Girl* (2004).

Germán Jaramillo (right) and Anderson Ballesteros *in Barbet Schroeder's* Our Lady of the Assassins *(2000).*

In Brazil, Hector Babenco, who had made *Pixote* (1981), a searing exposure of homeless children, directed the prison drama *Carandiru* (2003). The other well-known Brazilian director, Walter Salles, had hits with *Central Station* (1998) and *The Motorcycle Diaries* (2004), while Fernando Meirelles triumphed with *City of God* (2002). In a lighter vein was Andrucha Waddington's *Me, You, Them (E Tu Eles,* 2000), about a strong woman with three husbands, all living in the same house. Other countries not known for film production had successes, such as Juan Pablo Rebella and Pablo Stoll's *25 Watts* (2001) and *Whisky* (2004), from Uruguay; Barbet Schroeder's *Our Lady of the Assassins* (2000), from Columbia, and Rodrigo Bellott's *Sexual Dependency* (2003), from Bolivia, which uses a split screen throughout.

Juan Villegas plays an out-of-work mechanic *whose life is transformed when he is given a pedigree dog in Carlos Sorin's* Bombon, the Dog *(2004).*

Australia and New Zealand

Since the 1970s, Australian films have increasingly come to the world's attention, while Peter Jackson, director of *The Lord of the Rings*, put New Zealand on the map as a country in which popular big-budget fims could be made.

Mel Gibson continues *in his role as a vengeful futuristic cop in* Mad Max 2 *(1981).*

Australia has been making homegrown movies ever since *The Story of the Kelly Gang* (1906), believed to be the world's first feature-length film at 66 minutes. However, at first there was little incentive to make Australian movies because of the American and British exports, until World War I cut Australia off from European film imports. It began to turn out its own cheap productions, melodramas, and what were called "blackblocks farces," broad comedies of rural families.

NICOLE KIDMAN

Nicole Kidman (born 1967) made her US screen debut in *Dead Calm* (1989). She then co-starred with Tom Cruise in *Days of Thunder* (1990). The two stars were married the same year, becoming one of Hollywood's most celebrated couples. Together they made *Far and Away* (1992) and Stanley Kubrick's last film *Eyes Wide Shut* (1999) before they divorced in 2001. Kidman showed her acting range in *To Die For* (1995), *Moulin Rouge!* (2001), *The Hours* (2002), and *Dogville* (2003).

There was little attempt at art cinema, an exception being Raymond Longford's *The Sentimental Bloke* (1919), an adaptation of a popular series of poems and Australian cinema's first international success. Most other films transplanted Hollywood formulas, particularly the Western, to Australia.

By 1936, only four countries in the world were entirely "wired for sound": the USA, the UK, Australia, and New Zealand. The best-known director from the early sound era was Charles Chauvel (1897–1959), who made two successful war films: *40,000 Horsemen* (1940), based on the exploits of the Australian Light Horsemen in World War I, and *The Rats of Tobruk* (1944). The wartime documentary *Kokoda Front Line!* (1942) brought Australia its first Oscar. But until the 1970s, Australian films meant films made in Australia by foreigners. For Ealing Studios, Harry Watt made Aussie Westerns such as *The Overlanders* (1946) and *Eureka Stockade* (1948), which

Paul Mercurio *and Tara Morice win the Australian Pan Pacific Ballroom Dancing Championship in Baz Luhrmann's hit,* Strictly Ballroom *(1992).*

started a vogue for filming British films in Australia. Among the directors who made films there were Stanley Kramer (*On the Beach*, 1959), Fred Zinnemann (*The Sundowners*, 1960), and Tony Richardson (*Ned Kelly*, 1970).

In 1973, the Australian Film Development Corporation (AFDC) came into being and quickly bore fruit. The directors who emerged were Bruce Beresford (*The Getting of Wisdom*, 1977), Peter Weir (*Picnic at Hanging Rock*, 1975), Fred Schepisi (*The Devil's Playground*, 1976), Phillip Noyce (*Newsfront*, 1978), Gillian Armstrong (*My Brilliant Career*, 1979), and George Miller (*Mad Max*, 1979), all of whom went on to have parallel careers in Hollywood. Of the next generation, Baz Luhrmann is the most celebrated. His first feature, *Strictly Ballroom* (1992), won awards and became one the most profitable films ever in Australia. Perhaps the first well-known New Zealand director was the animator Len Lye, who invented the technique known as "direct film," or painting designs on film stock without using a camera (although he worked mostly overseas). Jane Campion is another high profile New Zealand director. *An Angel at My Table* (1990) launched her international career. While Campion, Roger Donaldson, and Geoff Murphy used their first films to gain entry to Hollywood, Peter Jackson managed to lure Hollywood to Wellington to shoot *The Lord of the Rings* trilogy (2001, 2002, and 2003).

WHAT TO WATCH

1975	Picnic at Hanging Rock (Peter Weir)
1977	The Getting of Wisdom (Bruce Beresford)
1978	Newsfront (Phillip Noyce)
1979	My Brilliant Career (Gillian Armstrong)
1979	Mad Max (George Miller)
1986	Crocodile Dundee (Peter Faiman)
1990	An Angel at My Table (Jane Campion)
1994	Heavenly Creatures (Peter Jackson)

Phillip Noyce's Rabbit-Proof Fence *(2002) follows three young aboriginal girls in 1931 attempting to make a 1,500-mile trek home.*

China, Hong Kong, and Taiwan

Until the 1980s, China, the world's most populous nation, produced relatively few internationally known films, whereas its neighbors, Hong Kong and Taiwan, were renowned for their martial arts movies. Today, China has become a cinematic force to be reckoned with.

China was one of the slowest countries in Asia to develop its own film industry. Many of the first films were derived from staged opera productions or light comedies. Although they attracted large local audiences, they were rarely more widely distributed. One problem was language. The main studios were in Shanghai, and when talking pictures arrived the films were made in Mandarin rather than the local dialect, and few members of the audience could understand them. Small companies in Hong Kong then started making films in Cantonese, which were distributed in China. The first Chinese film to be acclaimed internationally was Chu-sheng Tsai's *The Song of the Fishermen* (1934), about the daily hardships faced by the fishermen on the Yangste river.

When the Japanese invaded Shanghai in 1937, many film-makers left for Hong Kong or Taiwan. Others followed the government into exile in Chungking. The Japanese took over the studios in order to produce propaganda films, and very few Chinese films were made. After the war, left-wing groups produced the best films, such as Cheng Chun Li's *Crows and Sparrows* (1949), about a corrupt landlord and his tenants, who fight for their rights. One of the last fruits of a fertile period in the cinema of pre-Communist China, it was a landmark in its move toward a style not far from Italian neorealism.

Kaige Chen's landmark film, *Yellow Earth (1984), set in 1939, tells of a soldier's attempts to change the superstitious ways of a rural family.*

WHAT TO WATCH

1965	Two Stage Sisters (Jin Xie, China)
1969	A Touch of Zen (King Hu, Taiwan)
1972	Return of the Dragon (Bruce Lee, Hong Kong)
1984	Yellow Earth (Kaige Chen, China)
1989	City of Sadness (Hsiou-hsien Hou, Taiwan)
1990	Ju Dou (Zhang Yimou, Japan/China)
2000	Yi yi... (Edward Yang, Taiwan)

FILMS OF THE CULTURAL REVOLUTION

The first film to be made after the People's Republic of China was established in 1949 was the Soviet-Chinese documentary *Victory of the Chinese People* (1950), directed by Sergei Gerasimov. Jin Xie emerged as the brightest of the Chinese directors in the early 1960s with *Red Detachment of Women* (1960), based on the classic Chinese ballet, and *Two Stage Sisters* (1965). Both films revealed a vivid sense of color, composition, and inventive camera angles. The finely crafted *Two Stage Sisters*, although anti-Capitalist and pro-Feminist,

The young Gong Li *studies the barrels in her middle-aged husband's wine distillery in* Red Sorghum *(1987), Zhang Yimou's story of passion and murder.*

contained many elements of Hollywood melodrama. It was one of the last films made before the Cultural Revolution. Jin Xie was accused of "bourgeois humanism" and imprisoned for some years, and could only return to film-making in the late 1970s.

A mere six films were made during the Cultural Revolution, all of them crudely propagandistic, but visually striking, most of them revised versions of previously filmed Peking operas. *The White-Haired Girl* (1970) and *Red Detachment of Women* (1971) were supervised by Mao Tse-Tung's wife, the former film actress and dancer Chiang Ching.

After the Cultural Revolution, film production picked up, and films made were highly critical of that period. Jin Xie's *Legend of Tianyun Mountain* (1980), presented a bleak picture of a young girl pressured by the Red Guard to leave her intellectual lover for political reasons. Tian-ming Wu's *Life* (1984) was the first in a series of films that depicted a person's struggle to retain some individuality. Wu belonged to The Fifth Generation, those directors who graduated from the Beijing Film Academy in the late 1970s. The most

Three heroes *(Hsu Feng, Shih Chun, and Tien Peng) await their enemies in King Hu's martial arts classic A Touch of Zen (1969).*

Bruce Lee, *in his first starring role, displays his karate skills in* The Big Boss *(1971), the film which literally kick-started kung fu mania.*

famous of these were Chen Kaige and Zhang Yimou, whose first films, respectively *Yellow Earth* (1984) and *Red Sorghum* (1987), made them into the most widely known mainland Chinese directors ever. Chen's *Farewell my Concubine* (1993) was the first Chinese film to win the *Palme d'Or* at Cannes. Notable films from other Fifth Generation directors were Huang Jianxin's *The Black Cannon Incident* (1985), a witty satire on bureaucracy, and Zhuangzhuang Tian's *Horse Thief* (1986), filmed in Tibet.

HONG KONG

In Hong Kong, where most of the population spoke Cantonese, film production reached its peak in 1960 with over 200 films being produced, and the former British colony claimed to be "The Hollywood of the East." The mixture of musicals, detective films, and soft porn gave way in the late 1960s to new-style martial arts films, which brought huge profits from abroad, especially to the Shaw Brothers' film company.

TAIWAN

The first big sword-play hit was the Taiwanese production of *Dragon Gate Inn* (1966). The director King Hu, who worked in Taiwan, went on to make *A Touch of Zen* (1969). This was an exciting three-hour epic, set during the Ming dynasty, and one of the finest examples of the genre. The first *kung fu* (simply meaning "technique" or "skill") film to be given general release in the west was *Five Fingers of Death* (1972), directed by Chang-hwa Jeong. Cheh Chang reinvented the swordplay film with a trilogy: *One-Armed Swordsman* (1967), *Return of the One-Armed Swordsman* (1969), and *The New One-Armed Swordsman* (1971)—all three were quintessential tales of

heroic bloodshed. Meanwhile, Golden Harvest, a production company started by Raymond Chow, broke the Shaw Brothers monopoly with Bruce Lee "chop-socky" hits, starting with *The Big Boss* (1971). After Lee's premature death at the age of 32, the prolific director Chang Cheh continued the tradition, taking fight choreography to new heights. Chang's films influenced other directors, such as John Woo and Liu Chiau Liang, and made famous Hong Kong stars, such as Lung Ti.

Although Taiwan was associated with kung-fu movies, several directors made political and social dramas in a more cryptic style, the best known being Hsiao-Hsien Hou *(see page 309)*, whose work was close to the Japanese

Yi yi: A One and a Two... *(2000) by Edward Yang, a leading auteur of the New Cinema in Taiwan, is an epic story of a family seen from different perspectives.*

Chen Chang and Lisa Yang in Edward Yang's *A Brighter Summer Day (1991), young lovers living in the shadow of gang warfare.*

master Yasujiro Ozu. The most internationally celebrated Taiwanese director of the 1990s and beyond is Ang Lee *(see page 322)*, whose work ranges from an updated version of the Chinese *wu xia* (samurai-style) tradition of storytelling involving myth, swords and magic with *Crouching Tiger, Hidden Dragon* (2000) to Hollywood hits such as *Brokeback Mountain* (2005).

Bamboo canes *are chopped down with brilliance to form palisade-cages and improvized spears, one of the many dazzling, gravity-defying stunts in Zhang Yimou's* House of the Flying Daggers *(2004).*

Japan

Although Japan had been making films of high quality since the beginning of cinema, Japanese films remained virtually unknown in the west for over half a century. Since the 1950s, however, Japanese cinema has become very successful, both critically and commercially.

For most of its history, Japanese cinema was divided into two categories, *gendai-geki*—films in a contemporary setting—and *jidai-geki*—period films usually set in the Togukawa era (1616–1868), before the opening of Japan to western influence. A sub-genre was *shomin-geki* ("home dramas"), films about families, of which directors Yasujiro Ozu and Youjiro Shimazu were the most consistent practitioners.

The Seven Samurai *(1954) remade in Hollywood as* The Magnificent Seven *(1960), is still seen by many as a masterpiece for its characterization and skillful action scenes directed by Akira Kurosawa.*

At first, two theatrical traditions were carried over to the cinema: the *onnagata* (males in female roles), and the *benshi* (an actor who stood at the side of the screen and narrated the film). However, as films became more realistic, the *onnagata* looked out of place and, with the coming of sound, the *benshi* became redundant.

After an earthquake in 1923, which devastated Tokyo and destroyed its film studios, Japan had to rely upon foreign imports for some years. Slowly the industry recovered, though foreign audiences were still largely unaware of

A Page of Madness (1926, Teinosuke Kingasa), *one of the more radical and shocking early Japanese films, in which the main character works in a mental asylum where his wife is an inmate.*

Members of an audience *watch the performance of an onnagata (female impersonator) in Kon Ichikawa's* An Actor's Revenge *(1963), a study of opposites—love/hate, illusion/reality, masculinity/femininity.*

Japanese films. An exception was Teinosuke Kinugasa's *Crossways* (1928). Fragmentary close-ups, claustrophobic atmosphere of angst, and dark stylized décor are reminiscent of German expressionism, although the director had apparently not seen any German films up to that time.

The first Japanese talkie was Heinosuke Gosho's *The Neighbor's Wife and Mine* (1931), a delightful slice-of-life comedy. But as Japan became increasingly militaristic, more and more right-wing propaganda films were being made. Humanists such as Kenji Mizoguchi avoided government propaganda and, in his mature stage, delivered twin masterpieces, *Osaka Elegy* and *Sisters of the Gion* (both 1936), stories of exploited women in contemporary Japan.

WARTIME JAPAN

All Japanese cinema came under state control in 1939 and film production slowed down. However, some of the great directors continued to make films in their own way. Ozu made *There Was A Father* (1942), one of his most affecting films. The most popular war film was Kosaburo Yoshimura's *The Story of Tank Commander Nishizumi* (1940), which was not afraid to show the weakness and hardships that were associated with war.

WHAT TO WATCH

1952	Life of O'Haru (Kenji Mizoguchi)
1954	The Seven Samurai (Akira Kurosawa)
1958	Equinox Flower (Yasujiro Ozu)
1963	An Actor's Revenge (Kon Ichikawa)
1969	Boy (Nagisa Oshima)
1979	Vengeance Is Mine (Shohei Imamura)
1985	Tampopo (Juzo Itami)
1997	Hana-Bi (Takeshi Kitano)
1998	After Life (Hirokazu Koreeda)
2001	Spirited Away (Hayao Miyazaki)

AMERICAN OCCUPATION

Under American occupation, there were a number of *jidai-geki* films made to avoid censorship of contemporary issues. Despite the flood of American films, the problems of industrial disputes with Toho, the largest studio and relatively new directors such as Akira Kurosawa and Keisuke Kinoshita—who directed *Carmen Comes Home* (1951), the first Japanese color film—became established. The breakthrough came when Kurosawa's *Rashomon* (1950, *see page 435*) won the Grand Prix at Venice in 1950, thus opening up the floodgate of Japanese films to the west. Among the most celebrated films of that time were: *The Seven Samurai* (Akira Kurosawa, 1954), *Tokyo Story* (Yasujiro Ozu, 1953) and *Ugetsu Monogatari* (Kenji Mizoguchi, 1953). Others were Kon Ichikawa's anti-war films, *The Burmese Harp* (1956) and *Fires on the Plain* (1959), and Masaki Kobayashi's *The Human Condition* (1959–61), an impressive and harrowing socially conscious trilogy.

At the same time Ishirô Honda created *Godzilla* (1954), which led to a whole stream of movies featuring

Koji Yakusho as a gangster *who invades the ramen (noodle) bar owned by Nobuko Miyamoto in Juzo Itami's gastronomic comedy,* Tampopo *(1985).*

threatening prehistoric monsters and mutants formed as a result of radio-activity caused by nuclear bombs. The dubbing in the west was atrocious, but the special effects were spectacular.

The 1960s was an even richer creative time for Japanese cinema, beginning with Kaneto Shindo's *The Island* (1960), a tale—told beautifully on the wide screen without dialogue—about the hard life of a peasant family. Masaki Kobayashi's *Hara-Kiri* (1962) remained true to the traditions of the period film, while managing to criticize the rigid codes of honor that are basic to their subject. Kobayashi's *Kwaidan* (1964), one of the most expensive Japanese films up to that date, tells four tales of the supernatural using haunting imagery derived from Japanese art.

Among the new wave of Japanese directors, many of whom have explored eroticism and violence, were Shohei Imamura (*The Insect Woman*, 1963; *The Pornographer*, 1966); Hiroshi Teshigahara (*Woman of the Dunes*, 1964), Yoshishige Yoshida (*Eros plus*

Eihi Shiiha as a woman *who seeks to wreak vengeance on all men, especially on one particular middle-aged widower, in* Audition *(1999), Takashi Miike's psychological horror film.*

Massacre, 1969) and Nagisa Oshima (*Death by Hanging*, 1968). It was Oshima who took the sexual revolution still further with his *Ai No Corrida* (1976, *see page 462*).

1980 AND BEYOND

Old hands like Kurosawa, who made his two great spectacles *Kagemusha* (1980) and *Ran* (1985), and Imamura, whose *The Ballad of Narayama* (1983) won the Best Film at Cannes, continued to have success. Of the younger generation, Juzo Itami was the bright new meteor of Japanese cinema in the 1980s with his comic satires of Japanese culture, *Tampopo* (1985), *A Taxing Woman* (1987), and *A Taxing Woman Returns* (1988), all starring his wife Nobuko Miyamoto.

At the turn of the 21st century, Japanese films continued to win prizes at festivals and to attact large audiences. A dominant figure is Takeshi Kitano, whose films vary from violent *yakuza* (gangster) movies (*Hana-Bi*, 1997; *Brother*, 2000), to period films (*Zatoichi*, 2003) and sentimental comedies (*Kikujiro*, 1999). Credited as "Beat" Takeshi, he has also acted in many films, including his own. In Kinji Fukasaku's *Battle Royale* (2000), where a school forces its pupils to slaughter one another on an island, Takeshi plays the sadistic headmaster.

Japan has also produced some of the most effective horror films, many of which have been adapted by Hollywood. Hideo Nakata's *Ring* (1998), Japan's most successful horror film to date, led to a sequel, a prequel, and an American remake in 2002. Another Hollywood remake was *The Grudge* (2004), made by the same director, Takashi Shimizu, as the original chiller, *Ju-On* (2000). Also frightening, but more subtle, are the supernatural crime movies directed by Kiyoshi Kurosawa (no relation to Akira), such as *Pulse* (2001).

Other violent films included Takashi Miike's *Audition* (1999). In a different vein are Hirokazu Koreeda's films, which explore memory and loss, such as *Nobody Knows* (2004), and Hayao Miyazaki's charming *Spirited Away* (2001), which won the Oscar for the Best Animated Feature, a reflection of the rise in the huge popularity of Japanese anime films, first awoken in the west by *Akira*.

Akira *(Katsuhiro Otomo, 1988) features breathtaking animation; it shows a world in which biker gangs are at war, awaiting the arrival of a legend called Akira.*

Korea

Although Korean films now loom large in the world cinema landscape with international hits such as Park Chan-wook's *Sympathy for Lady Vengeance* (2005), they have only established a distinctive character and been truly visible since the mid-1990s.

The fact that Korea was under Japanese rule from 1903 to 1945 did not help the establishment of a film industry, although a number of silent Korean films were made. In 1937, when Japan invaded China, the Korean film industry was converted into a propaganda machine. However, after World War II, despite Korea regaining its independence, it was soon divided into the Communist North Korea and the Capitalist South.

Two of the most important Korean movies appeared in 1960: Kim Ki-young's *The Housemaid*, and Yu Hyun-mok's *Aimless Bullet*, both dark domestic melodramas dealing with family life and survival in the years following the end of the Korean War (1950–53).

In 1962, the Motion Picture Law mandated that film companies must produce at least 15 films per year. This resulted in an increase in films being made although few were seen outside Korea. The leading director of the period was Shin Sang-Ok, whose *My Mother and Her Guest* (1961), told through the eyes of a young girl who wants her widowed mother to marry again, is considered his masterpiece. Shin and his wife were kidnapped from their

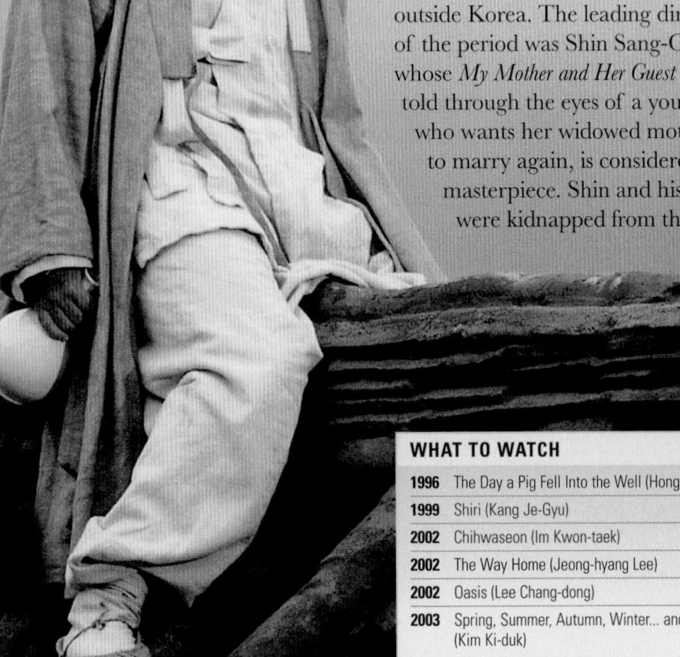

Chihwaseon *(2002) traces the life of an artist (Choi Min-Sik) known for his addiction to alcohol and women.*

WHAT TO WATCH

1996	The Day a Pig Fell Into the Well (Hong Sang-soo)
1999	Shiri (Kang Je-Gyu)
2002	Chihwaseon (Im Kwon-taek)
2002	The Way Home (Jeong-hyang Lee)
2002	Oasis (Lee Chang-dong)
2003	Spring, Summer, Autumn, Winter... and Spring (Kim Ki-duk)

native South Korea in the late 1970s and held for several years in North Korea to make movies for Kim Jong Il, son of the North Korean leader. They were granted asylum in the United States in 1986.

After a fallow period, there were some signs of revival in the 1980s when the first films of Im Kwon-taek began to appear at festivals. Im had made dozens of films since 1962. His breakthrough came with *Mandala* (1981), a film about Buddhist monks. Another film of Im's, *Adada* (1987), reflects the marginalized position of women in traditional Korean society. *Seopyonje* (1993), the story of a family of roaming *pansori* (a sort of Korean folk opera) singers' struggles in postwar Korea, became an unexpectedly huge hit in Korea. In 2002, Im won the Best Director award at Cannes for his magnificent *Chihwaseon*, about the life of a 19th-century Korean painter. In the same year, Lee Chang-dong's astonishing *Oasis* (2002), about a love affair between a mentally retarded boy and a girl with cerebral palsy, won a number of awards.

Oldboy *(2003), part of the "Vengeance" trilogy by Chan-wook Park, has taken Korean film to a new worldwide audience.*

Previously, Hong Sang-soo made his debut with the award-winning *The Day a Pig Fell Into the Well* (1996), which weaves the experience of four characters into a single story. The year 1996 also saw the debut of controversial filmmaker Kim Ki-duk, whose extremely violent films such as *The Isle* (2000) and *Address Unknown* (2001) were counterbalanced by the serene *Spring, Summer, Autumn, Winter... and Spring* (2003). Other huge successes for Korean cinema in recent years have been Kang Je-Gyu's espionage thriller *Shiri* (1999), Chan-wook Park's so-called "Vengeance" trilogy—*Sympathy for Mr. Vengeance* (2002), *Oldboy* (2003) and *Sympathy for Lady Vengeance* (2005). Two films by women directors, Jeong-hyang Lee's touching *The Way Home* (2002) and Jae-eun Jeong's bittersweet comedy *Take Care of My Cat* (2001), have also been at the forefront of Korean film.

Spring, Summer, Autumn, Winter... and Spring, 2003, *is a beautifully told multilayered fable about the Buddhist beliefs of life and reincarnation.*

India

India is the world's largest manufacturer of films—in the 1990s the country produced over 800 films annually. It is the only country that has a bigger audience for indigenous films than imported ones. It also boasts one of the biggest international audiences.

Indian films mean different things to different people. For the majority they mean Bollywood, and for others they mean exquisite art movies as exemplified by the work of Satyajit Ray. The films of "Bollywood," a conflation of Bombay, the old name for Mumbai, and Hollywood, are generally rigidly formulaic Hindi-language musicals, comedies, or melodramas. In the 1990s, Bollywood musicals, the staple of the Indian film industry, became more and more popular among non-Indians in the west, mainly for their kitsch qualities. Although Bollywood musicals came into being with the coming of sound, some of the plots were already apparent in the popular silent films.

The most prominent of the early, silent director-producers was Dadasaheb Phalke, who introduced the mythological film, peopled by gods and goddesses of the Hindu pantheon. All the roles were played by men, as women were forbidden to act at the time. But Phalke was ruined by the introduction of sound which, in a country with 18 major languages and more than 800 different dialects, inevitably resulted in the fragmentation of the industry and its dispersal into different language markets.

Bombay, the original center of the industry, continued to dominate by concentrating on films in Hindi, the most widely spoken Indian language. In the south, Madras developed its own massive industry with films in Tamil. The Hindi film in the north and the Tamil in the south constituted the mainstream of Indian cinema, both dominated by a Hollywood-style star system. Among minority language cinema the only one of importance is

Sunil Dutt as the rebellious son in Mother India *(1957), Mehboob Khan's classic tragic epic of rural life, known as India's* Gone With The Wind.

Jean Renoir's The River (1951) *opens and closes with shots of the Ganges, which runs through the film as a symbol of life, death, and renewal.*

Bengali, thanks mainly to Satyajit Ray's influence in the 1950s. The first talkie was *Alam Ara* (1931), directed by Ardeshir Irani with dialogue in both Urdu and Hindi. It contained several song and dance numbers and its huge financial success led to the formula of films being built around songs.

At the same time, Hindi cinema had also almost imperceptibly developed a tradition of socially aware films. Founded in 1934, the Bombay Talkies Studio produced a number of such pictures. However, it was only in the 1950s that Indian films began to be shown around the world. Among the first were *Aan* (1952), the first Indian feature in Technicolor, and *Mother India* (1957), both directed by Mehboob Khan and the latter starring Nargis, the supreme Bollywood star, who was nominated for a Best Foreign Film Oscar. Bimal Roy's *Two Acres of Land* (1953), about the bitter issue of caste, won the *Prix International* at the Cannes Film Festival.

Satyajit Ray *(behind the camera), the dominant figure of Bengali cinema, and Subrata Mitra, the brilliant cinematographer on ten of Ray's films.*

INFLUENCE ON WORLD CINEMA

When Jean Renoir came to Calcutta in 1950 to shoot *The River* (1951), he was assisted by the 29-year-old Satyajit Ray. Renoir encouraged Ray to fulfill his dream of making a film based on the popular autobiographical novel by Bhibuti Bashan Bannerjee, dealing with Bengali village life, called *Pather Panchali*. With the majority of money coming from the West Bengal government, Ray was able to make *Pather Panchali* (1955), the first in his "Apu Trilogy" five years later. Aside from Renoir's importance to Ray, the influence of *The River* cannot be overestimated. It was one of the first films from the west to bring back images of

WHAT TO WATCH

1955	Devdas (Bimal Roy)
1955	Pather Panchali (Satyajit Ray)
1957	Mother India (Mehboob Khan)
1964	Charulata (Satyajit Ray)
1969	Bhuvan Shome (Mrinal Sen)
1975	Sholay (Ramesh Sippy)
1988	Salaam Bombay! (Mira Nair)
1994	Bandit Queen (Shekhar Kapur)
2002	The Clay Bird (Tareque Masud)

India, other than as an exotic background to Kipling-style colonial adventures. It was only after *The River* that Fritz Lang visited India in 1956 to make *Taj-Mahal*, although the project was later abandoned. Roberto Rossellini also went there to direct *India* (1959). *The River* was a further inspiration to James Ivory who later made several films in India including *Shakespeare-Wallah* (1965) and *Heat and Dust* (1983). Another European director to be influenced was Louis Malle (*Phantom India*, 1969).

The success of Satyajit Ray's films proved that it was possible to work outside the commercial system. Those that benefited from this newly independent cinema, situated mainly in Calcutta, were Mrinal Sen and Ritwik Ghatak, both Marxists, who developed a new kind of social cinema in opposition to Ray's European humanism.

Sen, who has been called the "Bengali Godard," attacked the poverty and exploitation in Indian society in his films. "I wanted to make

Chanda Sharma as Sweet Sixteen, *a beautiful Nepalese virgin who has been sold into prostitution in Mira Nair's realistic drama* Salaam Bombay! *(1988)*

Seema Biswas as Phoolan Devi *in Shekhar Kapur's exciting* Bandit Queen *(1994), based on the real-life experiences of a modern Indian folk hero.*

disturbing and annoying films, not artistic ones," he claimed. Sen's *The Royal Hunt* (1976) and *And Quiet Flows the Dawn* (1979) are powerful unsentimentalized political parables which try to come to terms with the complexities of the country. Ghatak's best known films, *The Cloud-capped Star* (1960), *Komal Ghandhar* (1961), and *Subarnarekha* (1962), make up a trilogy based in Calcutta which address the subject of refugees.

In contrast, in Bombay, Hrishikesh Mukherjee's *Anand* (1970) laid the foundation of a genuine middle-class cinema. It tells of a terminally ill man who, determined to remain cheerful, brings about positive changes in the lives of those people around him. Meanwhile, Bollywood movies were improving in quality, both technically and artistically. Ramesh Sippy's *Sholay* (1975), starring one of the great Bollywood heroes, Amitabh Bachchan, is one of the most successful Hindi films of the 1970s.

In the 1980s, with Satyajit Ray's films becoming less frequent and of lower quality, Indian "art cinema" was not as visible. However, in 1988, Mira Nair's *Salaam Bombay!*, became a huge international success. Made in record time and for little money, it was an impressively assembled mosaic of Bombay's street life, its harsh cruelties and fleeting pleasures. Other critically acclaimed Indian films in recent years have been Shekhar Kapur's *Bandit Queen* (1994), an examination of caste discrimination, human suffering, and the role of women in India's changing culture; Deepa Mehta's *Fire* (1996), which references Indian mysticism and the epic poetry of the *Ramayana* as well as late-20th-century feminism, and Tareque Masud's *The Clay Bird* (2002), a touching picture of childhood in the 1950s and the first Bangladeshi film to win an award at Cannes.

India is the world's largest producer of feature films, most of them musicals, the soundtracks of which are released before the movie is released. Since the 1980s, the sale of music rights has generated income for the film industry equivalent to the distribution revenues.

AMITABH BACHCHAN

Amitabh Bachchan (born 1942) is India's greatest superstar. With his deep baritone voice and brooding personality, Bachchan was the archetypal "Angry Young Man" of the 1970s, replacing the blander heroes of the 1960s. His breakthrough came with *Zanjeer* (*The Chain*, 1973), in which he starred opposite his future wife Jaya Bhaduri. He continued to express his anger in such major hits as *Deewar* (1975) and *Don* (1978). He was as active and popular as ever when past middle age in *Khakee* (2004) and *Black* (2005).

A-Z OF DIRECTORS

The definition of a director's function has been accepted only comparatively recently. For many years, he or she was considered just an anonymous member of a team, generally subordinate to the producer. This has all changed. The director is preeminent in the perception of a film. Nowadays, most film lovers have an idea of the role of the director and know the names of the directors of many of the films they see.

In the early days, the general public was unaware of a director's name. People went to see movies on the strength of the stars and the subject. Gradually, certain directors became known because they made themselves visible. For instance, Cecil B. DeMille often introduced his films in trailers and Alfred Hitchcock made brief appearances in his films. This made them recognizable, and also encouraged the public to associate them with a certain genre, in this case, the epic and the thriller respectively. It was the influential French magazine *Cahiers du Cinéma*, which formulated the so-called *auteur* theory in the mid-1950s. Its writers argued that the film, though a collective medium, always had the signature of the director on it, and that directors should be considered in the light of thematic consistency. This formulation shed light on those directors, especially in the Hollywood studio system, who had never been considered within the "cinema as art" school of criticism, such as Vincente Minnelli, Howard Hawks, Nicholas Ray, and Otto Preminger. The theory was taken up by critics all over the world and the director was finally given his due as the principal creator of the film, if not the "onlie begetter."

Expressing the isolation *of a great director, John Ford seeks inspiration from the sea for the next shot of* Donovan's Reef *(1963).*

With the growth of film studies faculties in universities and the increased sophistication of audiences, many keen movie-goers are familiar with the names of such great directors of the past as Sergei Eisenstein, Luis Buñuel, Ingmar Bergman, Federico Fellini, and Akira Kurosawa. Nowadays, it is possible to hear non-specialist audiences referring to the latest Steven Spielberg movie rather than the latest Tom Hanks.

At the moment, there are directors emerging from obscurity, renowned ones adding to their filmographies, and new talent being discovered. This A–Z of Directors has tried to be as up-to-date as possible. It includes the young, the old, the quick, and the dead, international independent geniuses, Hollywood greats, cult figures, Developing World film-makers, underground, and experimental film-makers. The main criterion has been to include directors whose work has been widely shown internationally, either in commercial cinemas or art houses. The profiles are an attempt to give readers enough objective information to be able to assess the type, quality, content, and style of each director's work and then to discover or rediscover them for themselves.

Chantal **Akerman**

1950– BELGIAN 1968–

20 Avant-garde, Documentary

The essence of Chantal Akerman's minimalist style is a static camera, medium long shots, and monologues, as well as silences that get close to the heart of her alienated characters.

The most characteristic film by Akerman is *Jeanne Dielman, 23 Quai du Commerce, 1080 Bruxelles* (1975), which reveals the minutiae of three days (225 minutes of film time) in the life of a Belgian housewife and part-time prostitute (Delphine Seyrig). In *The Meetings of Anna* (*Les Rendezvous d'Anna*, 1978), the heroine is a Belgian film director in her twenties (like Akerman at the time), who travels to several European cities to publicize her latest film. *All Night Long* (*Toute une Nuit*, 1982) is a series of amorous fragments, its dislocated characters existing in impersonal hotel rooms and railway stations. More conventional but less effective was *The Captive* (*La Captive*, 2000), adapted from a novel by Marcel Proust.

Sylvie Testud *plays Ariane in* The Captive, *a film that is woven around the obsessive love a young man feels for a woman.*

WHAT TO WATCH

1975	Jeanne Dielman
1977	News From Home
1978	The Meetings of Anna
1982	All Through the Night
2000	The Captive

Robert **Aldrich**

1918–1983 AMERICAN 1953–1981

29 Melodrama, War, Western

The forceful, often bludgeoning style of Robert Aldrich — overhead shots, vast close-ups, and shock cuts — was most effective in genres like Westerns and war films.

A maverick in Hollywood terms, Robert Aldrich was his own producer in 1955 with *Kiss Me Deadly*, a classic multi-level film noir that uses a Mickey Spillane story to form a gripping allegory of America in the 1950s. Its portrayal of an immoral hero, use of real locations, and low-key photography influenced the French New Wave. Aldrich's characters tend towards the hysterical and his direction often matches them, such as the histrionics of film people in *The Big Knife* (1955), an adaptation of Clifford Odets' play about Hollywood; the Gothic extravagances of *What Ever Happened to Baby Jane?* (1962); and lesbian rivalries in *The Killing of Sister George* (1968). *Attack!* (1956), about an infantry company led by a cowardly commander, and *The Dirty Dozen* (1967), an action drama in which 12 American military prisoners are sent on a suicide mission, are bitter war films. Equally powerful are his pro-Native American films, such as *Apache* (1954), which follows a warrior fighting against white oppression, and the stark *Ulzana's Raid* (1972), about a band of Apaches on a rampage.

Joan Crawford and Bette Davis *play elderly sisters, "Baby Jane" and Blanche, in* Whatever Happened to Baby Jane?, *a black comedy and psychological thriller.*

WHAT TO WATCH

1954	Apache
1955	Kiss Me Deadly
1956	Attack!
1962	What Ever Happened to Baby Jane?
1967	The Dirty Dozen

Woody **Allen**

1935– AMERICAN 1969–

36 Comedy, Drama

Films directed by the prolific Woody Allen have amused adult audiences over many years. In the best of them, however, there is pain lurking beneath the comic surface.

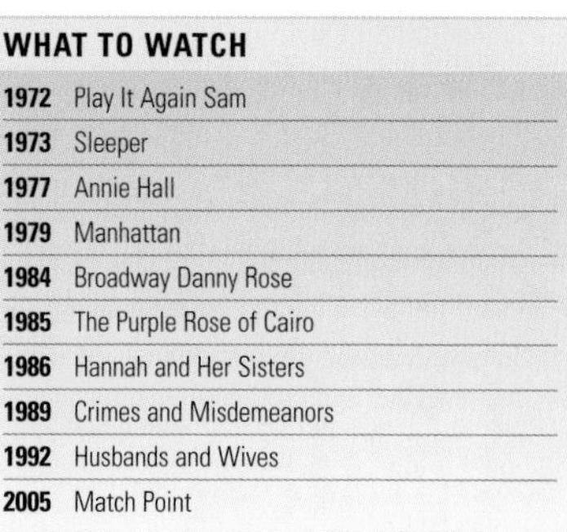

WHAT TO WATCH

1972	Play It Again Sam
1973	Sleeper
1977	Annie Hall
1979	Manhattan
1984	Broadway Danny Rose
1985	The Purple Rose of Cairo
1986	Hannah and Her Sisters
1989	Crimes and Misdemeanors
1992	Husbands and Wives
2005	Match Point

Before directing films, Woody Allen was a stand-up comic whose subject matter was his own obsessions — his relationships with women and his analyst, and death — which he elaborated on in his films. His first five movies were constructed as closely linked revue sketches, although in *Love and Death* (1976), a witty satire of 19th-century Russian literature, he paid more attention to form. *Annie Hall* (1977) was a breakthrough film, successfully showing a complex relationship (based on his own with Diane Keaton), while *Manhattan* (1979) is a stunning black-and-white tribute to New York, the city he loves. There is an autobiographical element in many of his films, most intensely in *Husbands and Wives* (1992), during the filming of which he broke up with Mia Farrow, his real-life partner. Among his wittiest comedies are *Take the Money and Run* (1969), *Bananas* (1971), *Play It Again Sam* (1972), *Sleeper* (1973), *Broadway Danny Rose* (1984), and *The Purple Rose of Cairo* (1985). Allen's admiration for Ingmar Bergman became clear in *Interiors* (1978), his first "serious" movie. Other homages to Bergman include *A Midsummer Night's Sex Comedy* (1982) and *Deconstructing Harry* (1997). He also used Bergman's favorite cameraman Sven Nykvist on *Crimes and Misdemeanors* (1989) and cast actor Max von Sydow in *Hannah and Her Sisters* (1986). *Sweet and Lowdown* (1999) and *Stardust Memories* (1980) were inspired by Federico Fellini. *Match Point* (2005) was a box-office hit and for Allen "arguably maybe the best film I've made." Although in the 1990s, his work lost some of its resonance, Allen has managed to speak to a small but loyal audience of intelligent fans.

Film poster, *1986*

Scarlett Johansson *plays the seductive Nola Rice, here with director Woody Allen on the set of* Match Point *(2005), the first film Allen made in the UK.*

Cecilia Roth *as the stage actress in* All About My Mother *(a reference to* All About Eve*), seen against a poster advertising* A Streetcar Named Desire.

Pedro **Almodóvar**

1949– | SPANISH | 1974–

16 | Underground, Melodrama

Pedro Almodóvar's outrageous and provocative films have made him the most internationally acclaimed Spanish filmmaker since the death of Franco in 1975.

"My films represent the new mentality... in Spain after Franco died...because now it is possible to make a film like *Law of Desire*." Despite its homoerotic sex scenes, *Law of Desire* (*La Ley del Deseo*, 1987) was heralded as a model for Spain's future cinema. Almodóvar's forté is in incorporating elements of underground and gay culture into mainstream forms with wide crossover appeal, thus redefining perceptions of Spanish cinema and Spain. His first feature film, *Pepi, Luci, Bom and Lots of Other Girls* (*Pepi, Luci, Bom y Otras Chicas del Montón* 1980), was made in 16mm and blown-up to 35mm for public release. Although his breakthrough export success was *Women on the Verge of a Nervous Breakdown* (*Mujeres al Borde de un Ataque de Nervios*, 1988), he hit his stride in Spain with *What Have I Done to Deserve This?* (*Qué he Hecho yo Para Merecer Esto*, 1984). In *Matador* (1986), he made the link between violence and eroticism, while in *All About My Mother* (*Todo Sobre mi Madre* 1999), *Talk to Her* (*Hable con Ella*, 2002), and *Bad Education* (*La Mala Educación*, 2004) he shows a warmth towards his characters.

WHAT TO WATCH

1984	What Have I Done to Deserve This?
1987	Law of Desire
1986	Matador
1988	Women on the Verge of a Nervous Breakdown
1999	All About My Mother
2002	Talk to Her
2004	Bad Education

Victoria Abril, *one of Pedro Almodóvar's favorite leading actresses, on the set of* What Have I Done to Deserve This? *with the director.*

Robert **Altman**

1925– AMERICAN 1955–

35 Satirical comedies, Drama

With an individualism that has gained him the reputation of being a difficult man for producers to work with, Altman tries something different with each film. An unusual director, he has refused to make formulaic pictures.

After four forgettable movies, Robert Altman was offered *M*A*S*H* (1970) when 14 other directors turned it down. Its iconoclasm struck a chord in a U.S. disenchanted with the Vietnam War. He later subverted traditional Hollywood genres with revisionist Westerns: *McCabe and Mrs Miller* (1971), in which the hero (Warren Beatty) is a pimp, while *Buffalo Bill and the Indians* (1976) reveals William S. Cody (Paul Newman) as a phony. *The Long Goodbye* (1973) presents private eye Philip Marlowe (Eliott Gould) as a shambling coward.

Altman likes to use the same actors, often getting performers to improvize their dialogues. He adeptly maps out areas in which a group of people are brought together for a purpose, allowing him to manipulate 24 characters in *Nashville* (1975), 40 in *A Wedding* (1978), and a huge cast in *Short Cuts* (1993), a mosaic of Raymond Carver stories, and *Gosford Park* (2001).

The experimental use of sound is an important feature of Altman's films. It includes the simultaneous conversations and loudspeaker announcements in *M*A*S*H*, the 8-track sound system in *California Split* (1974), and the absence of a music score in *Thieves Like Us* (1973). After the relative failure of *Popeye* (1980), and being fired from *Ragtime* (1981), Altman was forced to work mostly in television, but became the darling of Hollywood again with *The Player (1992)*.

Tim Robbins *as a hotshot studio executive in* The Player, *Altman's clever, sardonic satire on Hollywood, the dream factory that he never wholly embraced.*

WHAT TO WATCH

1970	M*A*S*H
1971	McCabe and Mrs Miller
1975	Nashville
1992	The Player
1993	Short Cuts
2001	Gosford Park
2006	A Prairie Home Companion

Robert Altman *directs Emily Watson on the set of* Gosford Park, *a sumptuous, old-fashioned British murder-mystery that weaves an elaborate tapestry of intrigue, satire, and brittle social commentary.*

Alejandro **Amenábar**

1972– | SPANISH | 1991–

6 | Horror, Thriller, Psychological drama

With only four feature films — each with a chilling story — behind him, the Chilean-born director-screenwriter-composer Alejandro Amenábar has justified his reputation as one of the most talented contemporary film-makers.

At 25, Amenábar gained international fame with his dazzling second feature *Open Your Eyes* (*Abre los ojos*, 1997), remade as *Vanilla Sky* (2001) starring Tom Cruise. The Spanish film, unlike the pale Hollywood copy, is an audacious mixture of romance, thriller, and science fiction, with Eduardo Noriega as the handsome playboy who is disfigured in an accident. Noriega also appears in Amenábar's first feature, *Thesis* (*Tesis*, 1996), a gripping horror movie about the media's fascination with violence, while Javier Bardem in *The Sea Inside* (*Mar adentro*, 2004), a passionate plea for euthanasia, is a quadriplegic struggling to have his life ended. *The Others* (2001), Amenábar's first film in English, starring Nicole Kidman, is an atmospheric ghost story made with authority.

Penélope Cruz *and Eduardo Noriega star in* Abre los ojos (Open Your Eyes), *in which Amenábar masterfully juxtaposes fantasy and reality in a multilayered plot.*

WHAT TO WATCH

1997	Open Your Eyes
2001	The Others
2004	The Sea Inside

Lindsay **Anderson**

1923–1994 | BRITISH | 1952–1987

6 | Drama, Satire

Unlike most of his contemporaries, Lindsay Anderson never made transatlantic blockbusters but remained English to the core, gaining a reputation as the keeper of British cinema's conscience.

Known as a harsh film critic, Lindsay Anderson became part of the Free Cinema movement, shifting from middle-class dominated British films to more naturalistic films about the working class. Anderson's excellent documentaries include *Every Day Except Christmas* (1957) about London's Covent Garden market. *This Sporting Life* (1963), his first feature, is set in the industrial north with Richard Harris providing an emotional power rarely attained in British films. *If* (1968) — inspired by Jean Vigo's *Zero de Conduit* (1933) — is a pungent critique of the British public school ethos, of which Anderson himself was a product. *O Lucky Man!* (1972) and *Britannia Hospital* (1982) are ambitious satires on the state of the British nation, while *The Whales of August* (1987) is a gentler story about old age.

Malcolm McDowell *and Christine Noonan star in* If..., *an exposure of hypocrisy in British society that proved to be a commercial success.*

WHAT TO WATCH

1963	This Sporting Life
1968	If...
1972	O Lucky Man
1982	Britannia Hospital
1987	The Whales of August

Paul Thomas **Anderson**

1970– AMERICAN 1997–

4 Drama

Perhaps the most ambitious American filmmaker of his generation, Paul Thomas Anderson grew up around movies and worked as a production assistant from a young age.

Anderson's father was a voice artist and presented horror movies on late night cable television. Influenced above all by Robert Altman, Anderson has two wildly ambitious, panoramic ensemble movies to his name; *Boogie Nights* (1997) is a requiem for the 1970s refracted through the story of porn star Dirk Diggler, and *Magnolia* (1999) is a three-hour epic, both pretentious and inspired, about a group of dysfunctional people over the course of one day and night. *Punch Drunk Love* (2002) is a change of pace, an expressionistic romantic comedy, with Adam Sandler as the quiet, awkwardly shy owner of a small business, who is terrorized by his seven sisters but finds love when a mysterious woman enters his life and transforms him.

WHAT TO WATCH

1997	Boogie Nights
1999	Magnolia
2002	Punch Drunk Love

Heather Graham *plays Brandy "Rollergirl," a school dropout who aspires to be a film star, in* Boogie Nights, *Anderson's darkly comic look at the porn industry.*

Theo **Angelopoulos**

1935– GREEK 1970–

11 Historical, Political, Epic, Drama

In 1975, after the seven-year military dictatorship in his country ended, Theo Angelopoulos emerged on the international scene with the most ambitious Greek films to date.

A portrayal of official incompetence that subtly undermines the "Colonels' regime," *Days of 36* (*Meres Tou 36*, 1972) is the first of an impressive trilogy, followed by *The Travelling Players* (*O Thiassos*, 1975) and *The Huntsman* (*Oi Kynighoi*, 1977), all allegories of Greek politics of the 20th century. Later, Angelopoulos used widely known actors — Marcello Mastrioanni in *The Beekeeper* (*O Melissokomos*, 1986), Harvey Keitel in *Ulysses' Gaze* (*To Vlemma tou Odyssea*, 1995), and Bruno Ganz in *Eternity and a Day* (*Mia aioniotita kai mia mera*, 1998). With the masterful use of slow pans and long takes, the films are rewarding metaphysical road movies. Other films of note are *Landscape in the Mist* (*Topio stin omichli*, 1988) and *The Weeping Meadow* (*Trilogia I: To Livadi pou dakryzei*, 2004), the first of a projected trilogy, which is stylistically breathtaking and vividly descriptive.

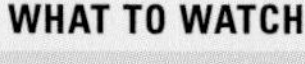

WHAT TO WATCH

1975	The Travelling Players
1988	Landscape in the Mist
1998	Eternity and a Day
2004	The Weeping Meadow

An exploration *of an inner journey,* Eternity and a Day *shows how time becomes a central concern for terminally ill Alexandre (Bruno Ganz).*

Michelangelo **Antonioni**

1912– ITALIAN 1950–

17 Psychological drama

The long tracking shots, set pieces, attention to design and architecture, and the relationship between the characters and their environment are hallmarks of Michelangelo Antonioni's meditations on contemporary angst.

A personal stamp was already noticeable in the elegance of Antonioni's first feature, *Chronicle of a Love Affair* (*Cronaca di un Amore*, 1950), but his style reached its maturity with *L'Avventura* (1960), which realigned the perception of time and space in cinema. *L'Avventura* was followed by *La Notte* (1961) and *L'Eclisse* (1962) to form a trilogy that examined themes of alienation. In *Il Deserto Rosso* (1964), Monica Vitti portrays a housewife, Giuliana, who is driven mad by the industrial landscape that surrounds her. Antonioni uses deep reds and greens to reflect the woman's neurosis, while brighter colours appear during her flights of fantasy. In his next four films, Antonioni cast his eye outside Italy: on China with a documentary, *Chung Kuo* (1972); on

WHAT TO WATCH	
1960	L'Avventura
1961	La Notte
1962	L'Eclisse
1964	Il Deserto Rosso
1966	Blow-Up
1975	The Passenger

Alain Delon *and Monica Vitti as the doomed lovers Piero and Vittoria in* The Eclipse.

"Swinging Sixties" London in *Blow-Up* (1966), with a fashionable photographer at the film's centre; on liberated American youth in *Zabriskie Point* (1969), which ends spectacularly with a materialistic civilization exploding, and on arid North Africa in *The Passenger* (*Professione: Reporter*, 1975). Back in Italy and reuniting with Vitti, his lover with whom he made four films, Antonioni made *The Oberwald Mystery* (*Il Mistero di Oberwald*, 1980), one of the first major films to be shot on video. He worked on video for the next few years, although *Identification of a Woman* (*Identificazione di una Donna*, 1982) was shot on film. In 1985, Antonioni had a stroke that partially paralysed him. Despite this setback, he made *Beyond the Clouds* (*Al di là Delle Nuvole*, 1995), which is based on his short stories.

Jack Nicholson *plays a reporter in* The Passenger, *a film that questions notions of reality and illusion.*

Gillian **Armstrong**

1950– AUSTRALIAN 1979–

12 Drama

Part of the "Australian New Wave," which emerged in the late 1970s, Gillian Armstrong places women at the center of her films, exploring the conflict they face between career, creativity, and marriage.

Armstrong directed the stylish and subtly feminist drama *My Brilliant Career* (1979), starring Judy Davis as a headstrong woman in Australia's outback at the start of the 20th century, who goes on to have an international career. In Hollywood, Armstrong made *Mrs Soffel* (1985) and *Little Women* (1994), again period tales of women who broke with convention. Back in Australia, with *The Last Days of Chez Nous* (1992) and *Oscar and Lucinda* (1997), she continued her examination of women who subvert their traditional roles to redefine their lives.

The March family *is portrayed by Winona Ryder, Trini Alvarado, Kirsten Dunst, Susan Sarandon, and Claire Danes in Armstrong's adaptation of the 1868 novel* Little Women.

WHAT TO WATCH

1979	My Brilliant Career
1994	Little Women
1997	Oscar and Lucinda

Richard **Attenborough**

1923– BRITISH 1969–

11 Biopics, War

After establishing a reputation as an actor, Richard Attenborough had a second career as a director, mostly of lavish biographical films.

A film based on World War I, *Oh! What a Lovely War!* (1969) was Attenborough's first directorial venture, but it was *Gandhi* (1982) that won him acclaim. It took him over 20 years to finance the film, which had Ben Kingsley in the title role and went on to win eight Oscars. He was able to express his anger at apartheid in South Africa in *Cry Freedom* (1987), about the black activist Steve Biko, and turned to another of his idols in *Chaplin* (1992).

Film poster, *1982*

WHAT TO WATCH

1969	Oh! What a Lovely War
1982	Gandhi
1987	Cry Freedom

Bille **August**

1948– DANISH 1978–

12 Drama

Bille August's refusal of US money and the suggestion he make *Pelle the Conqueror* (*Pelle Erobreren*, 1988) in English paid off when the film won the Foreign Film Oscar at Cannes.

A renowned cinematographer, August made his directorial debut with *In My Life* (*Honning Måne*, 1978). He made an international impact with *Twist and Shout* (1978) and *Pelle the Conqueror*, an unsentimental but moving epic of social exploitation in early 20th-century Denmark. It remains his best film, although *The Best Intentions* (*Den Goda Viljan*, 1992), with Ingmar Bergman's autobiographical script about his parents' marriage; *Les Misérables* based on Victor Hugo's novel of the same name; and *A Song For Martin* (2001), which treats the tragedy of Alzheimer's, are laudable successors.

WHAT TO WATCH

1988	Pelle the Conqueror
1992	The Best Intentions
1998	Les Misérables

Isak (Erland Josephson) *and Helena Ekdahl (Gunn Wallgren) share a moment of intimacy in* Fanny and Alexander, *Bergman's most autobiographical film.*

Ingmar **Bergman**

1918– | SWEDISH | 1946–

40 | Psychological, Metaphysical drama

The son of a pastor, Ingmar Bergman made films filled with religious imagery, which paradoxically express a godless, loveless universe. Bergman's entire oeuvre can be seen as the autobiography of his psyche.

Dividing his directing between the stage and screen, Bergman often introduced the theater into his films as a metaphor for the duality of the personality. At least five of his films take place on an island, a circumscribed area like the stage. The subject of his early work is the struggle of adolescents against an unfeeling adult world. The transient, sun-soaked Swedish summer days, the only period of happiness before the encroachment of a winter of discontent, are captured glowingly in *Summer Interlude* (*Sommarlek*, 1950 and *Summer with Monika* (*Sommaren med Monika*, 1952). The operetta-like comedy of manners, *Smiles of a Summer Night* (*Sommarnattens leende*, 1955), was the culmination of this first period. *The Seventh Seal* (*Det Sjunde inseglet*), set in cruel medieval times, and *Wild Strawberries* (*Smultronstället*, both 1957) consolidated Bergman's international reputation, as did *The Face* (*Ansiktet*, 1958), a Gothic tale. The trilogy on the silence of God: *Through a Glass Darkly* (*Såsom i en spegel*, 1961), *Winter Light* (*Nattvardsgästern*, 1963), and *The Silence* (*Tystnaden*, 1963), moved Bergman into a more angst-ridden world. With *Persona* (1966), the female face in close-up became his field of vision, although women have always been central to his work. A succession of psychodramas followed, including the emotionally charged *Cries and Whispers* (*Viskningar och rop*, 1972). In *Autumn Sonata* (*Höstsonaten*, 1978) the director points an accusing finger at parental neglect, while *Fanny and Alexander* (*Fanny och Alexander*, 1982) is a magical evocation of childhood. He announced this film as his final feature and, although he would continue to direct for television and the theater, it was a superlative climax to his 36 years as one of cinema's most profound artists.

WHAT TO WATCH

1950	Summer Interlude
1955	Smiles of a Summer Night
1957	The Seventh Seal
1957	Wild Strawberries
1958	The Face
1972	Cries and Whispers
1978	Autumn Sonata
1982	Fanny and Alexander

Scenes From a Marriage *(1973), German poster.*

Busby **Berkeley**

1895–1976 AMERICAN 1930–1970

21 Musical

Although he directed 21 features, it is Berkeley's creation of spectacular dance sequences that singles him out as an auteur.

When Broadway dance director Busby Berkeley came to Hollywood to stage production numbers for the Eddie Cantor musical *Whoopee* (1930), he concentrated on only one mobile camera. At Warner Bros. from 1933 to 1937, using a single dancing camera, Berkeley dollied in on the lines of identically dressed dream girls, forming erotic, kaleidoscopic effects with overhead shots from a mobile crane. There were also great narrative numbers such as "My Forgotten Man" (*Gold Diggers of 1933*) and "Shanghai Lil" (*Footlight Parade*, 1933). At MGM, he created fantastic aqua ballets for Hollywood's mermaid, Esther Williams.

WHAT TO WATCH

1933	42nd Street (dance director)
1935	Gold Diggers of 1935
1939	Babes in Arms
1943	The Gang's All Here

Judy Garland *and Mickey Rooney star in the lively musical,* Babes on Broadway *(1941).*

Claude **Berri**

1934– FRENCH 1967–

19 Drama, Comedy, Period

Although many of Claude Berri's films were based on his own life and times, his greatest success was with his compelling works, *Jean de Florette* and *Manon des Sources* (*Manon of the Spring*), which were set in rural France, far from his own world.

Berri's first feature was the amusing and touching *The Two of Us* (*Le Vieil homme et l'enfant*, 1966), based on his own experiences as the Jewish foster child of an anti-Semitic old man during the war. Also autobiographical were *The First Time* (*La Première fois*, 1976) about adolescence, *Marry Me! Marry Me!* (*Mazel Tov ou le mariage*, 1968) about marriage, and *The Man with Connections* (*Le Pistoné*, 1970) about military service in Algeria. Berri also returned to the war period of occupied France in *Uranus* (1990) and *Lucie Aubrac* (1997), which is based on a French Resistant's autobiography. *Jean de Florette* and *Manon des Sources* (both 1986), adapted from Marcel Pagnol's 1953 film, feature towering performances from Daniel Auteuil, Yves Montand, and Gérard Depardieu. The two films are linked in theme and narrative, with multi-dimensional characters enacting a tragic story of greed and revenge. Berri's version of Emile Zola's novel *Germinal* (1993) is epic in scale, telling the grim story of the struggle for the rights of coal miners.

Berri's powerful masterpiece Manon des Sources, *featuring Daniel Auteuil (left) and Yves Montand, explores the complexity of human relationships.*

WHAT TO WATCH

1966	The Two of Us
1986	Jean de Florette
1986	Manon des Sources
1993	Germinal

Bernardo **Bertolucci**

1940– ITALIAN 1962–

15 Epic, Political, Psychological drama

The son of a well-known poet, and winner of a prestigious poetry prize himself, Bernardo Bertolucci believes that "cinema is the true poetic language," a claim that many of his wide-ranging films justify.

Bertolucci directed his first film *The Grim Reaper* (*La Commare Secca*, 1962) at the age of 22. In his second film, *Before the Revolution* (*Prima della Rivoluzione*, 1964), he began to explore some important themes of his work — father-son relationships and the political-personal conflict, themes also evident in *The Spider's Stratagem* (*Strategia del Ragno*, 1969). *The Conformist* (*Il Conformista*, 1970) successfully brought together his Freudian and political preoccupations in pre-war Italy. But it was *Last Tango in Paris* (1972) that gained the director worldwide notoriety, mainly because of the loveless sex scenes between Paul, a middle-aged American (Marlon Brando), and Jeanne, a young Frenchwoman (Maria Schneider).

With *1900* (1976), a film about class struggle, Bertolucci turned away from the introspection of his previous films. *Tragedy of a Ridiculous Man* (*La Tragedia di un uomo ridicolo*, 1981), an ambiguous view of terrorism, failed to please the public and the critics. But *The Last Emperor* (1987), the first western film to be made entirely in China and covering 60 years of China's history (1906–1967), won nine Academy Awards, including Best Picture, Best Director, and Best Cinematography. *The Sheltering Sky* (1990), set in North Africa; *Little Buddha* (1994); and *The Dreamers* (*I Sognatori*, 2003) are other Bertolucci films of note.

Bertolucci directs *Debra Winger and John Malkovich in* The Sheltering Sky, *in which an American couple travel across North Africa to find meaning in their relationship.*

WHAT TO WATCH

1964	Before the Revolution
1970	The Conformist
1972	Last Tango in Paris
1976	1900
1987	The Last Emperor
2003	The Dreamers

Louis Garrel, *Eva Green, and Michael Pitt star in* The Dreamers, a story of troubled friendships *set against the backdrop of the 1968 student riots in Paris.*

Luc **Besson**

1959– | FRENCH | 1983–

9 | Thriller, Science Fiction

Even into his forties, Luc Besson was the *enfant terrible* of French cinema, looking towards comic books, Hollywood blockbusters, and pop videos for inspiration.

Besson's first contribution to the French "Cinema du Look" movement, in which style overrides content, was the flashy *Subway* (1985), set in a vividly imagined Paris metro that is inhabited by social misfits. The breathtaking *The Big Blue (Le Grand Bleu,* 1988), about two deep-sea divers, was a more personal project — Besson's parents were diving instructors. Both *Nikita* (1990), an homage to the American action movie, and *Léon* (1995), set in New York, are thrillers but also explore the themes of personal growth and morality. Besson's work reached its climax in the stylish science fiction *The Fifth Element* (1997), featuring spectacular special effects, about evil aliens out to destroy mankind. In contrast, the exquisite black-and-white film *Angel-A* (2005) is set in a hauntingly vacant Paris.

WHAT TO WATCH

1988	The Big Blue
1990	Nikita
1995	Léon
1997	The Fifth Element

Maiwen LeBesco *as Diva Plavalaguna, an alien opera singer performing in a concert on a spaceship, in the futuristic thriller* The Fifth Element.

Peter **Bogdanovich**

1939– | AMERICAN | 1967–1977

17 | Comedy, Drama, Pastiche

Although Peter Bogdanovich has probably had more flops than most, only some of these were merited. He has, unjustly, suffered from the reputation of being a curse on the box office.

Former critic and fanatical film buff, Peter Bogdanovich made an impressive debut with the suspense thriller *Targets* (1968), featuring Boris Karloff as a horror film star (one of Karloff's last films). Both *The Last Picture Show* (1971), which won two Academy Awards — Best Supporting Actor (Ben Johnson) and Best Supporting Actress (Cloris Leachman), and *Paper Moon* (1973) lovingly evoke in black-and-white the spirit of John Ford and William Wyler. *What's Up, Doc?* (1972) is an homage to Howard Hawks' screwball comedies. All these pastiches were extremely successful. Bogdanovich later made a sequel to *The Last Picture Show,* called *Texasville* (1990), in which the characters, now middle-aged, review their lives. *Daisy Miller* (1974), an adaptation of the novel by Henry James, was, however, poorly received, as was a musical, *At Long Last Love* (1975), and a slapstick comedy, *Nickelodeon* (1976). *Mask* (1985) and *Noises Off* (1992) redeemed his reputation somewhat, but he never returned to his former glory.

WHAT TO WATCH

1968	Targets
1971	The Last Picture Show
1972	What's Up, Doc?
1973	Paper Moon
1985	Mask
1992	Noises Off

The Last Picture Show, *starring Cybill Shepherd and Jeff Bridges, is an evocative and bittersweet film about growing up in an American small town in the early 1950s.*

John **Boorman**

1933– BRITISH 1965–

16 Action, Thriller, Crime

In over 40 years as a film director, John Boorman has made only 16 feature films, demonstrating a taste for the allegorical, and revealing a strength for visually distinctive story-telling.

Different genres have been taken on by John Boorman: war (*Hell in the Pacific*, 1968); science fiction (*Zardoz*, 1973); horror (*The Exorcist II — The Heretic*, 1977); the epic *Excalibur* (1981); the political (*Beyond Rangoon*, 1985; *The General*, 1998); and the spy thriller (*The Tailor of Panama*, 2001). *Point Blank* (1967) is a powerful crime thriller set in the concrete jungle of Los Angeles; *Deliverance* (1972) follows four urban men on a canoe trip who are terrorized by mountain men, while *The Emerald Forest* (1985) tells the story of a man seeking his kidnapped son in the Amazon jungle.

WHAT TO WATCH

1967	Point Blank
1968	Hell in the Pacific
1972	Deliverance
1981	Excalibur
1987	Hope and Glory
1998	The General
2001	The Tailor of Panama

Sebastian Rice-Edwards *and Geraldine Muir in a scene from* Hope and Glory *(1987), which draws on Boorman's childhood experiences during World War II.*

Frank **Borzage**

1893–1962 AMERICAN 1916–1959

100 Melodrama

With his penchant for sentimental love stories, Frank Borzage created films in which lovers battle with adversity in some form.

Three beautifully photographed silent romances with Janet Gaynor, who was the embodiment of sweetness on screen, were Borzage's triumphs. One of them, *Seventh Heaven* (1927), was the very first film to win Academy Awards (Best Direction, Best Actress). *A Farewell to Arms* (1932) was much softer than Ernest Hemingway's tough novel set in World War I. Better suited to Borzage's gentle gifts were the urban poetry of *Man's Castle* (1933), about a young couple looking for a ray of hope during the Depression; the pacifist *Desire* (1936); and *History Is Made at Night* (1937). His best work was with Margaret Sullavan: *Little Man, What Now?* (1934), *Three Comrades* (1938) and *The Mortal Storm* (1940) were all poignant and prescient love stories set against the growing threat of Nazism.

WHAT TO WATCH

1927	Seventh Heaven
1929	The River
1932	A Farewell To Arms
1933	Man's Castle
1934	Little Man, What Now?
1936	Desire
1937	History Is Made at Night
1940	The Mortal Storm

Frederic (Gary Cooper) *and Catherine (Helen Hayes) in Borzage's romantic recreation of Hemingway's classic novel,* A Farewell to Arms.

Robert **Bresson**

1907–1999 FRENCH 1943–1983

13 Metaphysical drama

Although Robert Bresson made only 13 films in 40 years, his oeuvre is impressively consistent: austere, uncompromising, and elliptical.

Of his insistence on using only non-actors in his films, Bresson declared: "Art is transformation. Acting can only get in the way." However, his first two films, *Angels of the Streets* (*Les Anges du Péché*, 1943) and *Ladies of the Park* (*Les Dames du Bois de Boulogne*, 1945), about the redemption of women, both used professional actors. *A Man Escaped* (*Le Vent Souffle où il Veut*, 1956), a testament to courage, is about a French resistance fighter while *Balthazar* (*Au Hasard Balthazar*, 1966), about the life of a donkey, is one of Bresson's most lyrical films. Many of his films, such as *The Trial of Joan of Arc* (*Procès de Jeanne d'Arc*, 1962), end in death. In 1969, with *A Gentle Creature* (*Une Femme Douce*), he started using color, and a more overt sensuality was noticeable. *The Devil, Probably* (*Le Diable Probablement*, 1977) brought the theme of pollution, literal and figurative, into Bresson's enclosed world.

WHAT TO WATCH

1945	Ladies of the Park
1950	Diary of a Country Priest (Journal D'un Cure de)
1956	A Man Escaped
1966	Balthazar
1983	L'Argent

Claude Laydu *and Nicole L'Admiral in* Diary of a Country Priest *(1950), the first truly Bressonian film in its use of non-actors, natural sound, and pared-down images.*

Mel **Brooks**

1926– AMERICAN 1968–

11 Comedy

In 2001, with the Broadway musical *The Producers*, the career of Mel Brooks (Melvin Kaminsky), came almost full circle, from his greatest film triumph, the 1968 movie of the same name, to the hit show that had been inspired by it.

The Producers plays fast and loose with "bad taste" and the ingenious idea of a producer (Zero Mostel) and his hysterical accountant (Gene Wilder) hoping to make more money out of a flop than a hit. After it, Brooks embarked on a series of movie pastiches, often with startling accuracy. These include the Western (*Blazing Saddles*, 1974); horror (*Young Frankenstein*, 1974, and *Dracula: Dead and Loving It*, 1995); Alfred Hitchcock (*High Anxiety*, 1977); Frank Capra (*Life Stinks!*, 1991); the epic (*History of the World-Part I*, 1981); sci-fi (*Spaceballs*, 1987); and swashbucklers (*Robin Hood: Men in Tights*, 1993). These energetic movies consist of so many hard-hitting jokes that some are bound to hit the target.

WHAT TO WATCH

1968	The Producers
1974	Blazing Saddles
1974	Young Frankenstein
1976	Silent Movie
1977	High Anxiety

Zero Mostel *as the scheming producer and Gene Wilder as the wide-eyed accountant in* The Producers.

Clarence **Brown**

1890–1987 AMERICAN 1920–1952

50 Melodrama, Drama

Typifying the MGM style of the 1930s and 40s, Brown's films are glossy entertainments, staying on the right side of sentimentality.

Clarence Brown carried over the pictorial qualities he had learned in silent cinema into his sound films, which were elegant dramas set in plush surroundings, shot in soft focus and high-key lighting. He directed seven of Greta Garbo's films, including the silent-film classics *Flesh and the Devil* (1926), *Anna Christie* (1930), and *Anna Karenina* (1935), and made idealistic and warm-hearted films for MGM, three of them with Mickey Rooney: *Ah Wilderness!* (1935), *The Human Comedy* (1943), and *National Velvet* (1944). Brown also directed *The Yearling* (1946), a lyrical boy-loves-deer tale, and *Intruder in the Dust* (1949), one of the first Hollywood films to deal with racism.

WHAT TO WATCH

1926	Flesh and the Devil
1930	Anna Christie
1935	Ah Wilderness!
1935	Anna Karenina
1940	Edison the Man
1944	National Velvet
1946	The Yearling
1949	Intruder in the Dust

National Velvet, *tells the story of Velvet Brown, a young girl who enters the Grand National, England's great racing event. The film made 12-year-old Elizabeth Taylor a star.*

Tod **Browning**

1880–1962 AMERICAN 1915–1939

64 Horror

The eerily atmospheric horror movies Tod Browning made with actors Lon Chaney and Bela Lugosi are his hallmark.

In 1918, Browning signed with Universal and made 17 films for them, including two in which Chaney had small roles. After Chaney became a star, the actor persuaded MGM to hire Browning. Together, the pair made eight horror movies, great vehicles for the "man with a thousand faces." After Chaney's death in 1930, Browning moved back to Universal to make *Dracula* (1931) with Lugosi. In the same genre are the campy *Mark of the Vampire* (1935) and the inventive *The Devil-Doll* (1936). In a way, *Freaks* (1932) is an anti-horror movie because it urges audiences not to be repulsed by the parade of monsters. This masterpiece was withdrawn from distribution for 30 years until it was rehabilitated at the Venice Film Festival only a few weeks before Browning's death.

Tod Browning *on the set of* Freaks *with Olga Baclanova (wearing a chicken skin) as Cleopatra, who is persecuted by "freaks" until she becomes one of them.*

WHAT TO WATCH

1925	The Unholy Three
1926	The Blackbird
1927	The Unknown
1928	West of Zanzibar
1931	Dracula
1932	Freaks
1936	The Devil-Doll

Luis **Buñuel**

1900–1983 | SPANISH | 1929–1977

32 | Surrealist drama, Comedy

Born with the 20th century, Luis Buñuel never wavered in his ideas and vision, establishing himself as perhaps the most mordantly comic and subversive of all the great directors.

In response to a bourgeois family upbringing and a Jesuit school education, Buñuel entered adulthood fervently anti-middle class and anti-clerical.

His first two films, *An Andalusian Dog* (*Un Chien Andalou*, 1928) and *The Golden Age* (*L'Age d'Or*, 1930), both made under the influence of André Breton's *Surrealist Manifesto*, contained many themes — Catholicism, the bourgeosie, and rationality — that would reappear in his later films. After *Land Without Bread* (*Las Hurdes*, 1932) — a stark documentary about the contrast between peasant poverty and the wealth of the Church — was banned in Spain, Buñuel did not make another film for 15 years.

In 1947, he moved to Mexico and made *The Young and the Damned* (*Los Olvidados*, 1950), a powerful, detached view of the cruel world of juvenile delinquents. He also made about a dozen cheap films for the home market, but still managed gems such as *Torments* (*El*, 1952), *Robinson Crusoe* (1952), in which he overturns Daniel Defoe's Christian message, and *Wuthering Heights* (*Abismos de pasión*, 1953). *Viridiana* (1961), the first film he made in his native land for 29 years, is a savage comedy about Catholic mentality and rituals, which was banned in Spain. Regardless, because of the film's critical success, Buñuel was welcomed back to the center of world cinema. *The Exterminating Angel* (*El Ángel exterminador*, 1962), made in Mexico, is a parable about guests at a sumptuous party who find it physically impossible to leave. In *The Discreet Charm of the Bourgeoisie* (1972), the wealthy characters are unable to get anything to eat. Two other superb French films are *Diary of a Chambermaid* (*Le journal d'une femme de chambre*, 1964), a cynical take on Octave Mirbeau's 1900 novel, and the witty, erotic, and subversive *Belle de Jour.*

Silvia Pinal *as the novice nun Viridiana, who fights a losing battle to remain true to her moral ideals and faith in* Viridiana, *which won the Best Film award at Cannes.*

WHAT TO WATCH

1928	An Andalusian Dog
1930	The Golden Age
1950	The Young and the Damned
1958	Nazarin
1961	Viridiana
1962	The Exterminating Angel
1964	Diary of a Chambermaid
1967	Belle de Jour
1970	Tristana
1972	The Discreet Charm of the Bourgeoisie

Catherine Deneuve *with Michel Piccoli in* Belle de Jour, *in which a middle-class wife leads a double life, playing out the fantasies of the rich.*

Tim **Burton**

1958– AMERICAN 1985–

11 Fantasy, Animation

The offbeat, yet mainstream films of Tim Burton depict a highly stylized visual evocative of cartoons, a consequence of his beginnings as a Walt Disney animator.

Tim Burton's first feature, *Pee Wee's Big Adventure* (1985), an episodic live-action cartoon of a nine-year-old boy in a grown up's body, relates to his later works such as *Edward Scissorhands* (1990), *Ed Wood* (1994), *Sleepy Hollow* (1999), and *Charlie and the Chocolate Factory* (2005), in which he spins fantastic tales of a misfit suspended between the adult world and one of childlike dreams. All these later films were built around the gentle and strange persona of Johnny Depp, in whom Burton found his perfect interpreter.

Edward Scissorhands — part fairytale, part suburban satire — is one of Burton's most personal films. A product of suburbia himself, he idolized Vincent Price, whom he cast in the film and about whom he made a short animated film (*Vincent*, 1982). *Ed Wood* is a sympathetic portrait of an outsider who is cheerfully unaware that as a film director he has no talent at all.

Film poster, *2005*

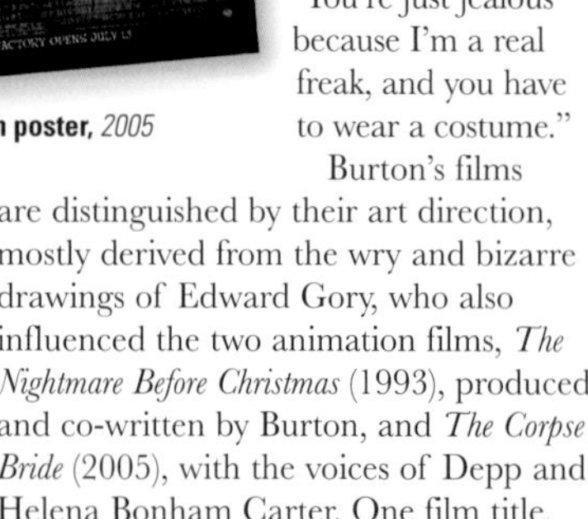

Burton became famous with *Beetlejuice* (1988), a landmark in supernatural comedy with zany, sometimes overwhelming, special effects. Its success enabled him to direct the first two Batman films, *Batman* (1989) and *Batman Returns* (1992), which are much darker than previous screen versions of the comic strip. This time, however, it is the hero who represents "normal society" while his various foes are the outcasts. As the Penguin, a character in the film, tells Batman in *Batman Returns*, "You're just jealous because I'm a real freak, and you have to wear a costume."

Burton's films are distinguished by their art direction, mostly derived from the wry and bizarre drawings of Edward Gory, who also influenced the two animation films, *The Nightmare Before Christmas* (1993), produced and co-written by Burton, and *The Corpse Bride* (2005), with the voices of Depp and Helena Bonham Carter. One film title, *Believe It or Not* (2006), sums up his work.

WHAT TO WATCH

1989	Batman
1990	Edward Scissorhands
1994	Ed Wood
1999	Sleepy Hollow
2005	Charlie and the Chocolate Factory

Johnny Depp *brings alive the passion, enthusiasm, and quirkiness of film-maker Edward D. Wood, Jr. in* Ed Wood, *Burton's biographical account of a man considered one of the worst directors in history.*

James **Cameron**

1954– CANADIAN 1984–

8 Action, Adventure, Thriller

A hugely successful Hollywood director, James Cameron virtually dropped out of movie-making at the height of his career to pursue his passion for deep-sea exploration.

A graduate of the Roger Corman school, James Cameron made one of the least auspicious directorial debuts ever with *Piranha Part II* (1981). Three years later, the sci-fi thriller *The Terminator* (1984) transformed his career (and that of Arnold Schwarzenegger, who portrays an iconic cyborg assasssin). *Aliens* (1986) consolidated his reputation as an action director, and *The Abyss* (1989) eschewed his usual apocalyptic nightmares in favour of imaginary benign alien life forms. By the time of *True Lies* (1994), the strain of constantly upping the ante on his own action sequences was beginning to tell. He bounced back with *Titanic* (1997), derided by the critics but becoming a smash hit on the scale of *Gone With the Wind*.

Leonardo DiCaprio *as Jack and Kate Winslet as Rose enact the fictional love story in* Titanic; *excellent cinematography and dazzling special effects made Cameron's film a fantastic visual treat.*

WHAT TO WATCH

1984	The Terminator
1986	Aliens
1991	Terminator 2
1997	Titanic

Jane **Campion**

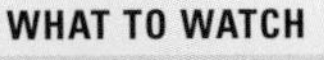

1954– NEW ZEALANDER 1989–

7 Costume drama, Drama, Thriller

Almost without exception, Jane Campion's films depict the lives of young women who, for one reason or another, find themselves outsiders within a society.

Jane Campion became the first woman director to win the Best Film award at Cannes with her third feature, *The Piano* (1993). This hauntingly beautiful tale of passion is about a mute, 19th-century Scottish woman (Holly Hunter), who is only able to communicate through her daughter (Anna Paquin) and finds liberation by playing the piano. Both Hunter and Paquin won Academy Awards for their performances, as did Campion for her screenplay. It consolidated her position as a leading director following *Sweetie* (1989), a black comedy about the problems of an overweight, over-emotional girl, and *An Angel at My Table* (1990), a portrait of Janet Frame, a plump, repressed child who became one of New Zealand's greatest writers. Campion's further depictions of women at the mercy of insensitive, predatory males who assault them physically and emotionally, such as *The Portrait of a Lady* (1996) have been less successful.

WHAT TO WATCH

1989	Sweetie
1990	An Angel at My Table
1993	The Piano
1996	The Portrait of a Lady

Ada (Holly Hunter), *with her daughter Flora (Anna Paquin), on her way from Scotland to New Zealand to marry a man she has never seen, in* The Piano.

Frank **Capra**

1897–1991 | AMERICAN | 1926–1961

37 | Comedy, Melodrama, Drama

From 1936 onwards, Frank Capra's films evoked the American Dream, through which any honest, decent, and patriotic American could overcome corruption and disappointment to prove the power of the individual.

Frank Capra began his movie career as a gag writer for comedian Harry Langdon. After directing movies at First National, he went to Columbia, where he made madcap comedies such as *Platinum Blonde* (1931), *American Madness* (1932), and *It Happened One Night* (1934), which won five Academy Awards and turned Columbia from a "Poverty Row" studio into a major one. Capra also made Barbara Stanwyck a star at Columbia with four movies, including *The Bitter Tea of General Yen* (1933). An early masterpiece was *Lady for a Day* (1933), filled with wonderful New York street characters. Capra's autobiography states

A scene *from Capra's highly acclaimed series of documentaries entitled* Why We Fight *(1943–45), which explained the US's participation in World War II.*

that an unknown man came to him in 1935 and told him to use his gifts for God's purpose. Following this advice, Capra lost the sensuality and anarchy in his films and replaced his central female characters with idealistic boy-scout heroes. The result was sentimental social comedies that were deemed "Capraesque." *Mr. Deeds Goes to Town* (1936), and *Meet John Doe* (1941) with Gary Cooper, and *You Can't Take It with You* (1938), *Mr. Smith Goes to Washington* (1939), and *It's a Wonderful Life* (1946), with James Stewart, glorify the little man's fight for what is right and decent. Politically naïve as they are, the films have comic pace and invention, splendid sets, as in *Lost Horizon* (1937), and outstanding performances.

Film poster, *1937*

WHAT TO WATCH

1931	Platinum Blonde
1933	The Bitter Tea of General Yen
1933	Lady for a Day
1934	It Happened One Night
1936	Mr. Deeds Goes to Town
1938	You Can't Take It with You
1939	Mr. Smith Goes to Washington
1946	It's a Wonderful Life

James Stewart *plays the eponymous hero in* Mr. Smith Goes to Washington. *The quintessential everyman is seen here with Clarissa Saunders (Jean Arthur).*

Jean (Jean Gabin) *and Nelly (Michèle Morgan), the doomed lovers who meet in a misty French port city, in* Port of Shadows *(1938).*

Marcel **Carné**

1909–1996 | FRENCH | 1936–1974

20 | Poetic realism, Costume drama

In Marcel Carné's *Hôtel du Nord* (1938), Arletty, looking at her dingy surroundings, cries, "Atmosphere! Atmosphere!" There is plenty of it in his best films, which, mostly written by Jacques Prévert and shot by Alexandre Trauner, were beautifully crafted, written, and played.

After assisting Belgian director Jacques Feyder on four of his best films between 1933 and 1935, Marcel Carné directed Feyder's wife, Françoise Rosay, in *Jenny* (1936). This was co-scripted by the poet Jacques Prévert, with whom Carné was to collaborate on six further films over the next decade. *Bizarre Bizarre* (*Drôle de Drame*, 1937), an eccentric comedy thriller set in an imaginary Victorian London, was followed by *Port of Shadows* (*Le Quai des Brumes*, 1938), the film that created the melancholic "poetic realism" associated with the director and his screenwriters. The slant-eyed Michèle Morgan together with the doomed Jean Gabin trying to grab happiness in a fog-bound port are typical images associated with the world-weariness in pre-war France. *Daybreak* (*Le Jour se Lève*, 1939), one of the most celebrated of the Carné-Prévert poetic realist films, made memorable use of the dark set and small room in which Gabin, wanted for murder, has barricaded himself. The Nazi Occupation of France forced Carné to make "escapist" films such as *The Devil's Envoys* (*Les Visiteurs du Soir*, 1942) — a medieval fairy tale — and *Children of Paradise* (*Les Enfants du Paradis*, 1945), a richly entertaining evocation of 19th-century Paris. *Gates of the Night* (*Les Portes de la Nuit*, 1946), which marked the end of the Carné-Prévert partnership, failed to take into account the optimistic post-war mood in France, and flopped at the box office. Carné tried to capture old glory with Jean Gabin in *La Marie du Port* (1949), and *The Adultress* (*Thérèse Raquin*, 1953), but he was a spent force and his reputation, despite some youth films, like *The Cheaters* (*Les Tricheurs*, 1958), was swept away by the French New Wave.

Film poster, *1938*

WHAT TO WATCH

1937	Bizarre Bizarre
1938	Port of Shadows
1939	Daybreak
1942	The Devil's Envoys
1945	Children of Paradise

John **Cassavetes**

1929–1989 AMERICAN 1959–1989

17 Drama

Actor-director John Cassavetes is remembered as the godfather of American independent film-makers. Although *Shadows* (1959), his breakthrough film, was not the first American movie made outside the system, it became a rallying point for future generations.

The searing domestic drama *Faces* (1968), which was self-financed, had a great impact when first released. It played for a year in New York and earned Academy Award nominations for its cast of unknowns.

Cassavetes was often labelled an improvisational film-maker, but his films were almost entirely scripted. Yet he had a preference for documentary-style camerawork and was obsessed with human interaction. His wife Gena Rowlands became his muse, appearing in *Minnie and Moskowitz* (1971), *A Woman Under the Influence* (1974), *Opening Night* (1977), *Gloria* (1980), and *Love Streams* (1984).

WHAT TO WATCH	
1959	Shadows
1968	Faces
1971	Minnie and Moskowitz
1980	Gloria

A gangster's moll *(Gena Rowlands) and six year-old Phil (John Adames) are chased across New York by crooks in* Gloria, *an action-packed, character-based film.*

Claude **Chabrol**

1930– FRENCH 1958–

53 Crime

The prolific Claude Chabrol has created an impressive oeuvre of ironic black comedies, and endless variations on the theme of infidelity leading to murder.

Murder, often seen as an inevitable act, is at the heart of most of Claude Chabrol's films. Chabrol mocks the complacency of bourgeois marriage with the added spice of Stephane Audran (his wife from 1964 to 1980) in the role of the victim or the cause of murder. Whatever is seething under the surface of his characters — guilt, jealousy, or crime — the niceties of life go on. Large meals at home or in a restaurant have become his signature scenes. Although Chabrol has always been happy in the mainstream, it was his *Le Beau Serge* (1958), made on location in his own village, that is considered the first film of the New Wave. After Audran, Chabrol found, in Isabelle Huppert, the ideal actress to portray his perverse heroines with murder on their minds.

WHAT TO WATCH	
1959	The Cousins (Les Cousins)
1960	The Good Time Girls (Les Bonnes Femmes)
1969	The Unfaithful Wife (La Femme Infidele)
1982	The Hatter's Ghost (Les Fantômes du Chapelier)
1995	The Ceremony (La Cérémonie)
2000	Nightcap (Merci pour le chocolat)

Stephane Audran *(right) and Bernadette Lafont (left) are the bored Parisian shopgirls longing for better lives in Chabrol's* Les Bonnes Femmes.

Artist extraordinaire *Chaplin behind the camera for* The Gold Rush. *Said to be his favourite film, one famous scene shows the poor hero reduced to eating his shoes.*

Charlie **Chaplin**

1889–1977 | BRITISH | 1921–1967

11 | Comedy, Drama

Born in the Victorian slums of Lambeth in London, Charlie Chaplin died in Switzerland as the wealthy Sir Charles. He became one of the most famous men in the world on the strength of over 60 silent shorts made before 1920, and only a handful of unforgettable features.

In 1913, Chaplin, the son of music-hall performers, went to Mack Sennett's Keystone Studios in Hollywood where he featured in dozens of short slapstick comedies. In *Kid Auto Races at Venice* (1914), he appeared for the first time as the Little Tramp, a character he was to play until 1936. Chaplin was soon directing and writing all his own films, gradually breaking away from the crude techniques of the Sennett comedies. He introduced pathos and a detailed social background into more structured and ambitious farces such as *Easy Street* (1917) and *The Immigrant* (1917). His first feature, *The Kid* (1921) was set in the London slums. *A Woman of Paris* (1923) starred Edna Purviance — his leading lady in almost 30 comedies — as a high-class prostitute. Critically acclaimed and an influence on German director Ernst Lubitsch, it failed at the box-office. The next three films were Chaplin's greatest: *The Gold Rush* (1925), *The Circus* (1928), and *City Lights* (1931) all manage to shift Dickens-like from satire to pathos to comedy.

Feeling that talkies would weaken his international appeal, Chaplin resisted dialogue for 13 years. In *Modern Times* (1936), his voice is heard for the first time — singing gibberish. *The Great Dictator* (1940), his first film to use sound fully, has many comic set-pieces as well as being an attack on Hitler. He continued to experiment with styles in *Monsieur Verdoux* (1947) and *Limelight* (1952), which contains a stunning music-hall sequence.

WHAT TO WATCH

1921	The Kid
1923	A Woman of Paris
1925	The Gold Rush
1931	City Lights
1936	Modern Times
1940	The Great Dictator

Film poster, *1921*

Cheng Dieyi *(Leslie Cheung), one of the male opera stars, plays a concubine in* Farewell My Concubine, *a film that discusses homosexuality and the plight of the individual, against a panorama of Chinese history.*

Kaige **Chen**

1952– CHINESE 1984–

8 Costume drama

Chen was a leading exponent of the "Fifth Generation" of film-makers, whose work after the Chinese Cultural Revolution earned a deserved international reputation.

When Chen Kaige's *Yellow Earth* (*Huang tu di*, 1984) was first shown in the west, it altered western perceptions about Chinese cinema. This heady mixture of music, poetry, dance, and drama told the tale of a soldier in a remote village trying to change traditional superstitious ways. This beautifully photographed film is also notable for its cinematography by Zhang Yimou. Chen continued with further well-conceived meditations on recent Chinese history in *The Big Parade* (*Da yue bing*, 1986), a film about young people preparing to take part in the National Day parade, and *King of the Children* (*Hai zi wang*, 1987), on a teacher in a remote district trying to get his pupils to understand the world around them. His most famous film is *Farewell My Concubine* (*Ba wang bie ji*, 1993), about the friendship of two Beijing Opera stars over 50 years of turbulent Chinese history. Chen is one of a new wave of Chinese film-makers; the often strong political statements in his films have caused the communist regime to ban some of his work.

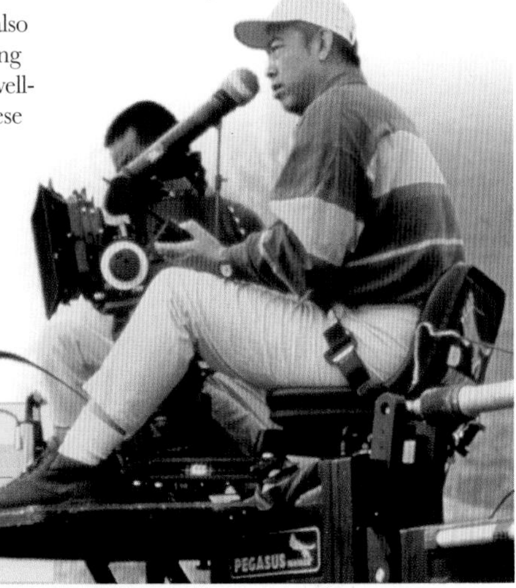

The director *at work on location for* The Empire and the Assassin (Jing ke ci qin wang, *1999); the film's battle scenes were shot at Bashan plateau near Inner Mongolia.*

WHAT TO WATCH

1984	Yellow Earth
1986	The Big Parade
1987	King of the Children
1993	Farewell My Concubine

Michael **Cimino**

1939– AMERICAN 1974–

7 War, Action

There are few more striking examples of a fall from grace in Hollywood than that of Michael Cimino, whose career plunged from universal acclaim with *The Deer Hunter* (1978) to total condemnation with *Heaven's Gate* (1980).

Cimino's second film, *The Deer Hunter*, won five Academy Awards, and caught the mood of the time — the need for the US to come to terms with the Vietnam War. *Heaven's Gate* (1980), made for $40 million, turned out to be the most expensive flop of the time. After critics trashed it, United Artists cut the film from 225 to 148 minutes, which made this sprawling Western even more incoherent. In 1983, it was released at its original length, and was greeted more favorably. "Since then," Cimino has said, "I've been unable to make any movie that I've wanted to make."

Heaven's Gate, *Cimino's sprawling epic set in 1890s Wyoming, was infamous for the extravagance of its vast sets. Compounded with United Artists' other losses at the time, the film's cost led to MGM buying out the studio.*

WHAT TO WATCH

1974	Thunderbolt and Lightfoot
1978	The Deer Hunter
1980	Heaven's Gate

René **Clair**

1898–1981 FRENCH 1923–1965

24 Comedy, Fantasy, Musical

The films of René Clair have the same reputation for gaiety as Paris, the city in which he was born. In the 1920s, he created some of the most original films of early French cinema.

Entr'acte (1924), a 20-minute surrealistic, but playful film shot in Paris and featuring modernist artists, such as Marcel Duchamp, earned Clair the reputation of being a member of the avant-garde. His adaptation of Eugène Labiche's 19th-century farce, *The Italian Straw Hat* (*Un Chapeau de Paille d'Italie*, 1927), in which he substituted many of the play's verbal jokes with visual ones, was made with clockwork precision. His first sound film, *Under the Roofs of Paris* (*Sous les Toits de Paris*, 1930) — one of the very first French talkies — uses songs, sound effects, and street noises (created in the studio).

The musical comedies *The Million* (*Le Million*, 1931) and *Freedom for Us* (*À Nous la Liberté*, 1931) influenced Hollywood musicals in the use of related action and songs, while the latter's satire on the dehumanizing effects of mass production inspired Chaplin's *Modern Times* (1936). Just before the war, Clair left France to work abroad. Whether in Britain (*The Ghost Goes West*, 1935) or in the US (*I Married a Witch*, 1942), he continued in his carefree way. His postwar films include *Beauty and the Devil* (*La Beauté du Diable*, 1950) and, his first film in France for over a decade, *Silence is Golden* (*Le Silence est d'Or* (1947) — a regretful look at silent cinema. Clair's gentle irony is evident in the comedy *Summer Maneuvers* (*Les Grandes Manoeuvres*, 1955), his first film in color.

WHAT TO WATCH

1927	The Italian Straw Hat
1930	Under the Roofs of Paris
1931	The Million
1931	Freedom for Us
1934	The Last Millionaire (Le Dernier Millairdaire)
1935	The Ghost Goes West
1943	It Happened Tomorrow
1952	Night Beauties (Les Belles de Nuit)
1955	Summer Manoeuvres

Film poster, *1932*

Henri-Georges **Clouzot**

1907–1977 | FRENCH | 1942–1968

11 | Thriller

Mainly because of ill health, Henri-Georges Clouzot only made 11 films, most of them exceptionally dark in character with a fine observation of human frailty.

Clouzot's second film, *The Raven* (*Le Corbeau*, 1943), about the effect poison pen letters have on a French village, took a bleak view of provincial life. In 1953, he made the hugely successful *The Wages of Fear* (*Le Salaire de la Peur*), about four truck drivers transporting highly dangerous nitroglycerine. *Diabolique* (*Les Diaboliques*, 1955) is a chilling tale of murder set in a private school. *The Picasso Mystery* (*Le Mystère Picasso*, 1956), which brilliantly captures the painter at work, is an intriguing documentary, while *The Truth* (*La Verité*, 1960) is an awkward coming together of the New Wave Brigitte Bardot with the "old guard."

Christina (Véra Clouzot) *looks on as Nicole (Simone Signoret) prepares to kill her husband by mixing poison in his whisky bottle in* Diabolique.

WHAT TO WATCH

1943	The Raven
1947	Quay of the Goldsmiths
1953	The Wages of Fear
1955	Diabolique
1956	The Picasso Mystery

Jean **Cocteau**

1889–1963 | FRENCH | 1930–1960

6 | Avant-garde, Fantasy

Poet, novelist, playwright, film director, designer, painter, stage director, and ballet producer, Jean Cocteau directed six films that form part of his work in other art forms.

For Cocteau, films were another form of poetry, and the poet is at the center of his *oeuvre*. Cocteau made his first film when he was 41 and already famous. *The Blood of a Poet* (*Le Sang D'un Poète*, 1930) contains all the signs and symbols of his personal mythology evident in his novels, poems, and drawings, such as the death and resurrection of a poet, the link between death and youth, the bullfight, and the living statues. The haunting, witty *Orpheus* (*Orphée*, 1950) is a perfect marriage between Greek myth and Cocteau's own ideas. It elaborates on the theme of the poet caught between the worlds of the real and the imaginary, as is the heroine in *Beauty and the Beast* (*La Belle et la Bête*, 1945). *The Testament of Orpheus* (*Le Testament d'Orphée*, 1960) is a poetic, semi-autobiographical evocation of the director's work.

WHAT TO WATCH

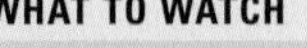

1930	The Blood of a Poet
1945	Beauty and the Beast
1950	Orpheus
1960	The Testament of Orpheus

Josette Day *plays Beauty and Jean Marais stars as the Beast in Cocteau's* Beauty and the Beast.

Joel and Ethan **Coen**

1955– (JOEL) 1957– (ETHAN) AMERICAN

1984– 11 Film noir, Comedy

When Joel and Ethan Coen first burst onto the film scene with *Blood Simple* in 1984, they immediately established their credentials as true descendents of the masters of the American film noir, while putting their own distinctive, often quirky stamp on their films.

The film *Blood Simple* helped ignite the indie film movement from the mid-1980s, representing the opposite of commercial studio film-making. Despite having their movies financed and distributed by major studios, the Coen brothers manage to remain true independents. Nominally, Joel directs and Ethan produces, but as Joel has explained, "We really co-direct the movies. We could just as easily take the credit 'produced, written and directed' by the two of us."

From the start, they showed how profoundly they were imbued with the spirit of the hardboiled school of writers such as James M. Cain, Raymond Chandler, and Dashiell Hammett. However, their films can be appreciated by those who get the references to the novels by these authors, as well as those who enjoy them on a less cerebral level. Crime is the core of their screenplays, but intrinsically they are fables of good versus evil. Most are films noirs disguised as horror (*Blood Simple*), farce (*Raising Arizona*, 1987), gangster movie (*Miller's Crossing*, 1990), psychological drama (*Barton Fink*, 1991), police thriller (*Fargo*, 1996), black comedy (*The Big Lebowski*, 1998), and social drama (*O Brother, Where Art Thou?*, 2000). *The Man Who Wasn't There* (2001), shot in black and white, is their most direct homage to 1940s film noir. However different they are on the surface, each film contains elements of the other: horror edging into comic-strip farce, violence into slapstick, and vice versa. Not content with the tools of conventional narrative, in film after film they have found the appropriate visual style for the subject.

WHAT TO WATCH

1984	Blood Simple
1987	Raising Arizona
1991	Barton Fink
1996	Fargo
1998	The Big Lebowski

John Turturro, *Tim Blake Nelson, and George Clooney star in* O Brother, Where Art Thou?*, an easy-going comedy about escaped convicts.*

Nicolas Cage *plays Hi, a hapless reformed convict who has to steal a baby for his wife in* Raising Arizona*, which features a cast of amusingly dim characters.*

Francis Ford Coppola *(right) pictured with Joe Mantegna on the set of* The Godfather III, *in which Mantegna plays Joey Zasa, a rival of the Corleones.*

Francis Ford **Coppola**

1939– | AMERICAN | 1962–

23 | Gangster, War, Drama

In a career that has been a rollercoaster affair, not only has Francis Ford Coppola always been torn between two extremes of film-making — the massive epic form, and the small, intimate film — but he has fluctuated between mammoth and modest hits as well as failures.

It was Francis Ford Coppola who led the way for other "movie brat" directors, such as Martin Scorsese, George Lucas, and Steven Spielberg, to emerge from film schools and storm into Hollywood in the 1970s. Coppola first worked as writer and assistant director to Roger Corman, who enabled him to direct his first movie, a gruesome cheapie called *Dementia 13* (1963). *You're a Big Boy Now* (1966), a lively comedy about a young man's sexual education, was very much a movie by a 26-year-old of the mid-1960s. In 1969, Coppola opened his own studio, American Zoetrope, after the unhappy experience of making the musical *Finian's Rainbow* (1968) for Warner Bros. *The Conversation* (1974), made for Zoetrope, is a post-Watergate thriller about a professional eavesdropper (Gene Hackman) being under surveillance himself. *The Godfather* (1972) made Coppola one of the world's most bankable directors, while *The Godfather: Part II* (1974) won six Oscars, and is one of the few sequels that is considered better than the original.

With *Apocalypse Now* (1979), Coppola succeeded in his desire to "give its audience a sense of the horror, the madness, the sensuousness and the moral dilemma of the Vietnam War." The film, costing $31 million, took three-and-a-half years to complete and five years to break even. The failure of *One From the Heart* (1982), a $27 million-dollar musical romance filmed on a gigantic set, led Coppola to scale down his ambitions with two teen films, *The Outsiders* and *Rumble Fish* (both 1983), the casts of which now read like a Who's Who for the Brat Pack. *Tucker: The Man and His Dream* (1988), about an entrepreneur's pursuit of a dream, then followed. Coppola returned to familiar territory with *The Godfather: Part III* (1990), concluding a saga that started off as "just another gangster picture" and ended up being one of the great achievements of postwar American cinema.

Film poster, *1979*

WHAT TO WATCH

1972	The Godfather
1974	The Conversation
1974	The Godfather: Part II
1979	Apocalypse Now
1983	The Outsiders
1988	Tucker: The Man and His Dream
1990	The Godfather: Part III

Roger **Corman**

1926– AMERICAN 1954–

46 Horror, Youth, Crime

The self-styled "Orson Welles of the Z movie," Roger Corman became a symbol of independent, low-budget movie-making.

In 1953, Corman started his own production company, and for some time produced and directed sensational movies, such as *She-Gods of Shark Reef* (1956) and *Attack of the Crab Monsters* (1957). In the early 1960s, he made adaptations of works by Edgar Allan Poe — stylish, garish, and amusing shockers in wide-screen and color. The best of these was *The Masque of the Red Death* (1964). Corman also started trends in comic-horror with *A Bucket of Blood* (1959) and *The Little Shop of Horrors* (1960), the latter with Jack Nicholson (his first break) as a masochistic dental patient. He made profitable "youth" movies, such as *Wild Angels* (1966) and *The Trip* (1967), but *The Intruder* (1962) — his only "message" film (about racism in the Deep South) — lost money.

WHAT TO WATCH

1959	A Bucket of Blood
1960	The Fall of the House of Usher
1960	The Little Shop of Horrors
1961	The Pit and the Pendulum
1963	The Raven

In the climactic *scene in* The Fall of the House of Usher, *Madeline (Myrna Fahey) rises from her "death" to kill her brother Roderick (Vincent Price).*

Constantin **Costa-Gavras**

1933– FRENCH 1966–

15 Political thriller

Drawn to political subjects — not so much by the ideas behind them, but by the effect those ideas have on people — Constantin Costa-Gavras believes that enlightenment comes with entertainment.

One of Costa-Gavras' first movies, *The Sleeping Car Murders (Compartiment Tueurs*, 1965) is a hypnotic thriller using breathtaking CinemaScope and black-and-white photography. However, his international success came with *Z* (1969), an exciting and effective condemnation of the right-wing regime in Greece, the country of his birth; it won the 1970 Academy Award for the Best Foreign Film. Because of the film's worldwide success, he was able to continue to make political thrillers. Yves Montand, who had been assassinated in *Z*, is tortured by the Czech police in *The Confession* (*L'Aveu*, 1970), and kidnapped in Uruguay in *State of Siege* (*État de Siège*, 1972). Costa-Gavras' first American film won him the Best Director award at Cannes — *Missing* (1982) depicts a father's anguish when he goes looking for his son who is arrested by the military junta in Chile. He took on another large subject in *Amen* (2002), which dealt with the silence of the Vatican and Pope Pius XII on the mass extermination of Jews.

WHAT TO WATCH

1965	The Sleeping Car Murders
1969	Z
1970	The Confession
1972	State of Siege
1975	Special Section
1982	Missing
1988	Betrayed
2002	Amen

In this chilling *scene from* Missing, *Beth (Sissy Spacek) and her father-in-law Ed Horman (Jack Lemmon) search for her missing husband among the dead in a morgue.*

Wes **Craven**

1939– AMERICAN 1972–

24 Horror

A former humanities professor with a masters degree in philosophy, Wes Craven is one of the more articulate and thoughtful of American directors. Surprisingly, perhaps, with only a couple of minor deviations, he has specialized in the horror genre.

Craven was a film editor in a post-production company before breaking into film-making through sex films, most notably *Together* (1971), co-directed with Sean S. Cunningham, who would go on to create the *Friday the 13th* series. Craven's independently financed *Last House on the Left* (1972) was a grotesque but fiercely intelligent horror movie loosely based on Ingmar Bergman's *The Virgin Spring*. A gang of sadists rape, torture, and murder two 17-year-old girls, then through a series of coincidences find themselves at the mercy of one of the girl's middle-class parents, who pays them back in kind. The divide between rich and poor, city and country, and young and old, and Craven's insistence on the brutalizing effects of violence, reflect the social turmoil of the period and are themes that are echoed in many of his subsequent movies, most obviously in the mutant Western *The Hills Have Eyes* (1977). Most of Craven's output from the 1980s is disposable, with the important exception of *A Nightmare on Elm Street* (1984), which features the bogeyman character Freddy Krueger (Robert Englund), a murdered child abductor who returns in the dreams of his killers' teenage offspring. It was the most original horror movie of the decade. Craven scorned the sequels, save for the smartly self-reflexive *Wes Craven's New Nightmare* (1994). Further in that vein, *Scream* 1, 2, and 3 (1996, 1997, and 2000), worked post-modern variations on done-to-death slasher movies, and *Red Eye* (2005) is a psychological suspense thriller that follows a young woman who is terrorized by a co-passenger on a late-night flight.

Film poster, *1984*

WHAT TO WATCH

1984	A Nightmare on Elm Street
1994	Wes Craven's New Nightmare
1996	Scream
2005	Red Eye

In Scream, *reporter Gale Weathers (Courtney Cox), and college students Randy (Jamie Kennedy) and Sidney (Neve Campbell) are terrorized by a killer in a ghost mask.*

David **Cronenberg**

1943– | CANADIAN | 1969–

18 | Horror, Drama

There is nothing warm or feel-good about David Cronenberg's films, which delight in stomach-churning imagery and voyeurism, linking sex with violence.

They Came from Within (1975), the first Cronenberg horror film to gain wide notice, is about sex-obsessed zombies. *Rabid* (1977) concerns a plague-carrying woman with a taste for human blood; *Scanners* (1981) is a combination of horror, sci-fi, and conspiracy thriller; and *Videodrome* (1982) deals with the effects of on-screen violence. *Crash* (1996), which turns car accidents into sado-masochistic turn-ons, and *A History of Violence* (2005) also explore themes of violence. Cronenberg combines phobias about aging, disease, and deformity, and the potential horrors of technology in *The Fly* (1986) and *Dead Ringers* (1988).

"Be afraid. Be very afraid" *is the tagline for* The Fly, *where a science experiment gone horribly wrong transforms eccentric scientist Seth Brundle (Jeff Goldblum) into a fly.*

WHAT TO WATCH

1981	Scanners
1982	Videodrome
1986	The Fly
1988	Dead Ringers
1996	Crash
2005	A History of Violence

Luisa (Ana Lopez Mercado) *and two teenagers (Diego Luna and Gael Garcia Bernal) learn about life, friendship, and love in the entertaining road movie,* Y Tu Mamá También.

Alfonso **Cuarón**

1961– | MEXICAN | 2001–

5 | Drama

After a stint in Mexican television, Cuarón made the break into Hollywood with his comedy, *Love in the Time of Hysteria* (1991), about a lothario misdiagnosed with AIDS by an ex-lover.

WHAT TO WATCH

1995	A Little Princess
2001	Y Tu Mamá También
2004	Harry Potter and the Prisoner of Azkaban

Cuarón's sensitive treatment of the Victorian children's story *A Little Princess* (1995) was widely admired in the industry (Warner Bros. gave the film a second release after it failed the first time). A modern *Great Expectations* (1998) with Ethan Hawke, Gwyneth Paltrow, and Robert De Niro was a misjudgement. But its failure may have been the best thing to happen to him. Cuarón returned to Mexico and came out with the earthy and liberating *Y Tu Mamá También* (2001), his first international box-office hit. Such versatility led Warner Bros. to entrust him with filming the third book in the Harry Potter series, *Harry Potter and the Prisoner of Azkaban* (2004).

George **Cukor**

1899–1983 | AMERICAN | 1930–1981

55 | Comedy, Musical, Drama

The name George Cukor on movie titles conjures up the image of a sophisticated dinner party where elegant people meet, and the conversation is pitched at exactly the right level — neither vulgar nor highbrow.

George Cukor's career got off to a shaky start when he was taken off an early film (the musical *One Hour with You*, 1932) and replaced by Ernst Lubitsch. Seven years later, Cukor was also taken off *Gone With the Wind*. At MGM, however, he distinguished himself with glossy, literate productions such as *Dinner at Eight* (1933), *David Copperfield* (1935), and *Romeo and Juliet* (1936). It was not long before he gained a reputation as a "woman's director," and even the titles of many of his films reflect this: *Little Women* (1933) and *The Women* (1939), with an all-female cast; *Camille* (1936) and *Two-Faced Woman* (1941) with Greta Garbo; *A Woman's Face* (1941) starring Joan Crawford; *Les Girls* (1957), and *My Fair Lady* (1964), which won him his only Academy Award. His favorite actress, Katharine Hepburn, whom he directed in her first film *A Bill of Divorcement* (1932), was at her most radiant in *Holiday* (1938), her wittiest in *The Philadelphia Story* (1940), and her most affecting in *Sylvia Scarlett* (1935).

Later, Cukor moved into harder-edged comedies such as *Adam's Rib* (1949), *Pat and Mike* (1952), and three Judy Holliday movies, the best of which was *Born Yesterday* (1950). Cukor reached his peak in the 1950s with *A Star is Born* (1954) starring Judy Garland and James Mason, in which his use of lighting, color, and costumes surpassed all other musicals on the CinemaScope screen.

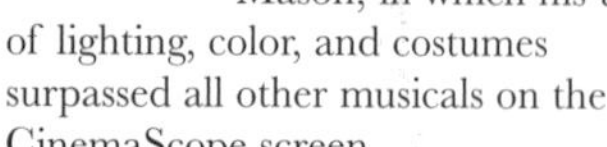

Film poster, *1964*

WHAT TO WATCH

1933	Dinner at Eight
1933	Little Women
1935	Sylvia Scarlett
1935	David Copperfield
1936	Camille
1938	Holiday
1939	The Women
1940	The Philadelphia Story
1949	Adam's Rib
1954	A Star is Born
1964	My Fair Lady

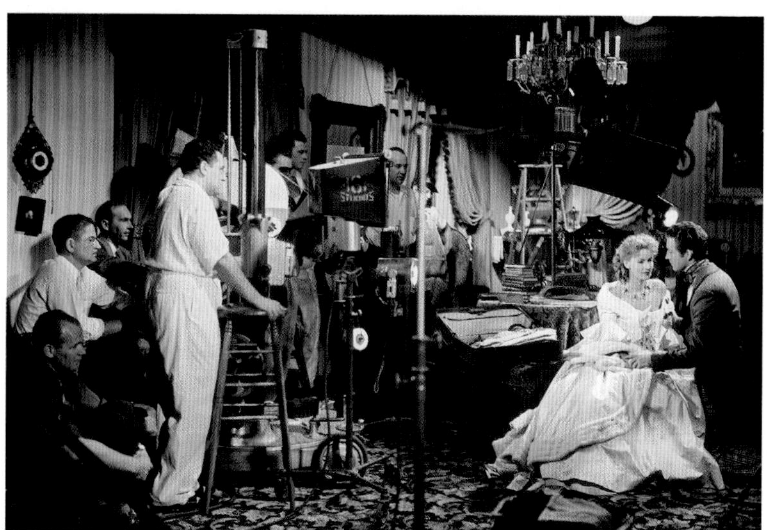

Greta Garbo *and Robert Taylor are directed by Cukor (standing behind the stool) on the set of* Camille. *At the camera is lensman William Daniels.*

Michael **Curtiz**

1888–1962 HUNGARIAN (AMERICAN) 1912–62

160 Drama

Representing the archetypal studio director of Hollywood's golden era, Michael Curtiz, under contract to Warner Bros. for 27 years, turned out more than 150 films of every genre.

During the 1930s and 1940s, Curtiz, who had made many films in Hungary and Austria, was the ideal Warner Brothers director, filming with economy, fluency, and pace. He made over a dozen pictures with Errol Flynn, including some of the star's best swashbucklers, such as *The Adventures of Robin Hood* (1938). He directed James Cagney in *Angels with Dirty Faces* (1938) and *Yankee Doodle Dandy* (1942), for which Cagney won his only Academy Award. Joan Crawford, too, won her sole Academy Award under Curtiz's guidance in *Mildred Pierce* (1945), a superb film noir. His touch was unmistakable in *Casablanca* (1942).

Clarence (William Powell) *and Vinnie (Irene Dunne), with their sons played by Johnny Calkins, Martin Milner, Jimmy Lydon, and Derek Scott in* Life With Father *(1947).*

WHAT TO WATCH

1937	Kid Galahad
1938	The Adventures of Robin Hood
1938	Angels with Dirty Faces
1942	Casablanca

Jules **Dassin**

1911– AMERICAN 1942–1980

24 Film noir, Drama

The reputation of Jules Dassin rests on five crime thrillers, three of which were made in Hollywood before he was forced to leave the United States for political reasons.

An ineffectual mixture of comedies and dramas characterized Jules Dassin's early films until he made *Brute Force* (1947), a tough prison drama. Realizing his talent lay in film noir, Dassin made *The Naked City* (1948) and *Thieves' Highway* (1949), both distinguished by their dramatic use of locations, as was *Night and the City* (1950), set in a sleazy London milieu. After Dassin settled in France, he directed *Rififi* (1956), a much-imitated heist movie celebrated for its tense, meticulously enacted 22-minute robbery sequence without dialogue. When he married Greek actress Melina Mercouri, his career changed direction. She was his star, in the role of a prostitute in both *He Who Must Die* (1957) and *Never on Sunday* (1960) — the latter remembered for its *bouzouki* music — and in updated Greek classics such as *Phaedra* (1962). In *Topkapi* (1964), a comedy-thriller about a hold-up in the Istanbul museum, he revisited the heist theme with great success.

Richard Widmark *in a scene from* Night and the City *(1950). Considered one of Dassin's best films, it shows a seamy side of London neglected by British directors.*

WHAT TO WATCH

1947	Brute Force
1948	The Naked City
1949	Thieves' Highway
1950	Night and the City
1956	Rififi
1957	He Who Must Die
1960	Never on Sunday
1964	Topkapi

Cecil B. **DeMille**

1881–1959 AMERICAN 1914–1956

72 Epic, Western, Comedy, Melodrama

A name that evokes the image of a larger-than-life showman is Cecil B. DeMille, who made grandiose Biblical epics. However, his films covered much wider ground during Hollywood's "Golden Age."

After a few Westerns, including *The Squaw Man* (1913), one of the first major films produced in Hollywood, Cecil Blount DeMille brought Metropolitan Opera soprano Geraldine Farrar from New York to play *Carmen* (1915). In 1918, he made a series of risqué domestic comedies, six of them starring Gloria Swanson. These were followed by *The Ten Commandments* (1923), which parallels the biblical story with a modern one. Sex and religion were bedfellows in *King of Kings* (1927), *The Sign of the Cross* (1932), and *The Crusades* (1935). His only musical, *Madam Satan* (1930), featured a bizarre party sequence on a Zeppelin. The milk bath in *Cleopatra* (1934) with Claudette Colbert highlighted his obsession with bathtub scenes.

DeMille's best period was from 1937 to 1947, during which he directed *The Plainsman* (1937), *North West Mounted Police* (1940), and *Unconquered* (1947), all starring Gary Cooper. Lively, unsubtle, patriotic celebrations of the pioneers of America, they extolled strength, perseverance, and forthright manliness. DeMille saw himself as a pioneer too, and he would narrate many of his films in a grandiloquent manner. He returned to the Bible with *Samson and Delilah* (1949). When receiving praise for the climactic destruction of the temple, DeMille claimed modestly, "Credit is due to the Book of Judges, not me." He was attracted to the circus, and *The Greatest Show on Earth* (1952) was his first film set in contemporary times since 1934. Before he died, he was planning *Be Prepared,* an epic story of the boy-scout movement.

WHAT TO WATCH

1915	The Cheat
1923	The Ten Commandments
1934	Cleopatra
1937	The Plainsman
1939	Union Pacific
1942	Reap the Wild Wind
1947	Unconquered
1949	Samson and Delilah
1952	The Greatest Show on Earth
1956	The Ten Commandments

Film poster, *1938*

Charlton Heston *as Moses in* The Ten Commandments; *DeMille's grandiose remake featured a cast of thousands and gigantic sets.*

Jonathan **Demme**

1944– AMERICAN 1974–

22 Thriller

A promising director for many years, Jonathan Demme finally broke into the big time with *The Silence of the Lambs* (1991).

Demme directed three low-budget movies before *Citizens Band* (1977) gained attention. He had successes with *Melvin and Howard* (1980), about the friendship between multi-millionaire Howard Hughes and a gas-station attendant, and *Married to the Mob* (1988), but nothing prepared the film world for *The Silence of the Lambs*, an eerie psychological thriller that manages, despite its gruesome subjects of serial killing and cannibalism, to avoid sensationalism. It gained five Academy Awards, including Best Picture and Best Actor. Demme followed this with *Philadelphia* (1993), the first mainstream movie to deal specifically with AIDS.

WHAT TO WATCH

1980	Melvin and Howard
1988	Married to the Mob
1991	The Silence of the Lambs
1993	Philadelphia
1998	Beloved

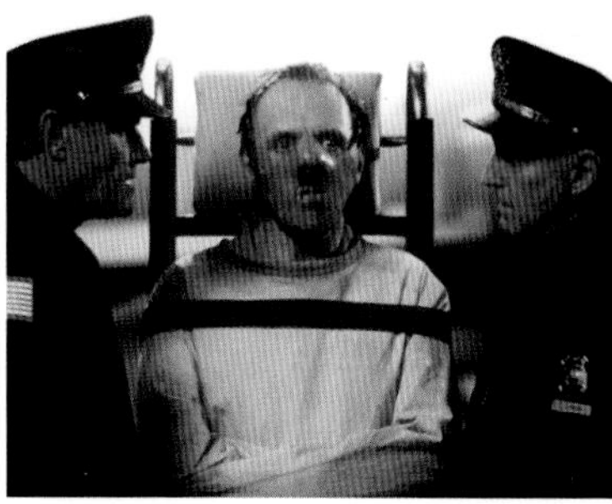

Anthony Hopkins *delivers an Academy Award-winning performance as Dr. Hannibal Lecter, a psychiatrist turned psychopath, who helps a female FBI trainee track a notorious serial killer in* The Silence of the Lambs.

Jacques **Demy**

1931–1990 FRENCH 1961–1988

12 Fantasy, Musical

A whimsical purveyor of modern fairytales, Jacques Demy was one of the rare French directors to make musicals.

Demy was brought up in Nantes (see his widow Agnès Varda's film, *Jacquot de Nantes*, 1991), where his first film, *Lola* (1961), was set. Its circular construction, frothiness, and long tracking shots are reminiscent of Max Ophüls, the film's dedicatee. It owes as much to Stanley Donen and Gene Kelly's musical comedy *On The Town* (1949), with its sailors on leave, chance meetings, and fleeting love. *The Young Girls of Rochefort* (*Les Demoiselles de Rochefort*, 1967) was a direct homage to the MGM musical, a fact that was underlined by the casting of Gene Kelly. In his enchanting musical, *The Umbrellas of Cherbourg* (*Les Parapluies de Cherbourg*, 1964), the dialogue is sung to Michel Legrand's music. In contrast, *Bay of Angels* (*La Baie des Anges*, 1963), a love story set on the French Riviera, is one of the most vivid evocations of gambling fever on film, while *Model Shop* (1969), Demy's only US film, continues the story of *Lola*.

Catherine Deneuve *and Anne Vernon in a scene from* The Umbrellas of Cherbourg, *Demy's colorful musical, which catapulted Deneuve to stardom.*

WHAT TO WATCH

1961	Lola
1963	Bay of Angels
1964	The Umbrellas of Cherbourg
1969	Model Shop
1971	Donkey Skin

Brian **De Palma**

1940– AMERICAN 1967–

28 Gangster, Thriller, Action

Early in his career, Brian De Palma gained a reputation as a "Hitchcock imitator," a description he gradually shook off with his own violent, kinetic thrillers.

The films *Sisters* (1973), *Carrie* (1976), *Obsession* (1976), *Dressed to Kill* (1980), *Blow Out* (1981), and *Body Double* (1984), all contain aspects of Alfred Hitchcock's *Psycho*, *Vertigo*, and *Rear Window* — girls in showers, voyeuristic killers, sexual obsessions, and women in peril. The films demonstrate a mature command of manipulative cinema, particularly cross-cutting and split-screen techniques. Among these, *Carrie*, which launched Sissy Spacek to stardom, was one of De Palma's greatest hits. Less Hitchcockian were his gangster movies, *The Untouchables* (1987), which won a Best Supporting Actor Academy Award for Sean Connery, *Scarface* (1983), and *Carlito's Way* (1993). These films showed a personal stamp, being full of tour-de-force sequences, and allowing actors like Al Pacino (in the latter two movies) to be at their most compelling.

The eponymous heroine *Carrie (Sissy Spacek) unleashes horrifying revenge in the final scene of* Carrie, *adapted from Stephen King's novel.*

Mission: Impossible (1996), adapted from the 1960s television series by De Palma, was a huge success. Typical of his flamboyant camera work is the opening scene from *Snake Eyes* (1998), in which a politician is assassinated in full view of the huge crowd at a boxing match.

Lobby card, *1993*

WHAT TO WATCH

1973	Sisters
1976	Carrie
1983	Scarface
1987	The Untouchables
1993	Carlito's Way
1996	Mission: Impossible

A publicity still *from* The Untouchables, *with Charles Martin Smith, Kevin Costner, Sean Connery, and Andy Garcia as the men who hunt down gangster Al Capone, played to perfection by Robert De Niro.*

Vittorio **De Sica**

1901–1974 ITALIAN 1940–1974

26 Neoralist drama, Melodrama, Comedy

The director *standing behind his cameraman at an outdoor shoot of* Umberto D.*, a poignant, lyrical tale about an old man's struggle to retain his dignity in the face of poverty.*

The neorealist films of Vittorio De Sica changed the face of Italian cinema, and the director claimed that, "my films are a word in favour of the poor and unhappy and against the indifference of society towards suffering."

A successful stage and film actor throughout the 1920s and 1930s, De Sica directed four light comedies before making a sudden breakthrough with the dramatic, humane, and sharply realistic *The Children Are Watching Us* (*I Bambini ci Guardano*, 1942), one of the first Italian neorealist films. It was De Sica's first important collaboration with the writer Cesare Zavattini, who worked on many of his films. Together they believed in the responsibility of the camera to observe real life as it is lived without the traditional compromises of entertaining narratives.

De Sica proved himself a sensitive director of children again in *Shoeshine* (*Sciuscià*, 1946), set in Rome during the Allied Occupation and dealing with the main theme of the neorealist — poverty in post-war Italy. Using non-actors in real locations, it was an international sensation, and the first non-English language film to win an honorary Academy Award (until 1956, foreign films were given non-competitive awards). Yet, De Sica had to raise the money himself for *Bicycle Thief* (*Ladri di Biciclette*, 1948), his most famous film. *Miracle in Milan* (*Miracolo a Milano*, 1951), set in a shanty town where the poor get all they desire, prefigured the work of Federico Fellini and Pier Paolo Pasolini. Following *Umberto D.* (1952), an ode to his father, De Sica returned to comedy. However, *Two Women* (*La Ciociara*, 1960), which gained Sophia Loren a Best Actress Academy Award, was a stark tale of a mother and her daughter trying to survive in Italy in 1943. His next notable film was *The Garden of the Finzi-Continis (Il Giardino dei Finzi-Contini,* 1970*)*, about Italy's involvement in the Holocaust — it won the Academy Award for Best Foreign Film.

WHAT TO WATCH

1946	Shoeshine
1948	Bicycle Thieves
1951	Miracle in Milan
1952	Umberto D.
1960	Two Women
1970	The Garden of the Finzi-Continis

Stanley **Donen**

1924– AMERICAN 1949–

27 Musical, Thriller, Comedy

A dancer and choreographer on Broadway, Stanley Donen came to Hollywood and made a spectacular success of staging numbers for MGM musicals, working with Gene Kelly on four films.

Having been given the chance to direct a film together, Stanley Donen and Gene Kelly came up with the joyous and innovative *On the Town* (1949). Conceived balletically, it follows three sailors on leave for 24 hours in New York — the opening number was actually shot in that "wonderful town." This was followed by one of the greatest Hollywood musicals; *Singin' in the Rain* (1952) and a third collaboration with Kelly, *It's Always Fair Weather* (1955), about three GIs who reunite after World War II, only to find they have nothing in common. His solo work includes the exuberant *Seven Brides for Seven Brothers* (1954) and *Funny Face* (1957), notable for their visual quality. With the demise of the Hollywood musical, Donen made two chic, effective Hitchcockian thrillers, *Charade* (1963) and *Arabesque* (1966), as well as entertaining comedies, such as *Indiscreet* (1958), *Surprise Package* (1960), and the comedy-drama *Two for the Road* (1967), which follows the marital ups and downs of a British couple.

Gene Kelly *and Stanley Donen hammer out the details on the set of* Singin' in the Rain; *Kelly not only played one of the leads but also co-directed the film with Donen.*

Albert Finney *and Audrey Hepburn sizzle as a married couple in* Two for the Road, *one of Stanley Donen's finest films.*

Film poster, *1954*

WHAT TO WATCH

1949	On the Town (with Gene Kelly)
1952	Singin' in the Rain (with Gene Kelly)
1954	Seven Brides for Seven Brothers
1955	It's Always Fair Weather (with Gene Kelly)
1957	Funny Face
1963	Charade
1967	Two for the Road

Alexander **Dovzhenko**

1894–1956 UKRAINIAN 1926–1948

13 Drama

The films of Alexander Dovzhenko, who was brought up on a farm in Ukraine, are lyrical panegyrics to the life and history of the area.

The first of Alexander Dovzhenko's films on which he had total freedom was *Zvenigora* (1927), an allegory, which was the last flowering of the exciting avant-garde Russian cinema. His next three films were political poems dedicated to his homeland. *Arsenal* (1929), about collectivization, greatly influenced movements abroad; *Earth (Zemlya,* 1930) a pastoral symphony, creates the indelible vision of a rural paradise gained with the blood of the peasants; and *Ivan* (1932), his first sound film, describes the building of a hydroelectric project. Despite bureaucratic interference, his later films still retain a brisk pace and luminous photography.

Earth, Dovzhenko's masterpiece, *in which the director lingers lovingly on the land and its people, bringing together lyrical images of birth, life, and death.*

WHAT TO WATCH

1927	Zvenigora
1929	Arsenal
1930	Earth
1932	Ivan
1935	Frontier (Aerograd)

Carl **Dreyer**

1889–1968 DANISH 1919–1964

24 Drama

In the relatively few films he made over half a century, Carl Dreyer used deceptively simple means to achieve powerful effects and a restrained emotional intensity.

One of the first of Dreyer's mature works, *Chained* (1924), is close to German Expressionism, while the feminist *Master of the House (Du skal ære din hustru,* 1925) is more naturalistic — yet they both have a formal beauty. This quality is clear in *The Passion of Joan of Arc (La Passion de Jeanne d'Arc,* 1928), his ground-breaking silent film, made in France. *The Vampire (Vampyr,* 1932) makes most other horror films pale into insignificance, and *Day of Wrath (Vredens dag,* 1943) follows a witch hunt in 17th-century Denmark, when a parson's wife is denounced for witchcraft. The film was thought to be an allegory for occupied Denmark, and Dreyer had to seek refuge in Sweden until after the war. *The Word* (*Ordet,* 1955), about a miraculous resurrection in a rural household, is an extraordinary expression of spiritual optimism. *Gertrud* (1964), which tells the story of an opera singer and her relationships with several lovers, was made after a ten-year break from directing. Dreyer's last film, it radiates a deep and affecting atmosphere of serenity.

WHAT TO WATCH

1925	Master of the House
1928	The Passion of Joan of Arc
1932	The Vampire
1943	Day of Wrath
1955	The Word
1964	Gertrud

In The Vampire, *Dreyer's brilliant use of shadow, light, camera movement, and settings creates an unnerving and chilling atmosphere of suspense.*

Clint **Eastwood**

1930– | AMERICAN | 1971–

25 | Western, Thriller, Action, Drama

After making his name as an actor in the 1950s and 1960s, Clint Eastwood emerged as a director in the early 1970s, gradually gaining admiration and awards for his range of movies, particularly his personal Westerns.

Clint Eastwood *plays Frankie Dunn, an aging trainer, and Hillary Swank plays Maggie, a waitress who takes up boxing to escape her past, in* Million Dollar Baby.

In Italy in the mid-1960s, three Sergio Leone Spaghetti Westerns launched Clint Eastwood's film-acting career. Back in the United States, he made five films for Don Siegel in which he continued to play loners, notably the diffident detective Harry Callahan in *Dirty Harry* (1971). There are elements of Leone and Siegel in his own films as actor-director. Siegel's influence is evident in his first feature, *Play Misty for Me* (1971), a chilling misogynistic thriller, and Leone's in *High Plains Drifter* (1973), a moody, stylishly self-conscious Western, in which Eastwood protects a town from outlaws. But Eastwood soon came into his own in Westerns with a vein of self-mockery, often revealing flaws in his macho image. *The Outlaw Josey Wales* (1976), *Bronco Billy* (1980), *Pale Rider* (1985), his most classic Western, and the Academy Award-winning *Unforgiven* (1992), are the summation of his career as director and star of the genre. Along the way, he showed his versatility by making cop movies: *Sudden Impact* (1983), in which he returned to his Dirty Harry character, *The Rookie* (1990), and *Mystic River* (2003); biopics: *Bird* (1987) about jazzman Charlie Parker, and *White Hunter, Black Heart* (1990) about film director John Huston (played by Eastwood); love stories: *The Bridges of Madison County* (1995); and a boxing drama, *Million Dollar Baby* (2004), another Academy Award winner.

Film poster, *1976*

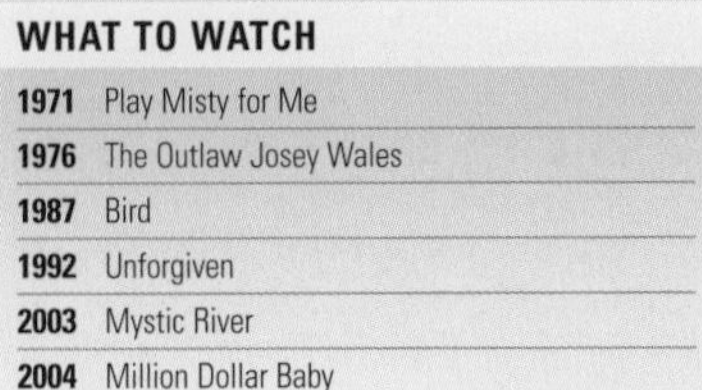

WHAT TO WATCH

1971	Play Misty for Me
1976	The Outlaw Josey Wales
1987	Bird
1992	Unforgiven
2003	Mystic River
2004	Million Dollar Baby

A devastated Jimmy *(Sean Penn) learns of his daughter's murder in* Mystic River; *Eastwood's standout direction makes this multi-layered film hauntingly real.*

Inspector Clouseau (Peter Sellers) *and his wife (Capucine) in* The Pink Panther. *Sellers' portrayal of the simple-minded French police inspector who speaks in a ridiculous accent was his most famous comic character.*

Blake **Edwards**

1922– AMERICAN 1955–

37 Comedy, Drama

Almost the whole of Blake Edwards' career is built on the *Pink Panther* movies and a number of bittersweet comedies starring his wife, Julie Andrews.

Among the first films Blake Edwards directed was *This Happy Feeling* (1958), a title that sums up much of his work. *The Pink Panther* (1964) started a series of eight films, six starring Peter Sellers as the clumsy Inspector Clouseau. Edwards also featured Julie Andrews in seven films, including *10* (1979) and *Victor/Victoria* (1982), one of the best gay comedies in both senses of the word. But it was *Breakfast at Tiffany's* (1961), a tender version of the Truman Capote short story, with an enchanting Audrey Hepburn as Holly Golightly, that made his name in cinema. A departure from comedy, *Days of Wine and Roses* (1963) is a surprisingly bleak, realistic portrayal of alcoholism, with Jack Lemmon in one of his meatiest roles.

WHAT TO WATCH

1959	Operation Petticoat
1961	Breakfast at Tiffany's
1963	Days of Wine and Roses
1964	The Pink Panther
1982	Victor/Victoria

AUDREY HEPBURN

The elfin-featured Audrey Hepburn (1929–93) provided an antidote to the trend for the fuller figure of the 1950s. In her first American film, *Roman Holiday* (1953), she received the Best Actress Oscar for her performance as the incognito princess who finds romance with a newspaperman. As an innocent, she was often courted by older men such as Humphrey Bogart in *Sabrina* (1954), Gary Cooper in *Love in the Afternoon* (1957), and Fred Astaire in Stanley Donen's *Funny Face* (1957). She was also perfectly cast as the childlike Natasha in *War and Peace* (1956) opposite her first husband, Mel Ferrer, and was effective as the Belgian nun who questions her faith in *The Nun's Story* (1959). She sang "Moon River" touchingly in *Breakfast at Tiffany's* (1961), but was dubbed for the songs in *My Fair Lady* (1964), although she was still ravishing in the role. Hepburn is remembered today for her sense of style as much as for her acting.

Sergei **Eisenstein**

1898–1948 RUSSIAN 1925–1944

7 Propaganda, Avant-garde, Epic

One of the undisputed geniuses of cinema, Sergei Eisenstein was not only a leading practitioner of his art, but its principal theorist. Despite strict Soviet government guidelines, he was able to set his personal stamp on the seven features he was allowed to complete.

In Eisenstein's first film, *Strike (Stachka*, 1924), many of his stylistic devices were already in evidence: caricature, visual metaphors, and shock cutting — a factory boss uses a lemon squeezer as police move in on striking workers and shots of a slaughterhouse are cut in as the police mow them down. What Eisenstein defined as "dynamic montage" (rapid cutting) is used to devastating effect in the "Odessa Steps" sequence in *The Battleship Potemkin* (*Bronenosets Potyomkin*, 1925).

The "intellectual montage," based on Eisenstein's editing technique, at which the audience must not only react emotionally but be shocked into thinking, was perfected in *October (Oktyabr*, 1927). The number of

The face *of a factory owner, who refuses workers' demands, is juxtaposed with that of a monkey in* Strike, *illustrating Eisenstein's use of visual metaphors.*

shots — 3,200 — was more than double those of *Potemkin* and more than probably any other film. The emotional and rhythmic composition shows the storming of the Winter Palace, the dismemberment of the Tsar's statue, and a dead white horse sliding off a drawbridge into the river. It completed Eisenstein's trilogy of the Russian Revolution through which several motifs reappear, especially that of turning wheels representing change, *Strike* ending in defeat, *The Battleship Potemkin* in partial triumph, and *October* in ultimate victory. However, *October* displeased those in power who felt that Eisenstein was unwise to allow himself to experiment with a film whose subject matter was as sensitive as that of the revolution. Eisenstein tried to appease

MONTAGE

In 1920, *The Birth of a Nation* was shown in Moscow and, according to Eisenstein, "It played a massive role in the development of montage in the Soviet film." Later, he went far beyond D.W. Griffith's use of cross-cutting and parallel action. Yet several years before Eisenstein, Lev Kuleshov was articulating what seems basic to us today — that the arrangement of individual shots in the cutting room (montage) is central to cinema. Kuleshov arrived at montage almost by accident because a shortage of film during the Civil War years led him to experiment with making new movies by cutting up and rearranging parts of old ones.

A woman shot in the face by Cossacks after protesting against the soldiers during the massacre on the Odessa Steps in *The Battleship Potemkin.*

the party with *The General Line (Staroye i Novoye, 1928)*, but could not restrain his ironic humor, such as in the mock marriage of a cow and a bull, and when the milk hovers for a moment in a cream-separator before it orgasmically splatters onto a woman's face.

In 1931, the left-wing American novelist Upton Sinclair agreed to finance *Que Viva Mexico* (1931), intended as a four-part semi-documentary on Mexican life and history, but Eisenstein overran the time and the budget. The money was withdrawn, and he never got to edit the material he had shot. Today it exists in various re-edited forms and its baroque images tinged with eroticism make one regret the loss. Charged with "formalism" in the unfinished *Bezhin Meadow* (*Bezhin Lug*, 1936), Eisenstein recanted by making the patriotic spectacle *Alexander Nevsky (Aleksandr Nevskiy*, 1938), a richly enjoyable epic with stirring images and a dramatic use of Prokofiev's music, especially in the famous "Battle of the Ice" sequence.

Eisenstein (fourth left) *directs the cast of* Ivan the Terrible Part II *during the winter of 1943 in Kazakhstan.*

Taking his imagery from grand opera, kabuki theater, and Shakespearean and Russian icons, Eisenstein embarked on the three parts of *Ivan the Terrible (Ivan Groznyy I, II,* 1944–1946), but only two were completed. Stalin approved Part I, but as Ivan's character became more complex, he turned against it, perhaps recognizing something of himself in it. Part II was not shown until 10 years after both Eisenstein's and Stalin's deaths. *Ivan the Terrible* is the peak of Eisenstein's achievement, fulfilling his ambitions of achieving a synthesis of all the arts.

Soviet leader Lenin *(Vasili Nikandrov) sits in conference with his comrades in* October. *Shot in documentary style, the film celebrates the 10th anniversary of the Revolution.*

WHAT TO WATCH

1924	Strike
1925	The Battleship Potemkin
1927	October
1928	The General Line (or The Old and the New)
1938	Alexander Nevsky
1944	Ivan the Terrible Part I
1946	Ivan the Terrible Part II (released 1958)

Rainer Werner **Fassbinder**

1946–1982 | GERMAN | 1969–1982

30 | Melodrama

Almost a one-man film industry, Rainer Werner Fassbinder made dozens of films in about 12 years: a surprising, consistent, entertaining, probing, and lively output.

With friends from the Munich Action Theatre Group, Rainer Werner Fassbinder began making films in 1969, rapidly becoming a part of the new generation of young directors who put German cinema back on the map after 30 years. Often starring his favorite actress Hanna Schygulla, Fassbinder's films reveal a heartless, avaricious postwar Germany. The characters tend to be frustrated by the barrenness of urban existence, sometimes turning to violence, as in *The Third Generation (Die Dritte Generation,* 1979), which focuses on a Berlin terrorist group. One of the many Fassbinder films to use Douglas Sirk's Hollywood melodramas as its prime model, *Fear Eats the Soul (Angst essen Seele auf,* 1973) borrows the plot from *All That Heaven Allows* (1955), showing a lonely ageing woman having an affair with a younger Arab man. Women are generally at the center of his films, and *The Marriage of Maria Braun (Die Ehe der Maria Braun,* 1978), *Lola* (1981), and *Veronika Voss (Die Sehnsucht der Veronika Voss,* 1982) all present women trying to survive in an ironically evoked Germany. A more flamboyant style is used in these recreations of an era than the static camera set-ups of his earlier films. Sexuality as a means for the strong to manipulate the weak is a frequent motif, whether showing heterosexuality — *Effi Briest* (1974) and *Lili Marleen* (1980) — or homosexuality — *The Bitter Tears of Petra Von Kant (Die Bitteren Tränen der Petra von Kant,* 1972), and *Fox (Faustrecht der Freiheit,* 1975).

Schygulla (Karin) *and Margit Cartensen (Petra) star in the beautifully visualized* The Bitter Tears of Petra Von Kant, *based on Fassbinder's own play about desire and power.*

WHAT TO WATCH

1971	The Merchant of Four Seasons
1972	The Bitter Tears of Petra Von Kant
1973	Fear Eats the Soul
1974	Effi Briest
1975	Fox
1975	Mother Küsters' Trip To Heaven
1978	The Marriage of Maria Braun
1978	In a Year of Thirteen Moons
1981	Lola
1982	Veronika Voss

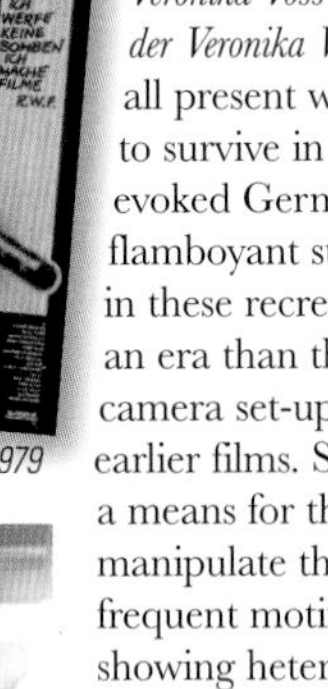

Film poster, *1979*

In his brief life, *Fassbinder directed more than 40 productions, including television and stage work. He also wrote, edited, photographed, and produced many of his films.*

Fellini directs *Richard Basehart as "The Fool" who walks the tightrope in* La Strada, *a film the director called "the complete catalogue of my entire mythological world." Anthony Quinn was the other American in the film.*

Federico **Fellini**

1920–1993 ITALIAN 1950–1990

19 Comedy, Drama

A magnificent ringmaster, Federico Fellini created a world that was rather like a circus, peopled by grotesque or innocent clowns.

For 12 years, after he came to Rome from his home town of Rimini, Fellini wrote film scripts, many for Roberto Rossellini. But unlike Rossellini, Fellini was never a neorealist, and established his own mythology when he started directing. He commented, "If the cinema didn't exist I might have become a circus director," and it could also be said that if the circus did not exist, he might not have become a film director. The circus as metaphor (and reality) plays an important role in his films. In *La Strada* (1954), Giulietta Masina (Fellini's wife) plays an innocent white-faced clown, brutally mistreated by a traveling strongman (Anthony Quinn), who realizes he loves her only when she dies. The film, the first to win the Academy Award for Best Foreign Language Film, made Fellini internationally known. Fellini used Masina's Chaplinesque persona as the "innocent" prostitute once again in *Nights of Cabiria*, (*Le Notti di Cabiria*, 1956). Marcello Mastroianni plays Fellini's alter ego in *La Dolce Vita* (1959) and in *8½* (1963), the title referring to the number of Fellini's films (including collaborations). This calculated self-portrait remains a compendium of every Fellini theme and stylistic device. An autobiographical aspect was also evident in *I Vitelloni* (1953), set in the seaside town of his birth; *Roma* (1972); and *Amarcord* (1973), an affectionate, dreamlike view of the past.

Mastroianni plays Guido Anselmi, *a film director with a creative block in 8½, in which Fellini creates a complex narrative, interspersing fantasy with reality.*

WHAT TO WATCH

1953	I Vitelloni
1954	La Strada
1959	La Dolce Vita
1963	8½
1965	Julietta of the Spirits (Giulietta degli Spiriti)
1972	Roma
1973	Amarcord
1976	Casanova

David **Fincher**

1962– AMERICAN 1995–

6 Thriller

In *Fight Club* (1999), David Fincher made arguably the most subversive mainstream movie of its time — an all-out anarchic assault on consumerism, capitalism, and even civilization itself.

If the themes for *Fight Club* were already in Chuck Palahniuk's cult novel, there is no doubt that Fincher (a very successful commercials director) heartily embraced the material. There is a similar morbid misanthropy in the ill-starred *Alien 3* (which Fincher disowned) and the dark serial killer thriller *Se7en* (1995), a singularly bleak and macabre film, with a "noir" twist reminiscent of the shocking endings of Argentinian writer Jorge Luis Borges's short stories. Borges might also have appreciated *The Game* (1997), about a live-action game taken too far, although he would have been in a minority. Fincher seemed surprised and stung by the hostile reception to *Fight Club*, which was released at a time when there was concern about movie violence, following shootings at Columbine High School in Littleton, Colorado. *Panic Room* (2002) was a retreat, a purely formal exercise in locked room suspense, but Fincher returned to the serial killer theme with *Zodiac* (2006).

WHAT TO WATCH	
1995	Se7en
1999	Fight Club
2002	Panic Room
2006	Zodiac

Film poster, *1995*

Robert **Flaherty**

1884–1951 AMERICAN 1922–1949

8 Documentary

Considered by many to be the father of the documentary film, Robert Flaherty expressed his view of the importance of primitive societies and the balance between man and nature in his silent era films.

Flaherty made his first full documentary feature, *Nanook of the North* (1922), by living with the Inuit for 16 months. Because of the film's huge success, Paramount asked Flaherty to make a "Nanook" of the South Seas. He spent two years in the Samoan Islands making *Moana* (1926) and filmed an Eden, unlike the cold hell of the Arctic, where noble savages hunt, fish, and cook.

Gainsborough Studios gave him a free hand on *Man of Aran* (1934), and he spent a further two years living with the Aran islanders off the coast of Ireland, documenting their harsh daily lives. Although uncompleted, *The Land* (1942) marked Flaherty's aesthetic departure from depicting exotic communities to documenting more known landscapes. It prepared the ground for *Louisiana Story* (1948), a poetic slice of Americana that describes the drilling for oil in the Louisiana swamplands as seen through the eyes of a young boy.

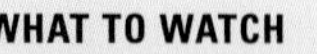

WHAT TO WATCH	
1922	Nanook of the North
1926	Moana
1934	Man of Aran
1948	Louisiana Story

Joseph Boudreaux *plays a young Cajun boy, with his pet raccoon, in* Louisiana Story, *which explores man's relationship with the environment.*

Victor **Fleming**

1883–1949 AMERICAN 1920–1948

45 Various

A first-rate craftsman, and part of an expert team, Victor Fleming happened to be at MGM at the right time to direct *Gone With the Wind* (1939) and *The Wizard of Oz* (1939).

Although Fleming is credited as director of two of the most popular films ever, they are seldom cited as his movies. The reason for this is that they are perceived as producer and studio-dominated creations: much of *Gone With the Wind* was conceived by producer David O. Selznick, George Cukor shot at least three long sequences, and Sam Wood completed it when Fleming fell ill during shooting. King Vidor directed the black-and-white sequences in *The Wizard of Oz*, but Fleming made an excellent job of the rest. Actors liked working with him, and he secured inspired performances from Gary Cooper in *The Virginian* (1929), Clark Gable in *Red Dust* (1932), and Spencer Tracy, who won an Academy Award for *Captains Courageous* (1937), as well as his leading actresses, such as Jean Harlow in *Red Dust* and *Bombshell* (1933).

Clark Gable and the sultry *Jean Harlow star in* Red Dust, *a steamy romance set in Indo-China. Gable became one of MGM's hottest properties.*

WHAT TO WATCH

1925	Lord Jim
1929	The Virginian
1932	Red Dust
1933	Bombshell
1934	Treasure Island
1937	Captains Courageous
1939	Gone With the Wind
1939	The Wizard of Oz

Dorothy (Judy Garland) *follows the Yellow Brick Road with the Tin Man (Jack Haley), the Scarecrow (Ray Bolger), and the Cowardly Lion (Bert Lahr) in* The Wizard of Oz.

John **Ford**

1895–1973 AMERICAN 1917–1966

122 Western, Drama

It was John Ford (Sean Aloysius O'Feeney) who, more than anyone else, gave the Western an epic stature, and raised it to artistic status. He created a personal, recognizable world that is an essential part of American culture.

The Westerns made by John Ford are romantic visions of the Old West. They are mythical views of America's past, where men are heroes, defending the lives of women and children in the fort, community, or homestead. The births, deaths, funerals, weddings, and dances are punctuated by songs (often sung by cavalry officers as they ride out against Indians) and drunken brawls. It was from 1939, with *Stagecoach*, that the true Ford Western emerged. His relatively few ventures out of America included two films set in Ireland: *The Informer* (1935), an atmospheric drama that takes place during the Irish Rebellion, and *The Quiet Man* (1952), a romance. These, and *How Green Was My Valley* (1941), set in Wales, won John Ford the Academy Award for Best Director.

At the climax of The Searchers, *Ethan Edwards (John Wayne) leaves his relatives' home to return to his lonely life in the great outdoors.*

WHAT TO WATCH

1939	Stagecoach
1939	Young Mr. Lincoln
1940	The Grapes of Wrath
1948	Fort Apache
1956	The Searchers
1962	The Man Who Shot Liberty Valance

In the 1930s, Ford used Henry Fonda's noble, youthful character to excellent effect as the epitome of American idealism, especially as *Young Mr. Lincoln* (1939) and as Tom Joad in *The Grapes of Wrath* (1940). During World War II, Ford made a series of morale-boosting documentaries, then returned to Westerns. Among the best were *My Darling Clementine* (1946), with Fonda, and *She Wore a Yellow Ribbon* (1949), with John Wayne, the leading light of the Ford Stock Company (as the group of actors most used by Ford was known). *The Searchers* (1956) was the culmination of Ford's frontier movies, with a vein of bitterness evident in Wayne's disillusioned officer searching for his niece who is captured by Indians. *The Man Who Shot Liberty Valance* (1962) was the last Western Ford made with John Wayne. Despite the substantial budget he had for it, he shot the film in black-and-white, probably to evoke a sense of nostalgia.

Milos **Forman**

1932– | CZECH, AMERICAN | 1963–

12 | Biopic, Comedy, Costume drama

The Czech films of Milos Forman reveal a gently mocking humour and a keen eye for the minutiae of human behavior, qualities he brought to bear on his American movies.

Using mostly non-actors, and a cinema-verité technique, Forman gave *Black Peter* (*Cerný Petr*, 1963) and *Loves of a Blonde* (*Lásky jedné plavovlásky*, 1965), both about young people in conflict with their elders, a comic freshness. *The Fireman's Ball* (*Horí, má panenko*, 1967), a satire on petty bureaucracy, brought him into conflict with the Czech authorities. Before the Russian invasion, he left for America, where he triumphed with *One Flew Over the Cuckoo's Nest* (1975). It won five major Academy Awards, including Best Film and Best Director, as did *Amadeus* (1984), a sumptuous visual and aural treat, much of it shot in the Czech Republic.

Tom Hulce *plays Mozart in* Amadeus*; Forman's compelling portrait of the legendary composer is filled with rich details, powerful drama, and a wonderful score.*

WHAT TO WATCH

1965	Loves of a Blonde
1967	The Fireman's Ball
1975	One Flew Over the Cuckoo's Nest
1984	Amadeus
1999	Man on the Moon

John **Frankenheimer**

1930–2002 | AMERICAN | 1957–2000

29 | Thriller, Drama

One of the first generation of television directors to make it to the big screen, John Frankenheimer brought realism and a liking for strong plots and situations to cinema.

The first two features directed by John Frankenheimer, *The Young Stranger* (1957) and *The Young Savages* (1961), dealt with juvenile delinquency, a popular subject at the time. Another aspect of youth was evident in *All Fall Down* (1961), which starred 24-year-old Warren Beatty, whose seduction of an older woman has tragic results. Most of *Birdman of Alcatraz* (1962) takes place in a prison cell, but the intensity of the direction and Burt Lancaster's mesmeric performance, brilliantly sustain it. *The Manchurian Candidate* (1962) incorporated social and political satire into a thriller plot, while *Seven Days to May* (1964) entered similar territory, with the imminent military takeover of the United States government. Lancaster starred again in *The Train* (1964), an intelligent and gripping war drama, which details the efforts of the French Resistance to prevent a trainload of French art from reaching Germany. *French Connection II* (1975) was, in many ways, a better film than its predecessor (William Friedkin's 1971 *The French Connection)*, proving Frankenheimer's credentials as a first-class action director.

Robert Stroud *(Burt Lancaster) is smitten by a fledgling sparrow in the* Birdman of Alcatraz*, a true story of a prison inmate who becomes a renowned bird expert.*

WHAT TO WATCH

1962	The Manchurian Candidate
1962	Birdman of Alcatraz
1964	The Train
1966	Seconds
1975	French Connection II

Stephen **Frears**

1941– BRITISH 1971–

16 Various

The films of Stephen Frears are brilliant studies of modern Britain. With the exception of *Dangerous Liaisons* (1988), the best screen version of Choderlos de Laclos's 1782 novel, he has been happiest on home ground.

After a start in television and a 13-year gap between *Gumshoe* (1971), his first feature, and *The Hit* (1984), Stephen Frears' breakthrough came with *My Beautiful Laundrette* (1985), which deals with sexual, class, and racial prejudices in Thatcherite Britain. *Sammy and Rosie Get Laid* (1987) continues the theme, while *Prick Up Your Ears* (1987) is about gay playwright Joe Orton in the 1960s. Frears' greatest successes have been his films made in Britain such as *Mrs. Henderson Presents* (2005), about the history of the "naughty" Windmill Theatre in London.

Judi Dench *plays Laura Henderson, the daring widow who shocked pre-war Britain by featuring naked women on stage in her theater, in* Mrs Henderson Presents.

WHAT TO WATCH

1985	My Beautiful Laundrette
1987	Sammy and Rosie Get Laid
1987	Prick Up Your Ears
1988	Dangerous Liaisons
2005	Mrs. Henderson Presents

Sam **Fuller**

1911–1997 AMERICAN 1948–1989

23 War, Thriller, Western

Often using a moving camera as a blunt instrument, Sam Fuller created direct and raw films that reflect his experience in tabloid journalism and in the U.S. army.

WHAT TO WATCH

1957	Run of the Arrow
1957	Forty Guns
1961	Merrill's Marauders
1963	Shock Corridor
1964	The Naked Kiss
1980	The Big Red One

Appearing as himself in Jean-Luc Godard's *Pierrot le Fou* (1965), Sam Fuller says, "film is like a battleground, love, hate, action, violence, death... in one word, Emotion." Among his "emotion" pictures are *Shock Corridor* (1963) and *The Naked Kiss* (1964), both high-pitched melodramas that pack a punch. But it is Fuller's war films that are his greatest achievement. *The Steel Helmet* (1950) and *Fixed Bayonets* (1951) were the first of his taut, tough, and truthful war films, which followed a group of multi-racial Americans fighting to survive. *Merrill's Marauders* (1961) shows them wiping out Japanese soldiers in Burma in a "war is hell" manner, while World War II in Europe is reduced to its essentials in the stylized *The Big Red One* (1980), Fuller's masterpiece.

Lee Marvin *plays a battle-hardened sergeant (right), with Mark Hamill as a rookie in* The Big Red One.

Abel **Gance**

1889–1981 FRENCH 1911–1971

42 Epic, Costume drama, Melodrama

One of cinema's great pioneers before the arrival of sound, Abel Gance reached his artistic climax with *Napoléon* (1927), a pyrotechnical display of almost every device of the silent screen.

At the start of his career, Abel Gance experimented with various techniques. In *The Folly of Doctor Tube* (*La Folie Du Docteur Tube*, 1915), he used a subjective camera and distorting mirrors for effect. *J'Accuse* (*I Accuse*, 1919; remake 1938), a pacifist statement in which a triangular relationship becomes a microcosm for the horrors of war, was actually shot during WWI with real soldiers under fire. It begins with infantrymen forming the letters of the title and ends with dead soldiers rising from their graves. This final scene is then contrasted, in a split-screen sequence, with a victory parade to the Arc de Triomphe. For *The Wheel (La Roué*, 1922), an ambitious production, he used rapid montage techniques — long before Sergei Eisenstein's experiments with editing. His most impressive film was *Napoléon* (1927), first shown at the Paris

WHAT TO WATCH

1918	The Tenth Symphony
1919	J'Accuse (I Accuse)
1922	The Wheel
1927	Napoléon
1936	The Life and Loves of Beethoven

Opéra in a five-hour version. It used hand-held cameras (one strapped to a horse's back), wide-angle lenses, superimposition, rapid cutting, and a triple screen. Sadly, Gance's romantic visual imagination was constrained with the coming of sound. Many of his later films are routine melodramas, although he sometimes used the same ideas and sequences from his silent films, such as the melodrama *The Tenth Symphony* (*La Dixieme Symphony*, 1918). Poignant and paradoxical is the sequence in *The Life and Loves of Beethoven* (*Un Grand Amour de Beethoven*, 1936) when the great composer loses his hearing, portrayed by silent shots of violins, birds, and bells. The loss of sound for Beethoven and the coming of sound for Gance were equally agonizing.

In the first version of J'Accuse *(1919), Gance's anti-war film, wounded soldiers are welcomed home from the World War I battlefields by the civilian population.*

Jean-Luc **Godard**

1930– FRENCH 1959–

39 Drama, Political drama, Satire

Always striving to go beyond films into other arts and politics, Jean-Luc Godard has formulated a truly revolutionary film language free from the dominant bourgeois culture in the west.

Breathless (*À Bout de Souffle*, 1960), Jean-Luc Godard's first feature, established him as one of stars of the French New Wave. His second, *The Little Soldier* (*Le Petit Soldat*, 1960), presents an ambivalent view of the Algerian war. *My Life to Live* (*Vivre sa Vie*, 1962) uses a Brechtian device of episodes with texts, quotations, and interviews, giving it a documentary tone. Color is used symbolically in *Pierrot le Fou* (1965), a stunning study of violence and relationships. *Two or Three Things I Know About Her* (*Deux ou Trois Choses que Je sais d'Elle*, 1967) refers to Paris, a city that has always inspired him, and *Weekend* (1967) is a devastating critique on modern French society. Godard broke away from commercial film-making to shoot a series of ciné-tracts in 16mm and video, but returned to more accessible film-making with *Tout va Bien* (1972). From 1980, a more mature Godard emerged, his films becoming contemplative poetic essays on contemporary issues, a challenge to audiences to think differently.

WHAT TO WATCH

1960	Breathless
1962	My Life to Live
1963	Contempt (Le Mépris)
1964	The Outsiders (Bande á Part)
1965	Alphaville
1967	Two or Three Things I Know About Her
1967	Weekend
1990	New Wave (Nouvelle Vague)
1999	In Praise of Love (Eloge de l'Amour)
2003	Our Music (Notre Musique)

Ferdinand (Jean-Paul Belmondo) *takes a break after a bizarre car chase, one among a series of wild adventures he shares with Marianne (Anna Karina) in* Pierrot Le Fou.

Anna Karina *plays Natascha Von Braun and Eddie Constantine plays Lemmy Caution, an American secret agent, in a sequence from* Alphaville, *set in a futuristic city, and shot with minimal lighting.*

Alejandro González **Iñárritu**

1963– MEXICAN 2000–

6 Drama

A disc jockey, film composer, and television producer before he became a leading figure in Mexico's advertising world, Iñárritu made a splash at Critics' Week in Cannes 2000 with his debut film, *Amores Perros*.

A collaboration with the writer Guillermo Arriaga, *Amores Perros* began as separate short films about the conflicting nature of life in Mexico City, but ended up as a triptych of loosely intertwined tales told with ferocity and compassion. The writer-director duo stuck with overlapping tragedies and social inequities for *21 Grams* (2003), but mixed up its structure, cutting between half a dozen major characters and time frames. Iñárritu goes for extreme contrasts and big emotions, but he has the talent to pull them off.

WHAT TO WATCH

2000	Amores Perros
2003	21 Grams
2006	Babel

Jorge Salinas *plays the violent Luis in* Amores Perros*; each of the three tales revolves around dogs to varying degrees, as implied by the original title, "Love's a Bitch".*

Peter **Greenaway**

1942– BRITISH 1980–

12 Avant-garde

Displaying haunting images of strange worlds akin to those of writers Jorge Luis Borges and Franz Kafka, Peter Greenaway's films feature his fascination with numbers, maps, the English landscape, birds, nudity, and expanses of water.

Greenaway began making experimental films until *The Draughtsman's Contract* (1982), an elegant deconstruction of a costume drama, became a hit. Going beyond the restrictions of cinema, Greenaway creates an intertextual world, which draws heavily on the other arts and media. Those who are prepared to jettison their notions of conventional narrative will find his films rewarding.

WHAT TO WATCH

1980	The Falls
1982	The Draughtsman's Contract
1985	A Zed and Two Noughts
1987	The Belly of an Architect
1988	Drowning by Numbers
1989	The Cook, the Thief, His Wife, and Her Lover
1996	The Pillow Book

Tomás Alea **Gutiérrez**

1928–1996 CUBAN 1962–1994

15 Political drama

Never afraid to be critical of his own country, Tomás Alea Gutiérrez is considered Cuba's leading film director. His reputation is justified by his wide-ranging and inventive films.

Although he made a documentary about coal-miners in 1955, it was only after the 1959 Cuban revolution that Gutiérrez could begin to make "revolutionary" feature films. After making *Death of a Bureaucrat (La Muerte de un Burócrata,* 1966), an amusing satire on red-tape, Gutiérrez directed his masterpiece, *Memories of Underdevelopment* (*Memorias del Subdesarrollo,* 1968), which subtly and ironically examines the role of the intellectual in the new Cuba. *Strawberries and Chocolate* (*Fresa y Chocolate,* 1993) bravely tackles Cuba's treatment of homosexuals in a non-didactic manner.

WHAT TO WATCH

1966	Death of a Bureaucrat
1968	Memories of Underdevelopment
1993	Strawberries and Chocolate

On the set of *Intolerance (1916), D.W. Griffith, loud hailer in hand, directs the cast in one of the film's four tales—the modern American story.*

D.W. **Griffith**

1875–1948 AMERICAN 1908–1932

33 Epic, Melodrama, Costume drama

With his epic Civil War drama *The Birth of a Nation* (1915), David Wark Griffith did much to convince the world that cinema is as valid an art form as any other.

WHAT TO WATCH	
1915	The Birth of a Nation
1916	Intolerance
1919	True Heart Susie
1919	Broken Blossoms
1920	Way Down East
1921	Orphans of the Storm

Griffith, the son of a Confederate soldier, started directing at Biograph Studios in 1908. Biograph was the first studio to shoot a movie in Hollywood—Griffith's *In Old California* (1910). With Billy Bitzer (the photographer of nearly all his films), Griffith turned out hundreds of one- and two-reelers, learning his craft as he went along. By 1911, he had used close-ups, changed the camera set-ups within one scene, and developed cross-cutting. Despite its reactionary attitudes, *The Birth of a Nation* remains a remarkable film in which all the technical innovations of his early work reached maturity. In order to answer critics of the racist elements in the film, Griffith's next project was the epic *Intolerance* (1916), containing four separate stories to illustrate his theme. Throughout this period, Griffith struggled to free himself from studio control, and a result of this was United Artists, which he co-founded in 1919 with Charlie Chaplin, Douglas Fairbanks, and Mary Pickford. He made some of his most endearing movies with the waiflike Lillian Gish, his favorite actress, notably *Broken Blossoms* (1919), *True Heart Susie* (1919), *Way Down East* (1920), and *Orphans of the Storm* (1921). But due to his narrow views, and the emergence of new directors and of sound, Griffith lost his popular appeal and his influence. His first talkie, *Abraham Lincoln* (1930), failed, and until his death in 1948, he led an obscure existence.

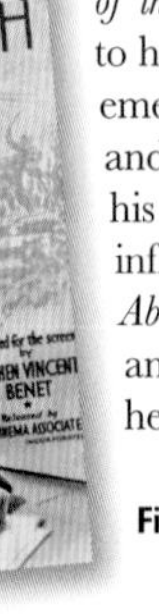

Film poster, *1930*

Lasse **Hallström**

1946– SWEDISH 1977–

17 Drama

On the strength of *My Life as a Dog* (*Mitt liv som hund*, 1985), which was an international success, Lasse Hallström was invited to make films in Hollywood, where he made his mark with his gentle talent.

My Life as a Dog is an enchanting tale of childhood set in a small country village in Sweden. Despite the lead being a charming 12-year-old boy dealing with his mother's death and separated from his dog, the film avoided cuteness and sentimentality. Some of its tone was present in his second Hollywood feature *What's Eating Gilbert Grape?* (1993), with Johnny Depp in the title role and an impressive young Leonardo DiCaprio as his autistic brother. Both this film and *The Cider House Rules* (1999), his adaptation of John Irving's novel starring Michael Caine, received critical acclaim.

WHAT TO WATCH

1985	My Life as a Dog
1993	What's Eating Gilbert Grape?
1999	The Cider House Rules
2000	Chocolat
2005	Casanova

Ingemar (Anton Glanzelius) *and the pet he loves in* My Life as a Dog. *Hallström received Oscar nominations for Best Director and Best Screenplay for the film.*

Michael **Haneke**

1942– AUSTRIAN 1989–

9 Psychological drama

Most of Michael Haneke's films shock, not so much with their violence, but with the cold and ambivalent depiction of that violence.

Haneke, one of Austria's most celebrated directors (although he works in France), intends his films to be critiques of European society and of American cinema. *Benny's Video* (1992) and *Funny Games* (1997) analyzed the cause and effect of violence on youth seemingly immune to sadistic practices. He attacked bourgeois behavior in *The Piano Teacher* (*La Pianiste*, 2001) and *Hidden* (*Caché*, 2005), expounding the philosophy that nothing we do in society is private.

Film poster, *1997*

WHAT TO WATCH

1997	Funny Games
2001	The Piano Teacher
2005	Hidden

Curtis **Hanson**

1945– AMERICAN 1987–

9 Thriller, Drama

A former film critic, Curtis Hanson came to directing like so many others—through the auspices of Roger Corman.

Starting out with B-grade movies, by the late 1980s Hanson was capable of fashioning tight, smart, unpretentious suspense pictures like *Bad Influence* (1987), *The Hand That Rocks the Cradle* (1992), and *The River Wild* (1994). Yet it was a big step up when he pulled off a streamlined but still authentic adaptation of James Ellroy's labyrinthine *L.A. Confidential* (1997), coaxing a host of star-making performances out of Russell Crowe, Guy Pearce, and Kevin Spacey. Since then Hanson has charted an unpredictable, but often rewarding, course with *Wonder Boys* (2000), *8 Mile* (2002), and *In Her Shoes* (2005).

WHAT TO WATCH

1992	The Hand That Rocks the Cradle
1997	L.A. Confidential
2000	Wonder Boys
2002	8 Mile

Howard **Hawks**

1896–1977 AMERICAN 1926–1970

41 Western, Comedy, Action

Since Howard Hawks' assured narrative style and handling of most genres was not immediately obvious as "art," he was not appreciated as a true auteur and a candidate for Hollywood immortality until years after his death.

Many of Howard Hawks' own personal interests feature in his films. A pilot in World War I, he brought authenticity to his four films about flying: *The Dawn Patrol* (1930), *Ceiling Zero* (1936), *Only Angels Have Wings* (1939), and *Air Force* (1943). A former designer and driver of racing cars, he recreated the excitement of the track in *The Crowd Roars* (1932) and *Red Line 7000* (1965). Energetic sportsmanship also inspired him to make *Hatari!* (1962) and *Man's Favorite Sport* (1963). Some of these films reflect the theme of the camaraderie of men who risk their lives, but it was the battle of the sexes and gender role-swapping that preoccupied him in his screwball comedies, *Twentieth Century* (1934), *Bringing Up Baby* (1938), *His Girl Friday* (1940), and later in *I Was a Male War Bride* (1949). Particularly remarkable was the sublime sexual byplay between Humphrey Bogart and Lauren Bacall in *To Have and Have Not* (1944) and *The Big Sleep* (1946), and the stunning opening number of *Gentlemen Prefer Blondes* (1953). Notable among his films is the pairing of John Wayne with Montgomery Clift in *Red River* (1948), with Dean Martin in *Rio Bravo* (1959), and with Robert Mitchum in *El Dorado* (1967).

John Wayne, *Hawks' favorite actor, plays Colonel Cord McNally, a Union Army officer who travels with his men to Texas in search of justice in* Rio Lobo *(1970).*

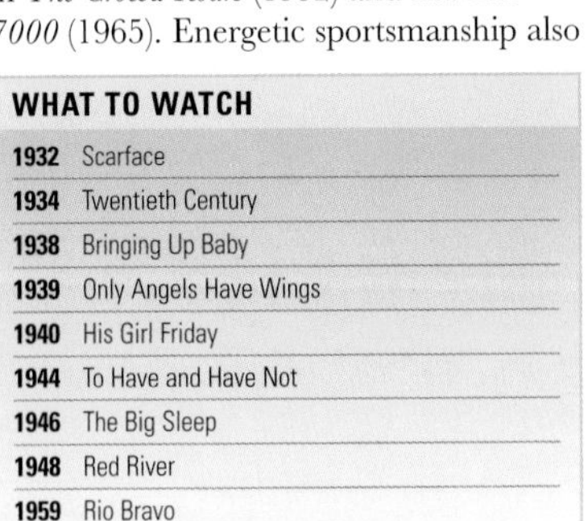

WHAT TO WATCH	
1932	Scarface
1934	Twentieth Century
1938	Bringing Up Baby
1939	Only Angels Have Wings
1940	His Girl Friday
1944	To Have and Have Not
1946	The Big Sleep
1948	Red River
1959	Rio Bravo

Lauren Bacall plays Vivien *and Humphrey Bogart stars as private detective Philip Marlowe in* The Big Sleep, *a hard-boiled thriller adapted from Raymond Chandler's novel.*

Werner **Herzog**

1942– GERMAN 1967–

19 Epic, Documentary

Known for going to any lengths to make a film, Werner Herzog (Werner Stipetic) is drawn to bizarre characters and situations set in stunningly photographed exotic surroundings.

Herzog's first feature, *Signs of Life* (*Lebenszeichen*, 1967), takes place during World War II on a Greek island where a German soldier recovering from wounds refuses to obey orders. This theme foreshadowed later preoccupations with outsiders refusing or unable to conform to society. *Fata Morgana* (1971), shot in the desolate Sahara desert, is an "outsider" film par excellence, while *Even Dwarfs Started Small* (*Auch Zwerge haben klein angefangen*, 1970) is set on an island populated by dwarfs, and depicts the problematic nature of the liberation of the spirit. *The Enigma of Kaspar Hauser* (*Jeder für sich und Gott gegen alle*, 1974), about a wild boy who appeared from nowhere in the early 19th century, also appealed to Herzog's fascination with social misfits. Herzog's greatest success was *Aguirre, Wrath of God* (*Aguirre, der Zorn Gottes*, 1972). Shot in the Peruvian Andes, it was the first of several films about obsessive heroes played by the manic actor Klaus Kinski. The odd relationship between Kinski and Herzog became the subject of the director's documentary, *My Best Fiend* (*Mein liebster Feind*, 1999), and *Fitzcarraldo* (1982) is about a turbulent trip by Kinski and Herzog into more untamed regions, this time the Amazonian jungle where Brian, the main character, is determined to build an opera house. "If I should abandon this film," Herzog said when conditions became difficult, "I should be a man without dreams... I live my life or end my life with this project."

The manual hauling of a *320-ton steamship over steep hills in the jungles of Peru in* Fitzcarraldo *was a feat accomplished without special effects, and is one of cinema's most astonishing scenes.*

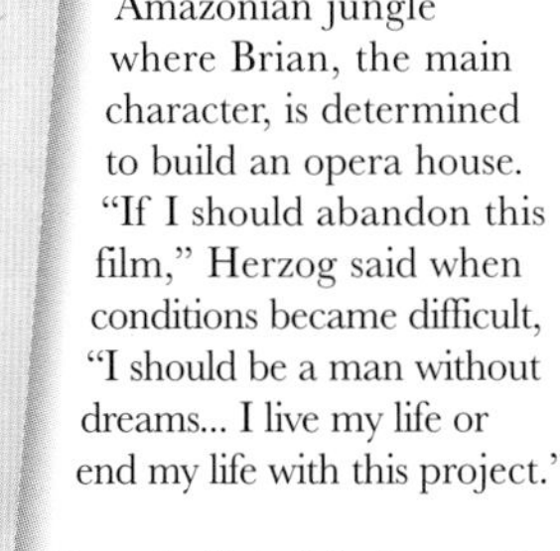

Film poster, Nosferatu the Vampyre, *1979*

WHAT TO WATCH

1967	Signs of Life
1971	Fata Morgana
1972	Aguirre, Wrath of God
1974	The Enigma of Kaspar Hauser
1982	Fitzcarraldo
1999	My Best Fiend

Alfred **Hitchcock**

1899–1980 | BRITISH | 1926–1976

58 | Thriller, Horror, Film Noir

For decades, Alfred Hitchcock was the only film director whose name and face were as famous as those of a film star. "Hitch" was dubbed the "Master of Suspense," putting his own unique stamp on the thriller genre.

Born in London's East End, Hitchcock was educated by Jesuits. He entered the film industry in 1920 as a designer of silent-film titles, but soon rose to become an art director, scriptwriter, and assistant director. Hitchcock directed nine silent films, including *The Lodger* (1926), in which he first explored his favorite theme of the innocent in danger. The film marked his first appearance in front of the camera, in one of the fleeting cameos that became a feature of all his subsequent films.

THE LURE OF HOLLYWOOD

In 1929, while *Blackmail* was in production, sound was introduced to cinema. The 30-year-old Hitchcock quickly demonstrated his understanding of this new technology. At one point in the film, he created a sound montage in which the word "knife" echoes over and over again in the guilty girl's mind the morning after the murder. Hitchcock followed *Blackmail* with a number of superb comedy-thrillers including *The Man Who Knew Too Much* (1934) and *The Lady Vanishes* (1938).

In 1940 David O. Selznick invited Hitchcock to Hollywood to direct the film of Daphne du Maurier's novel *Rebecca.* Hitchcock's first American film had a British cast that was headed by Laurence Olivier and Joan Fontaine. *Rebecca* was a triumph, winning the Oscar for Best Picture and launching Hitchcock's long career in the United States, where he lived for the rest of his life.

PSYCHOLOGY, PLOT, AND PURSUIT

Hitchcock claimed not to care about the morality, the subject, or the message of his films, only the manner in which the story was told. The obvious Catholicism in films such as *I Confess* (1953) and the blatant psychology of *Spellbound* (1945), *Psycho* (1960), and *Marnie* (1964) were no more than plot devices.

The pleasure of Hitchcock's films lies elsewhere, for example, in the picaresque pursuit of *Saboteur* (1942), in which a hapless bystander becomes involved in a crime and must prove his innocence while being chased by both police and criminals. Then there's the underlying sense of menace that emanates from unexpected places, evident in *The Birds* (1963). Hitchcock also had the remarkable ability

"I am a typed director. If I made Cinderella, the audience would immediately be looking for a body in the coach."

ALFRED HITCHCOCK, ***1965***

Paul Newman discusses *direction with Alfred Hitchcock on the set of* Torn Curtain *(1966).*

THE HITCHCOCK BLONDE

Hitchcock's ideal heroine was a "cool blonde," a woman who seems outwardly prim and proper, but responds in a more sensual way when aroused by passion or peril. In Hitchcock's own words his heroines were, "real ladies, who become whores once they're in the bedroom." Their appeal contrasted with the Marilyn-Monroe style of glamour, which was openly sexual.

Grace Kelly *plays Lisa in* Rear Window, *one of Hitchcock's best thrillers; her co-star in the film was a wheelchair-bound James Stewart.*

In Hitchcock's horror The Birds, *Tippi Hedren finds herself under a sustained and vicious attack from the most innocuous of sources.*

WHAT TO WATCH

1936	The 39 Steps
1938	The Lady Vanishes
1943	Shadow of a Doubt
1951	Strangers on a Train
1954	Rear Window
1958	Vertigo
1959	North by Northwest
1960	Psycho
1963	The Birds
1964	Marnie

to surprise his audiences, for example, audaciously killing off his leading lady (Janet Leigh) halfway through *Psycho*.

He demonstrated an extravagant sense of location, as shown with the shooting that coincides with a clash of cymbals during a concert at London's Royal Albert Hall in *The Man Who Knew Too Much* (1934 and 1956); the climactic chase on Mount Rushmore in *North By Northwest* (1959); and the strangulation in London's Covent Garden market in *Frenzy* (1972). From 1956 to 1966, all Hitchcock's films were set to Bernard Herrmann's distinctive pulsating music, which was particularly effective in *Vertigo* (1958), which many critics consider his masterpiece.

Mike **Hodges**

1932– BRITISH 1971–

10 Gangster, Science fiction

With his first feature, *Get Carter* (1971), Mike Hodges started the trend of hard-boiled and cold-blooded British crime movies set in seedy locations.

A familiar name in television, Mike Hodges has, in over three decades, made only nine feature films and a documentary about serial-killer movies, *Murder By Numbers* (2001). His debut feature *Get Carter* had a gritty reality rare in British gangster films of the time. After the pastiche thriller, *Pulp* (1972), Hodges made two vastly different science-fiction movies, *The Terminal Man* (1974), a downbeat film about a man causing violence due to computers in his brain, and the tongue-in-the-cheek *Flash Gordon* (1980). Hodges returned to thriller and gangster movies with *Croupier* (1998) and *I'll Sleep When I'm Dead* (2003).

Michael Caine *plays Jack Carter, a London gangster investigating the death of his brother in bleak Newcastle, in the gripping cult film* Get Carter.

WHAT TO WATCH

1971	Get Carter
1974	The Terminal Man
1980	Flash Gordon
1989	Black Rainbow
1998	Croupier

Ron **Howard**

1954– AMERICAN 1969–

17 Various

One of the most successful Hollywood directors for over 20 years, Ron Howard turns out well-made genre films that have wide audience appeal, yet no real personal signature.

To many people, Ron Howard will forever remain the lanky, ineffectual teenager Richie Cunningham in television's *Happy Days*. Howard once said that he became a director to avoid being typecast as an actor. He has also refused to be typecast as a director and, like the character Richie, he seems to be able to turn his hand to any subject. Howard has won plaudits for rather earnest features, such as *Apollo 13* (1995), *A Beautiful Mind* (2001), an exploration of the inner world of a genius that won him Academy Awards for Best Picture and Best Director, and *Cinderella Man* (2005). However, he has also shown a light touch in comedies, such as *Splash* (1984), *Cocoon* (1985), *Parenthood* (1989), and *Ed TV* (1999).

WHAT TO WATCH

1984	Splash
1989	Parenthood
1995	Apollo 13
1999	Ed TV
2001	A Beautiful Mind
2006	The Da Vinci Code

John Nash (Russell Crowe), *the mathematical genius and paranoid schizophrenic, is caught in his own delusional world, in* A Beautiful Mind.

Hajime **(Tadanobu Asano)**, *a bookseller who records train sounds as a pastime in* Cafe Lumiere (Kohi Jiko, *2005), Hou's tribute to Japanese director Yasujiro Ozu.*

Hou Hsiao-Hsien

1947– TAIWANESE 1979–

17 Drama

The films of Hou Hsiao-Hsien, the most internationally renowned director associated with Taiwan's 1980s New Cinema movement, are subtle and beautifully composed.

Most of Hou's films of the 1980s are semi-autobiographical. They depict the frustrations of growing up in rural Taiwan in the 1950s and 1960s, and the complex intertwining of different strands that shape individual lives, particularly within a family. *The Boys from Fengkuei* (*Fengkuei-lai-te Jen*, 1983), Hou's fourth feature, was not only a rite-of-passage piece but the coming-of-age of the Taiwanese film industry. The film, about three youths who leave a small fishing village to try to survive in the big city, had a more modern and universal approach than many previous Taiwanese movies. This was followed up by *A Summer at Grandpa's* (*Dongdong de Jiaqi*, 1984), where children have both amusing and frightening experiences, as seen through Hou's clear, unflinching eyes. In *A Time to Live, a Time to Die* (*Tong nien wang shi*, 1985), another family drama revolving around a child, Hou began to perfect his simplicity of style, building up a rich tapestry from small details. From *City of Sadness* (*Beiqing Chengshi*, 1989), a complex panorama of Taiwanese life, Hou further experimented with scrupulously composed master shots, long takes, and elliptical narratives. *Flowers of Shanghai* (*Hai shang hua*, 1998), set in a brothel in the 1880s, was Hou's first period film. Perhaps his most accessible, it is emotionally charged without ever becoming melodramatic or sentimental.

WHAT TO WATCH

1983	The Boys from Fengkuei
1984	A Summer at Grandpa's
1985	A Time to Live, a Time to Die
1989	City of Sadness
1998	Flowers of Shanghai
2005	Cafe Lumiere

John **Huston**

1906–1987 AMERICAN 1941–1987

38 Various

The films of John Huston express his wide masculine interests but, beneath the tough exterior, a tenderness and a romantic idealism is revealed.

Son of actor Walter Huston and father of Angelica and Danny — both actors too — John Huston led a varied life as painter, boxer, horseman, hunter, actor, and writer before becoming a director. *The Maltese Falcon* (1941), considered the first film noir, was his assured debut, starring his favorite actor Humphrey Bogart. He directed his father and Bogart in *The Treasure of the Sierra Madre* (1948), a saga of human greed. Greed is also the theme of *Key Largo* (1948) with Bogart and Lauren Bacall, and of *Beat the Devil* (1954), which parodies *The Maltese Falcon* and Bogart's persona. Most of his heroes are fiercely independent loners such as Toulouse-Lautrec (*Moulin Rouge*, 1953), Captain Ahab (*Moby Dick*, 1956), Freud (in the film of the same name, 1962), the defeated boxers in *Fat City* (1972), and the preacher in *Wise Blood* (1979). *The Misfits* (1961), starring Clark Gable, Montgomery Clift, and Marilyn Monroe, among others, was actually a film about losers. Fatalism and irony pervade his best films, which are rich in character and plot, and told in an incisive narrative style, one of the best examples being *The Asphalt Jungle* (1950). He made two excursions into the African jungle with *The African Queen* (1952), with Bogart and Katharine Hepburn making an unlikely pair, and *The Roots of Heaven* (1958), about doomed elephants. Huston's final film *The Dead* (1987), based on a James Joyce short story and filmed in Ireland where he had made his home, was a poignant valediction.

WHAT TO WATCH

1941	The Maltese Falcon
1948	The Treasure of the Sierra Madre
1948	Key Largo
1950	The Asphalt Jungle
1952	The African Queen
1954	Beat the Devil
1961	The Misfits
1967	Reflections in a Golden Eye
1972	Fat City
1987	The Dead

Film poster, 1950

Tim Holt, *Walter Huston, and Bogart are the prospectors brought together by greed in* The Treasure of the Sierra Madre, *for which Huston won the Best Director Oscar.*

Kon **Ichikawa**

1915– JAPANESE 1947–

80 Various

A consistent critic of Japanese society, Kon Ichikawa is noted for the visual beauty of his films: "I began as a painter and I think like one."

Although Kon Ichikawa's first features were mostly satirical comedies, there is nothing comic about the films that made his reputation in the west. Both *The Burmese Harp (Biruma no Tategoto*, 1956) and *Fires on the Plain (Nobi*, 1959) depict the anguish of the Japanese army's defeat in visionary black-and-white images; in *Conflagration (Enjo*, 1958), a man burns down a temple he feels has been polluted. Ichikawa used the wide-screen to magnificent effect in *Odd Obsession (Kagi*, 1959), *Alone in the Pacific (Taiheiyo Hitori-botchi*, 1963), *An Actor's Revenge (Yukinojo Henge*, 1963), and *Tokyo Olympiad (Tokyo Orimpikku*, 1965), a triumph of technical wizardry and creative genius.

Mizushima *(Shoji Yasui, extreme left) is a Japanese soldier in Burma who tries to bring the battalion to terms with the Japanese surrender in 1945 in* The Burmese Harp.

WHAT TO WATCH

1956	The Burmese Harp
1958	Conflagration
1959	Fires on the Plain
1959	Odd Obsession
1963	An Actor's Revenge
1963	Alone in the Pacific
1965	Tokyo Olympiad

James **Ivory**

1928– AMERICAN 1963–

21 Costume drama

The films of James Ivory are made by his own company set up with Indian producer Ismail Merchant, and mostly written by Ruth Prawar Jhabvala. Each film is literate, ironic, subtly intellectual, refined, and beautifully designed.

Ivory's first four features were made in India, showing the influence of E.M. Forster, Satyajit Ray, and Jean Renoir's *The River* (1951). The first, *Shakespeare-Wallah* (1965), follows an English theater company around India and is gently satirical about the cultural pretensions of both the British and the Indians. As the major theme of Ivory's films is the encounter between two cultures and the corruption of innocence, it was inevitable that Ivory should go directly to Henry James and E.M. Forster for inspiration. *The Europeans* (1979) and *The Bostonians* (1984) were more Jamesian than any other attempt on film. Even more successful were Forster's adaptations: *A Room with a View* (1986), *Maurice* (1987), and *Howards End* (1992). Ivory's adaptation of Kazuo Ishiguro's *The Remains of the Day* (1993), about the withering away of past grandeur and illusions as seen through the eyes of a butler, also received acclaim.

Emma Thompson *plays the housekeeper and Anthony Hopkins plays the head butler — both vestiges of another era — in* The Remains of the Day.

WHAT TO WATCH

1965	Shakespeare-Wallah
1979	The Europeans
1983	Heat and Dust
1984	The Bostonians
1986	A Room with a View
1990	Mr. and Mrs. Bridge
1992	Howards End
1993	The Remains of the Day

Naomi Watts *plays Ann Darrow, held for the last time by the computer-generated giant ape, King Kong, on top of the Empire State Building.*

Peter **Jackson**

1961– NEW ZEALANDER 1988–

9 Fantasy

With *The Lord of the Rings,* Peter Jackson established himself as the natural successor to fantasy film-makers Steven Spielberg and George Lucas — and all without leaving his native New Zealand.

The first feature that Peter Jackson directed was *Bad Taste* (1988), which he shot at weekends with a few friends. It is a story of an extra-terrestrial fast-food operation run by aliens prospecting for brain food on Earth, with only the Alien Investigation Defence Service to stop them. *Meet the Feebles* (1989), a vulgar parody of *The Muppets*, was his first film with writing partner Fran Walsh. *Braindead* (1992) was another black comedy, and is regarded as one of the most gory films ever made.

Heavenly Creatures (1994) is a surprising change of pace, and a sign that there was more to the mature Peter Jackson than mere gusto. Based on a notorious murder case from the 1950s, it is the story of Juliet and Pauline, teenage girls whose torrid fantasy life runs counter to the strict proprieties of the day, and ends in the murder of Pauline's mother. Turning down offers to direct sequels to various horror movie franchises, Jackson persuaded Hollywood to come to him. He built a sophisticated special effects studio in New Zealand to shoot the gothic horror *The Frighteners* (1996), then convinced New Line Productions to bankroll his epic adaptation of J.R.R. Tolkien's trilogy *The Lord of the Rings.* He emerged triumphantly three years later with a dazzling ten-hour series and won Academy Awards for Best Picture, Best Director, and Best Adapted Screenplay in 2004 for *The Lord of the Rings: The Return of the King* (2003).

Peter Jackson, *often nicknamed "The Hobbit" after Tolkien's fantasy creatures, directs with his usual intensity, wearing his trademark purple T-shirt.*

King Kong (2005) is an audacious remake of the 1933 original. Again, Jackson demonstrated scale and virtuosity but, although hugely successful, this time the material did not strike quite the same chord with audiences.

WHAT TO WATCH

1994	Heavenly Creatures
1996	The Frighteners
2001	The Fellowship of the Ring
2002	The Two Towers
2003	The Return of the King
2005	King Kong

Jim **Jarmusch**

1953– AMERICAN 1984–

10 Comedy

A true American independent director, Jim Jarmusch's off-beat, mocking, minimalist films have explored the American Dream through an interplay of outsiders, whether American or "strangers in a strange land."

Jarmusch's second feature *Stranger Than Paradise* (1984), winner of the Best First Film at Cannes, is a comic road movie in which two Hungarian émigrés are confronted with middle America. *Down By Law* (1986) tells the tale of two down-and-out Americans who have to adjust their views of their native land when thrown into jail. *Mystery Train* (1989) shows Memphis as seen through the eyes of a Japanese couple and *Night on Earth* (1992) takes place in taxis in Los Angeles, New York, Paris, Rome, and Helsinki. In Jarmusch's movies, characters are always on the move, including Don (Bill Murray) who goes on a cross-country search for the mother of his child (*Broken Flowers*, 2005).

WHAT TO WATCH

1984	Stranger Than Paradise
1986	Down By Law
1989	Mystery Train
1992	Night on Earth
1999	Ghost Dog: The Way of the Samurai
2005	Broken Flowers

Youki Kudoh *(Mitsuko) and Masatoshi Nagase (Jun) play a couple influenced by US popular culture in* Mystery Train.

Miklós **Jancsó**

1921– HUNGARIAN 1958–

47 Political drama

The films of Miklós Jancsó, from the mid-1960s to the mid-1970s, are brilliantly choreographed dramas. Jancsó traces the fight for Hungarian independence and socialism by using emblem and symbolism.

Jancsó's very personal style blossomed in *The Round-Up* (*Szegénylegények*, 1965), which contains many of the devices and themes of his later films. Set in a desolate plain in Hungary, some time after the 1948 revolution against Austrian rule collapsed, the film powerfully depicts the conflict between the political oppressor and the oppressed. Jancsó's films are subtly choreographed, with the camera fluidly tracking the movements of characters, emphasizing their relationship to the landscape. Color, especially red, is used symbolically in *The Confrontation* (*Fényes Szelek*, 1969), *Agnus Dei* (*Égi Bárány*, 1970), and *Red Psalm* (*Még Kér a Nép*, 1972). These are hymns of despair as well as celebrations of freedom, illustrated by Jancsó's masterful long takes and extended sequence shots.

WHAT TO WATCH

1964	My Way Home
1965	The Round-Up
1967	The Red and the White
1969	The Confrontation
1970	Agnus Dei
1972	Red Psalm
1974	Beloved Electra

Elektra *(Mari Törocsik) in* Beloved Electra, *Jancsó's take on the Greek myth, participates in a ritual with women in white, while awaiting her brother's return.*

Jean-Pierre **Jeunet**

1953– FRENCH 1991–

6 Fantasy, Comedy

Audiences have come to expect an astonishingly inventive visual style and black humour from the films of Jean-Pierre Jeunet.

Jeunet and designer Marc Caro began film-making with several prize-winning short films. The weirdness of their films became more extreme in their first feature,

WHAT TO WATCH

1991	Delicatessen
1995	The City of Lost Children
2001	Amélie

Delicatessen (1991), a bizarre comedy inspired by French comics and the films of David Lynch and Terry Gilliam. *The City of Lost Children* (*La Cité des Enfants Perdus*, 1995) is even more eye-boggling than its predecessor. The film's success led Jeunet to Hollywood and *Alien: Resurrection* (1997), in which he uses bold images to compensate for a weak storyline. Back in France, Jeunet made *Amélie* (2001) with Audrey Tautou. Whimsical and utterly delightful, it became a worldwide hit. Tautou also starred in *A Very Long Engagement* (*Un long dimanche de fiançailles*, 2004), which contains some extraordinary set pieces.

The gamine *Audrey Tautou plays Amélie, a waitress determined to bring cheer into others' lives. Jeunet imbues the film with bright reds and greens.*

Neil **Jordan**

1950– IRISH 1982–

14 Thriller, Drama

Proving himself to be a distinctive and visionary film-maker, Neil Jordan rose to prominence as part of the British cinema revival in the 1980s.

WHAT TO WATCH

1982	Angel
1984	The Company of Wolves
1986	Mona Lisa
1992	The Crying Game
1996	Michael Collins
1997	The Butcher Boy

With a stunning directorial debut, the almost surreal *Angel* (1982), Jordan attracted attention. The film stars Stephen Rea (who has appeared in nine of the director's films) as a jazz musician who swaps his saxophone for a machine-gun in Northern Ireland. *The Company of Wolves* (1984), a nightmarish fairytale, also owes much to surrealism, and *Mona Lisa* (1986), an accomplished British film noir, revolves around a small-time gangster's love for a prostitute. After unsuccessful excursions into Hollywood, Jordan returned happily to home ground with Irish subjects: the coming-of-age drama *The Miracle* (1991); *The Crying Game* (1992), a political drama with a sensational twist; *Michael Collins* (1996), a political biopic about the Irish rebel hero; and *The Butcher Boy* (1997), a dark view of childhood.

Ralph Fiennes *and Julianne Moore in* The End of the Affair *(1999), based on Graham Greene's novel.*

Aki **Kaurismäki**

1957– FINNISH 1981–

16 Comedy

The films of maverick Finnish director Aki Kaurismäki are mostly about taciturn losers in soulless jobs in bleak surroundings. However, their grimness is enlivened by his dry humor.

Kaurismäki's unsentimental sympathy with outsiders was noticeable early in his career. *Ariel* (1988), about a sacked miner, is the second of his "working-class trilogy," which also consists of *Shadows in Paradise* (*Varjoja Paratiisissa*, 1986) and *The Match Factory Girl* (*Tulitikkutehtaan Tyttö*, 1989) – tragi-comedies about proletarians. In *Leningrad Cowboys Go America* (1989), a group of inept musicians drive across the US. *Drifting Clouds* (*Kauas Pilvet Karkaavat*, 1996) and *The Man Without a Past* (*Mies Vailla Menneisyyttä*, 2002) reveal a new warmth for his quirky characters. Kaurismäki's philosophy is summed up in a line from *Drifting Clouds*: "Life is short and miserable. Be as merry as you can."

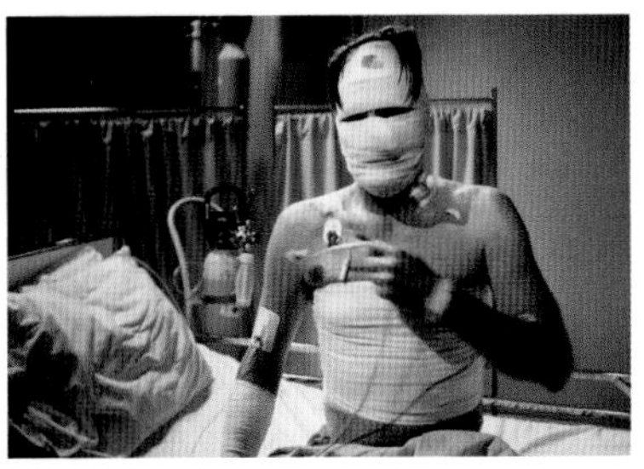

In A Man Without a Past, *an outsider (Markku Peltola as "M") gets a fresh start in life in a new city after he is beaten up and loses his memory.*

WHAT TO WATCH

1988	Ariel
1989	Leningrad Cowboys Go America
1994	Take Care of Your Scarf, Tatjana (Pidä Huivista Iinni, Tatjana)
2002	The Man Without a Past
2006	Lights in the Dusk

Elia **Kazan**

1909–2003 AMERICAN 1945–2003

150 Drama, Cult

All of Elia Kazan's films have strong social themes, a keen sense of location, and superb performances. Despite his betrayal of his friends at the McCarthy hearings in 1952, Kazan's reputation as one of the finest directors in the US has never wavered.

From his work in the theater and the Actors Studio, Kazan had great respect for actors, and he allowed them to develop their work during shooting. This trust inspired some outstanding performances, including those by Marlon Brando in *On the Waterfront* (1954) and Jo Van Fleet in *Wild River* (1960). Kazan made Brando a star with *A Streetcar Named Desire* (1951), "discovered" James Dean (*East of Eden*, 1955), and gave debut screen roles to Jack Palance (*Panic in the Streets*, 1950), Lee Remick (*A Face in the Crowd*, 1957), and Warren Beatty (*Splendor in the Grass*, 1961). He worked closely with Tennessee Williams (in *A Streetcar Named Desire* and *Baby Doll*, 1956), and John Steinbeck (in *Viva Zapata*, 1952, and *East of Eden*).

Vivien Leigh *plays the fragile and neurotic Blanche DuBois in* A Streetcar Named Desire — *here with Marlon Brando.*

WHAT TO WATCH

1951	A Streetcar Named Desire
1954	On the Waterfront
1955	East of Eden
1957	A Face in the Crowd
1960	Wild River
1961	Splendor in the Grass

Buster **Keaton**

1895–1966 AMERICAN 1920–1929

12 Comedy

Whether Buster Keaton, the great silent film comedian, co-directed or got no director's credit at all, he was responsible for the overall conception of his films, supreme examples of visual comedy allied to cinematic technique.

From 1920, Keaton was virtually his own director in dozens of shorts, before making features. The multitude of gags depended on cutting, camera set-ups, and brilliant timing. His first feature, *The Three Ages* (1923) parodied D.W. Griffith's *Intolerance*; in fact, the pictorial splendor and feeling for landscape of *Our Hospitality* (1922), *Go West* (1925), and *The General* (1926) owe much to Griffith. In *Sherlock Jr.* (1924), Keaton is a projectionist who finds himself in the films he is working on. Keaton's reputation declined with the coming of sound, but he was rediscovered in the 1960s.

Buster Keaton *as a brave, but foolish train engineer in pursuit of his passionately loved locomotive in* The General, *arguably his favorite movie.*

WHAT TO WATCH

1922	Our Hospitality
1924	Sherlock Jr.
1924	The Navigator
1925	Seven Chances
1926	The General
1927	College
1928	Steamboat Bill Jr.

Abbas **Kiarostami**

1940– IRANIAN 1974–

14 Drama

The fact that Iranian cinema is considered one of the best in the world is mainly due to Abbas Kiarostami, whose films play brilliantly with audiences' perceptions of cinema.

WHAT TO WATCH

1987	Where is the Friend's House?
1992	And Life Goes On
1994	Through the Olive Trees
1997	Taste of Cherry
1999	The Wind Will Carry Us (Bad ma ra Khahad Bord)
2002	Ten

Abbas Kiarostami had been making films for almost two decades before *Where is the Friend's House?* (*Khane-ye Doust Kodjast?*, 1987), a gently humorous film on a child's loyalty, became an international success. *And Life Goes On* (*Zendegi va Digar Hich*, 1992) follows a film director, after an earthquake, searching for the children who featured in one of his films, while *Through the Olive Trees* (*Zire Darakhatan Zeyton,* 1994), written and directed by Kiarostami, is about the filming of *And Life Goes On*. Kiarostami's trademark of people driving over long roads reaches its perfection in *Taste of Cherry* (*Ta'm e Guilass*, 1997), about Mr. Badii, a middle-aged man, who is bent on suicide. Desperately seeking for people to help him, he drives up and down winding roads asking passers-by to bury him in the grave he has already dug for himself. The car motif recurs in *Ten* (2002), a road movie that follows 10 conversations that take place in a car as it is navigated through the streets of Teheran. Although Kiarostami has said, "I don't invent material. I just watch and take it from the daily life of people around me," his realism is carefully constructed.

Set in *Siah Dareh, a remote Kurdish village, The Wind Will Carry Us is a parable about outsiders who pretend to search for a treasure in the village cemetery.*

Krzysztof **Kieslowski**

1941–1996 POLISH 1976–1993

10 Drama

Through his rather sardonic examinations of the conflict between the state and its citizens, Krzysztof Kieslowski has come to represent the "cinema of moral unrest" in Poland.

Politically active in the struggle for a more democratic Poland, Kieslowski expresses many of his ideas obliquely in his features. Nevertheless, his ironic humanism was not appreciated by the authorities and two of his films were suppressed: *Blind Chance (Przypadek,* 1981), which examines the effect of arbitrary fate on the life of a medical student, and *No End (Bez Konca,* 1984), which involves the ghost of a dead lawyer watching his family survive without him. It was on their release in 1986, followed by two short films made as part of a television series based on *The Ten Commandments* (*The Dekalog*), that Kieslowski was extolled abroad. *A Short Film About Killing (Krótki Film o Zabijaniu,* 1988*)* is a powerful anti-capital punishment film, which shows authorized killing is as disturbing as the murder of a taxi driver by a young drifter. In *A Short Film About Love (Krótki Film o Milosci,* 1988), a 19-year-old postal worker is obsessed with a woman in the apartment facing his own. With the fall of communism, Kieslowski chose to work in France where he directed *The Double Life of Véronique* (*La Double Vie de Véronique,* 1991) and the trilogy *Three Colors: Blue (Trois Couleurs: Bleu,* 1993), *Three Colors: White (Trois Couleurs: Bialy,* 1994), and *Three Colors: Red (Trois Couleurs: Rouge,* 1994).

Krzysztof (Henryk Baranowski) *is a university professor who believes in logic but is confronted with the unpredictability of fate, in* The Dekalog.

Irene Jacob *is Veronika, a Polish singer in* The Double Life of Véronique, *which follows the parallel lives of two young women in Poland and France, both played by Jacob.*

WHAT TO WATCH

1981	Blind Chance
1988	A Short Film About Killing
1988	A Short Film About Love
1991	The Double Life of Veronique
1993	Three Colors: Blue
1994	Three Colors: White; Three Colors: Red

Malcolm McDowell *plays Alex, head of a violent gang of teenagers, the Droods, in* A Clockwork Orange, *Kubrick's bleak view of a futuristic Britain.*

Stanley **Kubrick**

1928–1999 AMERICAN 1953–1999

13 Various

The scrupulous care with which he chose his subjects, his slow method of working, and his reclusive personality created a rare expectancy every time Stanley Kubrick made a film.

Deeply pessimistic and claustrophobic, Kubrick's films deal brilliantly with technical and textual complexities. *Lolita* (1962), based on Nabokov's novel about a pedophile, was an acerbic comedy full of "perverse passion." Kubrick's anti-militarism first revealed itself in the bitterly ironic and moving World War I drama *Paths of Glory* (1957) and continued in the black comedy *Dr. Strangelove* (1963). In *Full Metal Jacket* (1987), he powerfully depicts the brutal military training for a pointless war (Vietnam). His futuristic movies develop the theme of dehumanization. In *2001: A Space Odyssey* (1968) man is merely a machine controlled by a machine, while in *A Clockwork Orange* (1971) alienated youths are brainwashed into conformity. Madness is manifest in *The Shining* (1980), and sexual fantasies are explored in his final film, *Eyes Wide Shut* (1999). In contrast, *Barry Lyndon* (1975), inspired by the English landscape and portrait paintings of the 18th century, lovingly recreates the sensibilities of the time.

Film poster, *1987*

WHAT TO WATCH

1957	Paths of Glory
1962	Lolita
1963	Dr. Strangelove
1968	2001: A Space Odyssey
1971	A Clockwork Orange
1975	Barry Lyndon
1987	Full Metal Jacket

Kirk Douglas *produced and starred in Kubrick's epic* Spartacus *(1958).*

Akira **Kurosawa**

◒ 1912–1998 JAPANESE 1943–1993

31 Epic

The best-known Japanese director in the west, Akira Kurosawa has achieved an international popularity that comes from making films with a strong similarity to American movies as well as a deep fidelity to the Japanese tradition.

There has seldom been more cross-fertilization in the cinema than in the work of Akira Kurosawa. Three of his films have transferred easily into Hollywood Westerns. *Rashomon* (1950), the first Japanese film to be shown widely in the west, became *The Outrage* (1964); *The Seven Samurai (Shichinin no Samurai*, 1954) was turned into *The Magnificent Seven* (1960); and *The Bodyguard* (*Yojimbo*, 1961) into *A Fistful of Dollars* (1964). Some of Kurosawa's films are homages to American cinema, while others have literary sources: *Hakuchi* (1951) is based on Dostoevsky's *The Idiot*; *Donzoko* (1957) on Gorky's *The Lower Depths*; *Kumonosu Jô* (1957) on Shakespeare's *Macbeth;* and *Ran* (1985) on *King Lear*. The films work well on an extrovert level, although tragic contemporary tales like *To Live (Ikiru*, 1952), about a man dying of cancer, and *I Live in Fear (Ikimono no Kiroku*, 1955), a family drama, delve much deeper. Kurosawa's flamboyant samurai adventures mix comedy and rich imagery, such as *The Hidden Fortress (Kakushi-toride no San-akunin*, 1958), and *Sanjuro (Tsubaki Sanjûrô*, 1962). Widescreen and color are used magnificently to frame the epic grandeur of *Derzu Uzala* (1975), as well as *Kagemusha* (1980) and *Ran* (1985), with their glorious red sunsets, vivid rainbows, and multicolored flags.

WHAT TO WATCH

1950	Rashomon
1952	To Live
1954	The Seven Samurai
1957	Throne of Blood (Kumonosu Jô)
1958	The Hidden Fortress
1961	The Bodyguard
1962	Sanjuro
1975	Derzu Uzala
1980	Kagemusha
1985	Ran

Film poster, *1950*

A magnificent *battle scene in* Ran, *Kurosawa's cinematic ode to Shakespeare's* King Lear, *in which a warlord's lack of judgement leads to death and disaster.*

In The Seven Samurai, *a veteran samurai (Takashi Shimura, far right) gathers six out-of-work men to rescue a village from bandits.*

The extraordinary *Peter Lorre in one of cinema's most compelling performances, as Hans Beckert, the psychopathic child killer, both frightening and pathetic, in Lang's* M *(for "murderer").*

Fritz **Lang**

1890–1976 | GERMAN-AMERICAN | 1919–1960

46 | Film noir

Looking upon the world with grim detachment and a strong moral sense, Fritz Lang worked through two careers: in Germany (1919 to 1932) and Hollywood (1936 to 1956).

Lang's reputation grew in Germany with serials such as *Dr. Mabuse, The Gambler (Dr. Mabuse, der Spieler,* 1922), which is a masterly study of a decadent society. *The Nibelungen* (1924), a German saga in two parts, makes impressive use of stylized studio sets, while the huge sets of *Metropolis* (1927) represent the futuristic city-factory, where workers slave for rich masters. In his first sound film, *M* (1931), based on a real child-killer, an ironic social comment is made on justice, capital punishment, and mob rule — themes Lang took up in his first American film, *Fury* (1936). *Hangmen Also Die* (1943) was a fictionalized account of the assassination of Nazi Gestapo leader, Reinhard Heydrich — nicknamed the "Hangman" — in which Lang projected increasing public reaction against Nazi atrocities. Having fled Nazi Germany, Lang had to deal with dictatorial producers in Hollywood. MGM tacked on a happy ending to *Fury* and Warner Bros. did the same to *Cloak and Dagger* (1946). Yet, he managed to make splendidly dark films of murder, revenge, and seduction such as *The Woman in the Window* (1944) and *Scarlet Street* (1945); *Clash by Night* (1952), dealing with postwar dissipation; *The Big Heat* (1953) and *Human Desire* (1954), both film noirs, and *Beyond a Reasonable Doubt* (1956) — all of which have a spare, uncompromising visual style reminiscent of German expressionism.

WHAT TO WATCH

1922	Dr. Mabuse, The Gambler
1927	Metropolis
1931	M
1936	Fury
1943	Hangmen Also Die
1944	The Woman in the Window
1945	Scarlet Street
1952	Clash by Night
1953	The Big Heat
1954	Human Desire

Film poster, The Spies, *1927*

David **Lean**

1908–1991 BRITISH 1942–1984

16 Epic, Costume drama

After making several splendid films in the 1940s that epitomized the best of British cinema, David Lean directed five international blockbusters. From then on, his name became inseparable from gargantuan film-making.

David Lean co-directed his first film, *In Which We Serve* (1942), with Noël Coward, before going on to make three further films with Coward: *This Happy Breed* (1944), a saga of the doughty English lower middle-classe; *Blithe Spirit* (1945), a skilful adaptation of the supernatural farce; and *Brief Encounter* (1945). The last, based on a one-act play by Coward (who wrote the screenplay) must be one of the most telling juxtapositions of the romantic and the mundane in cinema. The script, beautifully balanced between the passionate narration and clipped dialogue, the performances of Trevor Howard and Celia Johnson, and fluid camerawork, make it Lean's greatest film.

He followed this with two of the finest screen adaptations of Charles Dickens, *Great Expectations* (1946) and *Oliver Twist* (1948), both with brilliant photography (by Guy Green), design, and acting. Lean's expertise was apparent in the three films he made with his wife Ann Todd, especially *The Sound Barrier* (1952). His films on a larger scale — *The Bridge on the River Kwai* (1957), *Lawrence of Arabia* (1962), *Doctor Zhivago* (1965), *Ryan's Daughter* (1970), and *A Passage to India* (1984) — won a total of 23 Academy Awards. Because of the magnitude of these enterprises, Lean made only five films in the last 27 years of his life.

Judy Davis *plays Adela Quested riding on an elephant with Dr Aziz (Victor Banerjee) on a fateful visit to the Malabar caves in* A Passage to India.

WHAT TO WATCH

1942	In Which We Serve
1945	Brief Encounter
1946	Great Expectations
1948	Oliver Twist
1954	Hobson's Choice
1957	The Bridge on the River Kwai
1962	Lawrence of Arabia
1965	Doctor Zhivago

Lean's epic Doctor Zhivago, *based on Boris Pasternak's novel, traces the life of surgeon-poet Yury Zhivago (Omar Sharif) before and during the Russian Revolution.*

Ang **Lee**

1954– TAIWANESE 1991–

8 Various

From being an art-house favorite, Ang Lee made an extraordinary leap to become a major studio director after only three films. He has demonstrated the crowd-pleasing touch in his character-driven studies of human nature.

The first two films of Ang Lee's trilogy of charming generation-gap family dramas are set in New York where Lee studied. *Pushing Hands* (*Tui shou*, 1991) is about an elderly man living with his son's family in America, and *The Wedding Banquet* (*Hsi yen*, 1993) deals with the farcical situation of a homosexual man making a marriage of convenience, but trying to convince his parents that his relationship is a genuine one. The third film is *Eat Drink Man Woman (Yin Shi Nan Nu,* 1994), which revolves around a widowed chef's relationship with his three daughters. Lee's only film to date shot entirely in Taiwan, it confirms his ability to create distinctive and believable characters who interact with emotion and humor. This led to his first mainstream Hollywood film, an elegant adaptation of Jane Austen's *Sense and Sensibility* (1995), which surprised many who held stereotypes of the themes that Asian directors could tackle.

WHAT TO WATCH

1994	Eat Drink Man Woman
1997	The Ice Storm
2000	Crouching Tiger, Hidden Dragon
2005	Brokeback Mountain

In The Ice Storm, *Kevin Kline, Joan Allen, and Christina Ricci play the dysfunctional Hood family, whose lives are upturned when bad weather hits town.*

This myth was further exploded by *The Ice Storm* (1997), which examines wealthy middle-class New Englanders in 1973 and a Western, *Ride with the Devil* (1999). He returned to an Asian subject with *Crouching Tiger, Hidden Dragon* (*Wo hu cang long*, 2000), renowned for its spectacular martial arts sequences. Lee's innate sensitivity was never more evident than in *Brokeback Mountain* (2005), which gently subverts the macho cowboy genre, making a case against sexual conformity.

Heath Ledger *as Ennis and Jake Gyllenhaal as Jack are doomed lovers who face challenges posed by social intolerance of homosexuality in* Brokeback Mountain.

In Jungle Fever, Spike Lee's *searing study of attitudes to race and the drug culture, Halle Berry makes her big-screen debut as a crack addict.*

Spike **Lee**

1957– AMERICAN 1983–

17 Political drama

The most significant turning point in black cinema was the emergence of Spike Lee, whose films explored a hitherto unknown range of themes from a black perspective.

It was black directors like Melvin Van Peebles, Gordon Parks, and Sidney Poitier in the 1970s who paved the way for Spike Lee in the following decade. But whereas their films catered mainly for black audiences, Lee's appealed to a wider spectrum of society, tackling potentially explosive subjects such as interracial sexual relations and drugs (*Jungle Fever*, 1991), black music (*Mo' Better Blues*, 1990), and black politics (*Malcolm X*, 1992), in terms of mainstream cinema. Lee's first feature, *She's Gotta Have It* (1986), was influenced by the French New Wave directors, and is about a sexually liberated young woman's relationship with her three lovers. Costing only $170,000, the film was a phenomenal box-office success. Lee's preoccupation with cultural identity was manifest in *Do the Right Thing* (1989), a story set in an Italian pizza parlor on a sweltering day in Brooklyn, where racial tensions are about to explode. In one controversial scene, characters shout racial and ethnic epithets directly to the camera. With the radical approach to the material, the brilliantly constructed set, the vibrant cinematography, and the complex (and loud) sound design, Lee showed full mastery of the medium. The film's succcess gave Lee the chance to direct *Malcolm X* after he condemned Warner Bros.' initial decision to hire Norman Jewison to do the job. This film, about the iconic African-American political activist, proved that Lee could fuse a popular form with significant social commentary on a large scale.

Denzel Washington *shone in his Oscar-nominated perfomance in* Malcolm X, *Lee's biopic on the controversial nationalist leader.*

WHAT TO WATCH

1986	She's Gotta Have It
1989	Do the Right Thing
1991	Jungle Fever
1992	Malcolm X
1994	Crooklyn
1995	Clockers

Mike **Leigh**

1943– BRITISH 1971–

9 Comedy

One of the most independent directors, Mike Leigh has developed individualistic working methods that produce hilarious and realistic critiques of mundane existences.

In the 17 years between his first feature, *Bleak Moments* (1971), and the second, *High Hopes* (1988), Mike Leigh built up a body of excellent television work. When he returned to cinema, Leigh worked with a group of actors, getting them to improvise and build up their characters, not knowing exactly where the film would go. The films, in which the characters are mostly sad losers, contain heightened language and imagery. They are also socially conscious without being didactic, when dealing with subjects such as racism (*Secrets and Lies*, 1996) and abortion (*Vera Drake*, 2004). His true period piece *Topsy-Turvy* (1999) is a celebration of the theatre.

Marianne Jean-Baptiste, *as Hortense, and Brenda Blethyn, as Cynthia, confront the past in* Secrets and Lies, *a compelling story of family and reconciliation.*

WHAT TO WATCH

1988	High Hopes
1990	Life is Sweet
1993	Naked
1996	Secrets and Lies
1999	Topsy-Turvy
2004	Vera Drake

Sergio **Leone**

1929–1989 ITALIAN 1961–1984

8 Western

The Italian Sergio Leone had the audacity to take on the sacrosanct American genre of the Western, branding it with his own ritualistic style in films of amoral mythic grandeur.

Sergio Leone's *A Fistful of Dollars* (1964), based on Akira Kurosawa's *Yojimbo* (1961), and his *For a Few Dollars More* (1965) were among a string of Italian-made movies known as Spaghetti Westerns. Recurring features of these films are: a taciturn hero patiently waiting for revenge, snarling faces in large, silent close-ups, circular tracking shots, and the Kabuki-like interruptions of Ennio Morricone's music. "When you have to shoot, shoot — don't talk," a line from *The Good, the Bad and the Ugly* (1966), which ends with an explosive showdown, seems to be the philosophy behind the films. After the success of *Once Upon a Time in the West* (1968) — a perfect example of Leone's style — he used a similarly grandiose approach to tackle crime in the drama *Once Upon a Time in America* (1984).

Clint Eastwood *plays Manco, a hardened bounty hunter in pursuit of a sadistic killer and his band of outlaws in* For a Few Dollars More.

WHAT TO WATCH

1964	A Fistful of Dollars
1965	For a Few Dollars More
1966	The Good, the Bad and the Ugly
1968	Once Upon a Time in the West
1984	Once Upon a Time in America

Ken **Loach**

1937– | BRITISH | 1967–

18 | Social drama

One of the foremost international film directors of his time, Ken Loach has never compromised on his socialist or aesthetic principles.

Loach made a name for himself in the 1960s, with social-realist television dramas, particularly *Cathy Come Home* (1966).

WHAT TO WATCH	
1967	Poor Cow
1969	Kes
1990	Riff Raff
1993	Raining Stones
1998	My Name is Joe
2006	The Wind That Shakes the Barley

Despite the relative commercial success of *Kes* (1969), he then found it difficult to get financing. His comeback in the 1990s showed confidence and maturity. *Raining Stones* (1993), *Ladybird Ladybird* (1994), *My Name is Joe* (1998), and *Sweet Sixteen* (2003) reveal Loach's understanding of and respect for his working-class characters, although he never sentimentalizes them. As he says, "I think it's a very important function to let those people speak, who are usually disqualified from speaking or who've become non-persons."

Film poster, *1969*

Joseph **Losey**

1909–1984 | AMERICAN | 1949–1984

31 | Various

A victim of the McCarthy witch-hunts, Joseph Losey, who made several taut movies in Hollywood, was forced into exile in England, where he became a sharp observer of the social mores of his new home.

Before being blacklisted for his leftist sympathies, Joseph Losey made five features in Hollywood, among them three low-budget thrillers, *The Prowler* (1951), *The Big Night* (1951), and *M* (1951), a worthy remake of Fritz Lang's classic. In England, he became part of the "new realism" movement of British cinema, although he developed a more baroque visual style using elaborate camera movements, shock angles, and dramatic set designs. Rather more restrained were his collaborations with playwright Harold Pinter on three pictures, *The Servant* (1963), *Accident* (1967), and *The Go-Between* (1970), all keen analyses of the English class structure. Based on Peter O'Donnell's comic strip, the pop-art *Modesty Blaise* (1966) is Losey's most enjoyable and relaxed movie.

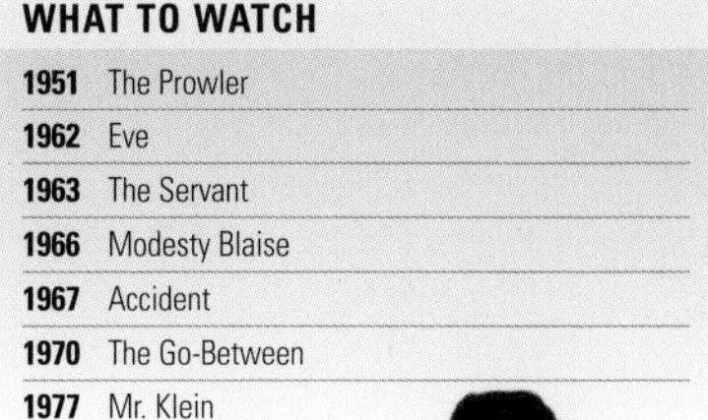

WHAT TO WATCH	
1951	The Prowler
1962	Eve
1963	The Servant
1966	Modesty Blaise
1967	Accident
1970	The Go-Between
1977	Mr. Klein

Dominic Guard *as Leo, a school boy, and Alan Bates as Ted, a tenant farmer, in* The Go-Between*, which deals with class distinction and its effect on a young boy.*

Emil Jannings *plays Louis XV and Pola Negri plays the king's mistress in* Madame Dubarry, *the film that launched both the director and actress into stardom.*

Ernst **Lubitsch**

1892–1947 | GERMAN (AMERICAN) | 1918–1947

46 | Comedy

Ernst Lubitsch brought continental manners and hedonism into puritan America. He established his own style of elegance, wit, incisiveness, and cynicism, perfectly suited to the varied themes he worked on, which came to be called the "Lubitsch Touch."

Lubitsch's features in Germany included a number of ironic historical romances such as *Madame Dubarry* (1919) with Pola Negri. His Hollywood career began with scintillating silent comedies, including *Lady Windermere's Fan* (1925). His musicals with Maurice Chevalier and Jeannette McDonald, as well as comedies *Trouble in Paradise* (1932) and *Design for Living* (1933), treated the audience as sophisticates — rare in commercial cinema. At the end of the 1930s, Lubitsch came up with a number of very entertaining romantic comedies: *Angel* (1937), starring a sparkling Marlene Dietrich; *Ninotchka* (1939), a witty tale of how a stern Russian commisar (Greta Garbo) is seduced by wicked, capitalist ways; and *The Shop Around the Corner* (1940), a charming comedy of errors starring James Stewart. Under the shadow of war, Lubitsch came up with one of Hollywood's great comedies, *To Be or Not to Be* (1942), which took on the Nazi occupation of Poland — of all subjects.

Film poster, *1937*

GRETA GARBO

The love affair between Greta Garbo's (1905–1990) extraordinary face and the camera remains unsurpassed, making her perhaps the greatest of all female screen legends. Her private life and public persona became inseparable; she was the enigmatic goddess who supposedly said, "I want to be alone." Garbo was famous for her classic tragic roles in *Queen Cristina* (1933), *Anna Karenina* (1935), and *Camille* (1937), so when she made *Ninotchka* (1939) MGM trumpeted, "Garbo Laughs!"

WHAT TO WATCH

1932	Trouble in Paradise
1933	Design for Living
1934	The Merry Widow
1936	Desire
1937	Angel
1939	Ninotchka
1940	The Shop Around the Corner
1942	To Be or Not to Be

George **Lucas**

1944– AMERICAN 1977–

6 Science fiction

Star Wars **(1977) changed everything, not least for the 33-year-old who wrote and directed it. He was George Lucas — among the first generation of film-makers to learn their trade at film school.**

Lucas entered Hollywood through his friendship with Francis Ford Coppola, documenting the shooting of Coppola's *The Rain People* (1969). When Coppola set up the American Zoetrope studio, Lucas was part of it. One of their first productions was a sci-fi film developed from Lucas's college project, *THX-1138* (1971), but the film's austerity alienated audiences.

With the war being waged in Vietnam, Lucas talked about going there to shoot a documentary-style feature film inspired by Joseph Conrad's *Heart of Darkness*. Instead, he made *American Graffiti* (1973), a nostalgic evocation of California teen life in the early 1960s: cars, girls, and rock'n'roll. Where *THX-1138* had been cold and cerebral, *Graffiti* was warm and emotional, the first substantial box-office hit to come out of "young Hollywood" since *Easy Rider*. Empowered by this success, Lucas determined to film his dream project, a sci-fi adventure film, in the spirit of the Saturday morning *Flash Gordon* serials he had loved as a child. The shoot was hard: Lucas reputedly has no affinity for actors, and the film's innovative special effects came through trial and error. It was a surprise to everyone when *Star Wars* broke open the blockbuster era. Lucas, who had retained merchandizing rights to the series, became the richest man in Hollywood. He devoted his energies to the special effects company he founded, Industrial Light and Magic (ILM), and turned producer. During the 1980s, his output varied from *Raiders of the Lost Ark* (1981) to *Howard the Duck* (1986). Although there were two more *Star Wars* films in 1980 and 1983, Lucas did not direct again until he revived the franchise in 1999 with three widely disparaged, but still popular, prequels.

Charles Martin Smith *plays a nerdy, 20-year-old, known as "The Toad," in* American Graffiti*; the character represents Lucas.*

WHAT TO WATCH

1971	THX-1138
1973	American Graffiti
1977	Star Wars
1980	The Empire Strikes Back
1983	Return of the Jedi
1999	Star Wars: Episode I — The Phantom Menace
2002	Star Wars: Episode II — Attack of the Clones
2005	Star Wars: Episode III — Revenge of the Sith

Anthony Daniels *as the golden droid C-3PO, locked in a metal suit, is directed by George Lucas in Tunisia for* Star Wars*; Daniels appeared in all six of the* Star Wars *films.*

Baz **Luhrmann**

1962– AUSTRALIAN 1992–

3 Musical, Drama

This flamboyant director defied prevailing fashions to produce three highly artificial romances, which he retrospectively dubbed his "Red Curtain Trilogy." (a reference to their overt theatricality)

The first film in Luhrmann's trilogy is *Strictly Ballroom* (1992), a love story set against the background of amateur ballroom dancing. In the climax, lovers Scott (Paul Mercurio) and Fran (Tara Morice) break from the rigidly regimented steps to create a thrillingly original routine. An iconoclast himself, Luhrmann went to Hollywood and pulled off perhaps the most unorthodox Shakespeare adaptation in cinema: his

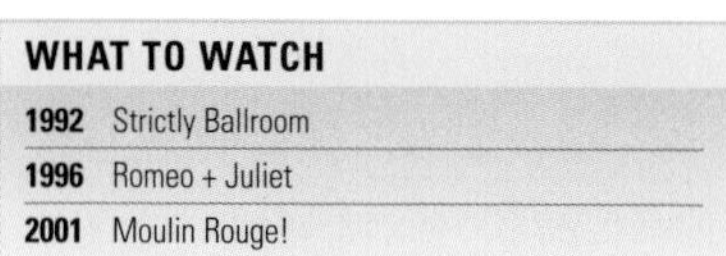

WHAT TO WATCH	
1992	Strictly Ballroom
1996	Romeo + Juliet
2001	Moulin Rouge!

Leonardo DiCaprio *and Claire Danes play the leads in* Romeo + Juliet*; the film's retro-modern style combines castles and armour, with bulletproof vests and boom-boxes.*

Romeo + Juliet (1996) retained the original verse, but relocated the action to a contemporary Mexican gang war.

Luhrmann's first musical, *Moulin Rouge!* (2001), was a kitsch celebration of bohemian Paris in the late 19th century. Stars Ewan McGregor and Nicole Kidman perform some of the film's musical selections themselves; for others, they lip-synch to a selection of karaoke classics by Elton John, David Bowie, and Marc Bolan. Luhrmann is likely to produce further work that reflects his talent for reinvention.

Sidney **Lumet**

1924– AMERICAN 1957–

42 Crime, Drama

Part of the first generation of television directors who transferred successfully to cinema, Sidney Lumet creates powerful films marked by naturalism and theatricality.

Seven of Lumet's first nine features were shot in black and white, the first, and best, being *12 Angry Men* (1957). Although confined to a jury room, the film is never static, due to Lumet's clever use of cutting and camera angles. There followed a trio of films adapted from plays by America's finest playwrights: Tennessee Williams (*The Fugitive Kind*, 1959), Arthur Miller (*A View From The Bridge*, 1961), and Eugene O'Neill (*Long Day's Journey into Night*, 1962). Always a New York director, however, Lumet is at his best among the cops, crooks, and corruption of the city, as with *Serpico* (1973), *Dog Day Afternoon* (1975), and *Prince of the City* (1981), all told against vividly realized New York settings.

WHAT TO WATCH	
1957	12 Angry Men
1962	Long Day's Journey into Night
1965	The Pawnbroker
1973	Serpico
1975	Dog Day Afternoon
1981	Prince of the City
1988	Running on Empty
1990	Q and A

Al Pacino *plays a NYC cop in* Serpico*, which is based on a true story. He is seen here with Barbara Eda-Young as his girlfriend, Laurie.*

David **Lynch**

1946– AMERICAN 1977–

11 Horror, Thriller

David Lynch has accumulated a huge following of audiences willing to enter his bizarre and labyrinthine dream world.

The first feature by David Lynch, *Eraserhead* (1977) was shot in black and white, almost entirely at night. A disturbing nightmare of a movie, ripped from the womb of Surrealist art and German Expressionist cinema, it appeals both to intellectuals and horror-movie fans as does much of his work. *The Elephant Man* (1980), a far more conventional film, evokes pity for the hideously deformed Victorian man, John Merrick (played by John Hurt, who wears layers of makeup).

WHAT TO WATCH

1977	Eraserhead
1980	The Elephant Man
1986	Blue Velvet
1992	Twin Peaks
1999	The Straight Story
2001	Mulholland Drive

Perhaps his most representative film is *Blue Velvet* (1986), which contains elements of satire, crime, and horror — features that are even more evident in the cryptic *Mulholland Drive* (2001). Lynch's most uncharacteristic film is *The Straight Story* (1999), which traces the slow progress of a man traveling hundreds of miles on a lawnmower.

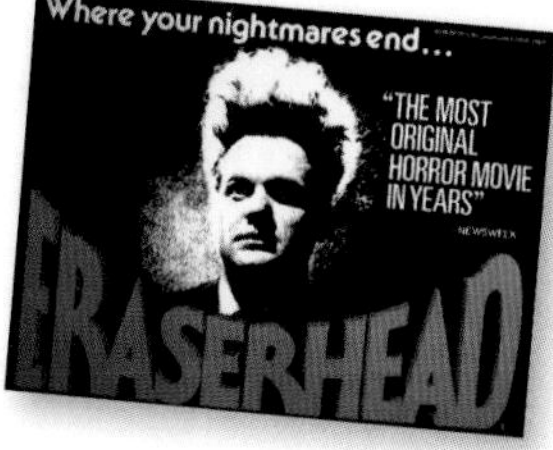

Film poster, *1977*

Leo **McCarey**

1898–1969 AMERICAN 1929–1961

24 Comedy, Drama

There were three phases to Leo McCarey's brilliant career as director: Laurel and Hardy shorts, zany wisecracking comedies, and sentimental romantic comedies.

Among the Laurel and Hardy shorts Leo McCarey directed from 1927 to 1931 is *Putting Pants on Philip* (1927), the first film the comedians made together as a real duo. Between 1932 and 1937, McCarey directed comedians Eddie Cantor (*The Kid From Spain*, 1932), W.C. Fields (*Six of A Kind*, 1934), the Marx Brothers (*Duck Soup*, 1933), and Harold Lloyd (*The Milky Way*, 1936), as well as Cary Grant in *The Awful Truth* (1937), one of the best screwball comedies ever made. The third phase of McCarey's career, after 1937, includes *Love Affair* (1939), remade as *An Affair to Remember* (1957), a shipboard romance. Bing Crosby appeared as a lovable priest in *Going My Way* (1944) and *The Bells of St Mary's* (1945), both handled with enough manipulative skill to bring an atheist to his knees.

WHAT TO WATCH

1933	Duck Soup
1934	Ruggles of Red Gap
1937	Make Way for Tomorrow
1937	The Awful Truth
1939	Love Affair
1940	My Favourite Wife
1944	Going My Way
1945	The Bells of St Mary's
1957	An Affair to Remember

Film poster, *1957*

Cary Grant *stars as Nickie, a wealthy bachelor who falls in love with Terry, an ex-nightclub singer (Deborah Kerr) during a sea voyage in* An Affair to Remember.

Alexander **Mackendrick**

1912–1993 AMERICAN (BRITISH) 1949–1967

9 Comedy

American-born Alexander Mackendrick joined Ealing Studios in London after World War II. He helped form their particular comedy style, whose effectiveness was rooted in realistic observation.

Mackendrick's first feature, *Tight Little Island* (1949), is set in Scotland's Outer Hebrides, on an island deprived of its lifeblood — whisky. *The Ladykillers* (1955), a black comedy about a gang of crooks trying to murder an old lady, was the last Ealing comedy. Mackendrick then made *Sweet Smell of Success* (1957), his first film in the country of his birth. A huge contrast to his previous work, it was a biting drama involving Burt Lancaster's powerful newspaper columnist and Tony Curtis's obsequious press agent, played out against dazzling black-and-white images of New York by night, set off with a jazzy score.

WHAT TO WATCH

1949	Whisky Galore
1951	The Man in the White Suit
1954	The Maggie
1955	The Ladykillers
1957	Sweet Smell of Success

Alec Guinness *(centre) plays Sidney Stratton in* The Man in the White Suit; *Stratton invents a fabric that will never wear out, thus incurring the clothing industry's wrath.*

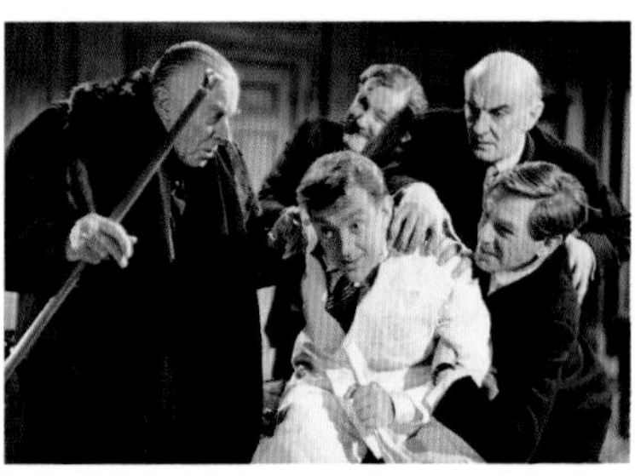

Dusan **Makavejev**

1932– SERBIAN 1966–

11 Experimental

An independent, anarchic, and ironic spirit, Dusan Makavejev creates films that are paradoxical essays. He uses collage methods, often juxtaposing a series of images in a humorous but dramatic manner.

For many years, Makavejev, who was virtually the only director from former Yugoslavia to be known internationally, met with disapproval from the authorities in that country. His first films, *Man is Not a Bird (Covek nije tica*, 1965) and *The Switchboard Operator (Ljubavni slucaj ili tragedija sluzbenice P.T.T.*, 1967) use clips from documentaries, lectures, and animal films to comment on the lives of fictional characters. *W.R.: Mysteries of the Organism (W.R. — Misterije organizma*,1971) refers to psychologist and philosopher Wilhelm Reich and his sexually liberating practices and represents a fusion of styles. Makavejev's exploration of eroticism continued in *Sweet Movie* (1974) and *Montenegro* (1981). For *Innocent Unprotected (Nevinost bez zastite*, 1968), he recut the first Serbian feature ever made (1942).

WHAT TO WATCH

1965	Man is Not a Bird
1967	The Switchboard Operator
1968	Innocence Unprotected
1971	W.R. – Mysteries of the Organism
1974	Sweet Movie

Montenegro is *a story about a community of former Yugoslav eccentrics living in Stockholm.*

Terrence **Malick**

1943– | AMERICAN | 1973–

4 | Drama, War, Epic

Since he made only four movies in 30 years, Terrence Malick's filmography is one of the slimmest in cinema history — yet each film is considered among the finest of its genre.

All four films directed by the enigmatic Malick are concerned with the corruption of innocence, the mythic expulsion from Eden, and the American propensity to violence. Each is a different genre and each is set in the past: the crime movie *Badlands* (1973), in the Midwest of the 1950s; the rural epic *Days of Heaven* (1978), in Texas just before the entry of the US into World War I; the war movie *The Thin Red Line* (1998) during the Pacific campaign of World War II; and the costume drama, *The New World* (2005), in early 17th-century Virginia, with the arrival of the first English colonizers. Each of these ravishing, meticulously crafted films is ironic, fatalistic, and allusive, with a variety of narrative strands, all dealing with the same situations from different viewpoints.

Colin Farrell, *as Captain John Smith, falls in love with O'Orianka Kilcher, as Pocahontas, in* The New World, *Malick's tale of the early colonization of the US.*

WHAT TO WATCH

1973	Badlands
1978	Days of Heaven
1998	The Thin Red Line
2005	The New World

Louis **Malle**

1932–1995 | FRENCH | 1956–1994

21 | Drama

Moving from France to the US with ease, Louis Malle was a "will o' the wisp" director, like the title of one of his films, *Le Feu Follet* (1963). He specialized in difficult or taboo subjects.

"I'm always interested in exposing a theme, a character, or situation which seems to be unacceptable," explained Louis Malle. His subjects included adultery in *The Lovers* (*Les Amants*, 1958), incest in *Murmur of the Heart (Le Souffle au Coeur,* 1971), and child prostitution in *Pretty Baby* (1978). In *My Dinner with André* (1981), he filmed 110 minutes of two people having a dinner conversation. *Lacombe Lucien* (1973) was one of the first French films to reveal some of the least savoury aspects of life in France under the German Occupation — its "hero" is a young laborer who turns Nazi collaborator. *Au Revoir, Les Enfants* (1987) is the culmination of Malle's themes — French collaboration with the Nazis, close mother-son relationships, and an unsentimental view of children.

WHAT TO WATCH

1958	The Lovers
1971	Murmur of the Heart
1973	Lacombe Lucien
1978	Pretty Baby
1980	Atlantic City
1987	Au Revoir, Les Enfants

Gaspard Manesse *and Raphael Fejto star in* Au Revoir Les Enfants, *based on Malle's own childhood.*

Joseph L. **Mankiewicz**

1909–1993 AMERICAN 1946–1972

19 Comedy, Drama

***People Will Talk* (1951) is one of the most appropriate titles in Joseph L. Mankiewicz's filmography. The screen was mostly a vehicle for his literate, witty, and satirical screenplays.**

Although Mankiewicz's films are dialogue-driven, they are not filmed plays. They have an elegant visual style, and many experiment with narrative form, being told from different points of view with an effective use of flashbacks. *A Letter to Three Wives* (1949) is a cleverly constructed story set in suburban America where three wives, Deborah (Jeanne Crain), Lora (Linda Darnell), and Rita (Ann Sothern) wonder which of their husbands is going off with the local vamp. The terse comedy is derived as much from the dialogue and acting as the meticulously observed milieu. *All About Eve* (1950), a poison-pen letter to the New York theatrical world, is a high comedy played to the hilt by Bette Davis as the bitching faded idol Margo Channing. *The Barefoot Contessa* (1954) is equally acerbic about the film industry. *Five Fingers* (1952) is an absorbing espionage tale told in a semi-documentary style. It stars James Mason, who also made a fine Brutus to Marlon Brando's powerful Mark Antony in *Julius Caesar* (1953), an intelligent reading of Shakespeare that avoids the temptation towards Hollywood spectacle, unlike the 45-million-dollar budget of *Cleopatra* (1963). Brando was also excellent in *Guys and Dolls* (1955), both his and Mankiewicz's only musical.

Film poster, *1959*

ELIZABETH TAYLOR

The ravishing raven-haired, sapphire-eyed English-born Elizabeth Taylor (born 1932) was one of the last stars to come out of the studio system in Hollywood. When she was 11, MGM signed her to a 20-year contract. After her triumph in *National Velvet* (1944), she never looked back. She went on to reveal her dramatic talents, winning two Oscars, as well as keeping the gossip columnists busy.

WHAT TO WATCH

1947	The Ghost and Mrs. Muir
1949	A Letter to Three Wives
1950	All About Eve
1952	Five Fingers
1953	Julius Caesar
1954	The Barefoot Contessa
1955	Guys and Dolls
1959	Suddenly Last Summer

Gambler Sky Masterson *(Brando) "corrupts" Save-a-Soul missionary Sarah Brown (Jean Simmons) in the stylish musical* Guys and Dolls.

Anthony **Mann**

1907–1967 AMERICAN 1942–1967

39 Western, Epic

Between 1950 and 1960, Anthony Mann directed 11 Westerns, full of tense love-hate relationships, violence, pain, revenge, and honor, and set against brooding landscapes.

Mann revealed a tougher and more bitter James Stewart in his Westerns than seen in other films, including his own *The Glenn Miller Story* (1954). Along with *Man of the West* (1958) starring Gary Cooper, the Westerns *Winchester '73* (1950), *Bend of the River* (1952), *The Naked Spur* (1953), *The Far Country* (1954), and *The Man from Laramie* (1955) are key films of the genre. The solemn rituals of the Western are not far from the chivalric tradition of *El Cid* (1961), which towers above most historical epics.

WHAT TO WATCH

1950	Winchester '73
1951	The Tall Target
1952	Bend of the River
1953	The Naked Spur
1954	The Glenn Miller Story
1954	The Far Country
1955	The Man from Laramie
1958	Man of the West
1961	El Cid

Legendary Spanish warrior, *El Cid (Charlton Heston), is comforted by his fiancée, Jimena (Sophia Loren), in* El Cid, *Mann's spectacular epic.*

Michael **Mann**

1943– AMERICAN 1995–

10 Adventure, Romance, Thriller

With the glossy 1980s TV series *Miami Vice*, Mann made his fortune. His career bears a superficial resemblance to those of directors of commercials who switched to feature films during that time.

Like contemporaries Tony Scott and Adrian Lyne, Michael Mann is a visual stylist with a penchant for modernist design. But while Scott and Lyne seem content to admire their reflections on the gleaming surface they create, Mann reveals himself as an old-fashioned existentialist, expressing an obsessive male social alienation in neo-noir thrillers like *Thief* (1981), *Manhunter* (1986), and his masterpiece, *Heat* (1995). *The Last of the Mohicans* (1992), the epic tale of adopted Mohican, Hawkeye (Daniel Day-Lewis), and his love affair with British colonel's daughter, Cora (Madeleine Stowe), is a realistic depiction of 18th-century colonialism and war in America. Looking to expand his reach, Mann took on a true-life whistleblower story, *The Insider* (1999), and invested it with his own preoccupations. *Ali* (2001) and *Collateral* (2004) struggle to match the excitement of the real-life situations on which they are based, but Mann remains a compelling contemporary film-maker.

WHAT TO WATCH

1981	Thief
1986	Manhunter
1992	The Last of the Mohicans
1995	Heat
1999	The Insider

Will Graham *(William Petersen), a young retired police officer, hunts down a serial killer in* Manhunter, *adapted from Thomas Harris' novel* Red Dragon.

Chris **Marker**

1921– FRENCH 1956–

18 Documentary

The creative use of sound, images, and text has made Chris Marker into one of the most inventive film-makers with his poetic, political, and philosophical documentaries.

In *Letter from Siberia* (*Lettre de Sibérie*,1958), Chris Marker (born Christian François Bouche-Villeneuve) questions the objectivity of documentaries by repeating one sequence three times, each time with a different commentary. The passionate and influential *Cuba Sí!* (1961) contains two long interviews with Fidel Castro.

WHAT TO WATCH

1958	Letter from Siberia
1961	Cuba Sí!
1963	Le Joli Mai
1962	La Jetée
1977	The Base of the Air Is Red (Le Fond de l'air est rouge)
1983	Sunless
1997	Level Five

In *Sunless* (*Sans soleil*, 1983), Marker tries to make sense of the cultural dislocation he feels in Japan, West Africa, and Iceland. He brings the same foreigner's-eye view to bear on his own city in *Le Joli Mai* (1963), which was compiled from 55 hours of interviews with the people of Paris. His only fiction film, *La Jetée* (1962), a 30-minute nuclear war story, is made up entirely of stills. In *Level Five* (1997), Marker extends the limits of the "documentary," making use of new video technology.

Helene Chatelain *in* La Jetée, *about an apocalyptic disaster; the brilliant use of still images and a sparse narrative make this film both compelling and haunting.*

Jean-Pierre **Melville**

1917–1973 FRENCH 1948–1972

12 Gangster, Film noir

It was his enthusiasm for the works of Herman Melville that made Jean-Pierre Melville change his name (from Grumbach). But it was the American gangster novel and film noir that were the greatest influences on his films, which, in turn, were to inspire several American independent directors.

Fever Heat (*Bob le Flambeur*, 1956) and *Two Men in Manhattan* (*Deux Hommes dans Manhattan*, 1959), Melville's first independent low-budget films, were shot on location in Paris and New York, respectively. His gritty freewheeling style brought something new to the crime thriller, and the eight made by him inhabit a world of sleazy bars, hotels, and nightclubs where double-crossings and killings are commonplace. *Le Samurai* (1967) follows the last day of a cold-blooded killer (Alain Delon) with a code of honor. Melville was in the French Resistance, and three of his films, including the tragic *Army in the Shadows* (*L'Armée des Ombres*, 1969), are about France under occupation.

Roger Duchesne *plans to rob a casino with his associates in* Fever Heat; *Melville's film is considered to be a precursor of the French New Wave.*

WHAT TO WATCH

1950	The Strange Ones (Les Enfants Terribles)
1956	Bob the Gambler
1963	Doulos – The Finger Man (Le Doulos)
1963	Magnet of Doom (L'Ainé des Ferchaux)
1966	The Second Breath (Le Deuxième Souffle)
1967	Le Samurai
1969	Army in the Shadows

Sam **Mendes**

1965– BRITISH 1999–

3 Drama

After rising rapidly in theater, Sam Mendes carried off the rare feat of winning the Academy Award for Best Director for his first film *American Beauty* (1999), which also won the award for Best Picture.

It was Steven Spielberg who offered Sam Mendes his chance to make *American Beauty* for his company Dreamworks after he saw Mendes' Tony-winning production of *Cabaret* in New York in 1998. Mendes' assured film debut was a bittersweet vision of suburban malaise revolving around dysfunctional family life, midlife crises, and teenage alienation. With the help of veteran cinematographer Conrad Hall, he used three distinct styles — tightly composed scenes for the narrative, fluid movements for the fantasy sequences, and hand-held video footage for the films shot by one of the characters. Hall also shot *Road To Perdition* (2002), Mendes' dark celebration of the Hollywood gangster movie of the 1930s. *Jarhead* (2005), an ironic view of the first Gulf War, further revealed Mendes' visual sense.

WHAT TO WATCH

1999	American Beauty
2002	Road To Perdition
2005	Jarhead

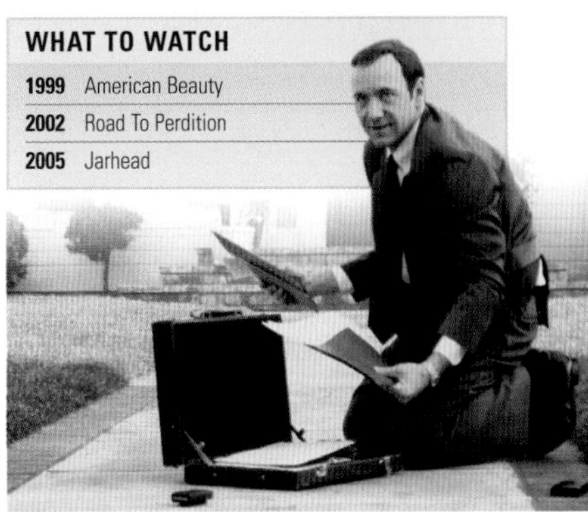

Kevin Spacey *as Lester Burnham, who learns to liberate himself from his "silly little life" in* American Beauty, *which explores themes of love, freedom, and family.*

Fernando **Mereilles**

1955– BRAZILIAN 1998–

4 Drama, Comedy, Thriller

Part of a remarkable resurgence of Latin American movies, Mereilles' *City of God (Cidade de Deus,* 2002) represented a stunning solo directorial debut that immediately placed him in demand outside his native Brazil.

After co-directing two features for an independent company he helped found — a children's movie, *The Nutty Boy 2* (*Menino Maluquinho 2: A Aventura*, 1998) and a comedy *Maids* (*Domésticas*, 2001) — Mereilles adapted a novel about violent gang warfare waged by young boys in one of the most deprived *favelas* of Rio de Janeiro (*City of God*, 2002). With harsh lighting, fast cutting, speeded-up action, jump cuts, and much use of a fluid hand-held camera, the film moves with lightning speed, capturing the fever-pitch life in the slums where life is precarious. Some of the same agitated style, in which Mereilles seems almost afraid to linger on any one thing, was carried over into the British-made *The Constant Gardener* (2005). The film, an effective depiction of drug companies and their ruthless pursuit of profit, is a social and political thriller based on the bestselling novel by John Le Carré.

Alexandre Rodrigues *as Rocket, a photographer who enjoys unrestricted access in the* favelas *to cover the brutal gang wars in* City of God.

WHAT TO WATCH

2002	City of God
2005	The Constant Gardener

Film poster, *2005*

Lewis **Milestone**

1895–1980 AMERICAN 1925–1962

37 Various

Although Lewis Milestone directed a vast range of films, he will always be associated with war movies because of *All Quiet on the Western Front* (1930), his most celebrated film.

WHAT TO WATCH	
1930	All Quiet on the Western Front
1931	The Front Page
1932	Rain
1936	The General Died at Dawn
1940	Of Mice and Men
1946	A Walk in the Sun
1946	The Strange Love of Martha Ivers
1959	Pork Chop Hill

Milestone was never to equal the Academy Award-winning *All Quiet on the Western Front*, one of the most devastating anti-war movies ever made, although his later war films *A Walk in the Sun* (1946), about World War II, and *Pork Chop Hill* (1959), about the Korean War, were also powerful. Among his best "peace" movies were *The Front Page* (1931), one of the first rapid-fire comedies; *Hallelujah I'm a Bum* (1933), an early musical about the Depression; and *Of Mice and Men* (1940), a great adaptation of John Steinbeck's story. Other notable films are *Rain* (1932) and *The Strange Love of Martha Ivers* (1946) — melodramas with strong performances by Joan Crawford and Barbara Stanwyck — and *The General Died at Dawn* (1936), an atmospheric thriller set in China.

George (Burgess Meredith) *and Mae (Betty Field) listen to the simple-minded Lenny (Lon Chaney, Jr.) in* Of Mice and Men, *a tale about unrealizable dreams.*

Anthony **Minghella**

1954– BRITISH 1991–

6 Drama

A talented playwright (and, briefly, an academic), Anthony Minghella spent several years writing for television before getting behind the cameras to direct films.

WHAT TO WATCH	
1991	Truly Madly Deeply
1996	The English Patient
1999	The Talented Mr. Ripley
2003	Cold Mountain
2006	Breaking and Entering

The first film made by Minghella for the BBC, *Truly Madly Deeply* (1991), was a very English riposte to the Demi Moore vehicle *Ghost*: cute and sentimental, but with recognizable heartache. His first Hollywood movie was the fluffy *Mr. Wonderful* (1993). He next teamed up with producer Saul Zaentz to take on Michael Ondaatje's World War II epic *The English Patient* (1996), a considerable leap in scale and ambition, but one he handled with great composure. Since then Minghella has carved out a niche for himself at the literary end of the middlebrow with *The Talented Mr. Ripley* (1999) and *Cold Mountain* (2003). All three movies earned Academy Award attention.

A thriller *about identity theft,* The Talented Mr. Ripley *stars Gwyneth Paltrow, Jude Law, and Matt Damon.*

Vincente **Minnelli**

1910–1986 | AMERICAN | 1942–1976

33 | Musical, Melodrama

The world of Vincente Minnelli is one of beauty, fantasy, brilliant colors, stylish set designs, and elaborate costumes, in which Fred Astaire, Judy Garland, Gene Kelly, Cyd Charisse, and Leslie Caron dance and sing entertainingly.

Seven of the screen's finest musicals were made by Vincente Minnelli for MGM. His film debut was the all-black musical *Cabin in the Sky* (1943), showcasing many of the era's legendary performers. Using Technicolor for the first time in *Meet Me in St. Louis* (1944), Minnelli portrays the life of a family in 1903 with a loving eye for period detail. The film highlights the songs of a radiant Judy Garland (who married Minnelli in 1945). *The Pirate* (1948) has stylized theatrical settings, but the performances by Garland and Gene Kelly prevent the film from being "stagey." Kelly (with Leslie Caron) shines in *An American in Paris* (1951), which ends with an audacious 18-minute ballet. *The Band Wagon* (1953), with Astaire in his finest screen role, which includes a number that sums up Minnelli's musicals: "That's Entertainment." Of the later CinemaScope movies, only *Gigi* (1958) is in the same league. Two of Minnelli's "straight" films, *The Bad and The Beautiful* (1953) and *Lust for Life* (1956), star Kirk Douglas, as a megalomaniac movie producer in the former, and as Vincent Van Gogh in the latter. *Some Came Running* (1959) was a lush, small-town melodrama, featuring Shirley MacLaine and Frank Sinatra.

Judy Garland *sings "The Trolley Song" with Tom Drake and a host of others in* Meet Me in St Louis *— an early Technicolor extravaganza.*

Film poster, *1958*

WHAT TO WATCH

1944	Meet Me In St. Louis
1948	The Pirate
1951	An American in Paris
1953	The Bad and the Beautiful
1953	The Band Wagon
1956	Lust for Life
1958	Gigi
1959	Some Came Running

Gene Kelly *and Leslie Caron sing and dance elegantly in a Paris setting created in Hollywood, in* An American in Paris*; the film won six Academy Awards.*

Kenji **Mizoguchi**

1898–1956 JAPANESE 1923–1956

89 Costume drama

Out of more than 80 films directed by Kenji Mizoguchi, only about a dozen have been seen in the west, but these are enough to establish him as one of the greatest directors of all time.

From 1922 to 1936, Kenji Mizoguchi was forced to make many films in which he had no interest, but he gradually developed his own style and themes. His humanist view of the brutality of feudal Japan is mainly concerned with the sufferings of women. Mizoguchi's style is one of long takes, long shots, and gentle camera movements, delicately avoiding the need for cutting by using slow dissolves and a minimum of close-ups. At moments of crisis or violence, the effect of moving away to a medium or long shot deepens the sympathy for the characters. His best-known films are *The Life of Oharu* (*Saikaku ichidai onna*, 1952), *Tales of Ugestsu* (*Ugetsu Monogatari*, 1953), and *Sansho the Bailiff* (*Sanshô dayû*, 1954), all poignant tales told in beautiful images.

WHAT TO WATCH

1936	Osaka Elegy
1936	Sisters of the Gion
1939	The Story of the Last Chrysanthemums
1946	Utamaro and his Five Women
1952	The Life of Oharu
1953	Ugetsu Monogatari
1954	Sansho the Bailiff
1956	Street of Shame

Women of the Night *(Yoru No Onnatachi, 1948) is an emotional drama about a drug dealer's mistress who learns that her lover is having an affair with her sister.*

Michael **Moore**

1954– AMERICAN 1989–

8 Documentary

Ever since he began making his personal documentaries, Michael Moore has been a thorn in the flesh of uncaring business corporations, rabid right-wingers, and unscrupulous politicians.

Moore has single-handedly taken documentaries out of the ghetto and placed them firmly in the mainstream. He usually puts himself at the center of his angry serio-comic investigations into social ills. In *Roger and Me* (1989), Moore is the "me" referred to in the title and Roger Smith is the chairman of General Motors, who was responsible for the closure of a plant in Flint, Michigan, the director's home town. In *Bowling For Columbine* (2002), Moore relentlessly pursues members of the gun lobby whom he almost accuses of being directly responsibile for the massacre at the high school in Colorado. *Fahrenheit 9/11* (2004) is another subjective attack, this time on "Stupid White Men," which is also the title of Moore's irreverent book on the 2000 US presidential elections.

WHAT TO WATCH

1989	Roger and Me
2002	Bowling for Columbine
2004	Fahrenheit 9/11

Michael Moore *(right) in a scene from the controversial* Fahrenheit 9/11, *his scathing take on the Bush administration and its much touted "War on Terror."*

F.W. **Murnau**

1888–1931 GERMAN 1919–1931

21 Drama, Fantasy

F.W. Murnau (Frederich Wilhelm Plumpe), with the very dissimilar Ernst Lubitsch, was one of the two great German directors in Hollywood. He was killed in a car crash on his way to Paramount Studios, leaving five masterpieces behind him.

Murnau's first features were supernatural tales, culminating in *Nosferatu* (*Nosferatu, eine Symphonie des Grauens*, 1922), the first Dracula film and one of the eeriest. *The Last Laugh* (*Der Letzte Mann*, 1924), although expressionistic in manner, moved nearer the *Kammerspielfilm* (chamber film), which dealt with ordinary people and events with an element of social criticism. The whole touching story of how an old hotel doorman (Emil Jannings) is reduced to a lavatory attendant is told without any intertitles. The camera tracking through the hotel corridors, the subjective shots, and the drunken dream sequences all make words superfluous. Jannings was also the imposing star of *Tartuffe* (*Herr Tartüff*, 1925) and *Faust* (1926), both studio productions with imagery derived from the Old Masters. In Hollywood, Murnau directed *Sunrise* (1927), a simple story of a farmer who tries to kill his devoted wife because of another woman. The blend of German and Hollywood techniques, the lighting, and the fluidity of the camera combine to make it a poetic masterpiece. However, a happy ending was imposed on it, and two more of his Hollywood films suffered from studio interference. As a reaction to this, Murnau (with Robert Flaherty) formed his own company and went to the South Seas to make *Tabu* (1931), the story of a young fisherman in love with a virgin dedicated to the gods, set in a Tahitian paradise. The film won an Academy Award for Best Cinematography.

Emil Jannings *as Mephisto tempts Gosta Ekman's Faust in order to settle a wager between God and Satan over the earth, in Murnau's 1926 film* Faust.

WHAT TO WATCH

1922	Nosferatu
1924	The Last Laugh
1926	Faust
1927	Sunrise
1931	Tabu: A Story of the South Seas

George O'Brien *plays Anses, a farmer, and Janet Gaynor is his wife Indre, in* Sunrise*; the farmer falls in love with a city woman, who suggests that he kills his wife.*

Mike **Nichols**

1931– AMERICAN 1966–

19 Comedy, Drama

Mike Nichols (Michael Igor Peschkowsky) triumphantly straddles both Broadway and Hollywood with sleek stage productions and streamlined movies, which are more thought-provoking and better crafted than most.

Nothing in Mike Nichols' career equalled the impact of his 1967 movie *The Graduate*, for which he won a Best Director Oscar.

WHAT TO WATCH

1966	Who's Afraid of Virginia Woolf?
1967	The Graduate
1983	Silkwood
1988	Working Girl
1990	Postcards from the Edge
1996	The Birdcage
1998	Primary Colors

The film, which made Dustin Hoffman a star, appealed to a young audience, and the songs by Simon and Garfunkel added to its attraction. After a number of flops, Nichols made a comeback with *Working Girl* (1988), a feel-good romantic comedy which also looks incisively at working women. *Postcards from the Edge* (1990) deals with the relationship between a Hollywood star and her unstable daughter, while *Primary Colors* (1998) is about a Clinton-esque politician.

Nichols started *his film career with his debut* Who's Afraid of Virginia Woolf?, *a multi-Oscar winner, starring Richard Burton and Elizabeth Taylor as a bitter middle-aged couple.*

Manoel **de Oliveira**

1908– PORTUGUESE 1942–

31 Costume drama, Documentary

Manoel de Oliveira is among the most original and profound artists working in the medium, and was never more prolific than after he turned 80, writing and directing one film a year until well into his 90s.

WHAT TO WATCH

1942	Aniki Bóbó
1979	Doomed Love
1981	Francisca
1988	The Cannibals
1993	Abraham Valley
1995	The Convent
2001	I'm Going Home
2003	A Talking Picture

While Portugal was under the dictatorial Salazar regime (1932–68), Oliveira was condemned to years of silence and inactivity. As a result, it was only in his 70s that he was able to fully explore his principal interests of desire, fear, guilt and perdition, underscored by the very Portuguese sentiment of the "consolation of melancholy." Many of his films are adaptations of literary works, which, while assuming the literary nature of the text, destroy conventional narrative with long and fixed shots or the repetition of such shots in beautifully composed colour images. Oliveira tantalizingly stipulated that *Memories and Confessions* (*Visita ou Memórias e Confissões*, 1982) is only to be released after his death.

Ema *(Leonor Silveira) is a sensual beauty who enters into a marriage of convenience in* Abraham's Valley, *a haunting portrait of privilege, passion, and loneliness.*

Lola Montès *tells the story of the daring but ruined Lola (Martine Carol), seen here with a circus ringmaster, brilliantly played by Peter Ustinov.*

Max **Ophüls**

1902–1957 GERMAN 1930–1955

21 Costume drama, Melodrama

Max Ophüls' main preoccupation was the transitory nature of love; his bittersweet, nostalgic films are set in the past with a tracking, circling camera suggesting the passage of time.

At the beginning of *La Ronde* (1950), the title being a clue to Ophüls' films, the Master of Ceremonies walks through a film studio onto a *fin-de-siécle* set, changes into an opera cloak, and spins a merry-go-round. He is Ophüls' alter ego and the films are merry-go-rounds moving to the sound of a waltz. A masked dancer sweeps into a dancehall in *House of Pleasure* (*Le Plaisir*, 1952), the camera moving with him, and he keeps whirling as the music gets livelier until he falls. In *Lola Montès* (1955), the ringmaster cracks his whip at the center of a huge circus ring as the heroine reminisces, and the camera revolves 360 degrees to reveal her past. Everything comes full circle as multiple couples keep changing partners in *La Ronde* and after the earrings of *Madame de...* (1953) are passed from hand to hand.

After five films in Germany including *Leiberlei* (1932), a story about doomed love, Ophüls went to the US. The only film he made there that suggests the European period was *Letter From an Unknown Woman* (1948). Returning to Paris in 1949, he made *La Ronde* with a terrific French cast; *House of Pleasure*, based on three Guy de Maupassant stories; *Madame de...*, a witty confection; and his final film, *Lola Montès*, the only one in colour and with an extraordinary treatment of space on the CinemaScope screen.

WHAT TO WATCH

1932	Leiberlei
1940	Mayerling to Sarajevo
1948	Letter From an Unknown Woman
1950	La Ronde
1952	House of Pleasure
1953	Madame de...
1955	Lola Montès

Anton Walbrook, *the worldly-wise raconteur, and Simone Signoret, the prostitute Leocadie, in* La Ronde *— a circular tale of relationships in Vienna set in 1900.*

Nagisa **Oshima**

1932– JAPANESE 1959–

26 Drama

The influence of the French New Wave is felt in Nagisa Oshima's films, which are mostly stimulating, disconcerting, and provocative metaphors of Japanese social values.

Both *Death by Hanging (Koshikei*, 1968), which earned international renown, and *Boy (Shonen*, 1969) critically dissect Japanese social life. The former deals with a condemned man, whose body refuses to die, while the latter relates how a boy's parents train him to get knocked down by cars so they can sue the drivers. Oshima equates sexual liberation with rebellion in *Diary of a Shinjuku Thief* (*Shinjuku dorobo nikki*, 1969), but his most notorious film is *In the Realm of the Senses (Ai no corrida*, 1976), focusing on obsessive sex between a gangster and a prostitute. *Empire of Passion (Ai no borei*, 1978) is equally steamy.

In an eerie *scene from Oshima's moody period piece* Empire of Passion, *Gisaburo (Takahiro Tamura), a murdered rickshaw driver, returns as a ghost.*

WHAT TO WATCH

1960	The Sun's Burial (Taiyo no hakaba)
1968	Death by Hanging
1969	Diary of a Shinjuku Thief
1969	Boy
1971	The Ceremony (Gishiki)
1976	In the Realm of the Senses
1978	Empire of Passion
1999	Taboo (Gohatto)

Yasujiro **Ozu**

1903–1963 JAPANESE 1927–1962

54 Drama, Comedy

It is difficult to describe Ozu's work without making it sound trivial but, within their chosen parameters, his films are rich in humor, emotion, and psychological and social insight.

The work of Yasujiro Ozu is marked by a certain consistency. He never married, yet, apart from his early films which were light, ironic comedies influenced by Hollywood cinema, he deals with middle-class family relationships, particularly the parent-child generation gap. He worked with the same actors and technicians throughout his career. Stylistically and thematically too, the movies of his mature period are very alike — even the titles are confusingly similar — and it was the interplay of characters that absorbed him rather than the plot. After 1930, he never used a dissolve and seldom moved the camera, which remained fixed a little lower than waist level. Each of his sequences is of great formal beauty, often punctuated by short external shots and intensified by music.

Keiji Sada *and Yoshiko Kuga take tea in* Good Morning, *which Ozu remade from his own first feature* I Was Born, But ... (1932)*; both are moving portrayals of childhood.*

WHAT TO WATCH

1947	The Record of a Tenement Gentleman
1949	Late Spring (Banshun)
1951	Early Summer (Bakushû)
1953	Tokyo Story (Tokyo Monogatari)
1956	Early Spring (Soshun)
1958	Equinox Flower (Higanbana)
1959	Good Morning (Ohayo)
1960	Late Autumn (Akibiyori)
1961	The End of Summer (Kohayagawa-ke no aki)
1962	An Autumn Afternoon (Sanma no aji)

Georg Wilhelm **Pabst**

1885–1967 GERMAN 1923–1956

31 Drama, War

Compelling depictions of human degradation in a corrupt society, Pabst's films came out of a Germany defined by rapid inflation and the rise of Nazism, and went on to inspire a major shift from expressionism to realism in the German cinema.

Despite the obvious unfairness to Pabst, it is temping to observe that in all his best films, the actresses, rather than the director, stand out: the 20-year-old Greta Garbo on the brink of prostitution in *Joyless Street* (*Die Freudlose Gasse*, 1925); Brigitte Helm as the lonely blind girl in *The Love of Jeanne Ney* (*Die Liebe der Jeanne Ney*, 1927); Lotte Lenya in *The Threepenny Opera (Die Dreigroschenoper*, 1931) and, above all, the American Louise Brooks in *Pandora's Box* (*Büchse der Pandora*, 1928) and *The Diary of a Lost Girl* (*Das Tagebuch einer Verlorenen*, 1929). *Pandora's Box* is a star vehicle for Louise Brooks, with her black bobbed hair framing her pale kittenish face, and her every gesture and expression imbued with eroticism. The character she created — Lulu, the woman who destroys men — became one of the icons of cinema, and inspired Pabst to produce his finest work, *Diary of a Lost Girl* (1929).

WHAT TO WATCH

1927	The Love of Jeanne Ney
1928	Pandora's Box
1929	Diary of a Lost Girl
1931	The Threepenny Opera
1931	Comradeship

The enigmatic *Greta Garbo plays Greta Rumfort, her second leading role, in* Joyless Street *(1925), a depiction of the dark side of life in Vienna after World War I.*

This film again explores the social and economic breakdown of post-war Germany, with its brutal depiction of a girls' reform school. Both *Westfront 1918* (1930), Pabst's sound film debut, and *Comradeship* (*Kameradschaft*, 1931) plead the cause of international brotherhood. The former ends with the hand of a French soldier clutching a dead German's hand; the latter tells of German miners rescuing their French comrades trapped in a shaft. Though Pabst's *The Threepenny Opera* is a slightly softened adaptation of the Bertolt Brecht/Kurt Weill musical, it retains plenty of anti-bourgeois bite.

Pabst made three historical films under the Nazis, including *Paracelsus* (1943). As a form of atonement, his later films, notably *The Trial* (*Der Prozeß*, 1948), are attacks on anti-Semitism.

Pabst's Westfront 1918 *gives a bitter, realistic view of the barbed wire and trenches of World War I, seen through the eyes of four young German recruits.*

Sergei **Paradjanov**

1924–1990 GEORGIAN 1954–1988

11 Costume drama

Sergei Paradjanov's poetic, pictorially breathtaking films explore not only the history and folklore of the great Georgian director's native land, but also his personal and idiosyncratic universe.

Born in Georgia to Armenian parents, Paradjanov was imprisoned for three years in the Soviet Union in 1974 for various "crimes." His first film to be shown in the west, *Shadows of Forgotten Ancestors* (*Tini Zabutykh Predkiv,* 1964), reveals his remarkable talent for lyricism and opulence.

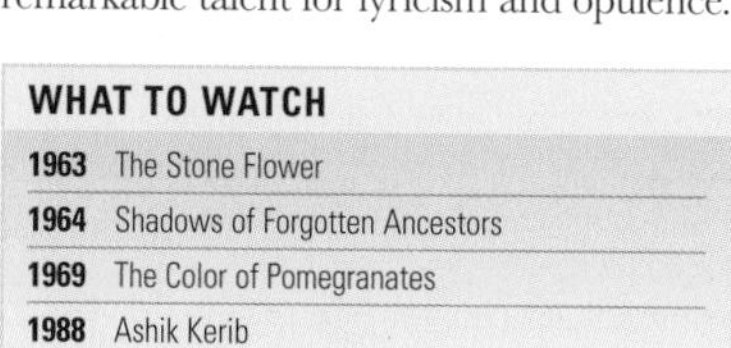

WHAT TO WATCH	
1963	The Stone Flower
1964	Shadows of Forgotten Ancestors
1969	The Color of Pomegranates
1988	Ashik Kerib

In Shadows of Forgotten Ancestors, *Ivan Mikolajchuk (centre), here wearing the traditional costume of the Ukrainian Hutsuls, plays a tragic hero.*

His love of music, dance, and costumes reached its peak in *The Color of Pomegranates* (*Sayat Nova,* 1969), its eloquent imagery illustrating — in a series of tableaux — the poems of the 18th-century Georgian poet Sayat Nova. In his final film *Ashik Kerib* (*Ashugi Qaribi,* 1988), each kaleidoscopic episode is ravishing; at the end, a white dove alights on a black camera, fluttering out of the past and into the present.

Alan **Parker**

1944– BRITISH 1976–

14 Musical, Thriller, Drama

The films of Alan Parker display technical bravura, strong, often contentious, stories, and an admitted preference for a "theatrical edge."

In the early 1970s, Alan Parker, a working-class Londoner, ran a successful advertising film company. His films reveal his training in attention-grabbing, and his talent for new and bold ideas. Parker's first film, *Bugsy Malone* (1976), featuring children playing Chicago gangsters of the 1920s, has well-staged numbers and a talented, appealing cast. The controversial *Midnight Express* (1978), Parker's biggest hit, is a brilliantly staged movie based on the true story of a young American jailed for drug smuggling in Istanbul. Also powerful, but more politically liberal, are *Birdy* (1985), set in an army hospital during the Vietnam War, and *Mississippi Burning* (1988), a civil rights drama. Balancing these is *Fame* (1980), a lively musical that follows eight young people at the American Academy of Performing Arts, and *Evita* (1996), a lavish adaptation of the stage musical. Curiously, only *Pink Floyd — The Wall* (1982) and *The Commitments* (1991) are set in the British Isles.

WHAT TO WATCH	
1976	Bugsy Malone
1978	Midnight Express
1985	Birdy
1988	Mississippi Burning
1991	The Commitments
1996	Evita

Madonna *plays the title role of Eva Peron in* Evita, *Parker's biopic. The film is based on Andrew Lloyd Webber's musical.*

Street urchin *Perkins (Ninetto Davoli) is an object of ridicule in Pasolini's sexually explicit rendition of* The Canterbury Tales. *The film was shot in Canterbury, UK.*

Pier Paolo **Pasolini**

1922–1975 ITALIAN 1961–1975

12 Satire, Drama

Although the uncompromising films of Pier Paolo Pasolini have their roots in Italian neorealism they are permeated in ideology and myth.

Pasolini was a well-known novelist, poet, and screenwriter before directing his first film, *Accatone* (1961). He drew on his knowledge of Rome for this realistic depiction of a derelict urban landscape, revealing his fascination with social outcasts. *The Gospel According to St. Matthew* (*Il Vangelo Secondo Matteo*, 1964) is a poetic attempt to present Jesus Christ as an ordinary Italian peasant. *Oedipus Rex* (*Edipo Re*, 1967), while faithful to Sophocles, has a prologue and epilogue set in modern Rome. Pasolini deals with the middle classes for the first time in *Theorem* (*Teorema*, 1968), which shows each member of a bourgeois family liberated sexually by a stranger (Terence Stamp). *The Decameron* (*Il Decameron*, 1971), *The Canterbury Tales* (*Il Racconti di Canterbury*, 1972), and *The Arabian Nights* (*Il Fiore Delle Mille e Una Notte*, 1974) form a trilogy of satires, which capture the free spirit of the classic original. The final 10 minutes of his last film *Salo, or the 120 Days of Sodom* (*Salò o le 120 giornate di Sodoma*, 1975), an updating of a de Sade novel, are among the most memorable in cinema.

WHAT TO WATCH

1961	Accatone
1964	The Gospel According to St. Matthew
1967	Oedipus Rex
1968	Theorem
1971	The Decameron
1972	The Canterbury Tales
1974	The Arabian Nights
1975	Salo, or the 120 Days of Sodom

Jesus Christ *(Enrique Irazoqui) is kissed by Judas (Otello Sestilli) in* The Gospel According to St. Matthew.

Sam **Peckinpah**

1925–1984 AMERICAN 1961–1983

15 Western

Associated with the rise of graphic screen violence in 1960s' Hollywood, Sam Peckinpah's lyrical films portray disenchantment. His Westerns, in particular, are explorations into moral ambiguities.

Born and brought up on a ranch in California, Sam Peckinpah attended military school and went through a spell in the Marines. His films reflect his background — a masculine world where one's manhood and independence are often expressed through violence. Hence the nostalgia for the Old West where men were heroes and women were subordinate. The recurring theme of "unchanged men in a changing land" is introduced in his second feature, *Ride the High Country* (1962), with Randolph Scott and Joel McCrea as aging gunfighters against an autumnal landscape. William Holden and his gang in *The Wild Bunch* (1969), set in 1914, try to live as outlaws from another age, although the scenes of

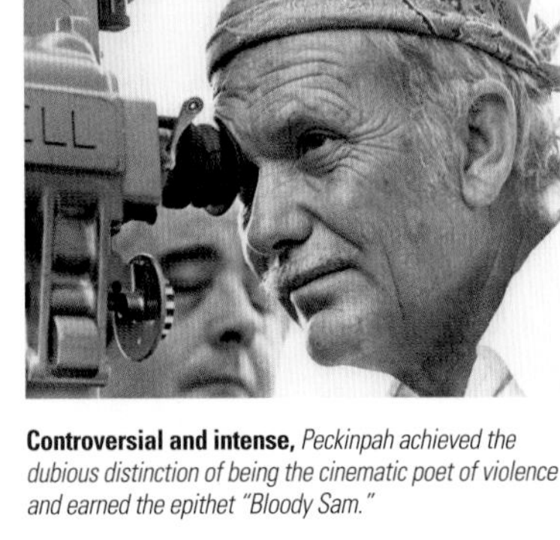

Controversial and intense, *Peckinpah achieved the dubious distinction of being the cinematic poet of violence and earned the epithet "Bloody Sam."*

carnage reflect the year the film was made. *The Ballad of Cable Hogue* (1970) is another elegy for the Old West, but with more of Peckinpah's edgy sense of humor. Steve McQueen as the title character in *Junior Bonner* (1972), rather touchingly, feels anachronistic (rather like the director himself) in the new-style West and follows his own moral code, living at the edge of society. Peckinpah continued a running battle with producers whom he saw as the bad guys. For example, he disowned *Major Dundee* (1965) when it was recut by others (a longer version, nearer the director's cut, was released in 2005). Away from the controlling mythology of the Western, his blood-dimmed vision was less coherent.

WHAT TO WATCH

1962	Ride the High Country
1965	Major Dundee
1969	The Wild Bunch
1970	The Ballad of Cable Hogue
1973	Pat Garrett and Billy the Kid
1974	Bring Me the Head of Alfredo Garcia

Billy (Kris Kristofferson) *and Pat (James Coburn), play old friends turned adversaries in the 1973 Western,* Pat Garrett and Billy the Kid.

Wolfgang **Petersen**

1941– GERMANY 1981–

13 Drama

More than competent when it comes to engineering suspense, but rarely inspired when choosing scripts, Wolfgang Petersen will do the best with what he is given.

Peterson's Hollywood work includes the absorbing Clint Eastwood vehicle *In the Line of Fire* (1993), the Homeric epic *Troy*, with Brad Pitt and Eric Bana (2004), and the mystery thriller *Shattered* (1991), which he also wrote. But *The Perfect Storm* (2000) was a disappointment, and *Air Force One* (1997) was inane. However, Petersen will always be remembered for one film, *Das Boot* (The Boat, 1981), which is a tense, gritty, claustrophobic U-boat drama that caused a sensation in Germany with its sympathetic portrayal of pragmatic mariners doing their job. Perhaps surprisingly, it was equally popular in the US, where it was nominated for six Academy Awards (Petersen was nominated for his direction and his screenplay). The film's reputation as a modern classic remains strong to this day.

WHAT TO WATCH

1981	Das Boot
1993	In the Line of Fire
2004	Troy

Das Boot, *originally a German TV mini-series, changed the direction of Petersen's career and propelled him into the world of Hollywood blockbusters.*

Roman **Polanski**

1933– POLISH 1962–

17 Drama

The turbulent life of Roman Polanski has influenced many of the subjects of his films. They offer a rather bleak view of humanity, but the stories are narrated with absurdist humor.

Born of Polish parents who were sent to concentration camp, Polanski revisited 1940s' Poland in the Academy Award-winning film *The Pianist* (2002), his first in his native country since *Knife in the Water* (1962). There is little distinction between nightmare and reality in many of his films. Mia Farrow screams "This is not a dream. It is reality" in *Rosemary's Baby* (1968) on believing that she has been impregnated by the devil. We witness the "reality" of Catherine Deneuve's breakdown as the walls of her room come alive in *Repulsion* (1965). Sex is a theme that runs through Polanski's films: sexual rivalry (*A Knife in The Water*), sexual disgust (*Repulsion*), sexual humiliation (*Cul-de-Sac*, 1965), and incest (*Chinatown*). The brutal murder of his wife Sharon Tate in 1969 was followed by his depiction of gruesome murders in *Macbeth* (1971), the most blood-soaked of all Shakespeare's plays.

WHAT TO WATCH

1962	Knife in the Water
1965	Repulsion
1965	Cul-de-Sac
1968	Rosemary's Baby
1974	Chinatown
1976	The Tenant
2002	The Pianist

Adrian Brody *plays Wladyslaw, a Polish Jewish pianist who witnesses Nazi persecution in* The Pianist.

Michael **Powell,** Emeric **Pressburger**

1905–1990 (Powell), 1902–1988 (Pressburger)

BRITISH (Powell), HUNGARIAN (BRITISH) (Pressburger) 1939–1972 (Powell), 1942–1956 (Pressburger) 50 (Powell), 16 (Pressburger)

Fantasy, Musical, War

The films that carry the unusual credit of "Produced, Written and Directed by Michael Powell and Emeric Pressburger" are eccentric, extravagant, witty fantasies. They contrast sharply with the realistic approach typical of British cinema of their period.

WHAT TO WATCH	
1943	The Life and Death of Colonel Blimp
1944	A Canterbury Tale
1945	I Know Where I'm Going
1946	A Matter of Life and Death
1947	Black Narcissus
1948	The Red Shoes
1948	The Small Back Room
1951	The Tales of Hoffman

In 1939, Michael Powell (as director) collaborated with the Hungarian Emeric Pressburger (as scriptwriter) for the first time on *U-Boat 29*, thus beginning one of the closest creative partnerships in cinema history. So close was their working relationship that, although Pressburger's contribution was mostly writing and Powell was in charge on the studio floor, they received joint directorial credit on their films from 1939 to 1956. This may account for their curious blend of the very British and the very Middle European. There is a mystical love for England in *A Canterbury Tale* (1944) and for Scotland in *I Know Where I'm Going* (1945), and British patriotism and courage in *One of Our Aircraft is Missing* (1942) and *Hour of Glory* (1948). However, the most sympathetic characters, enacted by different actors, are Germans in *U-Boat 29* (Conrad Veidt, 1939), *Pursuit of the Graf Spee* (1956, Peter Finch) and, most controversially, *Colonel Blimp* (1943, Anton Walbrook). Winston Churchill tried to ban the latter for "ridiculing the army" during wartime.

Film poster, *1959*

Stairway to Heaven (1946), *The Red Shoes* (1948), *The Tales of Hoffman* (1951), and *Oh! Rosalinda* (1955) are closer to the world of Vincente Minnelli's Hollywood musicals (influenced in turn by European design) than to any other British film. Each, however, examines the nature of cinema and its links with theatre, painting, and music. *The Red Shoes*, perhaps the duo's most popular film, is also an allegory of the artist's unswerving dedication to art in the person of Boris Lermontov (Anton Walbrook), the ballet-dancer impresario in the film. Out of the twelve films they made between 1943 and 1956, nine were in sensuous Technicolor (photography by Jack Cardiff

John Justin, *June Duprez, and Sabu in* The Thief of Baghdad, *an early Powell-Berger-Whelan film.*

or Christopher Challis) with flamboyant sets and designs (Hein Heckroth and Alfred Junge). Junge's studio sets for *Black Narcissus* (1947) create the atmosphere of a Himalayan convent, where nuns struggle against desire. A heady mixture of religion and eroticism also runs through the wondrously strange *A Canterbury Tale*, in which a man pours glue on the heads of girls who date servicemen.

The team broke up after the World War II adventure film *Night Ambush* (1956). Powell never had the same success alone, although the perverse *Peeping Tom* (1959), about a psychopathic murderer who photographs victims at the moment of death, is rich in levels of interpretation and has gained in reputation over the years. In the 1970s, Powell was "rediscovered" by Martin Scorsese and Francis Ford Coppola who set up projects with him. In 1981, he was appointed as advisor at Coppola's Zoetrope Studios, and he married Scorsese's editor Thelma Schoonmaker in 1984.

Moira Shearer *plays Victoria, a young dancer torn between love and her career, with Leonide Massine, in* The Red Shoes, *a romance set in the world of ballet.*

In One of Our Aircraft is Missing, *Robert Beatty, Emrys Jones, and Bernard Miles play bomber crew members desperate to survive.*

Otto **Preminger**

1905–1986 AUSTRIAN (AMERICAN) 1931–1980

37 Film noir, Thriller

The best films of Otto Preminger, made in the US from 1935, are moody crime melodramas, using a cool, interrogatory method.

As a young man, Preminger got to watch many trials because his father was a public prosecutor in Vienna. Many of his films are put together like pieces of evidence in a trial where the characters reveal themselves through their obsessions. In *Laura* (1944), a detective falls in love with a "dead" woman; murders and trials also occur in *Fallen Angel* (1945) and *Whirlpool* (1950). A whole town is put on trial in *The Thirteenth Letter* (1951), and trials are central to *The Court-Martial of Billy Mitchell* (1955), *Saint Joan* (1957), and *Anatomy of a Murder* (1959). These are considered the essential Preminger movies, along with *Daisy Kenyon* (1947), starring Joan Crawford. Preminger battled censorship for *The Moon is Blue* (1953) and *The Man with the Golden Arm* (1956). In the 1960s, he shifted to making blockbusters like *Exodus* (1960) and *Advise and Consent* (1962).

WHAT TO WATCH

1944	Laura
1945	Fallen Angel
1947	Daisy Kenyon
1956	The Man with the Golden Arm
1959	Anatomy of a Murder
1960	Exodus
1962	Advise and Consent

James Stewart, *Ben Gazarra, and Arthur O'Connell discuss the defense in* Anatomy of a Murder.

Vsevolod **Pudovkin**

1893–1953 RUSSIAN 1926–1953

13 Epic, Costume drama

At the forefront of the exciting experimental period in Soviet silent cinema, Vsevolod Pudovkin was, like others, forced to toe the Communist party line later in his career.

Pudovkin and his contemporary, Eisenstein, were among the first great theorists of cinema, who put their theories of dynamic montage into practise. A comparison was made when they both directed films on the same subject in the same location at the same time. Pudovkin's *The End of St. Petersburg* (*Konets Sankt-Peterburga*, 1927) is more human and less stylized than Eisenstein's *October*, showing the effects of the revolution of 1917 on an uneducated peasant boy. Pudovkin's first feature, *Mother, 1905* (*Mat*, 1926), adapts Maxim Gorky's rambling novel into a tightly constructed narrative. His last great silent film, the passionate *Storm Over Asia* (*Potomok Chingis-Khana*, 1928) tells the tale of Bair (Valeri Inkizhinov), a Mongolian nomad, who leads his people against the British occupying forces.

WHAT TO WATCH

1926	Mother
1927	The End of St. Petersburg
1928	Storm Over Asia

In this dramatic scene *in* Storm Over Asia, *Bair, the Mongol trapper, is captured by British soldiers.*

Joan Crawford, *here with Ben Cooper and Scott Brady, was one of two women starring in* Johnny Guitar *— the other was Mercedes McCambridge. The film is also a psychological study and a penetrating social commentary.*

Nicholas **Ray**

1911–1979 AMERICAN 1948–1963

20 Film noir, Western, Epic

Even within the context of the Hollywood studio, Nicholas Ray (Raymond Nicholas Kienzle) managed to make a number of off-beat movies, focusing on alienated characters, and using dynamic framing and dramatic colors.

A pre-credit sequence in *They Live By Night* (1948), Ray's first feature, introduces us to Cathy and Farley, doomed outlaw lovers, with the subtitle: "This boy, this girl were never properly introduced to the world we live in." This statement is applicable to most of Ray's characters. Among them are Nick (John Derek), the boy from the slums on trial for murder in *Knock on Any Door* (1949), Dixon (Humphrey Bogart), the isolated screenwriter with sadistic tendencies in *In a Lonely Place* (1950), and misanthropic cop Jim (Robert Ryan) in *On Dangerous Ground* (1951). They, with Jim, Judy, and Plato (James Dean, Natalie Wood, and Sal Mineo) in *Rebel Without a Cause* (1955), and Ed (James Mason) hooked on cortisone in *Bigger Than Life* (1956), are all loners, trying to make contact with the world, caught in extreme situations. As Johnny (Sterling Hayden) says in *Johnny Guitar* (1953), "I'm a stranger here myself." Ray's use of color and choreographed action sequences suggest a musical form, although he never made a musical. The anthropology in *The Savage Innocents* (1960), the ecology in *Wind Across the Everglades* (1958), and the neuroses of male leads, such as Jeff (Robert Mitchum), the lonely rodeo rider in *The Lusty Men* (1952), are all features that make these films unusual for the time. Ray's brooding romantic side was stifled in the epics, *King of Kings* (1961) and *55 Days at Peking* (1963). His final work *Lightning Over Water* (1980) is an account of his illness with brain cancer.

WHAT TO WATCH

1948	They Live By Night
1950	In a Lonely Place
1953	Johnny Guitar
1955	Rebel Without a Cause
1956	Bigger Than Life
1958	Wind Across the Everglades

Satyajit **Ray**

1921–1992 INDIAN 1955–1991

31 Drama

The films of Satyajit Ray, which mainly deal with the collision between traditional and modern beliefs, offer no easy answers, but reveal the human face of his vast country.

Pather Panchali (*Song of the Road*, 1955), *Aparajito* (*The Unvanquished*, 1956), and *The World of Apu* (*Apur Sansar*, 1959), known to the world as the Apu trilogy, established Ray's international renown. Most of his work's themes are in the trilogy, notably the effect of change on individuals. *The Music Room* (*Jalsaghar*, 1958) focuses on an ageing aristocrat trying to cling to bygone days, while in *The Chess Players* (*Shatranj ke Khilari*, 1977), a 19th-century nawab tries to stem the tide of change. *The Lonely Wife* (*Charulata*, 1964) and *Days and Nights in the Forest* (*Aranyer Din Ratri*, 1969), both subtle masterpieces, show the influence of Jean Renoir and Anton Chekhov, but the deceptively simple cinematic effects are the master Indian director's own.

In The Chess Players, *Nawab Wajid Ali Shah (Amjad Khan) confers with his prime minister (Victor Banerjee) before being ousted from his throne by the British.*

WHAT TO WATCH

1955	Pather Panchali
1956	The Unvanquished
1958	The Music Room
1959	The World of Apu
1963	The Big City
1964	The Lonely Wife
1969	Days and Nights in the Forest
1973	Distant Thunder
1975	The Middle Man
1977	The Chess Players

Carol **Reed**

1906–1976 BRITISH 1933–1972

28 Thriller

Directing a number of skilful dramas with excellent actors, Carol Reed created films that are rich in atmosphere and milieu.

Most of Carol Reed's successes were literary adaptations with complex lead characters. He brilliantly sustains the tension in *Odd Man Out* (1947), his first hit, which tells of the last hours of a wounded IRA gunman on the run. Reed reached the peak of his career in two films scripted by Graham Greene: *The Fallen Idol* (1948), an intensely claustrophobic drama with a child's perspective of the adult world, and *The Third Man* (1949), an atmospheric thriller set in the shadowy world of post-war Vienna. He made an attempt to recapture the atmosphere of his earlier films in *The Man Between* (1953), and returned to Greene with *Our Man in Havana* (1959). Some of his larger projects include the Academy Award-winning musical *Oliver!* (1968). Reed once commented: "I give the public what I like, and hope they will like it too."

Noël Coward, *Alec Guinness, and Burl Ives take instruction on the set of* Our Man in Havana, *a satirical comedy about espionage in Cuba.*

WHAT TO WATCH

1940	Night Train to Munich
1941	Kipps
1947	Odd Man Out
1948	The Fallen Idol
1949	The Third Man
1959	Our Man in Havana
1968	Oliver!

Jean **Renoir**

1894–1979 FRENCH 1925–1970

37 Drama, Farce, Musical

The career of Jean Renoir spans almost the history of cinema from expressionism to Neo-Realism. His films range from film noir to Hollywood studio productions, and from Technicolor period spectacles to fast television techniques.

Son of Pierre-August Renoir, the impressionist painter, Jean Renoir entered films in order to make his wife (Catherine Hessling, one of his father's models) a star. He displayed her strange stylized acting in his first five silent films. But Renoir only blossomed as a director with sound, which he used brilliantly. He directed the extraordinary Michel Simon in three of his first talkies, including *Boudu Saved from Drowning* (*Boudu Sauvé des Eaux,* 1932), where Simon, playing a tramp, is the spirit of anarchy trapped in a bourgeois marriage. Renoir's cinema is egalitarian: there are no heroes or villains. The three prisoners of war in *The Grand Illusion (La Grande Illusion*, 1937) are working class, middle class, and aristocratic, united in brotherhood. In *The Rules of the Game* (*La Règle du Jeu*, 1939), the servants are as important as their masters. "The terrible thing about this world is that everybody has his reasons," says a character in the film. In the US during World War II, Renoir managed to preserve his style, even persuading the studios to shoot *The Southerner* (1945) on location. On his return to Europe, he made three stylish operetta-like romances about the choice between the theater and life: *The Golden Coach* (*Le Carrosse d'Or*, 1953) with Anna Magnani; *French Can-Can* (1955) with Jean Gabin; and *Elena and Her Men* (1956) with Ingrid Bergman. Renoir's films are a unique blend of emotions and moods, realism, fantasy, tragedy, and farce.

WHAT TO WATCH

1932	Boudu Saved from Drowning
1936	The Crime of Monsieur Lange (Le Crime de Monsieur Lange)
1937	The Grand Illusion (La Grande Illusion)
1938	The Human Beast (La Bête Humaine)
1939	The Rules of the Game (La Règle du Jeu)
1945	The Southerner
1953	The Golden Coach (Le Carrosse d'Or)
1955	French Can-Can
1956	Elena and Her Men

Film poster, *1937*

Jean Gabin *and Simone Simon star in* La Bête Humaine, *a psychological thriller about a homicidal engine driver, based on the novel by Émile Zola.*

Alain **Resnais**

1922– FRENCH 1959–

15 Drama, Romance, War

Alain Resnais' best films mingle memory, imagination, past and present, and desire and fulfilment. They treat sound, words, music, and images on an equal basis.

In *Hiroshima Mon Amour* (1959), a French actress has an affair with a Japanese architect. Set in a rebuilt Hiroshima that is still traumatized by the horror of the atom bomb, images of the actress's past in wartime France flash into her mind. *Last Year at Marienbad* (*L' Année Dernière à Marienbad*, 1961) changed the concept of subjective time in cinema. *Muriel* (1963) seems more realistic on the surface, but it is as stylized and metaphysical as Resnais' previous films. These three masterpieces were never equalled, although *The War is Over* (*La Guerre est finie*, 1966), a portrait of an aging exile from Franco's Spain now living in France, and *Providence* (1977), a nightmare lived by a dying novelist, come close. In the 1980s, Resnais made a number of film adaptations of stage works with his own company of actors.

Elle (Emmanuele Riva) *and Lui (Eiji Okada), tormented by their past, console each other in* Hiroshima Mon Amour*; the film evokes Resnais' fixation with memory, history, and time.*

WHAT TO WATCH

1959	Hiroshima Mon Amour
1961	Last Year at Marienbad
1963	Muriel
1966	The War is Over
1974	Stavisky
1977	Providence
1997	Same Old Song

Tony **Richardson**

1928–1991 BRITISH 1959–1990

21 Adventure, Drama, Romance

At the start of his career, Tony Richardson was perhaps the most representative director of the new British realist "kitchen sink" drama. He later moved on to a number of literary adaptations.

As part of a group of playwrights, novelists, and film-makers labelled "angry young men," Tony Richardson, Karel Reisz, and John Osborne set up Woodfall Films in 1958 to produce movies concerned with social realism. Richardson's first two features were pungent versions of Osborne's plays, *Look Back in Anger* (1959) and *The Entertainer* (1960).

WHAT TO WATCH

1959	Look Back in Anger
1960	The Entertainer
1961	A Taste of Honey
1962	The Loneliness of the Long Distance Runner
1963	Tom Jones
1968	The Charge of the Light Brigade

Albert Finney *plays Tom, an 18th-century Englishman who loves women, food, and wild adventures in* Tom Jones*; he's seen here wooing Sophie (Susannah York).*

Richardson blended French New Wave techniques with his own for *A Taste of Honey* (1961) and *The Loneliness of the Long Distance Runner* (1962) — probably his best films. In vast contrast, *Tom Jones* (1963) turned Henry Fielding's mock heroic 18th-century novel into a freewheeling bawdy romp full of cinematic tricks. Richardson's last few films, made in the US, lacked that certain British stamp he brought to his earlier ones.

Leni **Riefenstahl**

1902–2003 GERMAN 1932–1944

5 Documentary, Propaganda

Despite Leni Riefenstahl's protestations that her documentaries celebrating the Nazi Party and the Berlin Olympic Games were merely records of historic events, she shaped them brilliantly into great propaganda spectacles.

Riefenstahl starred in her first feature, *The Blue Light* (*Das Blaue Licht*, 1932), a "mountain film" in which nature, especially dramatic mountains, played a key role. Hitler was impressed and supplied her with more than 40 cameramen to shoot the 1934 Nuremberg Rally under the title of *Triumph of the Will* (*Triumph des Willens*, 1935). In the film, Hitler is seen as a Wagnerian hero descending upon the medieval town, the sun shining on his head like a halo while ecstatic faces stare up at him. Riefenstahl was then commissioned to film the 1936 Berlin Games, which emerged as *Olympia* (1938) after two years of editing. Blacklisted by the Allies in 1945, she could not work for seven years, after which she completed *Lowlands* (*Tiefland*, 1944), begun in 1935, starring herself as a gypsy dancer.

Original German poster for Triumph of the Will. *Riefenstahl's innovative camera techniques and revolutionary approach to music and cinematography make this one of the greatest propaganda films.*

WHAT TO WATCH

1932	The Blue Light
1935	Triumph of the Will
1938	Olympia
1944	Lowlands

Jacques **Rivette**

1928– FRENCH 1960–

20 Avant-garde, Fantasy

The films of Jacques Rivette are challenging, intellectually enquiring, and uncompromisingly long. They are probably the most under-appreciated among the works of the French New Wave directors.

Ironically, for a director so steeped in cinema, theater dominates much of Jacques Rivette's work, one of the principal themes being the "play-within-a-film," which he explored in his first feature, *Paris Belongs to Us* (*Paris Nous Appartient*, 1961), where a group of amateur actors come together in a deserted Paris in summer to stage a performance of Shakespeare's *Pericles*. Paris is the constant background to his films, seen as realistically as possible, but where fantastic things take place. One of his most accessible films is *Céline and Julie Go Boating* (*Céline et Julie Vont en Bateau*, 1974), a brilliantly comic meditation on the nature of fiction. Rivette's exploration of the act of creation reaches its apex in *La Belle Noiseuse* (1991), which captures with painful lucidity the anguish of an artist struggling to express himself on canvas.

WHAT TO WATCH

1961	Paris Belongs to Us
1966	The Nun (La Religieuse)
1968	Mad Love (L'Amour Fou)
1974	Céline and Julie Go Boating
1991	La Belle Noiseuse
1994	Jeanne la Pucelle
2001	Va Savoir

Camille (Jeanne Balibar), *a stage actress, hunts for a missing ring in* Va Savoir, *a witty comedy, which, like many of Rivette's films, is located in a theatrical setting.*

Glauber **Rocha**

1938–1981 BRAZILIAN 1962–1980

10 Drama

The radical films of Glauber Rocha draw on the cultural traditions of Brazil. Often contrasting primitive and modern facets of his country, Rocha uses ritualized theatrical techniques and political texts.

Rocha was the leader of the group Cinema Novo, a cooperative set up in the late 1950s, whose aim was to free Brazilian films of American influence. *Black God, White Devil* (*Deus E o Diabo na Terra do Sol*, 1964) and *Antonio Das Mortes* (*O Dragão da Maldade Contra o Santo Guerreiro*, 1969) are set in the arid north-east of Brazil where the starving peasants are exploited by bandits, multinational companies, and the church. Forced into a ten-year exile by the military junta, Rocha made *The Lion Has Seven Heads* (*Der Leone have Sept Cabeças*, 1970) in Africa, its cry for international revolution represented by the five languages that make up the film's original title. Often evoking directors as diverse as John Ford, Sergei Eisenstein, and Luis Buñuel, Rocha's films moved increasingly into anarchy and madness.

WHAT TO WATCH	
1962	The Turning Wind
1964	Black God, White Devil
1969	Antonio Das Mortes
1970	The Lion Has Seven Heads

Geraldo Del Ray *is the peasant Manuel in* Black God, White Devil, *about a killer hired by the church and landowners in Brazil's impoverished hinterland.*

Nicolas **Roeg**

1928– BRITISH 1970–

14 Cult, Thriller

It is not surprising that the complex and elusive films of Nicolas Roeg, one of the very few great cinematographers to make a successful transition to film directing, should be visually stunning.

Roeg worked in the film industry as a cameraman for 12 years before co-directing (with Donald Cammell) his first feature, *Performance* (1970). The film is a bizarre psycho-sexual psychedelic drama with Mick Jagger as a faded rock-star and James Fox as a hitman on the run. Horrified by the kaleidoscope of sex and violence in the film, Warner Bros. delayed its release for two years. The film immediately made Roeg a cult director, and his followers were seldom disappointed by further offbeat films such as the supernatural thriller *Don't Look Now* (1973), the oddball sci-fi movie *The Man Who Fell to Earth* (1976), and *Bad Timing* (1980), about a sado-masochistic affair between Alex (Art Garfunkel), a psychoanalyst, and Milena, (Roeg's wife Theresa Russell), a young woman in Vienna.

John Baxter *(Donald Sutherland) recovers his daughter's drowned body in* Don't Look Now, *Roeg's powerful and puzzling thriller.*

WHAT TO WATCH	
1970	Performance
1970	Walkabout
1973	Don't Look Now
1976	The Man Who Fell to Earth
1980	Bad Timing

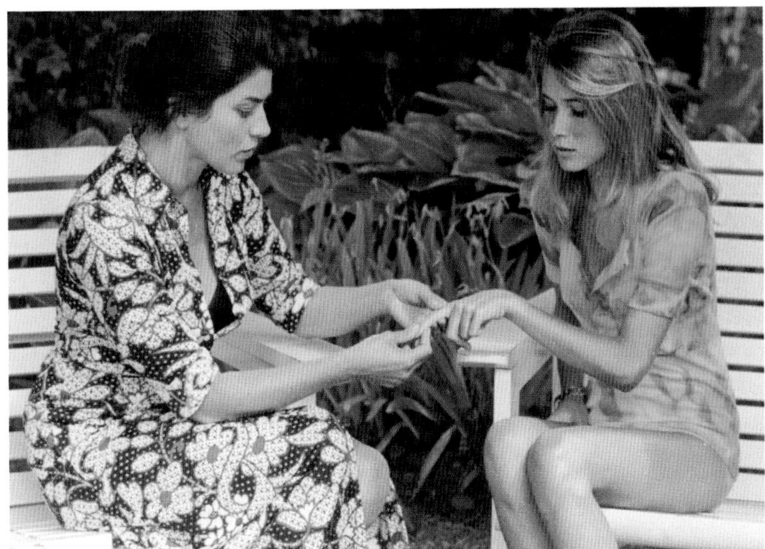

In this *scene from* Claire's Knee, *Aurora (Aurora Cornu), a novelist, chats with sultry teenager Claire (Laurence de Monaghan), whose knees are objects of fantasy.*

Eric **Rohmer**

1920– FRENCH 1959–

22 Comedy

In Eric Rohmer's words, "I'm less concerned with what people do than what is going on in their minds while they're doing it." Although most of his films are dialogue-centric, they are far from being conversation pieces.

The characters in Rohmer's delicious comedies of error are largely defined by their relationships with the opposite sex. The sumptuous, hedonistic settings and seductive characters are essentially what the conversations, narrations, and diary extracts in the plots are all about. For films that deal to a large extent with resistance to temptation, they are tantalizingly erotic. In each of the "Six Moral Tales" series, a man renounces sex with a woman for ethical reasons. In *The Collector* (*La Collectioneuse*, 1966), an intellectual rejects the advances of a promiscuous bikini-clad nymphet. (Young girls were to appear with increasing frequency in Rohmer's films as he got older.) In *My Night at Maud* (*Ma Nuit chez Maud*, 1969), a man spends a chaste night in bed with Maud, a beautiful woman. Jerome, a diplomat (Jean-Claude Brialy) spending summer in a lake resort, permits himself the exquisite pleasure of embracing a teenager's knee in *Claire's Knee* (*Le Genou de Claire*, 1970), as erotic a moment as any bedroom scene. In Rohmer's second series called "Comedies and Proverbs," characters are less articulate, but still analyze all their actions. His witty investigations into the illusions of love continued with "Tales of Four Seasons."

WHAT TO WATCH

1969	My Night with Maud (Ma Nuit chez Maude)
1970	Claire's Knee (Le Genou de Claire)
1980	The Aviator's Wife (La Femme de l'Aviateur)
1983	Pauline at the Beach (Pauline à la Plage)
1986	The Green Ray (Le Rayon Vert)
1989	A Tale of Springtime (Conte de printemps)
1992	A Tale of Winter (Conte d'hiver)
1996	A Summer's Tale (Conte d'été)
1998	An Autumn Tale (Conte d'automne)

Étienne (Didier Sandre), *a professor, and the young Rosine (Alexia Portal) pictured in* An Autumn Tale, *a bittersweet look at love and relationships in midlife.*

Roberto **Rossellini**

1906–1977 ITALIAN 1940–1977

30 Cult, Drama, Horror

Passion and humanity resonate through the films of Roberto Rossellini in the three phases of his career: neorealism, the Ingrid Bergman melodramas, and the films on saints and historical figures.

Although the term "Neo-Realist" was first applied to Luchino Visconti's *Ossessione* (1942), it was Rossellini's three films on the Resistance: *Rome, Open City* (*Roma, Città Aperta*, 1945); the Liberation: *Paisan* (*Paisà*, 1946); and postwar turmoil: *Germany Year Zero* (*Germania Anno Zero*, 1947), which established the style. Shot with minimum resources in natural surroundings, the films depict historic events in human terms with a striking immediacy. Children emerge as the nucleus of suffering: in *Germany Year Zero*, a young boy in occupied post-war Germany, who is unable to feed his family, throws himself off a ruined building. In 1950, Rossellini married Ingrid Bergman and instead of glamorous roles, cast her in intense ones. Bergman seeks salvation on top of a volcano in *Stromboli* (1950), tends the poor and the sick in *The Greatest Love* (*Europa '51*, 1952), witnesses a miracle in *Journey to Italy* (*Viaggio in Italia*, 1953), and is driven to suicide in *Fear* (*La Paura*, 1954)—all films about marriage in crisis. The sequence was interrupted by *The Flowers of St. Francis* (*Francesco, Giullare di Dio*, 1950), which illustrates the life of the saint. After his divorce from Bergman, Rossellini made historical and religious features, mainly for television. Among these were biopics on Socrates, Augustine of Hippo, the Medicis, and Alcide de Gasperi, Italy's first postwar president. *The Rise of Louis XIV* (*La Prise de Pouvoir par Louis XIV*, 1966), also released on the large screen, reveals how power resides in routine and ritual. *The Messiah* (*Il Messia*, 1976), on Christ, was his last film.

In Stromboli, *Karen (Bergman) realizes she has escaped a POW camp only to be imprisoned in marriage. The theme of displacement in Rossellini's war films is revisited here.*

Edmund *(Edmund Meschke), in* Germany Year Zero, *faces a burnt out Berlin where he must eke out a living. The low-angle shot points to the insurmountable task ahead of him.*

WHAT TO WATCH

1945	Rome, Open City
1946	Paisan
1947	Germany Year Zero
1950	Stromboli
1952	The Greatest Love
1953	Voyage to Italy
1959	General della Rovere (Il Generale della Rovere)
1966	The Rise of Louis XIV

John **Sayles**

1950– AMERICAN 1980–1996

15 Drama

A pioneer independent, John Sayles is one of the few directors who define "independent" film-making in a political sense.

Sayles has ploughed his own furrow, making low-budget films for which he writes the scripts himself and casts from a committed support group of friends and allies (including Chris Cooper, Angela Bassett, David Straithairn, and Kris Kristofferson). A novelist before he became a film-maker (he rewrote scripts for Roger Corman), Sayles rarely achieves the lifelike immediacy of, say, John Cassavetes. The dialogue can feel overly clever, while the visuals can seem like an afterthought. Nevertheless Sayles' intelligence is obvious, and his dedication to filming low-key blue-collar stories is admirable. His landmark films include *Return of the Secaucus Seven* (1980); *Matewan* (1987); *City of Hope* (1991); and *Lone Star* (1996).

Chris Cooper, *with Mary McDonnell as Elma, plays Joe, a union organizer in* Matewan. *Set in a 1920s West Virginian mining community, the film is beautifully conceptualized.*

WHAT TO WATCH	
1980	Return of the Secaucus Seven
1987	Matewan
1991	City of Hope
1996	Lone Star

John **Schlesinger**

1926–2003 BRITISH 1962–2000

17 Thriller, Drama

Moving as he did between America and Britain, John Schlesinger regarded himself as a "mid-Atlantic" director. His films reflects this cross-fertilization.

Schlesinger's first two films introduced young players, such as Alan Bates (*A Kind of Loving*, 1962), and Tom Courtenay and Julie Christie (*Billy Liar*, 1963), set in accurately depicted working-class surroundings. He replaced "kitchen sink" settings with those of "swinging London," and moved up in society with *Darling* (1965), a cynical morality play. *Midnight Cowboy* (1969), the first of his many American movies, is an insightful view of New York and American life. After the success of *Marathon Man* (1976), starring Dustin Hoffman — here pitted against a Nazi war criminal in New York — Schlesinger was encouraged to make further American thrillers. His British films, such as *Sunday, Bloody Sunday* (1971), a drama about a love triangle, are rather more personal and show a deep understanding of human behavior.

Dustin Hoffman *as conman Ratzo Rizzo and Jon Voight as "cowboy" stud Joe Buck enact memorable roles of amoral anti-heroes in New York's underbelly, in* Midnight Cowboy.

WHAT TO WATCH	
1962	A Kind of Loving
1963	Billy Liar
1965	Darling
1969	Midnight Cowboy
1971	Sunday, Bloody Sunday
1976	Marathon Man

Martin **Scorsese**

1942– AMERICAN 1968–

20 Gangster, Thriller

The exciting, dark, and obsessive talent of Martin Scorsese is seen at its best in his explorations into the Italian-American identity. He looks into its endemic machismo and violence that often manifests itself in crime.

Scorsese's inventiveness was first noticed as editor and virtual director of *Woodstock* (1970), the rockumentary. Roger Corman helped him to make his first feature, *Boxcar Bertha* (1972), an excellent apprentice work with a fine sense of locale. A restless, nervy man, Scorsese spent a bedridden asthmatic childhood in a Sicilian-Catholic family in Little Italy, New York. He gives the impression of being obsessed with his background, although he claims to have exorcised the demons of his childhood by making *Mean Streets* (1973). Filmed in dark tones, the film inhabits the twilight world of poolrooms, bars, and nightclubs, where two small-time crooks, Charlie (Harvey Keitel) and his sidekick "Johnny Boy," (Robert De Niro) try to survive. The smooth bonhomie between members of the Mafia, the pasta meals, Italian arias, religious and family rituals camouflaging the violence, and gun lore seething beneath, were to become familiar elements in Scorsese's thrillers. This milieu was revisited in *GoodFellas* (1990), where he expands and refines the examination of these dubious, ironically glamorized, members of the Mob, seen through the eyes of a young man, Henry (Ray Liotta), attracted to the false aura of power and success. In *Gangs of New York* (2002), Scorsese recreates the Manhattan of the mid-19th century on an epic scale,

WHAT TO WATCH	
1973	Mean Streets
1976	Taxi Driver
1977	New York, New York
1980	Raging Bull
1985	After Hours
1986	The Colour of Money
1988	The Last Temptation of Christ
1990	GoodFellas
1993	The Age of Innocence
2002	Gangs of New York

An unusual *film from Scorcese,* The Age of Innocence *nevertheless depicts his well-traversed theme of a man (Daniel Day-Lewis as Newland) caught between desire (for Ellen, played by Michelle Pfeiffer) and reality.*

Ray Liotta *(center) sizzles as "wiseguy" Henry Hill, who longs to be a gangster in* Goodfellas, *a hard-hitting, fast-paced, true-life mobster story set in 1970s New York.*

where the predecessors of the "goodfellas" operated. *Raging Bull* (1980), the story of Jake La Motta — world middleweight boxing champion from 1949 to 1951 — which alternates between professional fights and domestic ones, is another of Scorsese's powerful explorations into the close-knit Italian-American community with underlying codes of masculinity. Virtually an anti-biopic — unlike the more conventional one of Howard Hughes, *The Aviator* (2004) — it tells us nothing of La Motta's past, nor is there much use of narrative techniques. Rather, it presents us, in splendid black-and-white images, with the male animal's primitive emotions. Scorsese's favourite actor, Robert de Niro, won the Academy Award for Best Actor for the raw energy of his performance. If the New York of *Taxi Driver* (1976) is the city of the 1940s film noir, then *New York, New York* (1977) is the wonderful town of 1940s musicals. After playing a jazz musician in the latter, De Niro convincingly enacted the role of a disturbed would-be comedian in Scorsese's brilliant black comedy about show business fame, *The King of Comedy* (1983). Away from the violence that dominates many of his movies, he successfully entered Merchant-Ivory country with *The Age of Innocence* (1993) and courted controversy with *The Last Temptation of Christ* (1988).

In response to the criticism that his films contain pointless violence, Scorsese says: "There is no such thing as pointless violence. It's reality, it's real life, it has to do with the human condition. Being involved in Christianity and Catholicism when I was very young, you have that innocence, the teachings of Christ. Deep down you want to think that people are really good — but the reality outweighs that."

ROBERT DE NIRO

Intensity and relentless professionalism are key to the earlier part of the career of Robert de Niro (born 1943), the true heir to Marlon Brando. He excelled in the portrayal of outsiders, especially in the many films of Martin Scorsese, like *Taxi Driver* (1976), *New York, New York* (1977), *Raging Bull* (1980), and *The King of Comedy* (1983). After making these films he could easily have made his living as a cab driver, a saxophone player, a boxer, or a stand-up comic. De Niro was also superb as the younger Don Corleone in *Godfather II* (1974) and a Vietnam vet in *The Deer Hunter* (1978).

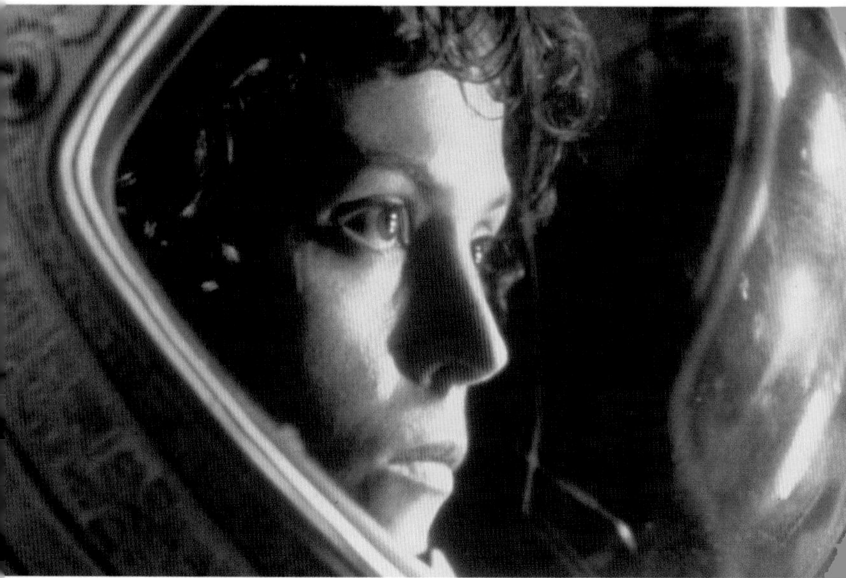

Ridley **Scott**

1937– BRITISH 1985–

17 Science fiction, Thriller

One of the supreme visual stylists, Ridley Scott is a graduate of the Royal College of Art, and came up through the British advertising industry along with his younger brother Tony, Alan Parker, and Hugh Hudson.

If his decorative pictorial style can produce breathtaking images, on a bad day Ridley Scott is also capable of virtually a parody of the over-designed advertising aesthetic, such as the blossom-strewn fantasy *Legend* (1985), which at times resembles a commercial for toilet paper. With *Alien* (1979), he redefined what space travel might look like, and *Blade Runner* (1982) went one better, imagining a dismal retro-fitted, dystopian future so authoritatively, it has become a cliché.

Ellen Ripley *(Sigourney Weaver as one of cinema's first female action heroes) is the sole survivor of the spaceship crew attacked by homicidal creatures in* Alien.

WHAT TO WATCH

1979	Alien
1982	Blade Runner
1991	Thelma and Louise
2000	Gladiator

Scott's best films have strong dramatic situations underpinned with either a mythic or broad political subtext, but he rarely delves very deep. Sometimes praised for his strong heroines (*Alien*; *Thelma and Louise,* 1991; *GI Jane,* 1997; and *Hannibal,* 2001), he seems to subscribe to sexual equality but reveals barely any interest in psychology. He is not a natural action director, but has the visual bombast to camouflage such deficiencies.

An up and down career hit a nadir with the Christopher Columbus movie *1492: Conquest of Paradise* (1992), but peaked with a costume epic, the Academy Award-winning spectacle *Gladiator* (2000). Surprisingly, his filmography consists of a few forgettable generic thrillers too: *Black Rain* (1989), *Someone to Watch Over Me* (1987), *White Squall* (1996), and *Matchstick Men* (2003).

In Thelma and Louise, *Susan Sarandon (Louise) and Geena Davis (Thelma) take their photograph before embarking on a weekend road trip that goes very wrong.*

Ousmane **Sembene**

1923– SENEGALESE 1963–

13 Comedy-drama

The comedy-dramas of Ousmane Sembane dig deep into African society and its colonial past. The director thought of himself as the modern incarnation of the *griot*, the tribal storyteller.

The favourite theme of Ousmane Sembene is the effect on his country of nearly 400 years of colonial rule. He joined the Free French Forces fighting in Senegal in 1942, and his wartime experiences contributed to the authenticity of two of his films, *God of Thunder* (*Emitai*, 1971) and *The Camp at Thiaroye* (*Camp Thiaroye*, 1987), which reveal aspects of World War II through African eyes. His second film, *The Money Order* (*Mandabi*, 1968), was the first feature ever made by an all-African crew in a native African language — Wolof, a widely spoken language in Senegal. Most of Sembene's intelligent and entertaining films are in Wolof, and they deliver social messages through wry humour and pathos.

Village women *fetch water in* Moolaadé *(meaning protection); the film critically analyses the practice of female circumcision still performed in parts of Africa.*

WHAT TO WATCH

1968	The Money Order
1971	God of Thunder
1974	Xala (The Curse)
1987	The Camp at Thiaroye
2004	Moolaadé

Bryan **Singer**

1965– AMERICAN 1993–

13 Thriller, Adventure

A serious-minded film-maker whose best-known work is derived from comic books, Bryan Singer appears well schooled in the rigours of popular entertainment.

Singer has a fluid, handsome camera style that was shown to best advantage in the teasingly atmospheric independent cult hit *The Usual Suspects* (1995). While borrowing from masters of film noir thrillers like Hitchcock and Scorsese, the film retains an originality that is Singer's own. Hardly the obvious choice for a director on the brink of a Hollywood career, *Apt Pupil* (1998) was a revealing follow-up, although in the end it was a rather ponderous adaptation of a Stephen King story about Todd (Brad Renfro), a teenager who becomes obsessed with a Nazi who lives next door. The film's themes of fascism and repression shed an oblique light on Singer's first two *X-Men* movies (*X-Men*, 2000 and *X2*, 2003), with their richly allegorical sympathies for myriad freaks and misfits. With the release of *Superman Returns* (2006), Singer returns to the comic book genre.

WHAT TO WATCH

1995	The Usual Suspects
2000	X-Men
2006	Superman Returns

Wolverine *(Hugh Jackman) bares his claws in* X-Men, *a stylish, witty sci-fi spectacle based on the 1960s Marvel comic book mutants.*

Douglas **Sirk**

1897–1987 | AMERICAN | 1934–1959

39 | Melodrama, Musical, Drama

Remembered, first and foremost, as the director of four rich Technicolor "women's pictures" of the 1950s, Douglas Sirk (Claus Detlev Sierk) made comedies, musicals, war films, and Westerns.

Born in Germany of Danish parents, Sirk made ten films in Europe under his real name before going to the US. In Hollywood, he attempted a range of genres, all of them created with impeccable style, paying attention to lighting, sets, and costumes. Sirk directed the suave George Sanders in three atmospheric period pieces—*Summer Storm* (1944), *A Scandal in Paris* (1946), and *Lured* (1947). His strength in soap operatics was first evident in a Barbara Stanwyck film, *All I Desire* (1953), but it burgeoned in the melodramas he made in Technicolor for Universal Pictures, beginning with *Magnificent Obsession* (1954).

Film poster, *1956*

In the film, Rock Hudson plays Bob Merrick, who becomes an eye-surgeon in order to restore the sight of Helen (Jane Wyman), whose blindness he had caused in an car accident. In *All That Heaven Allows* (1955), middle-aged widow Cary (Wyman) causes a scandal by marrying her much younger gardener Ron (Hudson). In *Written on the Wind* (1956), alcoholism, impotence, and disease are rife in the oil tycoon Hudley family. In *Imitation of Life* (1959), the close friendship between Annie (Juanita Moore), a black woman, and Lora (Lana Turner), a white woman, provides a weepy end to the golden age of Sirk's Hollywood melodrama. His fluid camerawork and inventive use of color, a genuine compassion for his characters, and an implicit condemnation of a hypocritical society transcend his soap opera material.

WHAT TO WATCH

1952	Has Anybody Seen My Gal?
1953	Take Me to Town
1953	All I Desire
1954	Magnificent Obsession
1955	All That Heaven Allows
1956	Written on the Wind
1957	The Tarnished Angels
1959	Imitation of Life

Bob (Rock Hudson) *comforts Helen (Jane Wyman) in* Magnificent Obsession.

Victor **Sjöström**

1879–1960 SWEDISH 1912–1937

54 Melodrama, Costume drama

The most influential director of early Swedish cinema, Victor Sjöström showed a preference for filming in natural settings, illustrating the relationship between the landscape and the psychology of his characters.

Sjöström became an international figure with *The Girl from Stormy Croft* (1917), the first of his adaptations of Selma Lagerlöf's novels, many about strong-willed women. *The Phantom Carriage* (1921), an eerie story shot mainly outdoors and starring himself, got him invited to Hollywood, where he directed nine films under the name of Victor Seastrom. He made his first MGM film, *He Who Gets Slapped* (1924), and directed Greta Garbo in *The Divine Woman* (1928). Sjöström returned to Europe and acting, and is best remembered for his role in Bergman's *Wild Strawberries* (1957).

WHAT TO WATCH

1917	The Outlaw and His Wife
1917	The Girl from Stormy Croft
1920	Karin, Daughter of Ingmar
1921	The Phantom Carriage
1924	He Who Gets Slapped
1926	The Scarlet Letter
1928	The Wind

In The Scarlet Letter, *Lillian Gish as Hester Prynne, emerges from prison holding her illegitimate baby; the letter A (for adultress) has been embroidered on her back.*

Steven **Soderbergh**

1963– AMERICAN 1989–

15 Drama

Although only 26 when his first feature, *sex, lies and videotape* (1989), unexpectedly won the Golden Palm at Cannes, Soderbergh had to wait until 2000 for an Academy Award.

After the intelligent, intimate low-budget *sex, lies and videotape*, Soderbergh pursued an ambitious path with *Kafka* (1991), set in 1919 Prague; *King of the Hill* (1993), set during the Depression; and the neo-noir *Underneath* (1995). He then unashamedly entered the mainstream with *Out of Sight* (1998), an amusing crime caper; *Erin Brockovich* (2000), an exposé film; and *Traffic* (2000), a complex drama about drug-dealing that won him the Academy Award for Best Director; and *Ocean's 11* (2001).

WHAT TO WATCH

1989	sex, lies and videotape
1998	Out of Sight
2000	Erin Brockovich
2000	Traffic
2001	Ocean's 11
2002	Solaris

Aleksandr **Sokurov**

1951– RUSSIAN 1987–

20 Political drama

Original and courageous, Aleksandr Sokurov is one of the most stylistically adventurous directors working at the beginning of the 21st century.

Sokurov first made his name with *Mother and Son* (1997), which was later followed by the equally brilliant *Father and Son* (2003). He also made an intriguing trilogy about three powerful political leaders of the 20th century: Hitler (*Moloch*, 1999), Lenin (*Taurus*, 2001), and Emperor Hirohito (*The Sun*, 2005). In 2002, he made the landmark film *Russian Ark*, a 96-minute film, which consists of a single take, shot using a specially designed steadycam.

WHAT TO WATCH

1997	Mother and Son
1999	Moloch
2001	Taurus
2002	Russian Ark
2003	Father and Son
2005	The Sun

Steven **Spielberg**

1946– AMERICAN 1975–

30 Adventure, Drama, Science fiction

One of the most famous Hollywood directors, Steven Spielberg has an intuitive sense of the hopes and fears of his audience. This quality and his showmanship have made him one of the greats, in the league of Cecil B. DeMille, Frank Capra, and Alfred Hitchcock.

WHAT TO WATCH

1975	Jaws
1977	Close Encounters of the Third Kind
1981	Raiders of the Lost Ark
1982	ET: The Extra-Terrestrial
1993	Jurassic Park
1993	Schindler's List
1998	Saving Private Ryan
2005	Munich

Spielberg's first films were influenced by Hitchcock's mechanics of suspense. *Duel* (1971) is a superior psychological thriller about road paranoia, while *Jaws* (1975) terrified viewers about horrors lurking in the ocean. But Spielberg was not interested in becoming the "new Hitchcock." Instead, the qualities repeatedly found in his films are those of childlike innocence and wonder. Two of these are about visitations from friendly aliens: *Close Encounters of the Third Kind* (1977) and *ET: The Extra-Terrestrial* (1982), which were huge hits. In addition, the throwback action-adventure films *Raiders of the Lost Ark* (1981) and its two sequels made Spielberg one of the most successful directors ever.

Clearly a prodigious talent, Spielberg is unencumbered by pretensions or politics. By the mid-1980s, after forming his own film studio, Dreamworks SKG, he was in a position to film anything he chose. He turned to books: *The Color Purple* (1985) by Alice Walker, with its tough subject matter of racism, sexism, and lesbianism in the US of the early 20th-century, provided meaningful themes to explore, although he veered towards sentimentality.

Empire of the Sun (1987), based on J.G. Ballard's wartime memoir, is a worthy film, but not a significant advance on the prisoner-of-war movies of previous decades.

Spielberg explored the persecution of Jews in Nazi Germany with conviction in *Schindler's List* (1993), based on Thomas Keneally's novel. A bleak, compelling account of the "Final Solution," it is probably his most important film, although, again, it is undermined by a residue of sentimentality. Another stark account of war, *Saving Private Ryan* (1998), with Tom Hanks as a US platoon commander in Normandy during World War II, displays the most intense combat scenes Hollywood has produced. Made at virtually the same time as *Schindler's List* (Spielberg edited one while shooting the other), *Jurassic Park* (1993) looked like his insurance policy: a groundbreaking computer-generated imagery (CGI) spectacle with dinosaurs more lifelike than ever seen before. It was pure showmanship, and another colossal box-office hit, but also a reminder that for all his technique, Spielberg has yet to invest his entertainments with the complexity and depth that, for example, Capra managed in *It's a Wonderful Life*, or that proved second nature to Hitchcock. *Artificial Intelligence: AI* (2001) is arguably the closest he has come to reconciling the two sides of his work — the cerebral side that wants to be respected and the entertainer who needs to be loved.

Liam Neeson *plays suave German businessman Oskar Schindler, whose conscience overcomes his greed during the Holocaust in* Schindler's List; *the film was shot in luminous black-and-white.*

Spielberg heralded *a special effects revolution with* Jurassic Park, *based on Michael Crichton's* The Lost World.

TOM HANKS

With his Academy Award-winning performance as the AIDS-stricken lawyer in *Philadelphia* (1993), Tom Hanks (born 1956) displayed a talent for serious roles. After Spencer Tracy, he became the first actor to win two successive Best Actor Academy Awards — the second for the title role of the simpleton in *Forrest Gump* (1994). In movies since 1980, Hanks was known at one time as the king of romantic comedy, largely due to three hits: *Splash* (1984), *Big* (1988), and *Sleepless in Seattle* (1993). He has continued to exploit his breezy personality in comedies, alternating them with meatier roles, as in Spielberg's *Saving Private Ryan* (1998) and in Ron Howard's *The Da Vinci Code* (2006).

Josef von **Sternberg**

1894–1969 AUSTRIAN 1925–1957

24 Melodrama

The iconographic figure of Marlene Dietrich was created by Josef von Sternberg (Jonas Sternberg). She appeared as the eternal femme fatale in different guises in seven of his films, among the most sensuous, bizarre, exotic, and unnaturalistic films in cinema.

WHAT TO WATCH	
1930	The Blue Angel
1930	Morocco
1931	Dishonored
1932	Shanghai Express
1932	Blonde Venus
1934	The Scarlet Empress
1935	The Devil is a Woman
1953	The Saga of Anatahan

The partnership of Josef von Sternberg and Marlene Dietrich is as iconic as that of, say, Laurel and Hardy, or Gilbert and Sullivan. Sans Dietrich, Sternberg made *Underworld* (1927), one of the few silent films to deal with organized crime, and *The Docks of New York* (1928), which treated urban squalor with poetic realism, achieved by soft, shadowy lighting (Sternberg's trademark).

In *The Salvation Hunters (1925)*, his first film, Sternberg states that "It is not conditions, nor is it environment — our faith controls our lives!" This is certainly true of his own life. Born in an impoverished family of Orthodox Jews, he spent his childhood in hunger and most of his teens on the streets. This experience is reflected in his film-making, which explores the motivations and faith of his characters. *The Last Command* (1928), with Emil Jannings as exiled Russian General Dolgorucki forced to become an extra in a Hollywood film about the Russian Revolution, sets up a strange double image between the exotic Russian past and the present studio set. Jannings also had a masochistic role as Immanuel Rath, a schoolteacher caught in the clutches of cabaret singer Lola in *The Blue Angel* (*Der Blaue Engel*, 1930), the film in which the world discovered Dietrich. Conjured up by make-up, wigs, costumes, and the subtle play of light and shadow, Dietrich next appeared as Amy Lolly in *Morocco* (1930), as Spy X27 in *Dishonored* (1931), Shanghai Lily in *Shanghai Express* (1932), Helen Faraday in *Blonde Venus* (1932), Catherine the Great in *The Scarlet Empress* (1934), and as Concho Perez in *The Devil is a Woman* (1935), inhabiting imaginary and fantastic countries. Nothing he did after he worked with Dietrich equalled these films, though *The Saga of Anatahan* (1953) showed what Sternberg could do with just a simple studio set and lighting.

Film poster, *1932*

Sternberg *(right) on the set of* Exquisite Sinner *(1926), a film from which he was fired, with cameraman Max Fábian, and actors Conrad Nagel, Matthew Betz, and Renée Adorée.*

George **Stevens**

1904–1975 AMERICAN 1933–1970

25 Various

Mainly because of multiple takes and shooting from every possible angle, George Stevens took 22 years to make his last eight films.

In the 1920s, Stevens directed Laurel and Hardy two-reelers, and in the 1930s and early 1940s, a wide range of polished films including three comedies with Katharine Hepburn, a couple of Fred Astaire musicals, and a colonial adventure film, *Gunga Din* (1939). His later films were more personal, his working methods slower, and his style more deliberate. *I Remember Mama* (1948), his first post-war movie, is a warm-hearted comedy-drama; *A Place in the Sun* (1951) contains luminous close-ups of Montgomery Clift and Elizabeth Taylor; the classic Western, *Shane* (1953), is seen through the eyes of a hero-worshipping boy; and *Giant* (1956) is an epic Western.

WHAT TO WATCH

1936	Swing Time
1939	Gunga Din
1942	Woman of the Year
1948	I Remember Mama
1951	A Place in the Sun
1953	Shane
1956	Giant

A sparkling *Elizabeth Taylor and Montgomery Clift star in the haunting film on lost love,* A Place in the Sun, *for which Stevens won an Academy Award.*

Oliver **Stone**

1946– AMERICAN 1986–

20 Action, Political drama, War

A controversial figure who likes it that way, Oliver Stone studied film under Martin Scorsese and famously learned about life in Vietnam.

Combative in everything he touches, Stone aims for hot issues, and approaches them from an overtly leftist perspective. Both *Platoon* (1986) and *Born on the Fourth of July* (1989) draw from his experience in Vietnam and attack American foreign policy. *Salvador* (1986) is sympathetic to the rebel cause; *Wall Street* (1987) satirizes the trader mentality; and *JFK* (1991) theorizes that a military-industrial complex was behind the shooting of John F. Kennedy.

The montage in an Oliver Stone movie is a battle zone of shock cuts and splintered frames. On a technical level, *Natural Born Killers* (1994) is as radical a merger of avant-garde and music television techniques as mainstream Hollywood has ever seen.

WHAT TO WATCH

1986	Platoon
1989	Born on the Fourth of July
1991	JFK
1994	Natural Born Killers

Woody Harrelson *and Juliette Lewis play an amoral couple on a cross-country killing spree in* Natural Born Killers, *Stone's lurid satire on the media, sex, and violence from a story by Quentin Tarantino.*

Erich **von Stroheim**

1885–1957 AUSTRIAN 1918–1933

9 Costume drama

Only the first two films of the nine directed by Erich von Stroheim (Erich Oswald Stroheim) were released without studio interference. Yet, despite the vandalism committed on his art, he remains one of cinema's great figures.

Born in Vienna of middle-class parents, Erich von Stroheim emigrated to the US and became an American citizen and an actor, adding the "von" to his name, and claiming to be an ex-army officer of noble descent. By playing a succession of brutal Prussian officers, he gained the title of "the man you love to hate." As a director, he was profligate with studio money (for example, he rebuilt a large part of Monte Carlo on the Universal backlot) so that Irving Thalberg, Head of Production, called him a "footage fetishist." But the luxury of the settings was essential to his vision of European decadence in his cynical, witty, erotic Ruritanian romances, rich in social and psychological detail. *Queen Kelly* (1928) is a truncated but nevertheless delirious sado-masochistic masterpiece, starring the silent movie diva Gloria Swanson. Even *The Merry Widow* (1925), based on the operetta, has a whiff of decay amidst the romanticism. Unlike his other silent films, *Greed* (1924) was filmed almost entirely on location. In its two-and-half-hour version (cut down from ten hours), it remains a masterpiece. Not long after being prevented from completing his only sound film, *Walking Down Broadway* (1933), he left for France where he spent the rest of his life, working as an actor. Returning briefly to Hollywood for Billy Wilder's *Sunset Boulevard* (1950), starring Gloria Swanson, he acted in his last role — as a faithful butler.

In Foolish Wives, *von Stroheim plays Sergius Karamzin, a Don Juan who swindles rich women; Maud George plays Princess Olga, his mistress and partner in crime.*

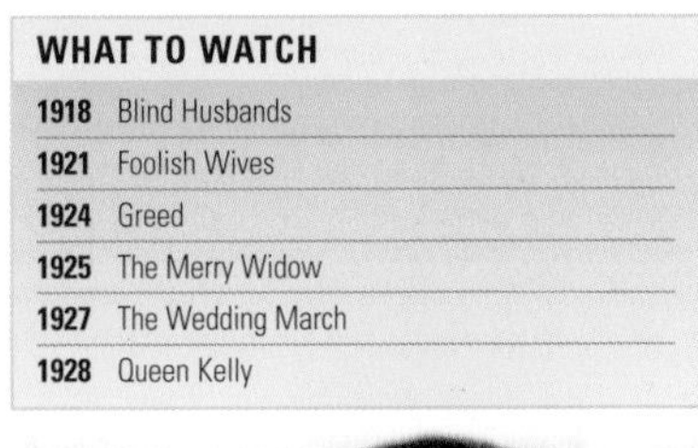

WHAT TO WATCH

1918	Blind Husbands
1921	Foolish Wives
1924	Greed
1925	The Merry Widow
1927	The Wedding March
1928	Queen Kelly

The winner *of a huge lottery, Trina (Zasu Pitts) becomes obsessive over the money in* Greed, *throwing her own life, and the lives of people around her, into turmoil.*

John **Sturges**

1911–1992 AMERICAN 1946–1976

43 Western, Action

Associated with action movies, particularly Westerns, John Sturges' cool style and interest in the individual pitted against outside forces, were particularly suited to the genres.

Both John Sturges' biggest hits, *The Magnificent Seven* (1960) — an invigorating Western transposition of Akira Kurosawa's *The Seven Samurai* (1954) — and *The Great Escape* (1963), featured Steve McQueen in prominent roles played with effectively controlled aggression. *Escape from Fort Bravo* (1953), with William Holden, has all the ingredients of a good Western, with intrigue, action, drama, and romance. Among his other robust Westerns are *Gunfight at the O.K. Corral* (1957) and *Last Train from Gun Hill* (1959), both with Kirk Douglas. One of Sturges' best films, *Bad Day at Black Rock* (1955), has Spencer Tracy as a one-armed stranger who descends on a small town to uncover its secrets. It is one of the few films to touch on the problems of Japanese-Americans during the war. Sturges' final effort was the action-packed war film, *The Eagle Has Landed* (1976).

WHAT TO WATCH

1953	Escape from Fort Bravo
1955	Bad Day at Black Rock
1957	Gunfight at the O.K. Corral
1959	Last Train from Gun Hill
1960	The Magnificent Seven
1963	The Great Escape
1976	The Eagle Has Landed

A stranger *in town, John Macreedy (Spencer Tracy), faces opposition from Hector David (Lee Marvin) and other residents in* Bad Day at Black Rock.

Preston **Sturges**

1898–1959 AMERICAN 1940–1957

12 Comedy

The USA of Preston Sturges is a giddy, corrupt, bustling country, full of eccentrics. The witty lines, visual gags, and comic timing form part of an acerbic view of American life, although his misanthropy is tempered with affection for his characters.

Sturges (Edmund P. Biden) worked as a screenwriter through the 1930s, and was one of the first directors to write his own scripts (he did so for all his films). Sturges was also the winner of the Academy Award for Best Original Screenplay in 1941 for *The Great McGinty* (1940). In *Sullivan's Travels* (1941), a director of comedies wants a firsthand experience of poverty in order to make a serious drama — but, over time, he realizes that making people laugh is his greatest achievement. Sturges' own mission to make people laugh was achieved in the screwball comedies *The Lady Eve* (1941) and *The Palm Beach Story* (1942). His satires on American small towns, *The Miracle of Morgan's Creek* (1944) and *Hail the Conquering Hero* (1944), exploit motherhood and patriotism for laughs.

Sullivan's Travels, *with Joel McCrea (as John Lloyd Sullivan) and Veronica Lake (as "The Girl"), has a clever script that sounds contemporary, even today.*

WHAT TO WATCH

1941	The Lady Eve
1941	Sullivan's Travels
1942	The Palm Beach Story
1944	The Miracle of Morgan's Creek
1944	Hail the Conquering Hero

Istvan **Szabó**

1938– HUNGARIAN 1964–

19 Historical drama

The principal theme of Istvan Szabó has been the agonies suffered by Middle Europe in the 20th century, particularly during the Nazi period.

Istvan Szabó's second feature, *Father* (*Apa*, 1966), is a masterful exploration of the younger generation's relationship to the past, symbolized by a growing boy's dreams of his dead father. Szabó's key work is a trilogy of visually splendid films: *Mephisto* (1981), about an actor who sells his soul by continuing to practise his art under the Nazis; *Colonel Redl* (*Oberst Redl*, 1984), in which the head of military intelligence in the Austro-Hungarian Empire has to hide the fact that he is both bisexual and Jewish; and *Hanussen* (1988), where an Austrian army corporal becomes a clairvoyant. All three feature the remarkable actor Klaus Maria Brandauer as a doomed character at odds with the powers that be. These films, along with *Sunshine* (1999), the inter-generational saga of a Jewish family, and *Taking Sides* (2001), on the life of Wilhelm Furtwängler during the Nazi era, reveal evil lurking beneath a glamorous surface.

WHAT TO WATCH

1966	Father
1976	Budapest Tales
1981	Mephisto
1984	Colonel Redl
1988	Hanussen
1999	Sunshine
2001	Taking Sides

Klaus Maria Brandauer *as the ambitious Alfred Redl in* Colonel Redl, *makes a dramatic entry in a masque, a metaphor for the deception and intrigue in the film.*

Quentin **Tarantino**

1963– AMERICAN 1992–

5 Crime

With his first two films, Quentin Tarantino's rise to fame was meteoric. This can be put down not only to a growing film audience and taste for bloodshed, but to his intelligent and playful approach to the rhetoric of film violence.

Tarantino received his education working in down-market video stores that rented ultra-violent movies, spaghetti Westerns, and kung-fu epics — the inspiration behind his films. He also drew on the American B-crime genre for *Reservoir Dogs* (1992), and Jean-Luc Godard's deconstructions of noir themes for *Pulp Fiction* (1994). In fact, he named his production company, A Band Apart, after Godard's *Bande à Part* (1964). *Four Rooms* (1995), a set of four interlocking stories, one of which Tarantino conceptualized and directed, derived from slapstick, an interesting departure from his staple of violent movies. In a return to his earlier themes, he made *Jackie Brown* (1997), a crime caper which revived the career of 1970s blaxploitation queen Pam Grier. *Kill Bill: Volumes 1* and *2* (2003, 2004), two parts of a hyperactive revenge tale, are the culmination of all that Tarantino loves in movies.

Violence is *satirized in this scene from* Pulp Fiction, *where a digital butterfly appears between hitman Vincent (John Travolta) and partner Jules (Samuel L. Jackson).*

WHAT TO WATCH

1992	Reservoir Dogs
1994	Pulp Fiction
1997	Jackie Brown
2003	Kill Bill: Volume 1
2004	Kill Bill: Volume 2

Andrei **Tarkovsky**

1932–1986 | RUSSIAN | 1962–1986

7 | Drama

Some of the most intensely personal and visually powerful statements to have come out of Eastern Europe for many decades are made in Andrei Tarkovsky's seven films.

The rich pictorial sense of Andrei Tarkovsky was already evident in his first feature, *Ivan's Childhood* (*Ivanovo detstvo*, 1962), the story of an orphan boy working for the partisans during World War II. His mastery of the medium was further confirmed in *Andrei Rublev* (*Andrey Rublyov*, 1966), eight imaginary episodes in the life of the great 15th-century icon painter as he journeys through feudal Russia, gradually abandoning speech, his art, and his faith because of the cruelty he witnesses. This measured, impressive parable of the artist's position in society was not allowed screening for some years by the Soviet authorities who felt it was too "dark." *Solaris* (*Solyaris*, 1972) — remade by Steven Soderbergh in 2002 — is a striking science-fiction film, which manages to be technologically convincing without relying on special effects. A different kind of science fiction was approached in *Stalker* (1979), which tells of a nightmarish journey through a forbidden wasteland undertaken by the shaven-headed stalker of the title and his two companions. Shot in eerie sepia colour, it haunts the mind long after it is over. *The Mirror* (*Zerkalo*, 1975) is full of dream-like images evoking memories and fantasies of Tarkovsky's private and public life in the form of a visual poem. Tarkovsky's last film was *The Sacrifice* (*Offret*, 1986), a post-apocalyptic drama, with an unbroken 10-minute take of a burning house as its climax.

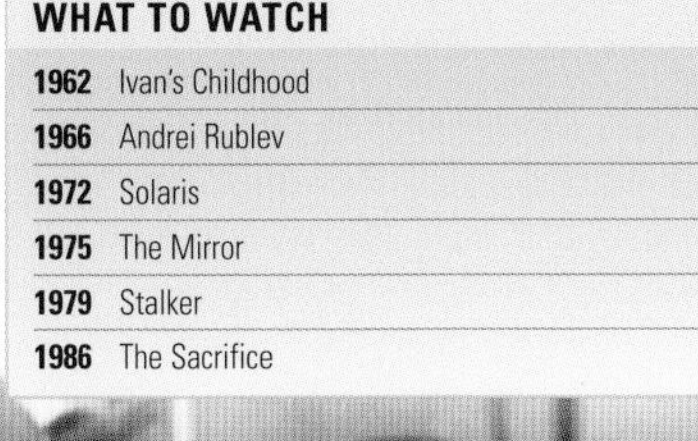

WHAT TO WATCH

1962	Ivan's Childhood
1966	Andrei Rublev
1972	Solaris
1975	The Mirror
1979	Stalker
1986	The Sacrifice

Ignat Daniltsev (Alexi) *walks with his mother (Margarita Terekhova) in* The Mirror; *his reflections as a dying man are poetically juxtaposed with Russian history.*

Tarkovsky directs *Donatas Banionis who plays Kris Kelvin, a psychologist sent to examine bizarre events aboard a space station in* Solaris.

Jacques **Tati**

1908–1982 | FRENCH | 1949–1973

6 | Comedy

As a brilliant observer of the absurdities of modern life and the idiosyncrasies of people, Jacques Tati restored the art of visual comedy, taking it to a different plane.

Unlike the films of Chaplin and Keaton, Tati's comedies are not built around himself. However, he is a memorable comic figure as the tall, socially awkward Monsieur Hulot, whose presence triggers off amusing incidents, as when he picks his way through a minefield of gadgets. Tati's films have little dialogue, but humor manifests itself in the body language of ordinary people, as well as in meticulously organized sound effects. *Monsieur Hulot's Holiday* (*Les Vacances de Monsieur Hulot*, 1953) shows people on holiday with comic realism, while *My Uncle* (*Mon Oncle*, 1958) and *Playtime* (1967) deal with the ridiculous aspects of the relationship of humans with machines and architecture.

WHAT TO WATCH

1949	Holiday
1953	Monsieur Hulot's Holiday
1958	My Uncle
1967	Playtime

Jacques Tati, *as Monsieur Hulot, saunters by beach huts in this scene from* Monsieur Hulot's Holiday.

Jacques **Tourneur**

1904–1977 | FRENCH | 1931–1965

36 | Horror, Western

The reputation of Jacques Tourneur was built on four horror pictures, in which the inventive use of light and shadow, as well as space and movement, suggested, rather than depicted, horror.

The son of the celebrated silent film director Maurice Tourneur, Jacques Tourneur went to Hollywood in 1934, subsequently becoming an American citizen. After turning out a few B-films for MGM, Val Lewton, a producer at RKO, hired him, and together they established a unique style of low-budget horror films. Without resorting to shock effects, a subtle evocation of the macabre gives *Cat People* (1942), *I Walked with a Zombie* (1943), and *The Leopard Man* (1943) a particular conviction. Tourneur returned to the genre 14 years later with *Night of the Demon* (1957). His other work consists of excellent Westerns and swashbucklers, and a classic film noir, *Out of the Past* (1947), with Robert Mitchum as the archetypal private eye ambling laconically through a murky atmosphere of double-cross and murder.

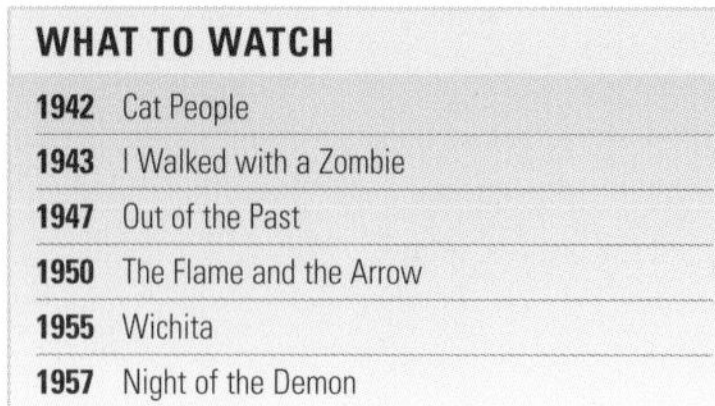

WHAT TO WATCH

1942	Cat People
1943	I Walked with a Zombie
1947	Out of the Past
1950	The Flame and the Arrow
1955	Wichita
1957	Night of the Demon

Night of the Demon *retained Tourneur's suggestive approach to horror; the monster was allegedly inserted by the film's producer.*

François **Truffaut**

1932–1984 FRENCH 1959–1984

21 Avant-garde

Enthusiasm, lucidity, and freedom of expression characterize the films of François Truffaut, a leading force in the French New Wave. They are obviously made by someone who wants to retain a certain innocence.

Julie Christie *performs a double role as Clarrise/Linda Montag in* Fahrenheit 451*; the science fiction parable set in a future dystopia was Truffaut's first work in color.*

Original film poster, *1966*

"Are films more important than life?" asks Jean-Pierre Léaud in *Day for Night* (*La Nuit Américaine*, 1973). For Truffaut the answer must be in the affirmative. The passion he feels for film-making communicates itself in his films, which are full of cinematic allusions: *Shoot the Pianist* (*Tirez sur le Pianiste*, 1960) is a homage to American film noir, *Jules and Jim* (*Jules et Jim*, 1961) makes references to Chaplin and Jean Renoir, and *The Bride Wore Black* (*La Mariée Etait en Noir*, 1967) is inspired by Hitchcock's work. But for all that, Truffaut is no mere imitator and many of his films have an immediacy and freshness uncluttered by ciné culture. This is best seen in his semi-autobiographical series of five films with Jean-Pierre Léaud playing his alter ego Antoine Doinel. The 12-year-old Doinel is sent to reform school in *The 400 Blows* (*Les Quatre Cents Coups*, 1959), as Truffaut himself was. The series follows Doinel as he grows older and falls in love in *Stolen Kisses* (*Baisers Volés*, 1968), marries and has a child in *Bed and Board* (*Domicile Conjugal*, 1970), divorces and finally becomes a writer in *Love on the Run* (*L'Amour en Fuite*, 1978). These seemingly lightweight films hide Truffaut's pain at the loss of youthful spontaneity and the difficulties of love. He demonstrates a wide range in terms of styles and subjects, from the futuristic nightmare of *Fahrenheit 451* (1966), the 19th-century period of *The Story of Adele H.* (*L'Histoire d'Adèle H.*, 1975) to France under Nazi occupation in *The Last Metro* (*Le Dernier Métro*, 1980).

WHAT TO WATCH

1959	The 400 Blows
1960	Shoot the Pianist
1961	Jules and Jim
1966	Fahrenheit 451
1967	The Bride Wore Black
1968	Stolen Kisses
1969	The Wild Child
1970	Bed and Board
1973	Day for Night
1978	The Green Room

On the *sets of* Love on the Run, *the last in the Antoine Doinel series, Truffaut directs Claude Jade, who plays Doinel's wife Christine.*

Gus **Van Sant**

1952– | AMERICAN | 1985–

11 | Drama

One of the leading independent directors to make his name in the 1990s, Gus Van Sant has flirted with the mainstream, but always returns to his "indie" roots, such as in *Gerry* (2002).

Gus Van Sant was able to force his way into world-wide distribution with his first two features, both refreshingly non-judgemental treatments of potentially uncommercial subjects: junkies in *Drugstore Cowboy* (1989) and male hustlers in *My Own Private Idaho* (1991). These movies immediately revealed his interest in doomed youth and misfits in American society. This interest manifested itself most forcefully in *Elephant* (2003), on the Columbine school massacre, in which two high-school students gun down their schoolmates; and *Last Days* (2005), about the troubled life of pop idol Kurt Cobain. *Good Will Hunting* (1997), about a mathematical genius who works as a janitor, again deals with an "outsider," but is less dark in tone.

WHAT TO WATCH

1989	Drugstore Cowboy
1991	My Own Private Idaho
1997	Good Will Hunting
2002	Gerry
2003	Elephant
2005	Last Days

In My Own Private Idaho, *Mike, an abandoned child (River Phoenix), walks long distances, searching for his mother and for some meaning in life.*

Agnès **Varda**

1928– | BELGIAN | 1954–

20 | Documentary

In 1956, Agnès Varda, a photographer, made *La Pointe-Courte*, although she claimed to have scarcely ever been to the cinema. The film gained her the reputation of being "the mother of the French New Wave."

Agnès Varda wrote, produced, and directed all her films, both fiction and documentary. *Cléo from 5 to 7* (*Cléo de 5 à 7*, 1961) observes two hours in the life of a spoiled nightclub singer as she waits for the medical verdict on whether she is to live or die. Every trivial incident takes on a new significance for her, and Paris is seen as if for the last (or first) time. *One Sings, the Other Doesn't* (*L'Une Chante, l'Autre Pas*, 1977) came out of Varda's involvement with the women's movement. Eight years later, she made *Vagabond* (*Sans Toit ni Loi*, 1985), one of her most successful features. In between her fiction films, Varda made imaginative documentaries, which were ciné-poetic essays, including tributes to her late husband, Jacques Demy.

WHAT TO WATCH

1961	Cléo from 5 to 7
1965	Happiness
1977	One Sings, the Other Doesn't
1985	Vagabond
1991	Jacquot de Nantes
2000	The Gleaners and I

Sandrine Bonnaire *is Mona, the outcast in* Vagabond, *which presents her as the epitome of the soul, free of social bondage.*

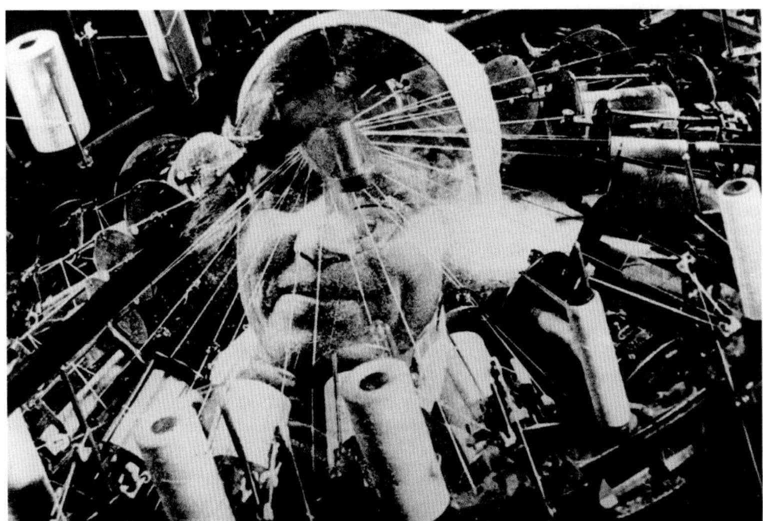

Dziga **Vertov**

1896–1954 RUSSIAN 1929–1954

4 Documentary, Propaganda

Dziga Vertov (Denis Kaufman) was part of the experimental art movement of the early Russian Revolution. His newsreels and documentaries echoed Lenin's plea that the function of Soviet cinema was to reflect "reality."

There were three Kaufman brothers: Denis, Mikhail, and Boris. Boris became a celebrated cinematographer in France (where he shot two of Jean Vigo's films), and in the US (winning an Academy Award for *On The Waterfront*). Mikhail was a cameraman in Russia, and Denis, while working for the Revolutionary Cinema Committee, changed his name to Dziga Vertov — Ukrainian words that mean "spinning" and "turning." He edited *Cinema Truth (Kino-Pravda)* and *Cinema Eye (Kino Glaz)*, a series of documentary films created from newsreel sequences, between 1922 and 1925. To these, Vertov added slow, speeded up or reverse motion, split screens, animation, text, and still photographs. All these techniques and more were used in Vertov's first full-length film, *The Man with the Movie Camera* (*Chelovek s kino-apparatom*, 1929). The title refers to Vertov's brother, Mikhail Kaufman, seen in action in this spectacular depiction of everyday life in the Soviet Union. Vertov then experimented with sound in *Enthusiasm* (*Entuziazm: Simfoniya Donbassa*, 1931), continuing to use mobile camerawork and unusual juxtapositions. The brilliance of his technique is also evident in *Three Songs about Lenin* (*Tri pesni o Lenine*, 1934). Vertov's films influenced the British documentary movement of the 1930s. His ideas were taken up by cinéma-verité directors in France in the 1960s, and Jean-Luc Godard formed the Groupe Dziga Vertov to promote his movies from 1968 and 1972.

This tilted shot *shows Vertov at work behind the camera; he strongly believed in the primacy of the camera eye* (kino-glaz) *over the human eye.*

This shot of *a spinning factory in* The Man with the Movie Camera *is a visual celebration of the integration of human and machine.*

WHAT TO WATCH

1929	The Man with the Movie Camera
1931	Enthusiasm
1934	Three Songs about Lenin

King **Vidor**

1894–1982 AMERICAN 1919–1959

57 Drama, Melodrama, Costume drama

The name of King Vidor is entered in the Guinness World Records as the film director with the longest career, spanning 67 years and over 50 films. His dominant personality, however, is stamped on many of them.

The Big Parade (1925) was one of the first films to deal with the horrors of World War I. It began "a series of films depicting episodes in the lives of the average American man and woman." In *The Crowd* (1928), John and Mary (starring Eleanor Boardman and James Murray) are a couple newly arrived in New York, whose high hopes are soon dashed by unemployment and poverty. *Hallelujah* (1929), Vidor's first sound film, was an innovative all-black musical, shot on location, that retained the visual poetry of silent cinema. His technical virtuosity is apparent in films as varied as *Stella Dallas* (1937), a melodrama with Barbara Stanwyck, the Western *Duel in the Sun* (1946), and the epic *War and Peace* (1956).

Barbara Stanwyck *plays Stella, a factory-town girl who sacrifices her own happiness for the sake of her daughter in* Stella Dallas, *a melodrama about class differences.*

WHAT TO WATCH

1925	The Big Parade
1928	The Crowd
1929	Hallelujah
1931	The Champ
1934	Our Daily Bread
1937	Stella Dallas
1946	Duel in the Sun
1949	The Fountainhead
1956	War and Peace

Jean **Vigo**

1905–1934 FRENCH 1933–1934

3 Drama

Few other directors with such a short filmography have had such a profound influence on other film-makers as Jean Vigo.

The son of an anarchist who died in prison in 1917, Jean Vigo (Jean Bonaventure de Vigo Almereyda) inherited his father's anti-authoritarian ideas. In *Zero for Conduct* (*Zéro de Conduite*, 1933), set in a dreadful boarding school, four boys organize an uprising. The film, based on Vigo's personal childhood experiences, presents a child's-eye view of authority, with adults seen as perverse, hypocritical, and oppressive members of the Establishment. The most celebrated sequence is the dormitory pillow fight that becomes a snowy wonderland of feathers in which a mock Catholic procession is enacted. Its influence on Truffaut and Godard is noticeable and it was a direct inspiration of Lindsay Anderson's *If...* (1968). Vigo died of tuberculosis aged 29 before completing *L'Atalante* (1934), an exquisite tale of a young man who takes his bride to live on a barge that travels the canals around Paris.

The pillow *fight sequence in* Zero for Conduct *is shot in slow motion; the film showcases Vigo's talent for mixing social commentary with unique imagery.*

WHAT TO WATCH

1930	À propos de Nice (short)
1933	Zero for Conduct
1934	L'Atalante

Luchino **Visconti**

1906–1976 ITALIAN 1942–1976

14 Drama, Spectacle

Aristocrat, Marxist, Neo-Realist, theatre and opera director, and decadence-monger, Luchino Visconti was a man of contradictions, a fact that is reflected in his work.

Despite being a Marxist, Luchino Visconti was always attracted by European bourgeois art. "Art is ambiguous. It is ambiguity made science," says the composer Aschenbach's friend in *Death in Venice* (*Morte a Venezia*, 1971). Visconti is both repelled and drawn to a decaying society, depicting it in loving detail. In *The Leopard* (*Il Gattopardo*, 1963), Prince Salina of Sicily reflects sadly on the death of the aristocratic world; Ludwig II of Bavaria (Helmut Berger) in *Ludwig* (1972) fights against the philistines who cannot appreciate Richard Wagner's genius; and in *Death in Venice*, cholera threatens to sweep away the luxury of the Hotel des Bains on the Lido. Although his reputation was gained as a Neo-Realist, only *La Terra Trema* (1948) actually comes close to the Neo-Realist ideal in its picture of the wretched conditions of Sicilian fishermen, shot in real locations with local people enacting their stories. It is through the conventions of opera that Visconti worked best, as in the lush Verdian spectacle of *Senso* (1954). *Rocco and his Brothers* (*Rocco e i suoi fratelli*, 1960), about a family who escape the poor South, is an attempt to return to Neo-Realism, despite its operatic dimensions.

Dirk Bogarde *delivers one of his finest performances as Gustav von Aschenbach, an ageing composer who is forced to take a convalescent holiday in* Death in Venice.

WHAT TO WATCH

1942	Ossessione
1948	La Terra Trema
1954	Senso
1960	Rocco and his Brothers
1963	The Leopard
1971	Death in Venice
1976	The Innocent (L'Innocente)

Concetta (Lucilla Morlacchi) *and Angelica (Claudia Cardinale) star in the stunningly photographed, designed, and costumed* The Leopard *(set in Italy of the 1800s).*

Lars von **Trier**

1956– | DANISH | 1984–

10 | Drama

The most famous Danish director since Carl Dreyer, Lars von Trier has as many fans as he has detractors. However, both would agree that he is an auteur with a strong personality.

Lars von Trier's directorial debut was with *The Element of Crime* (*Forbrydelsens element*, 1984), the first part of his "Europe in disintegration" trilogy, completed by *Epidemic* (1987) and *Europa* (1991). All three were shot in a mixture of black-and-white and color, with a post-apocalyptic atmosphere. *Breaking the Waves* (1996), his first English-language work — filmed like a home video — and *Dancer in the Dark* (2000) were unashamedly melodramatic. Von Trier's films set in an imaginary US, *Dogville* (2003) and *Mandalay* (2005), were interesting experiments in using minimalist theatrical sets. *The Idiots* (*Idioterne*, 1998) set out successfully to shock people into accepting mentally challenged people.

WHAT TO WATCH

1987	Epidemic
1991	Europa
1996	Breaking the Waves
1998	The Idiots
2000	Dancer in the Dark
2003	Dogville

In Dogville, *an allegory offering multiple readings, Grace (Nicole Kidman) is a fugitive who finds shelter in a small town with the help of Tom Edison (Paul Bettany).*

Andrzej **Wajda**

1926– | POLISH | 1954–

35 | Costume drama, War

In the 1950s, Andrzej Wajda's war trilogy became the voice of disaffected post-war youth. A generation later, Wajda was once again the voice of a Poland struggling to survive political and economic turmoil.

Wajda's war trilogy, *A Generation* (*Pokolenie*, 1954), *Canal* (*Kanal*, 1957), and *Ashes and Diamonds* (*Popiól i Diament*, 1958), were bitter and anti-romantic World War II films. Due to censorship, from the mid-1960s to the mid-1970s, Wajda was driven to adapt Polish allegorical novels, but even in these he subtly and ironically alluded to contemporary Poland. When censorship was slightly relaxed, he returned to overt political subjects, reflecting on the immediate past. *Man of Marble* (*Czlowiek z Marmuru*, 1976) depicted the life of a worker-hero of the 1950s who falls from official favour. Its sequel, *Man of Iron* (*Czlowiek z Zelaza*, 1981), made under enormous pressure, was about the struggle for solidarity.

WHAT TO WATCH

1954	A Generation
1957	Canal
1958	Ashes and Diamonds
1960	Innocent Sorcerers
1961	Siberian Lady Macbeth
1970	Landscape After Battle
1976	Man of Marble
1981	Man of Iron
1983	Danton

Danton *(with Gerard Depardieu in the title role) is set in the volatile Paris of the 1790s.*

Raoul **Walsh**

1887–1980 AMERICAN 1912–1964

134 Action, War, Western

Loud, extrovert, unpretentious, and fast-paced adventure movies were Raoul Walsh's forte, the best of which were vehicles for stars like James Cagney, Humphrey Bogart, and Errol Flynn.

Walsh's career was almost as long as the history of cinema, dating back to 1910 when he became an actor and assistant to D.W. Griffith. His outstanding silent films as director are *The Thief of Bagdad* (1924), which features magical trick photography, and *What Price Glory?* (1926), a comedy that turns into an anti-war drama. He never let a scene go on longer than necessary and was much given to the long shot. His assignments at Warner Bros. included *The Roaring Twenties* (1939), a documentary-style evocation of the gangster era with James Cagney as a bootlegger. *High Sierra* (1941) reveals a depth in Walsh's work and gave Humphrey Bogart his first three-dimensional role. Walsh remade the film as *Colorado Territory* (1949), a genuinely tragic Western. Errol Flynn starred in seven of Walsh's robust adventures, notably *They Died With Their Boots On* (1941) and *Gentleman Jim* (1942). Walsh's best period ended with *White Heat* (1949), in which murderer Cagney famously screams atop a blazing oil tank, "Made it Ma! Top of the world!"

Humphrey Bogart *and George Raft as truckers Paul and Joe meet Ann Sheridan as Cassie, a sassy waitress, in* They Drive By Night, *a mix of intrigue, drama, and romance.*

WHAT TO WATCH

1924	The Thief of Bagdad
1926	What Price Glory?
1930	The Big Trail
1940	They Drive by Night
1941	High Sierra
1942	Gentleman Jim
1949	Colorado Territory
1949	White Heat

A film noir *co-written by John Huston,* High Sierra *stars Bogart as Roy "Mad Dog" Earle, a criminal on the run, with Ida Lupino as Marie Garson, the only woman he can trust.*

Peter **Weir**

1944– AUSTRALIAN 1975–

15 Action, Adventure, Historical

A natural film-maker, Peter Weir displays an uncanny command of mood, pace, and nuance, creating a symphony of moving images.

Although it was not his first film, *Picnic at Hanging Rock* (1975) was the movie which introduced Weir to critics and film-goers around the world. It was a spellbindingly atmospheric and enigmatic story about the disappearance of several girls on a school trip in 1900. Weir's ability to imbue the film with an authentic sense of time and place caused many viewers to believe the plot was based on a true story (it was not).

The film put Weir at the forefront of the Australian New Wave, and the moving but relatively conventional *Gallipoli* (1981), his last Australian picture to date, sealed his reputation at home as a national totem. *The Year of Living Dangerously* (1982) is the first of a series of Weir's films that explore the clash between the modern western world and older cultures. In *Witness* (1985) Philadelphia cop Captain John Book (Harrison Ford) goes undercover in an Amish community. In *The Mosquito Coast* (1986), a self-styled inventor Allie Fox (Harrison Ford again) takes his family into the jungle to get back to nature, with disastrous results.

Weir's cinema arguably lacks the profundity (and certainly the solemnity) of Andrei Tarkovsky's, but their films share an aura of spirituality. In *Witness*, the generic cop story is soon forgotten, but a wordless sequence in which the community comes together to build a barn lingers long in the memory. *Fearless* (1993) is a haunting film about the survivors of an air disaster, and *The Truman Show* (1998) satirizes reality television while at the same time imbuing it with an existential melancholy.

WHAT TO WATCH

1975	Picnic at Hanging Rock
1981	Gallipoli
1985	Witness
1986	The Mosquito Coast
1989	Dead Poets Society
1993	Fearless
1998	The Truman Show
2003	Master and Commander: The Far Side of the World

Film poster, *1975*

Russell Crowe *traverses rough seas as Captain "Lucky" Jack Aubrey, in* Master and Commander.

Orson **Welles**

1916–1985 AMERICAN 1941–1975

14 Film noir, Drama

The idea that Orson Welles could never direct a film that could match the achievement of *Citizen Kane* (1941) persists. But few Hollywood directors can boast of a finer oeuvre.

Had Welles been a conformist, he might have been more successful — but his greatness would have been diminished. *Citizen Kane* (1941), his first full-length feature, went against the conventions of chronological narratives and techniques of film-making. In *F for Fake* (1973), Welles tells anecdotes about art forgerers with relish, demonstrating that "Art is the lie that makes us see the truth." Who, then, is a storyteller but a great liar? In the splendid comic poem and historical epic, *Chimes at Midnight* (1966), Falstaff — one of the magnificent liars of literature — is given dignity by Welles' portrayal. In *The Immortal Story* (1968), a wealthy merchant wishes to make a popular sailor's myth come true. Power is a sustaining motif of Welles' work, as evidenced in the character of megalomaniac newspaper tycoon Charles Kane in *Citizen Kane*; *Macbeth* (1948); *Othello* (1952); and the character of millionaire Gregory Arkadin in *Mr. Arkadin* (1955). A struggle for dominance is central to *The Lady from Shanghai* (1947) and *Touch of Evil* (1958). RKO edited down *The Magnificent Ambersons* (1942), but it remains a haunting portrait of a declining family in the late 19th century.

In the stunning *"House of Mirrors" sequence in* The Lady from Shanghai, *Michael (Orson Welles), having been falsely blamed for murder, confronts the beautiful Elsa (Rita Hayworth).*

WHAT TO WATCH

1941	Citizen Kane
1942	The Magnificent Ambersons
1947	The Lady from Shanghai
1948	Macbeth
1952	Othello
1955	Confidential Report
1958	Touch of Evil
1966	Chimes at Midnight

Orson Welles *is Captain Hank Quinlan in the classic film noir* Touch of Evil, *with Janet Leigh as Susie Vargas and "Uncle" Joe, a gang leader (Akim Tamiroff).*

William **Wellman**

1896–1975 | AMERICAN | 1923–1958

76 | Various

Although William Wellman's name is most often associated with action pictures, gaining him a reputation for working mainly with men, he brought his expertise to bear on a range of genres in the best Hollywood manner.

Wellman earned the nickname "Wild Bill" for his impatience with actors, his devil-may-care personality, and his spell as a pilot in World War I. He drew upon his wartime experiences for *Men With Wings* (1938), a story of the pioneers of the air; *Lafayette Escadrille* (1958), with his son playing himself; and *Wings* (1927), the first movie to win an Academy Award for Best Picture and one of the best flying films ever. Other than the he-man epics, such as *The Call of the Wild* (1935), *Beau Geste* (1939), and *Buffalo Bill* (1944), there was also *Wild Boys of the Road* (1933), a deeply felt Depression story of young people hopping trains. His original *A Star is Born* (1937) says more about Hollywood than its two remakes; *Nothing Sacred* (1937) is a hilarious, fast-paced satire; *Roxie Hart* (1942) is a cynical 1920s spoof (remade as the stage and screen musical, *Chicago*); and *Magic Town* (1947) is a Capraesque comedy about Grandview, a small town that represents all such towns in US. He also directed five movies with Barbara Stanwyck. It was thanks to Wellman that Robert Mitchum emerged as a star in the semi-documentary, *The Story of G.I. Joe* (1945), and James Cagney found stardom in one of the first of the Warner's gangster cycle, *The Public Enemy* (1931).

Jack (Charles Rogers) *and David (Richard Arlen) are two fighter pilots in love with the same nurse, Mary (Clara Bow), during World War I in* Wings.

Film poster, *1937*

WHAT TO WATCH

1927	Wings
1931	The Public Enemy
1933	Wild Boys of the Road
1935	The Call of the Wild
1937	A Star is Born
1937	Nothing Sacred
1939	Beau Geste
1942	Roxie Hart
1943	The Ox-Bow Incident
1945	The Story of G.I. Joe
1954	The High and the Mighty

Wim **Wenders**

1945– GERMAN 1970–

28 Drama, Musical

Wim Wenders is more aware than most contemporary German directors of the American cultural influence on post-war Germany, and his films, whether made in the United States or Germany, reflect this.

"The Yanks have colonized our subconscious," says one of the German friends in *Kings of the Road* (*Im Lauf der Zeit*, 1976), Wenders' complex, subtly comic road movie. His films neither condemn nor wholly embrace this idea. His characters are isolated and emotionally stunted — but when they take to the road, change becomes inevitable. The superbly photographed, leisurely odysseys reach metaphysical dimensions, as in *Paris, Texas* (1984), his greatest international success. He returned to the theme in *Don't Come Knocking* (2005).

WHAT TO WATCH

1973	Alice in the Cities
1976	Kings of the Road
1977	The American Friend
1984	Paris, Texas
1987	Wings of Desire
1999	Buena Vista Social Club
2005	Don't Come Knocking

Eliades Ochoa *and Ibrahim Ferrer perform in* Buena Vista Social Club*; Wenders' documentary follows a group of "lost" Cuban jazz musicians reunited by guitarist Ry Cooder.*

James **Whale**

1889–1957 BRITISH 1930–1941

20 Horror, Musical

The name of James Whale is almost always linked with Frankenstein's monster, which he brought to life in two horror film classics.

After staging R.C. Sheriff's play, *Journey's End* on Broadway, Whale was invited to Hollywood in 1930 to depict this World War I drama on film. He triumphed with his third film, *Frankenstein* (1931), for which he chose his compatriot Boris Karloff to play the title role. On the whole, Whale preferred to work with British actors: Charles Laughton in *The Old Dark House* (1932), Claude Rains in *The Invisible Man* (1933), and Elsa Lanchester in *The Bride of Frankenstein* (1935). It is perhaps his "Englishness" that frees his horror films, which are full of self-mocking humour, from the Germanic expressionism usually associated with early examples of the genre. He moved smoothly from Frankenstein to Hammerstein with the best of the three screen versions of *Show Boat* (1936). Interest in Whale revived when his life story became the subject of Bill Condon's *Gods and Monsters* (1998).

WHAT TO WATCH

1931	Frankenstein
1932	The Old Dark House
1933	The Invisible Man
1935	The Bride of Frankenstein
1936	Show Boat

Film poster, *1935*

Margaret (Gloria Stuart) *and her companions discover the dark secrets of an old mansion inhabited by an odd family in Whale's Gothic pastiche,* The Old Dark House.

Billy **Wilder**

1906–2002 AMERICAN 1933–1981

26 Comedy, Romance, Film noir

The films of Billy Wilder, which emphasize the importance of dialogue and the structuring of plots, derive from the satiric Viennese theatre, the witty elegance of Ernst Lubitsch, and the harsher screwball comedies of the 1930s.

Austrian-born Wilder began his Hollywood career writing films for Ernst Lubitsch and Mitchell Leisen in the 1930s. Writer, director, and producer, he made highly successful films in varying genres over the course of his long Hollywood career, receiving an incredible eight Academy Award nominations as Best Director (second only to William Wyler who had 12). Wilder was also nominated 12 times for his screenplays, which he usually co-wrote, first with Charles Brackett, and, from 1957, with I.A.L. Diamond.

Wilder's critically acclaimed films often reveal a romantic's bitterness that comes from disappointment — that life is not perfect, love is thwarted, people can be avaricious and cruel, and the world is not improving. *Sunset Boulevard* (1950) is the glorious swan song of the silent screen star Norma desmond (Gloria Swanson), dementedly thinking she is making a comeback. "I'm still big, it's the pictures that got small," she tells Joe Gillis (Holden), a world-weary screenwriter.

There are a number of heartless heroes in his work, such as the sensation-seeking reporter Charles Tatum (Kirk Douglas) in *Ace in the Hole* (1951), the slick insurance agent Walter Neff in *Double Indemnity* (1944), and the weak exploitative businessman J.D. Sheldrake in *The Apartment* (1960), both played by Fred McMurray. Others are Dino, Dean Martin's self-parodic crooner in *Kiss Me, Stupid* (1964), and Walter Matthau's crooked lawyer Willie Gingrich in *The Fortune Cookie* (1966). Wilder's attitude to them is condemnatory, and his tenderness is reserved for the female characters. Audrey Hepburn portrays all that is good in life as she tries to choose between the Larrabee brothers (Humphrey Bogart and William Holden) in *Sabrina* (1954), and when she is painfully smitten by middle-aged playboy Frank Flannagan (Gary Cooper) in *Love in the Afternoon* (1957). Marilyn Monroe is depicted as alluring but innocent, saving Richard (Tom Ewell) from adultery in *The Seven Year Itch* (1955), and poignantly telling

Film poster, *1955*

Barbara Stanwyck *and Billy Wilder on the set of* Double Indemnity, *a film noir classic about adultery, corruption, and murder based on a novel by James M. Cain.*

WHAT TO WATCH

1942	The Major and the Minor
1944	Double Indemnity
1945	The Lost Weekend
1950	Sunset Boulevard
1951	Ace in the Hole
1953	Stalag 17
1954	Sabrina
1959	Some Like It Hot
1960	The Apartment
1961	One, Two, Three

Humphrey Bogart, *in an unusual romantic role as the serious Linus, succumbs to the charms of Sabrina (Audrey Hepburn) in* Sabrina, *Wilder's sparkling comedy-romance.*

"Josephine" (Tony Curtis in drag) how much she loves Joe (Curtis in trousers) in *Some Like It Hot* (1959). Shirley MacLaine is rescued by C.C. Baxter (Jack Lemmon) in *The Apartment* (1960). *Fedora* (1978) explores a similar plot to that of *Sunset Boulevard* about a Garboesque star. Both films reflect and record a changing Hollywood.

The Lubitsch Touch is at play in Wilder's directorial debut *The Major and the Minor* (1942), in which working girl Susan (Ginger Rogers) pretends to be a 12 year old to save on train fare. The three acerbic comedies set in Germany: *A Foreign Affair* (1948) in a Berlin ravaged by war; *Stalag 17* (1953) in a prisoner-of-war camp; and *One, Two, Three* (1961) in a Berlin divided by the Wall, are also compassionate and extremely funny.

Some Like It Hot is a Prohibition-era gangster spoof, widely considered one of the funniest films ever. Wilder moved into the newly emerging genre of film noir with *Double Indemnity* (1944), a dark and pessimistic thriller portrayed with acid humour. *The Lost Weekend* (1945), one of the first films to deal seriously with alcoholism, is another grim and gripping depiction.

A scene *from* Sunset Boulevard, *Wilder's hard-hitting, cynical take on the vagaries of show business, with Gloria Swanson as Norma and William Holden as Joe Gillis.*

Robert **Wise**

1914–2005 AMERICAN 1944–1989

39 Drama, Musical

Although Robert Wise's most celebrated film was *The Sound of Music* (1965), shot in splendid Todd-AO and De Luxe Color, his forte was gritty, small-budget, black-and-white realistic dramas.

Robert Wise became one of Hollywood's leading directors by moving from genre to genre, from style to style, in a workmanlike manner. Although he did so without imposing any discernible personal stamp on his films, he directed some of the finest boxing dramas (*The Set-Up*, 1949), sci-fi movies (*The Day the Earth Stood Still*, 1951 — an intelligent, anti-war classic), and horror films (*The Haunting*, 1963).

Wise made his debut as a director making chilling horror films for Hollywood producer Val Lewton, such as the dreamy *The Curse of the Cat People* (1944). He then went on to make a number of tightly plotted suspenseful dramas, such as *Born to Kill* (1947), and an excellent Western with Robert Mitchum, *Blood on the Moon* (1948). *The Set-Up* is a metaphysical contemplation well suited to the angst of boxing melodramas, while *Somebody Up There Likes Me* (1956), a biopic of boxer Rocky Graziano (Paul Newman), is almost a direct riposte to it. Wise succeeded in combining realism and social commentary in the musical *West Side Story* (1961), for which he won the Academy Award for Best Director. He won the same award for *The Sound of Music* (1965), a Broadway musical, which he brilliantly introduced to the screen. He was back to sci-fi with *Star Trek: The Motion Picture* (1979), which became the fourth biggest earner in Paramount's history.

WHAT TO WATCH

1944	The Curse of the Cat People
1949	The Set-Up
1951	The Day the Earth Stood Still
1956	Somebody Up There Likes Me
1958	I Want to Live!
1961	West Side Story
1965	The Sound of Music

In West Side Story, *a New York teen gang, the Sharks, led by Bernardo (George Chakiris) perform a brilliant street dance.*

Aboard a mysterious *imaginary train in* 2046 *is an android played by Faye Wong. She also plays the part of Wang Jing Wen, the lost love of the protagonist, Chow Mo Wan.*

Wong Kar-Wai

1958– CHINESE 1988–

8 Avant-garde, Romance

One of the most original directors to emerge at the end of the 20th century, Wong Kar-Wai belongs to the Second New Wave of Hong Kong film-makers who have developed an innovative, non-realistic approach to films.

Wong's cinema is made up of dazzling images (usually of Hong Kong), with multi-layered, intricately structured plots. Added to this is mood and atmosphere, with nostalgic popular music on the soundtrack and alienated love-lorn characters. Wong achieved most of his cinematic effects with the assistance of cinematographer Chris Doyle, and actors William Chang, Maggie Cheung, Leslie Cheung, and Tony Leung. He consistently employs parallel narratives, where characters arbitrarily cross paths, a technique seen at its most extreme in *Chungking Express* (*Chung hing sam lam*, 1994) in which Wong has exceptional control over two separate storylines. The first is of a jilted cop's encounter with a heroin trafficker, and the second about a waitress's obsession with another cop. The Hong Kong of the 1960s is Wong's favourite setting. *Days of Being Wild* (*A Fei jing juen*, 1991), set in 1960, explores the fears of the territory's handover to China; *In the Mood for Love* (*Fa yeung nin wa*, 2000), his most approachable film, also takes place in the 1960s; while *2046* (2004) alternates between the 1960s and an imagined future in 2046. In all these films, Wong asks audiences to abandon their customary ideas of time and space. The ironically titled *Happy Together* (*Cheun gwong tsa sit*, 1997), about the stormy affair of two men, uses both monochrome and color and is one of Wong's few films shot outside China, in Buenos Aires.

WHAT TO WATCH

1994	Ashes of Time
1994	Chungking Express
1995	Fallen Angels
1997	Happy Together
2000	In the Mood for Love
2004	2046

Lovers Yiu-fai *(Tony Leung) and Po-wing (Leslie Cheung) go on the road to Buenos Aires in* Happy Together, *a film about the nature of love.*

Agent Sean Archer *(Travolta) fights terrorist Caster Troy (Cage) in the terse film* Face/Off, *which combines the action, sci-fi, and crime genres.*

John **Woo**

1946– | CHINESE | 1990–

36 | Action, Thriller

Hong Kong director John Woo moved to Hollywood in the early 1990s before the handover of the territory's British sovereignty to the Chinese. By that time he had reached the height of his creative powers.

Woo had struggled to define himself in the Hong Kong film industry's collection of martial arts quickies, but he virtually invented a whole new genre when he came up with *A Better Tomorrow* (*Ying hung boon sik*, 1986), a cops and robbers thriller in the style of the classical Hollywood gangster movie. The film merges hyperbolic violence with a floridly romantic — practically chivalric — take on male friendship and honor. Christened "Heroic Bloodshed" by fans, the genre would become a staple of Hong Kong cinema during the next 10 years, and Woo's action films are its finest exemplars.

Heavily influenced by Jean-Pierre Melville, Sam Peckinpah, and Vincente Minnelli, Woo creates highly choreographed action set pieces that have nothing to do with realism. Following his most extreme and personal film, the Vietnam-era gangster movie *Bullet in the Head* (*Die xue jie tou*, 1990), and the virtuoso shoot-'em-ups *The Killer* (*Die xue shuang xiong*, 1989) and *Hard-Boiled* (*Lashou shentan*, 1992), Woo gained a cult reputation in Hollywood. His flamboyant cinematic style comprising swooping crane shots, multi-angle coverage, and slow-motion replays — along with his trademark two-gun shoot-outs — was much copied in the 1990s. His best American film, *Face/Off* (1997), is a double-take on two adversaries Caster and Sean (Nicholas Cage and John Travolta), who switch identities. The stars' larger-than-life role-playing is typical of Woo's work, but it does not preclude his philosophical seriousness.

Jean-Claude Van Damme *promoted Woo (right) as the "Martin Scorsese of Asia," and thus Woo got to direct his first American film,* Hard Target *(1993).*

WHAT TO WATCH

1989	The Killer
1990	Bullet in the Head
1992	Hard-Boiled
1997	Face/Off
2000	Mission: Impossible II

William **Wyler**

1902–1981 | AMERICAN | 1926–1970

61 | Drama, Epic, Costume drama, Musical

The films of William Wyler are usually sturdy and tasteful Academy Award-winning entertainments that probe ethical issues.

Coming to Hollywood in 1924, German-born William Wyler worked his way up from prop boy to director of dozens of short Westerns, each made in a few days. Following these, he worked painstakingly, earning the nickname "99-take Wyler." His reputation as a film-maker of quality dates from his first encounter with cinematographer Gregg Toland on *These Three* (1936), Wyler's first version of Lillian Hellman's play *The Children's Hour* (He remade it in 1962 when he was able to mention lesbianism). Toland's camerawork, especially his deep-focus photography, gave Wyler's films a definition they might not otherwise have had. Producer Sam Goldwyn also helped him with some of his best work on *Dodsworth* (1936) and *Wuthering Heights* (1939). Other Goldwyn productions are *Dead End* (1937), a social drama about juvenile crime in New York, and *The Little Foxes* (1941), a lush Hellman drama with Bette Davis. Wyler also directed Davis excellently in *Jezebel* (1938) and *The Letter* (1940). *The Best Years of Our Lives* (1946), a moving and revealing portrait of post-war America, follows the lives of three soldiers on their return to civilian life, each representing a different armed service and social class. It won seven Academy Awards.

Film poster, *1946*

Wyler's meticulous style filled the canvases of *Friendly Persuasion* (1956), a gentle tale of a Quaker family forced to take up arms during the American Civil War; *The Big Country* (1958), a vast anti-Western; and the epic *Ben-Hur* (1959).

WHAT TO WATCH

1938	Jezebel
1941	The Little Foxes
1942	Mrs. Miniver
1946	The Best Years of Our Lives
1953	Roman Holiday
1956	Friendly Persuasion
1958	The Big Country
1959	Ben-Hur
1968	Funny Girl

Bette Davis *is the tempestuous heroine Julie and Henry Fonda is Preston — an engaged couple about to break up, in the compelling period drama* Jezebel.

Franco **Zeffirelli**

1923– | ITALIAN | 1957–

18 | Costume drama, Musical

Primarily a director of opulently mounted plays and operas, Franco Zeffirelli imbues his films with baroque imagery and sumptuous photography, sets, and costumes.

"We have no guarantee for the present or the future. Therefore the only choice is to go back to the past...I am an enlightened conservative continuing the discourse of our grandfathers and fathers," declared Zeffirelli, whose films are mostly set in the past or are adaptations of classical texts. His Shakespeare films are bustling and colorful: *The Taming of the Shrew* (1967) stars Elizabeth Taylor and Richard Burton in a raucous domestic duel; *Romeo and Juliet* (1968) has a youthful energy; and Mel Gibson makes a virile *Hamlet* (1990). The entertaining *Tea with Mussolini* (1999) is based on his own childhood.

Maggie Smith *as Lady Hester and Claudio Spadaro as Mussolini in* Tea with Mussolini, *in which five British and American women raise an abandoned child.*

WHAT TO WATCH

1967	The Taming of the Shrew
1968	Romeo and Juliet
1979	The Champ
1982	La Traviata
1990	Hamlet
1999	Tea with Mussolini

Robert **Zemeckis**

1952– | AMERICAN | 1984–

15 | Comedy

A protégé of Steven Spielberg, Robert Zemeckis is among the most technically savvy directors in Hollywood. He has made his name with a series of witty, mildly satiric comedies.

Zemeckis hit a home run with *Romancing the Stone* (1984), starring Michael Douglas, Kathleen Turner, and Danny DeVito, and oversaw the hugely popular *Back to the Future* series (1985, 1989, 1990) with rare acumen. In *Who Framed Roger Rabbit* (1988), he combines live action seamlessly with traditional animation to groundbreaking effect. Regrettably, as he has gotten older, the human elements in his movies have been displaced by a greater emphasis on technology; in 2004's *The Polar Express,* he uses digitalized motion-capture animation techniques that result in creepy, rather than lifelike, figures. Two of his films with Tom Hanks stand out. *Forrest Gump* (1994) is a deeply reactionary gloss on late 20th-century US history (and another huge hit), which won six Academy Awards, including Best Picture and Best Director among others. *Cast Away* (2000), on the other hand, is a salient modern-day Robinson Crusoe story, which can be considered the director's best work.

Chuck Noland *(Tom Hanks), a workaholic Federal Express inspector stranded on a remote Pacific island after a plane crash, re-examines his priorities in* Cast Away.

WHAT TO WATCH

1985	Back to the Future
1988	Who Framed Roger Rabbit
1994	Forrest Gump
2000	Cast Away

Zhang Yimou

1951– CHINESE 1987–

14 Costume drama, Melodrama

Among the first post-Mao film school graduates, Zhang Yimou dares to express moral ambiguity and an implicit reaction against authority in his films.

Reacting against the propagandist films he was subjected to in his youth, former cameraman Zhang recalled that at film school, "we swore...we would never make films like that." *Red Sorghum* (*Hong Gaoliang*, 1987), his first feature, lived up to that promise in its depiction of intricate relationships in rural China set in a beautiful landscape. *Ju Dou* (1990) is a passionate melodrama of adultery, recalling 1940s Hollywood film noir, although it takes place against the rich colors of a dye factory. *Raise the Red Lantern* (*Dahong Denglong Gaogao Gua*, 1991), *The Story of Qiu Ju* (*Qiu Ju da guan si*, 1992), and *To Live* (*Huozhe*, 1994) all deal with the position of women in Chinese society and star Zhang's former lover Gong Li. After they parted, his films lost some of their impact.

Flying Snow *(Maggie Cheung) and Moon (Zhang Ziyi) battle amid autumn leaves in the spectacular* Hero (2002).

WHAT TO WATCH

1987	Red Sorghum
1990	Ju Dou
1991	Raise the Red Lantern
1992	The Story of Qiu Ju
1994	To Live

Fred Zinnemann

1907–1997 AUSTRIAN (AMERICAN)

1942–1982 21 Various

Zinnemann's best features are humanistic and naturalistic movies. Although concerned with psychological, political, and social issues, they remain very entertaining.

Zinnemann was particularly sensitive to actors: Montgomery Clift (*The Search*, 1948), Pier Angeli and Rod Steiger (*Teresa*, 1950), Marlon Brando (*The Men*, 1950), Julie Harris (*A Member of the Wedding*, 1952), and Shirley Jones (*Oklahoma!* 1955) all made their debuts in his films. *High Noon* (1952), a classic Western, marks the apex of his career. *From Here to Eternity* (1953), a low-key film set in the days before Pearl Harbor, changed the images of Frank Sinatra and Deborah Kerr. *Oklahoma!*, the musical, the melodrama *The Nun's Story* (1959), and the costume drama *A Man for All Seasons* (1966) bear his distinctive stamp.

WHAT TO WATCH

1948	The Search
1948	Act of Violence
1950	The Men
1952	High Noon
1953	From Here to Eternity
1955	Oklahoma!

Cowboy Curly McLane *(Gordon MacRae) courts farmgirl, Laurey Williams (Shirley Jones) in* Oklahoma!*, Zinnemann's adaptation of the Rodgers and Hammerstein musical.*

TOP 100 MOVIES

It is always a challenge to produce a definitive list of "must-see" movies, because value judgments are, by definition, extremely subjective. However, the 100 handpicked films in this section have delighted, moved or educated audiences of all ages, all over the world. Over the last nine decades, these films have changed our perceptions of cinema, and most have left an indelible mark on film history.

The choice of the 100 movies was guided by various criteria. Although there are a handful of relatively recent films — some up-to-date, instant classics, one might say — the majority of these movies have been included because they have stood the test of time. Besides those films that are part of what is perceived as "the canon" — films that appear regularly on film historians and critics' all-time best lists and are an essential part of any Film Studies course — there are audience favorites as well.

Among the films in this section, you will find silent masterpieces from *The Birth of a Nation* to *The Passion of Joan of Arc*; comedies from *City Lights* to *Women on the Verge of a Nervous Breakdown*; musicals from *42nd Street* to *The Sound of Music*. There are horror movies, such as *Nosferatu*, cartoons — from the hand-drawn *Snow White and the Seven Dwarfs* to the computer-animated *Toy Story* — science fiction (*Star Wars*, naturally) and epics (*The Lord of The Rings* trilogy).

Among the films that are automatically on any list of "greats" are those that, regardless of personal likes and dislikes, have had a seminal effect on film history for both technical and esthetic reasons, such as *The Cabinet of Dr. Caligari*, *Nanook of the North*, *The Battleship Potemkin*, *Napoléon*, *Citizen Kane*, *Bicycle Thieves* and *Breathless*. Others have been significant in less obvious ways like *King Kong*, *His Girl Friday*, *L'Avventura*, *Bonnie and Clyde*, *Easy Rider*, *Taxi Driver* and *Annie Hall*.

The list has been limited to one film per director mainly because it would be easy to come up with 100 films that included only works by great directors, such as Alfred Hitchcock, Ingmar Bergman, Luis Buñuel, Federico Fellini, John Ford, Jean Renoir, Akira Kurosawa and Billy Wilder.

Any of the films we have chosen to represent the directors above could be replaced by another title; *North By Northwest*, *Psycho* or *Rear Window* instead of *Vertigo*; *Wild Strawberries*, *Persona* or *Fanny and Alexander*, in place of *The Seventh Seal*. Why not *Viridiana* or *Belle de Jour* for Buñuel? *Amarcord* or *8½* for Fellini? John Ford, the maestro of the Western, is represented by *The Grapes of Wrath*, a non-Western. Is *The Rules of the Game* better than *La Grande Illusion*? Is *Rashomon* better than *The Seven Samurai*? Is *Some Like It Hot* better than *The Apartment*? One could make a strong case either way.

It was from this embarrassment of riches that we have made a final selection of our top 100 movies.

Ziyi Zhang plays Jiao Long, *an impetuous, and physically skilled nobleman's daughter in* Crouching Tiger, Hidden Dragon, *Ang Lee' hit film from 2000.*

The Birth of a Nation | D.W. Griffith | 1915

The Birth of a Nation **was a landmark in the development of motion pictures and remains one of the most controversial films ever made. The epic story follows two families on opposite sides during and immediately after the American Civil War.**

At over three hours long, nothing on the scale of *The Birth of a Nation* had ever been attempted before in American cinema. All of the innovations of Griffith's earlier work — cross-cutting, close-ups, dissolves, and fades — reached maturity in *The Birth of a Nation.* One of its achievements was to integrate an intimate story within the progression of dramatically reconstructed historical events — for example the assassination of President Lincoln and the swirling mass of soldiers on the battlefields. Apparently, Griffith wrote no script, carrying the film's complex structure in his head. However, much of the latter part of the film, in which slaves gain freedom, the hero forms the Ku Klux Klan, and a black man pursues a white virgin who kills herself rather than succumb to his attentions, was, even in 1915, considered by many to be racially offensive. As a result, the National Association for the Advancement of Colored People (NAACP) picketed and boycotted the film. Despite its racism, the film is considered a technical masterpiece.

Film poster, 1915

CREDITS	
production	Epoch Producing Corporation
producer	D.W. Griffith
screenplay	D.W. Griffith, Frank E. Woods, Thomas Dixon Jr. Based on Dixon's novels *The Clansman* and *The Leopard's Spots.*
cinematography	G.W. "Billy" Bitzer

LILLIAN GISH

A delicate and beautiful actress, Lillian Gish (1893–1993) was the supreme actress of the silent cinema. She was D.W. Griffith's ideal heroine— a combination of virginal purity and spiritual strength, helping to lighten the heavy Victorian sentimentality of the many self-sacrificing heroines she played. Gish continued to make films into her 90s. Notable works included Victor Sjöström's *The Wind* (1928) and Charles Laughton's *Night of the Hunter* (1955). Her last film, *The Whales of August* (1987), also starred Bette Davis.

In The Birth of a Nation, *Lillian Gish plays the virginal heroine, Elsie Stoneman, who is rescued from a "fate worse than death" by the newly formed Ku Klux Klan, led by her lover.*

The Cabinet of Dr. Caligari | Robert Wiene | 1919

The deliberately distorted *perspective of the sets have an almost hypnotic effect on the audience, reflecting Caligari's control over his servant Cesare.*

Adapting its style from painting and the theater, *The Cabinet of Dr. Caligari (Das Kabinett des Doktor Caligari)* was considered the first true example of expressionism in the cinema (see box). It had an important influence on German films in the decade that followed its release, and on horror movies in general.

Caligari (Werner Krauss), a fairground showman, hypnotizes his servant Cesare (Conrad Veidt) so that he will commit murder. The somnambulist carries off the girlfriend, Jane (Lil Dagover), of the young hero (Friedrich Feher). The film, intended as a metaphor for the Great War, has Caligari representing a government that controls the will of its people. However, the ending shows Caligari as a benign director of a lunatic asylum, with the hero a patient who has imagined the murderous story. The distorted sets and grotesquely angled photography create a nightmarish atmosphere, a style that became known as "Caligarism." The film had a direct impact on James Whale's *Frankenstein* (1931) and *The Bride of Frankenstein* (1935), and influenced many later works, including those of Tim Burton, who modeled Johnny Depp's Edward Scissorhands on Veidt's character of the mesmerized slave.

CREDITS

producer	Erich Pommer for Decla
screenplay	Carl Mayer, Hans Janowitz
set design	Walter Röhrig, Hermann Warm, Walter Reiman
cinematography	Willy Hameister

GERMAN EXPRESSIONISM

Expressionism was a movement in the graphic arts, literature, drama, and film, which flourished in Germany between 1903–33. In film, the movement was characterized by the extreme stylization of sets, acting, lighting, and camera angles. Most of the major German directors of the silent period were influenced by The Cabinet of Dr. Caligari.

The Cabinet of Dr. Caligari was the classic expressionist film in Germany. The style inspired a series of horror fantasies known as "shadow films."

Nosferatu: A Symphony of Terror | F.W. Murnau | 1921

The film that marked the first appearance of Dracula the vampire on screen remains the eeriest and most magical of the multitude of film versions of this supernatural tale.

CREDITS	
production	Prana Film
producer	Albin Grau, Enrico Dieckmann
screenplay	Henrik Galeen, based on Bram Stoker's *Dracula* (uncredited)
cinematography	Fritz Arno Wagner

F.W. Murnau made his debut as a film director in 1919, the same year that *The Cabinet of Dr. Caligari* (*see page 399*) was released. He was clearly much influenced by that seminal work. However, unlike the stylized sets of the earlier film, much of *Nosferatu* was shot on location, with *chiaroscuro* lighting — a technique taken from the field of painting, in which the contrast between dark and light areas in an image is heightened (*see page 141*) — creating its gothic atmosphere. Murnau also used special effects, speeding up the frames and also using negative film to evoke a ghostly carriage ride. Murnau plundered Stoker's 1897 novel without permission and an action for breach of copyright was brought against him, but *Nosferatu* is an acknowledged classic of the horror genre.

The film's feeling of terror *is centred on the spectral, gaunt figure of Max Schreck's Vampire, who creeps through the film with menacing authority.*

Nanook of the North | Robert Flaherty | 1922

CREDITS	
production	Revillon Frères
producer	Robert Flaherty
screenplay	Robert Flaherty
cinematography	Robert Flaherty

Robert Flaherty's *Nanook of the North* had a great effect on the evolution of the documentary film. The film's strength lies in its basis in reality and the unprecedented rapport between the work's Inuit subjects and the man behind the camera.

In order to make this extraordinary document of hardship and endurance, Flaherty spent 16 months living with the Inuit of Canada's Hudson Bay. He concentrated on a year in the everyday life of a family — Nanook, his wife Nyla, and their children — depicting activities such as trading, fishing, hunting, and the construction of an igloo. However, Flaherty directed them to re-enact their roles for the camera, including a scene in which a walrus is hunted. To enable him to shoot inside an igloo, he had the dwelling built at twice the average size, with half of it cut away to permit sunlight to enter. Dubious as this sounds, such techniques allowed Flaherty to convey the drama and the struggle underlying the daily existence of these people, depicting a way of life threatened by encroaching civilization. It was a new approach to the presentation of reality on film, ennobling its subjects rather than exploiting them.

Nyla, Nanook's wife, *carries her son through the bleak Arctic landscape. Nanook died of starvation two years after Flaherty filmed him.*

The Battleship Potemkin | Sergei Eisenstein | 1925

Soviet cinema and Sergei Eisenstein were brought to international attention by this magnificent film. Although full of dramatic scenes, it swirls around a central denouement that is universally known as the "Odessa Steps" sequence — one of the most memorable and exciting pieces in all cinema.

Commemorating the 20th anniversary of the 1905 Revolution, *The Battleship Potemkin* focuses on an incident in which the crew of a battleship at Odessa mutinies rather than eat rotting food. The leader of the protest is fatally shot by an officer, prompting hundreds of civilians to pay homage to the dead man and lend their support to the mutiny. As many of them gather on the Odessa Steps to wave to the ship, they are mown down by the government troops. The soldiers march down a seemingly endless flight of steps, advancing on the fleeing citizens, the rhythm of their marching feet contrasting with the fall of injured and dying people, including a small boy trampled underfoot and an elderly woman shot in the face. With its rhythmic collision and contrast of images, the film was a splendid demonstration of Eisenstein's theory of montage (see page 291). What is sometimes forgotten, perhaps because of the film's revolutionary style, is that *The Battleship Potemkin* tells an exciting narrative through well-rounded characters.

A Russian poster *for the film is a fine example of the particular graphic style of the Soviet period, which was known as structuralism.*

CREDITS

studio	Goskino
producer	Jacob Bliokh
screenplay	Sergei Eisenstein, Nina Agadzhanova
cinematography	Vladimir Popov, Edouard Tissé

The Odessa Steps sequence *shows the horrifying moment when a pram hurtles down the steps towards certain destruction.*

Metropolis | Fritz Lang | 1926

The visual legacy of Fritz Lang's *Metropolis* can be seen from *The Bride of Frankenstein* (1935) to the *Batman* movies via *Modern Times* (1936), the *Star Wars* cycle, and *Blade Runner* (1982). It contained technical innovations that influenced Hollywood films of the 1930s and 1940s.

Metropolis is set in a futuristic city, where the downtrodden factory workers (living underground) are made to rebel against their masters by a malign robot created in the image of a saintly girl. Lang was given an unprecedented budget to create huge, realistic sets anticipating the 21st century, inspired by the New York skyline. To achieve futuristic effects, lighting cameraman Eugen Schüfftan introduced the Schüfftan process, which combined life-size action with models or artwork. Despite its ending — "Capital" and "Labor" reconciled by the love of the factory owner's son (Gustav Fröhlich) for a working girl (Brigitte Helm) — *Metropolis* can be seen as an allegory of totalitarianism. In 1984, composer Giorgio Moroder added a rock music score, tinted sequences, and optically enhanced several sequences, through which Lang's masterly control continues to astonish.

CREDITS	
studio	UFA
producer	Erich Pommer
screenplay	Fritz Lang, Thea von Harbou
cinematography	Karl Freund, Günther Rittaur
design	Otto Hunte, Erich Kettelhut, Karl Vollbrecht
special effects	Eugen Schüfftan

A German poster *shows the robot against the cityscape.* Metropolis *pioneered the use of science fiction to comment on contemporary society.*

The futuristic sets *created for* Metropolis *are still impressive decades after the film was made. Mirrors were used to create illusions, including the flying machine that glided between the huge buildings.*

Napoléon | Abel Gance | 1927

Abel Gance's most ambitious and personal film, *Napoléon* is a pyrotechnical display of almost every device of the silent screen and beyond. The use of a triple screen anticipates wide-screen techniques, such as Cinerama, which did not come into use for another 30 years.

Albert Dieudonné *plays Napoléon, here seen isolated after battle and surrounded by the dead and wounded. Such scenes typify Gance's desire to create a "richer and more elevated form of cinema."*

Director Gance's historical and historic film presents Napoléon Bonaparte in six episodes as a Nietzschean Superman, following his life from childhood, through his military schooling, his meeting with Josephine (Gina Manès), and his rise to power. With a dazzling use of visual metaphors, Gance shows the boy Napoléon as a brilliant budding military strategist during a snowball fight shot to resemble a military campaign, the split screen filling with snowballs in flight. The most famous set piece is the symbolic sequence in which Napoléon sails back to France from Corsica through stormy, rough seas that threaten to enter the boat, cut with scenes of a political storm raging in Paris. In order to gain his effects, Gance used hand-held cameras, wide-angled lenses, superimposed images, and rapid cutting. *Napoléon* was first shown at the Paris Opéra, in a version that lasted five hours. However, it was poorly received and was released in various truncated forms thereafter. In 1980, British film restorer Kevin Brownlow reconstructed the film, keeping as close to the original as possible. *Napoléon* finally received the recognition it deserved, amazing audiences everywhere.

CREDITS

production	West/Société-Générale de Films
screenplay	Abel Gance
cinematography	Jules Kruger
music	Arthur Honegger

Polyvision *was a revolutionary projection technique that used multiple frames to show a panorama of separate but thematically linked images.*

An Andalucian Dog (Un Chien Andalou) | Luis Buñuel | 1928

A balcony at night. A man (Luis Buñuel) sharpens a razor blade. He observes a small cloud moving towards the full moon. Then the head of a girl comes into view, her eyes wide open. The cloud now moves across the moon. The razor blade slices open the girl's eye.

Thus began *An Andalusian Dog (Un Chien Andalou)* — the title is unrelated to anything in the film — and the career of Luis Buñuel. It has one of the most startling openings of any film, retaining the power to shock. According to the French film

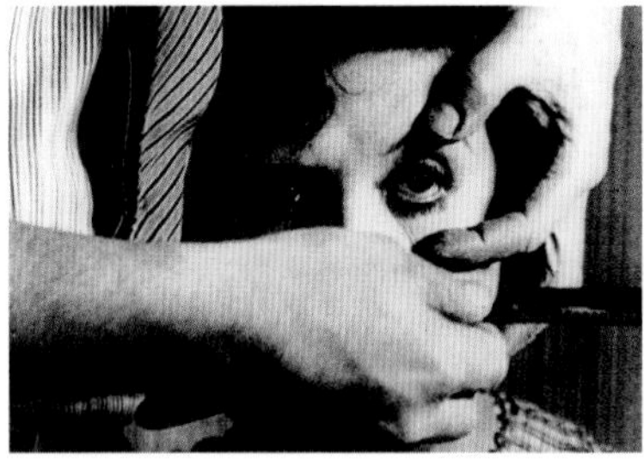

CREDITS	
producer	Luis Buñuel
screenplay	Luis Buñuel, Salvador Dali
cinematography	Albert Duberverger

director Jean Vigo, "The prologue… tells us that in this film we must see with a different eye." Made under the influence of André Breton's "Surrealist Manifesto," (1924) and co-conceived with the artist Salvador Dali, its series of unconnected incidents was intended to follow the logic of a dream: ants emerge from the palm of a disembodied hand (an archetypal Dali-esque image), priests are pulled along the ground, a woman's eye is slit open, and dead donkeys lie on two pianos. Although the film defies explanation, its rich supply of images from the unconscious can be read as a study of repressed sexual impulses.

The opening sequence, *in which a girl's eye appears to be slit by a razor, is the most memorable of 17 surrealistic images in the film that are designed to shock or provoke.*

The Passion of Joan of Arc | Carl Dreyer | 1928

***The Passion of Joan of Arc* is an intense depiction of individual suffering, a soul in torment transformed into cinematic images. It is the purest expression of Carl Dreyer's style, which he called "realized mysticism."**

Dreyer based his last silent film on transcripts of the 18-month trial of Joan of Arc (Renée Falconetti) before she was burned at the stake. By telescoping the events of the trial into one day, the screenplay provides the film with a formal intensity. Dreyer's constant and unforgettable use of long-held close-ups has led some critics to describe *The Passion of Joan of Arc* as a film consisting entirely of examples of this type of shot. In fact, the film also includes tilts, pans, medium

CREDITS	
production	Société Générale des Films
screenplay	Carl Dreyer, Joseph Delteil
cinematography	Rudolph Maté
costume design	Valentine Hugo

Reneé Falconetti *wore no make-up and had to crop her hair to play the lead role in Dreyer's film. Here, Joan is seen shortly before she is burnt at the stake.*

shots, and cross-cutting. The faces of the heroine's judges, wearing no make-up, are cruelly exposed to Rudolph Maté's camera. But it is the agonized face of Falconetti, in what was her only film, that burns itself into the mind. Dreyer fulfilled his intention to "move the audience so that they would themselves feel the suffering that Joan endured." But despite the agony, the film remains an uplifting experience.

All Quiet on the Western Front | Lewis Milestone | 1930

Based on Erich M. Remarque's best-selling novel of the same name, this devastating film was a landmark in anti-war movies, particularly as the narrative is viewed from the German perspective. The stark message that war is hell for both sides resulted in Germany and France banning the film for many years for fear that it would have a demoralizing effect on their armed forces.

Film poster, 1930

The powerful pacifist message of Lewis Milestone's film, made at the dawn of the sound era, transcends cultures and generations. The film follows seven German boys who leave school in 1914, full of patriotic fervor, to fight for their country. Their enthusiasm is soon dampened when they are thrown into the horror of warfare and experience the brutality of life in the trenches. Particularly effective are the tracking shots, which show the attacks and counter-attacks of both sides, and the appalling deaths suffered. So realistic were these battle sequences that some of them have been incorporated into documentaries about World War I. The famous climax, in which Paul Baümer (Lew Ayres) — the only one of the seven boys still alive — is killed as he stretches towards a butterfly, was shot some months after the film's completion. The director used his own hand — later to take hold of the Oscar for Best Director.

CREDITS	
studio	Universal Pictures
producers	Carl Laemmle, Universal Studios
screenplay	Lewis Milestone, Maxwell Anderson, Del Andrews, George Abbott, Erich Maria Remarque
cinematography	Arthur Edeson, Karl Freund
awards	Academy Awards: Best Picture, Best Director

Paul Baümer (Lew Ayres) *takes cover in a church cemetery under heavy shell fire from French forces counter-attacking a German bombardment.*

The Blue Angel | Josef von Sternberg | 1930

The first sound film made in Germany, *The Blue Angel* (*Der Blaue Engel*) was notable for introducing Marlene Dietrich, one of the screen's greatest stars, to the world. The film also marked the start of one of the most remarkable collaborations between an actor (Dietrich) and film-maker (Sternberg) that the cinema has ever seen.

The film depicts the downfall of an ageing and puritanical teacher, Professor Immanuel Rath (Emil Jannings), who becomes infatuated with a sultry nightclub entertainer named Lola Frohlich (Dietrich). She marries the hapless man, but goes on to deceive and humiliate him. *The Blue Angel* is an impressive tale of a decent man lured to his doom by *un amour fou*—exemplified in a startling scene that shows the cuckolded Rath crowing like a young rooster, while dressed as a clown. However, despite a moving performance by Jannings, *The Blue Angel* is Dietrich's film. Josef von Sternberg saw a sensuous, mysterious, and glamorous star potential in her, and she gives a splendid portrayal of an indolent, sluttish *femme fatale.* Sitting astride a chair and huskily singing "Falling in Love Again" while dressed scantily, Dietrich encapsulated an age and an impulse in German cinema. Shot concurrently in German and English, the film's seedy atmosphere is conveyed by Sternberg's masterful manipulation of lighting techniques.

MARLENE DIETRICH

The career of Marlene Dietrich (1901–92) can be divided into three unequal parts. Her early film and theatre work in the 1920s, the five years with Sternberg, during which he directed her as a femme fatale in seven masterpieces, and the years from 1935 in which her talent was often misused. Later films were Billy Wilder's *A Foreign Affair* (1948) and Fritz Lang's *Rancho Notorious* (1952).

CREDITS

studio	UFA
producer	Erich Pommerr
screenplay	Josef von Sternberg, Robert Liebmann, Karl Vollmöller and Carl Zuckmayer, from the novel *Professor Unrath* by Heinrich Mann.
cinematography	Gunther Rittau
music	Frederick Hollander

Dressed in top hat, *stiletto heels, and black stockings, Marlene Dietrich's Lola became one of cinema's most iconic images; the role was to launch her international career.*

City Lights | Charlie Chaplin | 1931

Four years after talkies had become *de rigeur*, Charlie Chaplin had the presumption to present a new silent film to the public. Only Chaplin—who not only starred in it as the beloved "Little Tramp," but also produced, directed, edited, and wrote the scenario, and composed the music—could have got away with it. Audiences loved *City Lights* and critics extolled it as his finest work.

Using his last cent, the Little Tramp (Chaplin) buys a flower from a blind girl (Virginia Cherill). Smitten, he determines to restore her sight, and is able to do so with money obtained from a drunken millionaire he saves from drowning. Seeing the rather ridiculous looking tramp for the first time, and unaware that he is her benefactor, the girl puts money in his hands, only to recognize his touch. Chaplin's unique stamp is unmistakable in this film, which shows his unerring ability to shift from satire to pathos. One of the funniest set pieces is a brilliantly choreographed boxing sequence in which Chaplin dances around the ring, keeping the referee between himself and his adversary. Although it had sound effects and music, *City Lights* was primarily a tribute to the art of silent screen comedy.

The Little Tramp, *Chaplin's trademark character, seen here with Cherill's blind flower girl, was inspired by Chaplin's poverty-stricken childhood in Victorian London. The character appeared in many of his silent movies, combining pathos with the sort of slapstick comedy that was enjoyed by early cinema audiences.*

Film poster, 1931

CREDITS	
studio	United Artists
producer	Charles Chaplin
screenplay	Charles Chaplin
cinematography	Gordon Pollock, Roland Totheroh, and Mark Marklatt

42nd Street | Lloyd Bacon | 1933

Although it was the archetypal "backstage" musical of the early 1930s, *42nd Street* added a new dimension to the genre with its hard-hitting references to the Depression, contrasting scenes of chorus girls slumming it in cheap apartments with Busby Berkeley's lavish kaleidoscopic production numbers.

This musical was the first of three that Warner Bros. released in 1933; the other two were *Gold Diggers of 1933* and *Footlight Parade*. Economical, fast-paced, and down-to-earth, these films revitalized the musical genre. While an advance on previous "backstage" musicals, such as *On with the Show!* (1929), and less escapist than its predecessors, *42nd Street* still contains all the essential elements of the genre, depicting the trials and tribulations of putting on a Broadway show and ending with the successful opening night. In this case, ingénue Peggy Sawyer (Ruby Keeler) takes over the leading role from Dorothy Brock (Bebe Daniels) at the last moment. The pep talk she gets from her director, Julian Marsh (Warner Baxter), just before going on stage has entered showbusiness lore. But what most people remember are Berkeley's extraordinary dance routines: "Shuffle Off To Buffalo," "Young and Healthy," and the title number, which, like the film, is "naughty, bawdy, gaudy, sporty."

CREDITS	
studio	Warner Bros.
producers	Hal B. Wallis, Darryl F. Zanuck
screenplay	Rian James, James Seymour
cinematography	Sol Polito
choreography	Busby Berkeley
costume design	Orry Kelly
musical numbers	Harry Warren, Al Dubin

"And Sawyer, you're going out a youngster, but you've got to come back a star!"

JULIAN MARSH (WARNER BAXTER) TO PEGGY SAWYER (RUBY KEELER)

Andy Lee (George E. Stone) *rehearses a tap routine with the chorus line; Peggy (Ruby Keeler), the lucky understudy, is at the front.*

Duck Soup | Leo McCarey | 1933

In their fifth film, the four Marx Brothers — Groucho, Chico, Harpo, and Zeppo – reached the height of their comic skills in this surreal satire that lampooned all authority and respectability, dictatorial leaders, war films (and war), and the Ruritarian musical romances of the period.

Rufus T. Firefly (Groucho Marx), *charms Gloria Teasdale (Margaret Dumont), the rich widow of the former President, at a party organized to welcome him as the new leader of Freedonia.*

The year 1933 was a time of immense social and economic upheaval: Hitler had seized power in Germany and the Great Depression was at its height in the US. So an outrageous comedy that begins with a political crisis and ends with a war would have seemed appropriate for its time. However, *Duck Soup* was both a critical and commercial failure when it was first released. Audiences were looking for reassurance, not the cynicism and anarchic humor of the Marx Brothers, hilarious as it is. In the film, Groucho plays the President of Freedonia, Rufus T. Firefly, who declares war on neighboring Sylvania, because he's "… already paid a month's advance rent on the battlefield." What follows is a series of lunatic set pieces, including the celebrated mirror routine during which Chico and Harpo, disguised as Groucho, all pretend to be each other's reflections. *Duck Soup* contains the essence of the Marx Brothers' comic genius (without the piano and harp solos that interrupted many of their other films). After this film, straight man Zeppo became an agent, and the three remaining Marx Brothers moved from Paramount to MGM, where they continued their lunacy, best seen in *A Night at the Opera* (1935).

The Marx Brothers — *Chico as Chicolini, Zeppo as Lieutenant Bob Roland, Harpo as Pinky, and Groucho as Firefly — pose for a promotional shot for their fourth feature* Duck Soup.

CREDITS	
studio	Paramount
producer	Herman J. Mankiewicz
screenplay	Bert Kalmar, Harry Ruby
cinematography	Henry Sharp
music	Burt Kalmar, John Leipold, Harry Ruby

King Kong | Merian Cooper/Ernest Schoedsack | 1933

Despite two remakes in 1976 and 2005, and many imitations, the original black-and-white *King Kong* retains its ability to charm and astonish. It became the yardstick against which monster movies would be measured.

CREDITS	
studio	RKO
producers	Merian Cooper, Ernest B. Schoedsack, David O. Selznick
screenplay	James Ashmore Creelman, Ruth Rose, Edgar Wallace
cinematography	Edward Linden, J.O. Taylor, Vernon L. Walker, Kenneth Peach
special effects	Willis O'Brien

Kong, a gargantuan ape, inhabits the prehistoric Skull Island. When he sees Ann Darrow (Fay Wray), who is part of an expedition to the remote spot led by showman Carl Denham (Robert Armstrong), his primal instincts are aroused and he goes on the rampage. He is eventually captured and taken to New York, where he meets a spectacular death — the image of Kong on top of the Empire State Building (holding a scantily dressed Wray moments before he is shot down) is one of the most iconic in cinema history. The film was made one frame at a time, using stop-motion photography (see box). Although he appears huge, Kong was a model made out of metal, rubber, cotton, and rabbit fur, only 46cm (18 inches) tall. Part of the movie's wonder is that the model seems to be a real actor, expressing human emotions.

Film poster, 1933

> **"It wasn't the airplanes. It was Beauty killed the Beast."**
>
> **CARL DENHAM (ROBERT ARMSTRONG) ON THE DEATH OF KONG.**

King Kong *swats at the biplanes buzzing around him, while balancing on top of the Empire State Building in the final sequence of the film.*

STOP-MOTION PHOTOGRAPHY

One of the first special effects techniques used, stop-motion photography allows an otherwise inanimate object to move and change position by exposing a single frame of film at a time. The object is moved very slightly between exposures so that when the film is projected an illusion of motion is created. Because it takes 24 frames to create one second of film, several minutes of footage can take months to complete. Willis O'Brien was a pioneer of this technology, his crowning achievement being *King Kong*. Stop-motion sequences using real scenes of buildings and people was a variation on this technique and can be seen most effectively in *Jason and the Argonauts* (1963). The process is still used in animated films, such as Tim Burton's *The Nightmare Before Christmas* (1993) and Aardman Animation's productions.

L'Atalante | Jean Vigo | 1934

Any précis of this film's seemingly simple story cannot do justice to the richness of director Jean Vigo's only feature-length film. Much of it was shot along canals around Paris and in severe weather, contributing to Vigo's tragic death from tuberculosis just weeks after the film's premiere.

A young barge captain, Jean (Jean Dasté), takes his city-dwelling bride, Juliette (Dita Parlo), to live on his boat — *L'Atalante* — which plies the waterways around Paris. Everyday life on the vessel is filled with magical moments, such as a waltz on a phonograph, the newlywed searching for his estranged sweetheart in water, and the joy of reconciliation. The film also contains rich characterization in the character of Père Jules (Michel Simon at his eccentric best), the master of the boat, who tells fantastic stories of his travels. Although ostensibly realist in setting and plot, the film has a surreal spirit, with a commitment to Freudian theories of dreams and the unconscious as well as the overthrow of bourgeois social and moral codes. Poorly received on its first showing, the film was badly edited and even the title was changed to that of a popular song. Happily, *L'Atalante* was restored to its original form in 1945, and has since gained the classic status it richly deserves.

Jean Dasté *plays Jean, and Dita Parlo his young city-dwelling bride, Juliette, who disappears after a quarrel but reunites with her husband in a moving final scene.*

CREDITS

production	Gaumont-Franco-Film-Aubert
producer	Jacques-Louis Nounez
screenplay	Jean Vigo, Albert Riéra, Jean Guineé
cinematography	Boris Kaufman
music	Maurice Jaubert

Jean and Juliette *stand at the prow of* L'Atalante, *the barge from which this haunting and beautifully visualized film takes its name.*

Snow White and the Seven Dwarfs | Walt Disney | 1937

Walt Disney took an enormous artistic and financial risk by making the first feature-length animation film in three-strip Technicolor. However, *Snow White and the Seven Dwarfs* confirmed his position as the master of the cartoon movie.

Rotoscoped figures, *such as Snow White, Prince Charming, and the Wicked Queen, appeared in a Disney film for the first time. The most lovable characters were the dwarfs, whose names were chosen by public poll.*

Initially dubbed "Disney's Folly," *Snow White and the Seven Dwarfs* was four years in the making and cost $1.5 million, a huge sum for the times. Many changes were needed to make a feature cartoon film rather than a short cartoon—the painted cells had to be enlarged to allow more detail in the images and about 750 artists worked on the two million drawings using drawing boards. The studio also devised a multi-plane camera, which enhanced the feeling of depth and could pan over each image without losing perspective. The result was possibly the most popular cartoon film ever, grossing over $8 million on its initial US release. The songs, such as "Whistle While You Work" and "Someday My Prince Will Come," became immediate hits. The film tells of how Snow White, the lovely stepdaughter of a jealous queen, flees the palace and takes refuge with seven dwarfs in their forest home. The queen changes into a wicked witch, and poisons Snow White, who falls into a deep sleep—until a prince finds her and wakens her with a kiss.

In 1938, Disney won a Special Academy Award for "a significant screen innovation that has charmed millions and pioneered a great new entertainment field for the motion picture cartoon." The success of *Snow White and the Seven Dwarfs* was followed by other Disney films including *Fantasia* (1940) and *Pinocchio* (1940).

CREDITS	
studio	Walt Disney Studios
producer	Walt Disney
screenplay	Ted Sears, Richard Creedon, adapted from the story by the Brothers Grimm
cinematography	Maxwell Morgan
supervising director	David Hand
award	Academy Award: Special Award

Olympia | Leni Riefenstahl | 1938

Riefenstahl's film on the 1936 Berlin Olympics is one of cinema's finest achievements. Nevertheless, admiration for its visual beauty is tempered by the fact that it was made as "a song of praise to the ideals of National Socialism" under Hitler's orders.

CREDITS	
production	Tobis
producer	Leni Riefenstahl
screenplay	Leni Riefenstahl
awards	Venice: Mussolini Cup, Best Film

Realizing the immense potential for propaganda through the Olympics, and its dissemination by means of cinema, Hitler gave Riefenstahl all the time and resources she needed to make this four-hour documentary. She had planes, airships, and 30 cameramen at her disposal and spent two years in the cutting room. It is easy to be seduced by the technical brilliance and the beauty of the film's images, including the slow and reverse motion used in the diving sequence; the marathon forming "an epic hymn to endurance"; and the yacht racing under a darkening sky. However, the film is clearly Nazi propaganda, and one cannot forget the horrific persecution of the Jews, which was taking place in Nazi Germany at the time.

The lighting of the Olympic flame *is the culmination of the prologue, which links the idea of beauty in Greek antiquity to those of the Third Reich.*

The Rules of the Game | Jean Renoir | 1939

Made on the eve of World War II, *The Rules of the Game* (*La Règle du Jeu*) is Jean Renoir's most complete film and his most complex in style. Inspired by the classic theatrical comedies of Pierre Marivaux, Pierre de Beaumarchais, and Alfred de Musset, the film reveals French society of the time being disemboweled from within.

Julien Carette, *giving a sly, comic performance as the poacher, Marceau, displays his quarry.*

The film takes place during a lavish weekend shooting party organized by the Count and Countess La Chesnaye (Marcel Dalio and Nora Gregor). During the party, sexual tensions become apparent, as relationships between aristocrats and servants are revealed in scenes set both above and below stairs. The structure, setting, and plot create a dynamic juxtaposition of tragedy, melodrama, and farce that imbue the film with its uniqueness. Apart from memorable performances, particularly Renoir's own as the lovable buffoon Octave, there are some outstanding set pieces, such as the rabbit and bird shoots and the after-dinner entertainment, which uses breathtaking tracking shots and deep focus. The film was a commercial disaster on its release and was banned because its exposure of class divisions in French society was "too demoralizing." It was only in 1956 that it was acclaimed as the masterpiece it undoubtedly is.

CREDITS	
production	Les Nouvelles Editions Françaises
producer	Claude Renoir
screenplay	Jean Renoir, Carl Koch
cinematography	Jean Bachelet
editor	Marguerite Renoir
production design	Eugène Lourié

Gone With the Wind | Victor Fleming | 1939

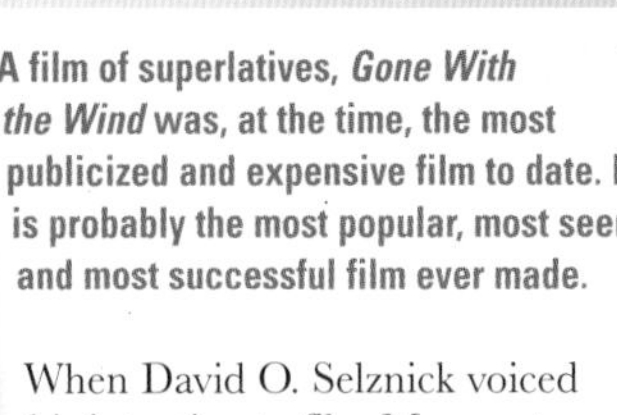

A film of superlatives, *Gone With the Wind* was, at the time, the most publicized and expensive film to date. It is probably the most popular, most seen and most successful film ever made.

Film poster, *1939*

When David O. Selznick voiced his intention to film Margaret Mitchell's bestselling novel about the US Civil War, for which he had bought the rights in 1936, Victor Fleming told him, "This picture is going to be the biggest white elephant of all time," while the usually astute producer Irving Thalberg commented, "...no Civil War picture ever made a nickel." Spectacular set pieces — such as the burning of Atlanta, the party at Twelve Oaks, and the sight of thousands of wounded Confederate soldiers — superbly evoked the Old South. The film's central relationship is between the roguish Rhett Butler and the willful Southern minx Scarlett O'Hara — a monument of passion brilliantly played by Clark Gable and British stage actress, Vivien Leigh.

CREDITS

production	Selznick International Pictures
producer	David O. Selznick
screenplay	Sidney Howard, from Margaret Mitchell's novel
cinematography	Ernest Haller
production	William Cameron Menzies
music	Max Steiner
costume design	Walter Plunkett
awards	Academy Awards: Best Picture, Best Actress (Vivien Leigh), Best Supporting Actress (Hattie McDaniel), Best Director, Best Screenplay, Best Use of Colour, Cinematography, Best Art Direction, Best Editing, Technical Achievement Award

CLARK GABLE

One of the most well-loved movie stars of all time, Clark Gable (1901–60) made some of his best movies with MGM during the 1930s, including *Red Dust* (1932), remade as *Mogambo* in 1953 and *Mutiny on the Bounty* (1935). The only film he made with Carole Lombard, whom he later married, was *No Man of Her Own* (1932). One of Gable's earliest film successes was *It Happened One Night* (1934) for which he won the Oscar for Best Actor. He considered his final film, *The Misfits* (1961), with Marilyn Monroe, his best work since *Gone With the Wind.*

Vivien Leigh, *as the tempestuous Scarlett O'Hara, runs away from an afternoon house party in the first part of the film.*

The Philadelphia Story | George Cukor | 1940

Although *The Philadelphia Story* has many of the elements typical of screwball comedy, the elegant, witty script and George Cukor's understated direction turned it into a sophisticated comedy of manners.

Film poster, *1940*

Katharine Hepburn scored a huge hit on Broadway as Tracy Lord in *The Philadelphia Story*, a role specially written for her by Philip Barry. She bought the film rights and chose her favorite director and co-stars. In a triumphant return to Hollywood, Hepburn plays a domineering, spoiled socialite, who melts in the arms of a cynical reporter, Mike Connor (James Stewart), who has been sent to cover her second marriage to the dull George Kittredge (John Howard). She eventually succumbs to the dazzling charms of her ex-husband, C.K. Dexter Haven (Cary Grant). The film sparkles right from the celebrated wordless opening scene when Grant is tossed out of the front door by Hepburn, along with his bag of golf clubs.

(Top) John Howard (George) *and Cary Grant (Dexter) look on as a tipsy Katharine Hepburn (Tracy) languishes in the arms of James Stewart (Mike) on the eve of her wedding, after a midnight dip in the swimming pool.*

KATHARINE HEPBURN

A true original and one of the all-time greats, Hepburn (1907–2003) was famed for her refusal to play the Hollywood game. Her film career began in the 1930s — she won the first of her four Academy Awards in 1933. After a string of flops she became known as "Box-Office Poison," a spell which was only broken by *The Philadelphia Story*. A series of films with her off-screen partner, Spencer Tracy, such as *Adam's Rib* (1949) and *Pat and Mike* (1952) capitalized on the chemistry between the pair and did well at the box office. Later roles in movies such as *The African Queen* (1951), *Suddenly Last Summer* (1959), and *The Lion in Winter* (1968) earned her further acclaim.

CREDITS

studio	MGM
producer	Joseph L. Mankiewicz
screenplay	Donald Ogden Stewart, based on the play of the same name by Philip Barry
cinematography	Joseph Ruttenberg
costume design	Adrian
awards	Academy Awards: Best Actor (James Stewart), Best Screenplay

His Girl Friday | Howard Hawks | 1940

Howard Hawks' scintillating adaptation of the Ben Hecht and Charles MacArthur Broadway comedy *The Front Page* is a fine example of screwball comedy with its breakneck pace, sexual innuendo, rapid-fire wisecracks, and absurd situations. But, it is also a pointed satire on political corruption and journalistic ethics, as well as a commentary on "a woman's place" in the professional world.

By changing the role of a main character — the star reporter — from a man (in the original play) to a woman, Hawks created sexual tension between the ruthless and wily newspaper editor Walter Burns (Cary Grant) and Hildy Johnson (Rosalind Russell), his employee and ex-wife. Hildy is about to leave the newspaper to marry meek insurance salesman Bruce Baldwin (Ralph Bellamy). The editor is determined to win her back, both to the newspaper and his bed, and hatches a plot, realizing that she will not be able to resist one final scoop. The twist works brilliantly in the film, especially as played by Grant and Russell, who give sharp and witty performances in this sparkling battle of the sexes. Most effective is the quick, intelligent repartee and the use of overlapping dialogue, while the characters are constantly on the move. Despite being limited mostly to two sets — the newspaper office and the pressroom at the jail, where the journalists await the execution of an anarchist for killing a cop — the film never feels staged. It eclipses Lewis Milestone's excellent earlier version *The Front Page* (1931) and Billy Wilder's tired remake (1974).

Rosalind Russell *as Hildy poses between co-stars Cary Grant and Ralph Bellamy in a promotional shot for the film.*

CREDITS

studio	Columbia
producer	Howard Hawks
screenplay	Charles Lederer, from the play *The Front Page* by Ben Hecht and Charles MacArthur
cinematography	Joseph Walker

Film poster, 1940

CARY GRANT

In a 34-year film career, Cary Grant (1904–1986), born Archibald Leach in Bristol, England, hardly varied his screen persona from that of a charming, elegant star with a good sense of irony and perfect timing. This made him ideal for the screwball comedies of the 1930s, such as Howard Hawks' *Bringing Up Baby* (1938), as well as for tongue-in-cheek adventures, such as *Gunga Din* (1939). Alfred Hitchcock took advantage of his playboy image in four thrillers, including *North By Northwest* (1959).

The Grapes of Wrath | John Ford | 1940

Dorris Bowden, *Jane Darwell, and Henry Fonda in their old jalopy face trouble on their way to California.*

John Steinbeck's great novel — a desolate vision of America during the Depression — provided John Ford with the material to make one of the few Hollywood films until then to reveal a genuine social conscience. With its unpatronizing treatment of ordinary people, it retains the themes of family and home — typical of many Ford films — while making a social statement.

This humanistic masterpiece follows the Joad family who, forced to leave their land in the dustbowl of Oklahoma, struggle to reach the "promised land" of California. Only exploitation, disappointment, and hardship await them at the end of their arduous cross-country journey, when they find that the meager wages paid to migrant workers are barely enough for survival. Although *The Grapes of Wrath* focuses on the recent past, the film has a nostalgic poetry in its bleak visual images and beautifully lit studio exteriors. Expert cinematographer Gregg Toland, who would go on to work in *Citizen Kane*, filmed it in documentary-style black-and-white textures and low-key lighting, recreating the look and feel of rural America in the 1930s. Henry Fonda gives one of his most sincere performances as Tom Joad, the grassroots American buffeted by fortune but willing to stand up for his rights. As he says to his mother: "I'll be all around... Wherever there's a fight so hungry people can eat... And when the people are eatin' the stuff they raise and livin' in the houses they build. I'll be there too." Producer Darryl F. Zanuck insisted on an upbeat ending, unlike the novel's bleak conclusion, with the indomitable matriarch Ma Joad, played brilliantly by Jane Darwell, proclaiming "They can't wipe us out. They can't lick us. And we'll go on forever, Pa, because we're the people," thus affirming the strength and human dignity of the individual spirit.

CREDITS

studio	20th Century Fox
producer	Darryl F. Zanuck
screenplay	Nunnally Johnson, from the novel by John Steinbeck
cinematography	Gregg Toland
awards	Academy Awards: Best Director, Best Supporting Actress (Jane Darwell)

The courage and strength *of Ma Joad (Jane Darwell) keeps her suffering family together.*

Citizen Kane | Orson Welles | 1941

In 1998, the American Film Institute (AFI) voted *Citizen Kane* first out of 100 of the greatest Hollywood films ever. It also tops *Sight And Sound*'s poll of best films every 10 years since 1962. Despite being burdened with the label of "greatest film ever made," *Citizen Kane* generally lives up to expectations.

As a newcomer to movie-making, the 25-year-old Welles is said to have broken rules he did not know existed. Working against chronological narrative conventions, his newspaper tycoon, Charles Foster Kane, is seen from many subjective viewpoints, providing a deeper understanding of the protagonist. The innovative use of wide-angle and deep focus lenses, the creative use of sound, the great set pieces, the titanic performance of Welles as Kane, were all in pursuit of the meaning of "Rosebud," the single word Kane utters on his death-bed at the beginning of the film. To facilitate the low-angle shots, nearly every indoor set had a visible ceiling, a device rare at the time. The newspaper magnate, William Randolph Hearst, tried to have the film banned, believing that Kane was a veiled portrait of himself. It was screened only after Welles threatened RKO with a lawsuit.

Orson Welles in the title role makes a speech in front of a giant poster of himself in Madison Square Garden during his campaign to become Governor of New York.

CREDITS

studio	RKO
producer	Orson Welles
screenplay	Orson Welles, Herman J. Mankiewicz
cinematography	Gregg Toland
editors	Robert Wise, Mark Robson
music	Bernard Herrmann
art director	Van Nest Polglase
awards	Academy Award: Best Original Screenplay

One of cinematographer *Greg Toland's high-angle shots depicts Kane (Welles) and his best friend, Jedediah Leland (Joseph Cotten) taking over a small newspaper, a shot echoed in the film's final scenes of Kane's amassed goods.*

The Maltese Falcon | John Huston | 1941

Considered the first film noir, *The Maltese Falcon* is one of the most assured directorial debuts and perhaps the greatest ever remake, effacing two other versions (1931, 1936) of Dashiell Hammett's classic detective novel.

In a hotel lobby, *Sam Spade (Bogart) confronts the hired gunman Wilmer Cook (Elisha Cook Jr.). Bogart is superb as the sentimental anti-hero living by his own code of ethics.*

Among the many firsts of this seminal film was the screen debut, at 61, of stage actor Sydney Greenstreet. He plays one of three people—the others being Joel Cairo (Peter Lorre) and *femme fatale* Brigid (Mary Astor)—searching for a treasured *objet d'art* named the Maltese Falcon. The trio hire private eye Sam Spade (Humphrey Bogart) to find it. Bogart's depiction of the laconic Spade pushed him into the top rank of stars, inaugurating a succession of thrillers featuring hard-boiled detectives. Huston created a brooding, shadowy world, often placing characters in the foreground, giving their mute reactions greater weight than was usual at the time.

Humphrey Bogart cornered the market in cool, streetwise investigators after his performance in *The Maltese Falcon*.

HUMPHREY BOGART

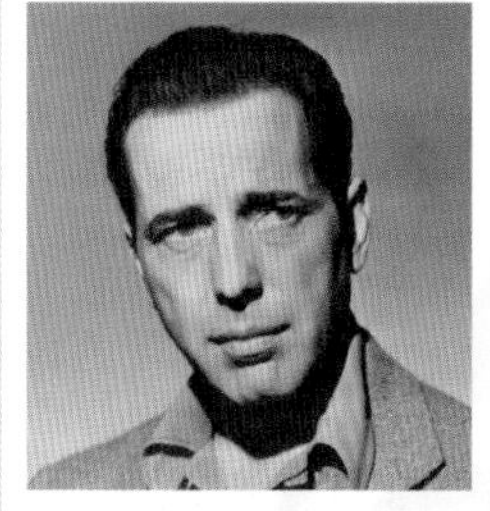

Humphrey Bogart (1899–1957) is today regarded as the archetypal anti-hero—tough on the outside, but sensitive at the core. *High Sierra* (1941) was the first film in which he played a sympathetic gangster. His persona was set forever in *The Maltese Falcon* (1941), *Casablanca* (1942), and in the four films he made with Lauren Bacall. He won his only Oscar for Huston's *The African Queen* (1951).

CREDITS

studio	Warner Bros.
producer	Hal B. Wallis
screenplay	John Huston, from the novel by Dashiell Hammett
cinematography	Arthur Edeson
music	Adolph Deutsch

The Little Foxes | William Wyler | 1941

Bette Davis was at her bitchy best and director William Wyler was as classy as ever in this remarkable cinematic adaptation of Lillian Hellman's lush, hothouse stage drama, which focued on an avaricious Southern family in the early 1900s.

Wisely resisting the temptation to "open up" Lillian Hellman's play, which was adapted by the playwright herself, William Wyler and his director of photography, Gregg Toland, were able to exploit the claustrophobic atmosphere of the house in which the Giddens family's power struggles take place. At its center is Bette Davis as the thoroughly nasty Regina Giddens — passionate, thwarted, tyrannical, and greedy. She conspires with her brothers in her bid to grab the family fortune for herself, only to deceive and blackmail them, too. Toland's use of deep focus photography is particularly effective in one tour de force scene in which Regina refuses to give her husband Horace (Herbert Marshall) his medicine although he is in the throes of a heart attack, choosing instead to watch him from the background as he struggles in the foreground. *The Little Foxes* was the last of three films Davis and Wyler made together, the others being *Jezebel* (1938) and *The Letter* (1940); each had a spark that perhaps came from the romantic involvement between the pair at the time.

BETTE DAVIS

Bette Davis (1908–89) thought of herself as a screen actress not a movie star. Her spoiled Southern belle in *Jezebel* (1938) won her a second Oscar. Other successes were *Dark Victory* (1939), *The Old Maid* (1939), and *Now, Voyager* (1942). Davis made a stunning comeback in *All About Eve* (1950) as an ageing actress.

CREDITS

studio	RKO
producer	Sam Goldwyn
screenplay	Lillian Hellman, from her play of the same name
cinematography	Gregg Toland

Regina (Bette Davis) talks business with her villainous brother Ben Hubbard (Charles Dingle), on the right, and industrialist William Marshall (Russel Hicks) over coffee in an Oscar-nominated performance.

To Be Or Not To Be | Ernst Lubitsch | 1942

As the world experienced the dark times of World War II, Lubitsch directed one of Hollywood's greatest comedies. *To Be Or Not To Be* took the Nazi occupation of Poland as its theme and, as anti-Nazi propaganda, it was more effective than many "serious" attempts.

CREDITS	
studio	United Artists
producers	Alexander Korda, Ernst Lubitsch
screenplay	Edwin Justus Mayer, Melchior Lengyel
cinematography	Rudolph Maté

In their finest performances, Carole Lombard and Jack Benny play Maria and Joseph Tura, a couple who head a troupe of Shakespearean actors trapped in Warsaw when Nazi troops march into Poland. When asked what he thinks of Joseph, the richly comic Gestapo chief, "Concentration Camp" Erhardt (Sig Ruman), says, "What he did to Shakespeare, we're now doing to Poland." Benny's darkly comic role sees him impersonating both a Nazi professor and a Gestapo officer. Although the jokes come thick and fast, and the Nazis are seen as incompetent clowns, the situation still comes across as horrific. When the film was released, no one was in the mood to laugh: Pearl Harbor had recently been attacked by the Japanese, the Nazis were sweeping across Europe, and Lombard had just been killed in a plane crash. However, over the years, the film has become a black-and-white classic.

Professor Alexander Siletsky *(Stanley Ridges) raises a glass to Maria (Carole Lombard). The Polish academic is actually a Nazi spy intent on destroying the Resistance.*

In Which We Serve | Noël Coward | 1942

Captain Edward V. Kinross *(Noel Coward) addresses his crew before their ship is sunk by enemy forces.*

A tribute to those serving in the Royal Navy in World War II, *In Which We Serve* captured the prevailing mood of Britain at the time. Noël Coward wrote the screenplay, as well as composing the score and starring in the film. David Lean edited the film and co-directed (his first film).

This "story of a ship" is told in flashback by the survivors of HMS *Torrin*, a bombed British destroyer, as they cling to a life raft. It is May 1941, and the *Torrin* has been patrolling Europe's coasts as part of Britain's defense against German warships. It is sunk by enemy action off Crete. Led by Noël Coward as Captain Kinross, an archetypal British commander, the crew hope and pray for rescue. Their stories and that of the ship is told in flashbacks, as some of them look back on the events of the war, including the 1940 evacuation of Dunkirk and the loss of many of their comrades. Permeating the film is a deep love for the ship, which symbolizes the unity of the nation without resorting to false heroics or flag waving. The behavior of the crew, all of whom "knew their places" on the social scale, was presented as the ideal model for the behavior of a society at war. The film is also notable for the debut of 19-year-old Richard Attenborough, playing a callow stoker who deserts his post.

CREDITS	
production	Two Cities Films
producers	Noël Coward, Anthony Havelock Allan
screenplay	Noël Coward
cinematography	Ronald Neame
awards	Special Academy Award: "outstanding production achievement"

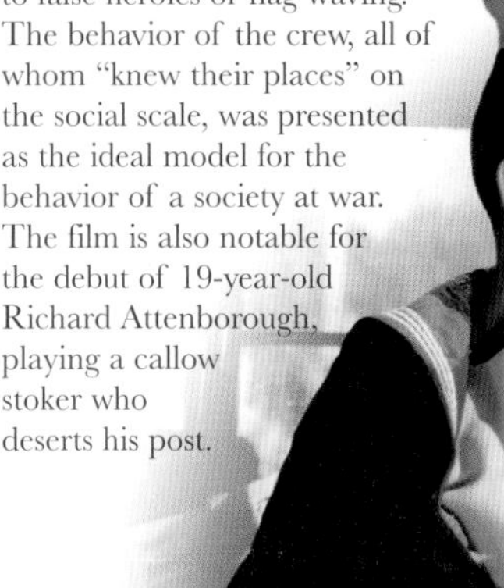

Ordinary Seaman *Shorty Blake (John Mills), one of the crew of HMS* Torrin*, begins a courtship with Freda Lewis (Kay Walsh) on a train.*

Casablanca | Michael Curtiz | 1942

The strong plot, the exotic setting, the quotable piquant dialogue, the cherished performances from a magnificent cast, and the emotional Max Steiner score—not forgetting Dooley Wilson as Sam playing "As Time Goes By"—have ensured that *Casablanca* remains the epitome of 1940s Hollywood romance.

The love between *Ilsa (Ingrid Bergman) and Rick (Humphrey Bogart) is rekindled as she makes one last effort to get the transit papers for her resistance fighter husband to be able to escape Casablanca.*

American forces liberated French North Africa in the same year that *Casablanca* was released, giving the movie a topical title. Most of the film takes place in and around the Café Américain, which is run by Rick Blaine (Humphrey Bogart), a cynical isolationist and gun-runner who gets involved in the Free French cause in order to help Victor Laszlo (Paul Henreid), a resistance leader and husband of Rick's former lover Ilsa Lund (Ingrid Bergman). The poignant and passionate team of Bogart and Bergman, with flashbacks to their love affair in pre-war Paris, is one of the most celebrated relationships in cinema history. Strangely, the most structured and beloved of films was made in a manner that left everyone on set confused as to what was happening. Everyone, it seems, except Michael Curtiz, who brought together all the subplots and huge supporting cast of this romantic war melodrama with his expert hand. As time goes by, *Casablanca* looks better and better.

Film poster, 1942

CREDITS

studio	Warner Bros.
producers	Hal B. Wallis, Jack L. Warner
screenplay	Julius J. Epstein, Philip G. Epstein, Howard Koch
cinematography	Arthur Edeson
music	Max Steiner
awards	Academy Awards: Best Picture, Best Director, Best Screenplay

INGRID BERGMAN

The healthy, unspoiled natural looks and personality of Swedish-born Ingrid Bergman (1915–82) made her a popular Hollywood star in the 1940s in films such as *For Whom the Bell Tolls* (1943), and *Gaslight* (1944), which won her the Academy Award for Best Actress. Other roles in the 1940s included Paula Alquist in Hitchcock's *Spellbound* (1945). Bergman, who had played a nun in *The Bells of St. Mary's* (1945) and *Joan of Arc* (1948), shocked Hollywood in 1949 when she left her family for Italian director Roberto Rossellini. Although it was years before she made another American movie, with *Anastasia* (1956) she won another Academy Award – which may have signalled Hollywood's "forgiveness."

"Round up the usual suspects," *says Claude Raines (second left) at the climax of* Casablanca *as Paul Henreid (centre), Humphrey Bogart and Ingrid Bergman await the result of the shooting of the Nazi officer.*

Ossessione | Luchino Visconti | 1942

Massimo Girotti *(Gino) and Clara Calamai (Giovanna) play illicit lovers whose relationship is beginning to descend into guilt and mistrust.*

Ossessione **was the first film to be labelled Italian Neo-Realist, a label given by critic Antonio Pietrangeli, one of the film's screenwriters. It was also the first film to be directed by Luchino Visconti, whose use of natural settings and working-class characters inspired other Italian film-makers.**

Gino (Massimo Girotti), a handsome drifter, and Giovanna (Clara Calamai), the beautiful and desperately unhappy wife of Bragana (Juan de Landa), an elderly and boorish inn-keeper, embark on an affair. Their passion leads them to kill Bragana, after which their relationship drifts toward inevitable tragedy. Visconti took James M. Cain's study of fatal lust in the rural US, *The Postman Always Rings Twice*, and brilliantly transplanted it to provincial Italy. Because it was wartime, Visconti was able to buy the rights of the novel and therefore retained only the outline of the original and introduced a new character, whose presence further disrupts the already guilt-ridden central relationship. Although having professional actors, a well-defined plot, and visual formality make it less neorealistic than its successors, the film's down-to-earth characters and evident sensuality contrasted vastly with the predominant bourgeois melodramas of the day. Initially cut and then withdrawn by the Fascist censors, the film only reappeared after the war. Cain's novel had already been made into a film in France—*Le Dernier Tournant* (1939). It was remade in Hollywood in 1945 and 1981, and then in Hungary in 1998, under the title of *Passion*.

Film poster

CREDITS	
production	ICI Rome
producer	Libero Solaroli
screenplay	Luchino Visconti, Antonio Pietrangeli, Giuseppe De Santis, Mario Alicata, Gianni Puccini
cinematography	Aldo Tonti, Domenico Scala

Children of Paradise | Marcel Carné | 1945

Marcel Carné described his film as a "homage to the theater" and the script breathes with the life and soul of the French theatrical tradition. The larger-than-life characters, the witty and profound dialogue, the narrative skill and sweep of the whole production have placed this on many critics' lists as one of the greatest films ever made.

Film poster, 1945

This film has the breadth and complexity of a novel, although its action and characters are confined to the world of Parisian theater in the 1840s. "*Paradis*" in the French title—*Les Enfants du Paradis*—refers to the upper seats in the theater where poorer spectators sat). Among the crowds that throng the boulevards in the film are the classical actor Frederic Lemaître (Pierre Brasseur), the mime-artist Debureau (Jean-Louis Barrault), and the criminal Lacenaire (Marcel Herrand)—all three are based on real historical figures. Each of these men is in love with the sensuous and free-spirited courtesan Garance (Arletty). Making her screen debut is Maria Casarès, as the wife of Debureau. The film came into being because the Nazi occupation of Paris forced Carné and scriptwriter Jacques Prévert to make "escapist" films, with no political content. Nevertheless, some commentators viewed the character Garance as a representation of Free France. Today, the film is seen as a richly entertaining and intensely romantic evocation of an epoch. Ironically, Arletty's career suffered owing to a liaison with a Nazi officer. She was put under house arrest, forbidden to work for three years, and was not invited to the film's premiere.

The great mime artist, *Baptiste Debureau (Jean-Louis Barrault), performs with his father Anselme (Etienne Ducroux), and the alluring Garance (Arletty).*

CREDITS	
production	S.N. Pathé Cinema
screenplay	Jacques Prévert
cinematography	Marc Fossard, Roger Hubert
production design	Léon Barsacq, Raymond Gabutti Alexandre Trauner
music	Joseph Kosma
costume design	Antoine Mayo

A Matter of Life and Death | Michael Powell, Emeric Pressburger | 1946

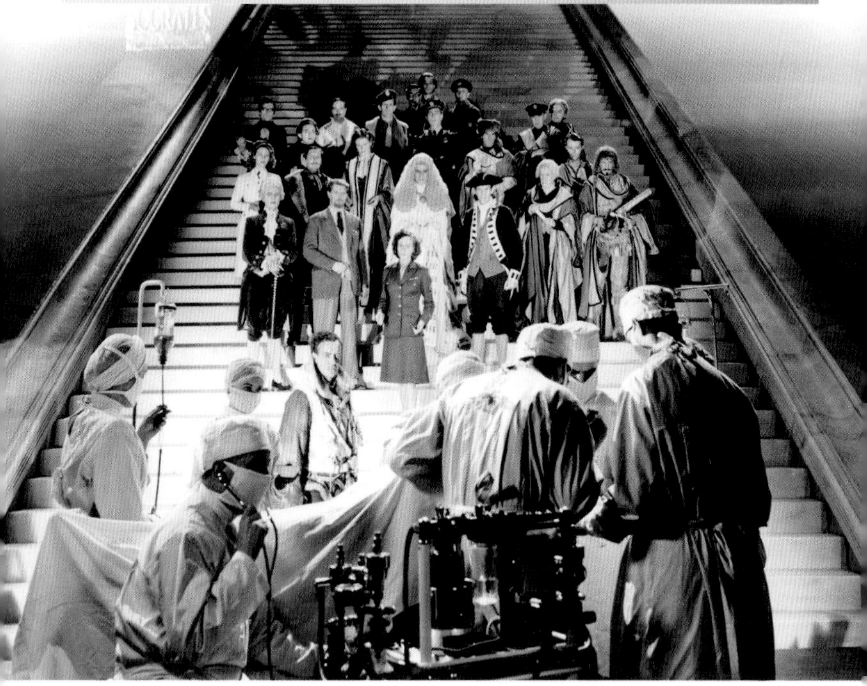

In the climactic sequence, *a celestial judge and jury use the "stairway to heaven" to visit the unconscious Peter Carter and decide his fate.*

In their fourth collaboration as producers, directors, and writers, Michael Powell and Emeric Pressburger delivered a richly comic film, which juxtaposed highly stylized fantasy with a morale-boosting version of Britain during World War II.

A British pilot, Peter Carter (David Niven) survives a plane crash only to discover that the powers above have made a mistake and that he was actually scheduled to die. As he fights for his life on the operating table under the loving eyes of June, an American radio operator (Kim Hunter), a debate takes place in Heaven about whether or not to save him. Avoiding the obvious, the directors decided to shoot the scenes on Earth in Technicolor and the sequences "up there" in black-and-white. The link between the two worlds, the one that exists in reality and the other in the mind of the pilot, is wittily represented by a mechanical staircase that uses modern technology to express a fantasy. One of the underlying intentions of the plot was to celebrate the Anglo-American alliance that prevailed during World War II.

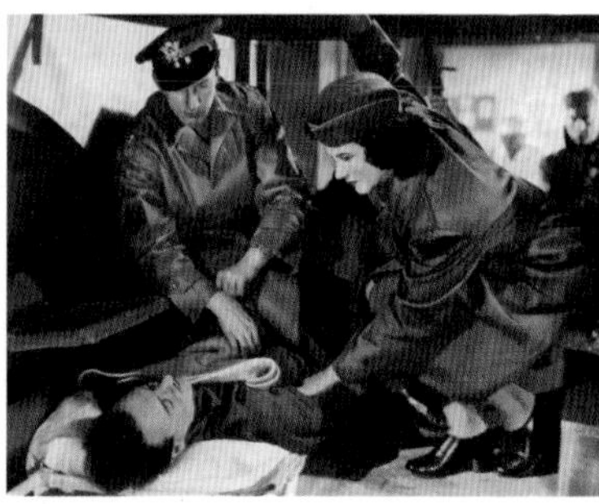

Back in the earthly realm, *here represented by color, June (Kim Hunter) comforts injured airman Peter Carter (David Niven) before he goes into the operating theater.*

CREDITS

production	The Archers
producers	Michael Powell, Emeric Pressburger
screenplay	Michael Powell, Emeric Pressburger
cinematography	Jack Cardiff
production design	Alfred Junge

It's a Wonderful Life | Frank Capra | 1946

Director Frank Capra called *It's a Wonderful Life* his favorite film and it is certainly loved by most audiences. Its story aims to impart the real meaning of the Christmas season and has similarities to Charles Dickens' *A Christmas Carol.* It has certainly justified its perennial screening during the festive season.

CREDITS	
studio	RKO
production	Liberty Films
producer	Frank Capra
screenplay	Frank Capra, Frances Goodrich, Albert Hackett, from the story *The Greatest Gift* by Philip Doren Stern
cinematography	Joseph Walker, Joseph Biroc
music	Dmitri Tiomkin

The impetus and structure of *It's a Wonderful Life* recall Capra's pre-war successes, including *Mr. Deeds Goes to Town* (1936) and *Mr. Smith Goes to Washington* (1939), in which the heroes represent a civic ideal only to be opposed by the forces of corruption until they are redeemed by society at large. The character of George Bailey (James Stewart) embodies the quintessential Capraesque "little man." He falls in love with Mary (Donna Reed), but financial troubles send him into a spiral of despair. He teeters on the verge of suicide when he is rescued by Clarence (Henry Travers), his guardian angel, who shows him how different the world would have been if he had never been born—Bedford Falls, the idealized small US town in which Bailey grew up, has become a cesspool of big city ways. The film was found too whimsical and sentimental for post-war audiences, and failed on its initial release.

In the celebrated final scene *of* It's A Wonderful Life, *Bailey (Stewart) realizes the value of the love of his family, having been rescued by his guardian angel.*

JAMES STEWART

James Stewart (1908–97), one of the screen's most natural actors, appeared so relaxed and easygoing that his very real talent was taken for granted. Tall, thin, and gangly with a slow distinctive drawl, his was a likeable film persona with which audiences found it easy to identify. Combining sensitivity with intelligence, Stewart was at his best with three directors: Frank Capra, who used his ability to express naivety; Alfred Hitchcock, who found his obsessive side; and Anthony Mann, who gave him the chance to reveal a rugged physicality in a series of Westerns in the 1950s.

Bicycle Thieves | Vittorio De Sica | 1948

Of all the films dubbed "Italian neorealist," Vittorio De Sica's *Bicycle Thieves* (*Ladri Di Biciclette*) is the most beloved and the most moving. The film is still as poignant today, despite improved social conditions in Italy, because it contains one of the most believable portrayals of a father-son relationship on screen.

Bewilderment and despair shows on the face of Bruno (Enzo Staiola). The boy joins his father as he searches for his stolen bicycle, showing his filial loyalty and trust.

Filmed on location in the working-class districts of Rome, *Bicycle Thieves* tells the simple story of an unemployed man who is offered a job as a bill sticker, provided he has a bicycle. He borrows money from a pawnbroker to buy a bike, but it is stolen on his first day of work. He then spends the day with his small son, desperately searching for it and the thief. He discovers that the thief was just as needy as he is and considers stealing a bicycle himself, thus conveying the message that anybody is capable of theft in certain circumstances. After De Sica's success in the US with *Shoeshine* (1946), David O. Selznick offered to produce *Bicycle Thieves* with a star like Cary Grant, but De Sica refused, raised the money himself, and continued to work with non-actors in real locations. It paid off because it was this un-Hollywood quality that gave the film its wide appeal.

CREDITS	
production	Produzioni De Sica
producer	Giuseppe Amato, Vittorio De Sica
screenplay	Cesare Zavattini, Oreste Biancoli, Suso D'Amico, Vittorio De Sica, Adolfo Franci, Gerardo Guerrieri
cinematography	Carlo Montuori
awards	Acadamy Award: Best Film in a foreign language

ITALIAN NEOREALISM

The origins of Italian neorealism can be traced to the "realist" or *verismo* style of writings of Verga and others. It influenced Italian silent cinema, which portrayed human suffering in natural settings. The neorealists of the 1940s returned to these themes, reacting against frivolity. Films, such as Vittorio De Sica's *Shoeshine* (1946), Roberto Rossellini's *Paisà* (1946), Luchino Visconti's *La Terra Trema* (1948), and Giuseppe de Santis' *Bitter Rice* (1949), dealt with the problems of working class people and the social conditions that caused them.

Roma, Città Aperta (Rome, Open City, 1945) *was an early neorealist film, shot in real locations, and using local people as well as professional actors.*

Letter from an Unknown Woman | Max Ophüls | 1948

The second of German émigré Max Ophüls' four Hollywood movies, *Letter from an Unknown Woman*, is set in a lovingly evoked turn-of-the-century Vienna. It is his only one that came close to capturing his sumptuous and sensuous European work. It is that rare thing — a Hollywood art movie.

Stefan *(Louis Jourdan), the self-absorbed concert pianist, finally realizes the consequences of his actions as he reads the deathbed letter from Lisa.*

In this bittersweet romance of unrequited love, Lisa Berndle, in a touching performance by Joan Fontaine, hero-worships her handsome, concert-pianist neighbor, Stefan Brand (Louis Jourdan), from a distance. After several years they meet and have a short-lived affair, but he disappears from her life again. The film, recounted in flashbacks, suggests that Lisa, blind to reality, occupies a romantic dream world in which her love can never be fulfilled. Seen from a female perspective, however, it also reveals the shallowness of many men's perception of women. Ophüls changed the original ending of Stefan Zweig's story by sending the hero to certain death in a duel. On its release in the US, the film was dismissed as too sentimental, but it was later celebrated as one of the most evocative "European" films ever made in Hollywood.

CREDITS

production	Rampart
producer	John Houseman
studio	Universal-International
screenplay	Howard Koch from the story by Stefan Zweig
cinematography	Franz Planer

"By the time you finish reading this letter, I'll be dead"

OPENING LINES

Lisa (Joan Fontaine), in her modest apartment, reflects on her glamorous encounter with Stefan.

Passport to Pimlico | Henry Cornelius | 1949

A tribute to the war effort and the British character, *Passport to Pimlico* exudes good humor and social observation. It is also an expression of hope in the post-war period.

CREDITS	
studio	Ealing
producer	Michael Balcon, E.V.H. Emmett
screenplay	T.E.B. Clarke
cinematography	Lionel Banes

In postwar Britain in Pimlico, a small district of London, a wartime bomb explodes and reveals treasures from Burgundy, France. Among these is a manuscript that claims, according to local historian Professor Hatton-Jones (Margaret Rutherford), that Pimlico is by ancient law a Burgundian possession. The inhabitants are no longer bound by wartime restrictions and austerity; instead they can operate outside British law by destroying their ration books and drinking at all hours. Border crossings are set up, and customs officers patrol local trains. An Ealing comedy, this delightful film shows ordinary people in a small community making extraordinary things happen. It pokes fun at the new Labor government, but is too gentle to be classified as satire; when Pimlico is forced to rejoin Britain, the spirit of compromise is celebrated.

Fire wardens Shirley (Barbara Murray) and Arthur (Stanley Holloway) discover a centuries-old document, which identifies Pimlico as French territory, not British.

EALING COMEDY

Although Ealing Studios, situated in west London's suburbs, made dramas and war films, they will always be associated with the particular brand of comedy they produced between 1947 and 1955. With rare exceptions, they used original scripts from the studio's own writers, principally T.E.B. Clarke, who wrote *Passport to Pimlico* (1949), *The Lavender Hill Mob* (1951), and *The Titfield Thunderbolt* (1953). They generally dealt with a small group of people in a naturalistic social setting, making much of the indomitable, if somewhat idealized, British spirit.

The Ladykillers (1955), starring Alec Guinness and Peter Sellers, marked the end of a short period of black comedy at Ealing Studios, which began with *Hue and Cry* (1947).

The Third Man | Carol Reed | 1949

One of the most effective British thrillers, the look of *The Third Man* derives from German Expressionism, Italian neorealism, and the work of Orson Welles. He appears for only about 20 minutes in the film, but his unforgettable presence is felt throughout.

Carol Reed *told Robert Krasker to keep the camera at an angle. This technique heightens the drama of the moment when Harry Lime (Orson Welles) reappears.*

Developed by Graham Greene from an idea jotted down on an envelope, this dark, yet playful, film studies the effect of post-war economic and social corruption on war-torn Vienna. It was the first British film to be shot almost entirely on location. The sense of locale, making the shattered city an integral part of the action, and the superb, moody, black-and-white cinematography all add to the film's very specific atmosphere. The moment, more than halfway through the film, when Welles — as the presumed-dead racketeer Harry Lime — reappears, is legendary. In the sequence, Holly Martins (Joseph Cotten) is searching for his friend through the nocturnal streets of Vienna. A cat miaows in a doorway. Martins turns and, as Anton Karas' exciting zither music swells, we see the cat licking a pair of shoes. The camera rises and Welles' face emerges into the light.

The film begins and ends with the same scene: the funeral and burial of Harry Lime. The first funeral pronounces him the unfortunate victim of an accident — but the second identifies him as an unrepentant mass murderer.

CREDITS	
production	British Lion, London Film Production
producer	Carol Reed
screenplay	Graham Greene
cinematography	Robert Krasker
art director	Vincent Korda
music	Anton Karas
awards	Academy Award: Best Black-and-White Cinematography; Cannes: Best Film

In the famous ferris-wheel showdown scene, Harry Lime offers Holly Martins (Joseph Cotten, see left) a partnership in his illicit penicillin trade.

Orpheus | Jean Cocteau | 1950

This witty and haunting film can be considered the centrepiece of Jean Cocteau's entire oeuvre. It forms part of his Orphic trilogy, along with *Blood of the Poet* and *The Testament of Orpheus.* Cocteau himself described *Orpheus* (*Orphée*) as "a detective story, bathed on one side in myth, and on the other, the supernatural."

Orpheus (Jean Marais) *presses his face against a mirror before he enters the Underworld through the glass to search for his wife Eurydice (Maria Déa).*

The poet Orpheus (Jean Marais) falls in love with the Princess of Death (Maria Casarés). In turn, her chauffeur (François Périer), the angel Heurtebise, is in love with the poet's wife, Eurydice (Marie Déa). Heurtebise takes Eurydice to the Underworld through a looking-glass, with Orpheus following to bring her back. "Mirrors are the doors through which Death comes and goes. Look at yourself in a mirror all your life and you'll see Death at work like bees in a hive of glass," says the angel. Although Cocteau uses reverse slow-motion and negative images to evoke the Underworld, the domestic life of Mr. and Mrs. Orpheus is filmed "realistically." This elaborates the theme of the poet caught between the real and the imaginary in a perfect marriage between Greek legend and Cocteau's own mythology.

CREDITS

production	Films du Palais-Royal
producer	André Paulvé
screenplay	Jean Cocteau based on his play of the same name
cinematography	Nicholas Hayer
production design	Jean d'Eaubonne

Orpheus (Jean Marais) *holds open a book, showing a photograph of Eurydice (Maria Déa). The presence of Eurydice in person and in a photograph reflects the subtle interplay of reality and illusion in the film.*

Rashomon | Akira Kurosawa | 1950

Akira Kurosawa's *Rashomon* was the first Japanese film to be shown widely in the west. This makes it significant beyond its indubitable qualities because it opened the way for even greater works by Kurosawa.

This combat scene *in a wood displays stunning light and shade effects.*

In feudal Japan, a samurai named Takehiro (MasaYuki Mori) travels through the woods with his wife Masako (Machiko Kyo). She is raped and he is killed by a bandit (Toshiro Mifune). At the trial, the incident is described in four conflicting, yet equally credible, versions by the bandit, the wife, a priest (Minoru Chiaki), and a woodcutter (Takashi Shimura), demonstrating the subjective nature of truth. The film's popularity was due to its intriguing story and the forceful performances, as much as for its unfamiliar background. By the time *Rashomon* (named after the ruined stone gate where the tale is told) awakened western audiences to Japanese cinema, Kurosawa was already an established director in his own country. The film was remade in Hollywood as the Western called *The Outrage* (1964), one of the three Kurosawa samurai movies to be adapted to the Hollywood genre.

CREDITS

studio	Daiei
producer	Minoru Jingo
screenplay	Akiro Kurosawa, Shinobu Hashimoto from two short novels by Ryunosuke Akutagawa
cinematography	Kazuo Miyagawa
awards	Academy Award: Honorary award for "most outstanding foreign language film released in the USA in 1951"; Venice: Best Film

POINT OF VIEW

Point of view (P.O.V.) is a shot filmed at such a camera angle that an object or an action appears to be seen through the eyes of a particular character. This is achieved by placing the camera beside the actor or at the spot he or she would occupy on set. The other actors look at the point where the character is supposed to be, rather than at the camera. One extreme example of P.O.V. was Robert Montgomery's *The Lady in the Lake* (1946), in which a subjective camera was used to tell the whole story as seen by the film's protagonist Philip Marlowe.

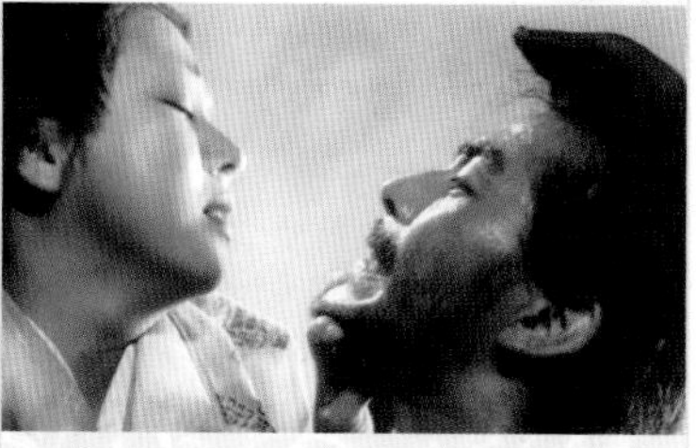

Masako cradles a *dying Takehiro. Viewed through the multiple perspectives of* Rashomon, *the events leading to Takehiro's death reveal the relativity of truth.*

Singin' in the Rain | Gene Kelly, Stanley Donen | 1952

Considered the apogee of MGM musicals, *Singin' in the Rain* is a delightful mixture of nostalgia and affectionate satire on the turmoil and triumphs that marked the transition from silent films to the talkies. The era is splendidly conjured up by the period settings and costumes, and a series of wonderfully staged numbers.

CREDITS	
studio	MGM
producer	Arthur Freed
screenplay	Betty Comden, Adolph Green
cinematography	Harold Rosson
music	Arthur Freed, Nacio Herb Brown, Comden, Green, Roger Edens

Producer Arthur Freed, the supremo of the MGM movie musical, brought together an expert team. Many of the songs he had previously written, along with Nacio Herb Brown, for Hollywood review of 1929 were integrated into the plot — including the liberating title number. This famous song showed off the balletic and hoofing skills of Gene Kelly as Don Lockwood to memorable effect. Kelly's skills were also in evidence in the "Broadway Ballet," while Donald O'Connor's electrifying comedy-dance routine, "Make 'Em Laugh," was the peak of his career. In one part of the plot, ingénue Debbie Reynolds, sparkling in her first major role as Kathy Selden, has to dub the voice of Lina Lamont, a movie star from the silent era (unforgettably played by Jean Hagen), because Lina's voice was found to be risibly squeaky for sound movies. Ironically, Debbie's singing voice was, in turn, dubbed by Betty Royce — who remained uncredited.

GENE KELLY

When Gene Kelly (1912–96) sang "Gotta Dance" in *Singin' In The Rain,* he was uttering his credo. He danced in 19 Hollywood musicals between 1942 and 1957, establishing himself, along with Fred Astaire, as one of the greatest dancers in motion picture history. Kelly also shone as a choreographer and director, continually widening his scope in films such as *Cover Girl* (1944) and *Anchors Aweigh* (1945).

Fantasy dance *sequence during which Don Lockwood (Gene Kelly) is bewitched by the shapely, seductive nightclub dancer and gangster's moll (Cyd Charisse)*

Tokyo Story | Yasujiro Ozu | 1953

Chishu Ryu *(left), Setsuko Hara, and Chieko Higashiyama in a domestic scene, shot at floor level.*

One of the finest films of Yasujiro Ozu's last decade, and one which continually appears in "best ever" lists of critics, *Tokyo Monogatari* (*Tokyo Story*) belatedly made the Japanese director's name in the west, mainly when it was released in the USA in 1972, almost 20 years after it was made.

An elderly couple (Chishu Ryu, Chieko Higashiyama), who live by the sea in south Japan, pay a visit to their children and grandchildren in Tokyo. No one shows them much affection, except for Noriko (Setsuko Hara), their widowed daughter-in-law. "Be kind to your parents when they are alive. Filial piety cannot reach beyond the grave;" so says a simple Japanese proverb. But instead, this old couple are made to feel a burden on their grown-up children. When they return home, the wife dies, leaving her husband to face an unknown future.

Tokyo Story was a prime example of *shomingeki*, defined as a family melodrama. Yet this radiant, gentle, heartbreaking, and perceptive investigation into the tensions within a family, the generation gap, old age, and the pressures of city life, is far from the west's idea of melodrama. There are remarkable performances in the film and a creative use of sound — the chugging boats, the noise of trains — and ravishing exteriors punctuating the subtle interior sequences. Ozu shoots his story with as little camera movement as possible, to attempt to make perfect the balance of every scene.

The poster *for the now-defunct Academy Cinema in London.*

CREDITS

production	Shochiku
producer	Takeshi Yamamoto
screenplay	Yasujiro Ozu, Kôgo Noda
cinematography	Yunharu Atsuta
music	Takanobu (or Kojun) Saitô

On the Waterfront | Elia Kazan | 1954

A shatteringly powerful melodrama of social conscience, *On the Waterfront* was shot on location in New York. It reveals Elia Kazan's mastery in dealing with realistic settings and personal conflicts, highlighted by a naturalistic, improvisational style of acting, which Kazan brought to cinema from the Actors Studio.

Edie (Saint) talks *to Terry (Brando) on a tenement rooftop beside a pigeon coop. The pigeon coop belonged to Edie's brother, for whose death Terry is partly responsible.*

The plot deals with a group of dock laborers in the clutches of an unscrupulous union boss (Lee J. Cobb), who eventually confront their exploiters with the aid of a former union henchman and washed-up boxer Terry Malloy (Marlon Brando, who at first balked at doing the role because Kazan had named sympathizers during the anti-Communist investigations at the time), a liberal priest (Karl Malden), and a courageous young woman (Eva Marie Saint). Brando's deeply felt characterization dominates the film. Especially memorable is the scene played in a taxi between Terry and his brother Charley (Rod Steiger), in which he speaks the poignant lines, "I coulda had class. I coulda been somebody. I coulda been a contender instead of a bum, which is what I am." Boris Kaufman's photography and Leonard Bernstein's music greatly enhance the mood of the film.

CREDITS

studio	Columbia
producer	Sam Spiegel
screenplay	Budd Schulberg
cinematography	Boris Kaufman
music	Leonard Bernstein
awards	Academy Awards: Best Picture, Best Director, Best Actor (Brando), Best Supporting Actress (Eva Marie Saint), Best Story and Screenplay, Best Art Direction (Richard Day), Best Editing (Gene Milford). Venice Silver Prize.

MARLON BRANDO

Modern film acting began with Marlon Brando (1924–2004). Unlike the stars of an earlier generation, Brando approached each part differently. Some of his performances may have been mannered, but he brought an intelligence and intensity to each role. Only Brando could have asked for £3 million for his ten-minute appearance in *Superman* (1978) and top billing for appearing just before the end of *Apocalypse Now* (1979).

All That Heaven Allows | Douglas Sirk | 1955

Although Douglas Sirk's *All that Heaven Allows* has the appearance of a lush soap opera, and is enjoyable at that level, it is also a thinly disguised, scathing critique of American suburbia and a potent analysis of a middle-class woman's social oppression.

Film poster, 1955

Cary Scott (Jane Wyman), a still attractive fortyish widow in a prominent social position in a New England town, is ostracized by her peers and condemned by her grown-up children when she becomes romantically involved with her gardener, Ron Kirby (Rock Hudson, Sirk's favorite actor), a much younger man. One of the most effective scenes is when Wyman's children, after trying to break up her relationship with Hudson, give her a television set as a Christmas present to occupy her time. The sequence ends with her reflection on the television's blank screen as she watches it in her empty house. The fluid camerawork, the inventive use of color, and the intensity of the performances transcend the usual "chick flick" format. Rainer Werner Fassbinder used the film as a model for his film *Fear Eats the Soul* (1973), and Todd Haynes' *Far From Heaven* (2003) paid direct homage to it.

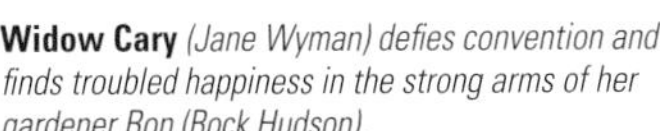

Widow Cary *(Jane Wyman) defies convention and finds troubled happiness in the strong arms of her gardener Ron (Rock Hudson).*

CREDITS	
production	Universal International
producer	Ross Hunter
screenplay	Peg Fenwick
cinematography	Russell Metty

Rebel Without a Cause | Nicholas Ray | 1955

***Rebel Without a Cause*, a disenchanted cry of youth, alienated from the adult world, will always be synonymous with its star, James Dean, in the role that did most to create his image and posthumous fame.**

The need to be loved and understood as an individual is at the core of this inappropriately titled film, which focuses on three youngsters: "Plato," (Sal Mineo) whose divorced parents have abandoned him, Judy (Natalie Wood), who feels her father has withdrawn his love, and Jim (James Dean), who is being "torn apart" by his domineering mother and weak father. Unlike many of the teen rebel films which followed, it places the blame on the parents rather than the teenagers. The main action takes place over one day, and includes a knife fight, a "chicken run," (a high-speed race in hot rod cars to the edge of a cliff) and a love affair between Jim and Judy. Nicholas Ray, making his first film in CinemaScope, a format in which he would become a master, caught the immediate and timeless qualities of frustrated adolescence. Strangely, all three of the film's young stars died violent and unnatural deaths: Dean was killed in a car crash, Mineo was murdered, and Wood drowned in mysterious circumstances.

JAMES DEAN

What is remarkable about the icon James Dean (1931–55) is that his fame rests on three movies — *East of Eden, Rebel Without a Cause*, and *Giant* — all made in the year of his death. In these, he was perfect as a complex young man, with his tortured postures, hesitant speech, and animal sensitivity.

CREDITS

studio	Warner Bros.
producer	David Weisbart
screenplay	Stewart Stern
cinematography	Ernest Haller

When Jim (James Dean), *far right, goes to the police station after Buzz, a teenage gang leader, has been killed in a "chicken run" with him, he meets Buzz's fellow gang members coming out.*

Pather Panchali | Satyajit Ray | 1955

Durga *(Uma Das Gupta) offers a stolen guava to her old aunt Indir Thakrun (Chunibala Devi).*

Out of an Indian film industry almost entirely dominated by formulaic, escapist musical films, Satyajit Ray suddenly appeared on the international scene with this masterpiece in the regional language of Bengali. *Pather Panchali* entirely altered notions of Indian cinema.

Shot in natural surroundings with non-professional actors, *Pather Panchali* revolves around Apu, a young boy who lives in a small Bengal village with his parents, his sister Durga, and aged aunt on the borderline of poverty. The title means "song of the little road," and the motif throughout is travel, of vistas beyond the confines of the tiny rural community. There are the traveling players viewed with wonder by the child, and the lyrical sequence when Apu and his sister run through the long grass towards the railroad line to see a train taking people to big cities. The boy was to take this journey himself in the film that followed — *Aparajito* (1956), the second part of the trilogy, which concludes with *Apur Sansar* (*The World of Apu*, 1959). Ray had difficulty raising funds for his debut film, and was about to abandon shooting after 18 months when he was rescued by the West Bengal government.

CREDITS

production	Government of West Bengal
screenplay	Satyajit Ray from the novel by Bibhuti Bhushan Banerjee
cinematography	Subrata Mitra
music	Ravi Shankar

Kanu Banerjee *(Harihar Ray), Apu's father, struggles to feed his family.*

The Night of the Hunter | Charles Laughton | 1955

The actor Charles Laughton's only film as director is an eerily beautiful parable of good and evil, its bold visual style derived from German Expressionism and American primitive paintings. The presence of Lillian Gish as Rachel, who represents the spirit of healing, echoes the rural dramas of D.W. Griffith.

With love and hate *tattooed on his hands, Robert Mitchum produces an unforgettable performance as a psychopath, posing as a pastor, hunting his prey.*

The plot focuses on Harry Powell, a psychopathic woman-hating preacher (Robert Mitchum) who obtains money for "the Lord's work" by marrying and murdering rich widows. Powell sets his sights on Willa Harper (Shelley Winters), whose imprisoned husband has hidden a huge sum of money. Only the couple's two children John (Billy Chapin) and Pearl (Sally Jane Bruce) know where the money is. The children flee from Harry and escape by river, finally finding refuge with an old woman, Rachel (Lillian Gish) who protects them with a rifle. Evil — Powell — is destroyed by the forces of good and innocence as represented by the old lady, the children, nature, and animals, all of which are atmospherically photographed. The extraordinary Mitchum pursuing the children through a nocturnal landscape, Gish guarding a brood of orphans like a mother hen, and the murdered Winters' hair streaming out underwater are some of cinema's most haunting images. Sadly, this unique film's failure at the box office dissuaded Laughton from ever directing another film.

CREDITS	
studio	United Artists
producer	Paul Gregory
screenplay	James Agee (rewritten by Laughton, uncredited) from the novel by Davis Grubb
cinematography	Stanley Cortez

The Seventh Seal | Ingmar Bergman | 1957

Ingmar Bergman's 17th film set him firmly in the pantheon of great directors. Shot in only 35 days, this powerful morality tale depicts in luminous images derived from early church paintings the cruelty of medieval life, including witch burning and flagellations, as well as the joy and noble aspirations of humankind.

Antonius Block (Max von Sydow), a 14th-century knight, returns from the Crusades with his earthy and cynical squire (Gunnar Björnstrand) to find Sweden ravaged by the plague. In his search for God, Block meets a group of strolling players, suffering peasants, and Death (Bengt Ekerot), with whom he plays a deadly game of chess in an attempt to save his life.

The Seventh Seal (Det Sjunde Inseglet), which Bergman called "a film oratorio," is one of the first in the director's mature works. It is shot in a highly individual style, full of religious imagery, which, paradoxically, expresses a Godless universe. The film also explores human morality, and Bergman uses the figure of Death to express his thoughts about existence and religion.

Tall, gaunt, and imposing, Von Sydow made his mark in cinema with his portrayal of a man in spiritual turmoil. Also in the cast was Bibi Andersson, who made 13 films with Bergman.

Silhouetted against *the sky, Death is seen holding his scythe and leading the knight and his followers in a medieval dance macabre.*

CREDITS

production	Svensk Filmindustri
producer	Allan Ekelund
screenplay	Bergman from his dramatic sketch *Wood Painting*
cinematography	Gunnar Fischer

Death (Bengt Ekerot) *plays chess with the knight (Max Von Sydow), who hopes to extend his time on Earth by beating the Grim Reaper.*

Vertigo | Alfred Hitchcock | 1958

In the opening scene, *James Stewart is a plainclothes police officer clinging to a rooftop gutter, frozen by fear.*

Although *Vertigo was* a commercial and critical flop when first released, the film's reputation has grown gradually over time, and it is now widely considered to be Alfred Hitchcock's finest achievement. The reassessment has come about because of a deeper understanding of Hitchcock's films, both in theme and style, of which *Vertigo* is a supreme example.

Private detective John "Scottie" Ferguson (James Stewart) quits the San Francisco police force because he has developed a pathological fear of heights. He is hired by a friend, Gavin Elster (Tom Helmore) to follow his suicidal wife Madeleine (Kim Novak) around San Francisco. Scottie falls in love with Madeleine as he watches her day after day, but is unable to prevent her fatal leap from a bell tower, because of his fear of heights. After she dies, the distraught Scottie meets Judy (also played by Novak) who reminds him of Madeleine. Scottie tries to remake Judy, a brunette, into the exact image of the blonde he had loved. *Vertigo* is an absorbing study of sexual obsession, which makes the twists in the plot almost irrelevant. With its central tragic love story, it is one of the few Hitchcock films to move audiences emotionally. *Vertigo* has also been acclaimed for its innovative use of camera techniques, such as forward zoom and reverse tracking shots, to intensify the atmosphere of suspense. Seldom has picturesque San Francisco looked so alluring as in the sharp-edged Technicolor photography of the film, nor has Bernard Herrmann's yearning music ever been so effective. Kim Novak's cool, somnambulist manner accords perfectly with the film's dreamlike atmosphere as she lures James Stewart to his doom.

CREDITS	
studio	Paramount
producers	Alfred Hitchcock and Herbert Coleman
screenplay	Alec Coppel and Samuel Taylor
cinematography	Robert Burks
music	Bernard Herrmann
title design	Saul Bass

Poster *designed by Saul Bass*

Ashes and Diamonds | Andrzej Wajda | 1958

Polish cinema burst upon the world with Andrzej Wajda's lively "War Trilogy" about the resistance in Warsaw carried out by young people. The third part, *Ashes and Diamonds (Popiól i Diament)*, which followed *A Generation* (1954) and *Kanal* (1957), is perhaps Wajda's finest work, its enigmatic twilight world communicating the "Polish experience" during World War II far beyond the country's frontiers.

The remarkable *Zbigniew Cybulski as Maciek, having been shot during a chase, besmirches white sheets hanging on a line with his blood.*

On the last day of World War II in 1945, Maciek (Zbigniew Cybulski), the youngest member of a Nationalist underground movement in a provincial Polish town, is ordered to kill Szczuka (Waclaw Zastrzezynski), the new Communist district secretary. As he waits in a hotel during the night, he meets and falls in love with a barmaid, Krystyna (Ewa Krzyzanowska) and learns that there is something more to life than killing — the possibility of love and happiness. He is soon torn between his conscience and loyalty to the cause he has lived for. The assassination scene, the climactic slow-motion dance to Polish music known as Polonaise, and Maciek's death scene are all stunningly realized. In a complex characterization, the brilliant Cybulski, his eyes hidden by dark glasses, embodies the sceptical new generation, establishing his reputation as "the Polish James Dean." The actor was killed while running for a train in 1967 at the age of 40.

CREDITS	
production	Film Polski
screenplay	Jerzy Andrzejewski, Andrzej Wajda from the novel by Andrzejewski
cinematography	Jerzy Wojcik
music	Jan Krenz, Michal Kleofas Oginski

The 400 Blows | François Truffaut | 1959

Truffaut's first feature film, made when he was 27, was based on his own deprived childhood. It was an immediate success, winning the Best Director's prize at Cannes. It also helped to launch the French New Wave and started a series of films following the character of Antoine Doinel (Jean-Pierre Léaud) through adolescence, marriage, fatherhood, and divorce.

Jean-Pierre Léaud *(fourth left) as Antoine Doinel lines up at the reform school, where he is sent for stealing a typewriter.*

A harsh critic writing for the magazine *Cahiers du Cinéma*, Truffaut was challenged by his movie-producer father-in-law to make a film himself. *The 400 Blows* was the triumphant result. A 12-year-old Parisian boy, Antoine Doinel (Jean Pierre Léaud), neglected by his mother and stepfather, plays truant and takes to petty crime. He is placed in a reform school, but escapes to the coast. The film has a wonderful free-wheeling quality as it follows its young hero through the streets of Paris. There was an extraordinary rapport between the director and Léaud, his alter ego, and much of the film's quality is due to the child's spontaneous performance. The freeze of his face as he runs towards the sea is one of cinema's most celebrated endings. The title comes from a colloquial expression *faire les quatre cents coups*, meaning "to get into a lot of trouble."

CREDITS

production	Les Films du Carrosse
producer	Georges Charlot
screenplay	Marcel Moussy from an original story by Truffaut
cinematography	Henri Decaë
music	Jean Constantin
award	Cannes: Best Director

NOUVELLE VAGUE

This term described the "new wave" of directors who made their first feature films in France in the years following 1959. The main impetus for the movement in France came from the critics-turned-directors of the influential magazine *Cahiers du Cinéma*, headed by François Truffaut and Jean-Luc Godard.

Jean-Luc Godard *was perhaps the greatest and most radical of the French New Wave directors.*

Some Like It Hot | Billy Wilder | 1959

A high watermark in American post-war comedy, Billy Wilder's *Some Like It Hot* is an amalgam of parody, slapstick, farce, and sophistication. Modern in its liberal sexual approach, the film is nostalgic in its tribute to the screwball comedies and gangster movies of the 1930s.

Two jazz musicians (Tony Curtis, Jack Lemmon), on the run from gangsters, disguise themselves as "Josephine" and "Daphne" and join an all-girl band on the way to Florida. On the train, they become friends with Sugar Kane (Marilyn Monroe), the band's singer. Complications occur when "Josephine" falls in love with Sugar, and "Daphne" is courted by millionaire Osgood Fielding III (Joe E. Brown). When "Daphne" finally admits he is a man, Osgood replies, in one of the most memorable punchlines in cinema, "Well, nobody's perfect." Curtis and Lemmon give two of Hollywood's best cross-dressing portrayals, with Curtis offering a triple treat — as his wise-guy self, as a woman with a dark wig and a high-pitched voice, and as an oil tycoon who sounds like Cary Grant. Lemmon, in high-heeled shoes, flapper's frock, and blond wig, is hilarious in his role, identifying himself closely with his female character. Monroe brings sensitivity to her role and sings two zippy 1920s' numbers.

Film poster, 1959

studio	United Artists
production	Mirisch Company
screenplay	Billy Wilder, I.A.L. Diamond
cinematography	Charles Lang
music	Adolph Deutsch
awards	Academy Award: Costume Design

MARILYN MONROE

The troubled life of Norma Jean Baker (1926–62) — her unhappy childhood, her marriages, and the tragic circumstances of her death — are probably as familiar as her films. Marilyn Monroe burst into the public consciousness and stardom in 1953 singing "Diamonds Are A Girl's Best Friend" in *Gentlemen Prefer Blondes*. In the same year she appeared in *How to Marry A Millionaire* alongside Betty Grable and Lauren Bacall and then made *The Seven Year Itch* (1955). By this time she was a box-office draw and her performances showed that she could not only sing but had a comic touch. In dramas, such as *Bus Stop* (1956) and *The Misfits* (1961), she revealed her special blend of vulnerability and sexuality that made her a screen legend, and she is as popular today as she was in her lifetime.

Sugar Kane *(Marilyn Monroe), in rehearsal with her band on the train to Florida, belts out "Runnin' Wild." Tony Curtis and Jack Lemmon can be seen over her right shoulder.*

Breathless | Jean-Luc Godard | 1960

This greatly influential film made the anarchic Jean-Paul Belmondo a star, revitalized Jean Seberg's career, and established 29-year-old Jean-Luc Godard, in his first feature, as a leading member of the French New Wave movement.

Patricia (Jean Seberg) *talks to petty criminal Michel (Jean-Paul Belmondo), who seeks refuge from the police in her Paris apartment.*

The story of Michel Poiccard (Belmondo), a young, dashing car thief who kills a policeman and goes on the run with Patricia Franchini (Seberg), his American girlfriend, was based on an idea by François Truffaut and dedicated to Monogram Pictures, Hollywood's all-B movie studio. *Breathless* (*A Bout de Souffle*) attempts to recapture the directness and economy of the American gangster movie by the superb use of location shooting, jump cuts (which eliminated the usual establishing shots), and a hand-held camera.

The cinematographer Raoul Coutard, who worked on many of the French New Wave films, was pushed around in a wheelchair, and used as a camera dollie, following the characters down the street and into buildings. In order to achieve an immediacy in the performances, Godard cued the actors, who were not allowed to learn their lines, during the takes. A former critic, Godard consciously broke film conventions but at the same time paid homage to what he regarded as worth emulating in Hollywood cinema.

Film poster

CREDITS	
studio	Impéria
producer	Georges de Beauregard
screenplay	Jean-Luc Godard
cinematography	Raoul Coutard
award	Berlin: Best Director

La Dolce Vita | Federico Fellini | 1960

CREDITS	
production	Pathé Consortium Cinema, Riama Film
producer	Guiseppe Amato
screenplay	Federico Fellini, Tullio Pinelli, Brunello Rondi, Ennio Flaiano
cinematography	Otello Martelli
music	Nino Rota
costume design	Piero Gherardi
awards	Cannes: Best Film

Causing a sensation when it was released, Federico Fellini's most (in)famous film is an impressive three-hour, wide-screen panorama of decadent contemporary society in Rome. It introduced into English the expressions "la dolce vita" and "paparazzi"— the latter now synonymous with intrusive photographers who chase celebrities.

The film's story follows jaded gossip columnist and would-be serious writer Marcello Rubini (Marcello Mastroianni) through seven nights and seven days, as he rootlessly and amorally wanders around the hot spots of Rome in search of himself. At the metaphoric ending, he glimpses innocence in the form of a young girl on the beach at dawn, but a stretch of water separates them and he cannot hear what she is saying. There is imaginative brilliance in the notorious set pieces—a vast statue of Christ is flown over Rome; Marcello and a bored heiress pick up a prostitute for a *ménage à trois*; a high society orgy takes place, at which the hostess Nadia (Nadia Gray) performs a striptease, and Marcello sticks feathers on a woman and rides her like a horse. Especially memorable is Anita Ekberg as blonde starlet Sylvia, who calls out to Marcello in seductive tones at the striptease party.

Film poster

Anita Ekberg, *as American starlet Sylvia, wanders tipsily into the Trevi Fountain in Rome.*

Saturday Night and Sunday Morning | Karel Reisz | 1960

Arthur Seaton (Albert Finney), *an amoral, disenchanted, blue-collar worker, goes to bed with the married Brenda (Rachel Roberts) while her husband is working a night shift.*

One of the key works of British cinema of the post-war period, and arguably the best and most honest of the British New Wave movies that dealt with working class life, Karel Reisz's first feature *Saturday Night and Sunday Morning* made Albert Finney, as the rebellious anti-hero, into a new kind of star.

"Don't let the bastards grind you down. That's one thing you learn. What I'm out for is a good time. All the rest is propaganda," says defiant Arthur Seaton (Finney), who works at a lathe in the Raleigh factory in Nottingham, in the north of England. He has an affair with Brenda (Rachel Roberts), the wife of his co-worker, who later finds out. Brenda gets pregnant and in the meantime Arthur has met Doreen (Shirley Anne Field) in a pub and marriage soon threatens him. Albert Finney's "angry young man" gives the film a punch as he reacts against his surroundings with energy and humor. The film, with well-rounded, recognizable working class characters rarely seen in British films until then, splendidly evokes the drab midland industrial setting — the factories and back streets, canal banks, and pubs — and its effect on human relationships.

CREDITS

production	Woodfall Film Productions
producer	Tony Richardson, Harry Salzman
screenplay	Alan Sillitoe from his novel
cinematography	Freddie Francis
music	Johnny Dankworth

FREE CINEMA

In the mid-1950s, a group of British film-makers challenged orthodoxy in society and cinema. They stressed the social responsibility of the artist to make films free from commercial considerations, and to express the "significance of the everyday." Karel Reisz, Lindsay Anderson, and Tony Richardson were connected with the "Angry Young Men" of literature and so-called "Kitchen Sink" drama in theatre.

This poster for Tony Richardson's *film adaptation of* Look Back In Anger *aptly reflects the impact of John Osborne's revolutionary play.*

L'Avventura | Michelangelo Antonioni | 1960

After five features in ten years, director Antonioni's style reached its maturity in *L'Avventura (The Adventure)*. A minimal plot, the long takes and slow tracking shots, limited dialogue, and strong relationship between the characters and their environment redefined views of time and space in cinema.

CREDITS	
producer	Cino Del Duca, Raymond Hakim, Robert Hakim, Amato Pennasilico, Luciano Perugia
screenplay	Antonioni, Elio Bartolini, Tonino Guerra
cinematography	Aldo Scarvarda
music	Giovanni Fusco

Anna (Lea Massari) and her fiancé Sandro (Gabriele Ferzetti) visit a Sicilian island with a group of wealthy people. After an argument with Sandro, Anna disappears. Her friend Claudia (Monica Vitti) joins Sandro in a search for her and they become lovers. The bitter ending is not a resolution of the conventional type. Antonioni's refusal to explain Anna's disappearance outraged and disconcerted many on its first release, although this did not stop the film from becoming a success. What matters in the plot is the effect the unsolved mystery has on the alienated characters, especially the ravishing Vitti in the first of many roles for Antonioni.

Best friends Anna (Massari), *left, and Claudia (Vitti) prepare to go off to spend a fateful few days on a Sicilian island, from where Anna disappears.*

Last Year in Marienbad | Alain Resnais | 1961

CREDITS	
producers	Pierre Courau, Raymond Froment
screenplay	Alain Robbe-Grillet
cinematography	Sacha Vierney
music	Francis Seyrig
awards	Venice: Jury Prize

By rejecting a chronological structure and objective reality, and by mingling memory and imagination, desire and fulfillment as well as past, present, and future, Alain Resnais, in his second feature, created one of the most enigmatic, haunting, and erotic of ciné-poems.

In a vast baroque mansion with geometrically designed gardens, X, an unnamed man (Giorgio Albertazzi) tries to convince A, a woman guest (Delphine Seyrig) that they had had an affair the year before, and that she should leave M, the man (Sacha Pitoëff), who might be her husband, for him. Although the style and structure puzzled many at the time, the interweaving of past and present, and the instant "flash-ins," instead of traditional slow flashbacks, have now become part of the vocabulary of contemporary film-making. Taken on one level, *Last Year in Marienbad (L'Année Dernière à Marienbad)* is a variation on the eternal romantic triangle, expanded from the old chat up line, "Haven't we met somewhere before?" The stylized dresses, the organ music, the tracking shots down endless corridors, the dazzling décor, and the mysterious Seyrig, are all unforgettable.

Delphine Seyrig *as A, the nameless woman who does not remember if she had an affair.*

Lawrence of Arabia | David Lean | 1962

One of the most intelligent and spectacular blockbusters ever made, *Lawrence of Arabia* is a travelogue, a history lesson, and an adventure movie. Above all, it is a study of an enigmatic and controversial military figure. Peter O'Toole in the title role became an international star overnight.

The playwright Robert Bolt brilliantly shaped much of the adult life story of T.E. Lawrence, a British army officer who fought in Arabia, into a manageable screenplay. Based on Lawrence's memoirs, *The Seven Pillars of Wisdom*, the film's narrative begins with the death of Lawrence (Peter O'Toole) in England in an accident. Then a flashback retraces the major stages of his tumultuous military career; his friendship with Sherif Ali (Omar Sharif), his support of Prince Feisal (Alec Guinness), his capture and torture by the Turkish Bey (José Ferrer), and the central role he played in the dismantling of the Ottoman Empire.

The story brought out the best in director David Lean, who responded, like his hero, to the beauties of the vast Sahara desert, splendidly caught in all its shifting moods by the camera of Freddie Young. The first sight of Sharif, initially a mere dot on the horizon, is perhaps the most striking sequence in this epic film.

Film poster, 1962

> **"...dreamers of the day are dangerous men...they may act their dreams out with open eyes...This I did."**
>
> **T.E. LAWRENCE**

CREDITS

production	Horizon
producer	Sam Spiegel
screenplay	Robert Bolt, Michael Wilson, based on the memoirs of T.E. Lawrence
cinematography	Frederick A. Young
music	Maurice Jarre
awards	Academy Awards: Best Picture, Best Director, Best Colour Cinematography, Best Colour Art Direction (John Box, John Stoll, Dario Simoni); Best Sound (John Cox); Best Film Editing (Anne Coates), Best Music Score

Peter O'Toole *plays Colonel Lawrence, a legendary war hero who leads the Arabs into battle in the campaign against the Turks in World War I.*

Dr. Strangelove | Stanley Kubrick | 1964

Stanley Kubrick's *Dr. Strangelove* elects to view nuclear annihilation as the ultimate absurdity. A satire on those who have stopped worrying about the bomb, this masterpiece of black comedy gets as close to a 20th-century catastrophe as possible, and is far more effective than more sombre efforts.

Kubrick had planned to make *Dr. Strangelove Or: How I Learned to Stop Worrying and Love the Bomb* as a serious drama about the inevitable heated ending of the Cold War. He changed the tone to a comic one during the early days of working on the script when he found he had to suppress some of the more absurd elements to keep it from being funny. The plot centers on frantic attempts by the US government to call back B-52s sent by mad Air Force Brigadier-General Jack D. Ripper to launch a nuclear attack on the Soviet Union. Sterling Hayden as Ripper, who is convinced the "Commies" are tainting the drinking water to reduce sexual potency, and George C. Scott as the hawkish General "Buck" Turgidson, embody Kubrick's antimilitarism.

Peter Sellers gives three brilliant caricature performances: as an RAF group captain; in the title role as a sinister, wheelchair-bound German scientist whose artificial arm involuntarily jerks into a Nazi salute; and as a liberal President of the USA. The ominous circular War Room, brilliantly designed by Ken Adam, is central to Kubrick's nightmarish vision. Through comedy Kubrick sought to bring about an awareness of the very real possibility of nuclear destruction.

Peter Sellers *(in dark glasses), in the title role as the mad scientist, gives advice to the President (Sellers again, offscreen) in the War Room.*

> **"Please gentlemen, you can't fight here, this is the War Room!"**
>
> **PRESIDENT MERKIN MUFFLEY**

CREDITS

production	Hawk Films
producer	Stanley Kubrick, Victor Lyndon
screenplay	Stanley Kubrick, Terry Southern, Peter George (based on his novel)
cinematography	Gilbert Taylor
production design	Ken Adam

The Battle of Algiers | Gillo Pontecorvo | 1966

Without recourse to any newsreel footage, director Gillo Pontecorvo achieved a naturalistic quality in this stunning film about the French–Algerian War, probably coming closer to the truth and the complexities of the situation than any documentary.

The guerilla war fought for Algerian independence from the French in 1954 is seen through the eyes of some of the participants, especially the central character Ali La Pointe (Brahim Haggiag), imprisoned for a petty theft. He joins the cause after seeing a fellow Algerian's execution and, recruited by the National Liberation Front, goes on to become a hero in the war. The film was shot in the actual locations, from the dingy backstreets of the Casbah to the tree-lined avenues of the French quarter. Except for Jean Martin as Colonel Mathieu, the cast are all non-professional, and the film mixes the grainy texture of a newsreel with hand-held camera movements, depth of field, and dramatic close-ups. Although banned in France for some years, its main strength lies in its scrupulous attention to the views and problems on both sides. The torture of Algerians by the French is shown, but so is a devastating scene in which a woman plants a bomb in a restaurant, knowing she will kill innocent people. In the late 1960s, *The Battle of Algiers (La Battaglia di Algeri)* was watched by Americans opposed to the Vietnam War, and the Pentagon reportedly held a screening early in the Second Gulf War.

A narrow alley *in the Casbah, the Muslim section of Algiers, where patrolling French soldiers pass by veiled women in an atmosphere fraught with tension.*

CREDITS	
production	Casbah/Igor
producers	Antonio Musu, Yacef Saadi
screenplay	Gillo Pontecorvo, Franco Solinas
cinematography	Marcello Gatti
music	Gillo Pontecorvo, Ennio Morricone
awards	Venice: Best Film

CINÉMA VÉRITÉ

Kino-pravda or "film-truth" was a concept evolved by Dziga Vertov in the Soviet Union in the 1920s. The term was adopted in 1960s' France to describe films by directors such as Jean Rouch and Chris Marker, who were attempting to capture truth on film by presenting reality without exercising directorial control. The improvements in 16-mm equipment – including the reduction in weight of the cameras – made it possible to reduce a film crew down to two people. The movement developed simultaneously in the USA as "Direct Cinema".

One of the recruits *in* Basic Training *(1971), directed by Fred Wiseman, which eavesdrops on life in a US Army training centre in Fort Knox, Kentucky.*

The Sound of Music | Robert Wise | 1965

This heart-warming musical features seven children, their handsome, wealthy widower father, and a fresh-faced singing governess. With its catchy Rogers and Hammerstein songs, the film, set in spectacular Tyrolean scenery and shot in magnificent Todd-AO and De Luxe Color, has become, for many audiences, one of their favorite things.

The plot centers on Maria (Julie Andrews), a young postulant nun who leaves the convent to take up a position of governess to the children of Captain von Trapp (Christopher Plummer). She marries her employer, and the family becomes the internationally celebrated Trapp Family Singers, but have to flee the country during the Nazi annexation of Austria. *The Sound of Music* is based on the true life story of the Trapp family as narrated in *The Story of the Trapp Family Singers,* written by Maria Augusta Trapp and published in 1949. Shot on location in Austria, and with a perfectly cast Julie Andrews radiating youthful charm — as well as showcasing a melodious voice — the film had an advantage over the 1959 Broadway musical. An unashamed escape from the harshness of contemporary life, *The Sound of Music* grossed almost $200 million worldwide on its first release.

Maria (Julie Andrews) *sings the opening sequence title song in a grassy, flower-filled meadow encircled by the Austrian Alps.*

CREDITS

production	20th Century Fox
producer	Robert Wise
screenplay	Ernest Lehman
cinematography	Ted McCord
choreography	Marc Breaux, Dee Dee Wood
music and lyrics	Richard Rodgers (music) Oscar Hammerstein (lyrics)
awards	Academy Awards: Best Picture, Best Director, Best Sound (20th Century Fox sound department), Best Film Editing (William Reynolds), Best Adapted Music Score (Irwin Kostal)

SING-A-LONG-A SOUND OF MUSIC

Since 1999, Sing-Along-A Sound of Music has played to packed houses all over the English-speaking world. It is interactive, fun entertainment in which audiences dress up as characters from the film, sing all the songs (helped by subtitles), boo the Nazis, and cheer and set off poppers when Captain von Trapp finally kisses Maria.

Andrei Rublev | Andrei Tarkovsky | 1966

This three-hour epic was shelved for some years by the Soviet authorities, who felt it was too "dark" for the October Revolution's 50th anniversary. But four years after it was made, it was released in the west to great acclaim.

CREDITS	
production	Mosfilm
producer	Tamara Ogorodnikova
screenplay	Andrei Tarkovsky, Andrei Konchalovsky
cinematography	Vadim Yusov
production design	Yevgeni Tcherniaiev

Eight imaginary episodes in the life of the great 15th-century icon painter Andrei Rublev (Anatoly Solonitsyn), as he journeys through feudal Russia, make up this film. Rublev leaves the peace and seclusion of a monastery and because of the cruelty he witnesses—rape, pillage, and famine—he gradually abandons speech, his art, and religious faith. Finally, inspired by a young peasant who assumes responsibility for making a huge bell, he learns that creativity is still possible in the worst of conditions, and regains his faith in the world.

Anatoly Solonitsyn *as the monk and artist Rublev; for director Tarkovsky, a horse was a "symbolic image," capturing the essence of life.*

The Chelsea Girls | Andy Warhol | 1966

A milestone of American Underground cinema, *The Chelsea Girls* marks the zenith of pop artist Andy Warhol's movie career and his breakthrough to national and international exposure. It features all the resident self-styled superstars of the "Factory," his art space in New York's Manhattan, such as "Pope" Ondine.

Consisting of twelve 35-minute reels, each representing the activities in one room of New York's Chelsea Hotel at 222 West 23rd Street, *The Chelsea Girls* is projected two reels at a time, side by side, bringing its six hours of footage to a running time of three hours. Each of the 12 reels, eight in black-and-white and four in color, consists of a single unedited shot in which personalities from Warhol's entourage (junkies, gays, transvestites, and rock singers) act out their fantasies, some of which involve sex and "shooting up." *The Chelsea Girls* is a consistently fascinating document of the counter-culture of the time.

Andy Warhol *prepares to film (from bottom to top) Mary Woronov, Nico, and International Velvet.*

CREDITS	
producer	Andy Warhol
screenplay	Andy Warhol, Ronald Tavel
cinematography	Andy Warhol
production assistant	Paul Morrissey
music	The Velvet Underground

Bonnie and Clyde | Arthur Penn | 1967

Gangsters *Buck Barrow (Gene Hackman), Clyde Barrow (Warren Beatty), and Bonnie Parker (Faye Dunaway) hold up a bank.*

One of the most influential American movies in its amoral attitude toward the outlaw, seen from a modern psychological and social viewpoint, *Bonnie and Clyde* also depicts a graphic violence rare in mainstream films of the time.

"They're young...they're in love...and they kill people..." was the effective publicity line of this most stylish and uncompromising of gangster pictures based on a true story. Faye Dunaway and Warren Beatty excel as Bonnie Parker and Clyde Barrow, infamous gun-toting criminals who roamed the American midwest during the late 1920s and early 1930s. They are joined by a boy who works in a gas station, C.W. (Michael J. Pollard), Clyde's brother Buck Barrow (Gene Hackman), and his wife Blanche (Estelle Parsons) in a crime spree that includes murder. In this film, the bank robbers are portrayed as heroic and as romantic—they are star-crossed lovers caught up in a whirl of violence and passion, meticulously evoked by posed photographs in sepia and carefully selected music and décor. The black comedy moves ineluctably toward the much imitated memorable ending: hundreds of bullets pump into the miscreant pair, who die in slow motion. The film gave two Genes, Hackman (Oscar nominated) and Wilder (in his screen debut), their first chance to shine. The script was earlier offered to Jean-Luc Godard and François Truffaut who turned it down, although the influence of the French New Wave is evident in Arthur Penn's bravura directing.

Film poster, 1967

CREDITS	
production	Tatira-Hiller; Warner Bros.
producer	Warren Beatty
screenplay	David Newman, Robert Benton
cinematography	Burnett Guffey
art director	Dean Tavoularis
awards	Academy Awards: Best Supporting Actress (Estelle Parsons), Best Cinematography

The Wild Bunch | Sam Peckinpah | 1969

On its release, *The Wild Bunch* caused a stir due to its amoral depiction of Texas outlaws as heroes and its graphic violence. Today it is seen as an elegiac examination of "unchanged men in a changing land" and a landmark in the Western genre.

CREDITS	
production	Seven Arts
studio	Warner Brothers
producers	Phil Feldman, Roy N. Sickner
screenplay	Walon Green, Sam Peckinpah, Roy N. Sickner,
cinematography	Lucien Ballard
editor	Louis Lombardo
music	Jerry Fielding

In 1913, Pike Bishop (William Holden) and his band of ageing outlaws are trying to live under the same codes as in the Old West when they find themselves stalked by bounty hunters, one of whom is Pike's former friend Deke Thornton (Robert Ryan). They flee into Mexico where, in the gory, surrealistically choreographed, slow-motion climax, the gang is riddled by bullets. *The Wild Bunch* takes a nostalgic view of the morals of the Old West and is a contemplation of the more romantic old Western. Beautifully photographed in wide-screen by Lucien Ballard, with multiple angles and elaborate editing — six Panavision cameras were run together at different speeds — the film emanates a lyrical disenchantment.

Outlaws *Ben Johnson, Warren Oates, William Holden, and Ernest Borgnine march across a Mexican town for the final shoot-out.*

Easy Rider | Dennis Hopper | 1969

CREDITS	
production	Columbia
producer	Peter Fonda
screenplay	Dennis Hopper, Peter Fonda, Terry Southern
cinematography	László Kovács

Made for less than $400,000, *Easy Rider* was a "sleeper" hit. The film's combination of drugs, rock music, violence, motorcycles, and its counter-culture stance caught the imagination of the young and earned over $50 million.

Two hippies, Wyatt (Peter Fonda) and Billy (Dennis Hopper), hit the road on motorcycles "in search of the real America." What they mostly find is hostility towards them from small-town bigots. The odyssey ends when the two trippers are shot down by a truck driver who despises their lifestyle. Stupidity, corruption, and violence are set against the potential freedom of America in Hopper's first feature as director (and Fonda's as producer). Derived from the American "Direct Cinema" documentary film-makers of the early 1960s, the film relied heavily on the expertise of cameraman László Kovács. The folk-rock music soundtrack featured Jimi Hendrix, The Byrds, Steppenwolf, Bob Dylan, and other "counter-culture" performers of the time.

Peter Fonda *(left) as Wyatt and Dennis Hopper as Billy, are hippie bikers from Los Angeles riding to New Orleans...and destruction.*

The Conformist | Bernardo Bertolucci | 1969

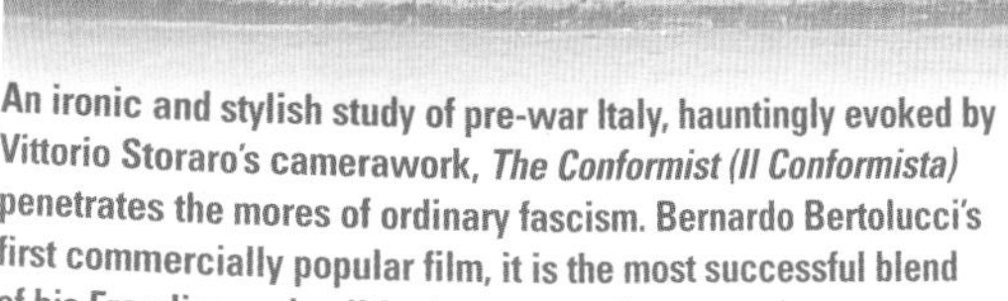

An ironic and stylish study of pre-war Italy, hauntingly evoked by Vittorio Storaro's camerawork, *The Conformist (Il Conformista)* penetrates the mores of ordinary fascism. Bernardo Bertolucci's first commercially popular film, it is the most successful blend of his Freudian and political preoccupations.

A professor in 1938 Italy, Marcello Clerici (Jean-Louis Trintignant) has suffered the childhood trauma of shooting a chauffeur who tried to seduce him. This experience, together with his own repressed homosexuality, contribute to his decision to enter into a bourgeois marriage with Giula (Stefania Sandrelli) and offer his services to the Fascist party. He is asked to assassinate his former teacher, Professor Quadri (Enzo Tarascio), leader of an anti-Fascist group, but then has doubts about his mission. *The Conformist* sees the full flowering of Bertolucci's flamboyant style — elaborate tracking shots, baroque camera angles, opulent colour effects, ornate décor, and the intricate play of light and shadow. Trintignant brings conviction to his role, and there are also enticing performances from Sandrelli and Dominique Sanda (as Anna, Professor Quadri's young wife), who dance a memorable tango together.

Jean-Louis Trintignant *(Marcello) carries flowers to a loved one along the streets of Rome.*

CREDITS	
producer	Maurizio Lodi-Fé
screenplay	Bernardo Bertolucci from the novel by Alberto Moravia
cinematography	Vittorio Storaro
music	Georges Delerue
costume design	Gitt Magrini

The Godfather | Francis Ford Coppola | 1972

CREDITS	
studio	Paramount
producer	Albert S. Ruddy
screenplay	Francis Ford Coppola, Mario Puzo from the novel by Puzo
cinematography	Gordon Willis
production design	Dean Tavoularis
set decoration	Philip Smith
music	Nino Rota
costume design	Anna Hill Johnstone
awards	Academy Awards: Best Picture, Best Actor (Marlon Brando), Best Screenplay (Coppola, Puzo)

In his shuttered room *during his daughter's wedding, Don Corleone (Marlon Brando) listens to one of several supplicants who want him to "deal with" their enemies.*

Film poster *(left).*

With this film, Francis Ford Coppola made the public "an offer it could not refuse." The story, covering the rise of the Mafia and the Corleone crime "family" in the 1940s, builds up a rich pattern of relationships, meticulously detailing the rituals of an enclosed group. The film was one of the biggest commercial and critical successes of the 1970s, making sequels (*The Godfather II*, 1974, and *The Godfather III*, 1990) seem inevitable.

Mafia boss Don Vito Corleone (Marlon Brando) is part of a society where murder is "nothing personal, just business." For all the excessive violence, justified by the plot and never arbitrary, the movie effectively conveys the codes of loyalty, love, masculine honor, and women's submissiveness that bind the family together. Even more than the killings, audiences seemed to have been shocked by the scene in which a Hollywood tycoon wakes up to find the bloody head of his horse in his bed. Coppola controls the material in a masterful manner with the help of extraordinary *chiaroscuro* photography of the interiors and the outstanding cast led by Brando, who creates an iconographic figure with his throaty voice and papal hand gestures as he switches from the stern Godfather to kindly paterfamilias. Brando famously sent a Native American woman to the Academy Awards in his place in protest about their treatment in the US.

AL PACINO

Al Pacino (born 1940) has gone from strength to strength as an actor since his dominating and pivotal performances as Michael Corleone in the three *Godfather* movies. Whether playing a gangster as in *Scarface* (1983) or Shylock in *The Merchant of Venice* (2004), he brings maximum power to the screen. Nominated eight times for an Oscar, he won it for *Scent Of A Woman* (1992).

Aguirre, Wrath of God | Werner Herzog | 1972

This film, featuring a megalomaniac hero, is a powerful, hypnotic, epic tale of the depravity of imperialism. Also known in German as *Aguirre, der Zorn Gottes,* Werner Herzog had to overcome difficult conditions filming in the Andes. The film's success, due mainly to the striking images, was proof that the hardships paid off.

CREDITS

production	Hessicher Rundfunk/Werner Herzog
producer	Werner Herzog
screenplay	Werner Herzog
cinematography	Thomas Mauch
music	Popol Vuh

In the wilds of Peru, a 16th-century Spanish conquistador, Don Lope de Aguirre (Klaus Kinski), with the assistance of native slaves, leads a hazardous expedition over the mountains and down an uncharted river in search of the mythical kingdom of El Dorado. The fascination of this morality tale, presented in the guise of a true historical account, derives from the jungle atmosphere and pictorial flair, as well as the intense performance of Kinski. This was the first of five films he was to make with Herzog. The opening long shot of the expedition weaving its way down the mountain through the fog is particularly effective, as is the final shot, in which the camera circles rapidly around a raft littered with dead bodies and overrun with monkeys. The narrative is a steady stream of images, accompanied by brief pieces of dialogue, which not only set the pace of the film, but the mood as well. It is the topography of the landscape—the film was shot on location in the Peruvian rainforest near Puerto Maldonado—that dictates the action, rather than the actors. Indeed, the actors react strongly to their surroundings, which reflect and mirror the growing madness and the feverish hallucinations of the doomed expedition.

Klaus Kinski *as the film's protagonist gives an enigmatic and frightening portrayal of human obsession and its consequences.*

Nashville | Robert Altman | 1975

This portrayal of one weekend in the lives of people involved in the music business in Nashville, Tennessee, in the US – the world's country music capital – is a tour-de-force in its manipulation of characters and sound.

In order to create this mosaic of characters, music, sights, and sounds, Altman used 16 tracks for the sound-producing conversations, as well as a continuously moving camera, rhythmic cuts, and on- and off-screen commentaries. Particularly remarkable is the opening sequence at Nashville airport during which all 24 characters are introduced. Conceived as a celebration of the US bicentennial anniversary in 1976, *Nashville* ironically reveals the dark side of the country, such as racial prejudice, selfishness, and vulgarity.

Karen Black *plays Connie White, a country singer who uses Barbara Jean's (the reigning queen of Nashville) period out of the spotlight to bolster her own career.*

CREDITS	
studio	Paramount Pictures
producer	Robert Altman
screenplay	Joan Tewkesbury
cinematography	Paul Lohmann
award	Academy award: Best Song: "I'm Easy" (Keith Carradine)

In the Realm of the Senses | Nagisa Oshima | 1976

Director Nagisa Oshima's first big commercial success, was, for many, in the realm of pornography. For others, it was a serious treatment of gender status and oppression, a link between eroticism and death, and an artistic breakthrough in the representation of explicit sex on screen.

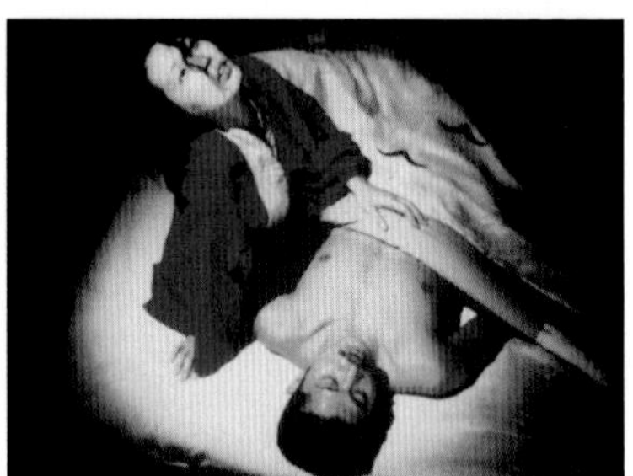

After strangling her lover, Kichizo (Tatsuya Fuji), while having sex, the geisha, Sada (Eiko Matsuda), prepares for a final, terrible act.

Kichizo (Tatsuya Fuji), a married man, and Sada (Eiko Matsuda), a geisha, retreat from the militarist Japan of 1936 into a world of their own where they obsessively act out their sexual fantasies. Finally, in a quest for the ultimate orgasm, Sada strangles and then castrates her lover. Based on a notorious murder case of the 1930s, Oshima's voyeuristic masterpiece is a blend of tenderness and brutality, spontaneity and ritual. The original title, *Ai No Corrida*, refers to a ritualized fight to the death — *corrida* means "bullfight" in Spanish. In the mid-1970s, the film created a storm of controversy, and encountered censorship problems in several countries. Although it still has the capacity to shock, when this sensational film was rereleased in the original uncut version in 2000, it caused hardly a ripple.

CREDITS	
production	Argos Films, Oshima Productions
producer	Anatole Dauman
screenplay	Nagisa Oshima
cinematography	Hideo Itoh
awards	Cannes: Best Director

Taxi Driver | Martin Scorsese | 1976

This deeply disturbing drama, which examines alienation in urban society by combining elements of film noir, the western, and horror movies, established Martin Scorsese as a major figure in world cinema and Robert De Niro as a star.

A Vietnam War veteran, paranoid loner, and taxi driver, Travis Bickle (De Niro) has no friends. He sees New York as "an open sewer" populated by "animals" and "scum" that need to be swept away. De Niro immerses himself in the complex character — his monologue to a mirror has become one of the most famous sequences from 1970s cinema. Bickle's diary entries — "Listen, you screwheads, here is someone who would not take it anymore" – force audiences into an ambivalent identification with him. Scorsese presents an apocalyptic view of the city, with steam hissing out of the streets, incessant traffic noise, and wailing sirens. This is contrasted with the haunting score by Bernard Herrmann (his last) that accompanies the film's bleak images.

"You talkin' to me?"

TRAVIS BICKLE TO HIMSELF IN A MIRROR

"On every street *in every city, there's a nobody who dreams of being a somebody..." The film's tagline describes Robert De Niro's character.*

CREDITS

studio	Columbia
production	Bill/Phillips Production, Italo-Judeo Production
screenplay	Paul Schrader
cinematography	Michael Chapman
music	Bernard Herrmann
award	Cannes: Best Film

JODIE FOSTER

Jodie Foster (born 1962) proved to be one of the most talented of child stars as the teenage prostitute in *Taxi Driver*. The film threw her reluctantly into the spotlight; John Hinkley Jr., who shot President Reagan, attributed his actions to his obsession with Foster in the role. This cast a shadow over her career until she won Academy Awards for *The Accused* (1988) and *The Silence of the Lambs* (1991). In 1991, she made her impressive directorial debut with *Little Man Tate*, after which she continued to move successfully between acting and directing.

Annie Hall | Woody Allen | 1977

Until *Annie Hall,* Woody Allen was considered one of America's brightest new funnymen whose films were little more than a series of revue sketches. He was catapulted into the big time with this "nervous romance," which won four Oscars, made a fortune, and gained a cult following.

Film poster, 1977

The script, about the on-off relationship between Alvy Singer (Woody Allen), a television and nightclub comic, and budding singer Annie Hall (Diane Keaton) is semi-autobiographical, based loosely on the stars' real-life affair (Keaton's real name is Diane Hall and her nickname is Annie). In the film, their friendship begins during an indoor tennis match of mixed singles which she wins, and continues through the Jewish Alvy's awkward and hilarious meeting with Annie's WASP family. The New York-loving Alvy then follows Annie to "mellow" California. The pair portray an intelligent, contemporary adult couple with wit, accuracy, and an undercurrent of anxiety. Highlights include media guru Marshall McLuhan, playing himself, who suddenly appears to refute what a phony, standing in line to see a Bergman movie, is saying about him. Keaton's unisex costume of baggy trousers, white shirt, black waistcoat, knotted black tie, scarf, and felt hat oozed character and was a strong influence on what the well-dressed, liberated woman was to wear in the late 1970s.

CREDITS

studio	United Artists
producers	Jack Rollins, Charles H. Joffe
screenplay	Woody Allen, Marshall Brickman
cinematography	Gordon Willis
awards	Academy Awards: Best Picture, Best Actress (Diane Keaton), Best Director, Best Screenplay

Diane Keaton (Annie) *and Woody Allen (Alvy) talk on the balcony of Annie's apartment; their real thoughts are seen in subtitles, contradicting the words actually spoken.*

Star Wars | George Lucas | 1977

In *Star Wars*, a young man, Luke Skywalker, is chosen by destiny to lead the resistance against the Galactic Empire. George Lucas's fantasy film inspired generations of audiences — and forever changed the way films are marketed.

Chewbacca (Peter Mayhew), *Luke (Mark Hamill), Master Kenobi (Alec Guinness), and Han Solo (Harrison Ford) set off to rescue Princess Leia from the evil clutches of Darth Vader, leader of the Galactic Empire.*

Lucas modeled his universe (a long time ago, in a galaxy far, far away) on the Saturday serials he enjoyed as a child, but he also studied Joseph Campbell's work on mythologies, and borrowed significantly from Akira Kurosawa's samurai film, *The Hidden Fortress*. The structure of *Star Wars* was substantial enough to fascinate adolescent boys — without complicating what is essentially a simple fable of good and evil. It was also able to hold two sequels and, 20 years later, three prequels. An unexpected hit (sci-fi wasn't considered box office at the time), *Star Wars* transformed the movie industry, ushering in a new era of special effects-driven cinema aimed at a youth audience, released on as many screens as possible, and with a marketing budget offset by merchandising. Lucas became a billionaire and established Industrial Light & Magic, the leading special effects company.

CREDITS

studio	20th-Century Fox
production	Lucasfilm
producer	Gary Kurtz, George Lucas
screenplay	George Lucas
cinematography	Gilbert Taylor
awards	Academy Awards: Best Art Direction (John Barry, Norman Reynolds, Leslie Dilley, Roger Christian), Best Costume Design (John Mollo), Best Effects, Best Film Editing (Paul Hirsch, Marcia Lucas, Richard Chew), Best Music (John Williams), Best Sound

THE RISE OF THE BLOCKBUSTER

The word "blockbuster," refers either to a big-budget Hollywood movie that catches the public's attention, or to a film that has broken box-office records, such as *Jaws* (1975), the first film to earn $100 million in domestic ticket sales. It ushered in the "blockbuster era" during which *Star Wars* became the biggest blockbuster of the 1970s. The blockbusters of the late 1970s and early 1980s were mostly fantasies, such as *E.T.* (1982) and *Back to the Future* (1985), while those of the 1990s, like *Terminator 2* (1991) and *The Matrix* (1999) were darker and more violent.

Darth Vader was first portrayed *in* Star Wars *(1977) by British actor David Prowse, with the voice of James Earl Jones dubbed over. Through the series, Darth Vader gradually develops from being a villain archetype to a more complex character.*

The Marriage of Maria Braun | Rainer Werner Fassbinder | 1978

Fassbinder's biggest international box-office success is his most effective onslaught on Germany's "Economic Miracle" of the 1950s, as well as being a dramatic and subtle picture of an indomitable woman.

Hanna Schygulla, *here seen with Karl Oswald (Ivan Desny), plays the seductive and scantily dressed Maria Braun, a strong woman who exploits the men in her life to prosper in post-war Germany.*

CREDITS

production	Albatros, Fengler, Autoren, Tango Film, Trio Film, WDR
producer	Michael Fengler
screenplay	Peter Märthesheimer, Pea Fröhlich
cinematography	Michael Ballhaus
music	Peer Raben
awards	Berlin: Best Actress (Hanna Schygulla)

Maria Braun (Hanna Schygulla) survives in wartime Berlin while her husband Hermann (Klaus Löwitsch) fights at the Russian Front. On his return, he is imprisoned for killing Bill (Greg Eagles), a black G.I. who had befriended his wife. Maria then takes up with industrialist Karl Oswald (Ivan Desny) and rises to a position of wealth and power. *The Marriage of Maria Braun* (*Die Ehe der Maria Braun*) is the first of Fassbinder's trilogy of women (*Veronika Voss*, 1982; *Lola*, 1981) struggling to survive in harsh post-war Germany. A successful blend of the elements of classical Hollywood melodrama with contemporary socio-political themes, the story, beginning in 1943, is filled with superbly conceived comic and soap-opera incidents. Effective use is made of the camera, which follows the heroine with long, sweeping movements as Schygulla gives one of her best performances in her 13th feature with Fassbinder.

NEW GERMAN CINEMA

Among the first of the new wave of German films to make an impression were Alexander Kluge's *Yesterday Girl* and Volker Schlöndorf's *Young Torless*, which were both made in 1966. The former is set in the 1950s, where a rebellious young East German girl escapes to the West, while the latter is set in a semimilitary boarding school for embryonic Nazis.

Angela Winkler greets Jürgen Prochnow (left) in *The Lost Honour of Katerina Blum* (1975), Volker Schlöndorf and Margarethe von Trotte's statement on terrorism.

The Deer Hunter | Michael Cimino | 1978

The first major American movie about the Vietnam War and its aftermath, *The Deer Hunter* won five Oscars. Because of the film's impact, Hollywood discovered that audiences were ready to accept the disastrous war as a subject, as testified by the number of films in the early 1980s that dealt with it.

Although there are a number of scenes set during the Vietnam conflict, the film's principal theme is friendship and the psychological and social effects of the war on a small community—a Pennsylvanian industrial town acting as a microcosm. Hunting and drinking buddies Mike (Robert De Niro), Nick (Christopher Walken), and Stevie (John Savage) volunteer to go to Vietnam together and are thrown into the hell of war, which affects their lives forever. Stevie ends up in a wheelchair, Nick shoots himself in the head, and Mike learns the dangers of the macho code he lived by. Director Cimino orchestrates the set pieces brilliantly—the wedding, the hunt, and the sequence when the American POWs are forced to play Russian roulette by their captors, which is a metaphor for the futility of war.

Mike (Robert De Niro) *hunts for deer in the mountains for the last time before going to Vietnam.*

MERYL STREEP

Meryl Streep (born 1949) is one of the few female stars of today who stands with the greats of the past such as Katharine Hepburn and Bette Davis. Her acclaim—she has been nominated for 13 Academy Awards, and has won two—is due to her versatility and ability to fully immerse herself in her roles. She won the Best Actress Oscar for her moving performance as a Polish survivor of Auschwitz in *Sophie's Choice* (1982), and is at her best playing mature and complex women, as in *The Hours* (2002).

CREDITS

production	EMI, Universal
producer	Michael Cimino, Barry Spikings, Michael Deeley, John Peverall
screenplay	Michael Cimino, Deric Washburn, Louis Garfinkle, Quinn K. Redeker
cinematography	Vilmos Zsigmond
music	Stanley Myers
awards	Academy Awards: Best Picture, Best Director, Best Supporting Actor (Christopher Walken), Best Editing (Peter Zinner), Best Sound (C. Darin Knight, William L. McCoughey, Richard Portman, Aaron Rochin)

E.T. The Extra-Terrestrial | Steven Spielberg | 1982

One of only a handful of live-action films to capture the imagination of generations of children and their parents, *E.T.: The Extra-Terrestrial* remains Steven Spielberg's best-loved movie. It may also be his most heartfelt.

Kicking off with a quick, precise sketch of a typical middle-class suburban California family household, much like the one in which Spielberg grew up, the film quickly gets down to the business of introducing young Elliott (Henry Thomas) to his new best friend. A brown, short, waddling creature with four rubbery limbs, a retractable neck and eyes the size of headlights, E.T. is basically playing the dog in this movie, but he's a dog with supernatural powers: telepathy, and telekinesis. If it doesn't really stand up to logical analysis (E.T. can build an interstellar communicator but seems to have nothing to say to earthlings), but from a child's (or E.T.'s) innocent viewpoint, the film works well on an emotional level. E.T. goes through an accelerated life-cycle with Elliott acting as his protector, teacher, and surrogate parent. The death scene is heartbreaking, but through the power of love E.T. is resurrected in time for the literally uplifting climax — and Elliott's own emotional education is complete.

The flying bicycle silhouetted *against a full moon was later adopted as the logo for Spielberg's Amblin Entertainment production company.*

CREDITS	
studio	Universal
producer	Kathleen Kennedy, Steven Spielberg
screenplay	Melissa Mathison
cinematography	Allen Daviau
awards:	Academy Award: Best Sound Effects (Charles L. Campbell, Ben Burtt), Best Visual Effects (Carol Rambaldi, Dennis Muren, Kenneth Smith), Best Music (John Williams), Best Sound (Robert Knudson, Robert Glass, Don Digirolamo, Gene S. Cantamessa), Best Sound Effects Editing (C. Campbell, B. Burtt)

"E.T. phone home," *E.T.'s repeated request, became the catchphrase of the film; here, Elliott and his vulnerable alien friend are about to part forever.*

Blade Runner | Ridley Scott | 1982

Deckard *(Harrison Ford) struggles to evade death in a scene from the film that brilliantly combines conventions of 21st-century sci-fi and 1940s detective film noir.*

Among the most discussed and influential science fiction films ever made, Ridley Scott's adaptation filters Philip K. Dick's novel, *Do Androids Dream of Electric Sheep?* through a retro noir sensibility appropriate to the Los Angeles setting.

Harrison Ford is Deckard, a "blade runner" hired to "retire" four rogue replicants — organic robots so lifelike they don't even know they're not human. In the course of his pursuit, Deckard falls in love with another replicant (Sean Young), and comes to question his own — ambiguous — humanity. Although the plot is thin, the movie's visuals are astonishingly layered. Scott's imagination knows no bounds here. The movie's spectacular cityscapes are reminiscent of Fritz Lang's *Metropolis*, while the street level scenes give equally vivid impressions of a social fabric torn every which way. A failure at the box office, *Blade Runner* became a key cult movie, and was among the first titles to benefit from a restored "director's cut" when it was re-released in 1991. This version was actually shorter than the original, dispensed with the lugubrious noir voice-over, and had a bleaker ending. Crucially, it also carried clearer intimations that Deckard himself might be a replicant. Ironically, this makes him all the more human because he finally realizes his brotherhood with the android combatant (Rutger Hauer).

HARRISON FORD

Harrison Ford (born 1942) starred in four of the 10 highest-grossing films of all time: as Han Solo in *Star Wars* (1977), *The Empire Strikes Back* (1980), and *Return of the Jedi* (1983), and as Indiana Jones in *Raiders of the Lost Ark* (1981). This was obviously attributable to the popularity of the films, but also to Ford's ability to embody plausible heroes, even in far-fetched tales. While continuing his fantastic exploits as Indiana Jones, in *Witness* (1985), *Regarding Henry* (1991), and *The Fugitive* (1993), Ford proved he could play characters with depth. He has also successfully starred in romantic comedies such as *Working Girl* (1988) and *Sabrina* (1995). It is hard to imagine that in the early 1970s, he gave up acting for carpentry until George Lucas, for whom Ford had played a small role in *American Graffiti* (1973), offered him *Star Wars*.

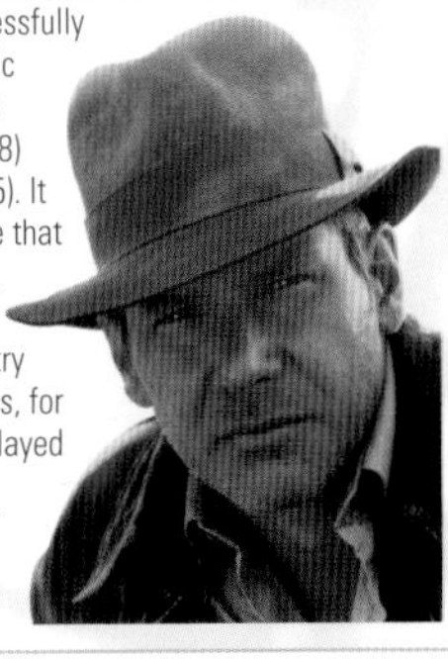

CREDITS

production	Ladd Company
producer	Michael Deeley
screenplay	Hampton Fancher, David Webb Peoples
cinematography	Jordan Cronenweth

Paris, Texas | Wim Wenders | 1984

A gaunt and *unshaven Travis (Harry Dean Stanton) wanders aimlessly across the bleak Texan desert.*

The title of the film suggests a meeting between the new and the old world, and *Paris, Texas* expertly reworks elements of both classical Hollywood and European art cinema in this successful collaboration between the German director Wim Wenders and the American writer Sam Shepard.

CREDITS	
production	Road Movies/ Argos
producer	Don Guest, Anatole Dauman
screenplay	Sam Shepard
cinematography	Robby Müller
music	Ry Cooder
awards	Cannes: Best Film

Wenders saw his chance to explore the vast American landscape — both urban and rural — in *Paris, Texas* and used it as the setting for the story of Travis, his lonely and lost protagonist. Brilliantly portrayed by the melancholy character actor Harry Dean Stanton, Travis does not speak for the opening 20 minutes, and is first seen walking alone in the Texan desert. Neither he nor the audience knows where he comes from or where he is going. Gradually we learn that he wishes to see Hunter (Hunter Carson), the son he left some years ago in the care of his brother Walt (Dean Stockwell), and is trying to find his estranged French wife Jane (Nastassja Kinski), hoping, in vain, to put the pieces of his life back together again. He does find his wife and son, only to lose them once again. Wenders, with the help of Ry Cooder's haunting score and Robby Müller's stunning camerawork, evokes a poignant world in which communication between people has become complex but not impossible.

Jane (Nastassja Kinski) *listens to Travis (Harry Dean Stanton), separated by a one-way mirror, as he talks about their life together in the past.*

Heimat | Edgar Reitz | 1984, 1992, 2005

Consisting of three series of 30 films, and running at 42 hours, Edgar Reitz's *Heimat (Homeland)* is an amusing, moving, and absorbing soap opera. Filmed in color and monochrome, it mirrors Germany's history from 1919 onwards through the eyes of ordinary people as the characters age and develop.

Part I, *A German Chronicle*, depicts life in the fictitious German village of Hunsrück. The central character is Maria (Marita Breuer), who marries into the Simon family. Part II, *Chronicle of a Generation*, moves to Munich in the 1960s, focusing on a group of young people; among them is Maria's son Hermann (Henry Arnold), who is struggling to become a composer. Part III, *A Chronicle of Endings and Beginnings*, starts with the fall of the Berlin Wall in 1989, as Hermann, now an internationally respected conductor, moves back to Hunsrück with his lover Clarissa (Salome Kammer). Particularly fascinating is the depiction of the Nazi era, when the film comes close to explaining how the evil of Hitler's ideology filtered down to taint otherwise decent citizens.

Hänschen *(Alexander Scholz), a one-eyed boy, aims at a prisoner in a concentration camp as a Nazi guard shows him how to sight the rifle — a chilling moment in Part III.*

CREDITS	
production	Edgar Reitz/WDR/SFB
producer	Edgar Reitz
screenplay	Edgar Reitz, Peter Steinbach
cinematography	Gernot Roll, Gerard Vanderbergh, Christian Reisz
music	Nikos Mamangakis

In Part III, A Chronicle of Endings and Beginnings, *Heiko Senst (center) plays Tobi, a young construction laborer from East Germany.*

Come and See | Elem Klimov | 1985

This moving and powerful film, the last to be directed by Elem Klimov, depicts the war in Belorussia in 1943, as seen through the eyes and heard through the ears of a 16-year-old boy, whose family and village have been destroyed by the Nazis.

The viewer is invited to "come and see" the teenage Florya (Alexei Kravchenko) as he wanders alone, gun in hand, witnessing an unbroken series of Nazi atrocities, until he joins a group of partisans as a hardened and active participant. Some of the unforgettable images include the agonising struggle through a swamp to reach an encampment of lamenting women, and the journey to find food, accompanied by a death's head effigy of Hitler. A sense of derangement is heightened by the film's soundtrack, most significantly when the bombing of a village damages Florya's hearing. Unlike many traditional war films, *Come and See* — or *Idi i Smotri*, the original Russian title — has no heroic catharsis or narrative symmetry. Instead, Klimov's apocalyptic vision, which mixes poetic and brutal imagery, focuses on the destruction of a young life and the horrors of war.

Alexei Kravshenko *plays Florya, a teenage boy scarred by his nightmarish experiences during the war, one of which is discovering his village destroyed and his family butchered by the Germans.*

CREDITS	
production	Byelarusfilm/Mosfilm
screenplay	Ales Adamovich, Klimov based on the works of Adamovich
music	Oleg Yanchenko
cinematography	Alexei Rodionov
awards	Moscow International Film Festival: Golden Prize

A group of partisans *terrify their new recruit, Florya, by pointing a pistol at him — while at the same time posing to have their photograph taken.*

Blue Velvet | David Lynch | 1986

David Lynch's radical fable is one of the seminal films of the 1980s — its influence was such that it spawned a number of inferior imitations. Initially a satire on the complacency of small-town America, it turns into a powerful parable of evil where corruption is found in the most unlikely places.

Gangster Dennis Hopper *snorts gas through an insect-like mask and forces Isabella Rossellini — a nightclub singer known as The Blue Lady — to have sex with him.*

Blue Velvet opens with dreamlike images of America: perfect houses with white picket fences and impeccably manicured lawns. A man collapses while watering his lawn, and the camera reveals a colony of swarming bugs between the blades of grass. A little later, a college student (Kyle MacLachlan) finds a severed ear in a field, and he and his girlfriend (Laura Dern) try to solve the mystery; it leads them to enter film noir territory with a femme fatale (Isabella Rossellini) and a sadistic villain (Dennis Hopper). "Are you a detective or a pervert?" asks Dern of her boyfriend at one point. The answer, perhaps, is that he, the director, and the audience are being a bit of both. The film is set in a rather vague time zone with Bobby Vinton's evocative 1963 hit title song juxtaposed with more contemporary music.

Kyle MacLachlan, a David Lynch favourite, plays Jeffrey Beaumont who, in his investigations, is half-forced to play a voyeur.

CREDITS	
production	De Laurentiis Entertainment Group
producer	Richard Roth
music	Angelo Badalamenti, David Lynch
screenplay	David Lynch
cinematography	Frederick Elmes

"See that clock on the wall? In five minutes you are not going to believe what I just told you."

JEFFREY BEAUMONT

Shoah | Claude Lanzmann | 1985

Lanzmann's monumental documentary, over eight hours long, on the calculated extermination of Europe's Jews by the Nazis is both a tribute to those who died and a warning. Although the film begins by saying, "This is an untellable story," it manages, as far as possible, to describe the indescribable.

CREDITS	
production	Les Films Aleph, Historia
cinematography	Dominique Chapuis, Jimmy Glasberg, William Lubtchansky
awards	Berlin: Caligari Film Award

In *Shoah*, survivors of the Nazi extermination camps (at Treblinka, Auschwitz, and elsewhere), Polish bystanders — who make no attempt to hide their past or anti-Semitism — and a handful of "former" Nazi officials, recall the Holocaust. Under Lanzmann's unwavering and detailed questioning, they reveal the barbarism of the atrocities and the minutiae of the planning that went into the Final Solution. The nightmarish conditions of the Warsaw ghetto are described and harrowing stories told. Lanzmann spent 10 years travelling and visiting the scenes of the crimes to amass his towering document, edited down from 350 hours of film. No archival footage is used in this terrible testimony, which is made all the more powerful for it.

An eyewitness *arrives at Treblinka by train, one of many who recount the horror and tragedy of* Shoah *(an Israeli word meaning "catastrophic upheaval").*

A Room with a View | James Ivory | 1985

The first (and best) of three adaptations of E.M. Forster novels filmed by director James Ivory, producer Ismail Merchant, and screenwriter Ruth Prawer Jhabvala, *A Room with a View* perfectly captures Forster's wit and idiom.

There was an ideal coming together when Ivory met Forster. *A Room with a View*, *Maurice* (1987), and *Howard's End* (1991) deal with the stultifying, hypocritical restrictions of Edwardian society. In *A Room with a View*, sheltered Lucy (Helena Bonham Carter), holidaying in Florence with her chaperone Charlotte (Maggie Smith), is kissed by bohemian George (Julian Sands). Back in England, she seems to settle for stuffy Cecil Vyse (Daniel Day-Lewis) although she really loves George. Ivory vividly contrasts the untamed landscape of Italy, which triggers Lucy's sexual awakening with the dampening effect of pastoral England.

Lucy Honeychurch *(Helena Bonham Carter) falls under the spell of Italy with free-spirited George Emerson (Julian Sands) in a lush field outside Florence.*

CREDITS	
production	Merchant-Ivory, Goldcrest
producer	Ismail Merchant
screenplay	Ruth Prawer Jhabvala from the novel by E.M. Forster
cinematography	Tony Pierce-Roberts
awards	Academy Awards: Best Adapted Screenplay, Best Art Direction (Gianni Quaranta, Brian Ackland-Snow, Brian Savagar, Elio Altramura), Best Costume Design (Jenny Beavan, John Bright)

Women on the Verge of a Nervous Breakdown | Pedro Almodóvar | 1988

Lucía (Julieta Serrano), *determined to kill her unfaithful husband, brandishes twin pistols in the "other woman's" apartment.*

Although Pedro Almodóvar had previously made seven features, it was this anarchic farce that broke through the barriers, becoming 1989's highest-grossing foreign film in North America and the most successful film ever in Spain, where it is called *Mujeres al borde de un ataque de nervios*.

Pepa — a smouldering Carmen Maura — is a volatile and attractive television actress who is pregnant by Iván (Fernando Guillén), her married philandering lover. Unaware of her condition, he blithely abandons her, leaving a message on her answering machine. As all her efforts to contact him fail, Pepa grows more and more hysterical, and is precipitated into a series of increasingly bizarre and surreal situations. As in the best of farces, the film's arrangement of irrational events is held together by an internal logic that is very funny, and, like many a French bedroom farce, most of the action takes place in one setting — Pepa's smart Madrid penthouse apartment, which becomes overpopulated with eccentric, desperate women. Among them is Iván's deranged wife Lucía (Julieta Serrano), intent on taking revenge on her husband, and Pepa's best friend Candela, who has fallen in love with a terrorist. Also making an appearance is the young, bespectacled Antonio Banderas as Carlos, Iván's 20-year-old son. There is a feminist message beneath the comic events, played out in true screwball comedy style, as all the women are frustrated by the childish egotism of the men with whom they get involved. Audiences were mainly attracted by Almodovar's campy brand of humor and distinctive visual style that was influenced by 1950s' Hollywood.

Spanish film poster

CREDITS	
production	Rank, El Deseo, Laurenfilm, Orion
producer	Pedro Almodóvar
screenplay	Pedro Almodóvar
cinematography	José Luis Alcaine
music	Bernardo Bonezzi

Cinema Paradiso | Giuseppe Tornatore | 1989

This heartwarming, nostalgic film looks at the lure of cinema and the death of the picture palace through the eyes of a child. Understandably, *Cinema Paradiso* has become one of the most popular Italian films of the last few decades, both outside and inside Italy.

Salvatore *(Salvatore Cascio as the young boy) learns how to edit films and run the projector from his mentor, Alfredo (Philippe Noiret).*

The story, told in flashbacks, of Salvatore (Salvatore Cascio), a little boy who lives with his harassed widowed mother in the grimness of a small, war-torn Sicilian village, and finds refuge from the daily misery of life by sneaking into Nuovo Cinema Paradiso, the local cinema hall. The projectionist, Alfredo (Philippe Noiret), soon becomes his friend and teacher. When Alfredo is blinded in a fire, he teaches the boy to take over his job, but ultimately encourages him to leave the stifling confines of the village. In his teens, Salvatore falls in love with a banker's daughter, Elena (Agnese Nano), and wins her over by taking Alfredo's advice to stand outside her window every night. Years later, when Salvatore (Jacques Perrin) has become a successful film-maker, he watches a montage, bequeathed to him by Alfredo, of all the scenes of kisses from the films shown at the Paradiso over the years — scenes that the priest (Leopoldo Trieste) of Salvatore's village insisted were cut from the movies. A poignant reminder, helped by Ennio Morricone's haunting musical score, of how personal the cinema experience can be, *Cinema Paradiso* is a film that stirs memories of childhood.

Father figure *Alfredo with the child, Salvatore, cycles down a village pathway in Sicily.*

CREDITS	
production	Cristaldifilm, Ariane, RAI, TF1
producers	Franco Cristaldi, Giovanna Romagnoli
screenplay	Giuseppe Tornatore
cinematography	Blasco Giurato
music	Ennio Morricone
awards	Cannes: Special Jury Prize; Academy Award: Best Foreign Film

Do the Right Thing | Spike Lee | 1989

A high watermark in US independent cinema and certainly the most important African-American film to date, Spike Lee's third feature is a stylized, provocative distillation of racial tensions in Brooklyn, New York, towards the end of the 20th century.

Film poster

Set over the course of a sweltering summer day, the film follows Mookie, a pizza delivery boy played by Lee himself, as he goes about the neighborhood. Along the way we encounter various black and Hispanic youths, such as Radio Raheem (Bill Nunn) and Buggin' Out (Giancarlo Esposito), their elders (Ossie Davis and Ruby Dee), and Mookie's employers at the pizzeria, Sal (Danny Aiello) and his sons, the racist Pino (John Turturro) and color-blind Vito (Richard Edson). Shot in bold, heavily saturated colors and using a blaring rap soundtrack (with band Public Enemy's "Fight the Power" prominent), the film bristles with energy and purpose. Tapping a rich vein of street comedy, Lee confronts racist attitudes before magnifying the tensions in a morally ambiguous climax reflecting contemporary controversies over police brutality. Although derided as inflammatory by some, the film is vibrant and searching.

CREDITS	
production	40 Acres/Mule Filmworks
producer	John Kilick, Spike Lee, Monty Ross
screenplay	Spike Lee
cinematography	Ernest R. Dickerson

Strolling in Brooklyn, *Bill Nunn as Radio Raheem, a quiet, easygoing character, prefers his boom box to do the talking for him.*

Raise the Red Lantern | Zhang Yimou | 1991

One of the first Chinese films to be widely shown in the west, *Raise the Red Lantern* (*Dahong Denglong Gaogao Gua*) was a great success. This can be ascribed to the gripping, humanistic story it tells, its exoticism, stunning visual imagery, and the radiant, stately beauty of its star, Gong Li, who was director Zhang Yimou's muse.

Gong Li *plays Songlian, the beautiful new bride of a feudal patriarch. Here she is bathed in the rich glow of the red lanterns in her bedroom, as she waits for her husband to come to her.*

CREDITS	
production	Century Communications, Era International, China Film, Salon Films
producers	Chiu Fu-Sheng, Hou Xiaoxian, Zhang Wenze
screenplay	Ni Zhen based on a short story *Wives and Concubines* by Su Tong
cinematography	Zhao Fei, Yang Lun

In the China of the 1920s, Songlian (Gong Li) becomes the fourth wife of Master Chen (Jingwu Ma), a rich and powerful landowner. It is the patriarch's tradition to light red lanterns outside the house of the wife he intends to join for the night. Most of the film takes place within one small compound where all four wives become rivals for their master's attentions. Intrigue and scheming mark the relationships between the wives and the young Songlian soon learns that she has to fight for her status in the convoluted domestic set-up. The house is seen through the seasons of a year, with the interiors of the four apartments in vibrant reds, oranges, and yellows, in spaces marked out for passion. The Chinese government banned the film from its homeland. The authorities obviously saw that, beneath the surface story, there is a parable of an authoritarian government, represented by the master, who allows no freedom of expression to the individual, represented here by Songlian.

Unforgiven | Clint Eastwood | 1992

The film that finally gave its director Oscar recognition after 40 years in the business, *Unforgiven* is a gripping Western, a genre in which Clint Eastwood made his name. In returning to the moral and thematic roots of the genre, the veteran actor gave the Western film a kiss of life.

Avenger *Bill Munny (Clint Eastwood) is tormented by memories of his past crimes, but when the sheriff kills his friend Ned, he forgets his remorse and goes on a blood-spattering killing spree.*

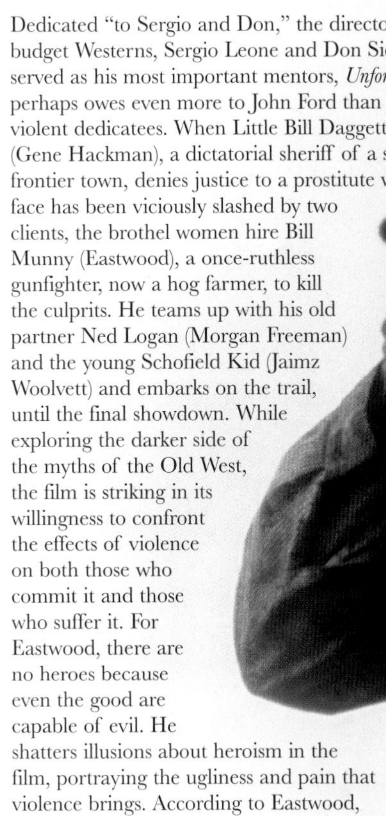

Dedicated "to Sergio and Don," the directors of low-budget Westerns, Sergio Leone and Don Siegel, who served as his most important mentors, *Unforgiven* perhaps owes even more to John Ford than its violent dedicatees. When Little Bill Daggett (Gene Hackman), a dictatorial sheriff of a small frontier town, denies justice to a prostitute whose face has been viciously slashed by two clients, the brothel women hire Bill Munny (Eastwood), a once-ruthless gunfighter, now a hog farmer, to kill the culprits. He teams up with his old partner Ned Logan (Morgan Freeman) and the young Schofield Kid (Jaimz Woolvett) and embarks on the trail, until the final showdown. While exploring the darker side of the myths of the Old West, the film is striking in its willingness to confront the effects of violence on both those who commit it and those who suffer it. For Eastwood, there are no heroes because even the good are capable of evil. He shatters illusions about heroism in the film, portraying the ugliness and pain that violence brings. According to Eastwood, *Unforgiven* "summarized everything I feel about the Western. The moral is the concern with gunplay."

CREDITS	
studio	Warner Bros.
producer	Clint Eastwood
screenplay	David Webb Peoples
cinematography	Jack N. Green
art direction	Janice Blackie-Goodine, Henry Bumstead
awards	Academy awards: Best Picture, Best Director, Best Supporting Actor (Gene Hackman), Best Editing (Joel Cox)

Reservoir Dogs | Quentin Tarantino | 1992

For many, the most distinctive and exciting voice to emerge in US movies in the 1990s, Quentin Tarantino announced himself with this bravura crime thriller. Smaller in scale than his subsequent output, *Reservoir Dogs* features the elements that would become fully-formed Tarantino staples.

Beginning in the middle of the story of a failed diamond robbery, and carving it into a series of chapters introducing each of the gangsters in turn, Tarantino borrows from the heist movie catalog — Stanley Kubrick's *The Killing*, Ringo Lam's *City on Fire*, and the underworld milieu of Jean-Pierre Melville — all but omitting the robbery itself. The aftermath is a bloody trial of conflicting loyalties and festering suspicions as the crooks convene to figure out what (or who) went wrong.

Tarantino's profane, pop-littered dialogue puts its own ironic spin on things — these heavies talk like movie-obsessed ordinary people, not like gangsters, but it is the disquieting ease with which post-modern cool shifts to blood-soaked violence, making it easy to overlook the emotional pain beneath, that caused a stir at the time.

Steve Buscemi *(on the floor) as Mr Pink and Harvey Keitel as Larry Dimmick alias Mr White, in the climactic shoot-out in a warehouse.*

Film poster, 1992

CREDITS	
production	Live Entertainment/Dog Eat Dog
producer	Lawrence Bender
screenplay	Quentin Tarantino
cinematography	Andrzej Sekula

Three Colors: Blue, White, and Red | Kryztof Kieslowski | 1993, 1994

The colors of the titles of Krzystof Kieslowski's trilogy, the Polish director's final work, refer to the colors of the French flag, while the themes are allied to the French revolutionary slogan "Liberty, Equality, Fraternity". All three films offer sensual, emotional, and spiritual experiences rarely so well depicted in contemporary cinema.

The trilogy is about people separated from those they love, but are different in tone, moving from meditative drama (*Blue*), through oblique social comedy (*White*), to a symbolic mystery-romance (*Red*). In *Blue*, after the deaths of her composer husband and young daughter in a car crash, Julie (Juliette Binoche) seeks to free herself from everyone and everything that reminds her of her past. In *White*, Polish hairdresser Karol (Zbigniew Zamachowski), returning to his homeland, makes a success of his life, aiming to avenge himself on the wife who spurned him. In *Red*, Valentine (Irène Jacob), a model, develops a relationship with an elderly, cynical judge Joseph Kern (Jean-Louis Trintignant). Kieslowski's stylish visuals and use of locations are a fitting epitaph to one of Europe's best directors.

In Red, which explores the nuances *of fraternity and platonic love, Valentine (Irène Jacob) models for a poster that visually illustrates the film's theme of loneliness.*

CREDITS	
production	CED, Canal +, Eurimages, France 3 Cinéma, MK2, TOR, TSR
producer	Marin Karmitz
screenplays	Agnieszka Holland, Slavomir Idziak, Kieslowski, Krzysztof Pisiewicz, Edward Zebrowski
cinematography	Slowomir Idziak (*Blue*), Edward Klosinski (*White*), Piotr Sobocinski (*Red*)
music	Zbigniew Preisner

In Blue, Kieslowski's film *about the imperfection of human liberty, Julie (Juliette Binoche) reflects on her vain search for freedom from the past.*

Through the Olive Trees | Abbas Kiarostami | 1994

Although Abbas Kiarostami had been making feature films since 1974, it was only in the 1990s with *Through the Olive Trees (Zire darakhatan zeyton)* that he was recognized as the leading force behind the extraordinary flood of Iranian films of quality that began to win prizes at international film festivals.

In 1992, Kiarostami made *And Life Goes On*, about a film being made on the survivors of an earthquake in Iran. *Through the Olive Trees*, set in the same area, is a comedy about a director casting and filming another film. The most fascinating aspect of this film-within-a-film is that the audience never knows what is real and what is fiction. The celebrated final sequence follows the two main actors, who are having a "real life" romance, in extreme long shot as the boy persuades the girl to marry him. The film, at once simple and complex, intimate and distant, is full of insights into film-making, society, and human relationships.

Fifteen-year-old Tahereh Ladanian *plays herself; here she is on the balcony of her grandmother's house, listening to pledges of love from her co-star Hossein Rezai (out of shot).*

CREDITS	
studio	Abbas Kiarostami productions, CiBy 2000, Farabi Cinema Foundation, Miramax
producer	Abbas Kiarostami
screenwriter	Abbas Kiarostami
cinematography	Hossein Djafarian, Farhad Saba

Four Weddings and a Funeral | Mike Newell | 1994

After the highs and lows that British cinema went through in the 1970s and 80s, it was this romantic comedy that hit the jackpot and made an international star of Hugh Grant.

Fashioned around an ingenious structural conceit, Richard Curtis's deftly polished script is a love story filtered across several months and five ceremonies. At the first wedding, the chronically self-effacing Charles (Grant) is surprised to find himself flirting with Carrie, a forthright American (Andie MacDowell) who is engaged to another man. Subsequent encounters only go to prove that "the course of true love never did run smooth." Reminiscent of the screwball comedies of the 1930s in its depiction of a wealthy class of socialites unencumbered with any cares but their own embarrassments, the film is an artful comedy of exquisite manners. Grant and Curtis reteamed with production outfit Working Title for *Notting Hill*, *Bridget Jones's Diary*, and *Love Actually*, all of them popular hits at home and abroad.

The habitually late Charles *(Hugh Grant) and room-mate Scarlett (Charlotte Coleman) race to the wedding of a friend, where Charles has been asked to be best man.*

CREDITS	
production	Channel Four/Polygram/Working Title
producers	Tim Bevan, Richard Curtis, Eric Fellner, Duncan Kenworthy
screenplay	Richard Curtis
cinematography	Michael Coulter

Toy Story | John Lasseter | 1995

The idea that a studio brand might define the quality and characteristics of a film bearing its logo disappeared in the 1950s. But starting with *Toy Story,* Pixar was an exception to this rule. It revitalized the form of digital animated technology, becoming a hallmark for witty, sophisticated productions.

CREDITS	
studio	Buena Vista/Walt Disney/Pixar
producer	Bonnie Arnold, Ed Catmull, Ralph Guggenheim, Steve Jobs
screenplay	Joss Whedon, Andrew Stanton, Joel Cohen and Alec Sokolow
awards	Academy award: Special achievement (John Lasseter)

The first feature-length blockbuster produced by the Pixar studio, a pioneer of computer-animated films in the mid-1980s, was *Toy Story*, which was also its first feature to be released in theaters. Based on one of director John Lasseter's earlier shorts, the story is about toys in the room of Andy, a six-year-old boy. Woody (voiced by Tom Hanks) is a cowboy toy and the favorite game in town — until his friend Andy gets a new Buzz Lightyear doll (voiced by Tim Allen) for his birthday and Woody finds himself gathering dust with the rest of Andy's cast-offs. Consumed with jealousy, he tries to get rid of his naïve rival — who still believes he really is a space explorer in some brave new world.

Lasseter's computer generated animation has a synthetic texture that is well suited to the subject of *Toy Story*, but also displays a fluidity and dynamism that the old animation style cannot match. However, Pixar's strengths go back to the drawing board: a rich story sense, fresh perspectives, and unforgettable characters created imaginatively and with originality. Pixar developed a corporate culture that nourished creativity and was rewarded with one hit film after another: *A Bug's Life* (1998), *Toy Story 2* (1999), *Monsters, Inc.* (2001), *Finding Nemo* (2003), and *The Incredibles* (2004).

Cowboy Woody *pretends to be friendly with Buzz Lightyear, a fancy high-tech action figure dressed in a spacesuit and outfittted with gadgets; the pretence is necessary because Woody feels threatened by Buzz.*

Fargo | Joel Coen | 1996

Brothers Joel and Ethan Coen hit the big time with their sixth film, *Fargo*, a cleverly plotted thriller effectively set in Minnesota "the abstract landscape of our childhood — a bleak, windswept tundra, resembling Siberia except for its Ford dealerships, and Hardee's restaurants."

Film poster, 1996

A desperate Minneapolis car dealer, Jerry Lundegaard (William H. Macy), in financial difficulties, hires two petty gangsters, Carl Showalter and Gaear Grimsrud (Steve Buscemi and Peter Stormare) to kidnap his wife so that his rich father-in-law Wade Gustafson (Harve Presnell) will pay a huge ransom. He plans to split the money with the kidnappers, but things go awfully wrong when they kill a state trooper, a murder which police chief Marge Gunderson (Oscar-winning Frances McDormand, Joel Coen's wife), seven months pregnant, investigates. Even though morning sickness overwhelms her, she conducts the murder investigation with astute aplomb. The role of Marge, played brilliantly by McDormand, is probably the best (and warmest) female part written by the Coens. The film, superbly photographed against a snowy background, moves seamlessly between black humor, violent crime drama, and genial comedy, while telling a good yarn. The semi-stylized dialogue, so important to the Coens' films, is here given another dimension by the "yah-yah" rhythms of the local Minnesotan dialect.

CREDITS	
production	Polygram/Gramercy/Working Title
producer	Ethan Coen
screenplay	Joel Coen, Ethan Coen
cinematography	Roger Deakins
music	Carter Burwell
awards	Cannes: Best Director; Academy Awards: Best Actress (Frances McDormand), Best Screenplay

Marge Gunderson *(Frances McDormand), chief of police, bends down in the snow to examine the scene of the crime after a shoot-out that kills a state trooper.*

Crouching Tiger, Hidden Dragon | Ang Lee | 2000

Posing as a warrior, *Ziyi Zhang as Jiao Long fights several men at once at a wayside station; her fiery passion shows that her fight is also for respect in a man's world.*

The Chinese tradition of *wuxia* storytelling combines swordplay, martial arts, and Tao Buddhist philosophy. The movies' greatest exponent of the form was the Hong Kong director King Hu, to whom Ang Lee pays tribute in this sweeping and romantic action film. This was the first Chinese language film to become a worldwide hit, making more than $100 million in North America alone.

Produced by Sony, the Japanese company, through Columbia, its Hollywood division — but with Chinese and European co-financing, a Taiwanese-born, US-based director, and both American and Chinese screenwriters — *Crouching Tiger, Hidden Dragon* was global entertainment not centered on the American dream — perhaps a sign of things to come. Measured and flamboyant, the movie pits a reckless, young couple Jiao Long and Luo Xiao Hu (Ziyi Zhang and Chen Chang) against two older, wiser souls, Yu Shu Lien and Li Mu Bai (Michelle Yeoh and Yun-Fat Chow) battling it out over love, duty, and the priceless jade sword "Green Destiny." For many western audiences, this was their first exposure to Hong Kong cinema's gravity-defying wire-work, a craft enabling swordsmen not just to leap through the air but to bound over rooftops. The climax is a duel between Chow and Zhang high among swaying bamboo trees, a scene at once perilous and mysteriously romantic. This scene was choreographed by Yuen Wo Ping, the kung-fu director who helped realize the director Ang Lee's vision.

Film poster, 2000

CREDITS	
production	Columbia Tristar
producers	Li-Kong Hsu, William Kong, Ang Lee
screenplay	Hui-Ling Wang, James Schamus, Kuo Jung Tsai
cinematography	Peter Pau

In the Mood for Love | Wong Kar Wai | 2000

A touching, atmospheric romance of unconsummated love, Wong Kar Wai's *In the Mood for Love (Fa yeung nin wa)* is set in a dreamy, impressionistic evocation of Hong Kong in 1962, and stars Tony Leung and Maggie Cheung, two of Asia's biggest stars.

Chow Mo-wan (Leung) and Su Li-zhen (Cheung) have rented rooms next to each other. They fall in love while trying to deal with the infidelities of their respective spouses whom they discover are involved with each other. Adultery has desecrated their lives: "For us to do the same thing, would mean we are no better than they are," Cheung says. What is unusual in a film about adultery is that we only see the wronged couple and not the adulterers. As the English title suggests, *In the Mood For Love* is a mood piece with nostalgic music in the background. Wong's skill in recreating Hong Kong of the 1960s is so assured that it is surprising to discover that the film was actually shot in Bangkok.

Maggie Cheung *and Tony Leung play two reluctant lovers struggling to repress their passion for each other. Christopher Doyle, Wong's favorite cameraman, imbued the film with deep colors of red, yellow, and brown.*

CREDITS

production	Block 2, Jet Tone, Paradis Films
producer	Wong Kar Wai
screenplay	Wong Kar Wai
cinematography	Christopher Doyle, Mark Lee Ping-bin
original music	Michael Galasso, Shigeru Umebayashi
production design	William Chang

Traffic | Steven Soderbergh | 2000

Unsuspecting Helena Ayala *(Catherine Zeta-Jones) and her young son watch in disbelief as federal agents arrest her husband, a high-level drug trafficker.*

CREDITS

production	Entertainment/USA Films
producer	Philip Messina
screenplay	Steven Gaghan
cinematography	Steven Soderbergh
awards	Academy Awards: Best Actor in a supporting role (Benicio del Toro), Best Director (Steven Soderbergh), Best Editing (Stephen Mirrione), Best Screenplay based on previous material (Stephen Gaghan).

At a time when American cinema seemed increasingly decadent and detached from the real world, director Steven Soderbergh took on the challenge of mapping out the drugs trade in this panoramic, multi-strand drama.

In Washington, the US President's drug czar, Robert Wakefield (Michael Douglas), plans a renewed "war on drugs," not suspecting that his teenage daughter is addicted to heroin. In San Diego, Helena (Catherine Zeta-Jones) is shocked when her husband Carlos (Steven Bauer) is arrested for trafficking — but realizes that the only way to preserve her standard of life is to carry on where he left off. Meanwhile, Tijuana cop Javier (Benicio Del Toro) puts his life on the line to enforce the law even as his superiors profit from smuggling. Inspired by a British television series but reconceived in American terms by Steven Gaghan, *Traffic* was one of a number of millennial movies that adopted a multi-story structure to address a bewildering sense of individual powerlessness.

Lord of the Rings | Peter Jackson | 2001, 2002, 2003

Released in three parts but filmed concurrently (with some additional shooting along the way), Peter Jackson's adaptation of J.R.R. Tolkien's saga of the land called Middle Earth was a massive undertaking, and a critical and commercial triumph. Using computerized special effects with great artistry, Jackson redefined the word "epic." For scale and spectacle, cinema-goers had never seen anything like it.

Immersing himself in Tolkien's richly imagined primordial world, inhabited by hobbits, elves, and other strange creatures, director Jackson exploits the natural wonder of his native New Zealand to full advantage and gets the details just right. But he never tarries for long — there are too many mountains, rivers, and valleys to traverse, armies to muster, and spells to cast. The narrative moves at a relentless pace as Frodo Baggins (Elijah Wood), a hobbit, is given a ring that gives its wearer great power. But is too dangerous to keep so Frodo has to travel with his friend Sam (Sean Astin) to Mordor, the only place where the ring can be destroyed. Understood as an anti-fascist allegory when Tolkien wrote it, *The Lord of the Rings* took on an unwelcome militaristic zeal when it was released during US campaigns in Afghanistan and Iraq, yet at root it remains a tribute to the resource and pluck of common men confronted with the evil lure of absolute power. In the grotesque, schizophrenic swamp creature Gollum, Jackson and actor Andy Serkis created a compelling character, computer-generated yet imbued with humanity.

Ian McKellen *plays Gandalf, the wizard who guides Frodo in his quest to destroy the evil ring; McKellen was nominated for an Academy Award for his performance.*

CREDITS	
production	Entertainment/New Line/Wingnut (Barrie M. Osborne, Peter Jackson, Fran Walsh)
producer	Grant Major
screenplay	Peter Jackson and Fran Walsh
cinematography	Andrew Lesnie
awards	11 Academy Awards for *The Return of the King,* including Best Director (Peter Jackson), Best Picture (Barrie M. Osborne, Peter Jackson, Fran Walsh), Best Art Direction (Grant Major, Dan Hennah, Alan Lee), Best Costume Design (Ngila Dickson, Richard Taylor), Best Editing (Jamie Selkirk).

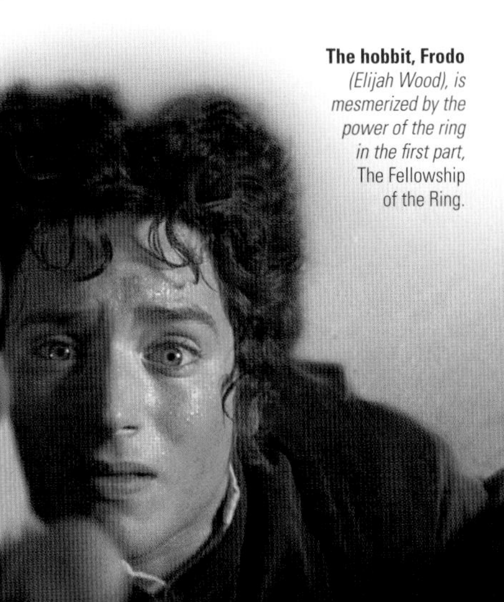

The hobbit, Frodo *(Elijah Wood), is mesmerized by the power of the ring in the first part,* The Fellowship of the Ring.

City of God | Fernando Meirelles | 2002

This searing, anecdotal account of growing up in the slums of Rio de Janeiro, Brazil, has a startling immediacy and a punchdrunk, charged camera style that leaves you reeling.

CREDITS	
studio	O2/Video Filmes
producer	Andrea Barata Ribeiro
screenplay	Bráulio Mantovani
cinematography	César Charlone

Working with a group of young non-professionals in front of the camera and creating episodes based on true stories, co-directors Fernando Meirelles and Kátia Lund recreate 15 years in the downward spiral of crime in Cidade de Deus, a Brazilian shantytown (*favela*) from the late 1960s to the 1980s. During this time, the cocaine trade had emerged in Brazil — and the *favelas* become the hideouts of drug gangs. Meirelles and Lund portray children growing up in these violence-ridden slums. They graduate from reckless but amusing hijinks to the ruthless terrorism of their neighborhood, with a new generation of preteen sociopaths following hard on their heels. The narrator of the film's story, Rocket (Alexandre Rodrigues), a poor boy, escapes life in the gangs by virtue of his criminal ineptitude and his passion for photography. It is his one-time friend Li'l Zé (Leandro Firmino), known as Li'l Dice (Douglas Silva) in the 1960s, who becomes a vicious, cold-hearted drug lord — with Rocket as his reluctant court photographer.

This powerful and fast-paced epic speaks the brutal language of the streets — in this respect, it is reminiscent of Martin Scorsese's *GoodFellas* and the Wachowski brothers' *The Matrix*. The film is a masterful depiction of urban violence and the chaotic combination of drugs, guns, and teenagers, and successfully portrays the horror of life in the *favelas*.

Film poster, 2002

This scene captures the violence *of life in a* favela, *as teenaged gangsters are chased by a rival gang down a street.*

Eternal Sunshine of the Spotless Mind | Michel Gondry | 2004

Clementine (Winslet) *with Joel (Carrey), who is reliving their first date on the frozen Charles river; her orange dyed hair indicates the scene is a memory of time gone by.*

This brainteaser of a love story proves there is something new under the sun. A successful second film from the screenwriter Charlie Kaufman (*Being John Malkovich*; *Adaptation*) and the inventive French pop video director Michel Gondry, *Eternal Sunshine of the Spotless Mind* drops you smack into an evaporating consciousness and demands that you make sense of what you are seeing.

Joel (Jim Carrey) gets on a train in the wrong direction and meets Clementine (Kate Winslet). He is reserved and conventional, while she is impulsive and extroverted. There is attraction, then there is heartache, resentment, and so much pain that they wonder if they ever really knew each other at all. If he could wipe all traces of her out of his mind Joel would do it — he can and he does, in this romantic comedy about memory erasure.

Original thinkers are rare in the movie business but Charlie Kaufman really does project out of the box. The theme of amnesia is hardly unfamiliar, and the notion of a firm — Lacuna, Inc. — specializing in memory loss is reminiscent of Philip K. Dick's science fiction. But the film's subjective stream of lucid and unconscious imagery is something else again — it is as if the movie is reinventing itself as it goes along.

CREDITS

production	Focus Features/Anonymous Content/This is That
producers	Anthony Bregman, Steve Golin
screenplay	Charlie Kaufman
cinematography	Ellen Kuras
awards	Academy Awards: Best Writing, Screenplay written for the screen (Charlie Kaufman, Michel Gondry, Pierre Bismuth)

KATE WINSLET

Although British actress Kate Winslet (born 1975) is most well known for her role as the rich American girl in love with poor boy Leonardo di Caprio in James Cameron's blockbuster *Titanic* (1997), she had already established herself in classical English parts. Winslet made a spirited Marianne Dashwood in Ang Lee's *Sense and Sensibility* (1995), was luminous as Sue Bridehead in Michael Winterbottom's *Jude* (1996), and was a poignant Ophelia in Kenneth Branagh's *Hamlet* (1996). She first made an impact in Peter Jackson's *Heavenly Creatures* (1994).

Reference

This section provides facts and figures from the world's greatest awards ceremonies, including the Academy Awards, or the Oscars, in the US, the BAFTA awards in the UK, and the most prestigious film festival of them all—Cannes, in France.

THE ACADEMY AWARDS

The best-known of all the awards ceremonies, the Oscars are watched by millions worldwide. Presented annually in Hollywood, they have a huge influence on the fortunes of the films involved.

ACADEMY AWARD WINNERS—BEST FILM

1927/8	Wings
1928/9	The Broadway Melody
1929/30	All Quiet on the Western Front
1930/1	Cimarron
1931/2	Grand Hotel
1932/3	Cavalcade
1934	It Happened One Night
1935	Mutiny on the Bounty
1936	The Great Ziegfeld
1937	The Life of Emile Zola
1938	You Can't Take It with You
1939	Gone With the Wind
1940	Rebecca
1941	How Green Was My Valley
1942	Mrs. Miniver
1943	Casablanca
1944	Going My Way
1945	The Lost Weekend
1946	The Best Years of Our Lives
1947	Gentleman's Agreement
1948	Hamlet
1949	All the King's Men
1950	All About Eve
1951	An American in Paris
1952	The Greatest Show on Earth
1953	From Here to Eternity
1954	On the Waterfront
1955	Marty
1956	Around the World in 80 Days
1957	The Bridge on the River Kwai
1958	Gigi
1959	Ben-Hur
1960	The Apartment
1961	West Side Story
1962	Lawrence of Arabia
1963	Tom Jones
1964	My Fair Lady
1965	The Sound of Music
1966	A Man for All Seasons
1967	In the Heat of the Night
1968	Oliver!
1969	Midnight Cowboy
1970	Patton
1971	The French Connection
1972	The Godfather
1973	The Sting
1974	The Godfather Part II
1975	One Flew Over the Cuckoo's Nest
1976	Rocky
1977	Annie Hall
1978	The Deer Hunter
1979	Kramer vs. Kramer
1980	Ordinary People
1981	Chariots of Fire
1982	Gandhi
1983	Terms of Endearment
1984	Amadeus
1985	Out of Africa
1986	Platoon
1987	The Last Emperor
1988	Rain Man
1989	Driving Miss Daisy
1990	Dances with Wolves
1991	The Silence of the Lambs
1992	Unforgiven
1993	Schindler's List
1994	Forrest Gump
1995	Braveheart
1996	The English Patient
1997	Titanic
1998	Shakespeare in Love
1999	American Beauty
2000	Gladiator
2001	A Beautiful Mind
2002	Chicago
2003	Lord of the Rings: The Return of the King
2004	Million Dollar Baby
2005	Crash

FILMS WITH MOST ACADEMY AWARDS

11 awards	Ben-Hur (1959), Titanic (1997), The Lord of the Rings: The Return of the King (2003)
10 awards	West Side Story (1961)
9 awards	Gigi (1958), The Last Emperor (1987), The English Patient (1996)
8 awards	Gone With the Wind (1939), From Here to Eternity (1953), On the Waterfront (1954), My Fair Lady (1964), Cabaret (1972), Gandhi (1982), Amadeus (1984)
7 awards	Going my Way (1944), The Best Years of Our Lives (1946), The Bridge on the River Kwai (1957), Lawrence of Arabia (1962), Patton (1970), The Sting (1973), Out of Africa (1985), Dances with Wolves (1990), Schindler's List (1993), Shakespeare in Love (1998)

ACADEMY AWARD WINNERS—DIRECTORS

1927/8 Frank Borzage *Seventh Heaven*
1928/9 Frank Lloyd *The Divine Lady*
1929/30 Lewis Milestone *All Quiet on the Western Front*
1930/1 Norman Taurog *Skippy*
1931/2 Frank Borzage *Bad Girl*
1932/3 Frank Lloyd *Cavalcade*
1934 Frank Capra *It Happened One Night*
1935 John Ford *The Informer*
1936 Frank Capra *Mr. Deeds Goes to Town*
1937 Leo McCarey *The Awful Truth*
1938 Frank Capra *You Can't Take It with You*
1939 Victor Fleming *Gone With the Wind*
1940 John Ford *The Grapes of Wrath*
1941 John Ford *How Green Was My Valley*
1942 William Wyler *Mrs. Miniver*
1943 Michael Curtiz *Casablanca*
1944 Leo McCarey *Going My Way*
1945 Billy Wilder *The Lost Weekend*
1946 William Wyler *The Best Years of Our Lives*
1947 Elia Kazan *Gentleman's Agreement*
1948 John Huston *The Treasure of the Sierra Madre*
1949 Joseph L. Mankiewicz *A Letter to Three Wives*
1950 Joseph L. Mankiewicz *All About Eve*
1951 George Stevens *A Place in the Sun*
1952 John Ford *The Quiet Man*
1953 Fred Zinnemann *From Here to Eternity*
1954 Elia Kazan *On the Waterfront*
1955 Delbert Mann *Marty*
1956 George Stevens *Giant*
1957 David Lean *The Bridge on the River Kwai*
1958 Vincente Minnelli *Gigi*
1959 William Wyler *Ben-Hur*
1960 Billy Wilder *The Apartment*
1961 Jerome Robbins, Robert Wise *West Side Story*
1962 David Lean *Lawrence of Arabia*
1963 Tony Richardson *Tom Jones*
1964 George Cukor *My Fair Lady*
1965 Robert Wise *The Sound of Music*
1966 Fred Zinnemann *A Man for All Seasons*
1967 Mike Nichols *The Graduate*
1968 Carol Reed *Oliver!*
1969 John Schlesinger *Midnight Cowboy*
1970 Franklin J. Schaffner *Patton*
1971 William Friedkin *The French Connection*
1972 Bob Fosse *Cabaret*
1973 George Roy Hill *The Sting*
1974 Francis Ford Coppola *The Godfather Part II*
1975 Milos Forman *One Flew Over the Cuckoo's Nest*
1976 John G. Avildsen *Rocky*
1977 Woody Allen *Annie Hall*
1978 Michael Cimino *The Deer Hunter*
1979 Robert Benton *Kramer vs. Kramer*
1980 Robert Redford *Ordinary People*
1981 Warren Beatty *Reds*
1982 Richard Attenborough *Gandhi*
1983 James L. Brooks *Terms of Endearment*
1984 Milos Forman *Amadeus*
1985 Sydney Pollack *Out of Africa*
1986 Oliver Stone *Platoon*
1987 Bernado Bertolucci *The Last Emperor*
1988 Barry Levinson *Rain Man*
1989 Oliver Stone *Born on the Fourth of July*
1990 Kevin Costner *Dances with Wolves*
1991 Jonathan Demme *The Silence of the Lambs*
1992 Clint Eastwood *Unforgiven*
1993 Steven Spielberg *Schindler's List*
1994 Robert Zemeckis *Forrest Gump*
1995 Mel Gibson *Braveheart*
1996 Anthony Minghella *The English Patient*
1997 James Cameron *Titanic*
1998 Steven Spielberg *Saving Private Ryan*
1999 Sam Mendes *American Beauty*
2000 Steven Soderbergh *Traffic*
2001 Ron Howard *A Beautiful Mind*
2002 Roman Polanski *The Pianist*
2003 Peter Jackson *Lord of the Rings: The Return of the King*
2004 Clint Eastwood *Million Dollar Baby*
2005 Ang Lee *Brokeback Mountain*

ACTRESSES WITH MOST NOMINATIONS

1 Meryl Streep (13)
2 Katharine Hepburn (12)
3 Bette Davis (10)
4 Geraldine Page (8)
5 Ingrid Bergman, Jane Fonda, Greer Garson (7)
6 Ellen Burstyn, Deborah Kerr, Jessica Lange, Vanessa Redgrave, Thelma Ritter, Norma Shearer, Maggie Smith, Sissy Spacek (6)

ACTORS WITH MOST NOMINATIONS

1 Jack Nicholson (12)
2 Laurence Olivier (10)
3 Paul Newman, Spencer Tracy (9)
4 Marlon Brando, Jack Lemmon, Al Pacino (8)
5 Richard Burton, Dustin Hoffman, Peter O'Toole (7)
6 Michael Caine, Robert De Niro, Robert Duvall (6)

ACADEMY AWARD WINNERS—BEST ACTOR

1927/8 Emil Jannings *The Last Command*
1928/9 Warner Baxter *In Old Arizona*
1929/30 George Arliss *Disraeli*
1930/31 Lionel Barrymore *A Free Soul*
1931/32 Wallace Beery *The Champ*
Fredric March *Dr. Jekyll and Mr. Hyde*
(this year there was a tie and two winners were announced)
1932/3 Charles Laughton *The Private Life of Henry VIII*
1934 Clark Gable *It Happened One Night*
1935 Victor McLagen *The Informer*
1936 Paul Muni *The Story of Louis Pasteur*
1937 Spencer Tracy *Captains Courageous*
1938 Spencer Tracy *Boys Town*
1939 Robert Donat *Goodbye Mr. Chips*
1940 James Stewart *The Philadelphia Story*
1941 Gary Cooper *Sergeant York*
1942 James Cagney *Yankee Doodle Dandy*
1943 Paul Lukas *Watch on the Rhine*
1944 Bing Crosby *Going My Way*
1945 Ray Milland *The Lost Weekend*
1946 Fredric March *The Best Years of Our Lives*
1947 Ronald Colman *A Double Life*
1948 Lawrence Olivier *Hamlet*
1949 Broderick Crawford *All the King's Men*
1950 José Ferrer *Cyrano de Bergerac*
1951 Humphrey Bogart *The African Queen*
1952 Gary Cooper *High Noon*
1953 William Holden *Stalag 17*
1954 Marlon Brando *On the Waterfront*
1955 Ernest Borgnine *Marty*
1956 Yul Brynner *The King and I*
1957 Alec Guinness *The Bridge on the River Kwai*
1958 David Niven *Separate Tables*
1959 Charlton Heston *Ben-Hur*
1960 Burt Lancaster *Elmer Gantry*
1961 Maximilian Schell *Judgment at Nuremberg*
1962 Gregory Peck *To Kill a Mockingbird*
1963 Sidney Poitier *Lilies of the Field*
1964 Rex Harrison *My Fair Lady*
1965 Lee Marvin *Cat Ballou*
1966 Paul Scofield *A Man for All Seasons*
1967 Rod Steiger *In the Heat of the Night*
1968 Cliff Robertson *Charly*
1969 John Wayne *True Grit*
1970 George C. Scott *Patton*
1971 Gene Hackman *The French Connection*
1972 Marlon Brando *The Godfather*
1973 Jack Lemmon *Save the Tiger*
1974 Art Carney *Harry and Tonto*
1975 Jack Nicholson *One Flew Over the Cuckoo's Nest*
1976 Peter Finch *Network*
1977 Richard Dreyfuss *The Goodbye Girl*
1978 Jon Voight *Coming Home*
1979 Dustin Hoffman *Kramer vs. Kramer*
1980 Robert De Niro *Raging Bull*
1981 Henry Fonda *On Golden Pond*
1982 Ben Kingsley *Gandhi*
1983 Robert Duvall *Tender Mercies*
1984 F. Murray Abraham *Amadeus*
1985 William Hurt *Kiss of the Spider Woman*
1986 Paul Newman *The Color of Money*
1987 Michael Douglas *Wall Street*
1988 Dustin Hoffman *Rain Man*
1989 Daniel Day Lewis *My Left Foot*
1990 Jeremy Irons *Reversal of Fortune*
1991 Anthony Hopkins *The Silence of the Lambs*
1992 Al Pacino *Scent of a Woman*
1993 Tom Hanks *Philadelphia*
1994 Tom Hanks *Forrest Gump*
1995 Nicolas Cage *Leaving Las Vegas*
1996 Geoffrey Rush *Shine*
1997 Jack Nicholson *As Good As It Gets*
1998 Roberto Benigni *Life is Beautiful*
1999 Kevin Spacey *American Beauty*
2000 Russell Crowe *Gladiator*
2001 Denzel Washington *Training Day*
2002 Adrien Brody *The Pianist*
2003 Sean Penn *Mystic River*
2004 Jamie Foxx *Ray*
2005 Phillip Seymour Hoffman *Capote*

ACADEMY AWARD WINNERS—BEST ACTRESS

1927/8 Janet Gaynor *Seventh Heaven, Stre*
1928/9 Mary Pickford *Coquette*
1929/30 Norma Shearer *The Divorcee*
1930/1 Marie Dressler *Min and Bill*
1931/2 Helen Hayes *The Sin of Madelon Claudet*
1932/3 Katharine Hepburn *Morning Glory*
1934 Claudette Colbert *It Happened One Night*
1935 Bette Davis *Dangerous*
1936 Luise Rainer *The Great Ziegfeld*
1937 Luise Rainer *The Good Earth*
1938 Bette Davis *Jezebel*
1939 Vivien Leigh *Gone With the Wind*
1940 Ginger Rogers *Kitty Foyle*
1941 Joan Fontaine *Suspicion*
1942 Greer Garson *Mrs. Miniver*
1943 Jennifer Jones *The Song of Bernadette*

ACADEMY AWARD WINNERS—BEST ACTRESS (continued)

1944	Ingrid Bergman *Gaslight*	**1975**	Louise Fletcher *One Flew Over the Cuckoo's Nest*
1945	Joan Crawford *Mildred Pierce*	**1976**	Faye Dunaway *Network*
1946	Olivia de Havilland *To Each His Own*	**1977**	Diane Keaton *Annie Hall*
1947	Loretta Young *The Farmer's Daughter*	**1978**	Jane Fonda *Coming Home*
1948	Jane Wyman *Johnny Belinda*	**1979**	Sally Field *Norma Rae*
1949	Olivia de Havilland *The Heiress*	**1980**	Sissy Spacek *Coal Miner's Daughter*
1950	Judy Holliday *Born Yesterday*	**1981**	Katharine Hepburn *On Golden Pond*
1951	Vivien Leigh *A Streetcar Named Desire*	**1982**	Meryl Streep *Sophie's Choice*
1952	Shirley Booth *Come Back Little Sheba*	**1983**	Shirley Maclaine *Terms of Endearment*
1953	Audrey Hepburn *Roman Holiday*	**1984**	Sally Field *Places in the Heart*
1954	Grace Kelly *The Country Girl*	**1985**	Geraldine Page *The Trip to Bountiful*
1955	Anna Magnani *The Rose Tattoo*	**1986**	Marlee Matlin *Children of a Lesser God*
1956	Ingrid Bergman *Anastasia*	**1987**	Cher *Moonstruck*
1957	Joanne Woodward *The Three Faces of Eve*	**1988**	Jodie Foster *The Accused*
1958	Susan Hayward *I Want to Live!*	**1989**	Jessica Tandy *Driving Miss Daisy*
1959	Simone Signoret *Room at the Top*	**1990**	Kathy Bates *Misery*
1960	Elizabeth Taylor *Butterfield 8*	**1991**	Jodie Foster *The Silence of the Lambs*
1961	Sophia Loren *Two Women*	**1992**	Emma Thompson *Howards End*
1962	Anne Bancroft *The Miracle Worker*	**1993**	Holly Hunter *The Piano*
1963	Patricia Neal *Hud*	**1994**	Jessica Lange *Blue Sky*
1964	Julie Andrews *Mary Poppins*	**1995**	Susan Sarandon *Dead Man Walking*
1965	Julie Christie *Darling*	**1996**	Frances McDormand *Fargo*
1966	Elizabeth Taylor *Who's Afraid of Virginia Woolf?*	**1997**	Helen Hunt *As Good As It Gets*
1967	Katharine Hepburn *Guess Who's Coming to Dinner*	**1998**	Gwyneth Paltrow *Shakespeare in Love*
1968	Katharine Hepburn *The Lion in Winter*	**1999**	Hilary Swank *Boys Don't Cry*
1969	Maggie Smith *The Prime of Miss Jean Brodie*	**2000**	Julia Roberts *Erin Brockovich*
1970	Glenda Jackson *Women in Love*	**2001**	Halle Berry *Monster's Ball*
1971	Jane Fonda *Klute*	**2002**	Nicole Kidman *The Hours*
1972	Liza Minnelli *Cabaret*	**2003**	Charlize Theron *Monster*
1973	Glenda Jackson *A Touch of Class*	**2004**	Hilary Swank *Million Dollar Baby*
1974	Ellen Burstyn *Alice Doesn't Live Here Anymore*	**2005**	Reese Witherspoon *Walk the Line*

THE BRITISH ACADEMY OF FILM AND TELEVISION AWARDS

Known as the BAFTAs, these awards were established in the UK in 1947 to honor international stars of stage and screen. The awards ceremony has outgrown its humble origins in a hotel room in Hyde Park, London, and the BAFTAs are now one of the film industry's most coveted awards.

BAFTA BEST FILM

1948	The Best Years of Our Lives
1949	Hamlet
1950	Bicycle Thieves
1951	All About Eve
1952	La Ronde
1953	The Sound Barrier
1954	Jeux Interdits
1955	The Wages of Fear
1956	Richard III
1957	Gervaise
1958	The Bridge on the River Kwai
1959	The Apartment
1960	Ballad of a Soldier
1961	The Apartment
1962	Ballad of a Soldier
1963	Lawrence of Arabia
1964	Tom Jones
1965	Dr Strangelove or: How I Learned to Stop Worrying and Love the Bomb
1966	My Fair Lady
1967	Who's Afraid of Virginia Woolf?
1968	A Man for All Seasons
1969	The Graduate
1970	Midnight Cowboy
1971	Butch Cassidy and the Sundance Kid
1972	Sunday, Bloody Sunday
1973	Cabaret
1974	Day for Night
1975	Lacombe Lucien
1976	Alice Doesn't Live Here Anymore

BAFTA BEST FILM (continued)

1977	One Flew Over the Cuckoo's Nest
1978	Annie Hall
1979	Julia
1980	Manhattan
1981	The Elephant Man
1982	Chariots of Fire
1983	Gandhi
1984	Educating Rita
1985	The Killing Fields
1986	The Purple Rose of Cairo
1987	A Room with a View
1988	Jean de Florette
1989	The Last Emperor
1990	Dead Poets Society
1991	GoodFellas
1992	The Commitments
1993	Howards End
1994	Schindler's List
1995	Four Weddings and a Funeral
1996	Sense and Sensibility
1997	The English Patient
1998	The Full Monty
1999	Shakespeare in Love
2000	American Beauty
2001	Gladiator
2002	The Lord of the Rings: The Fellowship of the Ring
2003	The Pianist
2004	The Lord of the Rings: The Return of the King
2005	The Aviator
2006	Brokeback Mountain

THE CANNES FILM FESTIVAL

An international film festival has been held in the French resort of Cannes every year since 1946 (apart from a couple of years when lack of funds prevented it from going ahead). Attended by writers, directors, and actors from all over Europe and the US, this glamorous festival generates a great deal of publicity—and not just for the films. Of the several prizes awarded at Cannes by a jury of movie professionals, the most valued and influential is the *Palme d'Or* (Golden Palm), which recognizes the year's Best Film.

CANNES PALMES D'OR WINNERS

1955	*Marty* (Delbert Mann, US)
1956	*Le Monde du Silence* (Jacques-Yves Cousteau and Louis Malle, France)
1957	*Friendly Persuasion* (Willian Wyler, US)
1958	*The Cranes Are Flying* (Mikhail Kalatozov, Soviet Union)
1959	*Black Orpheus* (Marcel Camus, France)
1960	*La Dolce Vita* (Federico Fellini, Italy)
1961	Joint winners: *Viridiana* (Luis Buñuel, Mexico) and *Une Aussi Longue Absence* (Henri Colpi, France, Italy)
1962	*O Pagador de Promessas* (Anselmo Duarte, Portugal)
1963	*The Leopard* (Luchino Visconti, Italy)
1975	*Chronique des Années de Braise* (Mohammed Lakhdar-Hamina, Algeria)
1976	*Taxi Driver* (Martin Scorsese, US)
1977	*Padre Padrone* (Vittorio Taviani and Paolo Taviani, Italy)
1978	*The Tree of Wooden Clogs* (Ermanno Olmi, Italy)
1979	Joint Winners: *Apocalypse Now* (Francis Ford Coppola, US) and *The Tin Drum* (Völker Schlondorff, Germany)
1980	Joint Winners: *All That Jazz* (Bob Fosse, US) and *Kagemusha* (Akira Kurosawa, Japan)
1981	*Man of Iron* (Andrzej Wajda, Poland)
1982	Joint Winners: *Missing* (Costa-Gavras, US) and *Yol* (Yilmaz Guney, Turkey)
1983	*The Ballad of Narayama* (Imamura Shohei, Japan)
1984	*Paris, Texas* (Wim Wenders, Germany)
1985	*When Father Was Away on Business* (Emir Kusturica, Yugoslavia)
1986	*The Mission* (Roland Joffé, UK)
1987	*Under Satan's Sun* (Maurice Pialat, France)
1988	*Pelle the Conquerer* (Bille August, Denmark)
1989	*sex, lies & videotape* (Steven Soderbergh, US)
1990	*Wild at Heart* (David Lynch, US)
1991	*Barton Fink* (Ethan Coen and Joel Coen, US)
1992	*Intentions* (Bille August, Sweden)
1993	Joint Winners: *Farewell My Concubine* (Chen Kaige, China) and *The Piano* (Jane Campion, Australia)
1994	*Pulp Fiction* (Quentin Tarantino, USA)
1995	*Underground* (Emir Kusturica, Yugoslavia)
1996	*Secrets and Lies* (Mike Leigh, UK)
1997	Joint Winners: *A Taste of Cherry* (Abbas Kiarostami, Iran) and *Unagi* (Imamura Shohei, Japan)
1998	*Eternity and a Day* (Theo Angelopoulos, Greece)
1999	*Rosetta* (Jean-Pierre and Luc Dardenne, France)
2000	*Dancer in the Dark* (Lars von Trier, Denmark)
2001	*The Son's Room* (Nanni Moretti, Italy)
2002	*The Pianist* (Roman Polanski, France)
2003	*Elephant* (Gus Van Sant, US)
2004	*Fahrenheit 9/11* (Michael Moore, US)
2005	*The Child* (Jean-Pierre and Luc Dardenne, Belgium)
2006	*The Wind that Shakes the Barley* (Ken Loach, UK)

THE VENICE FILM FESTIVAL

The oldest film festival in the world started in 1932 as part of the 18th Venice Biennale. The festival was not held every year and was not always competitive. Now, however, it is an annual competition held in Venice's Lido di Venezia. The top prize at the festival is the *Leone d'Oro*, or the Golden Lion, which was awarded from 1947 onwards. Before then, dual prizes were awarded to the best foreign film and the best Italian film.

GOLDEN LION AND MAJOR AWARD WINNERS

1934	*Teresa Confalonieri* (Guido Brignone, Italy), *Man of Aran* (Robert Flaherty, UK)
1935	*Casta Diva* (Carmine Gallone, Italy) *Anna Karenina* (Clarence Brown, US)
1936	*Squadrone Bianco* (Augusto Genino, Italy) *The Emperor of California* (Luis Trenker)
1937	*Scipione l'Africano* (Carmine Gallone, Italy) *Un Carnet de Bal* (Julien Duvivier, France)
1938	Luciano Serra Pilota (Goffredo Alessandrini, Italy) and *Olympia* (Leni Riefenstahl, Germany)
1940	*The Siege of Alcazar* (Augusto Genina, Italy) *Der Postmeister* (Gustav Ucicky, Germany)
1941	*La Corona di Ferro* (Alessandro Blasetti, Italy) *Ohm Krüger* (Hans Steinhoof, Germany)
1942	*Bengasi* (Augusto Genina, Italy) *Der Grosse König* (Veit Harlan, Germany)
1947	*Siréna* (Karel Steklý, Czechoslovakia) International Venice Award
1948	*Hamlet* (Laurence Olivier, UK) International Venice Award
1949	*Manon* (Henri-Georges Clouzon, France) Golden Lion
1950	*Justice est Faite* (André Cayatte) Golden Lion
1951	*Rashômon* (Akira Kurosawa, Japan)
1952	*Forbidden Games* (René Clément, France)
1953	Golden Lion not awarded
1954	*Romeo and Juliet* (Renato Castellani, Italy)
1955	*Ordet* (Carl Theodor Dreyer, Denmark)
1956	Golden Lion not awarded
1957	*Aparajito* (Satyajit Ray, India)
1958	*Muhomatsu, the Rikshaw Man* (Hiroshi Ingaki, Japan)
1959	*La Grande Guerra* (Mario Monicelli Italy), *Il Generale delle Rovere* (Roberto Rossellini, Italy)
1960	*Le Passage du Rhin* (André Cayatte, France)
1961	*L'Année Derniere à Marienbad* (Alain Resnais, France)
1962	Joint winners: *Cronaca Familiare* (Valerio Zurlini, Italy) *Ivanovo Detstvo* (Andrei Tarkovsky, Russia)
1963	*Le Mani Sulla Cittá* (Francesco Rosi, Italy)
1964	*Red Desert* (Michelangelo Antonioni, Italy)
1965	*Vaghe Stelle dell'Orsa* (Luchino Visconti, Italy)
1966	*The Battle of Algiers* (Gillo Pontecorvo, Algeria)
1967	*Belle de Jour* (Luis Buñuel, France)
1968	*Artists Under the Big Top: Perplexed* (Alexander Kluge, Germany)
1980	Joint winners: *Atlantic City* (Louis Malle, US), *Gloria* (John Cassavetes, US)
1981	*Die Bleierne Zeit (Marianne and Juliane)* (Margarethe von Trotte, Germany)
1982	*The State of Things* (Wim Wenders, Germany)
1983	*Prénom Carmen* (Jean-Luc Godard, France)
1984	*The Year of the Quiet Sun* (Krzysztof Zanussi, Poland)
1985	*Vagabond* (Agnès Varda, France)
1986	*The Green Ray* (Eric Rohmer, France)
1987	*Au Revoir, Les Enfants* (Louis Malle, France)
1988	*The Legend of the Holy Drinker* (Ermanno Olmi, Italy)
1989	*A City of Sadness* (Hou Hsiao-hsien, Taiwan)
1990	*Rosencrantz and Guildenstern are Dead* (Tom Stoppard, UK)
1991	*Urga* (Nikita Mikhalkov, Russia)
1992	*The Story of Qui Ju* (Zhang Yimou, China)
1993	Joint winners: *Short Cuts* (Robert Altman, US), *Three Colours: Blue* (Kryzsztof Kieslowski, France)
1994	Joint winners: *Vive L'Amour* (Tsai Ming-ling, Taiwan) *Before the Rain* (Milcho Manchevski, Macedonia)
1995	*Cyclo* (Anh Hung Tran, Vietnam)
1996	*Michael Collins* (Neil Jordan, UK)
1997	*Hana-bi* (Kitano Takeshi, Japan)
1998	*The Way We Laughed* (Gianni Amelio, Italy)
1999	*Not One Less* (Zhang Yimou, China)
2000	*The Circle* (Jafar Panahi, Iran)
2001	*Monsoon Wedding* (Mira Nair, India)
2002	*The Magdalene Sisters* (Peter Mullan, UK)
2003	*The Return* (Andrei Zvyagintsev, Russia)
2004	*Vera Drake* (Mike Leigh, UK)
2005	*Brokeback Mountain* (Ang Lee, US)

THE DIRECTORS GUILD OF AMERICA AWARDS

The Screen Directors Guild was founded by 13 film directors in 1936. It later merged with the Radio and Television Directors Guild to form the body that exists today. Apart from protecting the artistic and legal rights of directors, the guild also honors directorial creativity and achievement. Winners of DGA awards often go on to win Best Director at the Academy Awards.

DGA AWARDS FOR OUTSTANDING DIRECTORIAL ACHIEVEMENT

1939	Joseph Mankiewicz *A Letter to Three Wives*
1940	Robert Rossen *All the Kings Men*
1950	Joseph Mankiewicz *All About Eve*
1951	George Stevens *A Place in the Sun*
1952	John Ford The Quiet Man
1953	Fred Zinnemann *From Here to Eternity*
1954	Elia Kazan *On the Waterfront*
1955	Delbert Mann *Marty*
1956	George Stevens *Giant*
1957	David Lean *The Bridge on the River Kwai*
1958	Vincente Minnelli *Gigi*
1959	Willian Wyler *Ben-Hur*
1960	Billy Wilder *The Apartment*
1961	Robert Wise and Jerome Robbins *West Side Story*
1962	David Lean *Lawrence of Arabia*
1963	Tony Richardson *Tom Jones*
1964	George Cukor *My Fair Lady*
1965	Robert Wise *The Sound of Music*
1966	Fred Zinnemann *A Man for all Seasons*
1967	Mike Nichols *The Graduate*
1969	John Schlesinger *Midnight Cowboy*
1970	Franklin J. Schaffner *Patton*
1971	William Friedkin *The French Connection*
1972	Francis Ford Coppola *The Godfather*
1973	George Roy Hill *The Sting*
1974	Francis Ford Coppola *The Godfather Part II*
1975	Milos Forman *One Flew over the Cuckoo's Nest*
1976	John G. Avildsen *Rocky*
1977	Woody Allen *Annie Hall*
1978	Michael Cimino *The Deer Hunter*
1979	Robert Benton *Kramer vs. Kramer*
1980	Robert Redford *Ordinary People*
1981	Warren Beatty *Reds*
1982	Richard Attenborough *Gandhi*
1983	James Brooks *Terms of Endearment*
1984	Milos Forman *Amadeus*
1985	Steven Spielberg *The Color Purple*
1986	Oliver Stone *Platoon*
1987	Bernado Bertolucci *The Last Emperor*
1988	Barry Levinson *Rain Man*
1989	Oliver Stone *Born on the Fourth of July*
1990	Kevin Costner *Dances with Wolves*
1991	Jonathan Demme *The Silence of the Lambs*
1992	Clint Eastwood *Unforgiven*
1993	Steven Spielberg *Schindler's List*
1994	Robert Zemeckis *Forrest Gump*
1995	Ron Howard *Apollo 13*
1996	Anthony Minghella *The English Patient*
1997	James Cameron *Titanic*
1998	Steven Spielberg *Saving Private Ryan*
1999	Sam Mendes *American Beauty*
2000	Ang Lee *Crouching Tiger, Hidden Dragon*
2001	Ron Howard *A Beautiful Mind*
2002	Rob Marshall *Chicago*
2003	Peter Jackson *The Lord of the Rings: The Return of the King*
2004	Clint Eastwood *Million Dollar Baby*
2005	Ang Lee *Brokeback Mountain*

BFI CRITICS TOP TEN POLL

1	Citizen Kane
2	Vertigo
3	La Règle du Jeu
4	The Godfather *and* The Godfather Part II
5	Tokyo Story
6	2001: A Space Odyssey
7	Battleship Potemkin
8	Sunrise
9	8½
10 =	Singin' in the Rain
=	Our Daily Bread

BFI DIRECTORS TOP TEN POLL

1	Citizen Kane
2	The Godfather *and* The Godfather Part II
3	8½
4	Lawrence of Arabia
5	Dr. Strangelove
6	Bicyle Thieves
7	Raging Bull
8	Vertigo
9 =	Rashomon
=	La Règle du Jeu
=	Seven Samurai

THE GOLDEN GLOBES AWARDS

The Hollywood Foreign Press Association (HFPA) was founded more than 60 years ago by a group of Los Angeles-based journalists working for overseas publications. The aim of their award is to recognize outstanding achievement in film. The organization also funds scholarships for the film-makers of the future.

GOLDEN GLOBES

1944	The Song of Bernadette
1945	Going My Way
1946	The Lost Weekend
1947	The Best Years of Our Lives
1948	Gentleman's Agreement
1949	The Treasure of Sierre Madre *and* Johnny Belinda
1950	All the King's Men
1951	Sunset Boulevard
1952	A Place in the Sun
1953	The Greatest Show on Earth
1955	On the Waterfront
1956	East of Eden
1957	Around the World in 80 Days
1958	The Bridge on the River Kwai
1959	The Defiant Ones
1960	Ben-Hur
1961	Spartacus
1962	The Guns of Navarone
1963	Lawrence of Arabia and The Chapman Report
1964	The Cardinal
1965	Becket
1966	Doctor Zhivago
1967	A Man for All Seasons
1968	In the Heat of the Night
1969	The Lion in Winter
1970	Anne of the Thousand Days
1971	Love Story
1972	The French Connection
1973	The Godfather
1974	The Exorcist
1975	Chinatown
1976	One Flew Over the Cuckoo's Nest
1977	Rocky
1978	The Turning Point
1979	Midnight Express
1980	Kramer vs. Kramer
1981	Ordinary People
1982	On Golden Pond
1983	E.T.: The Extra-Terrestrial
1984	Terms of Endearment
1985	Amadeus
1986	Out Of Africa
1987	Platoon
1988	The Last Emperor
1989	Rain Man
1990	Born on the Fourth of July
1991	Dances with Wolves
1992	Bugsy
1993	Scent of a Woman
1994	Schindler's List
1995	Forrest Gump
1996	Sense and Sensibility
1997	The English Patient
1998	Titanic
1999	Saving Private Ryan
2000	American Beauty
2001	Gladiator
2002	A Beautiful Mind
2003	The Hours
2004	The Lord of the Rings: The Return of the King
2005	The Aviator
2006	Brokeback Mountain

TOP GROSSING FILMS US

1	Titanic
2	Star Wars: Episode IV—A New Hope
3	Shrek 2
4	E.T.: The Extra-Terrestrial
5	Star Wars: Episode I—The Phantom Menace
6	Spider-Man
7	Star Wars: Episode III—Revenge of the Sith
8	The Lord of the Rings: The Return of the King
9	Spider-Man 2
10	The Passion of the Christ
11	Jurassic Park
12	The Lord of the Rings: The Two Towers
13	Finding Nemo
14	Forrest Gump
15	The Lion King
16	Harry Potter and the Sorcerer's Stone
17	The Lord of the Rings: The Fellowship of the Ring
18	Star Wars: Episode II—Attack of the Clones
19	Star Wars: Episode IV—Return of the Jedi
20	Independence Day

TOP GROSSING FILMS WORLDWIDE

1	Titanic
2	The Lord of the Rings: The Return of the King
3	Harry Potter and the Philosopher's Stone
4	Star Wars: Episode I—The Phantom Menace
5	The Lord of the Rings: The Two Towers
6	Jurassic Park
7	Harry Potter and the Goblet of Fire
8	Shrek 2
9	Harry Potter and the Chamber of Secrets
10	Finding Nemo
11	The Lord of the Rings: The Fellowship of the Ring
12	Star Wars: Episode III—Revenge of the Sith
13	Independence Day
14	Spider-Man
15	Star Wars
16	Harry Potter and the Prisoner of Azkaban
17	Spider-Man 2
18	The Lion King
19	E.T.: The Extra-Terrestrial
20	The Chronicles of Narnia: The Lion, the Witch and the Wardrobe

Glossary

Given below is a selected glossary of the technical and critical terminology used throughout this book.

ABSTRACT FILM A type of non-narrative film that is organized around visual elements such as color, shape, rhythm, and size. Shots are related to each other by repetition and variation.

ACTION The movement that takes place in front of the camera, or the series of events that occurs in the film's narrative.

AMERICAN UNDERGROUND The world of films and film-makers that vary in production styles and exhibition venues from mainstream Hollywood film-making. Active in varying ways since the 1940s, the American underground has become noted for its inventive, usually low-cost methods of film-making and distributing, such as video film-making and online promotion.

AUTEUR The "author" of a film, usually referring to the director. The concept is the basis of the auteur theory, which originated with François Truffaut's theory of the *politique des auteurs* in *Cahiers du Cinéma* and was popularized in the US by critic Andrew Sarris.

AVANT-GARDE An inclusive term for many varieties of experimental art forms. Avant-garde films flourished in France, Germany, and the Soviet Union during the 1920s and part of the 1930s, each taking various paths.

CINEMA DU LOOK A group of late 20th- and early 21st-century French directors who eschew mainstream film-making and are informed by the image-centered art of Music Television (MTV).

CINEMA VERITÉ A type of film-making (its name means cinema truth) that aims to present truth by recording real-life events in an objective, unadorned manner. It originated with the ideas of Russian theoretician Dziga Vertov and practiced in the documentary work of US film-maker Robert Flaherty.

CINEMASCOPE A trademarked name for a wide-screen projection process developed in 1953 consisting of an anamorphic lens system drawn from an invention by Henri Chretien.

COMPUTER-GENERATED IMAGERY (CGI) Images created on a computer, often animated and combined with live action.

DEEP FOCUS The effect of having objects close to and away from the camera in focus. This increase in the depth of field is brought about by the deep-focus lens, developed in the 1930s.

DIGITAL EFFECTS Special screen effects made by reconfiguring movie frames or art stored inside a computer. Their uses include creating scenes, enhancing them, or representing change, as is done with the morphing of one type of creature into another. The images used to make these effects exist in binary digital form.

DIRECT CINEMA The term in the US since the late 1950s for *cinema verité*. Known through the work of Steven Leacock and Robert Drew as Living Cinema, it became Direct Cinema in the 1960s through the work of Albert Maysles and D.A. Pennebaker.

DIRECT FILM A film distribution system that bypasses traditional sales outlets such as television and periodicals to reach audiences through blogs and other online communications.

DIRECT SOUND Software that interacts with a computer sound card to allow applications to make sound effects and music.

DOLLY (OR DOLLIE) A platform on wheels mounted with a movie camera that makes tracking shots possible. They move by hydraulics, sometimes on tracks. To dolly in means to move the camera toward the subject; to dolly out means to move it away.

DYNAMIC MONTAGE The arrangement of intrinsically uncontroversial film images to offer polemical expression. This film-editing practice is often used for propaganda works.

ICONOGRAPHY The elements of a film that allow its identification with a certain genre or type. These elements may encompass plot formulas, subject matter, locations, and style; together, these elements distinguish a Western from film noir or science fiction, and for most viewers, simplify movie decoding.

INTELLECTUAL MONTAGE A type of film editing that eschews now-traditional Hollywood spatial and time continuity and instead employs unexpected, quick images out of standard time to make a point or have a certain emotional effect. Practiced by Russian director Sergei Eisenstein, these images often shock viewers.

MEDIUM LONG SHOT A film shot that places the main object of interest in the center of the composition, neither in the foreground or the background. Its angle is wider than a medium shot but not as wide as a long shot.

MISE-EN-SCÈNE Literally the "setting in scene," this term refers to the existence and placement of actors and objects within the frame. Drawn from the French theater, *mise-en-scène* may for some critics also refer to the tone and mood created by the film-maker.

MODERNISM An artistic movement of the late 19th- and 20th-centuries marked by its concentration on the presentation of the story rather than standard story components. Often, the term is applied casually in recent films; these films are considered modern because they explore feelings rather than follow plots.

MONTAGE The term referring to the juxtaposing of two opposing cinematic images to create a different meaning for the viewer. Deriving from the French word for assembling and mounting, montage was practiced most famously by Russian film-maker Sergei Eisenstein. Particularly in the 1930s, montage of calendar dates and photo images were used in US films to indicate the passage of time.

NEGATIVE IMAGE A reverse light capture of an image in photography and film-making, or the unsympathetic presentation of a screen character or issue.

PAINTED CELLS (OR CELS) The individual components of traditional animation, each of which has been painted on paper and later on acetate (originally celluloid) by an animation artist. Each cell represents a discrete movement of the character or characters; thousands are used for an animated film.

PAN A compression of the words "panorama" and "panoramic," a pan is a movement of the camera on a fixed plane from one part of a scene to another.

POSTMODERNISM An artistic movement arising in the late 20th-century concerned with the non-linear, non-traditional, and self-reflexive aspects of the arts. Postmodernist films often reflect an intimacy with non-cinematic forms, including computer art and literature.

PRODUCTION CODE The studio-generated self-governing system developed in 1930 to ensure acceptable levels of moral behavior and good taste in films. The Code was revised in 1966 and a movie ratings system was begun in 1968.

RAPID CUTTING The editing together of many very short film shots, often to create a heightened sense of excitement or danger. An example is the series of short cuts in *Psycho* (1960), which present a murder.

REVERSE SLOW MOTION A trick film effect in which a film is run backward in the camera at an accelerated rate. When projected, the action filmed appears to occur in reverse sequence and at a slow pace.

REVERSE TRACKING SHOTS A trick effect made by running the film backward in the dolly-mounted camera, which is itself moving backward, forward, in, and out of a scene.

SENSURROUND The trademark for a special-effects process developed by Universal in 1974 to increase the feeling of tremors during the watching of a film.

SHOCK CUTS A juxtaposition of widely varying images in a film to create a sensation of surprise or horror. Films employing the technique include *An Andalucian Dog* and *2001: A Space Odyssey*.

SHOT A single continuous action that is filmed or appears to be filmed in one take, from one camera setup. Many shots filmed are never seen by the audience: a single scene may be photographed from several different angles, with the director and editor selecting the ones that work best.

SLOW MOTION A film effect of making an action appear to occur more slowly than it would in reality. The effect is created by putting the film through the camera at an accelerated rate. When the film is projected at a normal rate, events run more slowly than usual.

SOUND EFFECTS (SFX) All sound in a film other than dialogue and music.

SPECIAL EFFECTS (SFX) Visual and mechanical effects used to create illusions on film.

STOP MOTION A film-making technique in which inanimate objects appear to have lifelike action. The effect is created by repositioning the inanimate figures for each frame. The sequence of manipulated images is projected, with the effect of character movement.

STORYBOARD A progression of sketches or photographs that outline the sequencing of a film. They are used by directors for planning scenes.

STRUCTURALISM A theory of film analysis in which meaning is acquired through the study of dual opposing images. For example, desire may be portrayed by a seemingly unconnected image of a person followed by an image of another person or a costly item.

SUPERIMPOSITION The practice of photographing or placing an image or set of words over an existing image. The superimposed images are viewed as one. Superimposition is often used to supply subtitles; when several images are projected in rapid succession, they convey a colloquial Hollywood form of montage, usually for time passage or romantic dissolves.

SURREALISM A 20th-century theory of art that pursues the expression of the irrational inner workings of the unconscious. Surrealist film-making draws upon fantasy and is often composed of a series of seemingly unrelated images.

TAKE An uninterrupted shot taken by a camera. Directors may film many takes of the same action.

TECHNICOLOR A film color process developed by Herbert Kalmus and Daniel Comstock during World War I and patented in 1922. Originally a two-color process, it was expanded in 1932 to a three-color process; represented in movies including *Gone With the Wind* (1939).

THREE-STRIP TECHNICOLOR Developed in 1932, this process is an advancement on the original two-color Technicolor that uses a custom-built camera and three strips of film in red, blue, and green to render more realistic color on screen.

TRACKING SHOT A shot created by a camera mounted on a dolly or track that follows the movement of an actor or action. The shot may move in any direction to follow action.

TRIPLE SCREEN A multiple-screen video display monitor for use in computer video editing.

VISTAVISION A wide-screen projection system developed by Paramount Pictures in the 1950s that creates its image through the technique of optical reduction from a large negative image to the standard release print image.

VISUAL FORMALITY The orderly arrangement of players and surroundings in the movie frame to convey a serious or settled tone to the film. Often the arrangement is meant to contrast with the world or characters in the film, as in the formality masking the disorder in *Ran* (1985).

Index

Page numbers in **bold** refer to main entries, *italic* numbers indicate illustrations.

A

B

N O

P

Q R

S

T

Acknowledgments

The Kobal Collection owes its existence to the vision, courage, talent and energy of the men and women who created the movie industry. In particular we collect, preserve, organize and make available the publicity materials issued by the film companies to promote their films and stars. The materials used in this work originated from the following companies and organizations. We apologize in advance for any unintentional omission and will be please to insert any amendments in future editions.

All images are supplied by The Kobal Collection except for those identified below:

Abbreviations key:
t-top; b-bottom; r-right; l-left; c-center; a-above, f-far

I MGM; 2–3 20th Century Fox; 4 Columbia/A.L. ('Whitey' Schafer); 5 Aquarius Library: Walt Disney; 6–7 RKO; 8 Paramount; 8–9t MGM; 8–9b Miramax/Universal; 10 MGM; 12 Hal Roach; 12–3Beijing New Pictures/Elite; 13 Walt Disney/Walden; 14–5 UA/Charles Chaplin; 16c Lumière; 16bl Photo12.com:–ARJ; 17t Amenica; 17b Melies; 18 Lasky Prods.; 19t Fox; 19b DK; 20l Paramount; 20r United Artists; 21no credit; 22t DK; 22b DK; 23 MGM; 24 United Artists; 25t Nero; 25b MGM; 26tl Corbis: Bettmann; 27 MGM; 28 MGM; 29 RKO; 30 VOG/Sigma/Raymond Voinquel; 31 Mosfilm; 32t Universal; 32bl Getty Images: A. E. French/Hulton Archive; 33 MGM; 34 MGM; 35t Columbia; 35c DK; 35b Pioneer Pictures; 36 MGM; 37 Crown Film Unit; 38 RKO; 39 Superstock; 40t Warner Bros.; 40b Rank; 41Columbia/Bob Coburn; 42 RKO George Hurrell; 43 Amenica; 44 United Artists; 45tr Getty Images: J. R. Eyerman//Time Life Pictures; 45b United Artists; 46t Gulu; 46b Getty Images: J. R. Eyerman/Time Life Pictures; 47t 20th Century Fox; 47b 20th Century Fox; 48 Warner Bros. 49t United Artists; 49b Columbia/Horizon; 50 Columbia; 51t Warner Bros.; 51b Columbia; 52–3 Columbia/Irving Lippman; 54 United Artists; 55t Mirisch/7 Arts/UA; 55b Mirisch/UA; 56 20th Century Fox; 57t Amenica; 57b Embassy; 58 Woodfall; 59t Eon/Danjaq/UA; 59b Eon/Danjaq/UA; 60t MGM/Hemmings/Veruschka; 61 Anouchka/Orsay/Sami Frey or Jean Claude Briarly?; 62 Debra Hill; 63 Universal; 64 United Artists; 64–5 Columbia; 65 Zoetrope/UA; 66 Warner Bros.; 67t Warner Bros.; 67b Warner Bros.; 68 Paramount; 69t Paramount; 69b UA/Fantasy Films; 70 United Artists; 71t Universal/Embassy; 71bLadd Co/WB; 72 Lucasfilm/Paramount; 73 Carolco; 74 Paramount; 75tl Corbis: Keith Dannemiller; 75b Constellation/Cargo/Alive; 76 Paramount/ Phill Caruso; 77 Castle Rock/Michael Weinstein; 78t Lazenne/Canal+/La Sept; 78b Working Title/Polygram; 78–9 20th Century Fox/Paramount/Merie W. Wallace; 79 Zentropa; 80–1 Polygram; 82 20th Century Fox; 82–3 Pathe/Sony Classics; 83tl SuperStock: age fotostock; 84 Anhelo/IFC; 85t Focus Features; 85b Basic/Media Asia; 86 Aquarius Library: Warner Bros.; 87 Lion's Gate; 88–9 Dreamworks/Paramount; 90 Amenica; 92 Samuel Bronston; 93 DK Images: Courtesy of the Museum of the Moving Image, London; 94–5t Corbis: Douglas Kirkland; 95bl Getty Images: Piotr Malecki; 96t MGM; 96b Archer Street/Delux/Lion's Gate Jaap Buitendijk; 97t Warner Bros.; 97b Lucasfilm/Paramount; 98t Universal; 98b Miramax/Universal/Laurie Sparham; 99 New Line Bob Marshak; 100 20th Century Fox; 101Dreamworks/Kelvin Jones; 100–1 Warner Bros./Blid Alabirk; 102t,c New Line; 102b 20th Century Fox; 103 MGM; 104tl Rex Features: Universal/Everett; 104–5 Universal/Wingnut; 105 20th Century Fox; 106–7 Warner Bros. 108t Charles Chaplin; 108b Corbis: Jim Sugar; 109tr Rex Features: Jonathan Player; 109b Corbis: Jim Ruymen/Reuters; 110–1b Corbis: Vincent Kessler/Reuters; 111t Corbis: Fred Prouser/Reuters; 112–3 Paramount; 114 Paramount; 116 Warner Bros.; 117t 20th Century Fox; 117 c Lucasfilm/Paramount; 117b Paramount; 118 MGM; 119t Aquarius Library: Walt Disney 119b Dreamworks/Aardman Animations; 120 Sony Classics; 121t Touhoku Shinsha; 121b Dreamworks; 122 Cinegraphic Paris; 123t Warner Bros.; 123b Fox 2000/Suzanne Tenner; 124t Sennett; 124b First National; 125 Hal Roach; 126t Hal Roach/UA; 126b United Artists; 127t MGM; 127b MGM; 128t Universal; 128b Miramax/Universal/Alex Bailey; 129t Handmade; 129b Prods Artistes Associés/Da Ma; 130 Pioneer Pictures; 131t Working Title; 131b Renn/France 2/D.A./Degeto; 132t Allied Artists; 132b Spinal Tap Prods; 133 20th Century Fox/Takashi Seida; 134 Gainsborough 135t Paramount; 135b YUFKU; 136 Leacock/Pennebaker; 136–7 CNC/ Canal+; 137 Alliance Atlantis/Dog Eat Dog; 138 20th Century Fox; 139t 20th Century Fox/Toho; 139b MGM; 140l RKO; 140r Paramount; 141t Monarchy/Regency; 141b Universal; 142t Warner Bros.; 142b Warner/First National; 143t Filmel/CICC/Fida; 143b Universal; 144 Bandai Visual; 144–5 Warner Bros.; 145 Miramax/Buena Vista; 146 Universal; 147t Universal; 147bRKO; 148 Kadokawa Shoten; 149t Golden Harvest; 149b Warner Bros./Concord; 150 Cineguild/Rank; 151t Killer Films; 151c RKO; 151bWarner Bros.; 152 MGM; 153t Warner Bros.; 153b MGM; 154 MGM; 155t MGM; 155c 20th Century Fox; 155b Warner Bros.; 156t Paramount; 156b 20th Century Fox/Sue Adler; 157Miramax/David James; 158tNero; 159t Walt Disney; 159b ICAIC; 160 20th Century Fox; 161t Allied Artists; 161b 20th Century Fox; 162t Paramount; 162b Toho/Columbia TriStar; 163Dreamworks/Paramount; 164t Universal; 164b Universal; 165 Lucasfilm/Paramount; 166t Columbia; 166b Universal; 167t Universal/Jasin Boland; 167b Universal; 168–9 MGM, 170 Maya Deren; 171t Paramount; 171b Pathé; 172t United Artists; 172b Assoc R&R/Paramount; 173t Warner Bros./Murray Close; 173b Dreamworks/David James; 174 Edison; 174–5 United Artists; 175 United Artists; 176t PEA; 176B Stanley Kramer/UA; 177t Orion; 177b Focus Features; 178–9 Yash Raj Films; 180 El Deseo/Miguel Bracho; 182t Mij Film Co/BAC Films; 182cDaiei–Kyoto/Brandon; 182bJet Tone; 183t Films Cisse/Govt of Mali; 183b Focus/Film4/Senator; 184 Duo/Arte France; 185t Moviworld/Mk2/Miramax; 185b Les Films Terre Africaine; 186t Lumen/Lama Prods; 186b Bac Films; 187t Makmalbaf Films; 187b Mk2/Makmalbaf; 188 Zespol Filmowy Kadr; 189t Film Polski; 189c Hungarofilm; 189b Hungarofilm; 190 Mafilm/Studio Objectiv; 190–1Czech TV/Total Helpart/Martin Spelda; 191 Portobello/Sverak; 192 CIBY; 193t 20th Century Fox; 193b Guney/Cactus Film; 195 YUFKU–Kino–Ukraine/Amkino; 196t Lenfilm; 196–7 Forafilm/Hermitage Bridge Studio; 197 Mosfilm; 198 MGM; 199t Svensk Filmindustri; 199b Europa Film; 200 Villealfa Productions; 201t Betzer–Panorama Film/Danish Filminst; 201b Bulbul Films/SFI/Erik Aavatsmark; 202 UFA; 203 UFA; 204 Seitz/Bioskop/Hallelujah; 205t Road Movies/Argos Films/WDR; 205b X Filme/WDR/arte/Bernd Spauke; 206t Gaumont; 206b Films Hakim/Paris Film; 208t UGC; 208b Fat Free Ltd/Miramax/David Appleby; 208–9 Spectra/Gray/Alterdel/Centaure; 209b Canal+/UGC/Wellspring Media; 210 Itala Film Torino; 211t 211b FC Rome/PECF Paris`; 212t RAI/BibiFilm; 212c RAI/BibiFilm; 212b Melampo Cinematografica/Sergio Strizzi; 213 Hepworth; 214t Korda/UA; 214b 20th Century Fox/Allied Stars/ Enigma; 215t Tiger Aspect Pictures/Giles Keyte; 215b Figment/Noel Gay/Channel 4; 216t Film 59; 216b Epoca/Talia/Selenia/Films Corona; 217 Elias Querejeta Prod.; 218t Canal+/Filmanova/Lucky Red/Teresa Isasi; 218b Trueba/Lola Films/Animatografo; 219t Zentropa Ent/GER/Mikado Films; 219b Madragoa/Gemini/Light Night; 220–1 Canal+/Miramax; 221t Victorious Films; 221b Alliance/Ego Film; 222t Amenica; 222b ICAIC; 223 Arau/Cinevista/Aviacsa; 224 Copacabana Films; 225 Glauber Rocha/Mapa; 226t Videofilmes/Mact Prod./Paula Prandini; 226b Guacamole Films/OK Films; 227t Film Four/South Fork/Senator Film; 227b Tucan Prod./Studio Canal+; 228t Warner Bros.; 228b Bazmark Films/20th Century Fox/Sue Adler; 229t M and A Film Corp.; 229b Miramax/Dimension Films/Penny Tweedie; 230 Guangxi Films; 231t Xi'an Film Studio; 231b Lian Bang; 232 Golden Harvest; 233t Yang & His Gang; 233b Atom Films/Omega/Pony Canyon Inc.; 234–5 China Film Group Corp./Bai Xiao Yan; 236t Toho; 236b Kinugasa Prod.; 237 Daiei; 238t Itami; 238b Omega; 239 Akira; 240 Taehung Pictures; 241t Egg Films/Show East; 241b LJ Films/Cineclick Asia; 242 Mehboob Prods.; 243t Priya; 243b United Artists; 244 Miraai/Jane Balfour; 245t Kaleidoscope/Arrow; 245b Excel Entertainment; 246–7 Touchstone; 248 Paramount; 250t Gemini Films/Canal+; 250b Warner Bros; 251t Orion; 251b BBC Films/Dreamworks/Clive Coote; 252t El Deseo/Renn/France 2; 252b Kaktus/Tesauro; 253t Spelling Films International; 253b USA Films/Mark Tillie; 254t Sogetel/Le Films Alain Sarde; 254b Memorial; 255t New Line G. Lefkowitz; 255b Theo Angelopoulos; 256t Interopa/Cineriz/Paris;

256b CCC/CIPI/MGM; 257t DiNovi/Columbia/Joseph Lederer; 257b Columbia/Goldcrest; 258t Svensk Filminstitut/Gaumont/Tobis; 258b Cinematograph AB Sweden/Cinema 5; 259t MGM; 259b Renn/A2/Rai–2; 260t Warner Bros; 260b Hachette Premiere/Kushner–Locke Co/Severine Brigeot; 261t Columbia/Tri–Star; 261b Columbia; 262t Columbia; 262b Paramount; 263t UGC/Roger Corbeau; 263b Embassy Pictures; 264t MGM; 264b MGM; 265t Films 59/Alatriste/Uninci; 265b Paris Film/Five Film; 266t Warner Bros.; 266b Touchstone; 267t 20th Century Fox/Paramount/Merie W. Wallace; 267b Jan Chapman Prods/Ciby 2000; 268t US War Department; 268c Columbia; 268b Columbia; 269 Cine Alliance/Pathé; 270t Columbia; 270b Paris Film Production/Panitalia; 271t United Artists; 271b First National/Charles Chaplin; 272t Tomson Films/China Film/Beijing; 272b Beijing Film Studio/H. Hattori; 273t United Artists; 273b Tobis; 274t Filmsonor/Mirkine; 274b Films André Paulvé; 275t Touchstone/Universal/Melinda Sue Gordon; 275b 20th Century Fox; 276t Paramount; 276b Zoetrope/United Artists; 277t AIP; 277b Polygram/Universal; 278t 20th Century Fox; 278b Dimension/Miramax; 279t 20th Century Fox; 279b Anhelo Prod/IFC Films; 280t Warner Bros.; 280b MGM/Frank Grimes; 281t Warner Bros.; 281b 20th Century Fox; 282t Paramount; 282b Paramount; 283t Orion/Ken Regan; 283b Parc Film/Madeleine Films; 284t United Artists; 284c Universal; 284b Paramount; 285 Dear Film; 286t MGM; 286bl 20th Century Fox; 286br MGM; 287t Yufku–Kino–Ukrain/Amkino; 287b Dreyer/Tobis/Klangfilm; 288t Warner Bros./Merie W. Wallace; 288c Warner Bros.; 288b Warner Bros./Merie W. Wallace; 289t United Artists; 289b Paramount; 290t Goskino; 290b Mosfilm; 291t Goskino; 291b Sovkino; 292t Tango; 292c Filmverlag Der Autoren; 292b Geria/Bavaria/Soc. Fr–De Prod.; 293t Ponti–De Laurentiis; 293b Cineriz; 294t New Line; 294b Flaherty Productions; 295t MGM; 295b MGM; 296 Warner Bros.; 297t Saul Zaentz Company; 297b United Artists; 298t BBC/Buena Vista International; 298b Lorimar; 299 Forrester–Parant; 300t De Laurentiis/Beauregard; 300b Chaumiane/Filmstudio; 301 Alta Vista; 302t Wark Producing Company; 302b UA/Art Cinema; 303t Svensk Filmindustri/AB Filmteknik; 303b Wega Film; 304t National General/Cinema Centre; 304b Warner Bros.; 305t Herzog/Filmverlag Der Autoren/ZDF; 305b Gaumont; 306b Paramount; 307t Universal; 307b Universal; 308t MGM; 308b Dreamworks/Universal/Eli Reed; 309 Shochiku; 310t MGM; 310b Warner Bros.; 311t Nikkatsu Corp.; 311b Columbia/Merchant Ivory/Derrick Santini; 312t Wingnut/Universal; 312b Wingnut/New Line/Pierre Vinet; 313t MTI/Orion; 313b Mafilm/Hunnia Studio; 314t UGC/Studio Canal+; 314b Columbia/Tri–Star; 315t Sputnik Oy; 315b Warner Bros.; 316t United Artists; 316b MK2/Abbas Kiarostami Prod.; 317t Zespol; 317b Sideral/Tor Studios/Canal+; 318bl Warner Bros.; 318br Bryna/Universal; 319t Daiei; 319c Herald Ace/Nippon/Greenwich; 319b Toho; 320t Nero; 320b UFA; 321t Columbia; 321b MGM; 322t Good Machine; 322b Focus Features; 323t Universal/David Lee; 323b Warner Bros.; 324t Ciby 2000; 324b Prod Eur Assoc/Gonzalez/Constantin; 325t Woodfall/Kestrel; 325b Associated British; 326t Paramount; 326bl MGM/C.S.Bull; 326br Paramount; 327t Lucasfilm/Coppola Co./Universal; 327b Lucas Film Ltd; 328t 20th Century Fox Merrick Morton; 328b Paramount; 329t AFI/Libra; 329c 20th Century Fox; 329b 20th Century Fox; 330t Ealing; 330b Viking/Europa/Smart Egg/New Realm; 331t New Line/Merie W. Wallace; 331b Nouvelles Editions/MK2/Stella/NEF; 332t Columbia/Robert Coburn; 332c Columbia; 332b Samuel Goldwyn/RKO; 333t Allied Artists; 333b De Laurentiis; 334t Argos; 334b OGC/Studios Jenner/Play Art/La Cyme; 335t Dreamworks/Lorey Sebastian; 335c Globo Films; 335b Focus Features; 336t United Artists; 336b Paramount/Miramax/Phil Bray; 337 MGM; 338t Shochiku; 338b Dog Eat Dog/Miramax; 339t UFA; 339b Fox Films; 340t Warner Bros; 340b Madragoa/Gemini/Light Night; 341t Gamma/Florida/Oska; 341b Sacha Gordine Productions; 342t Argos Films/Oshima Prod.; 342b Shochiku; 343t Sofar Films; 343b Nero; 344t Dovzhenko Films; 344b Cinergi Pictures; 345t Artistes Associés/PEA; 345b Arco/Lux; 346t Anglo–EMI/Rapid/Terra; 346b MGM; 347t Bavaria/Radiant; 347b Focus Features/Studio Canal/Guy Ferrandis; 348t Anglo Amalgamated; 348b Korda; 349t Rank; 349b British National; 350t Columbia; 350b Mezhrabpomfilm/Moscow; 351 Republic; 352t Devki Chitra; 352b Columbia; 353t Réalisations D'Art Cinematographique; 353b Paris Film; 354t Argos/Como/Pathé/Daiei; 354b Woodfall; 355t NSDAP; 355b CNC/France 2 Cinema/Studio Canal+; 356t Copacabana Films; 356b Casey Prods/Eldorado Films; 357t Films Du Losange; 357b Films Du Losange/La Sept Cinema; 358t Berit Films; 358b Tevere/UGC; 359t Red Dog/Cinecom; 359b United Artists; 360 Columbia/Phillip Caruso; 361t Warner Bros.; 361b Universal/Phillip Caruso; 362t 20th Century Fox/Bob Penn; 362b MGM/UA; 363t Les Films Terre Africaine; 363b 20th Century Fox/Marvel/Attila Dory; 364t Universal; 364b Universal; 365 MGM; 366 Universal/Amblin/Murray Close; 367t Universal/David James; 367b Castle Rock/Warner Bros/Ralph Nelson Jr.; 368t Paramount; 368b MGM; 369t Paramount; 369b Warner Bros./Sidney Baldwin; 370t Universal; 370b MGM; 371t MGM; 371b Paramount; 372t Mafilm/Mokep/ZDF; 372b Miramax/Buena Vista/Linda R. Chen; 373t Mosfilm; 373b Mosfilm; 374t CADV/Discina; 374b Columbia; 375t Anglo Enterprise/Vineyard; 375c Anglo Enterprise/Vineyard; 375b Les Films Du Carrosse; 376t New Line; 376b Films A2/Cine Tamaris; 377t VUFKU; 378t Samuel Goldwyn/RKO; 378b Jacques–Louis Nounez/Gaumont; 379t Alfa; 379b Titanus/20th Century Fox; 380t Zentropa Ent./Rolf Konow; 380b Films Du Losange/Groupe X/Gaumont; 381t Warner Bros.; 381b Warner Bros; 382t Picnic/BEF/Australian Film Commission; 382b 20th Century Fox/Universal/Stephen Vaughan; 383t Columbia; 383b Universal; 384t Paramount; 384b Samuel Goldwyn; 385t Road Movie Prods.; 385bl Universal; 385br Universal; 386t. 20th Century Fox; 386b. Paramount; 387t Paramount; 387b Paramount; 388 United Artists; 389t Columbia/Block 2/Jet Tone Films/Wing Shya; 389b Block 2; 390t Paramount/Touchstone/Stephen Vaughan; 390b Universal; 391t Samuel Goldwyn/RKO; 391b Warner Bros.; 392t Medusa/Phillipe Antonello; 392b 20th Century Fox/Dreamworks/Zade Rosenthal; 393t Beijing New Picture/Elite Group; 393b Magna/20th Century Fox; 394–5 RKO; 396 Columbia/Sony/Chan Kam Chuen; 398t Epic; 398bl Epic; 398brAmenica; 399t Decla–Bioscop; 399b Decla–Bioscop; 400t Prana–Film; 400b Flaherty; 401t Goskino; 401b Goskino; 402 Ufa; 403 SGF/Gaumont; 404t Bunuel–Dali; 404b Société Générale des Films; 405 Universal; 406t Paramount; 406b Ufa 407 Charles Chaplin/United Artists; 408 Warner Bros.; 409 Paramount; 410 RKO; 411 Gaumont–Franco–Film–Aubert; 412 Aquarius Library: Walt Disney; 413t Olympia/Tobis 413b Les Nouvelles Editions Francaises; 414 Selznick International; 415 MGM; 416 Columbia; 417 20th Century Fox; 418 RKO; 419 Warner Bros./Fist National; 420 RKO/Goldwyn; 421 UA/Romaine; 422 Two Cities; 423 Warner Bros.; 424–5 Warner Bros.; 426 ICI; 427 Pathe; 428 Archers/Independent/Rank; 429 RKO/Liberty; 430t PDS; 430b Excelsa/Mayer–Burstyn; 431 Universal; 432 Ealing; 433 London Films; 434 Andre Paulvé/Films du Palais Royal; 435 Daiei; 436 MGM; 437 Shockiku; 438 Columbia; 439 Universal; 440 Warner Bros.; 441 Govt of West Bengal; 442 United Artists; 443 Svensk Filmindustri; 444 Paramount; 445 Film Polski; 446t; 447l United Artists; 447r 20th Century Fox; 448 Credit – Aquaruis; 449 Raima–Pathé/Gray Film; 450 Woodfall; 451t Cine del Duca/PCE/Lyre; 451b Terra/Tamara/Cormora; 452 Columbia/Horizon; 453 Hawk Films/Columbia; 454 Casbah/Igor; 455cr Singalonga Productions Ltd; 455b 20th Century Fox; 456t Mosfilm; 456b Factory Films; 457 WB/Tatira–Hiller/7 Arts; 458t WB/7Arts; 458b Columbia; 459 Mars/Marianne/Maran; 460 Paramount; 461 Werner Herzog; 462t Paramount/ABC; 462b Oshima/Argos; 463 Columbia; 464 United Artists/Rollins–Joffe; 465 Lucas Film Ltd; 466–7 Lucas Film Ltd; 468 Trio/Albatros/WDR; 469 EMI/Universal; 470 Universal; 471tWarner Bros.; 471bLucasfilm/Paramount; 472 Road Movies/Argos; 473 Edgar Reitz/WDR/SFB; 474 Mosfilm; 475 De Laurentiis; 476t Films Aleph/Historia; 476b Merchant–Ivory; 477 El Desea–Lauren; 478 Cristaldi/Ariane/Rai; 479 Universal; 480 Era International; 481 Warner Bros.; 482 Live Entertainment/Dog Eat Dog; 483 Canal+/Mk2/CED/France 3/Cab/Tor; 484t Farabi/Kiarostami/Miramax; 484b Polygram/Woeking Title/Channel 4; 485 Aquarius Library: Buena Vista/Walt Disney; 486 Working Title/Polygram; 487 Columbia/Sony; 488t Block2/Jet Tone/Paradise Films; 488b Bedford Falls/Initial/USA Films; 489 New Line/Wing Nut/Saul Zaentz/Pierre Vinet; 490 Globo Films/Buena Vista; 491 Focus Features